Eighteen Minutes

WITI D1545610

WITHDRAWN

Other Books by Stephen L. Moore

Savage Frontier: Rangers, Riflemen, and Indian Wars in Texas. Volume 1: 1835–1837. Republic of Texas Press, 2002.

Savage Frontier. Volume 2: 1838–1839. Republic of Texas Press, forthcoming.

Taming Texas. Captain William T. Sadler's Lone Star Service. State House Press, 2000.

With William J. Shinneman and Robert W. Gruebel. *The Buzzard Brigade: Torpedo Squadron Ten at War.* Pictorial Histories Publishing, 1996.

Eighteen Minutes

The Battle of San Jacinto and the Texas Independence Campaign

Stephen L. Moore

REPUBLIC OF TEXAS PRESS

Dallas • Lanham • Boulder • New York • Oxford

Published by Republic of Texas Press
An imprint of The Rowman & Littlefield Publishing Group, Inc.
4501 Forbes Boulevard, Suite 200
Lanham, MD 20706

Distributed by NATIONAL BOOK NETWORK

Library of Congress Cataloging-in-Publication Data
Moore, Stephen L.
   Eighteen minutes : the battle of San Jacinto and the Texas independence campaign / Stephen L. Moore.
      p. cm.
   Includes bibliographical references and index.
   ISBN 1-58907-009-7 (alk. paper)
   1. San Jacinto, Battle of, Tex., 1836. 2. Texas—History—Revolution, 1835–1836.
I. Title.
   F390.M85 2004
   976.4'03—dc21

                                                                    2003013518

♾™ The paper used in this publication meets the minimum requirements of American National Standard for Information Sciences—Permanence of Paper for Printed Library Materials, ANSI/NISO Z39.48-1992.

Manufactured in the United States of America.

Contents

Acknowledgments

I must thank Lisa Struthers, Director of the San Jacinto Museum of History's Albert and Ethel Herzstein Library, for her assistance with this book. This newly remodeled museum library contains biographical information on all San Jacinto veterans, an exhaustive collection of Texana reference books, and an impressive photo and illustration archive. She was a vital source in my last-minute research and in allowing me to reproduce many of the illustrations for *Eighteen Minutes*.

Donaly Brice of the Texas State Library and Archives Commission in Austin has always been a trusted supporter. He has reproduced requested articles, looked up various requests concerning San Jacinto campaign participants and pointed me toward the important McArdle Notebooks on San Jacinto.

For the illustrations, John Anderson of the Texas Archives is greatly appreciated for his help. Other individuals and organizations who assisted in the artwork for this book include: Linda Peterson and Steven Williams of the Center for American History, The University of Texas at Austin; Russell Martin for the Travis illustration from Southern Methodist University's DeGolyer Library; Richard Sorenson of the Smithsonian American Art Museum; Dennis Medina of the University of Texas at San Antonio; and Mike Johnson, for his assistance in touching up old illustrations.

My parents, Marshall L. and Kathy Moore Jr., were always willing to take a trip in search of photos or information. Edwin G. Pierson Jr. provided research concerning his early Texas Ranger ancestors and numerous muster rolls of the Texas Revolution. Thanks also to my in-laws, David and Patsy Hunt, for enduring my many research trips while visiting in Houston.

Beyond those who have helped directly, I also credit those whom I did not contact personally. Louis Wiltz Kemp, the late San Jacinto proponent who worked diligently to make the monument and museum what it is today, left a wealth of information on the campaign veterans in the biographical sketches he compiled on each man. His work resides in the San Jacinto Museum and a second copy is in the Center for American History at the University of Texas at Austin.

For the inspiration to write history from the eye of the participant, I credit the late Walter Lord. His ability to take the reader into the action from numerous vantage points made reading history fun. His timeless treatments of such epic historic events as the Alamo, Pearl Harbor, the battle of Midway, the *Titanic* and the American Revolution have been in print for decades and should continue to be.

And, finally, to the resolve for independence shared by two of my ancestors who fought at San Jacinto, William Turner Sadler and John Morton, I dedicate this book.

Accounts by Campaign Participants

The following San Jacinto campaign participants added firsthand testimony to this book either through letters, dispatches, memoirs, legal depositions, audited military claims, pension papers or newspaper articles:

Allen, Capt. John Melville	Bryan, Moses Austin
Almonte, Col. Juan N.	Calder, Capt. Robert J.
Alsbury, Young Perry	Caro, Ramon Martínez
Baker, Capt. Moseley	Carper, Dr. William M.
Becerra, Francisco	Clopper, Andrew M.
Bennett, Lt. Col. Joseph L.	Coleman, Col. Robert M.
Benson, Ellis	Cooke, Francis Jarvis
Billingsley, Capt. Jesse	Cooke, Maj. William G.
Borden, John Pettit	Corry, Thomas F.
Borden, Paschal Pavolo	Crain, Roden Taylor
Bostick, James H.	Cravens, Robert M.
Bostick, Sion Record	Curtis, James, Sr.
Branch, Edward Thomas	Delgado, Col. Pedro
Brewster, Henry Percy	Denham, M. H.
Brooks, Thomas D.	Duncan, John
Brown, Oliver T.	Erath, George Bernard
Bryan, Luke O.	Farish, Oscar

Ferrell, John P.
Filisola, Gen. Vicente
Fitzhugh, Dr. John P. T.
Forbes, Major John
Franklin, Benjamin Cromwell
Giddings, Giles Albert
Gillaspie, Capt. James
Goodloe, Dr. Robert Kemp
Handy, Maj. Robert Eden
Hardaway, Samuel G.
Hardin, Benjamin F.
Harvey, John W.
Hassell, John W.
Heard, Capt. William J. E.
Hickox, Franklin B.
Hill, Isaac Lafayette
Hill, James Monroe
Hockley, Col. George W.
Horton, Col. Alexander
Hotchkiss, Rinaldo
Houston, General Samuel
Hunter, Robert Hancock
Irvine, Josephus S.
Jenkins, John Holland
Jones, Dr. Anson
Kelly, Connell O'Donnell
Kelso, Alfred
Kokernot, David L.
Kuykendall, James H.
Labadie, Dr. Nicholas D.
Lamar, Col. Mirabeau B.
Lane, Walter Paye
Lapham, Moses
Martin, Philip
Martin, Capt. Wyly
Mays, Thomas H.
McCullough, Benjamin
Menchaca, Jose Antonio
Menefee, John Sutherland
Mercer, Eli
Miles, Edward
Millard, Henry

Peña, Lt. Col. José E. de la
Perry, Maj. James Hazard
Phelps, Dr. James A. E.
Plunkett, John
Poe, George Washington
Portilla, Col. Nicolás de la
Rector, Elbridge Gerry
Roark, Leo
Roberts, George H.
Robinson, George W.
Robinson, James W.
Robison, Joel Walter
Rodriguez, Ambrosio
Roman, Capt. Richard
Rounds, Lyman Frank
Rusk, Col. Thomas Jefferson
Santa Anna, Gen. Antonio
Scates, William Bennett
Seguin, Capt. Juan N.
Shain, Charles B.
Sharp, John
Sherman, Col. Sidney
Shipman, Daniel
Smith, Dr. William P.
Snell, Martin Kingsley
Sparks, Stephen Franklin
Steele, Alphonso
Stevenson, Capt. Robert
Stout, William B.
Summers, William W.
Sutherland, George
Swearingen, William C.
Swisher, John Milton
Sylvester, James Austin
Tarlton, James
Taylor, Campbell
Taylor, William S.
Turner, Capt. Amasa
Urrea, Gen. José de
Usher, Patrick
Walling, Jesse
Wade, John Marshall

Walker, Capt. William
Wells, Maj. Lysander
Wharton, Col. John Austin
Whitaker, Madison Guess
Winn, Walter

Winters, James Washington
Woods, Samuel
Young, William Foster
Zavala, Maj. Lorenzo de, Jr.
Zuber, William Physick

"Daring Intrepidity"

Tired soldiers, fatigued from marching endlessly with little food or water, found themselves at their wits' ends. Few of these men had a uniform and some were even shoeless. Many cursed their commanding general for his lack of desire to engage the enemy. In return, their general was edgy, prone to shower bursts of profanity and threats upon some hapless soul who could not keep up during a march.

For forty-two days the army and its leader endured each other's differences of opinion. The Texas Army was a collection of regular soldiers, volunteer frontiersmen, cavalrymen, rangers, and recently arrived soldiers of fortune from the United States. They were led by forty-three-year-old General Samuel Houston, the ex-Governor of Tennessee and veteran of Andrew Jackson's Indian wars.

According to Texas historian Eugene C. Barker in 1901, the San Jacinto campaign covered just one month and ten days in the spring of 1836. Barker considered the campaign to begin with Sam Houston's assumption of command of the Texas Army on March 11, ending on April 21 with the battle of San Jacinto.

San Jacinto was the deciding moment in the Texas Revolution. The early Texas settlers had been basically loyal to the Mexican government until President Antonio López de Santa Anna Pérez de Lebrón in 1834 suspended the Constitution of 1824, driving them to rebel in order to defend their rights.

This book takes the reader on the campaign trail with the men of opposing generals Sam Houston and Santa Anna. Testimony from key Mexican participants and firsthand accounts related by more than one hundred of the Texans give perspectives of this campaign through the eyes of the commanders down to those of the lowliest private soldiers.

Each Texan company that fought at San Jacinto is profiled and at least one member from every company lends firsthand accounts. Some of these men wrote letters during the campaign or shortly thereafter. Others told their stories in complete memoirs or wrote in to the *Texas Almanac* years after the battle to share their experiences. Additional personal items of interest were found in men's service records, pension papers, and audited military claims.

Throughout the campaign and for decades to come, General Houston was often criticized for his perceived unwillingness to immediately take the fight to his enemy. Many among his army grumbled as their leader had them retreat from Gonzales and continue to pull farther away from the approaching Mexican troops. Even when the Texian army appeared to have a numeric advantage over a nearby division of Santa Anna's men, General Houston held his men at bay and had them fall back. From Gonzales to the battlefields of San Jacinto, his men would march a twisting route that would cover roughly 215 total miles.

Houston would write in defense of himself in 1855, "The army was not discounted, but a few weak and ambitious would-be leaders were. But why did not these heroic spirits urge on the General to call a council of war?" None of those eager to see someone lead them into fight sooner requested a council of war along the campaign trail.

Houston held no councils and offered little explanation for his constant retreats. His military experience and knowledge of Indian warfare convinced him that the best chance for victory for his outmanned little army was to lead his enemy toward the East Texas woodlands. There, he had more population to draw on than he did around the central Texas area. The long marches were also used to wear down his enemy's forces and to stretch its supply lines thin.

There is evidence that Sam Houston's decision to continue to fall back was influenced by others. Secretary of State Samuel Carson traveled to Louisiana, arriving April 13, with a plan he and Texas President David Burnet had hatched. They felt that they could draw General Edmond Gaines' U.S. forces into the Texas Revolution by showing that Santa Anna had incited Indian forces to commit depredations. In consequence to a treaty from the Florida Indian Wars, Gaines and the United States military were technically required to fight any Indian aggressors on either side of the border that threatened civilian life. Carson felt that Gaines would "maintain the honor of his country and punish the aggressor," in this case being Santa Anna's army.

Carson therefore sent a letter to General Houston on April 14 advising him to "fall back, if necessary, to the Sabine" to seek help from United States volunteer troops.

In the decades following the Texas Revolution, Sam Houston served as President of the Republic of Texas, as a United States Congressman and as Governor of the State of Texas. Before the public eye constantly, he was a great target for political mudslinging.

Criticized heavily by David Burnet, and former Texas Army officers Mirabeau Lamar and Sidney Sherman, Houston lashed back at them with a letter that was published in the *Central Texian* on September 22, 1855. He commented on all the specific charges that had been laid against him and he offered this stern opinion of how he had handled the San Jacinto campaign.

> The commander-in-chief was the only one of the officers who had ever witnessed an array of hostile armies, or been in a general battle; and it is not probable that he would surrender his opinions to those on whom no responsibility rested. If victorious, the victory would take the name of the place. If it were a defeat it would bear the name of the General, but not that of his subalterns!
>
> The battle was fought at the right time, and the right place, and had he met and vanquished the enemy at any point, on his retreat, the victory would have been indecisive.

By presenting enough sides to each controversy, the reader is left to make the decision as to how much of the attacks on Houston's character are warranted. One such debate has long been whether Houston planned to take the crucial fork in the road leading toward Harrisburg or whether he was coerced by the desires of his men or someone else's orders.

Another controversy of the San Jacinto campaign involves General Santa Anna's relations with a captured indentured servant girl named Emily West at the time that Texian troops were overrunning his campground. There is enough documentation to verify that Miss West was at San Jacinto but enough grey area to still debate on how much she gave for Texas.

Other basic facts of the campaign are in need of clarification. For example, General Sam Houston was shot in the left leg at San Jacinto. William Henry Huddle's famous 1886 depiction of Santa Anna's surrender, which hangs in the Texas Capitol, shows Houston lying with a wounded right ankle. Biographies of Houston and most previous accounts of the battle of San Jacinto have incorrectly listed his wound being in the right leg.

The number of men present during the campaign for Texas ranges widely based upon which source one has referenced. The figures range from as low as 743 to more than 900 Texans present on the battlefield. The estimates given by battle participants in their later years are less likely to be viewed as accurate.

An army adjutant officially counted 374 officers and men gathered at Gonzales on March 13 at the beginning of the San Jacinto campaign. Four days later, on March 17, General Houston gave his number as 420 "effective" men at Burnam's Crossing of the Colorado River. Many hundreds of other men joined and left his army during the next month. By April 21, best counts from all available sources indicate that he had 930 soldiers on the battlefield and another 255 men stationed at Camp Harrisburg.

Houston's 930 men attacked as many as 1,250 Mexican troops on April 21. After skirmishing with Santa Anna's forces on April 20, the Texian army finally forced the long-anticipated main engagement the following day. Per Sam Houston's report, it was only "about eighteen minutes" before his men had overrun Santa Anna's campground and put the Mexican army on the run.

"The hand of providence was with us," wrote Sergeant William C. Swearingen in a letter on April 22. Prior to Houston's battle report being written, Swearingen agreed that the battle was won in "time 18 minutes."

During the Texas Revolution, all of the Texas defenders at the Alamo in San Antonio had perished and their bodies had been burned. More than four hundred men under Colonel James Fannin had been taken prisoner and were later ordered to be executed by Santa Anna. With such atrocities fresh in mind, the Texans did not allow the battle of San Jacinto to end after the first eighteen minutes. The fleeing Mexican soldiers were pursued to the swamps and bayous and were slaughtered until order could be restored to the troops around sundown.

The men of the San Jacinto campaign were united by their common opposition to Santa Anna's failure to follow his own country's treaties. Many Tejanos were loyal to the Texas cause, and at least thirty served in the Texas Army at San Jacinto, including one all-Tejano company under Captain Juan Seguin.

Freed black men also played a role in scouting and fighting during the Texas Revolution. Peter Allen, a free black from Pennsylvania, served as a musician in Colonel James Fannin's command and was among those executed on March 27 outside of the Mission La Bahia.

James Robinson, an indentured servant to Robert Eden Handy, was at the battle of San Jacinto, but remained at the upper encampment at Harrisburg in obedience to orders. At least three blacks are credited with fighting under Sam Houston at San Jacinto: Maxlin "Mack" Smith, veteran scout Hendrick Arnold, and Dick, a free black who served in the army's little music corps.

Numerous veteran accounts of the San Jacinto campaign were published in the 1800s. The earliest complete account of the San Jacinto campaign was written in 1837 by Robert Coleman, one of Houston's staff members. Although it is key because of how early it was written, it must also be taken with a grain of salt. During 1837, Colonel Coleman was being held under arrest by order of the Texas government pending a court martial hearing.

In his anonymously written campaign pamphlet, Coleman takes many deliberate jabs, some apparently exaggerated, at Houston's character. Despite its malice, his manuscript remains important due to the simple fact that it is the very first documentary of the San Jacinto campaign written by a campaign veteran and printed in Texas. The only accounts preceding it into print were Houston's official battle report, various newspaper accounts and some letters of participants. Colonel Coleman's allegations are therefore presented here, along with what others witnessed at the same time. The reader is left to then interpret the true actions of those being critiqued.

This pamphlet was tagged as early as 1840 by the *Telegraph and Texas Register* as "Coleman's Pamphlet." This name was accepted by all, although some consider the pamphlet to have been ghostwritten to some degree by Algernon P. Thompson, John A. Wharton or ex-President David Burnet.

While Coleman's pamphlet was probably exaggerated as a political maneuver, much of its contents was later supported by other campaign veterans. Many of the Texans participating in the campaign, including officers, were critical of their commander-in-chief's leadership. Of Houston's officers, only Henry Millard, Alexander Somervell and Joseph Bennett continually defended their leader in their writings. At least two dozen other officers and key staff members denounced in writing Houston's action in the campaign and the battle of San Jacinto.

Another very early and detailed account is contained in Henry Foote's *Texas and the Texans*, published in 1841. This source is important in that Foote quotes from letters in his possession, written by participants and leaders of the San Jacinto campaign. Another early account of the campaign was written by Captain Jesse Billingsley and published in the September 19, 1857, *Galveston News*.

By 1859, accounts of veterans of San Jacinto began appearing in the *Texas Almanac*, a key early historical source. One of the more detailed of these was that of Dr. Nicholas Labadie, another sharp critic of Houston's. He also wrote enough damaging accusations against another of Houston's officers that the two ended up in an ugly late 1850s lawsuit that was not concluded until after the Civil War.

Other perspectives of the San Jacinto campaign can be found in the memoirs of several veterans. Some of these later memoirs, such as that of William P. Zuber, present certain episodes which the writer had obviously read in other printed accounts of the San Jacinto campaign. Some events Zuber does credit as having heard from others.

All controversies aside, the San Jacinto campaign was concluded with a decisive victory that ultimately provided the Republic of Texas its independence from Mexico. Those who fought on the historic grounds were considered heroes as brave as Davy Crockett and William Barret Travis.

Streets, schools, ships, and even a college have been named after San Jacinto. Hale County, Lamb County and Motley County were each named for a fallen Texan hero who gave his life for independence on the battlefields of San Jacinto.

Texas schoolchildren are now taught that Texas was once a part of Spanish Mexico. With the area around San Jacinto becoming more and more Hispanic demographically each decade, teachers cannot say "we won" at San Jacinto. In fact, many now show how Juan Seguin and other Tejanos played a significant role in the campaign.

All sides agree that San Jacinto was a key turning point for Texas, the battle eventually leading to a transfer of more than 700,000 square miles of territory from Mexico to the United States. The San Jacinto Monument, towering 570 feet above the center of the battlefield, has inscribed on its base the significance of this victory for Texas:

> Measured by its results, San Jacinto was one of the decisive battles of the world. The freedom of Texas from Mexico won here led to annexation and to the Mexican War, resulting in the acquisition by the United States of the states of Texas, New Mexico, Arizona, Nevada, California, Utah, and parts of Colorado, Wyoming, Kansas, and Oklahoma. Almost one-third of the present area of the American nation, nearly a million square miles, changed sovereignty.

The San Jacinto Monument won approval in the 1890s from the state legislature. Construction was under way in 1936, the battle's centennial. The building opened in 1939, billed as the tallest obelisk in the world.

The monument underwent a $10 million facelift in the late 1990s. It is topped by a nine-pointed star, which creates the illusion of a five-pointed Texas Lone Star when viewed from any direction. Also restored as of April 20, 2002, is a 300-acre section of the marsh beyond the Mexican campground. The marsh had largely subsided and became covered with silt over the years. Today, visitors can walk along a 510-foot interpretive boardwalk over a section of this marsh—an area where some of the heaviest fighting occurred after Texans pursued the fleeing Mexican army into the swamps.

Another effort will be to restore the actual battleground to its natural look, including the removal of a large reflecting pool that points toward the battleship *Texas*. On the day of battle, tall native grasses reached the soldiers' knees and helped the Texans pull off their surprise attack, coupled with the late afternoon sun which worked in their favor to help blind their opponents.

The battle is celebrated each year on the grounds of the San Jacinto Monument with reenactments to portray how our Texas independence was earned.

The victory was achieved with very little bloodshed on the part of the Texans but with heavy losses for the Mexican army. Sam Houston could not rely upon superior numbers or heavier firepower in his favor. In the end, his troops managed to catch Santa Anna's army completely off guard using the oldest military tactics around: surprise and, in Houston's own words, "daring intrepidity and courage."

CHAPTER 1

"Never Surrender"

March 3–5, 1836

> I took pride in being the first to strike in defense of the independence, honor, and rights of my nation.
> —*Major General Antonio López de Santa Anna Pérez de Lebrón*

Lieutenant Colonel William Barret Travis was not a fatalist but he was certainly beginning to believe that the fall of his defiant garrison was inevitable.

His men had taken up a defensive position across from the San Antonio River in an abandoned old Spanish mission that was known as the Alamo. This sprawling compound, covering more than three acres, included barracks, gun towers, an old church, a corral and was surrounded by a thick stone wall of about twelve feet in height.

At age twenty-six, Travis found himself in command of the Texian troops in the Alamo. This defiant young man already had a history of fighting the Mexican authority which had long ruled over Texas. Travis had put aside his law practice in San Felipe de Austin to raise a company of volunteers in June 1835. His men captured and disarmed a Mexican garrison which had occupied the coastal town of Anahuac. He continued to serve in the Texas Army during late 1835 and had risen to the rank of lieutenant colonel of cavalry during the first months of the Texas Revolution.

The most significant campaign of the revolution to date had been the struggle for San Antonio de Bexár. The volunteer army of Texas had made a determined assault on the eight-hundred-odd Mexican army troops stationed there under thirty-five-year-old General Martín Perfecto de Cos. More than 550 Texans stormed the city on December 5. By December 10 they had forced General Cos into a surrender. He promised that his people would never again take up arms against the Mexican Constitution of 1824. In return, Cos' men were allowed to withdraw toward Mexico.

Many of the Texas volunteers returned to their homes following the siege of Bexár. Lieutenant Colonel James Clinton Neill, a veteran of the battle of Horseshoe Bend under General Andrew Jackson, was placed in command of the troops remaining in the San Antonio area and the Alamo.

Even as the defeated General Cos was marching toward home in December, President Antonio López de Santa Anna Pérez de Lebrón was organizing his army in Mexico for an offensive thrust back into Texas.

Lieutenant Colonel James Bowie was sent from Goliad on January 17 with orders from General Sam Houston for Neill to abandon San Antonio, blow up the Alamo and move the artillery to Gonzales and Copano. Bowie had arrived on January 19 with about thirty men. Upon arrival, however, Bowie chose not to follow Houston's orders.

As intelligence was slowly gathered that the Mexican army was marching back into Texas toward San Antonio, the men under Neill had begun fortifying their position in the Alamo. Instead of carrying out his orders to destroy the place, Bowie was impressed enough to join the cause. He wrote to the ad interim governor of Texas, Henry Smith, telling him that "we will rather die in these ditches than give it up to the enemy."[1]

During early February 1836, other small groups of men arrived at the Alamo to join Colonels Bowie and Neill. Governor Smith sent twenty-five cavalrymen under a reluctant Lieutenant Colonel Travis to San Antonio. Soon after reporting for duty on February 3, however, Travis was equally empathic to the cause shared by Neill and Bowie.

On February 8, Alamo morale received another boost when legendary frontiersman David Crockett arrived with his Tennessee Mounted Volunteers. Clad in a buckskin shirt, coonskin cap and Indian moccasins, "Davy" had a reputation as a bear hunter and an Indian fighter. He had also served in the Tennessee Legislature and three terms in the U.S. Congress. At the Alamo, forty-nine-year-old Crockett refused to take rank, preferring to fight with the common men.

The volunteers were dejected when Colonel James Neill departed the Alamo on February 11 to handle illness that had struck his family. Neill vowed to return within three weeks and he transferred command of the garrison to Travis. Texas volunteer forces much preferred

Lieutenant Colonel William Barret Travis (1809–1836) was senior commander of the Texian forces gathered in the Alamo during the early days of March. This sketch is rumored to have been drawn in December 1835 by his friend Wyly Martin.
Courtesy of DeGolyer Library, Southern Methodist University, Dallas, Texas.

to elect their own commanders and so they did after Neill departed San Antonio.[2]

In the voting, the regulars voted for Travis but the volunteers voted for Jim Bowie. This thirty-nine-year-old had achieved a reputation along the Mississippi River valley as a frontiersman, land dealer and knife fighter. He had once slain an opponent with a large butcher knife and by the 1830s blacksmiths in the South were turning out so-called "Bowie" knives.

Bowie and Travis put aside their differences and ultimately agreed to serve as co-commanders of the Alamo, with Travis commanding the regulars. Mexican occupation forces began arriving and the siege against the Texas rebels within the Alamo began on February 23, 1836. The joint command of the garrison was short-lived, for by February 24, Jim Bowie was seriously ill with typhoid-pneumonia. He relinquished full command of the Alamo to Lieutenant Colonel Travis.

William Travis immediately put out urgent patriotic appeals to "the people of Texas & all Americans in the world" to come to his aid in defending San Antonio from the Mexican army. Although fired upon by his enemy this day, Travis promised, "I shall never surrender or retreat." He was aware that President Santa Anna was receiving more reinforcements daily, but pledged "Victory or Death."[3]

The fighting grew heavier on February 25 as Mexican soldiers advanced ever closer to the Alamo. Cannon and musket rounds were exchanged. That evening, Travis sent out another appeal, this time to the army's commander-in-chief, Sam Houston. Without aid from his

Modern view of the fabled Alamo in San Antonio. *Photo courtesy of publisher.*

countrymen, Travis wrote that "it will be impossible for us to keep them out much longer." Captain Juan Seguin, commander of the Tejano volunteers fighting for Texas, and his orderly Antonio Cruz were selected to carry this message down the Gonzales road that night.

The only spark of hope for the Alamo defenders had come on March 1, when thirty-two reinforcements from the town of Gonzales arrived. Accompanied by scout John W. Smith and returning defender Captain Albert Martin, Lieutenant George C. Kimbell brought his Gonzales Mounted Ranger Company through the main gate.

Travis expected that at least a sizable detachment of Lieutenant Colonel James Walker Fannin's command at Goliad would certainly come to his aid. He had even sent one of his loyal friends, Second Lieutenant James Butler Bonham, to Goliad to encourage Fannin to hurry it up.

By March 3, Lieutenant Colonel Travis' disappointment in the lack of further reinforcements showed in a letter written to the Independence Convention meeting at Washington-on-the-Brazos. He called for reinforcements and more provisions. "Col. Fannin is said to be on the march to this place with reinforcements, but I fear it is not true."[4]

Confirmation of Fannin's reluctance to immediately march to their aid arrived that very day. Courier James Bonham raced back into the Alamo at 11:00 a.m. on March 3 with the news that Fannin was *not* on his way from Goliad. In his defense, Fannin would explain to the government that he felt defending the fortress at Goliad was equally important.

The Alamo had been under siege ten days already. Major General Santa Anna himself was in town by March 3 and the number of Mexican troops present had risen to more than 2,400.

William Travis took up his pen again and wrote an appeal to the members of the General Convention of Texas at Washington-on-the-Brazos. He needed more ammunition and men. He believed in his cause, feeling that even if sacrificed his men would make the Mexican army pay dearly. "I am determined to perish in the defense of this place, and my bones shall reproach my country for her neglect," Travis wrote to his friend Jesse Grimes.[5]

Travis also promised in this message that he would fire his large cannon three times a day at morning, noon and night as long as he held the Alamo. This firing would be the signal that his men were still alive and in possession of the Alamo.

Around midnight of March 3, Scout John W. Smith saddled up his horse and prepared to carry Lieutenant Colonel Travis' latest appeal. A small party of Texans stirred up a gunfight with Mexican guards as a distraction so that Smith could race unseen from the Alamo gate. He rode hard into the dark night, bearing toward the convention in Washington.

While Travis' men remained secluded in San Antonio's Alamo compound, the provisional government of Texas worked on declaring this Mexican subprovince to be an independent nation. From the Mexican nation of some eight million people, the thirty-thousand-odd Texas colonists sought to remove themselves. Since Stephen Fuller Austin had been given permission in 1821 to bring in the first Anglo-American settlers, Texas had been under Mexican rule. This Mexican state was originally known as Coahuila y Texas. Settlers moved in from the United States, lured by the offer of free land and a chance to make a new start.

In some states, land was scarce enough that only the eldest son would receive inheritance land from his father. Landseekers, frontiersmen, farmers, slave traders, doctors, lawyers, politicians, soldiers of fortune and adventurers alike would come to make Texas their home by 1835. Cries to aid the revolutionary effort had brought the opportunity seekers.

The Mexican commander of the customs house at Anahuac—the principal port of Galveston Bay—helped further spread the seeds of discontent in June 1835. He arrested prominent colonists DeWitt Clinton Harris and Andrew Briscoe for not paying duties. Harris, whose family had founded the town of Harrisburg on Buffalo Bayou, was a merchant in partnership with Briscoe when the two were held. Harris was released but Briscoe was detained.

Harris returned to Harrisburg and helped organize a twenty-man company. The volunteers elected lawyer William Barret Travis as their captain and boarded the sloop *Ohio* with a six-pound cannon. They sailed to Anahuac and forced the Mexican command to surrender the town on June 30.[6]

General Martín Perfecto de Cos sent word, which was intercepted by Texians, that more Mexican troops would be sent to Anahuac to deal with the disturbance. Stephen F. Austin was returned from imprisonment in Mexico during August and he felt that war was inevitable.

His prediction came true in October 1835 when settlers at Gonzales clashed with Mexican forces over a cannon. Within two months, the Volunteer Army of Texas had cornered General Cos' troops in San Antonio de Bexar and assaulted the city. Cos was defeated and forced to retire from Texas. En route home, he met up with reinforcements led by his brother-in-law, who happened to be the president of Mexico— Antonio López de Santa Anna Pérez de Lebrón.

Santa Anna and the Texas Campaign

Santa Anna was born into a middle-class Spanish family in the Gulf Coast state of Vera Cruz in 1794. His military career began at age sixteen when he was a cadet in a Spanish infantry regiment, which was responsible for controlling Indian tribes. During the Mexican Revolution against Spain, he received his first wound in battle.

In 1829, he commanded a party of about two thousand Mexican soldiers in defending Tampico from a raiding party of about three thousand Spaniards. He emerged from the campaign with the title of "The Hero of Tampico."[7]

At five feet ten inches, Santa Anna was relatively tall, with handsome looks and a wide-shouldered build. He amused himself with wearing grandiose uniforms and Napoleonesque hats. His horses wore finely adorned saddles with gold-stamping and eagle-head saddle

Antonio López de Santa Anna Pérez de Lebrón (1794–1876) was elected president of Mexico in 1833. He advanced into Texas in 1836 with an army of more than 6,000 men to overthrow the rebellious settlers.
Oil portrait, courtesy of the San Jacinto Museum of History, Houston.

horns. Said to have a passion for opium and a love for violent gaming such as cockfights and bullfights, Santa Anna was very popular in his early years of command.

In 1833, he ran for president of Mexico as a liberal and won. It was the first of eleven times he would serve as Mexico's president. In 1834, Santa Anna abolished Mexico's Constitution of 1824, modeled after the U.S. Constitution, and declared himself dictator of Mexico.

Mexican Army's Organization
Entering Texas in February 1836

SENIOR COMMAND AND KEY STAFF

Antonio López de Santa Anna	Major General, Commanding
General Vicente Filisola	Senior Commander under Santa Anna
General Martín Perfecto de Cos	Brigadier General
Brigadier General Juan Arago	Major General
Brigadier General Adrián Woll	Quartermaster
Lt. Col. Pedro Ampudia	Commanding General of Artillery

VANGUARD DIVISION (REGULARS)   1,541 MEN
Brigadier General Joaquín Ramírez y Sesma
Lieutenant Colonel Eulogio González

Matamoros Infantry Battalion	Col. José María Romero
Jiménez Infantry Battalion	Col. Mariano Salas
San Luis Potosí Battalion	Col. Juan Morales
Dolores Regiment (cavalry)	Col. Ventura Mora
Artillery	Capt. Mariano Silva

FIRST INFANTRY BRIGADE   1,600 MEN
Brigadier General Antonio Gaona
Colonel Miguel Infanson   Lieutenant Colonel José Enrique de la Peña

Aldama Infantry Battalion	Lt. Col. Gregorio Uruñuela
Toluca Battalion	Col. Francisco Duque *(Killed March 6.)*
Querétaro Battalion	Col. Cayetano Montoya
Sapper Battalion	Col. Augustín Amat
Guanajuato Auxiliaries	Col. Ignacio Pretulia
Presidio Infantry	—
Artillery	Capt. Agustín Terán

SECOND INFANTRY BRIGADE   1,839 MEN
Brigadier General Eugenio Tolsa
Colonel Agustín Peralta

Guerrero Battalion	Col. Manuel Céspedes
Mexico City Battalion	Col. Francisco Quintero
Morelos Battalion	Col. Nicolás Condelle
Three Town Battalion	Col. Agustín Alcerrica
Guadalajara Battalion	Col. Manuel Cañedo
Artillery	Lt. José Miramón
Presidio Cavalry	

CAVALRY BRIGADE   437 MEN
Brigadier General Juan Jose de Andrade
Lieutenant Colonel Antonio Estrada

Tampico Regiment	Col. Francisco G. Pavón
Guanajuato Auxiliaries	Col. Julián Juvera

URREA'S DIVISION   601 MEN
Brigadier General José Urrea

Yucatan Infantry Battalion	—
Cuautla Cavalry Regiment	Col. Rafael de la Vara
Tampico Cavalry Regiment	Capt. José Ramírez
(Plus other actives from various units)	

Source: Vicente Filisola, *Memoirs for the History of the War in Texas*, II:149–52.

Freedom-loving citizens throughout Mexico were alarmed. Those Mexican citizens living in the territory of Texas were especially alarmed, and many of these Tejanos would join the rebellion against Santa Anna in 1835. When Santa Anna took acting command of the Mexican army in 1835, forty-six-year-old Miguel Francisco Barragán was appointed to serve as interim president of Mexico.

During late 1835, Santa Anna successfully defended his regime against Mexican federalists. Immediately after defeating these rebels, he organized his army in December 1835 in San Luis Potosí, north of Mexico City. His brother-in-law, General Cos, had been driven from Texas by the rebellious settlers. In order to further his regime and to set an example, Santa Anna as major general, commanding moved with his powerful army in early 1836 to literally crush all resistance.[8]

In his autobiography, Santa Anna outlined his rationale in personally leading this expedition.[9]

> I, as chief executive of the government, zealous in the fulfillment of my duties to my country, declared that I would maintain the territorial integrity whatever the cost. This would make it necessary to initiate a tedious campaign under a capable leader immediately. With the fires of patriotism in my heart and dominated by a noble ambition to save my country, I took pride in being the first to strike in defense of the independence, honor, and rights of my nation.

From Saltillo, he led more than six thousand Mexican troops toward the Rio Grande River. They endured harsh conditions through the desert areas of their country, suffering from insufficient water supplies and from raiding Indian parties.

Upon reaching the south bank of the Rio Grande on February 13, Santa Anna found that his army was strung out more than 300 miles. Further hardships greeted the Mexican army in the form of a two-day winter storm that assailed them with snow, sleet and gusting cold winds.[10]

It was not until February 23 that the first Mexican infantrymen moved into San Antonio to reoccupy the town. Offered the chance to surrender, Lieutenant Colonel Travis defiantly answered Santa Anna from the Alamo with a blast from his 18-pound cannon. The Mexican gunners responded by pounding the old mission with cannon shots in hopes of weakening its thick stone walls.

Thus began a historic thirteen-day struggle to remove the defiant Texan rebels from the Alamo compound. The Mexicans fortified themselves during the first few days and advanced their positions each day toward the Alamo while the remainder of their troops marched toward Bexar. Texas sharpshooters proved to be particularly deadly for any *soldado* not careful to keep his head down.

During the first days of sparring, El Presidente became bored and found himself taken with a seventeen-year-old San Antonio girl named Mechora Iniega Barrera. Legend has it that Santa Anna had one of his young officers pose as a priest so that he could take young Barrera as his wife in a mock ceremony. This lady was eventually sent back to San Luis Potosí in Santa Anna's private carriage.[11]

On March 5, Santa Anna called all of his senior officers together to analyze the Alamo situation. Many of them felt that the walls were weakening and that a few more days would force the rebels to surrender after their provisions ran out. Santa Anna, however, felt that an all-out assault should be mounted. Colonel Juan N. Almonte and General Joaquin Ramírez y Sesma agreed. The officers who were against the assault chose not to oppose their commander-in-chief's decision.[12]

Knowing well that he would likely take unnecessary casualties in such an assault, Santa Anna decided that his army would make its move against Travis the following day. He felt that the morale boost from such a crushing victory would infuse his troops with an indomitable triumph.

Sam Houston's Staff Departs Washington

When Samuel Houston rode into the dirty little river town of Washington-on-the-Brazos on February 29, news of William Travis and his Alamo defenders was in the air. The Mexican army had begun its attack on San Antonio. Rather than abandon the Alamo, Travis had pledged to "die like a soldier," promising "victory or death."

Having been elected as a delegate from Refugio to the General Convention, Houston now had the opportunity to help the other delegates in Washington make a difference for Texas. In the months prior, he had commanded the Texas Army and had given it up. Using his influence with this Convention, he hoped to soon have his command back.

At forty-two years of age, Sam Houston was already an old veteran of political and military battlefields. Born in Virginia, he had been

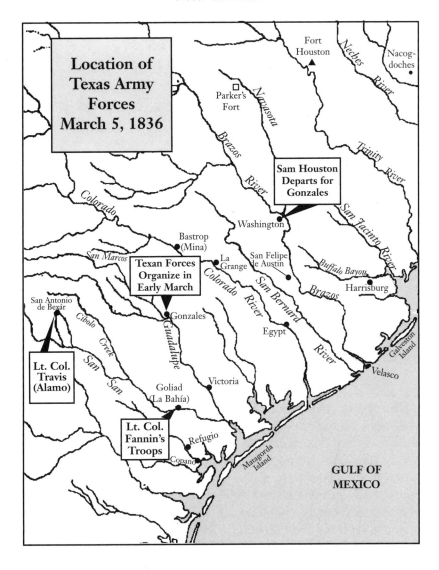

Location of
Texas Army
Forces
March 5, 1836

Sam Houston
Departs for
Gonzales

Texan Forces
Organize in
Early March

Lt. Col.
Travis
(Alamo)

Lt. Col.
Fannin's
Troops

GULF OF
MEXICO

raised by his mother in eastern Tennessee. After working a short time as a store clerk, Houston ran away from home and he lived with the Cherokee Indians until he turned eighteen. When he returned home, he began teaching school.[13]

The United States was fighting the War of 1812 against Great Britain at this time. At age twenty, young Sam enlisted in the army in March 1813. Within the year, he had been promoted to ensign and then to third lieutenant in his infantry division.

Major General Samuel Houston (1793–1863) shown wearing a cowboy duster in this early daguerreotype. A veteran of the early Indian wars under General Andrew Jackson and a former governor of Tennessee, Houston was commander-in-chief of all Texan forces during the San Jacinto campaign.
Texas State Library and Archive Commission.

During the battle of Horseshoe Bend with Creek Indians in March 1814, Houston had been wounded in the thigh by a barbed arrow. Despite his wound, he continued to fight until the Indians were driven back. In the course of the battle, Houston was also shot in the shoulder and in the upper part of his right arm. Such fighting spirit earned him the admiration of Major General Andrew Jackson and the two became lifelong friends.

Houston later served as a Congressman and for two terms as Governor of Tennessee. He married a young Tennessee woman named Eliza Allen, but the two later separated and Houston soon left Tennessee forever. In April 1829, he resigned as governor of Tennessee and went to live with the Cherokee Indians near present Fort Gibson, Oklahoma. He took an Indian woman named Tiana Rogers as his mistress.

He was particularly fond of whiskey and was even given the nickname of "Big Drunk" by the Cherokees. In 1832, Houston was commissioned by President Jackson to go to Texas to make treaties with some of the more hostile Indian tribes. He left Tiana behind and settled in Nacogdoches as a bachelor once again.

He arrived in Texas in December 1832. He towered above the average pioneer at six feet two inches tall and weighed 235 pounds. Aside from his military and political leadership abilities, he was a skilled gunsmith and blacksmith.[14]

Once the Texas Revolution commenced in October 1835, the provisional government met at San Felipe de Austin to organize its efforts. On November 12, Sam Houston was elected commander-in-chief of all Texan forces raised during the war. Major General Houston set up his headquarters at San Felipe to begin organizing his forces. His army was organized to defend the principles of the Constitution of 1824, which Santa Anna had gone against.

The Mexican army temporarily abandoned Texas after losing Bexar in December. The General Council determined that an attack on Matamoros would push the war in the enemy's direction. Governor Smith opposed the Matamoros expedition, but the General Council approved it over Smith's veto. James Fannin and Francis W. "Frank" Johnson were both commissioned separately to lead assaults on Matamoros. Governor Smith ultimately ordered Houston on January 6 to proceed to Goliad and take command of the troops there, and at San Patricio and Refugio, and lead them to Matamoros.[15]

Houston arrived in Goliad on January 15 to find the troops with little provision and unprepared for an expedition. Lieutenant Colonel James Clinton Neill sent a letter for help from the Alamo in San Antonio saying that he expected an attack from Mexico. Houston sent word to Neill to blow up the fortifications of the town of Bexar "and abandon the place." He considered it impossible for Neill to maintain his position with only volunteer troops.[16]

In contrast to Houston's orders, Neill did not abandon the Alamo, blow it up or move its armament on to Goliad and Copano. He was joined on January 18 by James Bowie and James Butler Bonham, who agreed that holding the Alamo at all costs was crucial to the defense of Texas.

General Houston and his Matamoros Expedition troops marched from Goliad to Refugio. Word arrived there on the night of January 20 that Governor Henry Smith had been deposed by the General Council in San Felipe. Fannin had been placed in charge of the Matamoros Expedition, thus effectively stripping Sam Houston of his command.

Houston and trusted staff aide George Washington Hockley set out immediately for Washington-on-the-Brazos. There they reported to ex-Governor Smith, but did not stay long in Washington. Houston moved on back to Nacogdoches to carry out a previous commission from Smith to negotiate a friendship treaty with the frontier Indians. After two weeks of negotiations, he and his aide John Forbes signed a treaty with Chief Bowles' East Texas Cherokees and their associated tribes on February 23, 1836.

Within days, Houston found that he had been elected as a delegate from Refugio and he returned to Washington to join the General Convention. William Fairfax Gray, a lawyer and land agent from Virginia, made note in his diary of the return of Sam Houston on Monday, February 29.[17]

> Houston's arrival has created more sensation than that of any other man. He is evidently the people's man, and seems to take pains to ingratiate himself with everybody. He is much broken in appearance, but has still a fine persona and courtly manners; will be forty-three years old on the 3rd of March—looks older.

By March 1, George C. Childress had penned the Texas Declaration of Independence at Washington and it was adopted with few changes. The vote on adopting this declaration was reportedly delayed one day to honor the forty-third birthday of the ever-popular Sam Houston. Whatever the true reason, the Texas Declaration of Independence was signed on March 3, 1836.

The following day, the Convention formed a committee for organizing the militia. During the morning of March 4, the committee voted to make Houston the superior commander-in-chief over all land forces in Texas, including regular army, volunteers, militia and rangers. Before he would command the army again, he was determined to make sure that his powers were absolute and that he would not again be deposed by the provisional government.[18]

That Sam Houston did not set out immediately on March 4 to aide Travis and Bowie in San Antonio became the subject of one of many complaints that would be lodged against his reign as commander-in-chief. His political opponents would later claim that the major general was stalling, avoiding taking command of the army and aiding the Alamo.

Robert Morris Coleman, a former ranger captain of 1835 and a veteran of the December Bexar siege, was among those who would criticize Sam Houston's actions. Coleman was present at Washington-on-the-Brazos as a constitutional delegate from the municipality of Mina. Deposed from his command of a ranger battalion in early 1837,

Coleman would ghost author a pamphlet on the San Jacinto campaign in which he bitterly attacked Sam Houston's character and his leadership throughout. He was among those who felt that Houston was neglecting his duties by not leaving Washington immediately.

After the delegates of the convention had formally given Houston command of the army on March 4, he stayed another day to settle other issues. Coleman later penned his biased version of General Houston's delayed departure.[19]

> When the Convention removed this frivolous excuse by a resolution declaring him Commander-in-Chief of the Texian Army, he still refused to depart, raising an objection more trivial than the former. In a long speech he advised the House that, during the past winter, a difficulty had arisen between the Council and Gov. Henry Smith, and that Smith had been ordered to answer certain charges that would there be presented against him.
>
> He said he could not leave for the army until this affair was settled, as he wanted to act a part in it. The Convention, however, determined to leave this matter for future investigation. What construction can we put upon this cowardly and procrastinating course of conduct? From the indecency of his actions during his stay, we have a right to infer, that the whiskey of the town of Washington had more charms for him, than the honorable service of his country, in the battle field.

On March 5, General Houston reappointed thirty-nine-year-old Major John Forbes as his volunteer aide de camp. Forbes, who had immigrated from Ireland to the United States in 1817, settled in Cincinnati before ultimately moving to the Nacogdoches area in 1835. There Forbes had been elected First Judge of the Nacogdoches Municipality. During January 1836, Judge Forbes administered the oath of allegiance to army recruits as they passed through Nacogdoches. Among those he swore in were Davy Crockett and his Tennessee volunteers, en route to their destiny at the Alamo.

Forbes was appointed as a volunteer aide to General Houston on February 17 and assisted him in negotiating the peace treaty with the Cherokees that month. He had thereafter accompanied General Houston back to the convention at Washington-on-the-Brazos. Forbes was described by another veteran of the San Jacinto campaign as "a stout-built, middle-sized man, with sandy complexion and sandy whiskers."[20]

On March 5, General Houston and aide-de-camp George Hockley ordered Major Forbes to "proceed forthwith to Velasco," where he would work with Colonel John Austin Wharton in forwarding troops and ammunition to the Texas Army. Forbes and Wharton were to send supplies and munitions no further south than Dimmitt's Landing at the head of Lavaca Bay.

News of the Mexican army reached Washington-on-the-Brazos late on March 5. An armed guard under Captain William Gordon Cooke arrived with two Mexican prisoners from Colonel Fannin's post at Goliad. One was an old priest and the other a former lieutenant of General Cos' army.[21]

Cooke, a twenty-seven-year-old raised in Virginia, had valiantly commanded the New Orleans Greys during the previous December's Bexar siege. When dispatched by Fannin on February 14 with the prisoners, he turned over his company to Captain Samuel Overton Pettus, who was now helping to hold the Alamo with Lieutenant Colonel Travis. Upon his arrival at Washington-on-the-Brazos, land agent William Gray found Captain Cooke to be "very badly off for a wardrobe." Cooke later wrote, "I arrived in Washington on the evening of the fifth of March and left the next day with General Houston, who had been elected Commander in chief by the Convention, for Gonzales." Provided with new clothing, Cooke was promoted to major on General Houston's staff as assistant inspector general of the army.[22]

The delegates at Washington were further made aware of the Alamo's situation when another courier rode into town on the morning of March 6 with what would prove to be Travis' final appeal for help. Nacogdoches delegate Robert Potter moved that the Convention adjourn to rush to his aid. Sam Houston called this motion "madness" and announced that he would ride to the front to organize troops while the Convention remained in session to create a new government.[23]

With his objections behind him and having the full support of the Consultation, General Houston was now ready to ride to join his troops. According to silent critic Robert Coleman, Houston had spent the previous night getting drunk one last time with a group in a Washington grog house.

Houston later stated that he left Washington in company with "two aides-de-camp, one captain and a youth." The proper count was actually *three* aides-de-camp, a captain and a youth: Colonel George Hockley, Major Alexander Horton, Major William Cooke, Captain James Tarlton and Richardson A. Scurry.[24]

Colonel Hockley, thirty-three, was born in Philadelphia and had previously served in Washington, D.C., as a clerk in the War Department. He had become acquainted with Sam Houston while the latter was a member of the House of Representatives in the U.S. Congress from Tennessee. Hockley also later resided in Tennessee while Houston was serving as governor. Houston made Hockley adjutant and inspector general of the army, with Major Cooke as his assistant.

Major Alex Horton, twenty-five, was born in North Carolina and later lived in Louisiana. He had come to Texas without a father, with his widowed mother and eight siblings, who settled in the present San Augustine area in 1824. At this time, he found Texas "so sparsely settled that there was no regulations in any legal form." Young "Sandy" Horton had already fought in the Fredonian Rebellion in Nacogdoches in 1827, served as sheriff of Ayish Bayou District and represented the San Augustine Municipality as its delegate in the 1835 Consultation.[25]

James Tarlton (who chose to drop the "e" from his name's original spelling of Tarleton) was a former Kentucky legislator who had come to Texas in November 1835 as captain of a thirty-six-man company of Kentucky riflemen. Once finding that San Antonio had been taken, his company disbanded. Captain Tarlton, forty-eight, had continued to serve as a courier between General Houston and Colonel Fannin at Goliad.[26]

The "youth" of the group traveling with General Houston from Washington was Richardson "Dick" Scurry, a twenty-four-year-old lawyer recently arrived in Texas from Tennessee.

With his staff organized, Sam Houston made his departure for the army on the afternoon of March 6. As he mounted his trusty horse in front of Mrs. Pamelia Mann's boardinghouse, Houston was invited to have one last drink. He reportedly announced to those present, however, that he would ride to the army completely sober.

Delegate Robert Coleman later wrote that the final drink "he refused, but taking from his pocket a phial filled with hartshorn and salts, and applied it to his nostrils, which seemed to raise his dejected spirits, and he summoned fortitude enough to bid farewell to those around him."[27]

CHAPTER 2

"Anxious for a Fight"

March 5–6

Let us all, with one accord, raise our hands to heaven and swear, "The Texas flag
shall wave triumphant, or we shall sleep in death."
—*Captain Moseley Baker on February 29, 1836, in a speech
before his volunteers assembling at San Felipe de Austin*

A Gathering at Gonzales Begins

José Antonio Menchaca was troubled by the Mexican army's invasion of San Antonio. Although his family was of Spanish descent, he had been born in San Antonio de Bexar in 1800 and had always considered this area his home. In fact, he had already fought in the Texas Revolution on the side of the Texas Army to defend his homeland.

He had been present at the Alamo when word arrived that Santa Anna's army was marching from Matamoros toward San Antonio. Menchaca served with Captain Juan N. Seguin's Tejano company. The commandant of the Alamo, Jim Bowie, held a council of war in February to discuss the arrival of the Mexican army. Bowie and Seguin made a motion to have Tony Menchaca move his family away from San Antonio, "knowing that they would receive no good treatment at Santa Anna's hands."[1]

Menchaca had met Santa Anna years before. Menchaca, a tall man at more than six feet in height, could speak and write English as fluently as he could Spanish.

He left San Antonio and moved his family to Seguin's ranch, where he remained for six days, preparing to journey on for help. He and his family made it to Gonzales on March 5, where they found that Texas soldiers were just beginning to arrive in answer to the pleas for help from the Alamo. In addition, there was a handful of locals.

18

San Antonio-born José Antonio Menchaca (1800–1879) was one of twenty-nine Tejanos who fought for Texas at San Jacinto.
H. A. McArdle Notebooks, Texas State Library and Archives Commission.

The town of Gonzales, located on the Guadalupe River about seventy miles east of San Antonio, was laid out similar to a huge Spanish cross. It contained wide avenues with cobblestoned plazas and roads of hard packed dirt. Due to the cool weather, the trees and grass were still dormant.

Menchaca arrived at the home of land empresario Green DeWitt "and there met up with Gen. Edward Burleson in command of 73 men, who had just arrived there."[2]

Menchaca hoped to move his family on eastward to safety, but the current crisis prevented his leaving DeWitt's.

> I slept there and on the next day [March 6] attempted to pass to the other side of the river with my family, but was prevented by Burleson, who told me that my family might cross but not me, that the men were needed in the army.
>
> There I also met fourteen Mexicans from San Antonio and they united and remained until a company could be formed. The Americans were gradually being strengthened by the addition of from three to fifteen daily.

Captain Billingsley's "Mina Volunteers"

Menchaca refers to Edward Burleson as "General" due to the fact that Burleson had most recently commanded the Texas Army. At the time he arrived at Gonzales on March 5, however, Burleson was merely passing time as a private in the volunteer unit of Captain Jesse Billingsley.

Captain Jesse Billingsley (1810–1880) was a wily frontiersman from Bastrop. His volunteer company was the first new unit to reach Gonzales on March 5. Billingsley would be wounded at the battle of San Jacinto.
Prints and Photographs Collection, Center for American History, University of Texas at Austin, CN Number 03725.

Burleson, a noted frontiersman, would soon enough have another formal command in the Texas Army. The call for support to San Antonio, however, had been strong enough to stir his fighting spirit.

His company had been formed in the Colorado River community of Mina, which later became known as Bastrop. The "Mina Volunteers" had first mustered into service on September 28, 1835, under command of Captain Robert Morris Coleman for the Texas Revolution. Billingsley and his neighbors fought during the Bexar siege under Coleman. After San Antonio had been secured, the company returned home and disbanded on December 17.

A little more than two months later, Bastrop County's residents were banded together again to answer Travis' call to return to San Antonio. The Mina Volunteers were reorganized on February 28 at the home of Edward Burleson and his uncle Joseph Burleson. Their family cabin was located on the Colorado River, about ten miles below present Bastrop. Edward, forty-three, and his twenty-year-old brother Aaron both enlisted as privates, although the elder Burleson had just recently commanded the Texas Army.

The volunteers elected Jesse Billingsley as their captain, Micah Andrews as first lieutenant and James A. Craft second lieutenant. Billingsley, twenty-six, was another able frontiersman already experienced in fighting both Indians and the Mexican army. Soon after the former Tennessean had settled in present Bastrop County in 1835, he had participated in Colonel John Henry Moore's late summer ranger campaign against the Tawakoni Indians. First Lieutenant Andrews, a twenty-seven-year-old from Alabama, had revenge on his mind. His older brother Richard Andrews had been the first Texan casualty of the Texas Revolution when he was mortally wounded at Concepcion on October 28, 1835.

Billingsley later wrote that "I had the honor of leaving Bastrop in command of the 1st company, in order to meet the invader of our country." The people of Bastrop were generous in supplying horses, oxen and provisions for their fighting men.[3]

The majority of his volunteers were men who had long since come to live in the Bastrop area, where the town was founded in 1829. Twenty-five-year-old Leander Calvin Cunningham was probably the first practitioner of law in Bastrop, where he settled in 1833 from Alabama. Wayne Barton and his family had arrived in Texas in 1830, settling forty-five miles farther up the Colorado River than any others at that time. Their remoteness was perilous, as Barton's brother Elisha was killed by Indians in 1833. George Green arrived in Texas in May 1835 and claimed to have literally swam the last mile to shore at Velasco when his boat was wrecked by a storm in the Gulf of Mexico.

Washington Anderson, nineteen, was the son of a Virginia doctor who had commanded a company in the Continental Army during the Revolutionary War. Land surveyor Thomas A. Graves had previously served in a short-lived ranger company organized by Captain Sterling Clack Robertson on January 17 to ward off Indian depredations.

Sixty-odd-year-old Sampson Connell, a veteran of General Andrew Jackson's victory at New Orleans, was the oldest enlistee of

Jesse Billingsley's unit. There was also fifty-nine-year-old Abijah M. Highsmith, who had moved his wife and kids from Missouri to Texas in 1827.

The youngest of Captain Billingsley's company, and now the youngest in the Texas Army, was thirteen-year-old John Holland Jenkins, who had tried without luck to get his mother's permission to join the Texas Army and fight in the revolution. Only after the siege of the Alamo and "with several friends to intercede in my behalf, we finally overcame her scruples and objections." Sarah Northcross, re-married to Methodist minister James Northcross in Bastrop in 1835, had already lost her first husband, Edward Jenkins, to Indians in 1833. Now she reluctantly gave up her oldest boy John, at age thirteen years and four months, to go fight the Mexican army as the youngest Texan soldier enlisted.[4]

"With all of a growing boy's appetite for good beef, bread, and ad-venture, I thought there had never been such fun as serving as a Texas soldier marching against Mexico," wrote Jenkins.

Captain Billingsley's Mina Volunteers marched out of town on March 1, bound first for Gonzales and then on to the Alamo. From Bastrop, Billingsley sent out David Halderman, Thomas McGehee and Martin Walker to scout out west toward San Antonio. These men were ordered to gather intelligence on the enemy's forces before join-ing the balance of the company again at Gonzales.

When Billingsley's men arrived at Gonzales on March 5, they were a welcome sight. They were the first newly organized unit to arrive as reinforcements for the Alamo. Few adult men remained in the area, as the town had sent most of its men to the Alamo the previous week as part of Lieutenant George C. Kimbell's Gonzales Mounted Ranger Company. Joined by a handful of other volunteers en route, Kimbell's men had entered the Alamo on March 1, the last company to make it into the besieged fortress.

Captain Hill's Washington Company

Gonzales was blessed with the arrival of another volunteer com-pany on March 5 that had been similarly raised along the river settle-ments. Eventually commanded by Captain William Warner Hill, this company was originally recruited by Captains Joseph P. Lynch and Philip Haddox Coe.

The core company was recruited by Captain Lynch from pioneers along the Colorado River. Many were enrolled into Lynch's company on March 1 and March 2 at the home of Asa Mitchell in present Washington County.

Muster roll information shows that Lynch's men came from a wide range of trades. Many were farmers trying to live off their newly acquired land, such as twenty-one-year-old James G. Wilkinson Jr., a Kentuckian who joined his family in Texas late in 1835. John S. Stump, thirty-six, was a house joiner. John Graham, at sixty-eight years old one of the oldest volunteers in Gonzales, had come to Texas from North Carolina in 1833 with the Swisher family, and was by trade a cooper. Twenty-seven-year-old Berry Doolittle from New York was a clothier and James Evetts, born in 1806 in Tennessee, was a blacksmith.

En route to Gonzales, Lynch and Hill's volunteer company was joined by another small group under Captain Phil Coe. Military service records show that Coe was enrolling men for army service along the Colorado River settlements. Brothers John and Francis K. Henderson, farmers originally from Illinois, were enlisted by Coe on March 1. The composite group had reached Gonzales on March 5, 1836, as twenty-one-year-old Kentucky native Allen Caruthers is shown in his military service records to have enlisted in Captain Coe's company at Gonzales on that date.[5]

Among Captain Lynch's company was Private John Milton Swisher. His brother Henry became the company's first lieutenant. In late February, John had joined a surveying party under Adolphus Hope for a two or three month expedition on the upper Brazos River. "We were all ready and were intending to start the next day on the expedition," he recalled. An express rider passed through their neighborhood with the famous "victory or death" appeal from Lieutenant Colonel Travis in the Alamo.[6]

Hope, soon to be second lieutenant of Hill's company, led his small party toward Gonzales, joining along the way with others under Lynch and Hill. Private Swisher recalls the lack of organization at Gonzales.

> We arrived at Gonzales on the fifth of March and found about 200 volunteers from the Colorado and the more contiguous points already there. These troops had no commander, save their company officers, and each captain seemed to be acting on his own responsibility. General Edward Burleson, who had been lately in chief command of all troops at Bexar, was drilling in

the ranks as a private soldier in Captain Billingsley's company of Bastrop volunteers. Our force was considered too small to justify a further advance in the direction of the Alamo; so we had nothing to do but remain in camp and await reinforcements, which were daily arriving in small squads.

Captain William Hill would be in command of the company within the week, as Captains Lynch and Coe left their men to recruit more volunteers. Records show that by March 11, Captain Coe had enlisted farmer Uriah Sanders at Asa Mitchell's. Among others, he would also sign David Smith Kornegay on March 15 and John Ingram on March 20, both on the Colorado River.[7]

Hill, twenty-nine, had migrated to the Washington County area of Texas in 1834. The former Kentuckian had then served as first lieutenant of a ranger company during a summer 1835 Indian expedition. When the call went out for volunteers from Washington County, he was among the first to volunteer on March 1 at the home of Asa Mitchell.

Captain Hill was an efficient leader of men. Throughout the San Jacinto campaign, his men would prove to be among the least rebellious of the companies.

Captain Sherman's Kentucky Riflemen

At the other extreme of discipline was the United States volunteer company which arrived at Gonzales on March 6. Captain Sidney Sherman's Kentucky Riflemen had traveled nearly one thousand miles in more than two months to join the freedom fight in Texas.

Sherman's company had been organized on December 18, 1835, in Newport, Kentucky, at a U.S. military post across the river from Cincinnati, Ohio. Thirty-year-old businessman Sherman sold his own cotton-bagging factory to cover costs of uniforming, equipping and supplying fifty men with ammunition, good rifles and food for the trip to Texas to join the war for independence.[8]

The citizens of the Cincinnati area, in fact, were very supportive of the Texas Revolution. A mass meeting presided over by Nicholas Clopper in November on behalf of Texas had, at the suggestion of Robert F. Lytle, decided to raise money for the purchase of arms and ammunition for the Texas colonists in their struggle for freedom from Mexico. Clopper, already a citizen of Texas, had returned to Kentucky to drum up support for the revolution. His son, Andrew M. Clopper, would soon join the cause and fight for Texas.[9]

Robert Lytle, James Allen and many other Cincinnati-area leaders helped the fund-raising campaign for Texas. Among the arms that their drive would eventually fund was a pair of cannon later dubbed the "Twin Sisters." These artillery pieces, which would reach the Texans late in the San Jacinto campaign, would prove invaluable on the battlefield.

The company organized by Sherman dubbed themselves the "Kentucky Riflemen." The men elected Sherman as their captain, William Wood the first lieutenant and Henry S. Stouffer the second lieutenant.

Captain Sherman's company was given a grand send-off with a ball at the mansion of one of the citizens of Cincinnati. During the gala, Sherman was presented a special flag while a fanfare was played by the

Captain Sidney Sherman's Kentucky Riflemen was the only Texian unit to carry a true flag into battle at San Jacinto. This banner was presented to Sherman's men by the women of Newport, Kentucky, in 1835. Today, the much-restored "Liberty or Death" standard hangs in the Senate Chamber of the Texas State Capitol in Austin. *Courtesy of the Texas State Library and Archives Commission.*

orchestra. It was presented by Mrs. Sherman and the ladies of New-port, Kentucky, where Sherman drilled his men during the unit's formation. It was made of white silk with a field of blue printed in the center. Bordered on three sides with a heavy gold fringe, the centerpiece of the flag was a half nude maiden clutching a sword over which a streamer draped bearing the words, "Liberty or Death." Sherman consigned the 6- by 3-foot silk flag to his company's ensign, James Austin Sylvester, a twenty-nine-year-old originally from Baltimore, Maryland.

Sergeant Oliver T. Brown, after arriving and fighting in Texas, wrote of the company's organization and early travels.[10]

> [William] Thompson stated to me that there was a Capt. Sherman of Newport, Kentucky making up a company of volunteers for Texas and he insisted on me going over and joining his company, getting at the rate of twenty dollars per month. I settled off with [Capt.] Scott and got my money and went over to Newport, Kentucky, just opposite Cincinnati, and joined Capt. Sherman's Company of Newport, Kentucky Riflemen and was furnished with a rifle and uniform.
> We had our company organized on the 18th Dec.—started for Texas on the 29th Dec., arrived at Louisville 30th . . . We spent that night and New Year's Morning with Mr. [John] Riddle and Mr. Dickey in great splendor and then we embarked on the *Augusta* for Natchitoches on Red River. We sailed to the mouth of Red River 250 miles above New Orleans and then we sailed up Red River 300 miles to Natchitoches, then took land.

Sherman's men entered Texas in January and proceeded to Nacogdoches, where they caused a stir on February 1 as elections were pending for members to attend the Texas provisional government's upcoming convention. Sherman's newly arrived men were on the side of independence and some spoke on February 1 to the voting crowd.

Captain Sherman was held up sick in Natchitoches, Louisiana, for two weeks and arrived in Nacogdoches only that day at the height of the controversy caused by his men. Colonel William Fairfax Gray, a recent arrivee to Texas, wrote in his diary that: "The company was drawn up with loaded rifles, and the First Lt. Wood swore that the men should vote, or he would riddle the door of the Stone House [Fort], where the election was held, with rifle balls."[11]

The elections proceeded without bloodshed the following day and Captain Sherman's company soon moved out for Washington-on-the-Brazos, the site of the Convention. As news of the Bexar siege reached the Convention site, Captain Sherman's company was gathered up and moved out of Washington on Saturday, February 27. With a baggage wagon to pull through roads muddied by heavy rains, the hundred-mile trek from Washington to Gonzales took a week.

Sherman's "Kentucky Rifles" company arrived in Gonzales on March 6. There, he found only about two hundred other men willing to join the cause to fight for the Alamo.[12]

Captain Seguin's Tejano Volunteers

Although the volunteer companies of Captains Billingsley and Hill were the first new units to reach Gonzales, there was one small company in town that had already been in service at San Antonio. Under Captain Juan Nepomuceno Seguin, this was the only all-Tejano unit present.

Captain Seguin was born in October 1806 in San Antonio. His father, a pure Castillian from the Canaries, was a friend of Moses Austin who had helped secure the original empresario contract for Texas settlement with Spain.[13]

Seguin had previously served as the political chief of the Department of Bexar and had been responsible for sending the only two

Juan Nepomuceno Seguin (1806–1889), born in San Antonio, was captain of the only all-Tejano company which participated in the San Jacinto campaign for Texas. One of the last to leave the Alamo before its fall, Seguin was painted here in the uniform he wore in 1837–1838 as lieutenant colonel of the Texas Cavalry.
Texas State Library and Archives Commission.

Tejano delegates to the Convention. He had commanded an all-Tejano company during the siege of Bexar from December 5–19, 1835. On December 20, he was elected captain of a company of cavalry by the General Council of the provisional government.

Juan Seguin was one of the Alamo messengers who departed on the evening of February 25, in company with his orderly, Antonio Cruz. He was at the Cibolo River, bound for Goliad, when he encountered one of Colonel James Fannin's officers, Captain Francis L. Desauque, who informed him that Fannin was en route to San Antonio and would reach the Cibolo in two days.

Seguin later wrote:[14]

> I therefore determined to wait for him. I sent Fannin, by express, the communication from Travis, informing him at the same time of the critical position of the defenders of the Alamo. Fannin answered me, through Lieutenant [Charles] Finley, that he had advanced as far as "Rancho Nuevo," but, being informed of the movements of General Urrea, he had countermarched to Goliad, to defend that place; adding, that he could not respond to Travis' call, their respective commands being separate.

Seguin managed to organize a group of twenty-five Tejanos, most being men who had departed San Antonio upon the arrival of Santa Anna's men. These men were sympathetic to the Texian cause, as they had been born in Texas territories themselves. Their families had sheltered on the Tejano ranchos outside of San Antonio, where they gathered up their belongings in carts should it be necessary to move quickly as the Mexican army swept in. By February 28, Captain Seguin's men were on the Cibolo River. He had been joined by another dozen men under Dr. John Sutherland, who had left the Alamo as a courier on February 23, and Dr. Horace Arlington Alsbury, whose wife Juana was in the Alamo.[15]

Learning that Colonel Fannin was not marching for Bexar, Seguin then moved his men from the Cibolo to Gonzales to look for more recruits to return to the Alamo. John Sutherland would serve the rest of the revolution as a courier and aide-de-camp to President Burnet. Dr. Alsbury and the other Anglo volunteers accompanied Seguin to Gonzales. Alsbury, for one, would serve as a mounted scout for the Texas Army and would be enrolled shortly in Captain Henry Karnes' company.

All of Juan Seguin's men save one had been born in Texas, most in and around San Antonio. The exception was Private Antonio Cruz, who had departed the Alamo with Seguin on February 25. Cruz had been born in Mexico and settled in the Bexar area in 1835. Shortly before arriving at Gonzales, Private Lucio Enriquez was enrolled to his company on March 4.[16]

Seguin's various accounts of his revolutionary service are somewhat conflicting as to which date he reached Gonzales, but his men were certainly in town by March 6. There, he added the fourteen Tejanos to his company that had not been previously assigned to a company. Salvador Flores became Seguin's first lieutenant and Tony Menchaca, the recent Gonzales arrivee who had been detained by Edward Burleson, was voted the second lieutenant. Menchaca's bilingual skills would come in handy translating for many of the company's non-English-speaking privates.[17]

Baker, McNutt and Rabb's Companies

The little gathering at Gonzales was further strengthened on the morning of March 6 as three new companies of Texas volunteers marched into town. They were commanded by Captains Moseley Baker, Robert McNutt and Thomas Rabb.

All three were organized in late February in response to the calls for aid to the Alamo. At San Felipe, the local neighbors organized themselves and elected Captain Robert McNutt, First Lieutenant Gibson Kuykendall and Second Lieutenant John Burleson as their officers. The service papers of most of Rabb's men show that they commenced service on March 1, 1836, the date the unit was likely mustered into service.

When Travis' dispatch made it to San Felipe at the end of the month, the government immediately ordered those companies which had begun forming to march out for Gonzales as the general rendezvous point.

Among those joining Captain McNutt was twenty-four-year-old Sherwood Young Reams, a former Tennessean who had recently been in the Alamo. He had participated in the "Come and Take It" skirmish on October 2, 1835, which had ignited the Texas Revolution, and in the siege of Bexar in December. Reams was promoted to second lieutenant of Captain Almeron Dickinson's artillery company in the Alamo, but he was discharged on December 28 for health reasons and returned to the Gonzales area to recover.

Many of McNutt's men were from present Washington County. McLin Bracey, thirty-nine, had come to Texas from Mississippi and settled in a present Austin County bend of the Brazos River now known as Raccoon Bend. Frederick Miller Grimes was a veteran militiaman who had fought Karankawas on the Texas coast and had served under Captain Bartlett Sims in an 1833 Waco Indian village battle. Basil Muse Hatfield, another Washington County settler, would in later years operate the steamboat *Washington* up and down the Brazos.

Another of McNutt's new recruits was James Hampton Kuykendall. He later wrote of the march of his company to Gonzales.[18]

> I enrolled myself in Capt. McNutt's company, which took up the line of march on the evening of the first day of March, 1836. On the morning of the 2d March, we formed a junction with Capt. Moseley Baker's company from San Felipe. Both companies were infantry, and each had a baggage wagon. The night of the third of March, we slept at Rocky Creek, twenty miles west of the Colorado, where we were joined by Capt. Thomas Rabb's company, from Egypt, on the Colorado, and on the morning of the 6th we reached Gonzales.

Captain Thomas Rabb's company of "Citizen Soldiers" numbered about forty-five men when he arrived at Gonzales. Rabb, forty-one, was one of Stephen F. Austin's "Old Three Hundred" original settlers who had arrived in the Austin Colony in 1821 from Pennsylvania. He settled near the community of Egypt, located on the Colorado River in present Wharton County. Captain Rabb had previously served as a first lieutenant in the colony militia and had fought at the battle of Mission Concepcion in the Texas Revolution.[19]

Assigned by the General Council of Texas to recruit men for the army, Rabb began gathering his first few men on February 1. Once the call went out from San Antonio in late February, Rabb's company was fully organized in Egypt.

Rabb's second-in-command was Lieutenant William Jones Elliott Heard, who was born near Knoxville, Tennessee, in 1801 and later lived in northern Alabama before coming to Texas in 1830. "I arrived on the Navidad, near Texana, in December, and located my headright league about six miles from Texana, now Jackson County," Heard wrote in 1872 for the *Texas Almanac*. "I lived there two years, and then moved to the Colorado and settled at Egypt, now Wharton County." According to Heard, Rabb's company "arrived at Gonzales on 6th March, 1836."[20]

The third senior officer of the "Citizen Soldiers" was Second Lieutenant William Mosby Eastland. A former Kentuckian who had fought under General William Henry Harrison in the War of 1812, Eastland was also a veteran of Texas campaigns. He had recently helped liberate San Antonio from the Mexicans in December and had previously served as an officer on Colonel Moore's 1835 ranger campaign. Eastland made his home in La Grange in present Fayette County, where he had opened a sawmill and was engaged in the lumber business.

Rabb's company was recruited along the Colorado River from present Fayette, Washington, Wharton and Colorado Counties. Two of his men, James Nelson and Hugh McKenzie, were members of Stephen F. Austin's "Old Three Hundred" settlers.

Although most had been born in North America, some of Rabb's "Citizen Soldiers" were relatively new to the continent. There was John McCrabb, born 1798 in Ireland. Christian Gotthelf Wertnzer had been born in Germany, and William Daniel Durham was from England. Forty-four-year-old Joseph Ehlinger, a cabinetmaker and carpenter by trade, had left his family in France and emigrated to New Orleans. In 1835, he had left Louisiana on horseback, bound for the new opportunities presented in Texas.

The third company of this group arriving in Gonzales was another San Felipe company under Captain Moseley Baker. His past was both brilliant and dark. Born in Norfolk, Virginia, in 1802, Baker moved to Montgomery, Alabama, and was later admitted to the bar. He was described as "a brilliant fellow, a lawyer and an editor." Moving away from law for a while, he founded the *Montgomery Advertiser* and became its first editor. He unfortunately lived beyond his means and in 1832 was accused of defrauding the Bank of Alabama of $21,000. Moseley Baker was arrested and carried to Tuscaloosa in chains, but he escaped and fled to Texas.[21]

Arriving in San Felipe, Baker had "but a single dollar in my pocket." He borrowed ten dollars and he settled down to practice law. "I resolved that I would rouse every energy" to make restitution to the bank and to convince the world that "I was a child of misfortune, not of crime."

Moseley Baker was an advocate of separating Texas from Mexico. He joined the Texas Army and was involved in the Grass Fight near San Antonio. After orders were received to retreat to Goliad, his company returned to San Felipe. When word came of the plight of the Alamo defenders, the town of San Felipe's militiamen hurriedly began organizing a new company on February 29.

To Gail Borden and the ladies of town, Baker thanked them for creating a "banner of independence" for his company to carry. Sporting a cross, stripes and a single star, this flag was promised to "never cease to cherish the pleasing and heartgratifying emotions produced by the recollections of this day." The cross represented the English jack, to show the origin of Anglo-Americans. Thirteen stripes represented that most Texan colonists were originally from the United States, and the single star was for Texas, as Baker wrote, "the only state in Mexico retaining the least spark of the light of liberty." He considered the "whole flag historic," being also tricolored to denote that Texas once belonged to the Mexican confederacy.[22]

In a letter thanking Borden and the ladies, Baker read before his companymen on February 29.[23]

> Fellow citizens, and citizen soldiers, behold the banner of your country. Before you waves the gift of two fair daughters of Texas. Your lot is fortunate and your distinction proud. First in your hands is placed the Texas flag: let you be the last to see it strike the invading foe: let no other feeling ever glow in your bosoms than that expressed in the motto on your banner, "our country's rights or death." He who refuses to surrender, if necessary, his life for its protection, let him be a dastard and a traitor for life, and let him have no inhabitation among the free. Let us all, with one accord, raise our hands to heaven and swear, "The Texas flag shall wave triumphant, or we shall sleep in death."

Captain Baker's company was mustered into service on March 1, 1836. The *Telegraph and Texas Register* of March 5 states:

> On Saturday last, the militia of this place held an election of officers. Moseley Baker, Esq., was elected captain, John P. Borden, first lieutenant, and E. B. Wood, second lieutenant. Captain Baker proceeded forthwith to organize the company, many of whom turned out as volunteers, who, with several gentlemen from the United States, constituted a company of thirty men.

Among his company was John Duncan, a former plantation owner who had operated a line of steamboats on the Alabama River. Second Corporal James Freele was a blacksmith recently arrived from Ireland. Companymates Robert Kleberg and Louis von Roeder had both arrived from Germany in late 1834. Their first taste of Texas was a wet one, as their schooner *Sabine* wrecked itself on sandbars off Galveston Island.[24]

Lieutenant John Pettit Borden and his brother, Private Paschal Pavolo Borden, shared a last name that was becoming well-known in

Texas. Their father, Gail Borden Sr., was one of the three founders of the first and only newspaper being printed in Texas, the *Telegraph and Texas Register*, whose first issue had been printed in San Felipe in October 1835. Their father made the Borden name even more recognizable when he patented the process for making condensed milk. Judge Joseph Baker, another of the three founders of the *Telegraph*, also joined Captain Baker's company at San Felipe.

Finally, Stephen F. Austin's own nephew, eighteen-year-old Moses Austin Bryan enlisted in Baker's company. He had made trips with his uncle into Mexico and during his early years had managed to master the Spanish language, a skill which would prove very valuable to the Texas Army.

On Monday, March 3, Gail Borden Jr., "in the name of two ladies of this jurisdiction, presented Captain Baker and his company with a stand of colors, accompanied with their earnest prayers that, under it, they and their children might be protected from the merciless invaders of their homes."

Gail Borden Jr. and two others were spared army service to attend to putting out the only Texan newspaper in existence. Captain Baker wrote of those remaining in San Felipe.[25]

> A great portion of the San Felipe company volunteered, and have marched. Maj. A. Somervell remained behind to superintend a draft of two-thirds of all who did not volunteer. Three of our printers were drafted; but the committee, deeming it all-important that the press should keep in operation, recommended Maj. Somervell not to call upon the printers, but to return them, subject to the payment of such sum as the authorities shall hereafter designate.

The companies of Baker, Rabb and McNutt comprised roughly 110 volunteers. These units marched into Gonzales on March 6 and nearly doubled the number of effective fighting men present.

"I found one hundred and sixty men here," Moseley Baker wrote on March 8, "which with our force, make about two hundred and seventy, fifty of which started yesterday for the Alamo. Our force now at this place is about 220 men."[26]

Baker's estimate of 160 men in Gonzales ahead of him sounds about right. This would be Captain Sidney Sherman with forty men, Captain Jesse Billingsley with about sixty, Captains Joseph Lynch and Philip Coe with a little over forty collectively and Captain Juan Seguin with a loosely organized group of Tejanos (who may not have been counted).

Captain Baker considered the new assortment of men in Gonzales to be "as brave men as ever shot the rifle, the most of whom had been in the Mexican and Indian fights of the country." Having heard the call to aid the Alamo in its plight, these men were "anxious for a fight."[27]

Baker was chosen by the heads of companies to take charge of the little force now assembled at Gonzales until the arrival of a superior army officer. The companies of Sherman and Billingsley had set up camp on the west bank of the river. The other companies under Baker, Lynch, Coe, Seguin, Rabb, and McNutt encamped in the river bottom, on the east bank of the Guadalupe, about a mile below the town of Gonzales, and less than half a mile below the ferry over the Guadalupe.[28]

Private James Kuykendall of McNutt's company describes the early days of camp at Gonzales as the Texas Army organized.

> On the west side of the river, opposite our encampment, was a bluff, which overlooked our position. This circumstance was noticed by Capt. Baker, who caused a number of trees to be felled and a circuit-shaped breastwork to be erected in front of our camp. The men rather sharply criticized this first essay of Capt. Baker in the art of fortification, and contended that the trees as they stood in the forest afforded much better protection.
>
> Notwithstanding our own perilous situation, and our anxiety about our friends in the Alamo, there was a good deal of life and merriment in our camp. Pork, corn meal, and vegetables were supplied us in abundance by the people of Gonzales, and we had brought a good supply of bacon and sugar and coffee from home. But our days of good cheer were fated to be few.

Captain Bennett's Company Heads Out

Joseph Bennett had been working on pulling a company together for more than a week and was impatient to get to the Alamo. On Sunday, March 6, he had his volunteers rendezvous at San Felipe. The fact that Captain Baker's San Felipe company had departed days before him made Bennett all the more eager to head for San Antonio.

Captain Bennett had seen his Texas in almost constant turmoil since settling in present Montgomery County in 1834. The site he chose for his unit's rendezvous on March 6 was the home of A. D. Kennard. From San Felipe's public stores, Captain Bennett drew muskets for those of his recruits who had none.

One of his most enthusiastic recruits was sixteen-year-old William Physick Zuber, whose parents had not allowed him to join the 1835

San Antonio campaign due to his young age. Captain Bennett convinced Zuber's father to allow him to join the patriotic calling he so desired. To his embarrassment, his parents accompanied him the four miles to Kennard's house for the rendezvous on March 6.[29]

> I saw my mother weeping and going from one to another of our men, talking with them. At first I thought that she was trying to influence them to induce me to stay at home, but, I soon learned that, having despaired of keeping me out of the army, she was begging them to keep me out of danger. They all promised to do so, including Captain Bennett.

Two of Bennett's other young recruits, Thomas Webb and Benjamin Johnson, lacked proper clothing for a military campaign. Several women of San Felipe promised to aid the company if they could delay marching. Captain Bennett agreed to wait three days before leaving. By the time his men departed San Felipe, he had twelve volunteers.

Twenty-seven-year-old Michael R. Goheen had previously served as a ranger captain on Colonel John Moore's 1835 Indian campaign and again during the Bexar siege. John Richardson had served in Captain Eli Hillhouse's original revolutionary ranger company during 1835 and early 1836. James Gillaspie, twenty-one, was born in Virginia and moved to Texas from Tennessee in 1835. Only two-thirds of Bennett's dozen-odd original company had horses. Four men—Zuber, Samuel Millett, Richard H. Chadduck, and William Stephens Kennard—were horseless. Captain Bennett's company moved out, stopping for the night at Henry Fanthorp's inn, located near the intersection of two main roads, en route to Washington-on-the-Brazos.

During the march to Gonzales, several more members joined up who had been part of the company's original organization on March 1. The company reached Washington on March 9 and took quarters in the Lott Hotel, run by John Lott. While in Washington, some of the company members stopped by the Convention hall where the Texas Declaration of Independence was being written.

While in Washington, Bennett's company received additional men who were assigned to him. Some, like Willis Ellis and William Ferrill, were new to Texas and had enlisted in the Volunteer Auxiliary Corps of Texas on January 14 in Nacogdoches. Another new enrollee into Bennett's was James W. Robinson, who was the ex-lieutenant governor of Texas during the 1835–1836 provisional government's tenure. Robinson had been sworn in as acting governor on February 12 and acted as such from Washington-on-the-Brazos until the delegates elected David Burnet as the new President of Texas. He joined with Zoroaster Robinson, an unrelated man who was a temporary resident of New Washington.

Another who joined Joe Bennett was eighteen-year-old Alfonso Steele, who had come to Texas from Hardin County, Kentucky. Prior to joining up, he had found work in Washington grinding corn on a steel mill "to make bread for the men who signed the Declaration of Texas Independence."[30]

Bennett's little company had grown appreciably. "Our company counted twenty-seven men," noted William Zuber. "This was considered a respectable number of men in a company in those crude days."[31]

The ragged collection of companies in Gonzales would certainly appreciate any and all new recruits that were en route to join the cause.

The Alamo's Fall

William Barret Travis' luck ran out when a final all-out assault on the Alamo began at dawn on March 6, 1836. The four Mexican army columns of attack were commanded by General Martín Cos and Colonels Francisco Duque, José María Romero and Juan Morales. According to Colonel Juan Almonte, "the columns were posted at their respective stations, and at half past 5 the attack or assault was made."[32]

According to First Sergeant Francisco Becerra, the Texans fought valiantly. Born in 1810 in the Mexican State of Guanajuato, he had entered the service of the Mexican military in 1828 and had been promoted to sergeant in 1835. In his recollections of the campaign in Texas, he admitted that Santa Anna's forces suffered heavy losses at the Alamo.[33]

> The firing of the besieged was fearfully precise. When a Texas rifle was leveled on a Mexican he was considered as good as dead. All this indicates the dauntless bravery and the cool self-possession of the men who were engaged in a hopeless conflict with an enemy numbering more than twenty to one.

True to his word, Lieutenant Colonel Travis fought to his death. Jim Bonham and Lieutenant Almeron Dickinson were killed at their cannon on the battery at the rear of the church. Davy Crockett's Tennessee Volunteers fought valiantly until being overwhelmed. Jim

Bowie, lying ill on a cot in the low barracks, went down firing from his cot.[34]

Although estimates range widely depending upon the source, it appears that no fewer than 183 Texan defenders died while defending the Alamo.

General Vicente Filisola, second-in-command under Santa Anna, acknowledged that there were "atrocious authorized acts" of killing once the Alamo had been seized. In his opinion, the "bloodshed of our soldiers as well as of our enemies was useless," serving only to show that Bexar had been reconquered by force of arms.[35]

Santa Anna later claimed that, "At the battle's end, the fort was a terrible sight to behold; it would have moved less sensitive men than myself."[36]

At least fourteen people survived the massacre at the Alamo, including one Mexican defender fighting for the Texas side who pleaded that he had been a prisoner of the Texans. The others were largely Mexican women and children. Juana Navarro de Alsbury had married Texan soldier Dr. Horace Arlington Alsbury in January 1836. With her husband away from San Antonio on a scouting mission, Juana had taken refuge in the Alamo with her sister and her sister's infant son when the siege began. Her husband, Dr. Alsbury, soon joined a mounted unit of the Texas Army and would serve throughout the San Jacinto campaign. The only American-born survivors were Susannah Dickinson (wife of an Alamo defender), her daughter Angelina and Colonel Travis' servant Joe.[37]

Joe, a stocky twenty-three-year-old, hid in the Alamo barracks until being taken prisoner by Mexican officers. A Mexican decree of 1829 had emancipated all slaves, although this order had been ignored by some Texas slaveholders. Travis and many other Texans had gotten around the decree by freeing their slaves and instead making them indentured servants for terms of up to ninety-nine years.

After dark, Santa Anna had the bodies of the slain Texans heaped in piles. Colonel Mora's cavalrymen brought in firewood. The wood and the bodies were piled in layers and set ablaze.

He allowed Susannah Dickinson to live, along with her child. He sent her, her young daughter and Colonel Almonte's cook, a freed black named Ben, eastward toward Gonzales on the morning of March 11. Joe, the ex-servant of Travis, managed to slip out of town and joined this trio en route.[38]

Fresh from the horrors of San Antonio, the two men were counting their lucky stars to be alive. For Santa Anna, the grieving widow and her young daughter were a fitting symbol for the rebel Texans who would find them of what could be expected for those who dared to stand up to his Mexican army.

CHAPTER 3

Houston Takes Command

> I found upward of three hundred men in camp, without organization, and who had rallied on the first impulse.
>
> —*General Samuel Houston, Gonzales, March 13, 1836*

Lieutenant Colonel J. C. Neill, commander of the Alamo, was returning to his command the day the garrison fell to Santa Anna's troops. Having been officially excused to attend to sick family, he had departed San Antonio on February 11 and had since been involved in raising funds to support the Volunteer Army of Texas.

Neill headed to the seat of government in San Felipe, where he received on February 28 from Governor Henry Smith "six hundred dollars of public money for the use of the troops at Bejar."[1] By early March, he was en route to San Antonio again.

He reached Gonzales on March 6 and found the assembled companies under Captains Baker, Rabb, McNutt, Billingsley, Lynch, Coe, Sherman and Seguin. From the local merchants, he purchased badly needed supplies for the Alamo garrison, signing his receipts as "col. comdt. of the Post of Bexar." From Stephen Smith, he purchased shoes, boots, shirts, suspenders, a coat and tobacco. He paid Horace Eggleston ninety dollars for medical supplies for the post and purchased 104 pounds of coffee from William Newland.[2]

As the senior officer present in Gonzales, Lieutenant Colonel Neill organized a group of these men to help him take the supplies to the Alamo. As a strong wind announced the arrival of a cold front on March 7, Neill and forty-eight men departed for San Antonio with the supplies. They were oblivious to the fact that they were already too late. Captain Moseley Baker, head of one of the newly arrived companies, wrote on March 8 of the 270-odd men he estimated to be in Gonzales, "fifty of which started on yesterday for the Alamo."[3]

While some of this group helped move the goods, another portion of the men moved ahead as scouts to ascertain Mexican strength. Among those going with Neill was Captain Juan Seguin's Tejano company. Seguin wrote, "I received orders to go to San Antonio with my company and a party of American citizens, carrying, on the horses, provisions for the defenders of the Alamo."[4]

Aside from Seguin's company, the others who headed for the Alamo with Neill were volunteers from the assembled companies. This party consisted of about twenty-eight men with Neill and another twenty-plus volunteers who served as scouts for the army. Lieutenant William H. Smith, a scout who had been given commission in the army in late November, called for those who would go to the aid of Travis and Bowie. Private Connell O'Donnell Kelly was one of those who joined Smith. "I was the only man out of Capt. Moseley Baker's company, along with 25 others, who volunteered to go," he wrote.[5]

The main body of Texas volunteers remained camped at Gonzales, waiting for the other troops that were en route and for their commander-in-chief. James Neill and twenty-seven other men would only get "within eighteen miles of Bexar before being driven back by a superior force."[6]

Although Neill's men turned back, Lieutenant Smith's group of scouts and Captain Seguin's men resolved to move closer to the Alamo and determine its status.

––––––––––

After the departure of James Neill's party, the volunteers gathered in Gonzales were still awaiting the arrival of General Sam Houston. Edward Burleson and Captain Moseley Baker proved to be the more senior leaders present. As the weather turned much colder this day, Baker wrote a letter to the Convention at Washington on March 8, requesting more men and ammunition be sent to hold against the Mexican army.[7]

> Send, as fast as possible, arms and ammunition. Some of my company are without guns, and no possible means of procuring them here. Not a pound of lead except what I brought, which I have distributed. Send these things, and speedily: and be assured, that unless Texas is victorious, I shall never return.

General Sam Houston had only reached Burnam's Crossing on the Colorado River by March 9, three days after departing Washington-on-the-Brazos. Oblivious to what was happening in Gonzales, he sent orders to Edward Burleson to unite with Lieutenant Colonel Neill in Gonzales. Burleson was to aid in forming a battalion, or regiment, according to the number of troops he found in Gonzales.[8]

Burleson, of course, was already in Gonzales, officially only a private in Captain Billingsley's company. Colonel Neill had since departed for San Antonio with his spies and provisions.

Houston's orders were sent by Colonel George Hockley via an express courier who was to find Colonel Neill first and then forward additional orders on to Colonel James Fannin in Goliad. Neill was to recommend a route for Fannin to take from Goliad in reaching a "point of cooperation" for these two commands. Fannin was "to march immediately" with two light pieces of artillery, fifty muskets and ten days provisions, leaving 120 men to protect the post at Goliad.

Aside from writing orders, Houston and his staff spent at least two days at Jesse Burnam's residence on the Colorado. William W. Thompson, in a sworn affidavit of 1840, claimed that "Gen'l Sam Houston was there on his way to the army at Gonzales."[9]

Thompson claimed that Houston lingered, declaring that Travis and Fannin's claims of Mexican forces were "lies" made as "electioneering schemes" to sustain their own popularity. Thompson swore that Houston showed

> no disposition of being in a hurry to the Army, much to the surprise of myself and others; for he remained at Capt. Burnam's all night and all that day, and all night again before he started for Gonzales, and this at a time, when anxiety for the relief of Colo. Travis and his brave comrades, appeared to fill the minds of everybody.

Thompson's affidavit was taken by a State Department official of Mirabeau Lamar and appears to be one of many attempts later made by political opponents to defame Houston.[10] Just days prior, he had predicted the arrival of Santa Anna in Texas. Before leaving Washington, he had sent Major Forbes to gather troops near the coast and to march them inland. The orders he wrote for Burleson, Neill and Fannin on March 9 clearly indicate that he was trying to organize his forces before he pushed on again to join whatever troops he might find mustered at Gonzales.

New volunteer soldiers trickled into Gonzales along with the prevailing cold northerly wind on March 10. Captain Sidney Sherman's Kentucky Riflemen company received new enlistees this day from another United States volunteer company which had recently disbanded.

Captain Carmic W. Vickery had organized a company at Natchez, Mississippi, to join the independence fight in Texas. They sailed into Matagorda Bay on January 10, 1836, and were formally mustered in on February 22. They had served under Captain Vickery until March 3, when Vickery and a number of his men decided to return to Mississippi.

From this company, Joseph Rhodes, Simon Peter Ford, Edward Miles and William Wallace Loughridge are known to have enlisted under Captain Sherman at Gonzales on March 10. At least three others who had previously served under Captain Vickery—Elijah Valentine Dale, William Griffin and Robert F. Howell—also joined Sherman's Kentucky Rifles.

Colonel George Hockley's courier from the Colorado River arrived in Gonzales on March 10, as did a dejected Lieutenant Colonel Neill. The former Alamo commandant had been forced to backtrack with his supplies and twenty-seven other men due to Mexican patrols around San Antonio.

Neill acknowledged receiving General Houston's orders and agreed to forward the additional orders on to Fannin at Goliad. Neill would "give him due time to concentrate his forces with mine at the time and place I shall designate."[11]

The Mexican Army Departs Bexar

Santa Anna set his forces in motion from Bexar on March 11. General Eugenio Tolsa arrived with his infantry brigade to bolster the forces around the newly captured Alamo. The First Infantry Brigade, under Brigadier General Antonio Gaona, would also remain in San Antonio until being dispatched for Nacogdoches on March 24.

Colonel Morales was sent with the Jiménez and San Luis battalions on March 11 for La Bahía, or Goliad. At Goliad, he would report to General Urrea. Morales had a twelve-pound cannon, an eight-pound cannon and one howitzer among his arsenal.[12]

The balance of the army, under General Joaquín Ramírez y Sesma and Colonel Eulogio González, left for San Felipe de Austin on March 11. Sesma's men, numbering about seven hundred, had been in San Antonio for twenty days at the time they marched out. Another of the senior army officers accompanying Sesma, General Vicente Filisola, wrote of the strength of this force:[13]

> Sesma left to move against the town of San Felipe de Austin with one hundred horses and the squadrons from Dolores, Veracruz and Tampico [all under Acting General Ventura Mora], the battalions from Aldama [under Lieutenant Colonel Gregorio Uruñuela], Matamoros [under Colonel José María Romero] and Toluca [under Colonel Francisco Duque], two six-caliber artillery pieces and the necessary equipment and supplies, the march to be made by way of Gonzales, the Guadalupe, Colorado and Brazos Rivers.

General Ramirez y Sesma's troops moved swiftly toward San Felipe. En route, they would pass directly through Gonzales where the Texian volunteers were gathering. Santa Anna would soon have solid information on any more rebels who dared to challenge his dictatorship.

Houston Arrives in Gonzales

Lieutenant Colonel Neill's failure to reach San Antonio with his additional men and supplies was a clear indication of just how grave the situation was for the Alamo defenders.

Captain Joseph Lynch departed Gonzales on March 11 to begin recruiting more men for the Texas independence cause. Muster roll records show that Robert Stevenson was recruited on the Colorado River by Lynch on March 20 in the area where the company was originally formed. Command of the unit passed to First Lieutenant William Hill, who became acting captain on March 11.

The bright spot of the day came in the afternoon when Major General Sam Houston rode into Gonzales with his staff and assumed command of the Texas Army. He arrived around 4:00 p.m. on March 11 with Colonel George Hockley, Major Alex Horton, Dick Scurry, Major William Cooke and Captain James Tarlton. Hockley, Horton and Cooke were thus the initial aides-de-camp of Houston's command staff. Of the other two new arrivals, Tarlton would serve as a private soldier in the company of Captain Moseley Baker and Scurry would eventually become an officer in the Texian army's artillery corps.

Major Alexander Horton (above left) and Major William Gordon Cooke (right) were two of Sam Houston's cabinet members who arrived in Gonzales with him on March 11. Horton (1810–1894) joined Houston's staff at Washington-on-the-Brazos and was later promoted to colonel. Cooke (1808–1847), former captain of the New Orleans Greys company, served as the assistant inspector general during the San Jacinto campaign. *Courtesy Texas State Library and Archives Commission.*

In contrast to the uniforms worn by the officers of the Mexican army, the major general of the Texan army was quite a sight. Houston wore a Cherokee coat, buckskin vest and high heeled boots adorned with silver spurs and three-inch rowels in the pattern of daisies. He wore a broad cap adorned with a feather. Around his waist he wore a belt pistol and a ceremonial sword presented to him by his Cherokee friends.[14]

As commander-in-chief of the army, he was in charge of all soldiers, be it regulars, militia, volunteers or rangers. What he found upon arriving at Gonzales was 300-odd frontiersmen, adventurers, Tejanos, and teenagers. Some had previous battle experience but few had the true military discipline that Houston desired.

"I found upward of three hundred men in camp, without organization, and who had rallied on the first impulse," he wrote.[15] The men were low on rations and had but two functioning cannon at their disposal. A third piece of artillery was in blacksmith John Sowell's shop.

General Houston proceeded to read the new Declaration of Independence and the orders appointing him as major-general of the Texas

Army. Thirteen-year-old Private John Jenkins of Captain Billingsley's Mina Volunteers found General Houston to be "a model of manliness and bravery, and my admiration knew no bounds."[16]

Listening to the general's introductory speech before several hundred other volunteers, Jenkins began to get a sense of what he was in for.

> Calling the men together at DeWitt's tavern in Gonzales, he delivered a short speech setting forth in stirring words the complications of troubles that threatened our Republic, finally closing with a rousing appeal to every Texan to be loyal and true in that hour of need and peril.
>
> Things began to wear a more serious aspect now that I comprehended more fully the situation in all of its bearings, and in the still hours of the night as we lay and listened to the low ominous rumblings of cannons at San Antonio, I felt that we were engaged in no child's play. I now began to take in all of the responsibility, danger and grandeur of a soldier's life.

New intelligence on the Alamo's situation began arriving soon after General Houston's appearance. The first new news came from two Tejanos of Captain Seguin's company who were shown anything other than respect for the intelligence they brought.

The two men were found and escorted back to Gonzales by Texas scouts, arriving there shortly after 4:00 p.m. on March 11. Each man had differing intelligence of the fall of the Alamo. Anselmo Bergara had been at large in the countryside near Bexar for thirteen days prior to the Alamo's fall. Being a Mexican by birth, he claimed to be able to move about freely and witness much of the events around San Antonio. The other Tejano arrivee, Andrew Barcena, stated that Bergara had fled to a nearby ranch at the arrival of the Mexican troops and actually knew only what he had been told.

These two men had entered the Alamo in February with Captain Seguin's company. Seguin wrote of Bergara and Barcena that "I had left for purposes of observation in the vicinity of San Antonio; they brought the intelligence of the fall of the Alamo. Their report was so circumstantial as to preclude any doubts about that disastrous event."[17]

Regardless of how Bergara and Barcena got their information, their stories were disturbing. The Alamo had been overrun, they said. All within the fortress had been killed, including seven who were taken alive. James Bowie was reported to have been in his bed sick during the final assault. Travis, they said, had even committed suicide rather than face the entire Mexican army. The bodies of the Texian defenders were reportedly stacked and burned. Another fifteen hundred Mexican troops were believed to be en route to support the twenty-five hundred at San Antonio.

Much of this information was later claimed to be exaggerated or fabricated. Some felt that the two Tejano messengers may well have been dispatched secretly by Santa Anna to spread word of Bexar's fall.[18]

Sam Houston knew well the danger that such stories could cause until better intelligence could be gathered on the state of affairs in San Antonio. He denounced the two men as "spies" and had them detained to keep them from further alarming the Gonzales citizens and his ragged collection of soldiers.

Citizen E. N. Gray wrote on March 11, "The contradiction of these two men makes me suspect that they are spies sent by Santa Anna; because, why should Bergara fly from Bexar after remaining so many days there undisturbed and enjoying himself?"[19]

Despite his intent to stifle such rumors, more bad news continued to arrive from the scouts. Lieutenant William Smith and other scouts who had left Gonzales on March 7 returned shortly after Bergara and Barcena had been detained. When Lieutenant Colonel Neill's men had been turned back by Mexican patrols, Smith's smaller party had pushed on ahead toward San Antonio. They had spent two nights hiding out in the woods within earshot of the Alamo.

They approached within eight miles, apparently the safest distance they could make. They waited in the area but did not hear any signal guns. Travis had said that he would fire signals three times each day that he was safe.[20]

Private Joseph Lawrence, a member of Captain Hill's unit, had ridden with Erastus Smith and Henry Karnes near the city. "We camped at the Powder House in sight of the city of San Antonio and waited for the signal gun to advance," he recalled.[21]

Captain Seguin's Tejano company was among the men who approached San Antonio to check Travis' condition. "Arrived at the Cibolo [River], and not hearing the signal gun which was to be discharged every fifteen minutes, as long as the place held out, we retraced out steps to convey to the General-in-Chief the sad tidings," Seguin wrote.[22]

Irishman Connell Kelly, who had originally come to Texas with the Mobile Greys in October 1835, had volunteered to go on the scout with Smith.[23]

We saw about one thousand Mexican camp fires, when they, the Mexicans, opened fire on us, and our party being too small, retreated to the Cibolo, under Capt. W[illiam] Smith, where we remained but a short time, and returned to Gonzales, when Gen. Sam Houston had just arrived from Washington, Texas. Our captain informed him that the Alamo had fallen.

The silence of the guns spoke volumes to General Houston. Smith, Seguin and the other scouts were loyal to Texas and their word was as good as gold.

Houston thus issued orders from Gonzales late on March 11 to Colonel James Fannin at Goliad. Fannin was to fall back to Victoria with as much of his artillery as could be moved. He was also to forward one-third of his effective men for Houston's use in the army. "Previous to abandoning Goliad, you will take the necessary measures to blow up that fortress," Houston ordered. Houston had already sent one set of orders on March 9 for Fannin to move out and rendezvous with other Texan forces. Despite these direct orders, Fannin would prove to be as much of an independent-minded soul as the late Jim Bowie and William Travis had been.[24]

In a separate note, Houston related the stories of the two Tejanos who had arrived from San Antonio. He concluded with, "I have but little doubt that the Alamo has fallen."

CHAPTER 4

"Flying in Terror and Agony"

March 12–19

No tongue can express the sufferings those fleeing families were called upon to endure.

—Captain David Kokernot, about the Runaway Scrape

The day after his arrival in Gonzales, Sam Houston took steps to organize his assembly of volunteer troops into a true military regiment. He named Edward Burleson the colonel commanding the First Regiment of Infantry on March 12. Burleson had commanded the army earlier in the revolution and was a well-respected leader of frontiersmen in Texas.

Sidney Sherman, commander of the rowdy Kentucky Rifles company, was promoted to lieutenant colonel of the First Regiment and Alexander Somervell was named major. Somervell, who had assisted with the recruiting at San Felipe, was a thirty-nine-year-old merchant by trade. Born in Maryland, he had arrived in Texas in 1833 and gone into the mercantile business at San Felipe with James F. Perry, a brother-in-law to Stephen F. Austin.

The eight companies present at Gonzales were originally enrolled under Colonel Burleson's First Regiment. As more units joined the army later in the campaign, some would eventually be reassigned. Lieutenant Colonel Sherman's former company, the earliest to organize, was designated as Company A. Lieutenant William Heard, second-in-command of Captain Rabb's company, wrote in 1872 that his "Citizen Soldiers" were originally "Company C, in Col. Burleson's regiment."[1]

The remainder of the original First Regiment was filled out by the companies under Captains William Hill, Juan Seguin, Jesse Billingsley,

48

Moseley Baker, Robert McNutt and Robert James Calder. The latter company under Captain Calder was actually organized on March 12.

Born in 1810 in Baltimore, Calder lost his father at a young age and had been raised by his mother and grandfather. He came to Texas with his family in 1832 and settled in present Brazoria County. During the battle of Concepcion, he had served as second lieutenant of Captain John York's company. Calder reenlisted in the army on March 1 in answer to the need to defend San Antonio.

He arrived at Gonzales on March 6, but he and many of the other straggling groups of volunteers were not formally organized into a company until March 12. Calder was elected captain by his two dozen new companymates, many of whom resided in present Brazoria, Fort Bend and Matagorda Counties.

Among Calder's Brazoria recruits was young John W. Hassell. He had joined the revolutionary effort to contest Santa Anna's army, which he felt was under orders "to exterminate every American citizen in the limits of Texas." When he joined the Texas volunteers at the Guadalupe River, he found that there were "about four hundred men in the field to contend against" thousands of enemy soldiers. Although outnumbered, Hassell was nonetheless ready for action, armed with a large holster pistol and and a trusty musket he affectionately called "old Betsy."[2]

Robert Calder's men were reckless seekers of independence. Kentucky native Andrew Granville Mills had participated in the battle of Velasco, a preliminary to the Texas Revolution, in June 1832. Irishmen Walter Lambert, thirty-four, and Thomas O'Connor, seventeen, and Pennsylvania native Charles Malone had been among the Goliad defenders who had signed a declaration of independence from Mexico on December 20, 1835.

Other men would continue to be assigned to Captain Calder throughout the San Jacinto campaign. John Plunkett, a twenty-six-year-old from Ireland, would join Calder at the Colorado River after his family had fled by boat for the United States.

Colonel Sherman's old Kentucky Rifles company elected First Lieutenant William Wood as its new captain on March 13, the day after Sherman's promotion. Wood, of course, had temporarily commanded Sherman's men during their journey to Texas when Sherman became ill. Joseph Rhodes became the new first lieutenant, who had only joined the company on March 10 from Captain Vickery's disbanded unit. Lieutenant Henry Stouffer, the Kentucky Riflemen's next most senior officer, had been selected to serve as adjutant to General Houston.

It is important to note that no cavalry companies were as yet designated. However, all of the infantry companies generally included cavalry. There were a few companies of pure infantrymen who did not have horses. One veteran recalled that during the San Jacinto campaign there were

> twenty-odd companies of volunteer infantry, with from half to three-fourths of each company mounted. All the volunteer infantry mustered and fought on foot, but, when marching, the mounted men rode by companies, like the cavalry, and the footmen walked by companies, infantry style.[3]

Houston sent orders late on March 12 to Captain Philip Dimmitt in Victoria on the Guadalupe River to join his command in Gonzales. Any companies in the area "whose services are not indispensible to the present emergencies of that section of the frontier" were to also report to Gonzales.[4] Dimmitt and his men would depart several days later. Upon their arrival in the Gonzales area, they would find that Houston's army was on the move. Dimmitt would then have his hands full dodging Mexican troops.

More volunteers continued to arrive in Gonzales each day. Captain David Kokernot, for example, arrived on March 12 in command of a small eight-man squad of mounted volunteers. Kokernot, thirty-one, had been born in Amsterdam, Holland, and came to the United States with his father at age twelve. During his youth, he had served as second mate aboard several sailing ships and had many grand adventures to speak of. After eventually settling in Texas, he became engaged in the Texian independence cause and was named second lieutenant of infantry on November 28, 1835. He thereafter had fought during the Bexar siege in December. "On the 8th [March], greatly to my surprise," wrote Kokernot, "I received a captain's commission in the regular army of the Republic of Texas from Gen. Sam Houston, commander-in-chief of the army."[5]

He immediately rounded up a "squad of brave comrades" and they rode from Lynchburg on March 8. Ironically, those of this squad that remained with the San Jacinto campaign would eventually find themselves back at Lynchburg for a fateful rendezvous. Captain Kokernot's men were Andrew Robison, David Johnson, James H. Spillman, Milton B. Atkinson, John Dorsett, Thomas W. Smith and James

Summary of General Houston's Forces at Gonzales
March 12, 1836

Company	Approx. No. of Men*	Notes
Capt. Jesse Billingsley	60	Arrived March 5 from Bastrop area.
Capt. William W. Hill	40	Arrived Gonzales March 5. Including men of smaller companies organized by Captains Philip Coe and Joseph Lynch.
Capt. Sidney Sherman[1]	52	Arrived March 6 from Kentucky.
Capt. Moseley Baker	110	Arrived March 6 in Gonzales.
Capt. Robert McNutt[2]	}	Arrived March 6 in Gonzales.
Capt. Thomas J. Rabb[3]		Arrived March 6 in Gonzales.
Capt. Juan N. Seguin	48	Organized all-Tejano company early days of March in Gonzales.
Capt. Robert J. Calder	27	Organized March 12 at Gonzales.
Scouts	12	Deaf Smith appointed recruiter of scouts on March 13; Captain William H. Smith assumes command of first spy company on March 16.
Unorganized	_25_	Capt. Patton's organized March 13.
	374 plus command staff	

General Sam Houston's command staff: Col. George Hockley, Lt. Col. James Neill, Major William Cooke, Major Alexander Horton, Lt. Henry Stouffer (adjutant), Col. Edward Burleson, Lt. Col. Sidney Sherman, and Major Alexander Somervell.

Note: Capt. David Kokernot's eight-man unit was merged with other companies.

[1]Later commanded by Captain William Wood.
[2]Later commanded by Captain Gibson Kuykendall.
[3]Later commanded by Captain William Jones Elliott Heard.
*Estimated numbers. Recruits alternated between companies and departed the service prior to the battle of San Jacinto.

Ferguson. "After four days' hard riding, we arrived in the town of Gonzales and were kindly received by the commander-in-chief," related Kokernot.

General Houston also moved the Texas camp two or three hundred yards away from the Guadalupe River to the edge of a prairie, where the men's tents were pitched in two parallel rows. The day passed without any further intelligence on the Alamo.

Captain Patton's Company Organized

Major General Houston, noting that the number of soldiers in Gonzales was approaching four hundred, ordered the men to prepare for organization at 10:00 a.m. on March 13.

For the first time since Houston's arrival, the Texas troops were counted. Lieutenant Colonel James Neill and Lieutenant Henry S. Stouffer, acting adjutant to General Houston, made a report of the total troops available at Gonzales on March 13:

Officers:		*Total:*
Captains	8	
First Lieutenants	8	
Second Lieutenants	5	21
Enlisted:		
Quartermaster Sergeant	1	
Sergeants	25	
Corporals	13	
Musicians	1	[Luke Bust, Comp. A, fifer]
Privates	313	353
Aggregate:		374

Twenty-five of the above as yet unorganized.[6]

At the time of Neill and Stouffer's mustering, there were eight companies under Houston's direction. By afternoon on March 13, he had created a ninth out of the men not formally assigned, giving command to Captain William Hester Patton. This twenty-eight-year-old Kentucky native had organized volunteers two weeks prior in Columbia in present Brazoria County and the group of men dubbed themselves the "Columbia Company." Patton's brother-in-law David Murphree was elected first lieutenant. Although Captain Patton had enlisted in the Texas Army on January 14, he was not promoted to captain of the Columbia Company until March 13.[7]

Patton had recruited men into his volunteer unit as early as March 1. Among the first enlistees were Tennessee-born brothers Claiborne, Pendleton and Elbridge Gerry Rector. Elbridge later related the early days of Patton's company in a personal sketch.[8]

> I was in Brazoria County at the breaking out of the war with Mexico. On the reception of the news that Santa Anna had entered San Antonio, I with others started in that direction. This news we received through the Travis let-

ter, who was at the Alamo. I was on the Guadalupe River at Gonzales when
General Sam Houston arrived.

The Columbia Company was small when enrolled into the army
on March 13, but would grow to well over sixty men as others were
enrolled in the ensuing weeks. Among the company's seasoned veterans were John Chenoweth, James Hayr, David Murphree, Sidney
Phillips and John Pickering, all of whom had fought in the December
Bexar siege.

Chenoweth had been promoted to captain during the Bexar siege
when Captain John W. Peacock fell mortally wounded during the battle. During early 1836, he continued to serve the army recruiting
troops and manning the coastal military post at Copano until receiving orders to join the main army, where he arrived with other enlistees
at Gonzales during March.

Most of Patton's company were already old-timers in Texas. There
was lawyer William Houston Jack, a former Alabama legislator and
University of Georgia graduate who had emigrated to San Felipe de
Austin in 1830. There was twenty-five-year-old Lewis Chiles, or-
phaned at an early age, who had left his other relatives behind and
came to Texas in 1833 to pursue work as a surveyor. Brothers Edmund
Calloway, Richard Brownfield and Emory Holman Darst had come to
Texas with their family in 1827, settling in present Fort Bend County.
Another man to later join Patton's company was Hinton Curtis, one of
the "Old Three Hundred" of Austin's colonists, who had received ti-
tle to a league of land in 1824 in present Matagorda County. Edward
Gallaher, born in Belfast, Ireland, had run away from home at age
fourteen and came to the United States, applying for land that year in
Austin's Second Colony.

Another colorful veteran of Captain Patton's company was former Alamo courier John Smith. Officer David Murphree later
stated in a deposition that Smith operated from the San Antonio
area with other couriers between San Antonio, Goliad and Gonzales. Smith accompanied one party from Gonzales "to relieve the
Alamo" and was "prevented from returning to Goliad and joining
his company." Smith then made his way back to Gonzales, where he
joined Captain Patton's company and was elected orderly sergeant
on March 20.[9]

William Patton himself had been in the Alamo as recently as February 5. He had commanded a small group of men during the Bexar

siege and had operated from San Antonio ever since. Captain Patton left the Alamo, apparently as a courier and likely in company with John Smith, sometime shortly before the arrival of Santa Anna's forces.[10]

Houston had sent out three of his best scouts on the morning of March 13 to gather intelligence on San Antonio. They were Erastus "Deaf" Smith, Henry Karnes and Robert Eden Handy.

Houston recognized these three as superb scouts. He held an enormous respect for the abilities of Erastus Smith, who at forty-nine was six years older than Houston. Although his hearing was failing him, Smith's other senses had sharpened dramatically. He could reportedly detect the presence of man or animal before others could see or hear one. Known as "Deaf" Smith to most everyone, he was confident and yet sensitive. Some of his contemporaries called him "Deef." Houston was one of the few who never called him "Deaf," but instead only "Smith" or "the wonderful Mr. E."[11]

Erastus had settled near San Antonio and married a woman of Mexican descent in 1822. Despite a long loyalty to those of Mexican descent, Smith was quick to enlist in the army of Stephen F. Austin when the revolution commenced. He participated in the battle of Concepcion and was wounded on December 5 while on top of the Veramendi House during the Bexar siege.

Even Henry Karnes respected the experience and abilities of Smith as a spy and scout. On March 13, Houston placed Smith in charge of recruiting for the cavalry, but when cavalry companies were properly organized, it would be Karnes and William Smith who would actually command them. Deaf Smith was much more valuable in the field leading a patrol than in commanding a large unit.

Karnes, twenty-four, was a short, heavyset man with bright red hair who had received little formal education while growing up in Tennessee. As a boy, he traveled across Arkansas and Texas with his father, who trapped fur-bearing animals for a living. Described by his friends as modest and generous and one not prone to cursing, Henry Karnes had also shown his bravery during the Bexar siege in securing advanced positions under fire.

Robert Handy, a twenty-nine-year-old lawyer from Philadelphia, soon became an esteemed aide-de-camp to General Houston. This solid horseman was also known as "the handsomest man in the Texas Army."[12]

Captain Henry Wax Karnes (1812–1840), a woodsman born in Tennessee, became captain of one of the two scout and cavalry units attached to the Texas Army during the San Jacinto campaign. He and two other scouts discovered the Alamo survivors en route to Gonzales on March 13, 1836.
Karnes sketch by early Texas painter Henry Arthur McArdle, courtesy of Texas State Library and Archives Commission.

Smith, Karnes and Handy were allowed to select the best horses in camp on the morning of March 13. Smith promised that they would make the trip to Bexar, entering the city if necessary, and be back in three days. The trio rode westward at high speed, but only made about twenty miles from Gonzales before encountering people on the road. They discovered Susannah Dickinson and her small party of Alamo survivors. They found the woman riding on horseback with her baby Angelina in her arms. She was accompanied by Colonel Almonte's servant Ben riding on a horse beside her and Travis' former servant Joe on foot.

Relieved that approaching riders were friendly, Susannah Dickinson related the news of the Alamo's fall. She also handed the scouts dispatches from Colonel Almonte. Henry Karnes was elected to race back to Gonzales and spread the news. Smith and Handy remained to ride back at a slower pace with the four Alamo survivors, Smith taking his turn at carrying young Angelina Dickinson for some time.

Karnes reached Gonzales between 8:00 and 9:00 p.m. and immediately started the panic. Smith, Handy and the Alamo survivors arrived at a slower pace after 11:00 p.m. Their arrival was visual testimony to the word already given by Karnes hours before. Fear immediately swept over the Gonzales townspeople and many among the army.

When the widow Dickinson reached Gonzales, wives of Lieutenant Kimbell's rangers quizzed her on their husbands' fates. By the time she finished describing the thoroughness of the execution, the women understood the painful truth that none of their men had survived.

Scout Robert Handy later wrote that, "Not a sound was heard save the wild shrieks of women and heart-rendering screams of their fatherless children." Handy found that both public and private grief was heavy and "it sunk deep into the heart of the rudest soldier."[13]

The wives of the men of the Gonzales Mounted Ranger company were grief-stricken at the realization that their husbands and sons were all gone. Young John Jenkins of Captain Billingsley's company recalled their pain.[14]

> Many of the citizens of Gonzales perished in this wholesale slaughter of Texans, and I remembered most distinctly the shrieks of despair with which the soldiers' wives received news of the death of their husbands. The piercing wails of woe that reached our camps from these bereaved women thrilled men and filled me with feelings I cannot express, nor ever forget. I now could understand that there is woe in warfare, as well as glory and labor.

Private John Swisher of Captain Hill's company found the news like a blow to the heart. "There was not a soul left among the citizens of Gonzales who had not lost a father, husband, brother or son in that terrible massacre." The arrival of the news brought a "mad agony" to the new widows of town. The soldiers immediately began a hasty gathering of their items in order to retreat. "The terrible massacre had, for a time, struck terror to every heart," wrote Swisher.[15]

General Houston was writing a letter to his friend, Colonel Henry Raguet in Nacogdoches when the news arrived. He hurriedly finished the letter, adding, "Tell the Red Landers to awaken and aid in the struggle!" The area of East Texas around Nacogdoches and San Augustine was referred to as the Red Lands because of the soil color.[16]

Houston dispatched couriers in all directions to spread the word of the Alamo's fall and his intent to pull the people back from the area. He needed to organize and concentrate his scattered forces, but it appeared for the moment that the Texas Army was best not caught in Gonzales.

The retreat did not begin immediately. The decision to retreat was being entertained soon after Karnes' arrival with Susannah Dickinson. According to Houston, twenty-five men deserted shortly after the scout's arrival. He called for their arrest and return, although he knew he was powerless to stop the terror these men would put into the citizens.

After the arrival of Smith, Dickinson and the Alamo survivors after 11:00, the decision came swiftly. Major Alexander Horton later wrote that after the arrival of the Alamo survivors, a council of war was held. During this meeting, Horton says

> it was decided that the troops must fall back at once. Orders was given for the women and children to retreat as fast as possible, assuring them that troops would cover their retreat and defend them as long as a man was left alive. The retreat was commenced about midnight, the troops following them.[17]

Houston wrote to James Collinsworth, head of the military committee at the Convention at Washington-on-the-Brazos, informing him of a change in plans. He had hoped to join Colonel Fannin's seven-hundred men to march to the Alamo. Fannin had taken up marching toward the Alamo to join Houston but had been turned back by "the breaking down of a wagon." Houston was further frustrated that Fannin had since indicated in letters that he would "march upon San Patricio, and also the occupation of Copano. So that I am at a loss to know where my express will find him."[18]

The news of the fall of the Alamo compelled Houston to change his plans, as he explained to the military committee. "The force under my command here was such as to preclude the idea of my meeting the enemy—supposing their force not to exceed the lowest estimate which has ever been made of it."

With but a few hundred men, some even lacking weapons, Houston thus chose to withdraw eastward to a point where he could gather proper reinforcements. While often criticized by his political opponents, he can hardly be faulted for not making a suicidal stand at Gonzales at this time. Santa Anna's troops vastly outnumbered his meager gathering. If he could compel Colonel Fannin to rendezvous with his troops, then his men would be better suited to challenge the Mexican army.

Gonzales Abandoned

Houston was still momentarily detained by the absence of two men of Captain Juan Seguin's company who had been sent by him to his rancho. They had not returned on the night of March 12 as expected, leaving Houston to deduce that "they have been taken by the enemy, or deserted."

Houston had learned that day that another company of roughly one hundred men from the Brazos area under Captain John Bird would join him by the following day. Putting Susannah Dickinson and her daughter under escort of Deaf Smith, Houston sent them on the road east to Nacogdoches.[19]

The citizens of Gonzales furiously packed up what they could carry away, fearful that Santa Anna's army might sweep into their town next at any moment. Rumor had it that two-thousand-plus Mexican soldiers would be momentarily marching into town. The ensuing rush of citizens fleeing eastward ahead of the slowly progressing Mexican army was a mass chaos that became known in Texas history as the "Runaway Scrape."

Houston wrote that "before 12, we were on the march in good order, leaving behind a number of spies."[20]

The retreat of the Texas Army was so speedy, in fact, that some of the spies did not get the word until after Gonzales had been evacuated. Private John H. Sharp was among those on patrol who was left behind. Fortunately, as he recalled, "Handy and Captain Karnes came back, in an hour or two, to relieve us."[21]

General Houston reportedly gave most of the $300 he carried with him to the distraught widows of the Alamo defenders. He also allowed three of his four supply wagons to be donated to the desperate citizens for use in hauling their belongings toward the Sabine River. Without these wagons, Houston was unable to transport his heavy artillery. The Texas Army's artillery, two brass 24-pounders, were thus thrown into the Guadalupe River to prevent the enemy from taking possession of them. One lone ammunition wagon was maintained, which was pulled by four oxen as the men began their retreat.

Without the other three wagons, it was also impossible to quickly haul all of the bulky camp gear and tents. If it could not be moved quickly, it should at least *not* provide shelter to the Mexican troops. In addition to the picket guard, at least several families were left in the rear during the initial retreat.[22]

Private James Kuykendall relates how the army gave up its baggage wagons and had to burn its own supplies.[23]

> The teams, which were grazing in the prairie, were yet to be found, and night had already set in. In the meantime, orders were issued to the army to prepare as fast as possible to retreat. As most of the companies (all infantry) had been deprived of the means of transportation, all our baggage and provisions, except what we were able to pack ourselves, were thrown into our

camp-fires. Tents, clothing, coffee, meal, and bacon were alike consigned to the devouring element. Tall spires of flame shot up in every direction, illuminating prairie and woodland.

Captain Jesse Billingsley protested to General Houston about retreating and being forced to leave many provisions behind. "General Houston came to me in person, and assured me that we would move only two miles or so, to a place more convenient for fighting, should an engagement ensue," Billingsley wrote.[24]

The troops moved past Gonzales, even as its citizens were hurriedly grabbing the last of their belongings. Some had fled ahead of the army with pack horses. Those without wagons or horses were forced to retreat on foot with little or nothing at all.

The night was very dark, although not particularly cold for a March evening. About a mile east of town, the trail moved into a post oak forest and the ground became increasingly sandy.[25]

Houston decided that Gonzales should not be left for the Mexican army's benefit. He ordered some of his scouts to stay behind and burn it. John Sharp, acting as a scout with Henry Karnes' group of spies, relates the burning of Gonzales.[26]

> Captain Karnes then told us that the orders were to burn the Town, and that not a roof large enough to shelter a Mexican's head was to be left, with everything else that could be of any service to the enemy. We divided ourselves into two parties, one party to commence at one end of the Town, the other at the other end, and meet.
>
> There were some four or five in each party, and we made rapid work of it. The houses were principally framed, covered with thin boards, split from the oak, similar to barrel staves. In the course of a few minutes the flames began their work of destruction, and by dawn every house was burning, or had crumbled to ashes.
>
> 'Twas a scene, the like of which I never before or since, have witnessed. I entered several houses, and found the beds yet warm, on which the inhabitants had, but a short time before, laid down, full of confidence and hope, and from which they had been awakened by the wild Tocsin of alarm and had fled, leaving all they had been for years collecting.

Horace Eggleston watched sadly as his home and storehouse went up in flames on the night of March 13. He had just received three thousand dollars worth of merchandise several days prior. His herd of seventeen cattle was also lost in the melee. Without a home, livestock or his business, Eggleston fell in with the army and served throughout the campaign.[27]

There was no disputing the fact that the retreat was hasty and included some chaos. All accounts seem to agree on this. Take the account of Lieutenant William Heard, second-in-command of Captain Rabb's men. Heard's account, cowritten by companymate Eli Mercer, was published in the 1860 *Texas Almanac.*

> On the night of the 13th, about the time the men were preparing their night's repast, Gen. Houston came down and ordered the horses to be got up, and the fires put out; after which, such a scramble and confusion commenced as I had never witnessed. About ten o'clock at night we were ordered to move, by whom I do not recollect; but I remember that Gen. Houston was in the front ranks.
>
> As to guards, we had none; there was no order or regularity in the retreat from there to Peach Creek, 10 miles east. The town of Gonzales was burnt; by whose order I do not know, but believe it was by Gen. Houston's, for the reason that it was generally talked and believed so to be in camp. Captain Byrd Lockhart, who arrived in Gonzales on the morning of the 14th, when it was on fire, told me that the men who were setting fire to the houses said they were left there by Gen. Houston to burn the town and gather up the horses.
>
> Some of the women and children had started before we did; some started with us, and we left others, crying and screaming in the town. Some we passed on the road that night between Gonzales and Peach Creek.

Captain Juan Seguin's Tejano company fell in as the rear guard for the retreating army. A portion of his company under Lieutenant Salvador Flores was ordered to help guard the fleeing families. Flores and his men would not rejoin Seguin during the San Jacinto campaign. Seguin wrote that Houston sent "Salvador Flores with 25 men of my company to the lower ranchos on the San Antonio River, to protect the inhabitants from the depredations of the Indians."[28] Captain Seguin specifically sent three men from his company to help his family evacuate their ranch.

As the Texas Army prepared to march out of Gonzales, Seguin sent word to the two Tejano delegates at Washington-on-the-Brazos, Francisco Ruiz and Jose Antonio Navarro, about the Alamo's fall.

José María Rodriquez, son of Corporal Ambrosio Rodriquez of Seguin's company, wrote that "we started with all our goods and chattels in ox-carts. The Flores and Seguin families were among those who went with us." Many of the young children rode in the carts. "Horses were very scarce, the army taking nearly all they could find," recalled Rodriquez.[29]

Captain Bird's Men Join Houston

Following the midnight flight from Gonzales, Sam Houston's army of 374 men marched all night into the early morning hours of March 14. General Houston paused just before sunrise at Bartholomew D. McClure's plantation on Peach Creek to collect his straggling array of retreating forces. The distance from Gonzales to Peach Creek was roughly ten miles.

In the darkness of the approaching dawn, the men halted to rest and have breakfast. Many men literally dropped and lay down on the ground.

Young John Jenkins was in need of a break by the time they reached Peach Creek. "After one day's steady march, carrying rifle, ammunition, and rations, tired and sleepy, I began to realize what endurance and fortitude are required in a soldier's life," wrote Jenkins.[30]

Campfires quickly sprang up to boil coffee and make breakfast. Back on the western horizon, a glowing light could be seen many miles away as the buildings of Gonzales continued to blaze. Many more of the fleeing Gonzales citizens caught up with the army during its predawn rest. Some citizens showed up with horses heavily weighted down with all the possessions they could retrieve before their homes and businesses were burned down.[31]

David Kokernot, commanding a small group of mounted volunteers, was moved by the plight of the "Runaway Scrapers."

> It was a sad thing to see the women and children plodding their way across the prairie, some on foot, some in oxcarts, and others on sleds, especially as the country was covered with water, making travel extremely difficult and unpleasant. No tongue can express the sufferings those fleeing families were called upon to endure.[32]

"While we were sipping our unsweetened coffee, two or three loud explosions in quick succession were heard in the direction of Gonzales," wrote Private James Kuykendall. Instinctively, most men assumed it was the booming of enemy artillery. Sidney Sherman recalled hearing an "explosion at Peach Creek," and remembered General Houston remarking that it was the bottles of "poisoned" liquor that some citizens had left behind at Gonzales for Santa Anna's men. The fires had now consumed these bottles.[33]

News of the fall of the Alamo and General Houston's decision to abandon Gonzales triggered a mass flight of settlers that became known as the Runaway Scrape. Houston donated three of his artillery wagons to the settlers, but most could only flee with what they could carry.
Charles Shaw painting, courtesy of the San Jacinto Museum of History, Houston.

While the army rested for two hours at Peach Creek, they were met by another volunteer company. One of Houston's soldiers noted that they were joined by a company of "mounted men, most of whom were from the Brazos and had passed the preceding night near the spot where the army bivouacked."[34]

There is a historical marker titled "Sam Houston Oak" 10 miles east of Gonzales on US 90-A. Although only a brief resting spot, the marker describes that an oak near this point, one-eighth mile north of the actual marker, was a brief headquarters of Houston's army. "Under this oak his small army was joined by many volunteers from the eastern settlements, who went with him to San Jacinto."[35]

The newly arrived company was under command of Captain John Bird, a forty-one-year-old former Tennessean who had brought his family to Texas to settle in 1829. He had fought with Andrew Jackson in the War of 1812 and had been active in defending Texas since his arrival. In 1832, Bird had led volunteers against hostile Comanches on the Brazos River. He had also participated in the late 1835 San Antonio campaign.

When word of Travis' plight got out in late February, John Bird began recruiting volunteers immediately and he organized his company at San Felipe.

Teenager Robert Hancock Hunter was at work nailing shingles on his father's corn ginning house with several others, including his brother John Calhoun Hunter, Pleasant D. McNeel, and Robert McNeel. A courier arrived calling for volunteers to join Captain Bird.

> The courier said that Capt. John Bird was making up a company at San Felipe and wanted every man that was going to meet him at midnight. This was about 4 o'clock in the evening and we had to go about 30 miles. We got our horses and extra suit of clothes and some grub and guns, and left for camp. We got there about 2 o'clock in the morning.[36]

Captain Bird's company was organized on March 5 and was mustered into service on March 6, 1836, the day the Alamo fell. Local merchant Nathaniel Townsend supplied most of the company's supplies with the expectation to be fully paid later. Townsend furnished clothing and other camp gear, including blankets, salt, two chopping axes, two coffee mills, and four large butcher knives. Captain Bird received these goods on March 6 "for the use of a volunteer company which I have raised for the defense of Texas."[37]

They departed the following morning, March 7, with about ninety men. As with Captain Moseley Baker's San Felipe company, Bird's men sported a fine new battle flag courtesy of two women from San Felipe. They marched as far west from San Felipe as the San Bernard River before making camp for the night.

En route, Captain Bird was met on March 13 by a courier from Sam Houston who brought news that the Alamo had fallen. The company made camp at Peach Creek to await the arrival of General Houston's troops.

Private Robert Hancock Hunter (1813–1902) was only twenty-two when he joined Captain John Bird's volunteer company at San Felipe in March 1836. Hunter left much colorful insight into the campaign in his 1860 memoirs. Robert, top left, is shown in this 1896 group portrait with brothers Thomas J., William A., and Thadeus W. Hunter.
Texas State Library and Archives Commission.

During the morning of March 14, Bird's men encountered two fleeing women whose husbands had been killed at the Alamo. They had left their supper on the table and fled with their children and only what they could carry. Bird had his own wagon and team, aboard which two proprietors, James Knight and Walter C. White had stowed two large boxes of tobacco. White and Knight operated stores in San Felipe and Ford Bend, respectively, and ran a schooner that moved between the two settlements. Bird called to Lieutenant John D. McAllister to throw all the boxes out of the wagon to make room for the women and children.[38]

"Bob, give me that ax," Bird then called to Private Bob Hunter, who was sitting on the wagon tongue.

> The boxes was too large for one man to handle, so he took the ax and chopped the boxes to pieces and thr[e]w it on the ground and called his men to come and get their tobacco. They took what they wanted.
> About this time General Houston's army came along and the Capt. hollered, "Boys, don't you want some tobacco?" They hollered out, "Yes." "Here, help yourselves," and they took all the tobacco.
> That gave room for the women and children, so we got them all aboard. General Houston's Army passed on, and we fell in rear guard.

Bird's men joined Houston just as the Texans were finishing their scanty breakfast and putting out their fires. With the full light of early morning, the troops marched eastward from McClure's. After covering four or five miles through an oak forest, they emerged from the trees into a wide prairie. The Texans marched to the principal eminence, known as "Big Hill," of this prairie and there halted for a short break.[39]

Private James Kuykendall took note of the difference in attire worn by his regiment's two senior officers, Colonel Edward Burleson and Lieutenant Colonel Sidney Sherman.

> [Burleson] wore a somewhat faded, blue home-spun round-jacket and pantaloons. He carried no sword or other arms, except a pair of small pistols in his belt. Sherman had a much more trim and military appearance. He wore a blue cloth round-jacket trimmed with silver lace, and a handsome dress sword was suspended at his side. Yet the former had seen much service, both in the United States and Texas, whilst the latter was then in his novitiate.

The break at Big Hill was brief. General Houston quickly ordered the troops to resume the march. He confidently announced that his troops now numbered eight hundred. "I have no doubt that he purposely exaggerated our strength in order to inspirit the men," thought

Kuykendall. Since adjutant Henry Stouffer's count the previous day of 374 men, only Captain Bird's ninety-man company had joined, bringing the army total to no more than 470.

Bird's company brought Colonel Burleson's First Regiment to ten full companies: Captains Bird, Baker, Seguin, Calder, Patton, Wood, Billingsley, Rabb, McNutt, and Hill.

The day's marching took its toll on some of the new recruits. John Jenkins, the youngest boy of the army, soon found himself exhausted from lack of sleep and hiking with all his provisions. During the hike on March 14, Jenkins was both impressed and then shamed by the command of General Houston. Noting "how tired I seemed" and the young age of Jenkins, Houston ordered Jenkins aboard one of the horses trailing him. He ordered his own indentured servant Willis down off his horse to let the boy ride a while on Willis' horse behind the general.[40]

The only problem was that young Jenkins had a "very spirited" horse and he soon became absorbed in the countryside. While so distracted, his feisty horse moved out a little too fast for General Houston.

"God damn your soul!" Houston suddenly roared at Jenkins. "Didn't I order you to ride right here?"

Jenkins immediately realized his carelessness and understood the general's need to rebuke him. Yet he felt that Houston's "passionate harshness and curse insulted and outraged my self-respect, young as I was." He immediately dismounted and passed the horse back to Willis, declaring that he would rather die than ride another step.

Falling back into the ranks, Jenkins had learned a hard lesson of military control. In one brief instant, his immediate initial admiration for Sam Houston "was turned into a dislike I could never conquer."

Being chewed out by a superior officer was not unknown in regular military life. Such reprimanding of common men only created bitterness with volunteers who were accustomed to fighting when they pleased and even having the freedom to elect their own officers.

As the Texas Army retreated from Gonzales, the Runaway Scrape grew in intensity. The sight of the refugees fleeing from Gonzales and surrounding farms was a pitiful sight to many. Captain Billingsley was disturbed by the sight of

> . . . families flying in terror from a foe well known as paying no regard to age or sex, striving to come up with those they regarded as defenders, but who, by

their hurried midnight march, seemed about to leave them exposed to all they so much dreaded—mothers carrying one, some two children, all flying in terror and agony, and nearly all on foot. There were no vehicles in the country, even if they had time to avail themselves of them (for at that day all had come to the country by water). There were also rivers to cross; and, for tender females with children, that was almost impossible. Men were flying barefooted in every direction, spreading terror and dismay all over the country—houses and property of all kinds unprotected—nay, they even left the tables spread out for the morning meal and fled leaving the food untasted.[41]

The marching continued throughout March 14 as General Houston put some distance between his men and Gonzales. Shortly after sunset, camp was made at Williamson Daniels' place on the Lavaca River. This spot is marked by a historical marker in the present town of Moulton in Lavaca County.[42]

The troops camped on the prairie, which was far removed from any woods. The only source of fuel with which to start their campfires was the fencing around the Daniels' homestead.

Shortly before camp was made, several cattle had been encountered. These were killed and slaughtered, so that there were some meat rations to distribute as the campfires sprung up that evening. With only a little coffee and no bread, most men were content to cook pieces of beef over the fires or eat from what remained of their personal provisions.

Using these fires, the men soon ate boiled or roasted strips of beef from the slaughtered cattle. Within some of the companies, the men had a portable corn grinder and ears of corn. Thanks in large part to the supply brought in by Captain Bird's company, there was ample chewing tobacco, which Sam Houston seemed to chew almost constantly.[43]

General Houston carried little food with him, save some ears of corn in his saddlebags. His love of alcohol was pushed aside for this campaign. In its place, he carried a vial of ammoniacal spirits made by distilling liquid from the shavings of deer horns. This ammonia, given to him by his Cherokee friends, was believed by Houston to prevent colds. He carried this vial in his breast pocket and was often seen to apply these spirits to his nostrils. Sleeping on the ground at night with only his saddle blanket, and his saddle for a pillow, the commander-in-chief did not take sick during the campaign. His frequent use of the hartshorn vial, however, caused some to believe that Houston was eating opium.

The all-night march, followed by another all-day march after only a two-hour break, was a rough experience for those not accustomed to soldier duty. John Swisher, a young member of Captain Hill's company, considered going into battle the great ambition of his life. By the night of March 14, Swisher was exhausted with army life.

> By this time I began to think soldiering was not the thing which I had supposed it to be. I could not perceive any of the pride, pomp and circumstance of glorious war. For all the night before the retreat, I had been on guard without sleep; the next night and all day I had marched on foot, carrying a heavy knapsack and rifle, and by the time we reached camp, I could scarcely drag one foot after the other. Forty-eight hours without sleep, and all the time on duty, was about as much as a sixteen-year-old boy could stand; and when I reached camp I did not even stop to cook my supper, but dropped down upon my blanket and fell into a sleep at once.[44]

Last Stand at La Bahiá: March 14
Despite previous orders from Sam Houston to evacuate Goliad and retire to Victoria, Colonel James Fannin had decided to act upon other priorities. Reports of General Jose Urrea's Mexican troops advancing upon the town of Refugio had prompted Fannin to send a small party under Captain Amon B. King south.[45]

King's men were to use their wagons to help evacuate the townspeople of Refugio in the midst of the Runaway Scrape. Captain King's men dallied in dealing with tories, or local *rancheros* who were sympathetic with the Mexican forces, and soon were confronted on March 12 with the advance forces of General Urrea's cavalry.

Captain King's men took shelter in Refugio's Mission Nuestra Señora del Rosario and held off the Mexican forces until Colonel Fannin was able to send Colonel William Ward's Georgia Battalion as reinforcements on March 13. Ward's men were unable to fight through the enemy lines to reach King's men. Under cover of the night, King's and Ward's men departed the Refugio area. King's men were reported to the Mexican army by the tories, however, and were soon captured.

The day after Houston's army departed Gonzales, Texan forces fought another battle with Mexican troops on March 14 at the old mission in Refugio. Fifteen Texans were killed and more than eighty enemy soldiers were killed or wounded. After dark, the Texas soldiers slipped out of the old mission and tried to escape. King's company was spotted by tories who reported them to General Urrea's troops. The Texans fought desperately for twelve hours, but were ultimately forced to surrender after suffering five casualties.

Ward's men fled southeast along the Copano Road and were fortunate to avoid the Mexican troops searching for them. Fannin sat tight in Goliad, waiting for word on the whereabouts of King's and Ward's men.

Urrea promised to treat Captain King's men as prisoners of war after their surrender. These men, however, were hauled back to the mission at Refugio. King's men were marched out of Refugio on March 16 onto the Bexar-Goliad Road and were executed by a firing squad.[46]

General Urrea, rationalizing that he had been "overcome by the difficult circumstances" surrounding him, had ordered these Texans killed. "I authorized the execution, after my departure from camp, of thirty adventurers taken prisoner."

Houston Marches Army to the Colorado

General Houston was not pleased with the discipline of his green army. Word came to him that one of his new sentinels, exhausted from the all-day march from Peach Creek to the Lavaca River, had fallen asleep at his post during the night. The guard was a young man named John B. Rhodes, a private of Captain McNutt's company. Upon learning of this charge, Houston placed him under arrest and swore that he would have Rhodes shot.[47]

During the morning, General Houston sent one of his aides-de-camp, Major William T. Austin, to the coastal town of Velasco at the mouth of the Brazos for munitions and supplies. Austin was to make a requisition upon Colonel John A. Wharton there for fifteen horses, six pieces of artillery "and an abundant supply of grape and canister shot." Austin was also ordered to forward 150 troops from Velasco to join him at Burnam's Ferry on the Colorado. Major Austin was to rejoin the army on the Colorado River within two weeks, an indication that Houston was preparing his men for conflict in the near future.[48]

Houston heard rumor of a poor blind widow, Mary Millsaps, and her seven children having been bypassed by the army. He sent "one guard thirty miles" to bring them in. The woman soon learned from Houston that her husband, Isaac Millsaps of the Gonzales Mounted Rangers, had perished at the Alamo.[49]

After breaking camp early, the army marched east from Daniels' league toward the Navidad River and on toward the Colorado River. En route, the men passed over Rocky Creek, a tributary to the Navidad River.

Private John Rhodes, marching as a prisoner in the forward section of the army, stopped in the middle of this stream to take a drink. This caused the men following him to halt. General Houston rode up to the crossing to find what the delay was about. Spotting his sleeping sentinel now holding up the army's progress in order to take a drink, Houston shouted, "Knock him down! God damn him, knock him down!"[50]

Another member of McNutt's company, Private Kuykendall, wrote, "Frightened by these imprecations, Rhodes instantly cleared the way without the necessity of being felled."

Sam Houston, throughout the San Jacinto campaign, was stressed with trying to keep unruly men motivated. He was subject to brief outbursts of cursing when such insubordination was present. He later admitted that "it was my habit, too frequently to indulge in profane language, as well as other bad habits."[51]

Houston had reason to be frustrated. He was angry with the two dozen men who had deserted the army at Gonzales when the word of the Alamo's fall had come in. He believed that they spread exaggerated reports which were producing "dismay and consternation among the people to a most distressing extent."[52]

Private Rhodes remained the ire of General Houston this day. Rather than court-martialing the young man and sentencing him to death, however, the commander-in-chief would instead reprimand him that night and order his release.

Captain Splane Joins

Shortly after noon on March 15, Houston's army received the welcome addition of another company of volunteers described by one soldier as "a squad of mounted men." Just before reaching the Navidad River, Captain Peyton R. Splane's Brazos-area mounted Texas volunteers joined the First Regiment as the eleventh company to participate in the San Jacinto campaign. Captain Splane, twenty-nine, came to Texas from Louisiana in 1829 and had previously commanded a company during the Bexar siege.[53]

Splane's "squad" was likely little more than a couple of dozen when it joined Sam Houston, but his company would grow to more than forty during the San Jacinto campaign.

Captain Splane's men were largely from around the coastal Brazoria area, and men such as Tilford C. Edwards had been enlisted by him as early as February 22. Private William P. Scott's military papers show that he enlisted in Captain Splane's company on March 15, the date of his unit's joining the army. Some of his men, such as thirty-six-year-old James Johnson, had been Texas settlers for years. Many others were new arrivals. First Lieutenant M. H. Denham of Tennessee and privates John B. Crawford, twenty-two, and Robert Crawford, twenty, of South Carolina had just arrived in Texas this year and had taken their oath of allegiance at Nacogdoches on January 14, at which time they voluntarily enrolled in the Volunteer Auxiliary Corps for six months. Two other soldiers originally enrolled by Lieutenant Denham in Nashville, George and Fielding Deadrick, also took the oath in January, but were soon reassigned from Splane's company to the cavalry. Denham raised recruits in Nashville on December 24, 1835, and moved to Nacogdoches by early January.[54]

Forty-one-year-old Dr. William P. Smith was a veteran of the War of 1812 who had also served as a sergeant in a Tennessee Mounted Volunteer Gunmen company in 1814–1815. Jesse Williams was another seasoned veteran, having participated in the Austin Colony militia, the battle of Velasco and in the recent Bexar siege. Jonathan and Freeman Walker Douglass came to Texas from Georgia. Jonathan, thirty-seven, was the eldest of five brothers, while his youngest sibling Freeman was now the youngest enlistee of the Texas Army. He had just turned thirteen in December!

Another of Splane's recruits was twenty-seven-year-old William W. Gant. He had arrived in Texas from Columbia, Tennessee, the previous year with his friend Asa Walker. When Walker had joined the rush to defend San Antonio de Bexar in November, he appropriated a rifle and overcoat from Gant. In his hurried note, Walker had penned, "The hurry of the moment and my want of means to do better are all the excuse I have to plea for fitting out at your expense." Walker stayed on in San Antonio, where he fell with Travis at the Alamo in March. Thus, Gant had lost not only a friend, but a $35 rifle and a $20 overcoat at the Alamo. He was certainly hopeful that Captain Splane's company would now be able to exact some revenge.[55]

After being joined by Captain Splane, the army continued its march until reaching the Navidad River around 1:00 p.m. Here, Houston wisely decided to rest his men and make camp early on William Thompson's land. His army, largely composed of teenage boys and frontiersmen not disciplined in military maneuvers, had marched roughly twenty-six of the past thirty-eight hours.

Santa Anna learned with delight on March 15 that the Texas Army had fled from Gonzales. Colonel Juan Almonte of his staff wrote in his diary that this intelligence was derived from a Mexican citizen. This man claimed that the Texans, "in number 500 fled as soon as they heard of the taking of the Alamo and the approach of our troops."[56]

Santa Anna also received a courier from Mexico this day with news of the serious illness of President Miguel Barragán. Jose Justo Corro had been elected by the government to fill Barragán's spot in the interim. "This election did not please Gen'l Santa Anna," wrote Almonte.

His Excellency thus made plans to pursue his enemy, but to do so slowly and methodically, while driving them on. He selected General Joaquín Ramirez y Sesma to move out from San Antonio for Gonzales with seven hundred infantrymen, two field pieces, one hundred horses and a great number of covered supply wagons. General Ramirez y Sesma was a loyal follower of Santa Anna and was thus well trusted to follow orders by his superior. "Sesma is a timid and irresolute commander, dilatory in his judgment and apathetic in his movements," wrote one of his fellow Mexican officers. "His plans are always exaggerated."[57]

The seven hundred men led by General Ramirez y Sesma reached Gonzales on March 14 and found the town completely vacated. Some of the buildings were still smoldering when they arrived.

This news was conveyed to President Santa Anna in San Antonio de Bexar. He elected to stay at Bexar and await better intelligence. On March 17, he sent General Eugenio Tolsa with six hundred men from his Guerrero and Mexico City battalions of the Second Infantry Brigade to join General Sesma on the Colorado River. The balance of Tolsa's Second Brigade, including a twelve-pound cannon, also marched on March 17 and were bound to reinforce General Jose Urrea at Goliad.[58]

General Ramirez y Sesma's forces did not linger long in Gonzales, but instead pushed on for the Colorado River in search of the rebels fleeing ahead of them.

Sesma was under orders of Santa Anna to prevent all aid to the rebel Texans of Goliad and to "do battle with any band of rebels that you may encounter along the way."[59]

From the intelligence received from the Gonzales area, Captain Joe Bennett decided that he would encounter Sam Houston's army soon enough. His twenty-seven-man company took up station at a key crossing on the Colorado River, waiting for the Texas Army to arrive.

On March 12, Bennett's camp had been a little north of Washington. From Convention Hall, James Collinsworth, Chairman of the Committee on Military Affairs, issued orders to Bennett to "proceed immediately to the headquarters of the commander-in-chief" and report for duty. Captain Bennett was authorized to purchase on credit such goods as his men might need en route and to press "such as may be absolutely necessary."[60]

Shortly before marching down the La Bahia Road, Bennett had appointed his noncommissioned officers, headed by former schoolteacher Samuel Millett as orderly sergeant. The company had then

Captain James Gillaspie (1805–1867) was originally first lieutenant of Captain Joseph L. Bennett's Washington Municipality company. When Bennett was promoted to lieutenant colonel on April 8, he became captain of the unit which would officially be the Sixth Company, Second Regiment. Gillaspie would later serve as the Superintendent of the Texas Penitentiary at Huntsville, Texas.
Courtesy of the San Jacinto Museum of History, Houston.

reached Moore's Fort on the Colorado, the site of present La Grange, about noon on March 13. They found the two-story frontier block-house deserted, the residents having moved to safety after word of the Mexican army had circulated.[61]

The company made camp on the east bank of the Colorado River near La Grange and awaited Houston's army. On March 14, the men elected lieutenants for their company. Those so promoted were First Lieutenant James Gillaspie and Second Lieutenant Matthew Finch, both volunteers from Tennessee who had joined the company at Washington.

Gillaspie, who would later move up to commander of this company, wrote of his experiences in the company.

> As soon as I heard of the disturbances in Texas, I hastened from home, leaving all my business there unsettled. I bore the expenses of three young men to this country.
>
> We left about the 25 of November 1835, was in Texas on Christmas and received the right of citizenship and enrolled our names as volunteers about the 15 January. We were then ready to do any service the country demanded. We remained, you know, in Nacogdoches some time and were furnished with means to move on towards the frontier of the country.[62]

Bennett's men attempted to fortify themselves near Moore's ferry on the Colorado. William Zuber describes the early trench his company dug to defend this crossing.

> We commenced to dig an entrenchment on the east bank of the river, in-tended for use in repelling any attempt by the enemy to cross it. We felled a large cottonwood tree, a few feet south of the landing at the ferry, so that it lay on the brink of the bank and parallel to it. We stuffed under the tree some brush from its branches. Then we dug a ditch about five feet east of the fallen tree, parallel to it, about two and a half feet deep and three feet wide. We piled the excavated dirt by the tree, saving a space about two feet wide be-tween the embankment and the ditch on which to stand or walk. Now our en-trenchment was complete. If a body of the enemy should attempt to cross the river, we could stand on the space, use the embankment for a breastwork, and fire upon them.[63]

By March 15, some of the fleeing citizens of Gonzales made their way to Moore's Ferry along La Bahiá Road and camped near Bennett's men. Among them was the elderly father of Captain Albert Martin, who had ridden back into the Alamo from Gonzales with recruits five days before the fortress was overrun. "He shed not a tear, but his whole body was convulsed in grief" over the loss of his son.

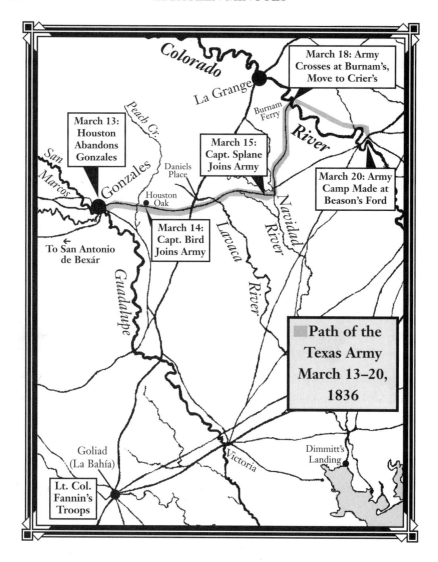

Path of the Texas Army March 13–20, 1836

Navidad to the Colorado

From the Navidad, General Houston made the curious move of marching his troops north on the morning of March 16. Rather than move straight toward Columbia-on-the-Brazos, he had his men swing north out of their way. This move indicates that Houston was wary of the movements of Santa Anna's forces and that he was dodging them by moving in a direction other than what they would first expect.

Feeling the need to better organize his mounted scouts and spies, General Houston created a twelfth company on this day. He promoted William H. Smith to "Captain of Cavalry" in command of the mounted scouts of the Texas Army. Smith, a veteran of the Bexar siege, had been paid as a Second Lieutenant, Infantry from December 2, 1835, through March 16, 1836.[64] Deaf Smith and Henry Karnes continued to lead small squads of spies out on patrols, and Karnes would soon be formally placed in command of his own cavalry company.

The march this day was largely without event. By 4:30 p.m., the troops had reached Burnam's Crossing of the Colorado River and halted on the west bank of this river. Jesse Burnam had in 1820 opened a trading post at this river crossing, located at the present town of Weimar in Colorado County.

Houston wrote the following morning that his rear guard was still "a few miles behind with the families, which were not known to be on the route as the army marched, and for which the guard was sent back."[65]

Major Alexander Somervell wrote to his friend James Perry from "Camp at Burnham's on Colorado" on the late afternoon of March 16. Like Houston, he exaggerated the strength of the Texian forces.

> We have retired to this place from Gonzales, followed as we suppose by a large Mexican force. We have every reason to believe that Santa Anna, at the head of a large army, will make a descent upon the lower country and sweep the coast, and really I do not see any prospect of arresting his progress for some time to come. We muster about seven hundred strong at this place.[66]

General Houston, writing to James Collinsworth during the night of March 16–17, estimated his total forces to be "about six hundred men." He noted that his army was now forced to deal with "several hundred women and children." He implored Collinsworth to put the word out to those east of the Trinity to "rush to us!" With fifteen hundred men, Houston vowed that he would fight Santa Anna's troops until they "lose all confidence from our annoyance."[67]

Both Somervell and Houston seem to have been counting a little on the high side, obviously including some of the Gonzales citizens who had not formally enlisted with any of the existing infantry or cavalry companies. With the addition of Captains Bird and Splane during the march from Gonzales, and other straggling volunteers who occasionally joined, Houston's little army now actually numbered just over five hundred men.

With dawn on March 17 came cool, drizzly rain upon the bivouacked soldiers at Burnam's Crossing on the Colorado River. The light rain slowly turned the west bank camp into a sloppy, muddy mess.

General Houston had decided to let his men rest sufficiently while the rear guard came up with all the terrified, fleeing civilians. He would pause long enough to ensure that the women and children had safely crossed the Colorado.

Some men received special furloughs to assist the women and children in the Runaway Scrape. For example, Captain Moseley Baker allowed Franklin Jefferson Starr of his company to return home to "make suitable disposition of his family" during the crisis. As approved by Colonel Burleson, Starr was to return to his company as quickly as possible. Starr moved his family from the Brazos County area to a safer haven at Nacogdoches.[68]

In orders written to Colonel Fannin on March 17 from the Colorado River, Houston listed his present force as numbering "four hundred and twenty effective men." If this number is to be trusted, this would indicate that only 46 additional men had joined him on the retreat from Gonzales to the Colorado River. The number is believable, as it is one of the lower estimates he had given in days. He had also lost about twenty-five men to desertion at Gonzales. It is also possible that his count of 420 men "present" did not include those out on scouting patrols.

When appealing to others to come to his aid, Houston had previously inflated his true numbers to make things sound better. On March 13, he had given his forces to the government's military committee as "more than four hundred" and to an East Texas troop organizer in another letter as "near 500." Both of these were written on a day when his adjutant had made an exact count of 374 officers and men present.[69]

On March 17, when Houston gave Fannin his strength as 420, he wrote another letter to the government's military committee saying that he had "about six hundred men." This figure obviously included all of the straggling families and children from Gonzales whom the rear guard of his army was protecting.[70]

Houston ordered Fannin to take a position on the Bay of Lavaca to protect the army's munitions at Cox's Point and Dimmitt's Landing. Should he be unable to defend these munitions, Fannin was to "fall back on the main army." Houston gave an important tip of the hat to Fannin of his own future plans: "The army now near Burnham's, on the Colorado, will remain for a time, and according to circumstances, fall down the river."

Houston also informed Fannin that he would "raise a company of spies to range the country from this [place] to Gonzales." His thoughts on this must have already been sent ahead to the new government in Washington, for new Secretary of War Thomas Rusk named an officer for this duty on March 17. Texas Declaration of Independence signer Andrew Briscoe was authorized that day to "organize a company of Rangers or Spies and observe the approach of the enemy and to communicate every day with this Department."[71]

Andrew Briscoe, twenty-five, was born in Mississippi, had attended Franklin University in Kentucky, studied law and came to Texas in 1833. He settled near the coast at Anahuac, where he engaged in the mercantile business, a job made more challenging due to the laws of Mexican authorities. The arrest of Briscoe and DeWitt Harris in 1835 had caused the scene in Anahuac in which Captain Travis' men had successfully demanded their surrender. During the Texas Revolution, Briscoe had commanded the Liberty Volunteers at the battle of Concepcion and during the Bexar siege. He had arrived at Washington-on-the-Brazos on March 10 with dispatches from Nacogdoches.[72]

Captain Briscoe utilized local revolutionary leader Colonel John Henry Moore to recruit and organize his spy company at Washington. The size of his company was likely very small, as they were required to move freely over open terrain and watch the enemy's movements. The service records of four men of this unit have original enlistment dates of March 17 and March 18. It is thus likely that John W. Cassidy, John Marner, William Patton and Daniel Richardson originally served as spies under Captain Briscoe. Briscoe would later take command of a regular army company.

At Burnam's the greenness of some of the new soldiers showed as they learned the routine of marching, standing guard duty and following orders. While passing beyond the guard lines this day, General Houston was hailed by a young sentinel who demanded his "pass." Houston asked the guard if he did not know that his general had the privilege to pass without challenge. The guard replied that his orders were to let no man pass the lines without written permission of the officer of the day.[73]

"Well, my friend," said the commander-in-chief, "if such were your orders, you are right." With that, Sam Houston seated himself upon a stump and waited until the officer of the day could remedy the situation.

The New Texas Government

The Convention at Washington-on-the-Brazos had taken the bold step on March 16 of passing a special ordinance to create a government *ad interim* for the republic. The grim news of the Alamo's fall, recounted by Sam Houston's intelligence, had reached the Convention hall in the late afternoon hours of March 15. The delegates had thus resolved to create the *ad interim* government to serve until a regular government could be established.

The Convention worked late electing the republic's leaders and a cabinet. These men were sworn into office at 4:00 a.m. on March 17.[74] Governor Henry Smith's provisional Texas government ceased to be when the fifty-eight delegates formally elected the men who would now run the free and sovereign Republic of Texas. The key elected officials were David Gouverneur Burnet as President, Dr. Lorenzo de Zavala as Vice President, Secretary of Treasury Bailey Hardeman, Secretary of Navy Robert Potter, Attorney General David Thomas, Secretary of State Samuel P. Carson, and as Secretary of War, Thomas Jefferson Rusk.

Burnet, forty-seven, was a native of New Jersey who carried a pistol in one pocket and a Bible in the other. A stocky man with bushy brown whiskers, he had fought in Venezuela in 1810 in an attempt to free this country from Spanish rule.

Vice President de Zavala, born in the Yucatan, was a founder of the Mexican republic who had supported Santa Anna up until the dictator had denounced the Constitution of 1824. Married to a New Orleans native, de Zavala had settled on a plantation along the San Jacinto River.

One of President Burnet's closest associates was Secretary of the Navy Robert Potter. A thirty-six-year-old from North Carolina, Potter had once served as a junior officer in the U.S. Navy. He was jailed in North Carolina for attacking and castrating two relatives whom he suspected of having sexual relations with his wife. He was later elected to the state's legislature but was run out of state for cheating at cards.

David Gouverneur Burnet (1788–1870) was sworn in as the President of the Republic of Texas on March 17, 1836. Burnet (above left) would soon become a bitter critic of General Houston's leadership. Vice President Lorenzo de Zavala (1788–1836), although born in Mexico, was a prominent organizer in the settlement of Texas and was a signer of the Texas Declaration of Independence. De Zavala's home near the San Jacinto battlegrounds would be used as a makeshift hospital.
Burnet courtesy of Texas State Library and Archives Commission. De Zavala painting courtesy of the San Jacinto Museum of History, Houston.

Soon after arriving in Texas in 1835, Potter had been elected to the Washington Convention as a Nacogdoches delegate. During Sam Houston's campaign, Potter would display a distinct distaste for the characters of both Houston and Secretary of War Thomas Rusk.[75]

Having elected a new government, the Convention adjourned and the delegates dispersed. President Burnet and most of his cabinet remained in Washington for several more days, while other members moved to join the army or their families.

On the day of his election, President Burnet showed his full confidence in Major General Houston's abilities to lead the Texas Army. Sending a circular from the Executive Department to "The People in Eastern Texas," he called on them to join the cause. "Gen. Houston is at his post on the frontier with eight hundred men and reinforcements constantly arriving," wrote Burnet. "Our army is in high spirits and full of confidence."[76]

Burnet's public display of confidence in Sam Houston had just reached its all-time peak.

_____

Texas Rangers Called to Join the Army

By mid-March 1836, there were nine companies of Texas Rangers operating in Texas. Most of these units had been called for by legislation from the General Council and conventions since late 1835. The most visible regiment of rangers was under the command of Major Robert McAlpin Williamson, who had been elected to command on November 28, 1835.[77]

Williamson, thirty, was a former Georgia lawyer who had emigrated to San Felipe de Austin in 1826. Fluent in Spanish, he had edited one of the first newspapers in Texas during his early years. An attack of white swelling had crippled him as a teenager. His right leg was drawn back at the knee, which forced Williamson to be fitted with a wooden leg from his knee to the ground. Known as "Willie" to friends, the wooden leg earned him the nickname "Three-Legged Willie."

His handicap had not stopped Williamson from participating in early expeditions against hostile Indians. In the summer of 1835, he had commanded a company of rangers from La Grange which participated in Colonel John Henry Moore's expedition.

After being named commander of a new ranger battalion, Major Williamson set up his headquarters at Bastrop during December and began the task of recruiting men for his service. He was authorized to raise three companies of rangers. The first two units to begin shaping up had been Captain Isaac Watt Burton's company along the Sabine and Captain John Jackson Tumlinson Jr.'s company. Tumlinson had mustered his men into service on January 17, 1836, at Hornsby's Settlement on the Colorado River, just below present Austin.

Tumlinson's men had fought a skirmish with Comanche Indians just three days later and had rescued a young boy being held captive by these Indians. His rangers had then constructed a blockhouse in present Leander on Brushy Creek. From this little fortification, they had ranged the Colorado River area during February.

Major Williamson received Colonel Travis' desperate appeal from the Alamo on February 25. He immediately sent orders to Captain Tumlinson, calling him in from the frontiers to guard Bastrop with his rangers.

Another ranger regiment was authorized by the Convention at Washington-on-the-Brazos on March 3. It was headed by Colonel

Jesse Benton Sr. and Lieutenant Colonel Griffin Bayne. Benton became involved in recruiting new men and working on a new military road that would lead from Robertson's Colony to the United States border at the Red River. Lieutenant Colonel Bayne was more actively involved with this ranger regiment during the San Jacinto campaign. His first company was organized in Milam on March 1 under Captain William C. Wilson.

Captain Tumlinson's ranger company operated from Bastrop during the early days of March under the direction of Major Willie Williamson. During the time that General Houston's troops were hurriedly evacuating Gonzales, Tumlinson posted several of his men as picket guards beyond Plum Creek on the road from San Antonio into Bastrop. Within days of Deaf Smith's party finding the Alamo survivors, the definitive word on the Alamo's fall reached Williamson in Bastrop.

General Houston sent orders to Bastrop for Williamson to monitor the movements of General Gaona's upper division of the Mexican army as it advanced toward the Trinity River. Williamson wrote to Houston that he had "received an additional order from Col. Burleson on the 18th of March," in which Burleson believed that Houston's army had "five hundred men."[78]

According to Captain Jesse Billingsley, General Houston "called on Col. Burleson to furnish a man from his regiment of volunteers to bear dispatches to Major R. M. Williamson, Comdr. of Rangers at Bastrop." Burleson detailed Jesse Halderman of Billingsley's unit to carry the orders to Captain Tumlinson's rangers and to rejoin the Texas Army near the Colorado River.[79]

The news of the Alamo spread fear among those still in Bastrop and the remaining townspeople began hurriedly evacuating. Major Williamson's rangers sunk all the ferryboats on the nearby Colorado River to prevent the Mexican army from crossing. Captain Tumlinson, his first lieutenant and several other men were allowed to take a leave of absence to move their families to safety. Second Lieutenant George M. Petty took acting command of the remaining twenty-two rangers.

Major Williamson's rangers remained near Bastrop until March 18, when the first advance of some six hundred Mexican troops appeared that morning across the Colorado River. The company then moved out toward the Brazos River, hoping to join the main Texas Army. Two men were without horses and this, coupled with muddy roads, slowed the advance of the whole unit. Major Williamson soon resolved to leave Petty's men to their own pace. Taking Privates Jimmy Curtis and Ganey Crosby with him, "Three-Legged Willie" rode on ahead toward Washington-on-the-Brazos.

Within days of Houston's evacuation of Gonzales, word had been sent to all ranger units in Texas of the Alamo's fall. The need to check Indian depredations mattered little when the army of Mexico was overruning Texas settlements. Captain Stephen Townsend's twelve-man ranger unit, camped on the east bank of the Colorado River in Robertson's Colony, received orders on March 16 to join the army.[80]

In present Anderson County, Captain William Turner Sadler commanded a ten-man mounted ranger unit that was occupied with finishing work on Fort Houston near present Palestine. According to Sadler's grandson, they were "working on the house when they got news that San Antonio had fallen." Sadler "and a party of men started to their relief."

He disbanded his company at Fort Houston just two weeks short of fulfilling their three-month service commitment. Private Daniel LaMora Crist later wrote that his little company was "discharged at Fort Houston by reason of the fall of the Alamo, when they were called to the Army of San Jacinto."

Seven of Captain Sadler's men remained with him, while two men chose to protect their families. Thus, eight of the "Houston Company" of rangers departed Fort Houston and moved down the old San Antonio Road to join the Texas Army. They crossed the Trinity River at the community of Randolph on March 19. Sadler wrote a promissory note to ferry keeper Nathaniel Robbins that his men had crossed the river "for the purpose of joining the army of Texas, for which we did not pay."

Captain Louis B. Franks, a veteran of the 1835 Bexar siege, operated a thirty-man ranger unit in Robertson's Colony during February and March. Unable to find battle with Indians and compelled to aid the plight of Texas, his unit was broken up by the end of March. Lieutenant Thomas Pliney Plaster of Franks' company would be enrolled in the Texas Army on April 1.

By March 16, Lieutenant Colonel Griffin Bayne was still recruiting men for his new ranger battalion in the old Robertson's Colony, which had been newly named the Municipality of Milam. By late March, Bayne and his recruits were on the move to join up with the Texas Army. Some of the rangers under Bayne and Captain William Wilson, such as Francis Weatherred and Daniel T. Dunham, would enlist in Sam Houston's army during the San Jacinto campaign. Other rangers helped escort the terrified settlers during the Runaway Scrape.

Including a new company recruited by Major Williamson, the various Texas Ranger companies in operation during March 1836 would contribute more than eighty new men to Sam Houston's army as the campaign progressed. As seasoned frontier fighters, these men would prove to be fierce soldiers in combat and invaluable scouts to help fill the ranks of the cavalry.

From Crier's to Beason's: March 18–19

The Texas Army assisted the straggling civilians with crossing over the Colorado River during the day on March 18. The five-hundred-man army also effected its own crossing, completing the ferrying across by around 3:00 p.m. Once firmly across on the east side, Houston moved his men a few miles farther down the river to Old Three Hundred settler John Crier's property.[81]

Rain returned on the morning of March 19, during which Houston marched his forces a few miles farther downriver. Due to the poor weather, camp was made early in the day in a thicket of post oaks while they awaited word from their cavalry scouts, which had been dispatched to scour the countryside for news of the advance of the Mexican forces.

This party included Henry Karnes, Deaf Smith, Robert Handy, Wash Secrest, John Sharp and David Murphree.[82] Karnes officially assumed command of the second company of Texas spies during this mission. At age twenty-four, Captain Karnes was less than half the age of forty-nine-year-old scout Deaf Smith, but he was an equally able frontiersman. Audited military claims of the Republic of Texas show him paid as "Captain of Cavalry" from March 20 to September 26, 1836.[83] Karnes' new company included a few men from Captain Hill's company and William Crittenden from Captain Rabb's. Other men rode with Karnes' company on scouting duties, although still officially attached to other units. Twenty-eight-year-old Churchill Fulshear Jr., for example, was a member of Captain John Bird's company who "was in the scouting service frequently" with Deaf Smith and Wash Secrest, "being detailed with others of his company" for such assignments as needed. Young Fulshear's family had come to Texas in 1823 as one of Stephen F. Austin's Old Three Hundred families.[84]

John Sharp wrote of the departure of Karnes' men to search for the Mexican forces.

> There was a call made for a cavalry company, who were to go back the way we had come, and see if they could find the enemy. I volunteered for one. We were to meet at Burnham's house in the afternoon, and start. When we mustered our forces, there were but nine of us. We got some provisions, and corn for our horses, in a wallet, which each of us carried on our saddles, and started.
>
> About one hour before night, we cooked our suppers, at the Navidad, and rode on to find a sleeping place, which we did, under a spreading post oak, some distance from the road, in the prairie, without a fire. We took this precaution on account of the Indians, or any straggling band of Mexicans, who might have been out, like ourselves, spying.[85]

CHAPTER 5

Sparring along the Colorado

March 20–23

> We pursued them, and, as we got nearer to them, fired our pistols off at them; but
> they kept ahead of us, until one of their horses was lamed by a shot from Col. Handy.
> —*Cavalry scout John Sharp*

Colonel James Fannin was finally forced to make a move from the old La Bahia Mission in Goliad. Despite direct orders from General Houston to blow up the mission, known as "Fort Defiance," and retire his forces further east to Victoria on the Guadalupe River, he had not.

Fannin was a man troubled by his command. Despite the repeated calls for help from San Antonio, he had clung to his original orders to hold the fort at Goliad. He had written several notes to Lieutenant Governor James Robinson in February asking to be relieved of command. In his final appeal, Fannin wrote, "If I am qualified to command an Army, I have not found it out."[1]

When he had made an attempt to march his men out for San Antonio on February 28, they had been turned back by broken-down supply wagons and a cold norther. His forces remained at La Bahia, many of the men growing more discontent with Fannin's lack of aggressiveness. After sending out Captain King's and Colonel Ward's troops to Refugio, he continued to hold out at Goliad awaiting their return.

"Fannin's great anxiety, alone, for the fate of Ward and King, and their little band, delayed our march," wrote Dr. Jack Shackelford, captain of one of Fannin's companies at Goliad.[2]

At 4:00 p.m. on March 17, news finally reached Fannin of the defeat and execution of King's and Ward's forces near Refugio. Still, he tallied in abandoning Goliad while organizing his forces on March 18 for the march out. When his four-hundred-odd men did fall back from

Goliad on March 19, they moved painfully slow toward Victoria while hauling nine cannon and some five hundred spare muskets.

Colonel Fannin's slow pace allowed General Jose Urrea to set up a trap for the Texian volunteers. Urrea's command had increased to at least 1,400 soldiers with his rendezvous the previous day with reinforcements from the Morales and San Luis battalions. In the afternoon of March 19, Urrea's cavalrymen approached Fannin's command in an opening near the Atasocita Road ten miles from Goliad and about two miles from Coleto Creek.

Among those retreating with Fannin's command was Private Charles B. Shain, a Kentuckian serving in Captain Burr H. Duvall's company. In a letter written to his father several months later, Shain described the ensuing battle of Coleto Creek.

> They still advanced until within about 400 yards, when at about 3 o'clock, they commenced firing with their muskets but still continued to advance. They marched toward us slowly until they got within 150 yards. We then commenced with our rifles and muskets. As soon as we opened our fire they fell back about 200 yards, and we kept up regular fire until nearly sundown, when they retreated.
>
> It was then proposed by some of the officers that we retreat to the woods, but some of the men objected on account of our wounded. We had about 20 or 25 men that would have been left. If our advance guard had not been cut off from us, we could have carried our wounded and made our escape to the woods and water, where we could have whipped the enemy with all ease.[3]

During the afternoon's fight near Coleto Creek, nine Texans had been killed and another 51 wounded. Colonel Fannin had been shot through the thigh but rose to his feet and shouted at his men to fight on. His men withstood pouring rain during the night, digging shallow trenches on the battlefield for cover behind the corpses of their slain team oxen.[4]

Daylight on the following morning, March 20, showed Fannin that his position was bleak and that his men were hopelessly surrounded by Mexican cavalry, infantrymen and artillery. Under a white flag of truce, he hobbled forward across the field and negotiated with General Urrea.

Urrea offered only terms of unconditional surrender. Fannin returned to his officers and assured them that the Mexican army had agreed to allow them to surrender with the promise that they would be marched to the United States in eight days to be paroled. With little option, they agreed to surrender.

The defeated Texans were then marched back to the Mission La Bahia at Goliad which they had just abandoned. Private Shain quickly found their conditions less than ideal.

> We then stacked our arms and marched in double file back to the fort. We arrived there late in the evening. They gave us nothing to eat that night and nothing till late next day. Then they gave us about as much for twenty-four hours as we could eat at one meal.[5]

Colonel Ward's Georgia Battalion, having avoided Mexican patrols, continued to try to locate Fannin's force. They encountered Urrea's men upon reaching Victoria on March 21. Many of Ward's men were killed or captured by the Mexican troops. Over the next few days, many more of his troops were surrounded, captured and marched back to Goliad to join Fannin.[6]

"We began to give away our things and also our little money for something to eat," wrote captive Herman Ehrenberg.[7] Santa Anna's previous orders to his officers were to treat all foreigners captured under arms as "pirates" and to summarily execute them. Fortunately for Fannin's and Ward's men, General Urrea hesitated on carrying out this directive. Clinging to the vain hope that they would be shipped to the United States for parole, the hundreds of Texian captives could only pray that Urrea would continue to lack the stomach to carry out Santa Anna's orders.

Karnes Takes a Prisoner

On the morning of March 20, Captain Henry Karnes' small party of spies awoke from their cold camp and rode until they were within a few miles of Rocky Creek, west of the main army's location at Burnam's Crossing.

Karnes knew that the main army planned to move downriver on the Colorado to the next major crossing point, Beason's Ferry (also known as Beason's Ford and Beason's Crossing). Located at the site of the present town of Columbus, Beason's was a river crossing ferry and boarding house operated by Benjamin and Elizabeth Beason. One of the area's major roads from Gonzales led directly to Beason's, and would thus be the natural place to encounter enemy troops moving eastward.

Beason's Crossing on the Colorado is located in present Colorado County. A historical marker three miles east of Columbus on Highway 90 marks the approximate area of one of the Texan camps. Another marker two miles west of Columbus marks the approximate campsite of General Sesma's Mexican forces.[8]

Karnes' scouts had no sooner struck the road that led to Beason's when they saw fresh horse tracks leading toward Beason's Ferry. Scout John Sharp describes the morning's encounter.

> Deaf Smith got off his horse, and examined them, and said, that at least ten or twelve horses had passed there, and not more than an hour before. Every man examined his arms, and put them in order for fighting. We started at a brisk gait, following them, and in a short time saw six soldiers, on a hill, some two or three hundred yards from the road, on horseback; two or three of them with led horses.
>
> They saw us, and immediately fled, leaving the horses they were leading, and scattering off in different directions. We pursued them, and, as we got nearer to them, fired our pistols off at them; but they kept ahead of us, until one of their horses was lamed by a shot from Col. Handy; and the fellow turned to make fight with his lance, and shot at Col. Karnes as he passed him, in pursuit of the others, with a pistol.
>
> Secrest came up to him, and shot him through the body, the fellow still resisting; when Secrest shot him through the head, and he fell. We still continued to pursue the balance of them, they making for the Navidad bottom, which, at this place, was a complete thicket of underbrush, so much so, that a man on horseback could not penetrate it.[9]

The Mexican soldiers, seeing that they could not ride through the thick brush, abandoned their mounts and plunged into the thicket on foot. Karnes' scouts were less than one hundred yards behind and they followed suit by abandoning their horses. In their haste, the Texans did not have time to tie their horses.

John Sharp jumped into Rocky Creek and was wading across when his panicked horse came crashing through the thicket and jumped into the creek also. "The first leap he made into the creek," recalled Sharp, "He struck me with his foot on the leg, and knocked me down in the creek, wetting myself and my gun all over."

Sharp was unhurt and quickly filled his gun with dry powder. He continued to search for the fleeing Mexican soldiers until he heard shouts from some of his companions to return. He found that Karnes, Deaf Smith and David Murphree had managed to subdue one of the enemy soldiers. They had difficulty gaining intelligence from the Mexican, who cried out to the Texans to spare his life.

Sharp continues:

> At last, by threats, and promises to spare his life, he told us that the Mexican army had encamped, the night before, at Daniels, on the Lavaca, and that this party had been sent out from the advance guard, at Rock[y] Creek, as a Spy Company; and that there were but six or eight hundred men in that division, with two pieces of artillery, and some sixty or seventy cavalry, all under the command of General Sesma.
>
> Karnes, Murph[ree], and myself, had lost our horses; though Karnes had taken one of the horses left by the Mexicans. We tied the prisoner's hands behind his back; and Murph[ree] and myself, with Deaf Smith, started back on the track of pursuit, and found two lances, one wallet of provisions, and two hats and cloaks, dropped by the Mexicans in their hurry to get off.[10]

Smith led the others back to the body of the Mexican shot by Wash Secrest. They took his sword and pistols but found that his horse was too badly crippled to ride. The trio then returned to the road and crossed the Navidad at Thompson's. There, they opened the wallets captured from the Mexican soldiers and had their first meal of the day. "We then burnt the house, and started, Murph[ree], myself, and the prisoner on foot, and Deaf Smith on horseback, for Beason's," wrote Sharp.

They were overtaken on their walk by the return of Karnes and Wash Secrest, who had gone out in search of the missing horses and had managed to catch two horses left behind by the fleeing Mexicans. One horse was complete with saddle and bridle, the other sporting nothing but a rope around its neck. En route back to their party, they encountered three other Texan scouts from the main army: Clark M. Harmon of Captain Patton's company, James D. Owen of Captain Splane's company, and Benjamin Cromwell Franklin of Captain Calder's unit.

Murphree and Sharp mounted the horses and their Mexican prisoner was lifted up behind Franklin, as John Sharp recalled.

> We hurried on towards the Colorado as fast as possible. We knew that the Mexican army could not be more than five miles behind us, and there were but six of us; so we had not time to spare.
>
> The horse I was on was one of those abandoned by the fugitives at the edge of thicket, and was completely broken down; and, after riding two or three miles, I was obliged to leave him and walk, occasionally relieved by some of those who were mounted. We arrived at Beason's about dark, and found a guard posted there by Captain Wiley Martin's company, who had been ordered to stop here for the army.
>
> Mr. Owen took the prisoner on to meet General Houston, who was on his way, with the army, coming down to Beason's. The balance of our party stayed at the river that night.

Colonel Juan Almonte of the Mexican army recorded in his diary several days later that the Texas scouts had "killed two men and wounded one" of Sesma's scouts. He, of course, did not know that the second man believed to be killed had in fact been taken prisoner.[11]

Karnes' men returned to the Texas camp on the afternoon of March 20. Private James Kuykendall watched as the scouts rode "into camp with a Mexican prisoner and created a lively sensation." Karnes' men reported that the enemy soldier killed was credited to Wash Secrest, "who exhibited the sword and pistols of his adversary."[12]

Colonel George Hockley wrote the following day that one of the horses captured by Karnes contained "a small portion of clothing belonging to some one murdered in the Alamo."[13]

McIntire, Martin, and Logan's Companies

On the morning that Karnes' scouts returned with their prisoner, Houston broke camp and put his men on the move a few miles down river again on March 20. They wound their way along the course of the river to the noted point on the east banks of the Colorado known as Beason's Ford. Beason's was reached about noon and the army set up camp near present Columbus.

As they approached Beason's Ford, the Texas Army was joined by a new company under the command of Captain Wyly (often spelled "Wiley") Martin. His company comprised roughly thirty men and had been formed on March 7 in the Fort Bend area.

Captain Martin, a sixty-year-old Georgian, was a fiesty fighter. Raised in Georgia, he had served as a schoolteacher and store clerk before he joined the United States Army in 1805. He had served under William Henry Harrison in 1812 and Andrew Jackson at the battle of Horseshoe Bend. Martin was promoted to captain for his gallantry in action. He later challenged a man to a duel and killed him, forcing Martin to resign his army commission and head for Texas in 1823.[14]

Wyly Martin was one of Stephen F. Austin's Old Three Hundred Settlers, receiving title to land in present Brazoria County in 1824. He quickly became engaged in Texas politics, serving on various committees and conventions. Martin had also served as alcalde and in 1835 was political chief at Gonzales.

Captain Martin's first lieutenant was veteran fighter Randall Jones, a forty-year-old from Georgia and Mississippi. He enlisted in the U.S.

Army for the War of 1812 and was made captain of a sixty-man unit. His company fought a battle with two groups of Creek Indians in Alabama and was praised for their valiant fighting effort. Jones made his way to Texas as one of Stephen F. Austin's Old Three Hundred settlers, settling along the Brazos near present Richmond. He was an early merchant, a member of the General Consultation of 1835–1836, the *ayuntamiento* of San Felipe and had served in the Anahuac Expedition of 1832. "On the organization of the company of volunteers from Fort Settlement under the command of Captain W. Martin, I was elected 1st Lieutenant on the 7th March," recalled Jones.

Jones' thirty-nine-year-old brother James Wales Jones was also a member of the company. The brothers were in Texas by 1822 and James had also settled in present Fort Bend County.[15]

Another forty-odd-man company joining Houston's army during this time was that of Captain Thomas H. McIntire. A native of Pennsylvania, McIntire arrived in Texas in February 1836 ready to fight, and by March 10, he had been appointed as first lieutenant by the Constitutional Convention at Washington-on-the-Brazos. He had recruited men from around the Washington Municipality, many of his men being Bexar siege veterans who were residents of the current Fort Bend and Brazoria County areas. McIntire's company was mustered into service on March 18. The unit had reached the Colorado River by March 20, where McIntire enlisted Jethro Thomas Bancroft, who had volunteered in the Texas Army on March 8 at Lynchburg, and former Mobile Grey soldier John L. Lowary.[16]

A third company joining the main body of the Texas Army on March 20 was Captain William Mitchell Logan's "Liberty Company."

This company was organized on March 11 in Liberty County. The date of this organization had been set in February at the home of Mr. James, who had just returned home from participating in the Bexar siege. At Mr. James' home, Isaac Moreland, another veteran of the siege related the facts of the recent San Antonio campaign, inspiring others and creating general enthusiasm. It was agreed that all volunteers to join the Texas Revolution would meet at Liberty on March 11, fully prepared and equipped to join the campaign.[17]

Born in North Carolina, thirty-three-year-old William Logan had settled in Texas in 1831. He had previously served as second lieutenant of Captain Andrew Briscoe's Liberty Volunteers in late 1835. Logan was motivated to begin organizing his company about the first of March 1836 when courier Joseph Dunman reached Liberty on horseback with a copy of Travis' appeal for help. The citizens agreed to quickly raise a volunteer company. Dunman rode on to Anahuac to spread the word while runners went out to other neighboring settlements to announce that Liberty was preparing a company.[18]

More volunteers came to Liberty in the next few days. Captain Benjamin J. Harper, thirty-six, arrived with a twenty-eight-man volunteer company which had been raised in Beaumont. Benjamin Franklin Hardin recruited another twenty men above Liberty. On March 6, the three units combined and elected as new officers Captain Logan, First Lieutenant Frank Hardin and Second Lieutenant Benjamin Harper.

One of the more experienced volunteers was Isaac N. Moreland, who had served as a captain of artillery during the Bexar siege.

Another volunteer arriving at Liberty was thirty-three-year-old Dr. Nicholas Descomps Labadie, a French Canadian who had studied medicine in St. Louis. His father had been married three times and Labadie was the youngest of twenty-three children. After his arrival in Texas in 1831 with a chest of medicine, Dr. Labadie had been appointed surgeon of the Mexican garrison at Anahuac by the post commander, John Bradburn. By June 1832, Labadie had moved his wife and family to a plantation on Lake Charlotte in Liberty County, where he enlisted under Captain Logan in 1836. He later wrote of his new company's organization.

> On the day appointed, all were promptly on the ground, and immediately went into an election of officers, when Wm. M. Logan, who had distinguished himself in resistance to Bradburn's attempt to set the slaves free, was chosen our Captain, and Harper, Hardin, and [Edward Thomas] Branch were chosen next in command, while Moreland was to act as Orderly, as he had acquired some knowledge in drill at San Antonio.
>
> Thomas Norman, son of Mrs. James, and the writer, were the only two from that neighborhood. The company embraced over seventy, composed of Beaumont and Liberty boys, and there was not in that campaign a more efficient company or a more fearless and determined set of men. After the election of officers, Wm. Hardin gave us a fine dinner, when we set forward to meet the enemy.[19]

Just as the men were beginning their march from Liberty, Baker M. Spinks, a member of the Committee of Safety for Liberty Municipality in 1835, drove up with a wagon load of bacon which he presented to the company. Captain Logan's company crossed the river on March 12 at Green's Ferry, where they met Juan Antonio Padilla re-

Dr. Nicholas Descomps Labadie (1802–1867), a French Canadian of Captain William Logan's company, was promoted to assistant surgeon of the Texas Army on April 18. Dr. Labadie wrote a lengthy account of the San Jacinto campaign, which was published in the 1859 *Texas Almanac* and subsequently landed him in a lawsuit with one of Sam Houston's officers.
Courtesy of the Prints and Photographs Collection, The Center for American History, University of Texas at Austin.

turning from the Convention at Washington-on-the-Brazos. They learned that Texas had been declared a free and independent nation.

En route to San Felipe, Captain Logan's company encountered an express rider who brought them the news that Travis' men had been slaughtered at the Alamo and that General Houston's army was retreating from Gonzales. Logan then ordered his men to make a forced march for San Felipe, not stopping for the night until forced by darkness.

"We camped under the six or eight tall pines there, using our saddles for pillows," wrote Dr. Labadie. The cold March weather took a turn for the worse overnight.

> During that night there came up a severe norther, accompanied with rain, and daylight found us all shivering with the cold and wet, and, to add to our disagreeable position, some of our horses could not be found. Upon this, Menard Maxwell, as brave a man as ever shouldered a rifle, cried out: "Captain Logan, give me three men, and I will go back for the horses to Roberts', for they have undoubtedly taken the back track, the cowardly devils."
>
> His request was granted, when they started back at a brisk trot, while we proceeded on our march in a slow gait. Towards evening Maxwell overtook us, having recovered the lost horses.

Upon reaching the Brazos River bottom, Captain Logan's company encountered scores of fleeing citizens of the Runaway Scrape. Women and children, some barefoot and others carrying their youngest, struggled with carts and wagons of their meager possessions. To Dr. Labadie, "the sight was the most painful by far, that I ever witnessed."

Logan's Liberty Company crossed the Brazos on the ferry near San Felipe. In town, they were able to purchase provisions and cooking utensils. The townspeople gave the company some rousing speeches and repeated cheers as they rode on out to join the Texas Army. En route to the Colorado, Logan's men recruited additional volunteers for the army and pressed spare rifles from families who were fleeing from Santa Anna.

Dr. Labadie was busy during the company's first ten days of service treating "cramps, colics and diarrhea" complaints from the men who had been exposed to the cold weather. "I therefore found the stock of medicines, with which I had filled my saddle-bags, very useful."

Captain Logan's Liberty and Beaumont volunteers marched into the army camp on March 20 and reported themselves to General Houston. The arrival of Captains McIntire, Martin and Logan brought Houston's command to sixteen companies. The total men present, including his staff, on March 20 was later believed by General Houston to be: "Six hundred and thirty-two men was the precise rank and file on the Colorado, and this I know to be true."[20]

Colonel Burleson had estimated to Major Willie Williamson on March 18 that the army comprised "five hundred" men. With the arrival of the three latest companies, Houston's count of 632 men on March 20 would be about right. It is probably short by fifty men, however, as Houston had detached Lieutenant Colonel Sherman on March 19 with a detachment of men under Captain William Patton. While the main army positioned itself to cover Beason's Ford on the Colorado River, Sherman had been ordered downstream to protect Mexican forces from using DeWee's Crossing.

Named for Texas pioneer William Bluford DeWees, this key crossing was located about twenty-five miles southeast of La Grange and seven miles south of present Columbus in what is now Colorado County.

On March 20, General Ramirez y Sesma's division began arriving on the opposite side of the Colorado River with two pieces of artillery. His men made camp in a bend of the river about midway between the two nearest key Colorado fords, Beason's and DeWee's. From the Texian camp at Beason's Ford around the twisting river down to DeWee's Ford was a distance of about seven miles. On a straight line crossing the river, the distance was little more than two miles.

Sesma had, according to General Filisola, 725 men when he encamped on the west bank of the Colorado near the Texans. Finding the river well defended, he made no immediate attempt to cross it. Sesma's men had suffered under heavy rains during their march from Gonzales to the Colorado River and their firearms had been thoroughly soaked. His men spent time drying and cleaning them to return them to proper working order.[21]

Captain Chance's Washington Guards

At Washington-on-the-Brazos, the Constitutional Convention adjourned on March 18 and its members scattered for their homes or to join the army.

Jefferson County delegate William Bennett Scates was not only a signer of the Texas Declaration of Independence, but he had been on a committee of five "to devise a flag" for the Republic of Texas. There is little evidence, however, that the flag mentioned ever flew. Vice President Lorenzo de Zavala's design was selected, and Scates made motion that it be accepted, which it was on March 11. Scates had drawn four sketches. The one selected for the Texas flag contained a "Rainbow and Star of five points above the western horizon; and the star of six points sinking below." With the breakup of the Convention, Scates moved toward the army, joining the Sabine company of Captain Benjamin Bryant en route on March 20.[22]

President David Burnet and his cabinet moved out of town and by March 20 had taken up station at Groce's Retreat plantation, located downriver from Washington in present Grimes County. Burnet's cabinet remained at Groce's Retreat for several days before moving on toward Harrisburg, where they had resolved to relocate.[23]

Among Burnet's cabinet was Colonel Thomas Jefferson Rusk, the new Secretary of War for Texas. Born December 1803 in South Carolina, Rusk had practiced law before coming to Texas in 1835. Soon after his arrival, he had organized a mounted company in Nacogdoches which fought bravely during the Bexar siege. He later served as Inspector General of the Army, before being elected to serve as the delegate from the Municipality of Nacogdoches to the Constitutional Convention.

Colonel Rusk was committed to protecting Washington-on-the-Brazos after the departure of the Texas government. On March 17, he had commissioned Captain Andrew Briscoe to organize a small spy company to watch the Mexican army's movements. Briscoe utilized local revolutionary leader Colonel John Henry Moore to recruit and organize a spy company at Washington. Briscoe had thereafter gone out on scouting duties, leaving Moore to organize a local company for the town's defense.

The volunteers that assembled at Washington-on-the-Brazos were organized into a company that was known as the "Washington Guards." According to the papers of John Campbell Hunt, who on April 7 would become first lieutenant of the Washington Guards, this spy company was organized by Colonel Moore and then command fell upon Captain Joseph Bell Chance, who was elected to command by his peers. Chance, a thirty-five-year-old former Tennessean, had served as a delegate to the Second Convention of Texas in San Felipe in 1833.[24]

By March 20, Major Willie Williamson had arrived in town with several of his Texas Rangers. He had ridden ahead of Lieutenant George Petty, acting commander of the remainder of Captain John Tumlinson's company, on the road from Bastrop. Williamson assisted John Henry Moore in organizing the Washington Guards company. With his power as ranger commander, he took supervisory authority of this unit. One of Tumlinson's former rangers, Henry P. Redfield, was assigned to Captain Chance's company. Redfield's audited claims show that he served under Lieutenant Petty until being reassigned to Captain Chance, as affirmed by Major Williamson, "Commanding the Rangers."[25]

Private James M. Manning, a twenty-four-year-old from New Hampshire, was a farmer who had been enlisted into the ranging service on February 11 by Captain Isaac Burton. Like Redfield, many of Captain Chance's volunteers had frontier experience. At least seven of his men—Ennes Hardin, David Wilson Campbell, James R. Childress, Calvin Brallery Emmons, John A. F. Gravis, Peterson Lloyd and Gilbert Wright—had recently served in other ranger companies during the Texas Revolution. Hardin had served as first lieutenant of Captain Daniel Boone Friar's ranger unit. Private Theodore Staunton Lee had served in Colonel Moore's 1835 ranger campaign and had participated in the battle of Gonzales, the Grass Fight and the battle of Concepcion.

Private Amos Gates later recorded that Chance's company was "to be under the command of Maj. R. M. Williamson [and] to remain at Washington and be [called] the Washington Guards." At the time the unit was mustered into service on March 20, Gates and several others were acting in "obedience to" the orders of Williamson. Gates and others "were detailed to go with the families" to the Trinity River, and thus missed out on the San Jacinto campaign.[26]

Colonel Rusk sent orders to General Houston on March 20 for him to post an officer at the ferry at Washington-on-the-Brazos with orders to let no man pass eastward who had a rifle, and to impress all powder, lead and horses possible.[27]

Major Williamson and Captain Chance's company thus fulfilled this duty at Washington, where they awaited further word from General Houston or sign of their enemy.

New Units Unite with Sherman's Division

March 20 proved to be a bonzana in recruiting new men into the Texas Army. In addition to the three new units which had reached Houston at Beason's Ford, Lieutenant Colonel Sherman was having his own good fortunes in gaining new soldiers. Along with a detachment under Captain William Patton, he had moved downriver to De-Wee's Crossing on March 19 and was joined the following day by five more small volunteer groups.

Sherman, the First Regiment's number two man, was joined by two ranger units, two volunteer companies and one regular army company at the shallow water ford of DeWees. Upon his arrival with Patton's men, he found the volunteer unit of Captain William Ware already posted there.

Ware, born in 1800 in Kentucky, was the son of a gunsmith who had settled near present Willis in Montgomery County in 1831. During the Bexar siege, he commanded a company and had been slightly wounded in the hand. Ware returned home from the campaign to look after his wife and three children until the call came to aid those in San Antonio once again. Due to his previous command experience, he was once again elected to lead the small unit which was raised.

Captain Ware's men included Jesse G. Thompson, who in late 1835 had served in the first officially sanctioned revolutionary Texas Ranger company, that of Captain Eli Hillhouse under the superintendence of Silas Parker.

Ware's eighteen-man original company also included two sets of brothers. William P. Cartwright, twenty-three, and Matthew Winston Cartwright, twenty-one, were born in Alabama and had settled with

James Washington Winters (1817-1903) served in the unit of Captain William Ware, which would become Second Company, Second Regiment. Winters returned to the San Jacinto battlefield in 1901 to help the Texas Veterans Association identify important locations.
Courtesy of the San Jacinto Museum of History, Houston.

their family in present Montgomery County during 1832. Nineteen-year-old James Washington Winters heeded the call to aid the Texas Army with two of his older brothers, William Carvin Winters, twenty-seven, and John Freland Winters, twenty-one. He had come to Texas with his parents, twelve siblings and George Lamb, who joined the family on horseback in Arkansas. They settled between the eastern and western prongs of the San Jacinto River in present Montgomery County. James Winters and his brothers, as he recalls, were among the first to join Captain Ware's company.

> On March 12, 1836, about eighteen of us organized a company on the San Bernard; we chose William Ware captain, Job Collard first lieutenant, George Lamb second lieutenant, Albert Gallatin first sergeant, William Winters second sergeant. We went to Dewees' Crossing on the Colorado with the intention of keeping the Mexicans from crossing. We acted independently, without instructions from any one. Houston, at Beason's on the Colorado, sent orders for us to fall back. We did so, marching to the prairie between the Colorado and the San Bernard.[28]

At DeWee's, Captain Patton was the senior officer under Lieutenant Colonel Sherman and became acting commandant of this little encampment. Sherman decided that his enemy should be deprived of any nearby fortification which might enable them to coordinate an attack on his division. He therefore sent Captain David Kokernot and another man across the river to burn the double log home of William DeWees on the opposite bank.

> Not expecting any danger, another man and myself got into a small dugout, crossed the river and set fire to the house and some corn and cotton pens. We had just pushed off on our return when about one hundred Mexican muskets were let loose at us, riddling the boat with holes, but we escaped unhurt, with a tight squeeze, the bushes being alive with the enemy.[29]

Kokernot and his small mounted unit had merged with the other Texas Army companies after arriving at Gonzales. Kokernot would serve under Captain William Hill. Most of his other men were sent on various assignments or left the army during the San Jacinto campaign. Two of Kokernot's men, James Spillman and Milton Atkinson, joined the company of Captain Patton and did serve throughout the campaign.

Shortly after Captain Ware had united with Sherman's men, this little camp was further swelled by the arrival of two more companies, the volunteer infantry unit of Captain Joseph Bennett, and the twelve-man ranger company of Captain Stephen Townsend.

Captain Bennett's men had defended the Moore's Ferry crossing upriver on the Colorado until receiving a dispatch from General Houston on March 19 which ordered them downriver. In their march downriver, they encountered Captain Townsend's rangers on the east bank of the river immediately opposite Jesse Burnam's residence, which was on the west bank.

Thirty-six-year-old Captain Stephen Townsend was one of eight brothers who were originally from the Marlboro District of South Carolina. He departed for Texas in 1833 with his older brother Thomas R. Townsend and a cousin. Stephen and his wife stopped in Louisiana for the birth of their first child. Soon thereafter, he brought his new family to the Colorado River settlements of Texas and settled near present Round Top in Fayette County.[30]

Stephen Townsend raised his small ranger company on February 1 in response to recent Indian attacks along the Colorado River and stationed his men at the head of Mill Creek. Foremost among his recruits were relatives who had also come to Texas to settle. Younger brothers Moses, William T. and Spencer Burton Townsend all enlisted, as did his nephew Stephen Townsend, a son of Captain Townsend's oldest brother Asa. Other members of Townsend's ranging unit included Bexar siege veteran James Bird and Napoleon Bonaparte Breeding.

Summary of General Houston's Forces
March 20–21, 1836: Beason's Ford on the Colorado River

Commander-in-Chief   General Samuel Houston

Command Staff
Col. George W. Hockley   Lt. Col. James C. Neill
Major Alexander Horton   Major William G. Cooke
Major Benjamin Fort Smith

First Regiment Texas Volunteers
Col. Edward Burleson   Lt. Col. Sidney Sherman
Maj. Alexander Somervell   Lt. Henry Stouffer, adjutant

Company	No. of Men*	Notes
Capt. Jesse Billingsley	60	Departed Gonzales March 13 with army.
Capt. Sidney Sherman[1]	51	Departed Gonzales March 13 with army.
Capt. Moseley Baker	110 ⎫	Departed Gonzales March 13 with army.
Capt. Robert McNutt[2]	⎬	Departed Gonzales March 13 with army.
Capt. Thomas J. Rabb[3]	⎭	Departed Gonzales March 13 with army.
Capt. Wiliam W. Hill	40	Departed Gonzales March 13 with army.
Capt. Juan N. Seguin	22	Departed Gonzales March 13 with army.
Capt. Robert J. Calder	25	Departed Gonzales March 13 with army.
Capt. Wm H. Patton	60	Enrolled March 13 at Gonzales.
Capt. William H. Smith	10	Took command of scouts on March 16.
Capt. Henry W. Karnes	15	Took command of scouts March 20.
Capt. John Bird	85	Joined army on March 14.
Capt. Peyton R. Splane	25	Joined army on March 15.
Capt. Wyly Martin	30	Reached main army March 20.
Capt. William Logan	80	Reached main army March 20.
Capt. Thomas McIntire	40	Reached main army March 20.
Capt. Daniel Perry	20	Reached main army March 20–21.
Capt. Joseph Bennett[4]	50	Reaches Sherman's camp March 20.
Capt. William Ware	27	Reaches Sherman's camp March 20.
Capt. Stephen Townsend	12	Reaches Sherman's camp March 20.
Capt. William Sadler[5]	8	Reaches Sherman's camp March 20–21.
Capt. Henry Teal[6]	40	Reaches Sherman's camp March 20–21.
	810	plus command staff

*Estimated numbers. Recruits alternated between companies and departed the service prior to the battle of San Jacinto.

[1] Later commanded by Captain William Wood.
[2] Later commanded by Captain Gibson Kuykendall.
[3] Later commanded by Captain William Jones Elliott Heard.
[4] Later commanded by Captain Gillaspie.
[5] Company later joins with Captain Leander Smith.
[6] Later commanded by Captain Andrew Briscoe.

Bennett's and Townsend's men had camped together on the night of March 19. A dispatch arrived that evening which ordered them to fall farther down the river. "We marched during all the night of the nineteenth, and just at daybreak on the morning of the twentieth we arrived at the encampment of a detachment of the army under captains Patton and Ware," wrote William Zuber of Captain Bennett's company.[31]

According to Zuber, the four-company detachment of Captains Patton, Ware, Bennett and Townsend embraced "about seventy-five men." Ware and Patton's companies had dug an entrenchment on the sandy beach of the Colorado River in the river's channel, near the water's edge. "This was designed as a defense in case of an attack by the enemy from DeWee's Bluff on the opposite side."

After arriving, Townsend's and Bennett's companies built, for their own defense, an extension of this entrenchment. As Sherman's four companies worked on their trenches, yet another small group of regular army soldiers arrived at DeWee's from Nacogdoches, according to Private Zuber.

> A company arrived from Nacogdoches, commanded by a lieutenant who was known by the appellation of "Black Hawk." They also went to work and built an extension of the entrenchment.

This company was that of Captain Henry Teal. Moving in to join the Texas Army from Nacogdoches, "Teal's company of regulars" was noted by General Houston as "not a full company." An examination of the service dates of Teal's men shows that he did have forty men under his charge as of March 20—a greater number than many of the army's volunteer companies.[32]

Henry Teal, born in 1800, came to Texas with his father and settled in present San Augustine County. He had been second lieutenant of Captain Thomas Rusk's company in the siege of Bexar, returning home afterwards. During early January 1836, Lieutenant Teal had recruited men for the regular army, enlisting them for periods of two years. Some of his men had arrived at Velasco aboard the schooner *Pennsylvania* on January 28 from New Orleans, while others had been recruited from around San Augustine. At least one man, John N. Taylor, had been transferred into Teal's company from Sidney Sherman's Kentucky company while in Nacogdoches on February 2.

Teal and Lieutenant Martin Kingsley Snell, a Pennsylvanian who had come to Texas in 1835 with Captain William Cooke's New Orleans

Greys, had enrolled more than thirty men before leaving Nacog-doches. They marched to the site of the Convention at Washington-on-the-Brazos, arriving March 15. By resolution of the Convention, Teal was appointed as a captain.

Captain Teal's company included two musicians, Frederick Lem-sky, a German immigrant, and Martin Flores, who had fought under Captain Thomas Rusk during the Bexar siege. The tallest man of the company at six feet four inches was undoubtedly Ohio native John Van Winkle. The shortest man, at five feet one and a half inches, was Ly-man Frank Rounds, who had been enlisted into the Texas Army on January 1 at San Augustine. A twenty-nine-year-old carpenter, Rounds was forwarded to Nacogdoches, where he was enrolled into Captain Teal's regular army company.

Rounds later wrote of the company's movements in catching up with the Texas Army.

> In March we left there to reinforce Col. Travis at the Alamo, but while Capt. Teal and myself was standing in the Hall of the Convention then sitting at Washington-on-the-Brazos, a courier arrived with the news that Travis and his whole party had been captured and cut to pieces. We then marched and joined Houston on the Colorado.[33]

Teal's company did not stay long at DeWee's Ford with Lieutenant Colonel Sherman. He was sent with dispatches to report in to General Houston at Beason's, arriving there on March 22.[34]

With the arrival of Captain Teal's regulars, Houston now had more military process about camp. For instance, tattoo and reveille were played by the musicians at dawn and in the evening on a regular basis to organize the men.[35]

Sidney Sherman remained fortified at DeWee's with his detach-ment under Patton, Ware, Townsend and Bennett. They were joined about March 21 by another small group of men, the remnants of Cap-tain William Turner Sadler's East Texas ranger company. His little Fort Houston ranger company had disbanded after getting the call to come to the Alamo's aid.

Sadler and seven of his men had crossed the Trinity River at Nathaniel Robbins' ferry on the morning of March 19. They then proceeded down the La Bahia Road toward San Felipe, apparently splitting off down the road which led to DeWee's Crossing.

According to W. T. Sadler's pension papers, his men joined the army "at or near the DeWees Crossing on the Colorado River." The

William Turner Sadler (1797–1884) disbanded his Houston County rangers in March 1836 to join the Texas Army. After riding more than 150 miles, he and seven of his men joined Colonel Sherman on the Colorado River. Sadler fought at San Jacinto as a member of the "Nacogdoches Volunteers," officially the First Company, Second Regiment. *Author's collection.*

other seven who accompanied Sadler to the Texas Army were Daniel Parker Jr., Dickerson Parker (both sons of the Daniel Parker who had brought the first non-Catholic church to Texas), John Crawford Grigsby, Philip Martin, James Madden, William Calvert Hallmark and John W. Carpenter. All of these men soon joined another company known as the Nacogdoches Volunteers near the Colorado River after that company's original formation date.[36]

Major Ben Smith's Brush with Sesma's Soldiers

With the army settled in at Beason's Ferry on the evening of March 20, many men feared for the safety of their families who were caught up in the Runaway Scrape. With the swell of new recruits joining the army that day, a few men were allowed to take furloughs.

Colonel Burleson allowed some men to return to help their families where there were special needs, such as the case of a son being the oldest male of a family where a father had died. From Jesse Billingsley's Mina Volunteers, he allowed privates Greenleaf Fisk, Edward Blakey, Walker Wilson and John Jenkins to depart from Beason's and return to Bastrop to assist their families.[37]

Houston was still frustrated by the men who had deserted him at Gonzales and he sent orders on March 21 to San Felipe to halt any deserters who were encountered. All persons leaving the country away from the enemy would be required to return or to have their weapons taken away for the army's use. Only one armed man per family moving to safety was to be allowed. "Victory is inevitable," wrote Houston, "if unity of action and good order is preserved."

Colonel George Hockley, the army's inspector general, wrote a report to Secretary of War Rusk from "Camp near Beason's" on March 21 of Captain Karnes' skirmish the previous day and of the Mexican soldier who had been captured. "The prisoner states that more than a thousand men are now on their march to this point," wrote Hockley, "and will probably be near us tonight." The prisoner also reported that the Mexicans had three artillery pieces and that a detachment of their army had also marched from San Antonio to attack Goliad.[38]

The Texan troops were "eager to meet the enemy." More importantly, "Our army are in very fine spirits, and good health, not having one on our sick list." The army's spies were "active and vigilant—and the enemy can gain no advantage over us." Hockley also added that "a detachment of one hundred men are now crossing the river to meet the enemy's advance—and every confidence may be placed in their entire success."

Lieutenant Colonel Sherman's detachment was downriver to hold DeWee's Crossing of the Colorado. Hearing of the closeness of Mexican troops, General Houston moved his men slightly off the main road at Beason's. He had the troops chop down some cottonwood trees on the east side of the Colorado to form breastworks for reinforcement.[39]

As mentioned in Colonel Hockley's note, Houston also sent a large force of men to size up the Mexican troops which were approaching his camp. In an army communication written on March 21, Houston stated that he "sent a force of two hundred men on the west side of the river. In a few days I hope to have force sufficient to capture the enemy before he can reach the Guadalupe."[40]

Major Benjamin Fort Smith was given command of several small companies to take on this mission. Smith, thirty-seven, was raised in Kentucky by the son of a Revolutionary War veteran and had fought under General Andrew Jackson in the 1815 battle of New Orleans. Later settling at Natchez, Mississippi, Smith served in that state's First Legislature and was thereafter appointed an Indian agent by President Jackson. He moved on to Texas in 1833 and settled in Brazoria County, where he engaged extensively in the purchase and sale of slaves. Having served with the Texas Army during 1835, Major Smith was appointed by General Houston to be the army's acting Quartermaster General and Adjutant General.[41]

Hockley gave Smith's detachment as "one hundred men" while Houston doubled that number in his correspondence. The true number was closer to one hundred and fifty men, half of whom had horses. The infantrymen were stationed by Major Smith at the boardinghouse of Benjamin and Elizabeth Beason.

His detachment included mounted men and infantrymen from the companies of Captains Henry Karnes, William Smith, John Bird, Robert Calder, Peyton Splane and William Logan. With General Ramirez y Sesma rumored to have pitched his camp on the opposite, west, bank of the Colorado, Dr. Nicholas Labadie was one of a dozen volunteers from Captain Logan's Liberty Company. Together with Major Smith, Labadie and a portion of the troops crossed over the Colorado River to reconnoiter the Mexican campground.[42]

General Houston also sent an aide to recruit volunteers who would proceed immediately to protect the next nearest river crossing from Beason's, the Atascocito Crossing of the Colorado. From Captain Robert McNutt's company, Privates Felix G. Wright, David Lawrence and James Kuykendall volunteered. To this was added John Ingram of Captain William Hill's company. The four went to Houston for instructions. They were asked to proceed cautiously to the Atascocito Crossing and remain stationed there until they could be relieved the following day.

Ingram led this little party out. By feeling their way along through the pitch blackness, the party reached the crossing around midnight. "Here we remained until after sunrise the next morning without seeing or hearing aught of the enemy," wrote Kuykendall. Relieved by another crew on March 22, his quartet had returned to the Texan camp the following morning.[43]

During the evening of March 21, Major Ben Fort Smith's men took up position near Sesma's camp. The following morning, March 22, he led approximately "one hundred men, to skirmish with the enemy," recalled Captain Calder.[44]

According to Dr. Labadie, the mounted party numbered sixty-four, but was accompanied by the company of Captain John Bird. "We were told we had to attack Sesma's camp of 600 men, and that Capt. Bird was to follow us, taking his position in the edge of the timber to cover our retreat." Labadie found Captain Karnes to be "brave" but not as experienced a leader as Major Smith, "having seen years of service in the U.S. Army."[45]

Karnes and some of his spies moved into the timber ahead of Major Smith's infantrymen. As they closed on General Sesma's campground, they were spotted by Mexican guards. Shots were fired at the Texans and the camp's cannon was even unleashed, sending Karnes' men racing from the vicinity.

As one of Karnes' cavalrymen raced from the woods, he shouted to Major Smith that the Mexicans were within sight and firing upon them. Having stirred up the enemy, Smith ordered his small force of men to fall back, as the cannon balls whistled by just overhead. He elected to recross the river and take up a defensive position from which he might be able to put up a fair fight. Smith's advance forces retreated back to the Colorado River. The cavalry stripped its horses and threw saddles, blankets and other gear into the ferry to hastily haul across the water.[46]

While his men crossed the river, Major Smith ordered one small group of his men to destroy anything that could be of assistance to the Mexican soldiers. Texas sentinels rounded up all the cattle that they could move from Beason's boardinghouse and then destroyed Beason's lodgings. Cavalryman John Sharp found himself once again faced with the unpleasant task of burning down dwellings of his fellow Texans before retreating.

> Beason had a large quantity of corn in his crib, and, attached to his gin was a mill, which might have been of service to the enemy, in grinding corn for the army; the house, also, was large, and would have accommodated a large body of the enemy, and have served to protect them, in case we had made an attack upon them. We therefore concluded to burn everything standing, and retreat across the river; which we did before the enemy had come in sight.

General Ramirez y Sesma, reluctant to cause a full-scale engagement with his division, did not immediately pursue the Texans as they made their way back across the Colorado. He did send a number of riflemen to the edge of the river to keep his enemy engaged.

Captain Robert Calder noted that Major Smith's men had scarcely made it back across the river before "some stragglers of the enemy appeared on the opposite side of the river." These Mexican troops "were fired upon by some of our men, not, however, with any perceptible effect, as they were beyond ordinary rifle range."[47]

Although Major Smith's surprise attack on the Mexican forces had not been successful, it had at least inspired the Texian troops. Many of them became even more eager for a fight.

In an effort to drum up more volunteers, Captain Moseley Baker wrote a letter from "Camp on the Colorado" to the editors of the *Telegraph and Texas Register* on March 22. He stated that the Mexican army was crossing the Colorado at DeWee's and that Houston had some 800 men at his disposal now. Baker called on the women of Texas "to permit no man to stay at home, but to bid them where duty and honor calls them." He also added that firing had just been heard between Major Smith's Texas spies and the Mexicans.[48]

Houston kept his camp across from Beason's burned boarding-house on March 23. Inspector General George Hockley's report to Secretary of War Rusk on this date gave the main army's location as "Camp near Beason's." He wrote that Houston "still maintains the position at this place, commanding the crossing of the Colorado at Mosely's, above Beason's," and that another small group held the crossing at Atascocito below. Hockley wrote that Houston "intends to remain stationary, unless offensive operations shall be justified by circumstances or reinforcements."[49]

Lieutenant Colonel Sherman's spies were kept on constant alert for signs that General Ramirez y Sesma's men were preparing for an assault. A group of his men had the good fortune to surprise three Mexican soldiers who were out foraging for food. These three prisoners were taken under a guard detail and marched along the river toward the main Texian camp.

On the morning of March 23, General Houston elected to send another hundred volunteers to strengthen Sherman's group. Among those volunteering was the majority of Captain Robert McNutt's company. Within five minutes, McNutt's men were en route to DeWee's Crossing to join Sherman. These volunteers passed the guard detail bringing in the new prisoners. Private James Kuykendall sized up Sherman's camp upon his arrival.

> We found Col. Sherman encamped in the bottom about sixty yards from the river, along the bank of which, and opposite the ford, he had dug a ditch. In the rear of the camp was a dense canebrake through which an opening had been cut to post sentinels. A prairie extended from the opposite bank of the river to the position of the enemy in the edge of the post-oak woods.[50]

When Sherman's prisoners arrived in Houston's camp in the afternoon of April 23, they were immediately interrogated. Moses Austin Bryan of Captain Baker's company helped to interrogate the prisoners. "I was sergeant of the camp guard and at the guard fire when Gen. Sam Houston sent for me to question the three Mexicans," he wrote.

Each prisoner was interrogated separately. Colonel Hockley informed Secretary of War Rusk of the intelligence garnered from the Mexican soldiers.

> They agree very nearly in their statements, an outline of which is as follows:—
>
> That General Sesma is on the opposite side of the river, about three miles from our encampment, with five or six hundred men—a hundred and fifty cavalry—and two small pieces of artillery. His troops are badly clad, and the state of the weather such as to render them almost ineffectual from cold. They are building a boat, and intend crossing near us.
>
> They are evidently checked by the skirmish with our spies (named in a previous letter). The prisoners say that General Sesma halted the next day to rest. With our reinforcements, we shall be able to anticipate any [men] the enemy may receive.[51]

Houston would soon send Sherman's latest prisoners and the Mexican soldier previously captured by Karnes' spies on to the government at Harrisburg under a guard company composed of Edwin Stanley, James McLaughlin and others.[52]

Houston wrote to Captain B. J. White on March 23 from "Camp at Beason's Ferry." He ordered White to "repair to Cox's Point, or Dimit's Landing and remove or secure the supplies at those places." Captain White was ordered to use all means to secure supplies and to remove families in this area and to move them safely to the east side of the Colorado. This message appears to have been sent with Benjamin Noble.[53]

Houston did receive more supplies on March 23. George Hockley wrote that "one wagon with arms, ammunition" arrived which included forty-eight muskets. To the troops, this "increased their anxiety and confidence, as they now find the promised supplies." Hockley still found that the army's need "for an efficient corps of cavalry" suffered from the want of good horses, sabres and pistols.[54]

From the prisoners' intelligence, Hockley expected the enemy to soon be crossing the Colorado. "From our present position, we can effectually command any point at which he may attempt it." Sherman's detachment "will be reformed in a thick wood on the bank of the river, and in a position that [is] highly favorable for observation and defense, its present flanks and front being well protected by felled trees, brush and timber."

Writing late into the night as March 23 turned into March 24, Hockley added that General Gregory of North Carolina, Colonel Willis Nibbs, "and some other gentlemen from Washington" had just arrived that moment in camp in company with Major George Washington Poe of the Texas Army's artillery. "They report about two hundred men on their march, who will join tomorrow."

Sam Houston received two letters from Tom Rusk this day from a courier named Walker. He noted that his "friend Hockley" had become his closest ally in camp. Houston offered Rusk congratulations on his new promotion to secretary of war, and thus the senior military commander in Texas. "I trust you will find in me a worthy subaltern," he wrote.

> You know I am not easily depressed, but, before my God, since we parted, I have found the darkest hours of my past life! My excitement have been so great, that, for forty-eight hours, I have not eaten an ounce, nor have I slept. I was in constant apprehension of a rout; a constant panic existed in the lines: yet I managed so well, or such was my good luck, that not a gun was fired in or near the camp, or on the march (except to kill beef), from the Guadalupe to the Colorado.[55]

Houston was bothered by the "panic struck" deserters, whose fears became "contagious, and all who saw them breathed the poison and fled." In anger he added, "Oh, curse the consternation which has seized the people!" Adding to the problem of the earlier deserters was the fact that he was now safekeeper of all the poor families of the Runaway Scrape. He could not swiftly move against an opponent without endangering many civilian lives.

As General Houston penned his letter to Rusk late on March 23, a courier brought news that Colonel Fannin had been attacked a few miles from La Bahia. The results of the battle were still unknown to him. Houston showed that he had no respect for the man who would not follow his orders and abandon Goliad.

> If what I have heard from Fannin be true, I deplore it, and can only attribute the ill luck to his attempting to retreat in daylight in the face of a superior force. He is an ill-fated man.

Houston was bolstered by the intelligence he had extracted from his Mexican prisoners this day. He knew that General Ramirez y

Sesma had no more than seven hundred men. Given more volunteers, Houston vowed "we can beat them." As for the retreat of the cabinet of the Texas government from Washington, "I am half-provoked at it myself."

Houston hinted that other Texian forces were being unnecessarily deployed. For example, he felt that Captain Chance's entire company at Washington-on-the-Brazos was overkill. "Why do you keep more than a sergeant's or lieutenant's guard at Washington?" he asked.

"I am writing in the open air," Houston wrote. "I have no tent, and am not looking out for the luxuries of life." He hoped only to be "useful to my country and the cause of liberty."

Despite the news of Fannin's defeat, the latest reinforcements on March 23 had Houston's spirits high.

> Men are flocking to camp, and I expect, in a day or two, to receive two hundred volunteers and regulars. Forty-eight muskets and a supply of ammunition came opportunely last night. In a few days my force will be highly respectable.

CHAPTER 6

Falling Back

March 24–27

> There are times when it requires more courage to retreat than to stand and fight, and this was the case at the Colorado. There is no doubt but that nine-tenths of the army was anxious to fight.
>
> —*Private John Milton Swisher, Company H, First Regiment*

Sam Houston was certainly aware of the growing desire of his men to attack General Ramirez y Sesma's forces across the Colorado River. There is some indication that Houston did plan to carry out such an attack at one point. He later indicated to Colonel Rusk that he was contemplating this move, although he spoke this to no one.

The Texian army was holding three key river crossings of the Colorado River, but the majority of the men were on the eastern banks. To attack Ramirez y Sesma's men, they would have to cross back over and risk coming under fire while doing so.

Sidney Sherman, in command of the division of men guarding De-Wee's [also called Moseley's] Crossing, sent a request to General Houston that he be allowed to lead an attack. He had more than three hundred men at his disposal.

He felt strongly that his men could rout Sesma's force of roughly six hundred with small loss. Lieutenant Colonel Sherman reportedly stated that he would "rout the enemy or not return alive." His request was refused and he was ordered not to provoke an attack.[1]

Orderly Sergeant Tony Menchaca of Captain Juan Seguin's Tejano company was among those ready to challenge Ramirez y Sesma at the Colorado.

> As soon as the Americans saw that the Mexicans were trying to draw them into an attack, the Americans prepared themselves to attack. But Houston

told them that not a single man should move out, that the Mexicans were only trying to draw him out and ascertain his strength, which he did not intend to let them know.

The Americans murmured, whereupon Houston told them that such was his determination, and that nothing would tempt him to depart from it.[2]

Captain Robert Calder's company was equally prepared to attack General Ramirez y Sesma.

> There was a strong desire on the part of a large portion of the army to attack this division of the enemy, numbering about seven hundred men, and a considerable murmuring was heard at the Commander-in-chief's refusal to gratify this desire. That we might have routed them, I have *no doubt*. I think our muster-rolls showed that we had some fourteen hundred men at the time.[3]

Calder's company was reinforced with the addition of some new volunteers on March 24. Among them was thirty-eight-year-old Dr. Anson Jones, a future president of the Republic of Texas. Born in Massachusetts, Jones had received his degree of Doctor of Medicine from the Jefferson Medical School at Philadelphia. After practicing there and at New Orleans, he had arrived in Texas in 1833 aboard the schooner *Sabine* and settled in Brazoria.[4]

Jones arrived with Colonel John Austin Wharton, Dr. James Hazard Perry and several other Washington area citizens. Wharton, a Nashville-raised lawyer, had practiced his trade in New Orleans for three years before joining his older brother, William Harris Wharton, in Texas in 1833. General Houston had appointed John Wharton a Texas Army agent in December 1835 and sent him to New Orleans to secure supplies. Recently returned, Colonel Wharton had made his way back to the main army and now joined Sam Houston's staff as adjutant general, the position that Major Ben Smith had been filling in the interim.[5]

Dr. Perry was a volunteer from New York who had left aboard a brig on November 21, 1835, with volunteer soldiers under Major Edwin Morehouse. Upon reaching Texas soil, Perry made his way to the Texas Army and introduced himself to Sam Houston. Taking the advice of new Texas President Burnet, Houston appointed Perry to a position on his command staff.

> He came to the camp on the Colorado with letters of introduction from the President and other members of the cabinet to the Commander-in-Chief, recommending him as a graduate of West Point, or having been a student

there. Being a good looking gentleman, plausible in his manner, unembarrassed by diffidence, not very cultivated, still would do well for a soldier or officer, the general appointed him a member of his staff.[6]

Among other promotions, John Sharp, a cavalryman of Captain Henry Karnes' company, was elevated to first lieutenant of Captain Calder's company on March 24. Irregardless of rank, Sharp would continue to be a vital courier for General Houston, a man unafraid to run the gauntlet of enemy troops to deliver important news.

The next evening, in fact, Lieutenant Sharp was ordered by Sam Houston out on an express mission to Major William Austin, commandant of the post at Velasco. Sharp carried words of encouragement from his commander-in-chief.

> Whilst receiving my papers, General Houston told me to tell the people down in that part of the country not to run any further. They were safe; there would be no more retreating; and that the next news they would hear from the army would be of a battle, the result of which no one could doubt.[7]

Sharp encountered many settlers during the Runaway Scrape. He noted "great alarm prevailing among the people, many of them flying with their families to the United States." He estimated the Texan forces on the Colorado at this time to number "from 1,000 to 1,200 men, and reinforcements hourly coming in."[8]

Sharp's estimate of Texan forces may have been a little high, but he was equally bold in his statements: "Our army will never leave the Colorado to go westward," he wrote. "Every day will bring news of a fresh victory, until not a Mexican soldier, opposed to us, can be found this side of the Rio Grande!"

Sharp reached Brazoria by March 27. En route, he noted that "several small companies" were pushing toward Houston's camp from the eastward sections of Texas. He believed that "from 300 to 500 men" were on their way toward Houston's camp.

Among the small companies of men that joined Houston on the Colorado River was that of Captain Daniel Perry, who had arrived in Texas in June 1832. His volunteer company had been organized in present Fort Bend County on March 6, 1836. Perry's company was passing San Felipe on March 18, when Second Lieutenant Ebenezer R. Hale acquired tools and horses for the use of the army.[9]

General Sesma's seven hundred troops on the Colorado River were joined on March 24 by another division under General Eugenio Tolsa. Tolsa brought with him the Guerrero and Mexico City battalions, fifty more horses and an additional fieldpiece. The combined strength of Sesma and Tolsa's union was now 1300 troops, two artillery pieces and 150 cavalry.[10]

Sesma estimated the opposing Texian forces to number about 1,000 men when he first arrived at the Colorado. He estimated to Santa Anna on March 28 that another two hundred rebels had joined during the next few days. With high water and no easy crossing of the river available to him, Sesma maintained his station across from the Texans and kept a close watch.

Houston Calls for a Retreat

In Sidney Sherman's large lower Colorado camp, a Texan named Peter Kerr arrived on the night of March 25 from Goliad. Major Alex Horton considered him to be "a man well skilled in the Mexican affairs." Kerr reported that Colonel James Fannin's command had been overtaken and captured by the enemy. Kerr had been held a prisoner at the ranch of Martin de Leon, and escaped after hearing of the defeat of Fannin.[11]

This news was disturbing to the Texas soldiers. Private William Zuber of Captain Bennett's company wrote, "Then it was certain that Houston's personal command was the last and only hope for Texas."[12]

When Kerr's report made it to Houston later, he would accuse Kerr of being a spy. "General Houston judged that, as a matter of course, his men were intimidated by Kerr's report, and, to preserve their courage, he affected to disbelieve it," wrote Zuber.

"We all, however, believed his report to be true, and it was corroborated by others the next day," wrote Dr. Labadie of Captain Logan's company, "after which the numbers in our camp began to diminish rapidly."

Indications are that Houston actually knew of Fannin's defeat as early as March 23, but word did not circulate through the masses until Kerr's report arrived late on March 25. Whatever thoughts he had entertained of making a stand on the Colorado River were soon dropped after this intelligence.

Houston decided to move his troops out again the next day. He would continue to wait for the right opportunity to make a decisive fight. Prior to Kerr's intelligence, Houston's "intention was to have attacked him on the second night [March 27] after the day on which Fannin's destruction was reported by Kerr." He also expected "the march of strong reinforcements" to Ramirez y Sesma.[13]

Ever since the Texas cavalrymen had been fired on while approaching Sesma's camp several days before, men such as Sidney Sherman were eager to bring on a general fight with Sesma's men. Prior to Kerr's report, Houston felt that his men had been "keen for action."

Why did Houston decide to refrain from attacking the Mexican forces at the Colorado? He knew that Major General Santa Anna controlled infantrymen, cavalry, and artillery in the divisions which were moving down from Bexar. If he faced these forces at this time, he would do so without artillery. With so many untrained and largely undisciplined volunteers, he did not reasonably expect a good outcome in conflict at this point.

He partially felt that a battle with only General Sesma's seven hundred men would have been an indecisive victory and that he had no means of transporting wounded soldiers in a retreat after battle. He was also unsure whether his untrained and unruly Texian force could handle more than one serious fight.[14]

The reason for moving camp cited by Sam Houston to his men was the need to find new grass for the horses and mules to graze upon.[15]

Houston issued an army order on March 26 from "Camp near Beason." He wrote that "the Army is moving out of the post oaks, and probably may fall back towards the Brazos. Troops coming from lower country after today ought to fall back on Columbia, and the mouth of the river as well as supplies."[16]

Although he had a number of key staff members, Houston consulted none in his decision to have the army fall back. He wrote that "The Army will march slowly" and that great caution should be used. For newly arriving troops in Matagorda, he ordered that they "act in defense of the coast."

Houston's unwillingness to engage Sesma at the Colorado was disappointing to most. The men felt that their numbers were strong enough to overpower the Mexican forces. The exact number of Texan troops gathered at the Colorado River as of March 26 will likely never be known due to the volume of men coming and going during these days of the campaign. Most of the surviving muster rolls for the San Jacinto campaign do not list all of the men who originally served with each company, making a true count virtually impossible.

There are a number of estimates given by the San Jacinto campaign participants, and these vary by hundreds of men. One such estimate was offered in 1860 by Major Ben Fort Smith.[17]

> The number of men mustered in the army under Gen. Houston, at the time of the retreat from the Colorado, was about 1360; and the men, to a man, were ready and eager for battle.

Captain William Heard felt that there were between fifteen and sixteen hundred Texans at Houston's disposal on March 26. "I believe this, because the issuing Commissary told me that morning that there were 1600 [who] drew rations." Heard also felt that the men were "more anxious to engage the Mexicans than I ever saw one set of men to engage another, except at San Jacinto." Ben C. Franklin felt that there "were at least fourteen hundred men in the army" at the time of the retreat from the Colorado River. Another soldier who joined the army on March 26, believed that "Houston's army was 1,372 men."[18]

Dr. Anson Jones, the newly arrived member of Captain Calder's company, gave an assessment of the number of troops which agrees closely with Heard's figures.

> On the morning we retreated from the Colorado, we had, by the official report of the day, over 1500 effective men (I think 1570). I assisted Col. John A. Wharton, the Adjt.-General, in making up his report. On the same morning, there were at least 100 men in camp who had not enrolled themselves in any company, but were ready and willing to fight. On the same morning, there were many on the way to join the army, enough to have increased the number to 2000 or more in ten days. On the same day, we were opposed by General Sesma, with only six to seven hundred men.

The total Texian troops and refugees in camp definitely numbered more than one thousand as of March 26. Major Smith's assessment of 1,360 seems to be a pretty fair estimate. Houston was joined by about three hundred new recruits as he was preparing to and beginning to fall back from the Colorado River.

Sam Houston was in a rush to move the men out from the Colorado River on the morning of March 26. "General Houston was here, there, and everywhere, hurrying up and giving orders preparatory for a start," wrote scout Daniel Shipman.[19]

One man not so eager to move was wagon driver James Wilson, a heavyset six-foot-four volunteer under wagon master Conrad Rohrer.

Although considered to be a "true, warm hearted, good natured back-woodsman," Jim Wilson was also prone to become "a perfect hyena when aroused to anger."

Shipman recalled that Wilson had worn out his shoes by the time he had reached the Colorado and the sawbrier plants had torn up his bare feet and ankles. "Jim was heard swearing most profainly" the previous evening that he would not move his oxen team again until he had been supplied with a pair of shoes. "Our mess encamped next to Jim and we anticipated a rich time in the morning," wrote Shipman.

Sure enough, General Houston had his confrontation with Wilson the next morning when he found his wagon team not moving. Cursing mightily, he ordered the wagon driver to move his team. Wilson pointed at his feet and barked back, "Do you think I am going to drive a wagon for a damned little one-horse army and my feet in that fix?"

True to his style, Houston had a way of motivating even the most belligerent of men in most cases. According to Shipman, Houston even offered up his own boots for the sake of getting the army moving. Apparently moved by this gesture, Wilson took up his whips and decided he would drive his wagon once again without shoes.

As word circulated that Houston was retreating from the Colorado, the men were resentful. James Tarlton of Captain Moseley Baker's company later wrote of this "shameful retreat." Tarlton had brought a company of Kentucky volunteers to Texas in 1835. Most had eventually returned home, but he had stayed throughout the Texas Revolution to fight, joining up with Baker at San Felipe. Tarlton said that "every man who had a wife or mother or sister, left the army, to place them beyond the reach of an enemy who had sworn to 'take no prisoners.'"[20]

During the days that Houston and Sesma sat across the river from each other, the soldiers in the Texas Army had been eager to fight. Private John Swisher:

> Much fault was found with General Houston for not giving battle to Sesma's division on the Colorado; and for years after, it was the fruitful theme of discussion between his friends and enemies. . .
>
> There are times when it requires more courage to retreat than to stand and fight, and this was the case at the Colorado. There is no doubt but that nine-tenths of the army was anxious to fight; our ranks were full; we outnumbered the enemy immediately opposing us nearly two to one.[21]

Some would brand Houston a coward for choosing to retreat. Few could think that he might have a great strategy behind his movements of the troops. Many men thus chose to leave the army. According to

Captain Baker, Houston lost "some three or four hundred men" who moved to take care of their families once the army retreated from the Colorado. The actual number of men leaving was probably closer to two hundred.[22]

As when Houston hastily abandoned Gonzales on March 13, the retreat from the Colorado River was swift on March 26. Again, it was so swift that some of the outlying sentinels did not receive word to move out. Such was the case of twenty-seven-year-old Moses Lapham of Captain Moseley Baker's company.

Captain William Heard later wrote:

> When the army commenced retreating from this place, a man called Moses Lapham, and two others, were left on picket guard, and remained in this condition several days without provisions, and frequently in sight of the enemy. For many days, the friends of poor Lapham believed him to have fallen a victim, but he afterwards came up to the camp [and] fought at San Jacinto.[23]

Houston's troops marched about seven miles on the afternoon of March 26 before making camp for the night. They were joined on the march by many civilians, including Benjamin and Elizabeth Beason, who left behind their ferry and the charred remains of their once-proud farm and boardinghouse.

The Nacogdoches Volunteers

At his encampment, Lieutenant Colonel Sherman ordered an extra supply of beef to be slaughtered on the morning of March 26, but did not order it to be cooked.[24]

His three-hundred-odd troops were joined that morning by a new East Texas company, Captain Leander Smith's Nacogdoches Volunteers. The company had organized in its namesake town on March 6 and consisted of citizens from around the Nacogdoches Municipality, an area that encompasses areas as far as present Houston and Anderson Counties. They arrived at Sherman's camp on March 26 after a steady march from Nacogdoches down the La Bahia Road and the Coushatta Trace road.

Captain Smith was a brother-in-law of Colonel Thomas Rusk. During the San Jacinto campaign, his company would include six sets of brothers. There were Levi and Martin Pruitt, John and Jesse

Walling, Daniel Jr. and Dickerson Parker, and Alfred M. and William Calvert Hallmark. There were enlistees Joseph Randolph and John Swason Yarbrough Jr., who joined with their father, John Swanson Yarbrough Sr. There were also brothers John Andrew, Nelson A., Stillwell and Thomas Griffin Box, plus their cousin James Edward Box. Another notable company member was David Rusk, the twenty-two-year-old brother of Secretary of War Rusk. The company included one Tejano, Jose Molino, who also went by the American name of Jose Palonio Lavigna.

"The first captain elected to command our company was Leander Smith on the Trinity River near Robbins' Ferry," wrote Madison Guess Whitaker, a twenty-five-year-old veteran of the Bexar siege, in his pension papers.[25] This date was March 13. Captain Smith's company then "joined the main army commanded by Gen. Houston on the Colorado River in the latter part of same month."

By March 23, the Nacogdoches Volunteers were at Cole's Settlement, Texas at the Asa Hoxey Plantation. There, Smith's men took on corn, fodder and bacon, the receipt being signed by thirty-year-old Lieutenant Hayden Arnold, a native of Tennessee who had enlisted in the volunteer auxiliary corps on January 14 in Nacogdoches.[26]

Along the company's march to join the Texas Army, Smith's company heard the bad news. Private John Harvey, a twenty-six-year-old former Tennessean, later wrote that his company "met an express with intelligence of the fall of the Alamo and the massacre of Fannin and his men. This news augmented our courage and hurried us on." Harvey noted that Smith's company joined Colonel Sherman on the Colorado River "the same day Sherman rec'd orders from Houston to retreat."[27]

After arriving at DeWee's Crossing, Captain Smith's Nacogdoches company was supplemented by the eight former rangers under William Sadler. The pension papers of Sadler show that he was assigned by Sherman as "a private soldier in the company commanded by Captain Leander Smith."[28]

Muster rolls and audited claims for Sadler's former rangers generally give March 6—the date the Nacogdoches company was organized—as the date that they joined Smith's company. Pension papers and other documents, however, show that they had actually joined up nearly three weeks later. Philip Martin, for example, wrote to Sam Houston in 1855 that "I joined the army on the Colorado, and in its march to San Jacinto I joined Captain Hayden Arnold's company."[29]

Shortly after Captain Smith's Nacogdoches men arrived, an express rider came into camp with a message from General Houston. Colonel Sherman handed the message to his adjutant Henry Stouffer to read to him. The message called for Sherman's men to fall back from the Colorado to a point where there was plenty of fresh grass for the animals.[30]

As the retreat orders from Houston were read, Sherman's command immediately expressed criticism. His men, however, reluctantly took up the line of march away from the Colorado River. They loaded their freshly slaughtered beef into sacks and onto their pack animals and departed without knowing exactly where they were going. They assumed that they were headed to join with General Houston's main body of the army.

"About sunset our little division was in motion," wrote James Kuykendall, one of the men who had joined Sherman's division on March 22. "After marching six or seven miles we lay down our arms without fire."[31]

Sherman's forces marched out of the Colorado bottomlands until about midnight on March 26–27. They halted in a thicket of dead saplings, some of which were hacked down and used to fuel the evening campfires. The men used wooden rods to cook the beef they had killed that morning. For some, it was their only meal of the long day.[32]

Sherman Joined by Forbes Battalion

Sidney Sherman had his men back on the march shortly after their morning coffee on March 27. Strengthened by Captain Smith's Nacogdoches company the previous day, he was soon joined by three additional companies under the supervision of Major John Forbes.

These three companies numbered at least 136 men and as many as 150. The first company, under Captain Amasa Turner, had arrived at 11:00 a.m. on March 26 as Sherman prepared to follow Houston's orders to retreat. The companies of Captains William S. Fisher and Richard Roman arrived during the overnight hours of March 26–27.

The companies of Captains Roman and Turner were largely men from the United States who had been recruited to fight in the Texas Revolution. The man most instrumental in recruiting had been Amasa Turner. Given a commission as a lieutenant by the General Council of Texas, Turner had returned home to Mobile to recruit. He had little luck in Alabama, however, and moved to New Orleans in search of volunteers. Using the *New Orleans Bee*, he printed two hundred handbills inviting "farmers" to go to Texas with him. Commissioners John Wharton and Stephen F. Austin, also in New Orleans to recruit, frowned on Turner's recruiting methods.[33]

Undaunted, Lieutenant Turner had posted his handbills all over town, asking people to meet him at a popular saloon on Levee Street. The next morning, Turner found a crowd in the saloon awaiting him. He climbed up on the bar and delivered a speech, and announced that a vessel would be ready at a wharf by nightfall to receive them. Learning of Turner's successful effort, John Wharton procured provisions, clothing, ammunition, muskets and even the schooner *Tamaulipas*.

The schooner departed New Orleans, skirted rough weather, and landed at Velasco in January 1836. One of Turner's volunteers, Vermont-born Ellis Benson, wrote, "We started out on the schooner *Tamaulipas*, intending to sail around to Corpus Christi and thence march to join the Texans at San Antonio. In going over the bar our vessel was wrecked. This stopped us." They then transferred to the schooner *Pennsylvania*, the *Tamaulipas* was freed and the group sailed on to the Gulf Coast port of Velasco.[34]

The *Telegraph and Texas Register* of February 20 carried an item about the arrival on January 28 in Velasco of a group of ships. First was the armed Texian schooner *Liberty*, under Captain Jeremiah Brown. Also arriving on the 28th was Captain William E. Mingle's schooner *Tamaulipas*, the cargo and public stores schooner *Caroline* and finally Captain Holt's public stores schooner *Pennsylvania*, the latter containing "one hundred men commanded by Captain A. Turner."

From the one hundred volunteers aboard her, twenty-six-year-old Richard Roman was elected captain of the volunteers. Roman, who had studied medicine in Kentucky, was now broke. He had to borrow thirty-five dollars from Turner just to get his baggage returned from his New Orleans hotel, which had seized his belongings due to his being in arrears on rent. Roman had served during the Black Hawk War, rising to the rank of captain.

Off-loading from the *Pennsylvania* on January 28, these United States volunteers were formed into companies the following day. To their number were added other individuals from the Brazoria Municipality who had gathered at Velasco.[35]

One regular army company, enlisted for two years as "Permanent Volunteers," elected Captain John Hart and First Lieutenant Richard

Captain Amasa Turner (1800–1877) came to Texas from New Orleans during the Texas Revolution. Turner commanded Company B of the regular army at San Jacinto. *Author's collection.*

Roman as its senior officers. Forty-eight men appear on the unit's original muster roll. Roman was soon elected captain of the company after Captain Hart's departure on February 13. His first lieutenant became George M. Casey and Nicolas Mosby Dawson became second lieutenant. Roman's company was transported on February 19 from the port town of Quintana to the home of Major Nathaniel Whiting aboard the steamboat *Yellow Stone*.

The men of Captain Roman's company had varied backgrounds and countries of origin. Many had been born in the United States, although twenty-six-year-old John Angel hailed from England and Andrew M. McStea, a twenty-two-year-old clerk by trade, had been born in Ireland. Privates Harvey Homan and James Conn were carpenters by trade. Corporals William P. Moore, a twenty-three-year-old New Orleans native, and James D. Egbert, a forty-one-year-old from New York City, were skilled in the printing business. Finally, musically talented George J. Brown became the company's drum major.

The second company organized at Velasco in late January formed for a two-year-period as "Regulars" under Captain Amasa Turner. Most of his men were new arrivals to Texas, although Private John Belden was a former member of the New Orleans Greys company which had fought during the Bexar siege. Belden was recovering from serious wounds he received from a cannon explosion on December 8, 1835.

Most of Captain Turner's other men were fresh from New Orleans sporting a rich cultural blend. There were forty-two-year-old Prospero Bernardi, originally from Italy, and thirty-year-old George Washington Browning, who had been born in Scotland. David Harvey had come over from England while Ferdinand Leuders was born in Mecklenburg, Germany.

Private Felix Wardzinski, thirty-five, was born in Poland and fought as an officer in the Polish Insurrection of 1830–31. After its downfall, he and many others crossed over into Austria, where they were arrested. Wardzinski and 234 other Poles were deported to the United States in 1834 by the Emperor of Austria. Arriving in New York City, he eventually made his way to New Orleans, where he enlisted in the Texas Army under Captain Turner to join an insurrection in another country.

Major John Forbes, an aide-de-camp of General Houston, moved from Washington-on-the-Brazos on March 5 with orders from Houston to forward troops and ammunition to the army. At Velasco, he helped complete the men's organization. Upon his arrival, he found Captain George Washington Poe in temporary command of the New Orleans-raised infantry companies.

Forbes found Captains Roman and Turner's companies to be "commanded by excellent officers, fully armed and equipped and under good discipline." He also found Velasco to hold "a considerable quantity of munitions of war." Major Forbes also quickly found that Colonel John Wharton was at Matagorda. In Wharton's absence, Forbes immediately took up the effort of recruiting an additional company for his little battalion.[36]

The new company was created on March 8, 1836, solely of the many volunteers who had been assembling at Velasco. The men elected William S. Fisher, the collector of customs for the Port of Brazos, as their captain. Captain Fisher was a Virginia native who had come to Texas in 1834 and had previously served as a delegate to the 1835 Consultation at San Felipe before being appointed in December to head the Brazos port at Velasco.

As with Roman's and Turner's units, Captain Fisher's company contained men with varied countries of origin, such as George W. Mason from England, Henry Tierwester from France and Joseph Sovereign from Portugal. Fisher's men had been in Texas longer than most of the men of the two New Orleans-raised companies. Occupations ranged from farmer to carpenter to even one Baptist minister from

Major John Forbes (1797–1880) reached the Colorado River with three new companies. As the army's commissary general, Forbes later came under review for his conduct on the San Jacinto battlegrounds. *Texas State Library and Archive Commission.*

Georgia, thirty-five-year-old Benjamin Franklin Fry. Privates George Mason, Adam Mosier and Samuel McKneely were already Texas Revolution veterans, having participated in the December siege of Bexar.

Dubbed the "Velasco Blues," Captain Fisher's company would be further reinforced later in the campaign with men from Captain Daniel Perry's small company.

Major Forbes thus had become the senior commander of the three infantry companies under Roman, Turner and Fisher. His battalion seized a cargo schooner in Velasco in late March, but newly arriving intelligence compelled the men to abandon this ship and march out immediately on foot. Forbes later described the movement of his troops.

> When I arrived at Velasco, there was no sea-going vessel at the port, but a few days after a large schooner arrived with freight to McKinney & Williams. As they were both absent, I had an interview with their agent to obtain the use of the vessel, to carry out the General Orders, and was flatly refused.
>
> Deeming it my duty to act promptly, a detachment of Capt. Roman's company was ordered up under arms, the vessel was impressed, and taken possession of (a very unpleasant duty, but unavoidable in our then trying crisis). I had just commenced to discharge its cargo, when received the intelligence through a reliable source (not official) of the unhappy defeat, and massacre of Col. Fannin's command at Goliad by the Mexican Army, and of their advance in strong force.
>
> I immediately abandoned my intention of proceeding by sea to Dimmitt's Landing and gave up the vessel after an hour's detention, without injury to the consignees and determined on my own responsibility to join Gen. Houston's Army wherever it was, by an overland route with the 3 companies of infantry, and as large a quantity of munitions of war as could be transported.
>
> I accordingly proceeded with the troops and munitions up the Brazos River to Columbia as a starting point, selecting the old contraband trace leading from there to the Colorado, as the line of march to Headquarters. By the aid of the patriotism and liberality of the citizens of Brazoria, Columbia and

neighboring planters of Brazoria County, a sufficient number of wagons and ox teams were procured for the use of the companies and transportation of munitions of war.

Major Forbes' troops continued a relentless forced march from Columbia. Due to the pace of the munitions wagons, he forged on ahead with the company of Captain Turner at a faster pace to locate the army. On the night of March 24, Turner's company camped at the farthest point of the timbers skirting the prairie west of the Brazos

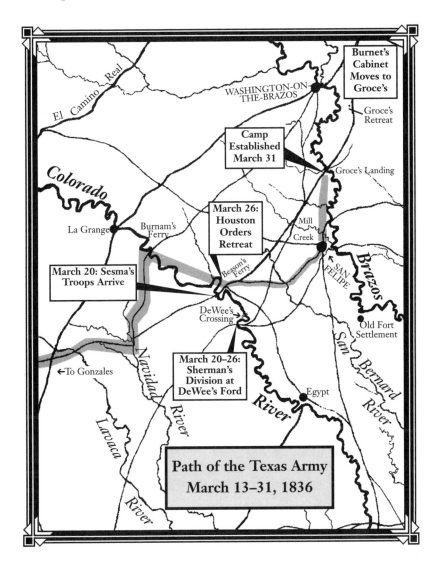

River. By the next evening, Forbes' and Turner's men had camped in the timbers of the Colorado River three miles from the Atascocito Crossing near present Columbus.

Captain Turner's company then reached Sidney Sherman's division of the Texas Army by 11:00 a.m. on March 26, "on the day that it fell back from the Colorado upon San Felipe," wrote Forbes. The trailing companies under Captains Fisher and Roman continued their forced marches with the ox teams and wagons, reaching Sherman's division at 2:00 a.m. on March 27.

Captain Robert Calder rode for a time in company with General Houston as the main body of the Texas Army marched from Beason's Ferry toward San Felipe. They exchanged views on the movements of the Texas Army thus far. Calder felt that the army could have whipped Sesma's division at the Colorado, but he guessed that Houston was hoping to draw the enemy deeper into the heart of Texas before fighting.[37]

Houston agreed, adding that it would offer him more supplies and more reinforcements. The inevitable wounded and killed would have been impossible to transport away from the Colorado area. Houston added to Calder, "You may tell those fellows who are so damned anxious to fight, that before long they shall have it to their heart's content."

Lieutenant Colonel Sherman's and General Houston's forces were united during the late morning of March 27, making for an impressive size Texas Army.

Sherman's companies arrived at the San Bernardo River about an hour before noon. There, they found and slaughtered a large cow, which was immediately put to fire for a fresh lunch. As the men sat around roasting their fresh kill, General Houston arrived with the main body of the army.[38]

Private William Zuber of Captain Bennett's company was quite impressed by the approach of Houston's men.

> Soon we saw their front guard, a small body of horsemen, emerging from the timber at the west end of the prairie. Then came the wagon train, consisting of six wagons drawn by oxen, then the unmounted infantry, and, lastly, the mounted infantry. The cavalry, being divided into two parts, formed the flank guards on the right and left of the central column. Looking down the

line, not much more than half a mile long, I was stricken with admiration for what I thought was a great assemblage, since I had previously never seen more than three hundred persons at one time.[39]

Captain Amasa Turner, commanding one of the two new United States companies, later gave his estimate of the total forces now.

> In relation to the number of men which composed the army at the time Gen. Houston left the Colorado, I am confident I am not mistaken. The morning report, including Sherman's command, was 1464, rank and file. Roman's and Fisher's companies joined at the first camp (after the retreat), five miles from the Colorado. These would swell the number to 1568, at the five-mile camp.

The Texas Army continued to retreat throughout the day. General Houston's main forces formed a marching battalion on the road, while Sherman's battalion, instead of joining the main column, marched thirty or forty paces to the right through the tall prairie grass. Ben Fort Smith rode among Sherman's troops during some of the march, gathering their opinions on the commander-in-chief's apparent reluctance to fight. Yet, no one made an attempt to suggest a mutiny.[40]

During the fallback on March 27, a small party of men formerly under Colonel Fannin reached the Texas Army. A large portion of Captain Albert C. Horton's mounted company had escaped the main action on March 19 at Coleto Creek and managed to avoid capture. Horton's men retreated toward Victoria before making their way toward Houston's army to join up. At least three of these men reached the army and would enlist in new companies for the balance of the San Jacinto campaign.

Thomas Jefferson Adams, a twenty-four-year-old who hailed from Mississippi, joined Captain Thomas Rabb's company of "Citizen Soldiers." Another of Horton's men, Garret E. Boom, was enrolled on March 27 into Captain Jesse Billingsley's "Mina Volunteers."

The third man was Dr. John Walker Baylor, nephew to the namesake of Baylor University. Although a member of another company, he had accompanied Captain Horton's men out at the time of the Coleto Creek battle and thus also escaped capture. Known to his friends as Walker, he was also called "Doctor" and "Dock" due to the fact that he had studied medicine in Mississippi. Aside from his surgical skills, "Dock" Baylor had attended West Point during the administration of President Andrew Jackson, who was a close friend of his father's. After reaching Houston's army and joining Captain Patton's Columbia

Company, his prior military training would prove handy, as Baylor became a drillmaster for his new company and helped to put it into good fighting trim.[41]

It was a long day's march of about twenty miles. The army stopped around 9:00 p.m. near the home of Samuel Mays Williams, located on Spring Creek less than two miles west of San Felipe. The fencing of Williams was used as firewood, as the timber was too far distant for men to fetch.[42]

Food on the evening of March 27 in most cases was again beef on a stick seared over a campfire. Since abandoning their camp on the Colorado, the men had marched with little rest. Some were so exhausted that they ate their meal and went to sleep on the ground without even struggling to erect their tents.

The Palm Sunday Massacre

The few former Fannin soldiers who reached General Houston on March 27 would soon find they had much to avenge. Their comrades had been captured at Coleto and held prisoner at the old La Bahia Mission at Goliad. The fate of the hundreds of Texian prisoners took a dark turn on Palm Sunday, March 27, however.

Word was passed to execute the rebel Texans. Even General Jose Urrea was turned off by the orders. Lieutenant Colonel Nicolás de la Portilla, the military commandant at Goliad, sent word to Urrea that "he had received orders from His Excellency, the general-in-chief, to shoot all the prisoners." By the time Urrea received this dispatch, the orders had been carried out. Urrea felt that these orders were a harsh sentence yet "they were the inevitable result of the barbarous and inhuman decree which declared outlaws those whom it wished to convert into citizens of the republic."[43]

Some 370 Texans were marched out in four separate groups, some being told that they would be marched to Matamoros. Colonel Francisco Garay spared four men from this march due to their medical training—Doctors Joseph H. Barnard, Jack Shackleford, James E. Fields and Joseph G. Ferguson. Private Andrew Michael Boyle was also spared because his family had sheltered Colonel Garay in their home several weeks prior.[44]

The men of Fannin's command never saw the United States border or Matamoros. After marching a short distance from Mission La

Goliad Massacre Survivors
March 27, 1836

Captain Uriah Irwin Bullock's Company
Samuel T. Brown, Third Corporal*

Captain David M. Burke's Mobile Greys
Neill John Devenny   Thomas Kemp[1]
Herman Ehrenberg*

Captain Burr H. Duval's Kentucky Mustangs
Thomas G. Allen*   William Mason*
John Crittenden Duval   Charles B. Shain[2]
John J. Holliday   Augustus V. Sharpe
Sidney Van Bibber

Captain Albert C. Horton's Mounted Rangers
William Haddin   Daniel Martindale

Captain Samuel Overton Pettus' San Antonio Greys
William Brenan[2]   David J. Jones[3]
William Lockhart Hunter, Sgt.   John Rees*
Benjamin H. Holland, Capt. (Artillery)

Captain Jack Shackelford's Alabama Red Rovers
Zachariah S. Brooks   Isaac D. Hamilton, Second Sgt.*
Dillard Cooper   Wilson Simpson

Captain Peyton Sterling Wyatt's Louisville Volunteers
Bennett Butler   Milton Irish

Company Unknown
Nathaniel C. Hazen[2]   Joseph W. Hicks
Daniel Murphy[2]   John Williams

*Escaped massacre but were recaptured. Each of these men eventually escaped again or were released.
[1] Joined Houston's army. Served as baggage guard at Harrisburg.
[2] Joined Capt. Patton's company and fought at San Jacinto.
[3] Joined Capt. Chance's company. Fought at San Jacinto with Capt. Stevenson.

Note: At least another eighteen Texans not marched from La Bahia were spared on March 27 for their medical service, translation abilities or through the intercession of others. These men later escaped at various times.

Key Source: Hopewell, Clifford. *Remember Goliad. Their Silent Tents.* Austin, Texas: Eakin Press, 1998.

Bahia, the four groups of Texans were halted near the San Antonio River and the Mexican soldiers began firing into them at point-blank range. Miraculously, at least twenty-eight men would manage to survive this execution.[45]

As the Mexican soldiers commenced firing into the helpless Texans, artillery Captain Benjamin Holland struck the soldier nearest him with his fist in desperation. Suffering a serious wound to his left hand, Holland still managed to wrench the soldier's rifle from his hand and race for the river. At the first volley, John C. Duval was knocked over by the body of the man collapsing in front of him. He stayed down until the Mexican soldiers charged after those that fled. He made it to the river without serious injury and soon joined fellow survivors John J. Holliday and Samuel T. Brown.[46]

Sergeant Isaac D. Hamilton was hit by a musket ball that tore through his left thigh on the first volley. He fled, suffering a bayonet wound to his right thigh in the process. He made his way into waist-high prairie grass and then to the timber, where he eventually joined companymate Zachariah Brooks. These two later joined with survivors Wilson Simpson and Dillard Cooper and made their way toward friendly settlements.[47]

"I glanced over my shoulder and saw the flash of a musket," recalled Private Cooper. "I instantly threw myself forward on the ground, resting on my hands." Unlike Hamilton, he and Simpson escaped without serious injury. Cooper found Brooks to be "severely wounded" and that Sergeant Hamilton had painful wounds in both thighs, "one made by a gun-shot and another by a bayonet."

William Haddin, a young member of Captain Albert Horton's company, survived the first volley and fled for his life with three others. The Mexican cavalry pursued them and struck down the escapees with lances. Haddin and his three companions plunged into the river and swam. "One was killed in the water, one upon the bank, and the fate of the third is unknown." It was not until April 7 that Haddin managed to make his way to Harrisburg and relate the horrible events of the Palm Sunday Massacre. Upon his arrival those present felt that "he alone escaped."[48]

William L. Hunter was shot, stabbed with a bayonet, clubbed with the butt of a gun, stripped of his clothing and finally had his throat cut. Despite all this, he miraculously crawled away after nightfall. He eventually was hidden in a thicket and cared for by a kindly Mexican woman who brought him food and water until he had healed enough to travel for help.

Some 370 captured Texans were marched outside of the Mission La Bahia at Goliad to be executed on March 27, 1836, by order of General Santa Anna. Only twenty-eight of Colonel Fannin's men survived the Goliad Massacre. Seven of them reached the Texas Army during the San Jacinto campaign, thus later spawning the battle cry of "Remember Goliad" in addition to "Remember the Alamo."
Norman Price "Remember Goliad" illustration, Texas State Library and Archives Commission.

Charles Shain, a young soldier who also survived this horrible massacre and later fought at San Jacinto, wrote a full account of his ordeal soon after the San Jacinto campaign. In this, he gives a glimpse into his personal trauma.

> They divided us into three divisions. The first division was led out on the Victoria road; the second, the division I belonged to, was taken out on the San Antonio road; as for the other, I do not know where they were taken, but I think that they were killed in the fort, as none of that division escaped.
>
> The division to which I belonged had proceeded as far as a brush fence, when a firing commenced in, or near the fort. Our guards immediately ordered us to halt; but the rear had not halted before I heard somebody say, "Prepare!" The enemy all leveled their guns and fired. They were within three or four feet of us when they fired.
>
> They missed me and I ran to the river and swam over. While I was swimming, they shot five times at me, at a distance of not more than fifty yards. John Duval, John Holliday, Daniel Murphy, Nat Hazen, and myself and several others swam the river together, but a good many were killed after they had reached the opposite shore.[49]

It appears that twenty-eight men escaped the massacre and made it to safety. Others escaped, but were hunted down and killed before they made it very far. Of these twenty-eight escapees, six would make their way to General Houston's army during the next two weeks.

They were Shain, Thomas Kemp, David J. Jones, William Brenan, Nathaniel C. Hazen and Daniel Murphy. Unaware of the others who survived the massacre, Shain wrote in a letter on April 11 that "I, with six others, out of 521, escaped."[50]

Twenty-eight-year-old Nat Hazen had come to Texas in January 1836. The *Telegraph and Texas Register* on January 11, 1837, related the fact that Hazen had "escaped from the horrid massacre" on March 27 and "with great exertion and fatigue he joined our army on the Brazos."[51]

Daniel Murphy was a Kentucky rifleman volunteer who had been sent in February to reinforce Colonel Fannin. He, fellow survivors Hazen and Jones and six others under Lieutenant Samuel Sprague had gone from San Felipe on February 9 to reinforce Fannin. Colonel Rusk certified that Murphy

> was in the Battle of Coleto, taken prisoner with Fannin, and afterwards marched out to be shot, miraculously made his escape, was wounded in his left knee and with a few of his unfortuante companions made his way to the Head Quarters of the Army then on the Brazos, where he reached almost naked and starved.[52]

The massacre was trying even on the hearts of some of the Mexican soldiers. Approximately 341 Texians had been slain. Inside the mission, Colonel Fannin was unable to walk due to his leg wound. Upon being informed that he was to be shot, he simply requested his executioners to blindfold him, give him a Christian burial and to send his pocket watch to his family. Fannin also requested that he be shot in the chest so that the powder would not burn his face. He then calmly tied on his own blindfold and faced the firing squad seated in a chair.[53]

The Mexican officer in charge of the execution pocketed Fannin's gold watch. Against his other requests, he was shot through the face and his body was later thrown upon a funeral pyre with other victims.

Lieutenant Colonel de la Portilla, hoping to be seen as a humble servant, followed orders to carry out the executions against his better wishes. Following this deed, Portilla wrote a note to General Urrea.

I feel much distressed at what has occurred here; a scene enacted in cold blood having passed before my eyes which has filled me with horror. All I can say is, that my duty as a soldier, and what I owe to my country, must be my guarantee. . .

Being but a subordinate officer, it is my duty to do what is commanded me, even though repugnant to my feelings.[54]

Had Santa Anna spared these men and kept them prisoners, he could have deposited them on United States soil demoralized, defeated and yet appreciative of the humanity of their Mexican captors. Instead, by ordering the shooting and butchering of entire companies of Texans and United States volunteers new to Texas, Santa Anna only painted himself as the most barbaric of killers.

CHAPTER 7

"Intensely Hungry, Weary and Wet"

March 28–April 2

> On my arrival on the Brazos, had I consulted the wishes of all, I should have been like the ass between two stacks of hay. Many wished me to go below, others above. I consulted none—I held no councils of war. If I err, the blame is mine.
> —*General Sam Houston*

Following breakfast at the Samuel Williams homestead, the Texian army was again on the march early on the morning of March 28. By the time it arrived at San Felipe that day, the army would have zigzagged more than 120 total miles from Gonzales.

Prior to leaving camp, General Houston had ordered Captain Moseley Baker to post a small guard at the key Brazos River crossing at San Felipe. While the army was breaking camp, Third Corporal Isaac Lafayette Hill and six men moved on ahead to take command of the ferryboat. Captain Baker could only assume that Houston thus planned to cross the Brazos after reaching San Felipe.[1]

Another small volunteer company had caught up with General Houston's army by the time it had neared San Felipe. Captain Jacob Eberly, a store owner from Columbia-on-the-Brazos, had organized roughly two dozen men into a unit at Columbia on March 20.

Jacob Eberly's audited claims show him to be paid as a captain from March 20 to June 20, 1836. He had also previously organized a volunteer company in Columbia on September 28 and had joined the army at Gonzales on October 5. His company fought in the San Antonio campaign, being discharged by Colonel Burleson in December 1835.[2]

William Preston Stapp, a former Kentuckian approaching his twenty-fourth birthday, was elected as Captain Eberly's second lieutenant. Stapp had fought Indians in 1831 and had served in Captain

Thomas Alley's Lavaca volunteer company during late 1835. Eberly's second sergeant was thirty-two-year-old Basil G. Ijams, a former North Carolinian who had also previously served in the Texas Revolution during 1835.

From Williams' place, Sam Houston's army covered the remaining mile and a half into San Felipe de Austin and there took on much-needed supplies. Surviving records show that merchants Joseph Urban and Nathaniel Townsend furnished food and clothing to many of the ragged soldiers. Urban was issued a promissory note for $885.66 on April 9 to cover the goods he had furnished Houston's men on March 28, 1836, without pay.[3]

This supply included:

$3.00 furnished to L. Smither by order of Capt. Calder for use of army on March 28, 1836;

$8.75 furnished to Wyly Martin, "Capt. of Volunteers," for 35 pounds of coffee at 35¢ per pound;

$28.58 worth of goods for David Halderman by order of Capt. Wyly Martin;

$57.50 worth of goods furnished to Quartermaster Pinckney Caldwell;

$9.50 for cooking supplies, three small kettles, 1 coffee kettle, two tin buckets, and one dozen bowls, to Capt. Jacob Eberly "for the use of my company";

$12.08 to Capt. William Fisher for a pair of shoes, twenty pounds of sugar, one yard domestic fabric, plugs of tobacco and paper;

$44.00 to Capt. Juan Seguin for furnishing twenty-two pairs of shoes "for the use of my company" at the cost of two dollars per pair;

$14.50 of supplies furnished Capt. William Wood, by order of General Houston; and

$713.75 worth of supplies furnished to Quartermaster Edward H. Winfield, including 107 pounds of bacon hams, thirty-six pairs of shoes and eight boxes of "Havana brown sugar" on March 29.

Fellow San Felipe merchant Nathaniel Townsend similarly took promissory notes for the goods he supplied to General Houston's companies. Captain Wyly Martin took on $46.25 of fabric for his company's use in making tents and clothing. Captain Fisher received one coffee mill and 140 yards of domestic fabric. Captain Jesse Billingsley's unit took on fabric, thread, needles, four gross of buttons, four dozen hair combs and three dirk knives.[4]

Captain Eberly's men took on 45 pounds of bacon ham, one barrel of flour, 72 pounds of sugar, 16.5 yards of twilled bagging, thirteen pounds of coffee, twelve short-handle frying pans, two large tin pans, coffee boilers, 24 tin cups and other camp supplies between March 29 and early April. David D. Barry of Eberly's also took on sugar, coffee, a blanket and a handsaw. Three other of Eberly's men—David M. Jones, Lewis H. Peters, and Hector McNeill—were furnished rifles by Townsend.

From San Felipe, General Houston ordered all coastal companies to remain and fortify their areas at some safe point. On March 28, he sent Colonel Edward Harcourt as his "principal engineer of the army" down to the coast near Velasco to help with the erecting of fortifications "at the most eligible point of defense. I place at his disposal the resources of the lower country for its defense and protection."[5]

North up the Brazos

The provisioning stop was brief at San Felipe. Sam Houston passed the word on March 29 that he was moving his men north of San Felipe instead of taking up a defensive station in town.

He had decided to move upriver from the San Felipe area to one of the settlements of the Austin Colony's richest man, fifty-four-year-old former Virginian Jared Ellison Groce Sr. Groce's Landing was located about fifteen miles (although a twenty-mile march along the river) from San Felipe, where the commander-in-chief hoped to find ample food supplies. Houston also had intelligence that the steamboat *Yellow Stone* was at Groce's Landing, where it was taking on cotton to transport down the Brazos.[6]

Two company commanders, Captain Wyly Martin and Captain Moseley Baker, refused to follow General Houston up to Groce's. James Tarlton of Baker's company wrote:

> We reached San Felipe on the Brazos and encamped. The next morning the troops were ordered to resume the march up that river. Capt. Baker demurred to this movement, and requested permission to remain at San Felipe, and guard that pass.[7]

Upon hearing that Houston planned to march the army north of San Felipe, "I indignantly refused longer to follow," wrote Captain Baker.[8]

As the companies were formed up for marching, Lieutenant Colonel Sherman learned that Baker's and Martin's men refused to come into line. Dr. Nicholas Labadie recalled that Sherman "sent a message to that effect to Houston, who had gone in advance with his staff." General Houston sent back Colonel Hockley to order Sherman to get the army moving and "if subordinate commanders were going to disobey orders, the sooner it was ascertained the better."[9]

Houston quickly found that Martin and Baker had no intention of giving in. Martin, at age sixty, was seventeen years older than Houston. Further, he had been a captain when he fought under Andrew Jackson at Horseshoe Bend, where Houston had been a lieutenant. Perhaps he now found it difficult to continue to retreat under a leader who had once been his junior.[10]

At this crucial time, the strategy Houston chose to employ was to not directly challenge such blatant insubordination from his junior officers. The mutinous actions of Baker and Martin were a direct challenge to his command. Therefore, to avoid dividing his meager army by challenging his officers to take sides, Houston issued them orders that ran parallel to their demands.

Captain Baker recalled that Houston "rode back to me in person and gave me orders to take post opposite San Felipe with my command." Baker, of course, had already sent Corporal Hill and six men to defend this crossing during the early morning hours.[11] The main contingent of Baker's command would guard the San Felipe crossing of the Brazos River and would help insure that all fleeing citizens made it safely across the river to the east bank. Army orders issued on March 28, 1836, include one from Houston to Captain Baker ordering him to post his command on the east bank of the Brazos, opposite San Felipe, and to obstruct the passage of the enemy.[12]

Captain Martin was given orders to move downstream about twenty-five miles from San Felipe to protect the key crossing at Fort Bend, or Old Fort (now Richmond in Fort Bend County). Martin's men were on station by March 30, on which date Hiram Thompson suppled eighteen bushels of corn for the "Fort Settlement" volunteers under Captain Martin.[13]

Some of Captain John Bird's company also stayed behind at San Felipe. Bird "found a barrel of whiskey" at San Felipe and "stayed with it to take care of it," reported Private Bob Hunter. In his absence, Lieutenant John McAllister took the balance of Bird's company and joined with Captain Baker to guard the river crossing. One such man was Private John Carr, who joined Captain Baker's unit on March 28.[14]

Of those who remained with Captain Bird, none would rejoin General Houston during his campaign. Some of his volunteers, such as First Lieutenant Robert Stewart and Private Nathan Brookshire, were later given furloughs on April 15 to remove their families from harm's way. Privates John M. Hensely and George Herder later attested to the fact that Peter B. Dexter was elected to the position of first lieutenant and that he assumed command of Bird's company. Lieutenant Dexter's men served throughout the San Jacinto campaign "on detached service under general's orders." Others from Captain Bird's unit continued to serve the army on special detail. Private George H. Roberts, for example, later recorded, "I was employed as a scout during the greater part of my service by the express order of Genl. Houston."[15]

Captain Juan Seguin wrote that his company was also detached at San Felipe "to cut off the enemy from the passage of the river." Shortly thereafter, Seguin's men were given new orders to occupy one of the Groce plantation houses while the army moved northward.[16]

Thirty-year-old Leonard Waller Groce, eldest son of Jared Groce, lived in the plantation homestead east of the Brazos River known as Bernardo. Jared Groce had constructed Bernardo in 1822 on a high bluff above the banks of the river about four miles south of present Hempstead and just across the river from Groce's Landing. Aside from the Bernardo home, the plantation also boasted a separate kitchen, a doctor's house, a bachelor hall for guests, a dairy and a servants' quarters.

Leonard Groce's father, Jared, had found this Brazos swampland to be unpleasant and had retreated northward up the river to another of his plantation homes to escape malaria. Jared Groce's more northerly homestead, in present Grimes County, was known as "Groce's Retreat," and had been a brief stopping point for the Texas cabinet on its retreat from Washington.

Captain Jesse Billingsley's company was another unit which preferred to stay and fight at the river crossing versus marching north.

> I, in common with others, earnestly entreated the General to give us permission to aid Baker, but he refused to the great grief of a large portion of the army. He then took up his line of march eastward, the army growing less and

less every day, many leaving the ranks imagining that Houston would not come to an engagement with the enemy.[17]

Houston's move up north had thus caused some mutiny and further fragmentation that was tough to afford in this campaign. He continued to tell his men that he had communications out to the United States and he hoped to soon join with these reinforcements. At San Felipe, his army is estimated to have numbered 1,400 men—its largest size of the campaign.[18]

He lost some two hundred or more to desertion as discontent grew with Houston's unwillingness to fight. Dr. Nicholas Labadie felt that the arrival of new troops had grown the Texas Army "from about 600 to 1600 men. In this I know I am correct, as we paraded every day, which gave me an opportunity of making a record of the numbers on the ground, and I made an entry in my journal."[19]

Second Sergeant William C. Swearingen of Captain Turner's Company B had arrived in Texas from New Orleans with many others of Turner's and Captain Roman's companies. He felt that the Mexican army was "3,000 strong" that trailed them. "Houston's army was, including our two companies, 1,372 men," Swearingen wrote on April 22. "The next day after we joined him, he commenced a retreat back on the River Brazos."[20]

Printer Gail Borden Jr. wrote to President David Burnet that due to the Texian army retreating from the Colorado "it has become necessary to move our press. I shall endeavor to put it over the river today." Borden asked that the government send a large wagon or team, without which, Borden would be forced to put his press in the river bottom.[21]

News that the Texas Army had retreated from the Colorado River to the Brazos had continued to fuel the Runaway Scrape. News that Houston's men were moving north of San Felipe and that the town had been burned added to the excitement. Further, President Burnet and his cabinet had fled from Washington to Groce's Retreat. By March 21, these government officials had moved down to Harrisburg on Buffalo Bayou, located within the present city limits of Houston.

The cabinet had taken up residence in the home of the widow Jane (Birdsall) Harris, mother of the town's founder. Staying there were Burnet, de Zavala, Rusk, Potter, Samuel Carson and David Thomas. De Zavala and Burnet had then moved down south on March 23 to visit their families near Galveston and San Jacinto Bay, returning late the following day.[22]

San Felipe Is Burned

Captain Baker was left with about forty men to protect San Felipe's main crossing along the public highway of Texas. He crossed his men on the ferryboat over to the east bank of the river and began fortifying his position. "I went forthwith to cutting down trees and digging ditches, determined to protect the crossing at all hazards," wrote Baker.[23]

Corporal Isaac Hill wrote that the company

> began to dig a ditch the entire length of which, when completed was one hundred and twenty-four yards. It was in the form of an L, the longer part fronting the river. The shorter part was below the road and extended eastward. The dirt was thrown outside the ditch. The work occupied us until the evening of the 31st.[24]

Texas scouts were out on March 29 while the army marched northward toward Groce's. Deaf Smith and John York returned that day, saying that they had seen the Mexican advance guard within a few miles of San Felipe. The report later turned out to be false. The men had apparently mistaken a drove of cattle in the distance for a squadron of cavalry. This report, however, was the cause of San Felipe being immediately set fire and destroyed.[25]

Captain Baker testified in 1838 that Houston had given him orders written in pencil to burn the town. Baker wrote again in 1844 that Houston had given him "orders to burn the town on the approach of the enemy." Houston would flatly deny ordering Austin's town burned.[26]

Private Sion Record Bostick of Baker's company wrote, "General Houston ordered us to cross over the river and burn San Felipe. The people had already abandoned the place, leaving everything they had in the houses and stores." Captain Baker's orderly sergeant, Joseph Baker, confirmed later that his captain acted under orders. Another San Jacinto veteran, Sergeant William Swearingen, wrote several weeks later on April 22 of San Felipe: "Gen. Houston had [it] burnt."[27]

The burning of San Felipe, Stephen F. Austin's original town, would become another of the little controversies that would be political fire for Sam Houston in the years to come. Irregardless of who actually decided to burn the settlement, the fact of the matter is that Santa Anna's forces would have looted and burned it within days anyhow.

Corporal Isaac Hill later gave an account of the burning of San Felipe.

> Capt. Baker paraded and informed the men that he had received intelligence that the Mexican army had crossed the Colorado and was advancing on San Felipe; that he had been instructed by Genl. Houston, upon the approach of the enemy, to burn the town, and that in obedience to said order the company would proceed to reduce it to ashes. We crossed the river after night and it was about eight o'clock when we arrived in the street of San Felipe.[28]

Baker asked Third Sergeant Moses Bryan to superintend the burning of San Felipe. Bryan, however, wanted no part in it.

> I was then a sergeant, and was ordered to take six men and burn the town, when John York and Deaf Smith reported the advance of the enemy at Bernardo, and I begged Captain Baker to excuse me from that duty, as I did not want to be the one who destroyed the first town my uncle Stephen F. Austin had laid out in the beginning of his colonization enterprise, and Edward O. Pettus, a sergeant, attended to the burning, after removing the balance of the meat in the smoke-houses. The goods had all been previously crossed over to the west bank of the river.[29]

According to Hill, Moseley Baker himself "commenced the work of destruction by setting fire to his own office with his own hands."

Moses Austin Bryan (1817–1895), nephew of Stephen F. Austin, in an 1850 photo with his son. This Spanish-speaking sergeant was not happy to watch his uncle's town of San Felipe de Austin reduced to ashes on March 29.
H. A. McArdle's San Jacinto Notebooks, Texas State Library and Archive Commission.

The wooden buildings flared up almost immediately and soon the entire town was a raging inferno. Hill adds:

> It was nearly midnight and the town was almost consumed when the company returned to camp.
>
> A large amount of goods were destroyed by this conflagration. All the merchants, with the exception of William P. Huff, had previously left the place but were represented by their clerks.[30]

Jeremiah D. Cochran was upset to see his town go up in flames. A member of Captain Baker's company, Cochran had already lost his brother, Robert E. Cochran, in the Alamo. Now he watched as the store of his brother James Cochran, an 1825 San Felipe settler from New Hampshire, went up in flames.[31]

After San Felipe was successfully destroyed, the company crossed back over the river, accompanied by the remaining clerks who had still been in town. Some of these men joined up with Baker's company for the remainder of the campaign.

If he had indeed given the orders, General Houston would not openly admit to such an unpopular military decision. Soon hearing the uproar about San Felipe's businesses being burned, he reportedly asked Isaac Moreland of Captain William Logan's company if he had heard any direct orders given to burn the town.[32]

"General, I have no recollection of it," stated Moreland.

"Yet they blame me for it," said Houston.

———————

About the time that Houston elected to move north of San Felipe on March 29, rains set in and continued for days. Leaving Martin, Bird and Baker's men behind, Houston's men spent the next two days covering the eighteen to twenty miles back through flooding creeks to where a camp was set up. Heavy rains left the roads in terrible condition, rendering some routes almost impassable. Wagons bogged in the muck. Deep mud tugged at boots and hooves like quicksand.

James Kuykendall of Captain Robert McNutt's company recalled:

> As we marched through Mill Creek bottom, floundering through mud and water and pelted by the pitiless storm, General Houston rode along slowly close to the company to which I belonged. He wore a black cloth dress coat, somewhat threadbare, which was rapidly absorbing the rain. He complained of having no blanket. He said he had a very good one, but some scoundrel had stolen it from him.[33]

After sunset on March 29, the army encamped about a mile north of Mill Creek and three miles above Cummins' mill. The relentless rain continued throughout the process of making camp. Amidst the darkness and storm, some men managed to run down and kill some cattle for beef. Fortunately, the rains died down a couple of hours after nightfall. Huge fires soon sprang up around camp and men were roasting the new beef and drying their clothing and blankets for the next few hours.

From "Camp near Mill Creek" on March 29, General Houston wrote to Colonel Rusk. He sharply advised Rusk not to fall back to Harrisburg with the rest of the government. "Your removal to Harrisburg has done more to increase the panic in the country than anything else that has occurred in Texas, except the fall of the Alamo." He wrote that there was "much discontent" on March 28 because he would not fall on down the river. His decision to move camp to Groce's Landing was not popular.

> On my arrival on the Brazos, had I consulted the wishes of all, I should have been like the ass between two stacks of hay. Many wished me to go below, others above. I consulted none—I held no councils of war. *If I err, the blame is mine.* I find Colonel Hockley, of my staff, a sage counselor and true friend. My staff are all worthy, and merit well of me.[34]

Despite the confidence he held in most of his staff, General Houston was content to silently endure the pains of making the decisions. He had taken much grief over not attacking General Ramirez y Sesma when the Texans held a numerical advantage. He felt, however, that he would only have been fighting a portion of Santa Anna's army where even a victory would have been indecisive in the grand scheme of the revolution.

Further, Santa Anna's divisions were much more disciplined, being organized into artillery, cavalry and infantry. Houston's men were a motley collection of frontiersmen, farmers, adventurers and teenage boys who had little to no military training or discipline. He struggled daily to keep these men from deserting camp in mass force or from taking it upon themselves to go in search of the enemy.

Houston now hoped to receive replacement artillery pieces for the cannon he had been forced to throw into the Guadalupe River when abandoning Gonzales. To be an effective offensive force, he now needed such armament. The downfall was that his men would have to move these heavy pieces through the swamps, rivers and muddy roads to their final place of battle.

Houston gave notice to Rusk that he had called for the arrests of Don Carlos Barrett and Edward Gritten. These men were to be held subject to the future orders of the Texas government. Houston felt that they should be detained "and tried as traitors and spies." He had reviewed seized papers which showed that Gritten had served as a spy of Santa Anna, but that Gritten had since lost the confidence of the Mexican leaders.[35]

Gritten, a former assistant editor of the *Telegraph and Texas Register*, declared his innocence, stating that he had been accused due to a charge from Captain Moseley Baker. Houston demanded that Gritten be sent to the army for questioning, but President Burnet refused to send him from Harrisburg. After questioning him, Burnet ordered that Gritten be sent to Colonel Morgan's place near Galveston for safekeeping.[36]

Houston had also become suspicious of the stories being told by Peter Kerr, the former Goliad soldier who had made his way to Captain Baker's camp on March 25 with the news of Fannin's defeat. Kerr had since remained in Baker's camp, but General Houston decided that he was a spy and sent a guard to that camp on March 29 to retrieve Kerr and return him to the main army for further questioning.[37]

The Texas government was apparently not yet aware of how many men had separated from Houston's command when he began his move northward to Groce's Landing. From Harrisburg on March 29, Elisha Marshall Pease wrote home. In a letter carrried by Major Norton, Pease wrote that, "I feel confident that if we can whip the army now in Texas, they will not be able to send another soon, and the war will then be on the seas." Employed by the government, Pease estimated that General Houston's total forces amounted "to about 1300 and increasing daily."[38]

The move upriver along the Brazos from San Felipe was anything but easy on the men. Troops worked during the second day out from San Felipe clearing a road wide enough for the baggage wagon, but progress was slow.[39]

The exhausting marches, poor diet, wet and cold conditions began affecting some men. Private Felix G. Wright of Captain McNutt's company became gravely ill during the first night out.

Felix Wright suffered along with his company, but he died after reaching camp the next night. According to Colonel George Hockley, the first Texian death of the San Jacinto campaign was "caused by great exposure to snow and cold when crossing Mill Creek."[40]

The previous morning, Wright had been detailed to fatigue duty. Without breakfast, he worked all day without food, helping to lift and pry the wagons from the mud in the creeks. Companymate William Zuber recalled poor Private Wright's condition.

> That night, intensely hungry, weary, and wet, he went to the camp of his mess, where he ate bountifully of charred raw beef. Then he lay down and tried to sleep. During the night, a severe case of cholera morbus ensued, which could not be allayed, and on the morning of the twenty-ninth he could not walk. He was hauled on a wagon to our next encampment, and died sometime during the following night.[41]

Wright's fellow soldiers dug a grave for him in the camp. Lieutenant Colonel Sherman had the victim wrapped in his blanket and stitched it to prevent it from unwrapping. He was laid in his watery grave, into which water from the saturated ground had seeped since its digging. A platoon of riflemen fired a salute. Long sections of bark peeled from green hickory trees were laid upon Wright before his grave was covered over. Once the march resumed on the following morning, he was left buried in the midst of the little oak grove forest in a solitary unmarked grave.

Arrival of Captains Kimbro and Bryant

This death and the bitterly cold weather took their toll on the men's spirits. Morale was improved en route to Groce's Landing, however, when Houston's army was joined by more volunteer troops from eastern Texas.

In Houston's correspondence of March 29, he had written that he expected that day to "receive ninety men from the Redlands. I can not now tell my force, but will soon be able." Colonel Hockley estimated that about "80 men from the Red Lands" were received.[42] The so-called Redlands was the area around Nacogdoches and San Augustine in East Texas, so known because of its red soil content.

The first Redlands company was that of Captain William Kimbro, whose men upon arrival were ordered by Houston to go assist Captain Baker's men in holding San Felipe. Kimbro was a stout man "fond of good toddy" who had moved to San Augustine from Tennessee in 1831. He had organized his company on March 15.[43]

One of Kimbro's men was Anderson Buffington, a thirty-year-old sawmill operator who had previously gained his education in Nashville, Tennessee, while working as a printer. There was also Roden

Taylor Crain, another former Tennessean just shy of his seventeenth birthday, and his cousin, Joel Crain. Crain recalled others of San Augustine who joined his company to be George Hancock, Newell W. Burditt, William Buck Burditt, John Harmon, Ben Thomas Jr., Andrew Caddell and Daniel McGary.[44]

The other Redlands company joining the Texas Army was that of Captain Benjamin Bryant, who had just celebrated his thirty-sixth birthday on March 15. He had arrived in Texas in 1834 and settled with his wife, child and nephew Hardy Price in present Shelby County, about fifteen miles east of San Augustine.

The recruits of his small company were largely from present Sabine, Shelby, and San Augustine Counties. Few of the families represented by these men were wealthy. Private Chester B. Rockwell, twenty-four, made a living as a hatter prior to the revolution. Private Josephus Somerville Irvine, a sixteen-year-old youth, had arrived in the Sabine County area in 1830 almost destitute. His family had set out from Tennessee for Texas, but his father died of yellow fever en route. This situation left "my mother with five children (all boys), strangers in a strange land, without a dollar of money in the world," wrote Irvine. "But by picking out cotton for a planter, near Alexandria, we obtained money enough to bring us to Texas."[45]

After serving in the army in 1835,

> I returned home during the winter, and remained at my mother's until March 1836, about which time the news reached the Red Lands that Santa Anna, with his murderous legions, were on the march for Texas. An urgent call was made for volunteers. My brother James T. P. Irvine and myself enlisted in a company from Sabine County, commanded by Capt. Benjamin Bryant. In March 1836, our company started for the seat of war; found and joined the Texas army under the command of Gen. Sam Houston at Groce's ferry, on the Brazos River.

Bryant's men crossed the Brazos at Washington and were informed of the location of Houston's main body by the troops stationed there. Private Irvine noted that the citizens were hurriedly packing and fleeing Washington at this time. "It was impossible even to get something to eat, for on two of us going to the tavern to get our dinner," he wrote, "we were informed that we could not get any from the fact that they were packing up to leave and had not time to prepare it."[46]

Camp Moves to Groce's Landing

The army marched about seven or eight miles across the prairies on March 30 and set up camp near the edge of the Brazos River bottom. This area was west of the Brazos River in heavy wooded bottomlands of present Austin County near the little community of Raccoon Bend. Peter Kerr, the soldier from Gonzales judged to be a spy by Sam Houston, was brought back into camp during the morning from San Felipe.

According to Houston, the most damning piece of evidence found on Kerr was "a letter from on board the [armed warship] *Montezuma*, written by a lieutenant, recommending said Kerr to the general favor of Mexican officers."[47]

A thirty-man work party under Lieutenant Nicholas Lynch was organized on March 31. His men were ordered to cut a road a mile and a half long, going east through a dense bottomland to a small lake near the west bank of the Brazos River. Houston intended for Lynch's men to clear a proper camping ground for the army near the banks of this lake. The party started working on an old abandoned narrow road, cutting trees and brush to widen it. Clearing the campground proved very laborious that afternoon, as many wild grapevines had to be cut and burned. Despite their hardships, Lynch's men arrived back in the Texan camp that night and reported their work complete.[48]

While an improved camp area was being cleared, General Houston wrote a circular at 4:00 p.m. on March 31. He announced that, "My intention never has been to cross the Brazos; and the false reports spread are by men who have basely deserted the army of Texas." He tried to calm fears that the enemy had as many as 30,000 troops. Only 1,500 had attacked Colonel Fannin, who had been overwhelmed with "only 320 men" and surrendered.[49]

Perhaps to prevent unpopular rumors, Houston further took no credit for burning San Felipe. "The citizens of San Felipe, when they heard it rumored that the enemy had crossed the Colorado, immediately set fire to their own houses and reduced the place to ashes."

In a letter written the same afternoon to Colonel Rusk, Houston insisted, "The citizens of San Felipe reduced it to ashes. There was no order from me for it." Obviously not counting the men who had stayed downriver to fight, he gave the strength of his army "somewhere between seven and eight hundred effective men." Colonel Hockley similarly estimated the Texas forces at Groce's Landing to be "750 to 800" men.[50]

Houston confided in Rusk that the news from messenger Peter Kerr, coupled with the arrival of Mexican troops on the Colorado, had dampened the spirits of his men. "I hope I can keep them together. I have, thus far, succeeded beyond my hopes," the general wrote. "Be assured, the fame of Jackson could never compensate me for my anxiety and mental pain."

Houston also made a call for flour, sugar, and coffee to be forwarded as soon as possible. He strongly recommended Colonel Rusk send these goods on packhorses versus wagons, probably due to the speed that a wagon could make on the rain-soaked "dreadful roads."

By late afternoon, one of Houston's spies had returned "and reports that he went ten miles beyond the St. Bernard, on the road to Beason's, and saw nothing of the enemy." Two more of Houston's spies had moved further on, saying "they would see the enemy if they had to cross the Colorado." His favorite spy, Deaf Smith, also remained out in the field. "If living, I will hear the truth and all important news," wrote Houston.

Houston sent his March 31 messages out to Harrisburg via express rider William Sweeney of the cavalry. Sweeney reached Harrisburg the next day and there encountered several more men who were ready to volunteer. Two of those who followed him back to camp were nineteen-year-old Thomas F. Corry and James Harris, who had journeyed up from Matagorda to join General Houston. They had been helping "terrified women and children" of the Runaway Scrape to board shipping for passage out of Texas. "We went up to the army with him, and joined his company," wrote Corry.[51]

In camp, Corry ran across Major John Forbes, whom he had known years before in Cincinnati. "While a boy I knew [Forbes], who was a keeper of a grocery store in this city," Corry said. Forbes presented both of the new volunteers to General Houston. Service records show that Harris and Corry were enlisted in Captain William Patton's company on April 2 near the plantation of Leonard Groce.

Late in the evening of March 31, Houston did hear news from Captain Moseley Baker, who had command at San Felipe. Baker reported the arrival of two spies who claimed that the enemy had crossed the Colorado River at Atascosito Crossing and were then in order of march. Upon hearing this news, Houston defiantly wrote in his March 31 circular, "We will whip them soon."[52]

This false report got the Texan camp stirred up for a short while. Other spies arrived during the night, however, with the clarifying intelligence that the Mexican troops were further away.

By the evening of March 31, Lieutenant Lynch's work party had successfully cleared out a new camp area for the Texas Army. Some of the troops began setting up at this location in the evening hours, while the balance of the army moved forward on April 1. Captains Smith and Karnes kept their spies busy during the overnight in scouting out the enemy.

Dr. Labadie of Captain Logan's company found that the new camp was pitched "near a deep ravine, which had the appearance of having once been the bed of the river, and which miserable hole was our hiding-place for about two weeks."[53]

Houston's new camp from March 31 to April 12 was located in present Austin County, west of the Brazos River, *opposite* Groce's Landing. The march from San Felipe had been roughly 20 miles due to the twisting river but was only 15 miles above San Felipe as the crow flies. A historical marker entitled "Sam Houston's Camp, West of the Brazos" is located 9 miles northeast of Bellville (Austin County) on State Highway 159, then right for 2 miles on a county road. This marker is on private property, but archaeological work has confirmed this site. An older marker on the east side of the river along Farm Road 1887 is incorrect.

According to Colonel George Hockley, the new permanent encampment was

> in a secure and effective position with excellent water from a lake immediately ahead, and one of the most beautiful parts of the timber of the Brazos River which is ahead about ¼ of a mile off in the road leading to Col. Groce's ferry. The weather for the last four days has been wet, and the men have undergone great fatigue from that circumstance and the road being in many places almost impassable for our waggons—so soon as they can wash their clothing and arrange their arms of an entire organization of camp duty and discipline will be established.[54]

Tents were erected and the men were put to work on detail parties. Some of the refugees from the Runaway Scrape continued to tag along with the army, including at least one widowed mother and her daughter of about twelve years. They were given a tent and the two women sewed shirts for the soldiers to help support themselves.[55]

Houston kept up strict rules in his new camp. Among them was that no liquor or playing cards were to be allowed "within ten miles" of his camp. Houston felt that card playing "impairs health, destroys rest, and renders men doubly liable to surprise and defeat."[56]

There was no music in the Texas camp, save for the drum that was beat for reveille an hour before dawn and for tattoo at night. General Houston often tapped out the calls himself, an art he had learned from a mounted gunman company in Tennessee in his early years. He spent his hours during the day inspecting the troops and writing dispatches to the government and to his allies. When time permitted, he whittled or turned the pages of two books—*Gulliver's Travels* and Caesar's *Commentaries*—which he had brought along in his saddle-bags from Washington.[57]

An important benefit of this new camp was the fact that Captain John E. Ross' steamboat *Yellow Stone* had arrived at Groce's Landing, where it was taking in cotton from the Bernardo plantation of Leonard Groce. Now almost completely loaded, the *Yellow Stone* was pressed into the service of the army by General Houston in case it became necessary to cross the river to rapidly act upon the enemy. Major William Cooke of Houston's staff "and a sufficient guard" was placed aboard her until her services were needed.[58]

Captain Ross, who also served as the boat's pilot, had come down from Tennessee and had been involved with riverboats since at least 1832. He had also brought the little steamer *Cayuga* to Galveston from New Orleans in 1834. The *Yellow Stone* had come to Texas during the revolution carrying a company called the Mobile Greys, many of whom had now perished in the Alamo on March 6.[59]

Crew of the Steamboat *Yellow Stone*

Captain:	*Firemen:*
John E. Ross	William Cooke
Engineer:	M. M. McLain
Lewis C. Ferguson	Martin Shackles
Clerk:	Ira Tate
James H. West	Thomas Smith
Deck Hands:	*Stewards:*
James Ferns	Robert Mosely
Robert Hall	Mrs. Mosely
Dyer Horton	Ira Armstrong
Thomas Lubbock	*Cook:*
John McKinney	Benjamin Sherman

Source: Donald Jackson, *Voyages of the Steamboat Yellow Stone*, 124–27.

The 144-ton *Yellow Stone*, 120 feet in length with a 20 foot beam, had been constructed in Missouri in 1831 for approximately four thousand dollars. She had no whistle, but instead a bell ordered from Pittsburgh. Built of pine, yellow poplar and white oak, she was powered by a pair of massive boilers to turn her waterwheels.[60]

Captain Ross' boat sported a seventeen-person crew. This included engineer Lewis Ferguson, a clerk, five deckhands, five firemen to tend the boilers, three stewards and a cook. His vessel was of United States registry, although it had lately been employed by merchant partners Thomas F. McKinney and Samuel M. Williams of San Felipe for hauling people and provisions up and down the Brazos River.

Captain Ross was not without his reservations. If captured by the Mexican army, his men could be considered prisoners of war for assisting the rebel Texas Army.

Houston wrote a promissory note the following day, April 2, to Ross that he and his crew would be paid for their time while pressed into "public services of Texas." Houston also promised that each person aboard "shall be entitled to one-third league of land and the officers a proportionately larger quantity. You are not required to bear arms."

It is possible that the steamboat's chief engineer, Lewis C. Ferguson, was less inclined to take sides in the Texas Revolution, for Sam Houston on April 2 was inclined to commit "one league of land [4428 acres], in consideration that he will act agreeably to my directions."[61]

Travels of the Twin Sisters

With the exception of the one death during the march north from San Felipe, the Texian troops had been in generally good health during the San Jacinto campaign. The last days of March and the first days of April, however, had been an endless misery of cold, rainy days. A few cases of measles were now reported, and General Houston ordered a hospital established on the other side of the Brazos River on April 1. These sick men were sent across to it.

The time spent north of San Felipe helped Houston instill discipline in his troops. Some manual exercise and company drilling was conducted. More importantly, thought Captain Robert Calder, was to "teach them as soldiers of obedience, which most of us had never been taught before in any former service in our country."[62]

Houston worked with his undisciplined troops on bringing them up to speed on nineteenth-century warfare tactics. Through hours of practice, he drilled them on the basics of forming a line, firing by volley and advancing on an enemy by quickstep. To those already disenchanted with Houston for his perceived unwillingness to engage the enemy, the constant drilling became an added distaste. But Houston did instill the fundamentals of battle formation into his army.[63]

Within the new campground, there was reorganization of some units. Captain Philip Coe's little unit, long married to Captain William Hill's company, was disbanded and the remaining men joined Hill's muster.

Also, Captain Leander Smith of the Nacogdoches Volunteers was promoted to Major of Artillery on April 1. Command of Smith's company of Nacogdoches Volunteers passed to Captain Hayden Arnold, previously the unit's first lieutenant. According to Private Madison Whitaker, "In the Brazos bottom, Hayden Arnold was made Capt. and continued in service as such until our discharge."[64]

Captain W. T. Sadler and his former ranger unit had joined Captain Smith's Nacogdoches company at the Colorado. According to one of Sadler's men, they now were formally "enlisted about the first day of April 1836 for the term of three months" in Captain Arnold's Nacogdoches Volunteers.[65]

Major Smith was promoted due to important news received by General Houston that a pair of much-needed cannon were actually en route to the army!

It appears that the first word Houston received of the existence of available artillery pieces was from Captain John Melville Allen. From Brazoria, located along the Brazos River north of Quintana and Velasco, Captain Allen had written to Houston on March 31.

> I have now been three days at this place with forty men, two fine field pieces—and one howitzer with 160 shells and 880 round shot—four hundred stands of muskets with a large quantity of powder, cannon and rifle, three hundred barrels of provisions, two hundred knapsacks, and a quantity of tents, all of which I intended to have forwarded immediately to the army.[66]

The two "fine field pieces" reported by Allen were a pair of cannons that had been cast in Cincinnati, Ohio. Their journey had been long and was still far from over. Sidney Sherman's Kentucky Riflemen had organized across the river from Cincinnati in Newport, Kentucky, in December 1835. At the suggestion of Robert F. Lyttle, Cincinnati's townspeople had also chosen to aid the Texans in their independence struggle by casting the two pieces of "hollow ware." William M. Corry, William Tatam, Pulaski Smith, David Bolles and other leading citizens of Cincinnati helped transport the artillery pieces down the Ohio and Mississippi Rivers to New Orleans.[67]

From New Orleans, the two cannon were loaded aboard a ship for passage to the Texas Gulf Coast. Aboard the packet which transported the cannon from New Orleans to Texas was the family of one Dr. C. C. Rice. Family tradition claims that someone aboard the vessel suggested a formal presentation of the cannon be made and that Rice's twin daughters should act as sponsors, thereby leading to the cannon to be dubbed the "Twin Sisters."[68]

The so-called Twin Sisters from Cincinnati arrived in the coastal port of Velasco, were unloaded and moved just up the Brazos River to Brazoria. Captain Allen had hoped to forward these cannon to General Houston, but he was frustrated by conflicting orders he received from his immediate superiors.

Before Allen's forty-man company could move out with all of the supplies and cannon, he had been met by the army's quartermaster general, Colonel Almanzon Huston, on March 30. Huston informed Captain Allen "that he had orders from the Government to send everything in shape of arms and provisions" back to Galveston Bay.[69]

Huston ordered Captain Allen's company to march to Galveston Bay. Just the day prior, Allen had been ordered by a different officer to march his men to Velasco to "assist in fortifying that place." Completely frustrated, Allen allowed the cannon, supplies and arms to go back to Velasco. With contradictory orders from different officers and "no orders from the Commander in Chief," he chose to ignore both and instead "march my men onto the army." Cannonless, Captain Allen's company vowed to "proceed up the river as far as Columbus" to join the army. Colonel Huston arranged for the schooner *Pennsylvania* to haul the badly needed supplies and the Twin Sisters from Velasco to Galveston Island.[70]

The journey of these little fieldpieces was not yet over. Their mere presence, however, was a powerful shot in the arm for Sam Houston. He could use the promise of their impending arrival to keep his weary troops motivated and to continue to train them during the idle time near Groce's.

Santa Anna on the Offensive

From San Antonio, President Santa Anna had dispatched the majority of his troops during late March. On March 24, he had sent out General Antonio Gaona toward Nacogdoches with artillery and a brigade of about seven hundred men, which included Colonel Nicolás Condelle's Morelos battalion and the Guanajuato auxiliaries under Colonel Julián Juvera.[71]

On March 27 he had sent out the Sapper Battalion and most of the Guadalajara Battalion, both under Colonel Augustin Amat, with orders to march toward San Felipe.[72]

Santa Anna planned to have General Gaona's troops move against the Texans from the northeast. General Urrea's thirteen-hundred-man division would move up from the south through Victoria. General Sesma's men would continue to follow right behind Sam Houston in a central sweep. Thus, the great "Napoleon of the West" hoped to pen in Houston's troops from all sides and crush them just as they had the rebels at the Alamo.[73]

With all infantry now marching through various areas of Texas, Santa Anna inspected his troops during the next two days and prepared them for departure. Counting twenty dragoons, and the assorted picket guards from all of the battalions that had already marched out, he had some 550 total men and one howitzer at his disposal. Commanding this assembly of troops was Lieutenant Colonel José Enrique de la Peña of the First Infantry Brigade. At 4:00 p.m. on March 29, de la Peña led his troops from San Antonio de Bexar toward the Colorado River.

> We had with us fifty boxes of ammunition, half rations of *condochi* [a thick corn tortilla] and beans, and one hundred *fanegas* [about 250 bushels] of corn, with a definite order not to touch them. On that day we camped at the Salado Creek after a march of seven miles.[74]

Heavy rains set in on March 30, keeping El Presidente in Bexar another day. President Santa Anna and his staff departed San Antonio on March 31, in company with his second-in-command, General Vicente Filisola. He left only a cavalry contingent under General Juan Andrade in San Antonio to hold that key town. "I went with my Béxar group on the appointed day with my staff and an escort of thirty dragoons," he wrote.[75]

Santa Anna's little force moved toward Gonzales to the Guadalupe River, catching up with Colonel Amat's Sapper and Guadalajara battalions and Lieutenant Colonel de la Peña's division there on April 2. Lieutenant Colonel Pedro Ampudia trailed this whole procession by two days with his collection of artillery and divisional provision wagons.

"I planned to advance swiftly against the rebellious colonists," wrote Santa Anna later, "as I felt that the campaign should be finished before the spring floods."[76]

Swift movement, however, was limited by the incessant rains of early April. "Since the Guadalupe River was on a rise," Santa Anna recorded, "it was not possible for troops and the train to cross in the brief time necessary, and a delay of three or four days was unavoidable."[77]

Leaving General Filisola behind to work with de la Peña and Ampudia in moving the wagon trains and artillery across the swollen Guadalupe River, Santa Anna pushed on toward General Ramirez y Sesma's men at the Colorado River.

News of Houston's whereabouts during the early days of April would be scarce for Santa Anna. In his memoirs, he later wrote that, "Houston, learning of the approaching Mexican army, completely disappeared."[78]

In his new camp near Groce's Landing, General Houston continued to await solid word of his enemy's movements. His spies were out and active, but he found the Mexican forces moving slowly. During the night hours of April 1–2, a Mexican soldier who had deserted his own forces was seized by the Texan guards. Houston wrote:

> A deserter invaded in our camp, from that of the enemy last night. He confesses information before me as to numbers &c and places beyond a doubt, the fact of great dissatisfaction being provident in his camp—and their great want of the necessities of life—they have no bread stuffs whatever—and beef very scarce.[79]

Houston wrote to "Major Wylie Martin" at Fort Bend on April 2 of this captured enemy deserter. "I shall confidently rely upon you to place the point you now occupy in the best possible state of defense—in case the enemy should advance—and be active and vigilant to observe his movements as within your power." Houston also warned that some individuals in the area of Fort Bend, "particularly part of [a] family by the name of Johnson" had openly declared their intention to march under a white flag to go join the Mexican troops. Houston

asked Martin to determine the actual truth of this report and to arrest
such traitors if they were encountered.

Houston sent messages to Martin and Baker via Private Christopher Columbus Bruff, a regular army soldier of Captain Amasa
Turner's unit.[80]

Across the river from the main army, Dr. James Aeneas Phelps was
struggling with trying to run a makeshift hospital for General Houston's
troops. Born in Connecticut in 1793, he had come to Texas in 1822 as
one of Stephen F. Austin's Old Three Hundred Settlers. The two-story
log house and plantation of Dr. Phelps, named "Orozimbo," stood
about ten miles northeast of present West Columbia. He and fellow
doctor Anson Jones had joined the army together the previous week.[81]

Doctor Phelps had gone across the Brazos aboard the *Yellow Stone*
with the sick men and those who had been injured in various ways
along the campaign trail. On the east bank of the river, he established
a field hospital at Leonard Groce's Bernardo plantation. He quickly
found that they were in need of all basic provisions: cooking utensils,
coffee, sugar, rice, bacon, potatoes, pork, medicinal brandy, salt, pep-
per, candles, soap, and fruit. Dr. Phelps requested these and other
items from the army's main commissary department prior to setting
up the new field hospital.

By April 2, Dr. Phelps was disgusted with the response he was getting and he penned an angry note from Bernardo to Secretary of War
Thomas Rusk in Harrisburg.

> I have assigned to the commissary's department for stores for this de-
> partment, and since have received nothing but insult in return. The sick and
> wounded are entirely destitute of all provisions, and consequently are justly
> and loudly complaining of the neglect with which they are treated. If they
> cannot be supplied, I must distribute them among their companies, and re-
> sign my station.[82]

Likely hearing of the frustration of his field doctors in securing
supplies, General Houston took matters into his own hands. On April
2, he promoted his aide-de-camp Major John Forbes to Commissary
General of the Texas Army with the rank of colonel.

There was also the second change of command in company commanders in as many days. Captain Thomas Rabb of the "Citizen Soldiers" from Egypt was granted furlough from the army on April 2 to
protect his family. Lieutenant William Heard succeeded him as captain of the company and William Eastland became first lieutenant.[83]

Also Lieutenant Ebenezer R. Hale of Captain Daniel Perry's company was given orders on April 2 to move to Columbia-on-the-Brazos. There he would join a new battalion of New York volunteers which was marching up from Matagorda. Hale had reached Columbia by April 8, at which time he fell under the orders of Major Edwin Morehouse.[84]

The remaining men who did not join Hale blended into Captain Fisher's company, including Captain Perry, who took the rank of private.

Fannin Survivors Reach Baker's Detachment

Captain Moseley Baker's company, since refusing to follow Houston north to the Brazos bottoms, had set up camp on the river opposite San Felipe. From this camp, Baker wrote to General Houston on April 2. One of Captain Bird's scouts, Moses Shipman, arrived this day and informed Baker that the Mexican army was still encamped on the other side of the river but was building rails to cross upon. Shipman considered the enemy troops to be one thousand strong, but were in "great disorder, wandering about the woods and prairie and to all appearance have out no guard or spies."[85]

Four men previously under the command of Major William Ward arrived in Baker's camp on April 2. They told of Mission La Bahia being attacked by "about 1000 Mexicans who they repulsed three times and continued to whip as long as their ammunition lasted." One of these men, Samuel G. Hardaway, informed Baker that Ward "became confused in a swamp" where he and three other men were detached by Ward "and have since heard nothing from him."

Major Ward had originally been sent by Colonel Fannin to relieve Captain Amon King at Refugio on March 13. Ward's men were later attacked by a Mexican force, which greatly separated these men and forced each to flee on his own. Most of Ward's men were captured, but a few survived. During his survival journey, Hardaway escaped on the Guadalupe River on the night of March 21. He eventually joined up with two other fellow Fannin force survivors from Captain Munroe Bullock's company, Joseph Andrews and James P. Trezevant, and a survivor from Captain William A. O. Wadsworth's company, M. K. Moses.[86]

After a close encounter with a Mexican army encampment, the quartet next encountered six horsemen charging toward them. Hardaway wrote of their experience two months later.

> We discovered they were Americans and did not run—they came up, and much to our relief, we found they were spies from Gen. Houston's camp. Their names were Cawmack and Johnson from Tennessee, Shipman and [Moses] Lapham of Texas, and two others that I did not know.
>
> They were astonished to see us at that place, and when I say we were glad to see them, I but feebly express the feelings of my heart. I was then, without hat or shoes, and only a few rags for clothing. While we were narrating our adventure, and waiting for one of the company whom we had got to go back a short distance after Andrews, we were attacked and fired upon by a small scouting party of Mexicans, but at such a distance as to do us no injury; but upon seeing that we had got among some trees and were preparing to give them a fire, they retreated and left.
>
> We then left that place, and the spies carried us to Gen. Houston's army, where we arrived, I think, on the 2d day of April, our appearance being such as to excite the sympathy of every soldier—and on meeting some gentlemen who had known us in this country, the noble tears of compassion were seen to trickle freely on their cheeks.

Hardaway was moved with "all the kindness" shown to him and joined Captain Moseley Baker's company for the remainder of the San Jacinto campaign.

Captain Baker's company was determined to hold the Brazos River crossing near San Felipe and constructed breastworks for defense. Baker informed Houston that "one hundred men can defend the crossing against the whole army. The few now here will also do it if it is possible."

Baker's company was joined at the San Felipe river crossing by Captain William Kimbro's San Augustine company, which had been ordered to help by Houston.

"Our force now amounted to one hundred and twenty or one hundred and twenty-five men," wrote Corporal Isaac Hill, "including, however, several merchants, clerks, and others only temporarily attached to the command."[87]

Court-Martial of Privates Scales and Garner

One of the more interesting events of the Texas Army while camped near Groce's was a court-martial held on April 2. Charges were levied against Private Abraham Scales of Captain Amasa Turner's Company B of the regular army and against twenty-seven-year-old Private John T. Garner of Captain William Wood's Company A of the First Regiment for his conduct over the past week in the army.[88]

The members of the court-martial board were a good cross-representation of the companies under General Sam Houston's immediate command in his new camp. Serving as president was Lieutenant Colonel Henry Millard, with Dr. Anson Jones serving as the judge advocate. The other members of the panel were Captains Jesse Billingsley, Richard Roman, William Hill, William Fisher, Joe Bennett, Amasa Turner, First Lieutenant George M. Casey (Captain Roman's), First Lieutenant Micah Andrews (Captain Billingsley's), First Lieutenant John W. Carpenter (cavalry), Second Lieutenant Robert P. Stewart (Captain Bird's) and Second Lieutenant Ebenezer Hale (Capt. Perry's).

The court-martial board opened at 10 a.m. on April 2, and began by reading Captain Turner's three specific charges of mutiny and desertion against Private Scales. The first incident had occurred on March 25 when the army began crossing from the Colorado River to the Brazos.

During the march that day, First Lieutenant William Millen of Turner's company had commanded the rear guard. Private Scales and two others stopped at a stream, whereupon Millen ordered them to proceed. Two of the men obeyed, but Scales replied that he was thirsty. Millen gave the soldier sufficient time to drink his water and then ordered him once again to begin marching. When Scales refused, Lieutenant Millen shoved him to make him move.

At that moment, Private Scales turned and brought his gun to bear on the officer. Other witnesses felt that he even cocked the gun, which was believed to be loaded. Scales advanced on Lieutenant Millen "in a threatening manner" until the officer backed off.

The second charge against Scales happened two nights later near San Felipe on March 27. First Sergeant John Smith of Captain William Patton's company was the duty officer this night and he ordered Private Scales to take on guard duty. According to the testimony of Smith, the "prisoner refused and said he would not until he was court-martialed." Smith added that Scales "has seldom been on duty," often excused due to sickness.

Finally, Scales was charged with deserting the guardhouse on the night of March 27. Corporal Asberry Snyder of Captain Turner's company reported that as he made his rounds that night, he noted Scales to be missing and could not locate him in the Texan camp. On orders from Captain Turner, Snyder set out with two others and managed to locate Scales near a branch between 8 a.m. and 9 a.m. His knapsack was found at a house outside the camp lines and his gun in another place.

Camp surgeon Dr. William Bomar testified that Private Scales "has been fit for duty" ever since Bomar first encountered him at Velasco. Scales protested to the court that Captain Turner, a member of the court-martial board, was prejudiced against him, but the court unanimously overruled and pronounced the prisoner guilty of the charges against him.

Lieutenant Colonel Millard's court next proceeded to try Private John Garner of Captain Wood's Company A of the First Regiment. This prisoner was charged with desertion and disobedience to orders.

Garner was a former member of Captain Ira J. Westover's regular army company at Fort Goliad during early March. Garner had been assigned by Westover to detail with the company's first lieutenant, Francis W. Thornton, who thereupon ordered him to help another soldier round up horses. The other soldier returned within three days, but Garner departed. Lieutenant Thornton departed Goliad and found Private Garner when he came into the Texas camp on the Colorado River in late March.

Captain Henry Teal ordered Garner to join his company, but the soldier refused. Dr. William Mottley was called upon by the court to verify that this soldier had indeed left Fort Goliad without leave. Lieutenant Thornton further charged that Garner refused his order to join Teal's company and that he "gave insolent language."

In consideration of the evidence, Lieutenant Colonel Millard's court also pronounced Private Garner guilty of the charges against him. After adjourning at noon for lunch, the court-martial board convened again at 2:00 p.m. to pass sentence upon the prisoners. Both Scales and Garner were sentenced to "suffer death by shooting" between the hours of 10:00 a.m. and 3:00 p.m. The prisoners were unanimously recommended to the commander-in-chief for mercy.

Publicly, Sam Houston would make an example of these two soldiers and try to put the fear of God into the other young men of his unruly army. He approved the proceedings of the court-martial board and ordered the sentences to be carried out by a firing squad the following day, April 3, at noon. Captain Richard Roman's First Regiment company was ordered "for detail to carry the sentence into effect."[89]

Captain Amasa Turner and Lieutenants Millen and William Summers petitioned Houston formally the next day for his official pardon of Private Scales. They promised that he was "very penitent, and has made a promise of a faithful performance of his duty as a soldier in the future for his term of service."[90]

After reviewing the proceedings, Houston elected to spare the life of Private Abraham Scales. Houston felt "compelled to assure the army that it is an exception to the general rule, which is resolved to preserve. Subordination can only be maintained by a strict observance of the rules and articles of war."

Having enlisted in the Texas Army on February 13 for two years or the duration of the war, Scales was granted his petition by General Houston to continue to fulfill his service requirement.

Houston felt that Scales' unruliness paled in comparison to the charges against Garner. "The man who abandons his post is more dangerous to the security of the army than twenty out of our lines."

Scales was thus spared and the execution of Private Garner was planned for the following day. "The punishment for delinquency must be proportional to the fault of the individual," wrote Houston.

Less than a week after his pardon, Private Scales would successfully desert the Texas Army again.[91]

CHAPTER 8

Camping in the
Brazos Swamps

April 3–10

The enemy are laughing you to scorn. You must fight them. You must retreat no further. The country expects you to fight. The salvation of the country depends on your doing so.
—*President David G. Burnet to General Houston*

The weather at Groce's Landing was as poor as the moods of the court-martialed men. Since camp had been properly secured on March 31, the rains had not ceased. The campground was pitched in a secure location, but rising waters soon threatened to invade this area by April 3. Sam Houston soon feared that he would have to move his men back to the prairie or cross the Brazos to a more secure higher ground.

After previously charging members of the government with being cowards for fleeing from Washington-on-the-Brazos, General Houston had received letters from some of them defending their actions.[1]

Writing to Secretary of State Samuel Carson, he explained that his anger in the cabinet's leaving Washington was with "the effect it produced on the public." Houston sent his camp servant, a Spanish-speaking black named Willis, to Carson with a cumbersome load of the general's private and public papers for safekeeping. Houston asked him to keep Willis and use him as a servant, while continuing to send daily expresses to the main army to advise of the government's actions.

Captains Smith and Karnes' spies returned to camp on the afternoon of April 3 and reported the Mexican troops to be "about one thousand strong on the Colorado, without pickets, and only a small campground." General Houston wrote to Secretary of War Tom Rusk that he expected a small detachment of his men to attack this camp during the night hours.[2]

162

Houston had sent twenty men under Captain William Patton, one of his acting aides-de-camp, on this mission. He considered Patton's men "among the best hearts of the army."

Houston told Rusk that if he did decide to move his troops across the river, he would move down to Fort Bend or some similar position. In his estimation, the enemy would not be able to cross the swollen Brazos without the aid of a steamboat such as the one he had pressed. He would then leave his "most effective cavalry" on the west side of the Brazos to gather intelligence.

Houston sent his intelligence to Colonel Rusk in Harrisburg via Nathan Este. Este was sent in charge of two prisoners, Peter Kerr and Anselmo Bergara, the latter one of the two Tejanos who had arrived from San Antonio on March 11 in Gonzales with news of the Alamo's fall. "I have nothing pointed against them; but suspicion has fallen upon them," wrote Houston, "and they are to be secured." Houston would learn several days later that Kerr had in his possession a letter in which a Mexican lieutenant indicated that Kerr "had befriended the Mexicans."[3]

Houston was unaware that Colonel Rusk had departed Harrisburg on April 1. President Burnet had held a meeting of his cabinet and Secretary of War Rusk was ordered to join Houston's army. Burnet informed Major William Austin that Rusk's job was "to stop a further retreat of our army, and to bring the enemy to battle." Colonel Robert Potter, the Secretary of the Navy, read aloud the orders for Rusk. According to Austin, Burnet had Rusk "sent to the field with authority to take charge and command of the army, if necessary to carry out the policy indicated in the order."[4]

Lorenzo de Zavala Jr., son of the vice president of the Republic of Texas, arrived in camp on April 3 and reported for duty to Sam Houston. He brought news that Rusk would arrive shortly. De Zavala was a native of Merida, the capital of the Mexican State of Yucatan, and he had been formally educated in New York and Massachusetts. He was appointed by General Houston to serve as an aide-de-camp on his staff.

On April 3, General Houston did follow through on his plans to guard the key Brazos crossings. He ordered Captain William Kimbro's company to report to "some position near to San Felipe and unite his command with that of Capt. M. Baker, and remain until further orders." Captain Benjamin Bryant's company was ordered to cross over the river and join the main army on the west side. Bryant was ordered to leave "his horses and sick with his heavy baggage in charge of a suitable guard, with strict orders for their regulation."[5]

Houston viewed Captain Moseley Baker as the "senior officer in date of appointment" and therefore appointed him in command of all troops gathered east of the Brazos. Any new or extra personnel in Baker's camp were to join up with one of the companies stationed there or be reported as a deserter. Captains Bryant and Kimbro were ordered to "make daily reports of the strength and state of their commands" to Houston. All of Baker's companies were advised by the commander-in-chief to respect all private property. "It is the soldiers' duty to protect the property of the citizen and not to waste or destroy it."

Prisoner Execution Spared

It was a sobering day for many Texian army soldiers in the Groce's Landing camp on April 3. Captain Richard Roman's company was detailed to serve as a firing squad for one of the two men who had been court-martialed the previous day. General Houston had granted clemency to Private Scales, but Private John Garner of Company A, First Regiment was to be executed at noon for his insubordination.

Captain Robert Calder found the preparation for the execution to be a "solemn and impressive" ceremony. Private James Kuykendall remembered that "Very little sympathy was felt by anyone for Garner, as he was not only an insubordinate soldier, but a hardened villain."[6]

Sixteen-year-old John Swisher, so excited to search out his first combat, found the court-martial process of the military somber indeed.

> The day appointed for the execution found many sad hearts. It was our first experience of the kind, and not without many a shudder among the more tender-hearted, was the entire army paraded and marched to the place of execution, to the music of muffled drums accompanying the ill-fated prisoner.[7]

Private Bob Hunter and several of Captain John Bird's men on the sick list had stayed with the main Texas Army when the balance of their men had gone with Lieutenant McAllister and Captain Baker to Fort Bend. Hunter was equally affected by the scene playing out before him. "The whole army was marched out to the ground, and the grave was dug and a coffin was there," he recalled. The army formed in a half circle around the fresh grave as Hunter gazed at the condemned man.

The man was blindfolded, and made to kneel on the ground by the coffin, and there was 12 men to shoot him. The officer gave command. He said, "Present arms, take aim." Just at that moment, Colonel Hockley was coming in a lope from camp, hollering, "Halt! Halt! Halt!" And the officer said, "Order arms."[8]

Hockley arrived without a second to spare, clutching a folded paper from General Houston. "Garner snatched the bandage from his eyes and staggered to his feet, not more glad in his heart, nor more grateful to the general than the majority of his comrades," wrote Private Swisher.[9]

In this reprieve, Sam Houston wrote that he had shown Private Garner mercy with the hope and belief that this act would "guarantee for his future good conduct and obedience to the rules and regulations of the army." He advised, however, that any further prisoners found guilty by a court-martial board of mutiny and desertion "will suffer the penalty of the law."[10]

Garner did, in fact, remain true to General Houston and stayed with the army throughout the San Jacinto campaign. He would come to play an important role late in the campaign.

———

Secretary of War Rusk moved up from Harrisburg and reached San Felipe on April 3. There he sent a note to Captain Wyly Martin at Fort Bend on the Brazos congratulating him on holding this key crossing. Rusk hoped that Martin's stand would "be of great service in stopping many who are on the retreat towards the Sabine." He encouraged Martin to send a courier east to Harrisburg and beyond to spread the word that the troops were holding their enemy back. Rusk hoped that "many men will be induced to turn back" and join Martin in the fight.[11]

The terrible word of the Fannin massacre reached General Houston via express on the night of April 3 at Groce's camp. He learned that the prisoners were marched out after eight days and then shot down in cold blood, "killing all but one who made his escape." William Haddin, the first survivor to encounter friendly forces, was originally believed to be the only survivor.[12]

General Houston's army received some welcome supplies on April 4. Acting Secretary of War David Thomas in the War Department in Harrisburg sent Captain John W. Moore to the army with 192 pairs of

Summary of General Houston's Forces
April 8, 1836

Groce's Camp West of the Brazos:

Commander-in-Chief
General Samuel Houston

Secretary of War
Colonel Thomas Jefferson Rusk

Command Staff
Col. George Washington Hockley
Col. John Forbes
Col. Robert Eden Handy
Major Alexander Horton
Major James Hazard Perry
Major Lorenzo de Zavala Jr.

Col. John Austin Wharton
Col. Robert Morris Coleman
Lt. Col. James Clinton Neill
Major William Gordon Cooke
Major Ben Fort Smith
Major James Collinsworth

Regular Army
Lieutenant Colonel Henry Millard

Companies
Capt. Henry Teal

Capt. Amasa Turner

First Regiment Texas Volunteers

Col. Edward Burleson
Maj. Alexander Somervell

Lt. Col. Sidney Sherman
Lt. Henry Stouffer, Adjutant

Companies
Capt. William Wood
Capt. Jesse Billingsley
Capt. William J. E. Heard*
Capt. William S. Fisher
Capt. Robert James Calder
Capt. Daniel Perry

Capt. Richard Roman
Capt. Robert McNutt
Capt. William W. Hill
Capt. Peyton R. Splane
Capt. Henry Wax Karnes (cavalry)
Capt. Stephen Townsend

* Assumed command on April 2 after Capt. Rabb's furlough.

Second Regiment Texas Volunteers

Col. Sidney Sherman
Maj. Lysander Wells

Lt. Col. Joseph L. Bennett
Sergeant Major Bennett McNelly

Companies
Capt. Hayden S. Arnold
Capt. William H. Patton
Capt. James Gillaspie
Capt. Alfred H. Wyly
Capt. William H. Smith (cavalry)

Capt. William Ware
Capt. Thomas H. McIntire
Capt. Juan N. Seguin
Capt. William M. Logan
Capt. Joseph Bell Chance

On Extra Duty:

Company	*Stationed:*
Capt. Wyly Martin	At Fort Bend/Thompson's Ferry
Capt. Moseley Baker	At San Felipe Crossing
Capt. William Kimbro	At San Felipe Crossing
Capt. Benjamin F. Bryant	Camp East of Brazos
Capt. John Bird	Camp East of Brazos
Capt. William Walker	Camp Cartwright East of Brazos

shoes and twenty-four bridles. Thomas was unable to fulfill Houston's request for flour, sugar and coffee. He promised to send a vessel from Galveston Bay to New Orleans to procure some, however. Due to the retreat of the army, Colonel Warren C. Hall had ordered all ammunition and public stores around to the east end of Galveston Island. Houston's location on the west side of the swollen Brazos made it difficult to obtain public stores from the other coastal Texian supply locations at Matagorda, Cox's Point or Velasco.[13]

President Burnet had appointed Colonel James Morgan to command the important coastal post of Galveston, where all foreign supplies and volunteers were directed to land or at nearby Velasco. Thomas also wrote to Colonel Morgan on April 4. He had learned that "some cannon from Brazoria" had arrived. These, of course, were the "Twin Sisters" of Cincinnati, the pair of new cannons destined for the Texian army. Burnet ordered Morgan to have the artillery pieces sent immediately upriver from Galveston via steamboat along with all the coffee, sugar and flour that could be had.

Rusk Arrives at Groce's

Sam Houston was up on the morning of April 4 sending orders to his various scouting units. From his camp east of Mill Creek, he ordered Lieutenant Benjamin Noble to "proceed in company with Daniel Kincheloe and Harvey Hall to the west of Mill Creek and range between that and the Colorado." This trio was to observe the movements of the enemy "and in the event of any discoveries they will transmit the earliest information on to Head Quarters."[14]

Houston sent word to Captain William Smith to "take up your quarters at Foster's with four of your company." First Lieutenant James Cook would command the spies in camp in Smith's absence, keeping a regular guard over the camp to protect property, to avoid goods from being wasted and to mind the horses in this vicinity. Smith was to send out a scout and report back to Houston "anything of importance."[15]

Houston wrote to Colonel Rusk on the morning of April 4, informing him of the news of Fannin's massacre which had reached him the previous night. "Humanity must recoil at the perfidy which has been exercised towards the brave and heroic men who have perished in the unequal conflicts with the enemy when they were always more than six to one," wrote Houston.[16]

Colonel Thomas Jefferson Rusk (1803–1857) was the Texas Secretary of War and senior military official of the republic. A former lawyer and a signer of the Texas Declaration of Independence, Rusk joined General Houston's troops at Groce's for the duration of the campaign.
Late 1840s daguerreotype, courtesy of the Chicago Historical Society, ICHi-12355.

The days in the Groce's Landing camp were largely rainy and often accompanied by cold winds. Disease crept in among the men in their wet and unhealthy campground. General Houston, however, would pull down his hat, wrap himself in a blanket and continue to train his little army.[17]

Campaign veterans would later relate how Houston worked with the greenest of foot soldiers to help train them in soldiering. Private George Bernard Erath, an immigrant from Vienna, Austria, who was already a veteran ranger and now a member of Captain Billingsley's Mina Volunteers, remarked that the time in this camp "had a good effect in disciplining us, and giving us information about military tactics."[18]

One young soldier approached the commander-in-chief with a wet gun that would not fire. Houston patiently lectured the youth to use his pocket handkerchief, and warm it by the fire. "Open the pan, wrap the handkerchief around the lock and let it remain a few seconds," he coached. After repeating this several times, the youth was to pick a little dry powder into the touchhole and then he would be able to easily remove the bullet.[19]

Conditions were tough in camp. The campsite and the entire countryside were virtually flooded from the constant rains. The men's tents were open. They gathered brush and straw to sleep on, to avoid lying directly in the mud. Few had more than one thin blanket. Those with only deerskin moccasins for shoes had the added discomfort of

During the two weeks of camping under trying conditions at Groce's Landing on the Brazos River, General Houston drilled his men on army basics.
Charles Shaw painting, courtesy of the San Jacinto Museum of History, Houston.

shrinking material to contend with. The animal skins were often soaked from sloshing through water. Once they began to dry, the skins contracted and tightened angrily around one's feet.[20]

Private George Erath later wrote an excellent summary of the conditions experienced by the men of the San Jacinto campaign.

> Their supplies were beef principally, scant of salt, an ear of corn for a man a day, which had to be ground on a steel mill. Generally every company had one, which, after marching the whole day, was fastened to a tree for each man to grind on, and then to be cooked into what is called mush, as there were no facilities for baking bread, frying pans and tin cups being the only cooking utensils. Many were sick, the discipline exacted by General Houston severe, often half at a time on guard, those not permitted to leave the guard fire for twenty-four hours; all this was to do when the men spent the greater part of the day knee-deep in water.

Thomas Rusk joined Sam Houston at Groce's camp on the evening of April 4. Colonel Rusk quickly became a supporter of General Houston, a move which helped to allay some of the rampant concern in the army that their leader was not of the mind to fight. Rusk, who had the power to take command of the army if he so desired, likely realized that Houston's strength of character was enough to see him through the tribulations of holding together such a motley bunch of adventurers and soldiers.

On April 5, Sam Houston sent orders to Captain Moseley Baker at San Felipe via express rider Lieutenant Ben Noble. Houston was concerned over reports he had received that Baker's men were wasting and destroying goods, stores and public property. "Every means in your power should have been used to preserve and protect the stores, until such were ordered to be destroyed," wrote Houston.[21]

Houston also sent orders to Major Ira Ingram to proceed on a recruiting drive to eastern Texas to round up more volunteers. He sent word that he expected a "short and decisive campaign." Those whom Major Ingram could enlist would need to move swiftly to Houston's aid or the battles would be fought and won "by the little band now at Head Quarters."[22]

Before Lieutenant Noble left with these dispatches, Houston had a guard detail accompany him with another man he had detained on suspicions of being a spy. John Joseph Linn, who had served as the alcalde of Victoria until the Runaway Scrape had commenced, had been detained at the insistence of Major Ingram during late March. Linn had left his wife and young children at a Tejano friend's ranch for safekeeping and then had ridden out on his horse to find Sam Houston's army. Upon reaching the Colorado River, he ran into Ingram, an old enemy of his. "At his instance I was speedily arrested as a spy," wrote Linn, "solely at his instigation, I repeat, and without the shadow of a single specific charge."[23]

Justice of the peace Samuel Fisher had Linn marched up to Houston's army at Groce's under the watchful eye of guard Major George P. Digges. According to Linn, "General Houston expressed astonishment at the story of my persecution." Despite the claim that he trusted Linn's patriotism, Houston still had Major Digges escort Linn from the Texas camp to Harrisburg to "deliver him safely to the supreme authorities of the Republic." Digges and Linn headed for Harrisburg in company with express courier Ben Noble. After arriving there, Digges had additional orders to proceed on to East Texas to round up new recruits.

Lieutenant Meriwether W. Smith tendered his resignation "as first Lieutenant in the Legion of Cavalry to which I was elected by the first council" to General Houston on April 5 in camp. Smith had recruited twenty-one men in the United States who had arrived in Velasco in early 1836 with many of the other regular army recruits. He resigned as he had "not enjoyed a single day's health since I left Tuscaloosa about the middle of February." Smith promised to rejoin Houston as soon as his health had been recovered.[24]

Lieutenant Smith turned over to the army the twenty-five men who currently comprised his company. He sent his men and his resignation under Sergeant Charles A. Foard. With Foard, he sent his recommendations for Privates Henry Percy Brewster and Alexander S. Mitchell. General Houston made Brewster his private secretary for the balance of the campaign. Sergeant Foard and many of the others became attached to Captain Henry Teal's regular army company.

Colonel Rusk appointed his own staff member, Moses Austin Bryan, to be his staff secretary and interpreter. A nephew of Stephen F. Austin, Bryan spoke fluent Spanish.

Also arriving at the Texas camp was a volunteer ammunition guard from Victoria. This detached group was placed under Allen Larrison and ordered to Dimmitt's Landing on March 15. On April 5, Larrison's small group joined the company of Captain Robert Calder.[25]

In Harrisburg, Secretary David Thomas received prisoners Peter Kerr and Anselmo Bergara, who had been sent from the Texian camp by Houston on April 3. Thomas reported that he was detained for some time in reading Houston's dispatches, as the courier, Nathan Este, had dropped the letters in the bayou as he rode in during the evening of April 4.

Thomas H. Hill in Harrisburg also took into his care Sam Houston's public and private papers collection on April 5, as Samuel Carson had moved on toward the Trinity River. Hill promised General Houston that he would look after Houston's servant Willis and "keep him safe subject to your orders."[26]

On the night of April 5, a deserter from the Mexican army was brought into the Texas camp. The prisoner was interrogated. General Houston wrote that he reported "the miserable condition of their troops; and adds that much dissatisfaction prevails in their ranks, from the severity of treatment and deprivation of the necessaries of life."[27]

Major Smith Raises New Company

The Texas Army was still awaiting its promised pair of cannon on April 4. Major Leander Smith, newly promoted into the artillery division on April 1 when General Houston first received news of the Twin Sisters, had since departed the Groce's camp to bring the fieldpieces to the army.

The next news Houston had heard of the artillery probably arrived about April 5. Colonel Edward Harcourt, whom Houston had appointed as the army's chief engineer, had gone to work on constructing breastworks at Velasco "with the aid of some citizens and sixty Negroes from some plantation." Secretary of the Navy Robert Potter had then ordered Harcourt down to Galveston. On April 3, Colonel Harcourt wrote to Houston that he "found two complete field pieces with ammunition" aboard the schooner *Pennsylvania*.[28]

Harcourt immediately began work on having the Twin Sisters moved up to Harrisburg. There, his word also made it to the attention of Secretary David Thomas, who was now serving the government as acting secretary of war in Thomas Rusk's absence. Captain John Allen had arrived in Harrisburg late on April 4 from Velasco, from which he had marched after the Twin Sisters were sailed from Brazoria to Galveston. Shortly before arriving at Harrisburg, he had met up with Major Leander Smith, who had been en route to Brazoria to fetch the cannon.[29]

Upon hearing the news that the Twin Sisters were in Galveston Bay, Secretary Thomas immediately dispatched the steamboat *Ohio* downriver to get the cannon and haul them to Harrisburg. Thomas also hoped that the steamboat could return with "flour, sugar and coffee" that the army was requesting. Thomas promised that he would send the artillery and supplies with Captain Allen's company as soon as it arrived.

General Houston was likely getting mixed signals over where the cannon truly were. Captain Allen had sent a note to Houston on April 4 stating that he was en route to the army from Velasco. Upon receiving this, Houston would pen a reply on April 8 that Allen's company should "use all possible expedition in reinforcing us with your command and the cannon."[30]

Upon arriving in Harrisburg to retrieve the cannon, Major Leander Smith had pressed a small American horse from citizen Edward Gritten for use in hauling the artillery. Smith also took the liberty of organizing another volunteer company for the Texas Army on April 5. Originally assigned to the army's First Regiment, this new company elected Captain Alfred Henderson Wyly into command.[31]

A muster roll of "Return of men raised for 3 months by Majr. L. Smith, April 5th, 1836" shows that he enlisted thirty-five men on this date. Among these men were Tennessean brothers John and Hezekiah Benjamin Balch. John Balch, twenty-four, had served in the Bexar siege, and then briefly served under Captain Philip Dimmitt. Dimmitt's company was ordered to join General Houston at Gonzales, but soon found that Houston had retreated. The company had then narrowly avoided being captured by the Mexican scouting patrols. Dimmitt's company was thereafter disbanded, leaving Balch and his brother to make their way to Harrisburg.

According to John Balch's pension papers, several of Dimmitt's former men were among those recruits "organized at Harrisburg" on April 5 under Captain Wyly. His brother, Hezekiah Balch, was elected first lieutenant of the new unit.[32]

By April 6, Major Digges arrived at Harrisburg with his prisoner, suspected spy John Linn, and delivered him to the War Department for detainment. Acting Secretary of War David Thomas noted that, "The steamboat has not yet arrived from Galveston."[33]

Thomas also noted that Major Smith "has got thirty or forty men to enroll themselves for three months service." Smith and Captain Wyly were planning "to start this morning for the army," wrote Thomas. "But I thought it best for him to remain today at least for the arrival of the cannon and provisions as he could be serviceable in getting them on having a number of them here to be employed for that service."

"I hope a just and wise God, in whom I have always believed, will yet save Texas," Sam Houston wrote to President Burnet on April 6. Apparently bitter over a recent harsh note received from Burnet, Houston's return volley was particularly sarcastic.

> I am sorry that I am so wicked, for "the prayers of the righteous shall prevail." That you are so, I have no doubt, and hope that Heaven, as such, will help and prosper you, and crown your efforts with success in behalf of Texas and humanity.[34]

Colonel Rusk wrote to President Burnet also, reporting that he was on his third day in camp. "I find the Army in fine spirits, ready and anxious to measure arms with the enemy," he wrote. Rusk estimated the army's strength to be fifteen hundred men, "though not all at this point." Rusk urged that Captain Wyly Martin at Fort Bend be "immediately reinforced from the ranks of those who are retreating towards the Sabine."[35]

Rusk wrote that he had helped interrogate the prisoner captured the previous evening. The prisoner reported the Mexican troops to be "much disheartened" from their lack of supplies and lack of full pay.

> We have correct intelligence of four hundred of a reinforcement, being on the road between this and Nacogdoches. The Trinity being high has detained them very much, but they will be in in a few days from this time. Good order and discipline prevail in Camp; there is some little sickness, one death today, [George W. Scott] the son of Capt. Scott [the captain of a steamboat at Galveston]. I hope you will lose no time or opportunity in procuring munitions and provisions.

The sickness was becoming more of an issue than Houston's letter acknowledges. According to Dr. Nicholas Labadie, the army's medical staff was organized on April 6 at the camp near Groce's Landing. Other promotions were made and some shuffling of men also occurred. Captain Logan was unhappy that his Liberty Company was reduced from nearly eighty men to about fifty in the shuffle.[36]

Labadie felt that much of the sickness was caused by "using stagnant water from the old bed of the river." In order to avoid further alarm and the spread of infections, Houston had the hospital established on Groce's nearby Bernardo plantation. The sick had been sent to the spot over the previous days to keep them isolated, yet the illnesses increased.

The army's conditions in the swamp camp west of the Brazos had only added to the health problems. Men drank stagnant water from an old river bed, adding dysentery to the measles outbreak that was already sweeping through the lines.

Dr. James Phelps was placed in charge of the main hospital. Dr. Alexander Ewing, a twenty-seven-year-old Irishman who had studied medicine at Edinburgh, was appointed as the army's surgeon general on April 6. Ewing then appointed Doctors William Bomar and Nicholas Labadie to be the surgeons of the regular army regiment of Colonel Henry Millard. Other surgeons were appointed to handle the various volunteer corps. Colonel Burleson appointed Doctors William Davidson and John Fitzhugh of Nacogdoches for his regiment. Colonel Sherman appointed Dr. Anson Jones and Dr. Shields Booker of Brazoria for the Second Regiment.

Jones was adamant that he still be considered a soldier.

> I made it a condition of accepting that I should be permitted to resign so soon as the necessity of my acceptance of that place should cease; and

that, in the mean time, I should be permitted to hold "my rank" as a private in the line.[37]

Dr. Labadie set to work organizing his medicine chest the next day and working on his new duties. "Owing to the state of inactivity and the increase of diarrhea in the army, great discontent and murmuring were manifested among all the officers and men," he wrote.[38]

Aside from organizing the army's medical corps, General Houston also detached the First Regiment company of Captain Jacob Eberly to move to his hometown of Columbia-on-the-Brazos. One of Eberly's men, Sergeant Basil Ijams, remained with the army and became second lieutenant of Captain Thomas McIntire's company on April 7. In addition to guarding that crossing and protecting citizens of the Runaway Scrape, Captain Eberly was given orders by Houston on April 6 to raise "fifty-six men or more, for the service of the Army of Texas, and employ them to the best advantage in that service, until further orders."[39]

Eberly's men arrived at Columbia and there became subject to the orders of Major Edwin Morehouse's newly arrived New York battalion. Private John T. White, nineteen, affirmed that he was "a soldier in Capt. Eberly's company under Col. Morehouse on the Brazos from about the last day of March 1836 until after the battle of San Jacinto."[40]

Captain Eberly found that his store in Columbia and its goods had been destroyed. He would later file a claim for the loss of $362 worth of liquor that had been destroyed on March 27 by the orders of Sam Houston.[41]

Major Morehouse, born in New York in 1801, had been given a commission in November 1835 to return to his home state to raise volunteers. The battalion he raised sailed from New York in November 1835, aboard the brig *Matawamkeag*. Morehouse's ship was captured by the British cruiser *Serpent* and his 174 men were detained as pirates for a month at Nassau in the Bahamas. Finally, under escort by a convoy of the Texas Navy, the *Matawamkeag* sailed into Matagorda Bay in late March 1836.

Only two men of Morehouse's battalion, Algernon P. Thompson and Major James Perry, managed to join the Texas Army during early April. From the coast at Matagorda, the balance of Morehouse's men marched quickly to Columbia-on-the-Brazos, arriving there exhausted on April 6.[42]

Morehouse sent a note to General Houston via Captain Edwin H. Stanley on April 6 that he had arrived "with a detachment of troops composed of volunteers and regulars." Their move up from Matagorda had been slowed in assisting fleeing families of the Runaway Scrape.[43]

At Columbia, merchant Nathaniel Townsend supplied Major Morehouse. Townsend, whose shop had been lost when San Felipe was burned, had the further misfortune of his next load of supplies being aboard the schooner *Santiago*, which wrecked at the mouth of the Brazos in early April. These supplies were put to the use of the army, however, as Morehouse's command—including Eberly's company— drew a large number of supplies from Townsend between April 6 and April 10.[44]

Santa Anna Captures a Texan

President Santa Anna had caught up with General Ramirez y Sesma's troops on the Colorado River on April 5. Noticing that there was only one canoe with which to cross the river, Santa Anna ordered General Adrián Woll to direct the Aldama battalion in constructing rafts "to facilitate the progress of the section that had remained with General Filisola."[45]

According to the latest reports from his officers, Santa Anna believed General Urrea to be moving toward Brazoria and General Gaona's men to be heading toward San Felipe de Austin. He therefore moved forward with Ramirez y Sesma's division on April 6 to San Bernard Creek. Resting for the night, their forces then marched into San Felipe at dawn on April 7.

The torching done by Captain Baker's company was all too evident. "This town, located on the west bank of the Brazos River, was no longer in existence because the enemy had burned it," Santa Anna later wrote.

Upon his arrival, the Mexican commander-in-chief had the good fortune of capturing a luckless Texan soldier who provided Santa Anna with useful intelligence.

> Among the ruins, an armed Anglo-American was arrested, and he stated that he belonged to a detachment of about one hundred fifty men located on the other side to protect the crossing. He said that the towns were burned to keep the supplies away from the Mexicans by orders of General Sam Houston, who was in a woods at Gross Pass, fifteen leagues distant from our left with only eight hundred men that he had left. His intention was to withdraw to the Trinity River if the Mexicans crossed the Brazos River.

Private Bill Simpson of Captain Moseley Baker's company was the luckless Texan captured by the Mexican army on April 7 at the Brazos River. Baker's company had already burned San Felipe and had dug trenches on the east bank of the Brazos River. Since his arrival, General Houston had reinforced him with the companies of Captains William Kimbro and Benjamin Bryant. Baker's command had also moved all the boats and rafts in the area to hiding places on the eastern banks. Several hours before the Mexican troops arrived, Captain Baker sent several men back to San Felipe to serve as pickets to warn him of the Mexicans' approach.[46]

Corporal Isaac Hill wrote that he, James M. Bell and Bill Simpson were selected for this mission. Using a canoe, they crossed the river and locked their canoe to a tree. During the night, they posted themselves on a gentle eminence in the prairie just west of the main town of San Felipe and about three-quarters of a mile from the ferry. Bell and Hill stood the first two watches during the night. Corporal Hill relates the story.

> The third and last was assigned to Simpson, as Capt. Baker had ordered us to return to camp very early next morning. Bell and I, when we lay down, requested Simpson to wake us at daylight.
>
> This, however, he neglected to do and we were roused at sunrise by the clattering of horses' feet. "What is that?" said I. Bell rose and exclaimed, "Mexicans, by God!"
>
> There were about a hundred cavalry, the advance guard of the Mexican army. Though not more than seventy or eighty yards distant they had not yet perceived us.[47]

Isaac Lafayette Hill (1814–1889) was among a detachment of Captain Baker's command which was posted on the east side of the Brazos River on April 7. Hill and another soldier escaped across the river, but one Texan was taken prisoner by the Mexican army. *Courtesy of the San Jacinto Museum of History, Houston.*

The Mexican horsemen descended upon Simpson and captured him quickly. Bell and Hill raced furiously for their canoe. Bell implored Hill that they should turn and fight, but Hill knew that the two would only be killed or captured against such superior numbers. "We had scarcely got into the canoe and pushed it from the shore when the Mexicans were on the bank and shooting at us," wrote Hill.

The Mexican soldiers fired several rounds at the fleeing Texans and shouted for them to "bring back that boat!" Private Simpson became a prisoner of war. Major James Perry of General Houston's staff wrote on April 9 that Simpson was "caught with a lasso during a comfortable snooze which he was taking whilst on post as a sentinel."[48]

Santa Anna makes no mention of what tactics his men used in extracting information from Simpson, but he appears during interrogation to have told what little he knew of General Houston's movements.

From the east side of the river, Captain Baker's men at first supposed the approaching horsemen to be Texan spies. Once he saw his sentinels under fire in the little boat, Baker ordered his men to return fire. The Mexican cavalry retired with its prisoner. Baker spread his men out during the afternoon, maintaining a force in the ditch that they had dug and posting sentinels along the riverbank above and below the main entrenchment. During the afternoon hours, Santa Anna maintained a sniper who fired on the Texans with a rifle from a fortified position on the west bank.

Santa Anna noted that Captain Martin's Texans had a well-protected entrenchment from which they fired across the river. El Presidente was only too happy to oblige the hostile Texans.

> I had a trench dug facing them and placed two six-caliber cannon which were fired upon constantly, without any mishap at all on our side. I immediately reconnoitered the river bank to the left and to the right up to two leagues distance looking for a crossing to surprise them during the night. But it was a fruitless search; the river is wide and deep and was on a rise, and not a canoe was to be found.

Santa Anna's personal secretary, Ramón Martínez Caro, in his campaign account published in 1837, disagreed with the commander-in-chief on casualties. Caro admitted that two soldiers and a mule driver were killed in the firing across the Colorado River.[49]

From the main Texas Army camp, Colonel Henry Millard wrote on April 7 of the skirmish that morning with Mexican forces at San Felipe. "A company of our men had a brush with them this morning across the river, killing 2 of their number." He was critical of those who would not turn out to defend their country. "Our countrymen are slow in coming to our assistance," Millard wrote. "Our army is not more than 1000 strong and we shall have to fight more than double our number."[50]

From the east bank of the Brazos opposite Fort Bend, Captain Wyly Martin sent a message to General Houston. His spies had learned through a free black named Wilson that Santa Anna was with the advancing portion of the Mexican army.[51]

General Houston wrote to friend Henry Raguet on April 7 in Nacogdoches that Colonel Rusk was in camp and that there "is the most perfect harmony in camp." He considered Rusk "a patriot and a soldier." Rusk's spoken sentiment was "Victory and Independence!" Houston sent his word to Raguet via Major Ira Ingram as messenger.

While encamped near Groce's Landing, Houston continued to receive intelligence from Texas Ranger forces which fell under his supervision. Major Willie Williamson, commander of a small government-authorized ranger battalion, was still operating from Washington-on-the-Brazos as of April 7. Williamson busied himself enlisting recruits for General Houston and sending out spy patrols for the purpose of gathering information on the approaching Mexican army.

The remaining members of Captain John Tumlinson's former ranger company were still trying to make their way to the Texas Army since Williamson had left them behind. High waters and enemy patrols frequently taxed their journey, and this group under Lieutenant George Petty was never able to catch up with Williamson during the San Jacinto campaign.

Major Williamson sent two letters to General Houston on April 7 on the activities he had been engaged in at Washington. He sent with Major Robert Barr a list of the new recruits he had put together in this town, including those of Captain Joseph Chance's Washington Guards.

When Barr departed, he traveled in company with four men whom Williamson had enlisted as volunteer rangers. Three were considered dutiful soldiers who were acting as guards over the fourth man named Murphy. This man had apparently pleaded guilty to petty larceny and disobedience of orders from Williamson. When this man was sent to Houston, Williamson sent a note which requested that Houston should "release him and make a soldier of him. I believe he will do his duty as such, for he is much alarmed."[52]

Williamson sent a second letter to General Houston in the afternoon. He wrote that one of his ranger spies, Daniel Gray, had returned that morning from an overnight scout. Gray had been chased by eight mounted men whom he believed were Mexicans. Williamson actually felt that his scout was mistaken; he noted that "five men are still out in the same direction and well mounted and have had time to report." Williamson noted to Houston of this chase, "I take them to be a party of your spies that have given chase—in a few hours we will know the truth."[53]

General Houston and Secretary of War Rusk were displeased to learn that drunken men under Major Williamson's command had killed two Mexican soldiers who were captured during a scouting mission. Rusk and Houston therefore sent new orders to Williamson via one of Houston's aides-de-camp, Major James Collinsworth.

They ordered Williamson to report himself to their headquarters "forthwith." Williamson relinquished his command at Washington to Major Collinsworth and headed to join the Texas Army to face Sam Houston. Collinsworth, who had been given specific new orders for using the rangers, took temporary command at Washington.

> He has orders to keep out spies and to adopt such measures as he may see proper for the safety of the place. I disapprove the killing of those two Mexicans. They should have been sent to me for examination. I have no idea, but that they were deserters from the enemy and important information might have been obtained from them. I order without exception the destruction of all ardent spirits at Washington and wherever it may be found. I have not delegated any power to any person or persons to arrest and try persons for offenses. The discretionary powers given to Maj. Collinsworth are the first issued by me. I wish Col. [William] Pettus to repair to camp and report to me. Major Collinsworth has power to call all persons into service, and to act to his discretion, saving life.[54]

Along with Major Collinsworth, Houston sent Quartermaster Edward Winfield to Washington-on-the-Brazos to secure much-needed additional blankets and fabrics for sewing tents and clothing.[55]

Baker Detachment versus the Mexican Army

Captain William Walker wrote to General Houston from "Camp Cartwright" on April 7. He signed as "Capt. of Family Guards, East Side Brazos." Walker sent his muster roll of fifty-four names, of which "some are sick and some very old men. There is not more than thirty effective men in the whole number. At present I have urged all young men to join the main Army." Walker had taken steps to prevent the wasting of corn left by his friends on the east side of the Brazos. Twenty of his men left for the army on April 5. The balance with him were the older, less able men who were guarding their families.[56]

Of those that left Captain Walker to join the Texas Army, fourteen men joined with Captain Moseley Baker's detachment and would serve through the balance of the San Jacinto campaign. Most of these men would serve under Captains Baker, William Heard and William Patton, arriving in the Texas camp on April 9. They were led to Baker's Brazos River camp across from San Felipe by George Sutherland, a thirty-nine-year-old former delegate of the conventions of Texas and previous captain during the 1835 Bexar siege.

Baker's men were pleased to receive any reinforcements, for Santa Anna's men had not let up on them. His Texian forces were still under cannon fire from the two Mexican cannon across the river.

Corporal Isaac Hill awoke in his pallet in the ditch right at daybreak on April 8. "I was startled by the booming of a cannon which had been planted near the head of a ravine opposite the ferry," he wrote.[57]

"Many rounds of roundshot, grape and canister were discharged at us, throwing the sand upon us and knocking the bark from the cottonwood trees that extended their branches over us," remembered Hill. Added to the occasional roar of cannon this day came a new sound, that of men busily hammering and chopping at logs.

Santa Anna had ordered two flatboats to be constructed in order to cross the swollen Brazos. Using logs and planks secured from homes above San Felipe, the Mexican soldiers busied themselves on April 8 with building these boats while their comrades continued to fire on Baker's rebels across the river.

From the San Felipe ferry landing, Moseley Baker sent General Houston his latest news.

> The enemy have all day been busily engaged chopping and hammering on the opposite side of the river, and but little doubt, can be entertained of their intention to attempt a crossing. We are about 95 strong [including Bryant's and Kimbro's men] . . . if this position is to be maintained—more force ought to be sent and sent speedily.[58]

Captain Baker also informed the general that "One man was killed by cannon shot this morning." Private John Bricker suffered a head wound from a copper ball on April 8. Major James Perry wrote that, "One of our men was killed by a grape shot through the head."[59] Corporal Hill witnessed the death of Bricker.

> John Bricker, of Capt. Baker's company, after having been relieved of his post below the entrenchment started up to the camp, but loitered on his way to pick up cannon balls and was struck by a canister shot. Almost instant death ensued, though the ball had barely buried itself in his temple.[60]

Private Bricker thus became the first Texian casualty of the San Jacinto campaign. Another soldier, Roden Taylor Crain of Captain Kimbro's company, was wounded in the action. He later reflected in the 1872 *Texas Almanac*.

> I was slightly wounded in the head, by an escopeto ball, at San Felipe, when Santa Anna's army first arrived at that place. Our company joined Houston at Groce's, and was ordered down to San Felipe, to guard that crossing. There were two other companies at the place to keep the Mexicans from crossing, Capt. Moseley Baker commanding the whole guard. We burned the town, crossed over to this side and entrenched.

Baker's men kept up enough fire that the two flatboats built by the Mexicans were not able to be launched that day. The Mexican soldiers looked up and down the Brazos for an easier crossing spot. Baker's men had previously sunk the ferryboat to prevent their enemy from crossing the river.

Santa Anna grew frustrated with the difficulty in crossing the swollen river and with the slow progress of his men in building rafts. "This loss of time seemed to me to be an irreparable evil since considering the situation of the army of the Republic the ending of the campaign before the rainy season was very important," he later wrote.[61]

As this small group bravely fought Santa Anna, the cannon fire could be heard plainly miles upriver in the Texan camp. Every cannon shot "was distinctly heard at our camp," recalled Private James Kuykendall. Secure in this location, Sam Houston chose to send out his scouts for intelligence, all the while facing increasing pressure from his commanders to attack.[62]

From Fort Bend, Captain Wyly Martin wrote to General Houston on April 8 with intelligence from two men who had arrived from above San Felipe. "They state that one division of the enemy has passed above, pointing the head of their column for Nacogdoches; the other column below, aiming for Matagorda."[63]

Houston Creates Second Regiment

During the days of camping in the Brazos River bottoms, Sam Houston continued to drill his men and encourage them with the promise that artillery pieces were on their way from Galveston. He and Colonel Rusk took time on April 8 to tighten up the organization of their army.

They created the Second Regiment of Infantry, which was placed under command of Colonel Sidney Sherman. Captain Joseph Bennett was elected its lieutenant colonel. In Bennett's place, First Lieutenant James Gillaspie was promoted into command of his company.

General Houston had scheduled these elections the previous evening, giving his leading men time to carefully consider whom they would elect to fill key positions. The captains comprising the First Regiment voted before noon on April 8. They elected Major Alexander Somervell to fill Sherman's old billet of Lieutenant Colonel of the First Regiment of Texas Volunteers.[64]

Captain Robert McNutt was elected to fill the open spot of major of the First Regiment and Gibson Kuykendall was elected to take command of McNutt's company. Captain William Patton was promoted to major on General Houston's staff and command of his company would pass to twenty-four-year-old Captain David Murphree. The oldest of eleven children, Murphree had come to Texas in 1834 and fought during the Bexar siege in December 1835.

Colonel Burleson's First Regiment now included the companies of Captains William Wood, Richard Roman, Jesse Billingsley, Moseley Baker, William Heard, William Hill, William Fisher, Robert Calder, Peyton Splane and Gibson Kuykendall.

Colonel Sherman's Second Regiment included the companies of Captains Hayden Arnold, Juan Seguin, William Kimbro, Benjamin Bryant, James Gillaspie, Thomas McIntire, William Ware, David Murphree, and William Logan. To this would be added Captain Alfred Wyly's newly recruited unit, which was still at Harrisburg on this date. Major James Collinsworth would move from Washington and rejoin Houston's army within the next week. With him would come Captain Joseph Chance's Washington Guards ranger company, which was ordered to operate with the Second Regiment.

Captain Daniel Perry's small volunteer company was broken up as the army was reorganized. Perry and the few who would remain, such

Colonel Edward Burleson (1789–1851), commander of the army's First Regiment of Texas Volunteers. A soldier under General Andrew Jackson in the Creek War, Burleson had already distinguished himself in Texas as a fearless Indian fighter and army commander. He would later be the first person to be buried in the Texas State Cemetery in Austin.
Courtesy of the Archives and Information Services Division, Texas State Library.

Colonel Sidney Sherman (1805–1873), was promoted into command of the new Second Regiment on April 8, 1836. An aggressive leader from Kentucky, Sherman had been previously promoted from captain of Company A to lieutenant colonel of the First Regiment under Burleson.
Courtesy of the San Jacinto Museum of History Association.

as John F. Stancell, took the rank of private and joined Captain Fisher's First Regiment company. Second Lieutenant Ebenezer Hale was released from Captain Perry's company on April 8 and was reassigned to Columbia-on-the-Brazos. Hale and other men would join Major Morehouse's New York battalion.[65]

The army now consisted of cavalry and scouts, a division of regular soldiers, the First Regiment of Volunteer Infantry and the Second Regiment of Volunteer Infantry.

Lieutenant Colonel Henry Millard, a twenty-nine-year-old from Mississippi, was in command of the regular army. This consisted of the two companies under Captains Amasa Turner and Henry Teal.

The cannon fire from San Felipe could be heard throughout the Texian camp in the Brazos bottoms. General Houston faced some problems in camp with others wanting a commander who was ready to fight, as Dr. Labadie recalled.

One day [Joseph] Kuykendall came into camp, and stated that he had
been taken prisoner by some Mexicans while eating his dinner in his own
house; that he had been taken before Santa Anna, who received him kindly,
and then gave him his liberty, telling him to go and hunt up General Houston, and tell him that he, Santa Anna, was tired of hunting after him and his
army, like so many Indians in the woods, but that if he would come out of his
hiding-place, he would give him a fight in the open prairie.

The challenge was a little too much for the Texas boys, and the desire
to meet the enemy became almost uncontrollable. Col. Sidney Sherman
had been elected Colonel of the Second Regiment, to which the Liberty
Company belonged, and while all were saying it was time to be doing something besides lying in idleness and getting sick, upon hearing this challenge
it was declared to be necessary that the army should have another commander, and Colonel Sherman was pointed out as the man calculated to
meet the emergency. This came to the ears of General Houston, who at
once caused notices to be written and stuck on trees with wooden pegs, to
the effect that the first man who should beat for volunteers, should be
court-martialed and shot.[66]

Dr. Labadie noted that one of these notices was pinned to a hickory tree within six feet of the tent of the Liberty Company. Major Ben
Fort Smith, Dr. Alexander Ewing and Isaac Moreland, a close friend
of Houston's, made the rounds encouraging others not to consider going against Houston's command, as they expected that "the camp
would break up within a few days" to pursue the enemy.

The steamboat *Ohio* arrived at Harrisburg during the early evening
hours of April 8. David Thomas wrote to General Houston at 10:00
p.m. that the two fieldpieces had finally arrived "with some ammunition." Thomas promised to forward these goods in the morning.
Colonel Huston, the army's quartermaster general, arrived in a steamboat from Galveston that evening also with flour, sugar and coffee,
which would be forwarded to the army in the morning.[67]

Thomas also informed Houston of the recent successes of the
Texas Navy. Captain Jeremiah Brown's *Invincible* had fought a duel
days before with the Mexican armed vessel *Montezuma*, driving her
ashore and leaving her in a sinking condition. Brown brought the
Montezuma safely into Galveston complete with her cargo and many
documents written in Spanish which gave details of Santa Anna's
movements from Bexar.

In the Brazos bottoms Texas camp, the wet weather had taken its
toll on men's health. In a letter written April 9, Major James Perry,
a New Yorker who had joined Houston's staff at the Colorado, paints

a graphic description of the scene. Perry stated that the army was "very badly provided with breadstuffs" and had not a single barrel of flour.

> We continue to occupy the same ground, but should the river rise much higher we shall be compelled to seek some more elevated position. Even now we are under the necessity of swimming to reach the prairie, and are almost flooded in our encampment. The camp is situated on a small lake or pool of stagnant water which serves as the general washing and watering place for men, animals and clothes, and as the ground we occupy gradually descends towards the lake it naturally becomes the receptical of all offals and filth, which necessarily collects in large quantities around the tents &c in the vicinity of an army.
>
> We have now about 300 men sick and not more than twice that number reported for duty. In addition to these there is about 90 men at Fort Settlement and a few more at Brazoria and Columbia. This forms the whole of the available force, that Genl. Houston will be able at any time to bring into the field.[68]

General Houston's report to Secretary Thomas on April 9 shows that the fighting continued near San Felipe. "The enemy are firing at San Felipe today," Houston wrote. "I reinforced the post by forty-five men. They now have at least one hundred and fifty men." The reinforcement party to the San Felipe ferry was led by newly promoted Lieutenant Colonel Joe Bennett of the Second Regiment. Houston kept his men tucked away back in the timber near Groce's and "our numbers increase."[69]

On April 9, Houston sent out another scout party "well versed in the use of the horse." He expected the Brazos waters to "fall in the course of a day or so." He reported that his army had two organized regiments. One of his spies, Jim Wells, had returned this day and reported, after examining signs at the enemy's parade grounds, that the nearest enemy forces numbered "six or seven hundred men."

Santa Anna Pushes On

Taking about 500 grenadiers and 50 infantrymen, Santa Anna on April 9 rode down the west bank of the Brazos, away from Groce's. He left General Ramirez y Sesma and about 850 men to continue fighting Captain Baker's men and building rafts. Sesma was waiting on the arrival of new columns under Generals Filisola, Urrea and Gaona.[70]

After departing San Felipe, Santa Anna's troops were observed by several Texas spies, who were chased but managed to escape down the road to Thompson's Ferry. En route, Santa Anna's advance force stopped at a little farm. Colonel Antonio Treviño found a mulatto man named Wilson and his wife in one of the houses and took them prisoner. He was told by the couple that a small group of Texans held Thompson's Crossing.[71]

Santa Anna's secretary, Ramón Caro, wrote that the president offered the mulatto one hundred pesos to return to Thompson and inform this party that he had seen Santa Anna's force but that they had taken a different route. "The mulatto fulfilled his mission, going to Thompson's immediately and returning at once to serve as guide," wrote Caro.

The army remained camped at this farmhouse overnight, waiting for the return of Wilson. He returned in the afternoon, bringing news that Texans were indeed camped on the banks opposite from Thompson's. Despite his return, Wilson was never paid his promised one hundred pesos. At 4:15 p.m., Santa Anna took up the march for Old Fort on the road from Brazoria.

Around 5:30 p.m. of April 10, Santa Anna's advance force stopped on the San Bernard River at the inn of widow Elizabeth Powell. She had not fled during the Runaway Scrape and was now forced to house the Mexican troops. Santa Anna held a council of war at Powell's tavern, unaware that her young son Joseph understood Spanish. Joseph Powell later rode from the inn and spread the word that Santa Anna's men were moving toward Fort Bend.[72]

Major General Santa Anna did not allow the troops to rest long at Powell's, but pushed on toward the Brazos River and Thompson's Ferry. He allowed his men to take another rest at 9:30 p.m. By the early morning hours of April 11, Santa Anna was moving forward again, as recorded in the diary of Colonel Juan Almonte.

> At 2 in the morning, we commenced the march on foot, from the President down to the soldier, leaving the baggage and cavalry, for the purpose of surprising the enemy who defended the crossing place before daylight.
>
> We did not succeed, as we found the distance double what we supposed it to be. Day broke upon us at a quarter of a league from the ferry and frustrated our plan. We then placed the men in ambush.[73]

From his camp opposite the Brazos River from San Felipe, Captain Moseley Baker held a conference with the other captains present.

His meeting included Captain William Kimbro, Captain Benjamin Bryant, J. W. E. Wallace and George Sutherland, the latter in charge of about fourteen men newly arrived from Captain William Walker's command.[74]

The captains found their force to be "about 85 strong and the enemy probably about 1200." They decided that their breastworks and ravine were "no longer tenable" as both were in striking range of the Mexican cannon. In a report to Houston, Captain Baker noted that "one half of our whole force is continually standing guard." Their campground was nearly surrounded by flood waters, leaving only the main road as their course of retreat.

> We have no position on the river to fight from without being exposed to the whole of the cannon.
> Wherefore we advise that the companies fall back to Iron's Creek & then fortify and make all suitable preparations for fighting the enemy through the swamp to the creek and to resist them at that crossing at all hazards.

Baker's camp was therefore moved and "Camp Iron's Creek" was established by mid-afternoon on April 9. Two of Baker's spies, Peter B. Dexter and Charles D. Ferris, returned in the afternoon to report that the Mexicans had departed San Felipe after the Texan forces withdrew to Iron's Creek.

Dexter reported from "Camp Salvation" near San Felipe that the enemy had left that town. Ferris, on the east side of the Brazos Ferry at San Felipe, found that the enemy had "removed to some other point, whose locality we have not been able to ascertain, leaving a small guard and but one piece of artillery." Baker's small group of spies remained near San Felipe on alert until they could be relieved by a picket guard from Captain John Bird's company.[75]

Captain Baker sent this intelligence from Camp Iron's Creek at 4:00 p.m. on April 10 to General Houston.

In Harrisburg, the Twin Sisters cannon had been started for the army on the morning of April 9. Major Leander Smith, in company with Captains John Allen and Alfred Wyly, was in charge of moving the artillery and supplies toward the main army camp on the Brazos. The movement of the Twin Sisters is shown in an April 10 note from the War Department in Harrisburg, from acting Secretary of War David Thomas to General Houston.

> An express just arrived here from Capt. Walker who says that he has been ordered by Maj. Martin to march his command to Fort Bend as the enemy

has appeared in force in ten miles below San Felipe that his spies had driven in. It may be the army is following down the river. Should that be the fact it would be better to have sent the cannon to some point below. It has been two days gone.[76]

Thomas sent Dr. William Carper to Houston's army to serve as regimental surgeon of cavalry. Carper was a newer arrival to Texas who had been recruited to serve in the Texas Army.

Captain Walker's express to Harrisburg had also inspired President Burnet to send a harsh note to Houston on April 10. "As soon as it was communicated to me, by Capt. Walker, of Fort Bend, that the enemy were preparing to cross the Brazos at that point, I wrote, by express, to the Secretary of War," wrote Burnet.[77]

Burnet was very direct with General Houston. He had word that "the enemy had jeeringly threatened to *smoke him out*" of his Brazos bottomlands campground at Groce's Landing. Burnet was also upset that Colonel Rusk had been in camp for a week now and had been unable to convince Houston to get his men moving. Burnet handed the express rider a letter that contained language which he hoped would inspire the Texas general.

> *The enemy are laughing you to scorn.* You must fight them. You must retreat no further. The country expects you to fight. The salvation of the country depends on your doing so.

Although received by Houston, it is unclear how much influence Burnet's stinging words may have had in getting the forces moving to fight. According to Branch Tanner Archer, Houston would approach Burnet later in the year and reproach him for giving such direct orders to fight and retreat no further "while he, then President Burnet, was luxuriating in the town of Harrisburg."[78]

Burnet and Houston, in fact, would share no love for one another. Burnet later wrote of Houston: "The army regarded him as a military fop, and the citizens were disgusted at his miserable imbecility." In return, the scramble of Burnet and his cabinet from Washington-on-the-Brazos was sarcastically described by Houston as "the flight of the wise men."[79]

CHAPTER 9

"I Will Avenge the Death of My Brave Friends"

April 11–12

At this crisis, the shafts of envy or malice should rest in the quiver. I am worn down in body by fatigue, and really take my rest most in the morning, for I watch nearly all night. Instead of being in a state of insanity, I fear I am too irritable.
—*General Houston on April 11, defending his command to President Burnet*

In his camp in the Brazos River bottoms opposite the charred town of San Felipe, Lieutenant Colonel Joe Bennett held command of some 150 Texian soldiers. By April 11, he had clear intelligence that the Mexican army had crossed the Brazos.

Bennett and his reinforcements had reached Captain Moseley Baker's camp on April 10 to monitor the enemy's movements and to help protect the crossing. His first new intelligence was sent by courier Thomas J. Sweeney back to General Houston, who remained in command of the army's main body on the west side of the Brazos.

Captain William Walker moved his men to Fort Bend in compliance with the orders he had received from Captain Wyly Martin. Having seen Mexican forces crossing the river, Walker sent out riders on the afternoon of April 11. Twenty of his ablest young men had already departed on April 5 to join the main army. Allowing the balance of his volunteer company to break up, Captain Walker soon joined Captain William Hill's First Regiment Company H as a private soldier.

Captain Andrew Briscoe, who had been placed in command of a small mounted spy company on March 17, took another rider and went out on the night of April 11 to reconnoiter and to check the enemy's movements.[1]

One of Captain Walker's couriers reached Lieutenant Colonel Bennett in his camp opposite San Felipe. Another went on to Harrisburg to report to the War Department and the acting secretary of war. Walker sent word that some of the Mexicans had crossed over at Morton's Ferry. Daniel Perry also rode into Harrisburg late on the night of April 11 and announced to Secretary of War Thomas that "about fifty had crossed over and taken possession of Morton's house."[2]

Joe Bennett sent Private Sanford Holman of Captain Kimbro's San Augustine company on to Sam Houston on April 11 with the news that the enemy was crossing at Thompson's Ferry, held by Captain Martin's company. "Our men and them [are] actually fighting," he wrote. "Some of our men are killed." Bennett figured that at least five hundred enemy troops were on the other side of the Brazos from him. "My force is only 150 efficient men."[3]

Bennett's news arrived at the main Texas Army camp as General Houston was writing a letter to President Burnet. At the bottom, he scrawled a postscript that, "I will cross the river soon and meet the enemy on the east side of the river if they are really crossing below."[4]

Houston informed Burnet of a mutinous letter he had found that day in camp. One of his volunteer aides-de-camp, Major James Perry, had written a letter concerning General Houston's leadership. While on a furlough to Brazoria, Perry became acquainted with Colonel Robert Potter, the Texas Secretary of Navy. "I presume their intercourse suggested the character of the letter," wrote Houston.

Houston had a standing order that all letters being sent from camp should be examined by the commanding general. As the express was preparing to head for Burnet with the day's mail on April 11, Houston noted Perry's letter, which had been written two days prior. "Finding this one sealed, I opened it, not suspecting the contents."

Major Perry was critical of the officers in command of the Texas Army and felt that the enlisted men "are entirely without discipline." Some of the company commanders were lacking proper military training in tactics and leadership, therefore displaying a "most culpable disregard of their duties to their country." Perry felt that some of those in charge had more interest in their own self-promotion than the good of their country.

> These individuals appear to have joined the army for no other reason than to gain popularity by the most-fawning and obsequious conduct towards all around them. . . .
>
> In the manner affairs are at presently conducted the men are not likely to become better disciplined than an ordinary mob. Indeed, in an election

riot in the United States, I have seen the contending parties much better organized than I ever expect to see this army until some more efficient officers are appointed.[5]

Major Perry did not spare Sam Houston in his criticism. He felt that men "disgusted with the inactivity and want of energy in the General" were each day departing the filthy, flooded Texas Army campground.

> Our men are loitering about without knowing more of military tactics at evening than they did in the morning. While the General, either for want of his customary excitement (for he has entirely discontinued the use of ardent spirits) or as some say from the effect of opium, is in a condition between sleeping and walking, which amounts nearly to a constant state of insanity.

If Houston had been seen using any drug which picked him up, it was likely the Cherokee hartshorn powder he carried and not opium. This medicine, a commercial patent compound of ammonium carbonate, was given to him by Chief Bowles' granddaughter Mary and was used by the general to ward off colds.[6]

Colonel Rusk, who had organized the express and who was to take the messages to Burnet, noticed the effect that the Perry-to-Potter letter had on the army's commander-in-chief. "It contained some comments upon the movements of the army, and the conduct of General Houston, which seemed to be offensive to him," recalled Rusk.[7]

Houston sent this bitter letter of James Perry on to President Burnet. Houston defended his own angry persona and attributed much of his own behavior to lack of sleep.

> You can judge of them. I will only remark that at this crisis the shafts of envy or malice should rest in the quiver. To whom his remarks apply beside myself, I am worn down in body by fatigue, and really take my rest most in the morning, for I watch nearly all night. Instead of being in a state of insanity, I fear I am too irritable for my duties.
>
> Our crisis is too important to indulge in any feeling but honorable emulation to save our country. I pity the man who loves office—God help him. I wish more would deserve office, and we would have more men to defend it.

Major Perry remained attached to the command staff, although General Houston now kept a close eye on him. "From that moment, the General became the deadly and bitter enemy of Major Perry," wrote another of Houston's staff members, Colonel Robert Coleman.[8]

While such events were troubling to the general, they did not deter him from his goal of being prepared for the enemy. In order to safeguard the Texian campground, he placed Captain Henry Karnes in command of all the camp's horses. When out on one of his regular scouting missions, Karnes was directed to "leave the proper directions for their safety and management."[9]

Houston also made plans for his troops to cross the Brazos River via the steamboat *Yellow Stone* which he had earlier pressed into the service of Texas. In consultation with Secretary of War Rusk, he decided to cross the river the following morning.

On the evening of April 11, Captain John Ross sent a note to the general requesting that he be able to keep his bales of cotton aboard. He still felt he could move five hundred men and their baggage in one haul with the cotton aboard. Ross wisely had the most vital parts of his steamboat—the boilers, engine and pilothouse—protected with the large bales he had available. These bales were capable of stopping the enemy's rifle fire and even grape shot from a cannon. During the Civil War, the Confederate navy would use the term "cottonclad" for a vessel armored with baled cotton.[10]

"I have four cords wood on board and everything ready to 'go ahead,'" wrote Captain Ross. Houston acknowledged Ross' readiness and had him stand by for further orders.

Houston ordered the apprehension of another man on April 11 whom he suspected of being a spy, Joseph Powell. Houston was alarmed that this man had made his way across the lower areas of Texas into the camp of Captain Wyly Martin. Powell had passed close by the army of General Urrea without harm. The fact that this man could move so freely past the enemy caused Houston to wonder if Powell might have "some assurance of their favor."[11]

Captain Martin had Powell sent to the main army camp, calling his statements "lies." General Houston in turn forwarded Powell and another prisoner under guard to acting Secretary of War David Thomas in Harrisburg. Among the guards was Private Connell Kelly, formerly of Captain Baker's company. "I was sent to Harrisburg with prisoners," he wrote. Kelly was appointed commissary at Harrisburg but would rejoin the Texas Army later as a member of Captain McIntire's company.[12]

As for Powell, General Houston noted to Thomas, "You will find him a panic-maker, and in my opinion, a spy." He recommended that . Powell be forwarded to Galveston to Colonel James Morgan, where he could be watched without suspecting it. The general felt that "Lynn and Kerr ought to be well watched."

"The high waters have interrupted us much," Houston informed Thomas. As his men prepared to cross the Brazos on the *Yellow Stone*, he kept up his guard for signs of Santa Anna. "I have ordered spies everywhere."

Arrival of Fannin's Survivors

On April 10, some of the Goliad Massacre survivors were encountered by members of the Texas Army's scout patrols. At the home of James Cummings (or Cummins) at Mill Creek north of San Felipe, the spies found Daniel Murphy, Thomas Kemp, Charles Shain, David Jones, William Brenan, and Nat Hazen. Murphy and Shain had joined soon after crossing the river. Shain says they met John Williams and the three hid out overnight, then joined two more of their companions the next day, one from their division and one from the other. During the next week, they made their way back toward the settlements and encountered four other survivors.

The spies brought horses to the Palm Sunday Massacre survivors and the pitiful-looking men rode to the spy camp. "That night we stayed in our picket guard camp, four miles from Cummings' and four miles from General Houston's camp," wrote Private Shain.[13]

The scouts made their way back to the camp of the main Texas Army, bringing along the Goliad Massacre survivors they had found. They arrived during the morning of April 11. Dr. Nicholas Labadie recalled that Fannin's former men were "wounded, barefooted, and ragged" when they made it into camp.[14]

Colonel Robert Coleman wrote that they "immediately detailed to the General the particulars of that unfortunate affair." When led before Houston, he was lying in a tent with his head upon the lap of Pamelia Mann, a Runaway Scrape refugee attached to the army, who was combing his hair.[15]

Houston jumped at the sight of the pitiful men, causing Mrs. Mann to exclaim, "Why, General, you nearly made me put the comb into your head."

These survivors drew some new clothing, hat and shoes from the quartermaster's department. Some of the other Texans shared garments with these men. "As soon as I arrived," wrote Charles Shain,

"Colonel Benj. F. Smith sent for me and gave me some clothes and told me that his negro boy [Mack Smith] would wait on me till I was well."[16]

Survivor David Jones joined Captain William Hill's unit, while Shain, Murphy, Hazen, Brenan and Kemp were enrolled into Captain William Patton's Columbia company.

Suspecting that conflict was soon approaching, some men took the chance to write home. Private Shain penned a letter to his father from "Groce's Crossing on the Brazos." He wrote that, "We have near 1500 men in camp, and expect to attack the enemy in a few days." Although Texas had been overrun by the Mexican army, Shain felt "I shall live to see her free."[17]

Shain related to his father the story of the massacre of his entire company with Colonel Fannin.

> We thought it best to surrender on the terms offered to us—which were, to treat us [as] prisoners of war, and according to the rules of Christian warfare. But how sadly we were deceived, the sequel will show.
>
> After starving us for a week, they ordered us out, saying we were going after beef, but when we had marched about half a mile from the fort we were ordered to halt. The Mexicans marched all on one side of us, and took deliberate aim at us, but I, as you have seen, was fortunate enough to escape.
>
> I have, however, had monstrous hard times, having nothing to eat for five successive days and nights, but at length arrived safely here this morning, after a travel of two weeks through prairies and dangers during which time I had some narrow escapes, especially the night before last on the line of the picket guards of the Mexican force, I was nearly killed or taken.

Although half-starved, exhausted, and sore-footed from walking the prairies barefooted, Shain hoped to rest a few days. But he had one further goal which he professed to his father, "I will try to avenge the death of some of my brave friends. All of my company were killed."

———

Martin's Men Abandon Fort Bend

Captain Andrew Briscoe and one of his men returned to Harrisburg on April 12 after an overnight scout. They had ridden twenty miles out from town to Stafford's Point. Acting Secretary of War David Thomas wrote that Briscoe had "received intelligence on which he thinks he can rely that four hundred Mexicans had crossed over and were on this side of the Brazos in the bottom of the river."[18]

Thomas sent another rider to Houston's camp informing him that the Mexicans were now crossing the Brazos and had nothing to stop them from marching through Harrisburg and on to Galveston. Thomas was blunt with General Houston, writing:

> The country expects something from you. The Government looks to you for action. The time has now arrived to determine whether we are to give up the country and make the best of our way out of it or to meet the enemy and make at least one struggle for our boasted independence.

Captain Wyly Martin's men at Fort Bend could certainly confirm the intelligence of the Mexican troops. Shortly after sunrise on April 12, the Mexicans fired on a party of Captain Martin's men who had crossed the Brazos River for corn. "They effected their retreat without loss," Martin wrote. "Shortly afterwards the enemy appeared in great force opposite us at Thompson's ferry."[19]

Hearing the firing from his position at Fort Bend, Martin sent Lieutenant Randall Jones to the assistance of his men at Thompson's Ferry. Martin was frustrated with his situation, "my whole force being 46 men with four crossings to defend." He had only been joined by twelve men from Captain William Walker's company, "less than one-fourth of what I expected."

Together with Captain Walker's dozen men, First Lieutenant James Moore of Walker's company and Lieutenant Samuel Stone of Martin's company proceeded "to give the enemy battle." The enemy continued crossing in great numbers during the day until Captain Martin decided that his men could no longer hold the various crossing points. They "retreated to the prairie where I threw myself in the rear of the retiring families."

Randall Jones (1786–1873), one of Austin's Old Three Hundred settlers, was first lieutenant of Captain Wyly Martin's company. He and his companymates fought to prevent the Mexican army from crossing the Brazos River.
Texas State Library and Archives Commission.

Martin stopped his troops after nightfall, sent word of the Mexican army's advance, and awaited further orders. General Houston wrote a note back to Martin the following day which stated, "I am proud to feel in favor of your conduct and the brave men who acted under your command."

Houston also ordered Martin to take up the line of march with his men "and proceed as expeditiously as possible after the receipt of this order" to the house of Charles Donoho on the road from Groce's to San Felipe. Martin was to there encamp and await further orders.

Also moving to join Captain Martin's command on April 12 was Major Edwin Morehouse's New York battalion. "I received orders to take up my march for Head Quarters on the river Colorado," wrote Morehouse, "and had made some three days march when by express I was ordered to change my march for Columbia on the Brazos River."[20]

They had arrived in Columbia on April 6, whereupon Major Morehouse sent a courier to report his presence to General Houston. The courier returned on April 9 "with orders that I should reinforce Capt. W. Martin at Fort Bend." Morehouse's battalion departed Columbia on April 10 and had reached Marion (Old Fort Settlement) by April 12. "I am now about crossing the river at this place, for the purpose of joining Major Martin's command, at Fort Bend, as ordered," he wrote.[21]

His men would find that the Mexican army had crossed the river and that Martin had moved out ahead of them. Major Morehouse's command, which had been joined by Captain Jacob Eberly's Columbia company, conducted reconnaissance missions from the Fort Bend area during mid-April but did not make contact with Santa Anna's troops. By late April, he had moved his command back to Columbia-on-the-Brazos to await further instructions from Sam Houston while Captain Eberly's men moved down to Galveston.[22]

Morehouse must certainly have been a frustrated man. Five months after sailing from New York, he was finally in Texas but was now chasing orders to various spots—each time only to find that Sam Houston's troops had moved again. It is with no wonder that one historian dubbed Morehouse's men "the Lost Battalion of the San Jacinto campaign."[23]

Twin Sisters Reach Bernardo Plantation

In Harrisburg, President Burnet was becoming increasingly disgusted with General Houston. He was still stinging from Houston's latest remarks, feeling that "a flying Cabinet is an odious term, which we by no means covet." He wrote to Colonel Rusk on the afternoon of April 12.

> It were perhaps hyperbolical to say, "The eyes of the World are upon him—" but assuredly the People of Texas are looking towards him with an ardent and anxious gaze. They regard his present conduct as decisive of the fate of their country. I do certainly consider it as of vital importance to the country and pregnant with momentous consequences. The cry has for some been for a battle. A further retreat without a fight would be infinitely disastrous. Houston's force is numerically greater than his antagonists.[24]

Preparing to cross the Brazos River, General Houston sent courier Major George Digges—recently returned from Harrisburg—toward the Trinity River. Digges, carrying the news that Santa Anna's men were crossing the Brazos, had orders for incoming East Texas volunteers to halt at the Trinity. Digges reached a group of sixteen volunteers under Colonel John A. Quitman around April 17. Quitman was accompanied by some Texans under Lieutenant James Smith of Nacogdoches. Some of those so ordered did turn back to guard their home areas, but Quitman proceeded on in crossing the Trinity. He would later find to his ire that he was just too late to find action.[25]

One of Houston's motivations to move the troops on this day was word arriving on Santa Anna's movements. The council of war at Powell's inn on the night of April 10 had been overheard by Elizabeth Powell's son, who understood Spanish. Once the Mexican forces had departed, word was sent to the Texas Army that Santa Anna was bent on reaching Harrisburg.[26]

Houston later wrote of his campaign plans in 1855, saying that he sent orders to his various forces to congregate within a few days at the plantation of Charles Donoho near present Hempstead.

> I resolved to cross to the east side of the Brazos, feeling assured that Gen. Santa Anna must have effected a crossing at some point below, and would advance on Harrisburg, to which place the seat of Government had him removed. With a hope to meet him, I ordered the troops at Washington to join me at Donoho's, as well as the troops opposite San Felipe and below there on the Brazos. At the same time, I sent orders to meet the troops expected from the east of the Trinity to form a junction with the army twenty-two miles in advance of Donoho's, and on the direct route to Harrisburg.[27]

During the early morning of April 12, his army was packing up camp. By 10:00 a.m., Captain John Ross' firemen had lit their boilers and raised steam on the *Yellow Stone* in preparation for crossing the

The steamboat *Yellow Stone* played a key role in the San Jacinto campaign by moving Houston's army and its baggage across the swollen Brazos River on April 12 and 13. The *Yellow Stone* is shown on the Missouri River in this 1832 George Catlin painting "St. Louis from the River Below."
Courtesy of Smithsonian American Art Museum, Gift of Mrs. Joseph Harrison, Jr.

Texas Army over the swollen Brazos River. Their little riverboat would act as little more than a giant raft, with her engines using only enough power to combat the angry river's swift currents.

The first division of the First Regiment under Colonel Burleson remained on the west bank as guards of the horses as the first of the troops crossed to the east bank on the *Yellow Stone*.

Colonel Robert Coleman noted men "emerging from their hiding places crimson with the Brazos mud, in which they had been wallowing during the last fifteen days."[28]

The army commenced crossing the river at 10:00 a.m. on April 12 and continued until afternoon of the following day. At noon on April 13, Sam Houston wrote to acting Secretary of War Thomas.

> I commenced crossing the river, and from that time till the present (noon) the steamboat and yawl (having no ferry-boat) have been engaged. We have eight or ten wagons, ox-teams, and about two hundred horses, belonging to the army; and these have to pass on board the steamboat, besides the troops, baggage. This requires time; but I hope in one hour to be enabled to be in preparation. I had sent an express evening before last to all the

troops of Washington, and above this point to meet me here by a rapid march.[29]

General Houston confided that, "I have, under the most disadvantageous circumstances, kept an army together."

After crossing the river, the companies moved to Leonard Groce's Bernardo plantation on the east side, where the Texian army doctors had previously established their field hospital.

As General Houston's men crossed over the Brazos, they found a welcome surprise awaiting them. Major Leander Smith, with Captains John Allen and Alfred Wyly, had arrived at Bernardo from Harrisburg with the long-promised twin six-pound iron cannon from Cincinnati, the Twin Sisters.

At least five of Major Smith's assistants were from Nacogdoches. Stephen Franklin Sparks was just sixteen years old when he and several companions had joined Captain Wyly's men with the Twin Sisters at Harrisburg. They had originally joined a volunteer company in Nacogdoches in March and moved to Washington-on-the-Brazos, but this company was disbanded during the Runaway Scrape. Sparks, later a president of the Texas Veterans Association, and his companions had remained active in government service over the ensuing weeks, pressing horses and guns from fleeing civilians for the army's use.[30]

"We asked the authorities to let us go with Captain Wyly, and join Houston's army," wrote Sparks. They marched with Wyly's men and

Modern view of the Brazos River where it divides present Grimes and Austin Counties. Slightly north of this area, the Texas Army crossed the flood swollen river aboard the steamboat *Yellow Stone* from its heavily wooded eastern bank campground. *Author's photo.*

arrived at Groce's Retreat on April 12 "about two o'clock in the afternoon." Sparks found that upon their arrival "nearly all the army had crossed to the east side of the river."

Stephen Sparks and his fellow soldiers "looked around for the Nacogdoches company, and after finding them, we joined them." Sparks, Howard W. Bailey, Henry M. Brewer, schoolteacher Thomas D. Brooks, and Henry S. Chapman were enrolled into Captain Hayden Arnold's Nacogdoches Volunteers on April 12.

Various San Jacinto campaign veterans agree that the Twin Sisters reached the Texas Army on April 12. "We crossed the Brazos and camped on its east banks near the Groce house. Here we received two pieces of artillery, six pounders, called 'Twin Sisters,'" wrote Private James Swisher.[31]

General Houston wrote that on April 12 the army "crossed the Brazos, where we met two small pieces of artillery, and the only artillery which was ever used in the army." President Burnet wrote a formal thank-you letter in July 1836 to the citizens of Cincinnati for their "free-will offering to the cause of human liberty." He felt that "the voices of the 'Twin Sisters of Cincinnati' will send their reverberations beyond the Rio Grande, and carry unusual terror into many a Mexican hamlet."[32]

Private James Winters of Captain Ware's little company admired the new "iron 6-pounders" that had arrived. After crossing the river, "We camped on the other side and worked all night preparing cartridges for the cannon."[33]

At Groce's Bernardo plantation, Dr. Labadie on April 12 met Jared Groce, who had moved downriver to his son's home from his own Groce's Retreat plantation to greet the army. "Standing before Mr. Groce's house, and on entering the house we found several ladies of the house and neighborhood employed in making flannel bags, while my friend Moreland was tying them. This was about noon on Sunday."[34]

Dr. Anson Jones shared dinner with General Houston on the night of April 12, "the evening of the day we crossed the Brazos at Groce's." They ate with some relatives of Jared Groce who were occupying his house temporarily. Houston commented on the fact that there was a "traitor" in the army among his officers and challenged Dr. Jones to guess the man's identity.

Dr. Anson Jones (1798–1857) was a private of Captain Robert Calder's Company K who became the Second Regiment's head surgeon. Jones would later serve as the last president of the Republic of Texas. *H. A. McArdle San Jacinto Notebook, Texas State Library and Archives Commission.*

Without hesitation, Jones correctly guessed Major Perry, who had been "endeavoring to have the command taken" from Houston. Jones commented that he felt Perry was "a reckless fool." He felt "there was a deep and growing dissatisfaction in the camp, and that Perry's conduct was but an index of that feeling."[35]

Dr. Jones advised that "if the retreating policy were continued much longer, he would be pretty much alone." To this, General Houston expressed that he hoped to yet gain "a bloodless victory."

This was an interesting strategy talk between two men who would both later serve as presidents of the Republic of Texas. As their dinner was concluded, Anson Jones later wrote that their conversation concluded with "an expression of an earnest hope on my part, that the next move he made would be *towards* the enemy."

CHAPTER 10

"The Last Hope of Texas"

April 13–15

> I have decided to leave for Harrisburg with one section, where the principal lead-
> ers of the rebellion are located, and to which place the so-called General Houston is
> marching with the band which he calls the "Army of Texas."
> —*Major General Santa Anna to General Urrea*

Another future president of Texas arrived in the new Texan camp without the fanfare given to the arrival of the Twin Sisters. Thirty-seven-year-old Mirabeau Buonaparte Lamar presented himself for service before General Houston at Bernardo.

Of medium height with large blue eyes, Lamar was a highly literate man with a background as both an editor and a poet. He had first visited Texas in 1835 and had returned home to Georgia briefly. In March 1836, he reached Velasco aboard the schooner *Flash*. He left Quintana, at the port of Velasco, for Harrisburg on March 27 with several others. Thomas F. McKinney wrote to President Burnet on March 28 that he found Lamar to be "a worthy and patriotic gentleman and highly trustworthy."[1]

Lamar and several other U.S. volunteers arrived in the Groce's Retreat camp on foot, walking from Harrisburg, a distance of about 50 miles. Sergeant Tony Menchaca recalled that Lamar arrived "at about 8 o'clock" with Peter Bell, Captain John Allen, and other volunteers who "reported to General Houston for duty."[2]

The future president of Texas was ready for the fight. He wrote to his brother before departing Harrisburg on April 10.

> A dreadful battle is to be fought in three or four days on the Brazos, de-
> cisive of the fate of Texas; I shall of course have to be in it. Wm. D. Redd of

Columbus is with me. Texas is in a dreadful state of confusion; the Mexicans thus far are prevailing. San Antonio has been retaken by them and every man in the fort murdered.[3]

Lamar was carrying a large sum of money with which to purchase land, but was unable to do so in the midst of the Runaway Scrape "in the present confused state of things." Preparing to go into battle, Lamar entrusted his six thousand dollars cash to Vice President Lorenzo de Zavala, using William Redd, Robert Potter and President Burnet as witnesses. "In the event of my falling" in battle, Lamar had Redd agree to send the money back to Lamar's brother, Jefferson J. Lamar in Macon, Georgia.

Shortly after arriving in camp, Private Lamar began showing signs of the influence he could exert on others. He was eager to fight and even talked of taking men out aboard the *Yellow Stone* to conduct guerrilla raids on the enemy's forces near the riverfront.[4]

A late enlistee into the San Jacinto campaign, Lamar would not be long in making his presence felt.

Mirabeau Buonaparte Lamar (1798–1859), a former Georgia newspaperman and poet, reached the Texas Army at Groce's Landing and enlisted as a private. Within a week, his valor would earn him the position of colonel of cavalry. He would later serve as president of the Republic of Texas.
Courtesy of the San Jacinto Museum of History Association.

Movements of Santa Anna's Men

Santa Anna's advance force had arrived near Thompson's Ferry during the early morning of April 11. Shortly after dawn, his men went into hiding along the road leading to the ferry. They did not have long to wait, according to Colonel Juan Almonte.

> A negro passed at a short distance and was taken. He conducted us to the place he had crossed at, and having obtained a canoe we crossed without being perceived, a little below the principal crossing place. In the meantime the cavalry arrived at Marion [Old Fort Settlement] and took possession of the houses.
>
> The enemy retired on the other side, and kept up a fire for a long time, until the Cazadores under command of [Colonel Juan] Bringas crossed at the lower ford [Morton's Ferry], and ascending the river, and were about to take them in the rear, when they abandoned Marion, and we remained in possession of the ferry, one canoe, and a flat boat.[5]

Almonte and his fellow soldiers obtained the flatboat by tricking the black servant of Brazos resident Joseph Kuykendall. One of the Mexicans who spoke good English, likely Almonte, called over to the servant, "Bring over the boat!"[6]

Apparently mistaking the men on the opposite bank for some of Captain Martin's men, the servant brought the boat over to them. As many men as could stand in it then crossed over to the east side. Kuykendall, a crippled man who could not serve the army, was at his home with his wife and children. His family fled but Kuykendall and a young man were captured and held prisoner while the Mexican army crossed the river.

The rebels under Captain Martin did manage to wound "one grenadier and our bugler," according to Santa Anna. Stationing Bringas' fifty men at Morton's house on the opposite side of the ferry, he sent a courier back to General Ramirez y Sesma with word that he had captured the ferryboat and two canoes at Thompson's Ferry. Sesma was ordered to bring his entire command to join him at Old Fort Settlement.

Sesma left Captain Baker's company at San Felipe and rushed downriver with his men. They arrived on April 13 and crossed with Santa Anna and found the troops working on repairing the ferryboat. Sesma reported that the slow-moving columns under Filisola and Gaona had not yet reached San Felipe when he departed.[7]

General Filisola's division struggled to catch up with Santa Anna's men during the first two weeks of April. He ultimately left some of the supply wagons behind when he encountered difficulty in crossing the Navidad River. Mules were used to carry baggage and ammunition, but they were constantly bogging down in the mud.[8]

"When the road was good we made moderate marches," wrote Lieutenant Colonel de la Peña, "but the march had to be forced when the road was impassable."

The straggling companies and supply trains would spend the better part of four days in crossing the troublesome Colorado River. By April 13, the companies of the Matamoros, Aldama, Guerrero, Toluca, Mexico and Guadalajara battalions had successfully crossed. They were accompanied by a six-pound cannon commanded by Lieutenant Ignacio Arrenal and fifty mounted men from Tampico and Guanajuato. This whole crossing force consisted of about six hundred men.[9]

At his headquarters at Thompson's Pass, Santa Anna left orders for General Filisola, second in command of army operations, on April 13. He ordered Filisola to send General Martin Cos with five hundred infantrymen to seize Fort Velasco. Lieutenant Colonel Pedro Ampudias was to accompany Cos as commander of two eight-pound cannon and a howitzer.[10]

Having no word from General Gaona, Santa Anna ordered Filisola to send "from forty to fifty cavalrymen" out to San Felipe to attempt contact with Gaona. He also ordered Filisola to station a small detachment near Thompson's Crossing to guard the ford and to watch for the steamboat *Yellow Stone*, which was still up river. "It would be very useful to capture it," wrote Santa Anna.

General Filisola would encounter the *Yellow Stone* near San Felipe during the early morning hours of April 15. Her pulsing engine could be heard as she chugged around the bend, certainly a frightful sight to many Mexican soldiers who had never seen such a river creature!

Lieutenant Colonel de la Peña was writing notes in his tent at 7:00 a.m. when the *Yellow Stone* approached.

> I heard voices of alarm and left my tent hurriedly. Its cause was the passing of an enemy steamboat, which had not been even remotely anticipated. The soldiers forming the advance posts on the river, who belonged to the Guadalajara Battalion, were dumfounded by the sight of a machine so totally unfamiliar and unexpected. The other soldiers who saw it were likewise surprised. Few in the camp were acquainted with steamboats, so all was in con-

fusion. Immediately a detachment was dispatched to that bank of the river away from the woods, which was like running after a bird.[11]

Colonel Juan Almonte, the well-traveled chief of staff, reportedly ordered the troops to fire into her boilers and de la Peña says that at least one shot was fired from a cannon. Captain Ross, counting on the effective use of the cotton bales for armor, maintained speed and plowed down the Brazos River with his ship's bell clanging. The cotton prevented damage to his precious boilers and pilothouse, leaving only his tall cylindrical chimneys to withstand the shots of musket balls from the numerous infantrymen who fired on his steamer.[12]

From his temporary headquarters at Fort Bend, Santa Anna learned that the Texas government's cabinet was working out of Harrisburg. He wrote:

> By means of some colonists who appeared, one of them a Mexican, I found out that in the town of Harrisburg, twelve leagues distance, located on the right bank of the Buffalo Bayou, resided the well known government of Texas, Don Lorenzo Zavala and the other directors of the revolution, and their capture was certain if a few troops marched on them quickly. The news was important, and even more so the movement indicated, the success of which would disconcert completely the revolution.[13]

General Filisola's division was still moving toward San Felipe and would not reach Fort Bend until April 17. Santa Anna had ordered General Jose Urrea to insure that Matagorda was safe and then to establish his general headquarters at Brazoria. He also gave Urrea word that he was pushing forward.

> I have decided to leave for Harrisburg with one section, where the principal leaders of the rebellion are located, and to which place the so-called General Houston is marching with the band which he has and which he calls the "Army of Texas."

The decision to further fragment his army by personally chasing President Burnet's cabinet insured that Santa Anna could not easily or quickly gather all of his forces. One factor motivating him to head this chase was news received from Mexico City. His loyal supporter and acting president, Vice President Miguel Barragán, had died on March 1 of putrid fever. The Mexican government had selected Jose Justo Corro to serve as acting president in Barragán's place. Without such loyal support in office, Santa Anna was suddenly unsure of his political strength back home. Instead of rushing home, he decided to complete his campaign in Texas and return home the battle hero. Barragán's death may have given Santa Anna an anxiety to end the Texas campaign that would make him become a little careless.[14]

Had he maintained his troops in one large body and simply continued his pursuit of Sam Houston's rebels, he would likely have brought them to battle with the entire strength of his command. The possibility of defeat or his own capture while leading one of the smaller commands apparently never entered General Santa Anna's mind.

Planning to end the rebellion by capturing the Texas government leaders, Santa Anna thus crossed the Brazos River on April 14 for Harrisburg. He had with him some seven hundred and fifty of his top grenadiers. His procession also included his staff, cavalry escort, mule drivers and some female camp followers who served as cooks and aides.

According to Colonel Pedro Delgado, Santa Anna left his baggage, and that of other officers, with General Ramirez y Sesma. His force departed the Fort Bend area at 4:00 p.m., expecting to return for Sesma in three days.[15]

Just crossing the Brazos bottomlands proved a hazardous chore for Santa Anna's force. His force reached a creek that created a challenge for the horses. The infantry easily crossed over on a fallen tree, passing over the ammunition by hand.

Secretary Ramon Caro later wrote that His Excellency had a profound fear of water that would affect his conduct more than once in the San Jacinto campaign. It had already slowed him from rushing across the river at Fort Bend to attack Captain Baker's rebels. At this swollen creek, Santa Anna dismounted and cautiously inched across the log while one of his soldiers swam his horse across. Remounted on the opposite bank, he quickly assumed the role of an impatient commander.

Colonel Delgado wrote in his diary for April 14:

> His Excellency, to avoid delay, ordered the baggage and the commissary stores to remain packed on the mules. However, the water was soon over the pack-saddles, and the opposite bank was steep and slippery. Several mules fell down, interfering with each other, which resulted in a terrible jamming of officers and dragoons, pack-mules and horses. This, together with shouts and curses, completed a scene of wild confusion, which His Excellency witnessed with hearty laughter.
>
> Several officers and dragoons fell in the water; the stores were damaged and two mules were drowned. So much for the precipitation of this march.

"You Must Fall Back"

From camp on the morning of April 13, Sam Houston took time to respond to the harsh letters from Secretary Thomas and President Burnet. He sent a letter from his camp on the Brazos "to the citizens of Texas." He boldly announced that the enemy troops had indeed crossed the Brazos but were now "treading the soil on which they are to be conquered."[16]

Houston stated that "twenty men in number checked the force of the enemy in crossing the Brazos at Fort Bend." He called on others to join his cause to save their country and their families. "Join the troops now in the field, and your enemy is certainly in your power," he wrote. "Come and free your country at once; and be men!"

Houston had good order of his army, as evidenced by his daily orders (see illustration) on April 13. Daily duties were assigned for guards and horse details and incoming messengers were to report to Houston, as were incoming new recruits.

Colonel Tom Rusk was equally vocal in calling for help in the fight for Texan independence. He was openly bitter that so many Texans were "flying before your enemy" while "people are flocking from the U.S. to your assistance." Disgusted with the lack of response to previous pleas, Rusk felt compelled to urge for help once again.

> Will you desert the principles of liberty? You entail upon yourselves and your children eternal infamy and disgrace, if you will not march at once to the field, join the army now on the line of march to meet the enemy, and conquer him, or die nobly in the cause of liberty and their country.[17]

The Texian army completed its crossing of the Brazos by the afternoon of April 13, when Colonel Sherman brought over the last of the army's baggage. The sight of the Twin Sisters was encouraging to each new group which disembarked the *Yellow Stone*. Only two yoke of oxen had been lost in the river crossing, being taken down by the strong current of the high river.[18]

San Felipe resident Gail Borden Jr., cofounder of the *Telegraph and Texas Register*, wrote from Harrisburg on April 14 that Houston's army was now "hastening down the river to stop the progress of the enemy." In his account of the army's recent actions, Borden was supportive of Houston's move in retreating his forces to Groce's plantation. In fact,

Army Orders: April 13, 1836
Groce's, Texas

1. Roll call at reveille (5 o'clock), retreat (sunset) and Tattoo (9 o'clock), when all lights will be put out except in the tents of the Officers employed on duty.
2. Silence is to be preserved after Tattoo.
3. At the first taps of the Drum, each man will take his place in line.
4. In case of an alarm, the men will form on their ground and await orders.
5. The Officer of the Day will make the Guard rounds at 9, 12 and 4 o'clock in the night. He will receive the Watch Word from the Commanding Officer and communicate the same.
6. Guards to be mounted and relieved at 9 o'clock a.m.
7. When a relief is leaving the Guard fire, the remainder of the Guard will remain under arms until its return.
8. No Sentinel will sit down on post, unless ordered.
9. The Guard will be responsible for all prisoners put in Custody.
10. To Desert or Sleep on Post, will be death by Law.
11. The Guard will form wherever the different calls take place.
12. Any person quitting camp, without leave, will be regarded as a deserter and treated as such.
13. No man is to pass the Lines with arms, unless passed by a Field Officer.
14. The Field Officers of the regiment, the General and his Staff only have power to pass persons through the lines.
15. The men always to parade with arms, and to sleep with their arms in their reach.
16. No shooting within one mile of Camp, or on march without leave.
17. Each mess will cook for its members on Guard, and take their provisions to the Guard fire.
18. All horses are to be brought within the line of Sentinels before dark.
19. All expresses arriving in Camp, and all intelligence, will first report to the Commander in Chief.
20. All Horses on arriving in Camp, will be staked down, tied, or close hobbled. Those that may not be attended to, will be liable to be condemned to the public use.
21. Persons arriving in Camp will immediately report to the Colonel and be attached to some Company for duty.
22. The Sick of each Company, platoon or Squad, will report themselves to their respective Officers, who will report them to the Surgeon.

It is ordered that the above regulations be strictly observed and obeyed.

Sam Houston,
Com'r in Chief.

he felt that the ragtag assemblage of Texan settlers, U.S. volunteers and fleeing refugees was "an army that was the last hope of Texas."[19]

On the morning of April 14, this army of salvation was camped near the eastern bank of the Brazos and preparing to march again. Private James H. Bostick of Captain Kuykendall's company wrote to his family during the idle moments in camp. "We will in a few hours take up the line of march, but I don't know where to but eastward, I presume." Bostick urged his family to move quickly out of harm's way. "We will soon know the fate of our country," he wrote. "If we don't do something in a few days, the army will dissolve in my opinion."[20]

Even as Houston prepared to move his men beyond the Brazos River camp, others were working on organizing more men from the United States. Secretary of State Samuel Carson had arrived at Natchitoches, Louisiana, on March 13 and met with General Edmond Pendleton Gaines at Fort Jessup. Acting upon the wishes of President Burnet, he was hoping to get Gaines to join the Texas cause in fighting the Mexican army. The United States troops could not officially engage unless acting upon enemies who had incited hostile Indians to commit depredations on either side of the national line. Hoping to "satisfy Genl. Gaines of the facts," Carson tried to show that the Mexican army was already working with Texas Indians.[21]

Carson believed that he could provide sufficient proof that Santa Anna had stirred up the Indians to commit depredations. "The proofs will, I have no doubt, be abundant, by the time he reaches Sabine, in which case he will cross and move upon the aggressors." Carson felt that Gaines would "maintain the honor of his country and punish the aggressor," in this case being Santa Anna's army.

Burnet and Carson's strategy was clever, hoping to draw the strength of thousands of United States troops against the Mexican army via a technicality. Carson also called on the governor of Louisiana to send a brigade of mounted volunteers and sent similar requests to the governors of Tennessee, Mississippi and Alabama. These states would indeed furnish a large number of volunteer soldiers, although most would arrive too late to help Houston's immediate cause.

Carson wrote to Houston on April 14 that "volunteer troops will come on in numbers from the United States." Carson also urged Houston not to fight yet if he could avoid it. "You must fall back, and hold out, and let nothing goad or provoke you to a battle, unless you can, without doubt, whip them, or unless you are compelled to fight."

Carson's advice was for the army to keep moving. "My view is, that you should fall back, if necessary, to the Sabine. I am warranted in saying that volunteer troops will come on in numbers from the United States."

General Gaines did, in fact, march six hundred troops from Fort Jessup on April 15 to the Sabine River, where he set up camp at Gaines' Ferry. He resolved not to enter Texas until circumstances justified his doing so. He would wait for an express that clearly showed him the necessary information that Indian forces had committed depredations on settlers that allowed him to cross onto Texas soil.[22]

Secretary Carson's one letter summed up the catch-22 faced by General Houston throughout the San Jacinto campaign. On the one hand, he was being openly ridiculed by fellow officers and government officials, including President Burnet, for not aggressively attacking the Mexican army. Other voices of reason, such as Sam Carson, urged Houston to hold off making his big stand against Santa Anna until more volunteers from the United States arrived.

In choosing to so delay battle with Santa Anna, Houston ran two large risks. The first was that the promised American volunteers would indeed show up soon in substantial numbers. The other, much greater, daily risk was that his army would completely disintegrate during the retreat.

Thus, the retreat continued as Houston waited for either the right moment to whip his enemy or for more men. Being unacquainted with the route from Washington-on-the-Brazos toward Harrisburg, Sam Houston had procured a guide, William McDermott.[23]

Ready to move, Houston released his hold on the steamboat *Yellow Stone* on April 14, after having initially detained her for army business on March 31. The army thus left Captain John Ross and crew to their own fate on a river that was believed to have enemy troops stationed downriver.[24]

An added challenge for the army was moving the newly arrived Twin Sisters from Groce's plantation. Infantryman Stephen Sparks recalled that, "The road was new and boggy, and the prairies covered with water. We had but few wagons, and our teams were insufficient to travel very fast, so we soon began to bog down."[25]

The six-pound Twin Sisters were smoothbore cannon because the insides of their barrels were not rifled (grooved to cause the projectile to spin). A six-pounder had a barrel whose six-inch bore diameter would thus accommodate a projectile just slightly under that size. The average weight of a solid cannonball generally matched the cannon's bore diameter, but could weigh up to a couple pounds more. In the absence of cast-iron round balls, the gun crews of the Texas Revolution often melted and molded available metal into solid shot balls.

In addition to the larger solid shots—effective in destroying fortified walls or other structures—the Twin Sisters were capable of firing packed smaller round shots such as canister or grapeshot. Grapeshot was small round shot often packed in a tightly wrapped cloth rag, which gave the appearance of clusters of grapes. Both canister and grapeshot scattered after departing the cannon muzzle and were used primarily against troops at close range.

Among the key artillery crew members on the battlefield were the gunner, loaders, spongers, and powder monkeys. The sponger used a wooden cylinder, covered on one end with lambskin, which was dipped in water and inserted into the barrel. This sponge would quench any sparks remaining from the previous shot and could be twisted in the barrel to clean the gun. Once the barrel was cleaned, a black powder cartridge was rammed into the barrel followed by the projectile. A six-pound ball would generally be paired with an equivalent six pounds of powder.

Lieutenant Colonel James Neill, the former commander of the Alamo, had been placed in command of the artillery. Each of the two six-pounders required a crew of nine to haul, load and quickly maintain them for battle. Neill found more than enough men willing to volunteer to join his new artillery corps. A proper company of men to man and transport the Twin Sisters was organized before leaving Groce's. Neill placed Captain Isaac N. Moreland in command of the artillery.

Among Neill and Moreland's men was John M. Wade, who had joined Captain Ware's company at Washington-on-the-Brazos in March. Wade was a native of New York who had "set type beside Greeley and Kendall when a mere boy." He wrote for the 1872 *Texas Almanac*, "At Groce's I was detailed, by Gen. Houston, with Dick Scurry, Ben McCullough, Tom Green, T. O. Harris and others, to man the Twin Sisters, which the lamented I. N. Moreland was appointed to command."[26]

Dick Scurry, who had traveled to Gonzales with Sam Houston, was assigned as first sergeant of Captain Moreland's company on April 14. Ben McCullough, a future Texas Ranger captain, future Confederate general and former Tennessee backwoodsman, bear hunter and trapper, had joined the Texas Army at Groce's. He was assigned to Moreland's company by Captain George Poe, one of two artillery captains in the army.[27]

Private James Swisher for one thought that the organization of the Texas artillery corps was impressive. "When these [men] took their position in the ranks they gave our little army a much more war-like appearance."[28]

General Houston had previously sent word for his various troops in Washington and those near San Felipe and along the Brazos to meet up at the plantation of Charles Donoho. With his artillery company organized, he set his troops to marching again on the afternoon of April 14. Trooping eastward, some men grumbled that Houston intended to retreat all the way to Nacogdoches. From Groce's Bernardo plantation, they moved south of present Hempstead about six miles in an easterly direction before evening began to approach.

Camp was made at Charles Donoho's plantation within the stockade walls of his enclosure. The site is currently four miles southeast of present Hempstead on FM 359 in Waller County.

Finding the trees too green to use for firewood, the men tore down all of the wood railing around the Donoho home for their fires. The Texas Army was rejoined that evening by the companies of Captains Moseley Baker and Wyly Martin, whose men had been busy skirmishing with the Mexican army at the various river crossings in the past two weeks.[29]

Lieutenant John McAllister and some of Captain Bird's men who had fought with Baker also rejoined the army and enlisted in other companies. Baker's company had marched fifteen miles up the Brazos on the east side toward Groce's plantation, after he had judged that Santa Anna would advance on Harrisburg. Believing that Houston was now committed to engaging the Mexican army at Galveston Bay, Baker "overlooked the past" and joined with Old Sam again. When he reached Donoho's camp on the evening of April 14, however, Captain Baker was not afraid to openly criticize Houston for failing to come fight the Mexicans along the riverfront.[30]

At Fort Bend, Wyly Martin had also given up trying to hold his crossing. They had left Fort Bend on April 12 and were ordered on

April 13 to march to Donoho's plantation. While Santa Anna's men crossed the river that day, Captain Martin's remaining companymen marched up the east side of the river and reached Donoho's camp the following night.[31]

Guards stood watch throughout the night at Donoho's camp. General Houston and Colonel Hockley twice made the rounds during the night, testing the sentinels on their preparedness.[32]

The town of Nacogdoches had been completely abandoned by mid-April. Thousands of women and children and older men had gone into hiding in the woods along both sides of the Sabine River. Many fled from San Augustine also. John A. Quitman, a former judge from Natchez, wrote on April 15 that he had seen "at least 300 men, with arms in their hands," among those heading east and adding to the panic.[33]

Robert A. Irion gave orders for several volunteer companies to stay and protect Nacogdoches. This included men under Captains William D. Ratliff and James Smith and Captain James Chesher's Jasper Volunteer Company, which had been mustered into service on March 23.[34]

At Harrisburg, Thomas Hardeman, Bailey Hardeman and David Thomas were the only cabinet members of the Texas government left in town. President Burnet and Vice President de Zavala had departed on April 13 to attend to their families. Secretary of Navy Robert Potter was at Galveston Bay attending to the affairs of the Texas Navy.

Attorney General and acting Secretary of War Thomas had gathered enough intelligence from incoming men to believe that Santa Anna's forces had crossed over the Brazos and were now near Fort Bend. Several men from Captain Baker's Iron's Creek camp came into Harrisburg and reported "that the Mexicans had entirely disappeared from" San Felipe.[35]

Secretary Thomas received a report from a young indentured servant who had just arrived from Thompson's farm near the Brazos crossing. He had seen the Mexican forces camped there and believed their number to be one thousand, with "a great many on the other side." Thompson's servant was told that the Mexican army would attack Houston's forces in three or four days' time.

Thomas gave Houston clear advice that may well have influenced Old Sam in when and where he might best challenge Santa Anna.

> It is my opinion that if you cannot meet the enemy before he gets out of the Brazos bottom, the best movement would be to face down towards Galveston, where you would be near the provisions and munitions of War, and prevent if possible Galveston falling into their hands. All our vessels are in the Bay and the fortifications are progressing as rapidly as possible.

Thomas sent this intelligence to General Houston on April 14. His courier was William Houston Jack, a thirty-year-old lawyer who had graduated from the University of Georgia in 1827. An early settler of San Felipe, Jack had joined Captain William Patton's Columbia company on March 1 and had been sent by Houston with an express to Harrisburg several days prior.

Colonel Sidney Sherman had his Second Regiment formed into line by daybreak on April 15. His men were first to take up the line of march on the road from Donoho's that led toward the Samuel Mc-Carley homestead, some twenty miles distant. Following him were Colonel Edward Burleson's First Regiment infantrymen and then Lieutenant Colonel Henry Millard's regulars. Lieutenant Colonel J. C. Neill's artillerymen brought up the rear with their ammunition wagon. The mounted men of each infantry company rode ahead as front guard while their horseless companymates formed the rear guard of each division. William Smith's and Henry Karnes' cavalry companies formed the flank guards, half on the right side and half on the left side.[36]

Before leaving Donoho's, General Houston had been forced to once again deal with insubordination from his junior officers. He had ordered an early march this day but soon found that Captain Wyly Martin's freshly arrived company refused to move until they had had their breakfast. His men and those of Captain Moseley Baker had only caught up to the army during the night, after having fought the Mexican army along the Brazos.

Tired of shepherding the pitiful citizen refugees and dealing with Baker and Martin's continued insubordination, Houston had had his fill. He furiously ordered Captain Martin to feed his men as quickly as possible and then leave the army, detailing this company to steer the Runaway Scrape families to safety.[37]

The general later explained his decision.

> Captain Baker was not disposed to march; for the reason that there would be no fighting, and Captain Martin refused to march for various reasons. Perceiving a spirit of mutiny, [I] made a virtue of necessity, and ordered Capt. Martin to Robbins Ferry on the Trinity, to assist and protect the women and children. Thus was the insubordination gotten over. Capt. Baker fell into line.[38]

Wyly Martin's company thus was separated from the Texian army and his men moved down toward Nacogdoches County with the citizens. At least two of Martin's men, Jesse Thompson and David Scott, remained with the army and joined Second Regiment companies.

At this critical juncture, the army left the fleeing civilians to make it on their own for Nacogdoches. It is estimated that as many as three or four hundred men left the army at this point. Sergeant William Swearingen of Captain Turner's company later wrote:

> Gen. Houston had been compelled to give furloughs to upwards of 200 men to go and carry their families beyond the Trinity River for security and one entire company that was left opposite San Felipe went home instead of joining us on our march.[39]

The balance of the army fell into line and marched along the road toward McCarley's. The pace was slow due to the cannon and there was little of interest to see along the road. Those on foot in the rear did what they could to pass the time, joking amongst each other. Private William Zuber of Captain Gillaspie's company found himself "a little homesick and melancholy" during the marching. William F. "Buck" Williams of Captain Arnold's company finally rallied Zuber to laughter by poking fun at young Zuber's large teeth, teasing him as "the pretty little man with a mouthful of bones."[40]

The weather was awful during the march. "A heavy Texas rain poured upon us," wrote Dr. Labadie, who was in charge of the medicine cart. He gave discharges to about eight men who were suffering with extreme cases of the measles. He even gave his cloak to one young son of a Mr. McLaughlin who had suffered through the rain and cold coatless with the measles. Mr. McLaughlin was allowed to take his sick sons home to recover. Another of those discharged was Private Leo Roark of Captain John Bird's First Regiment company. "I was taken sick at Groce's Retreat in the Brazos bottom with pneumonia," wrote Roark, "and was granted sick furlough to go home by General Sam Houston, and did not rejoin Capt. Bird's company again."[41]

The march on April 15 took the Texans across great open prairie lands along the well-traveled road from Washington-on-the-Brazos. Each passing mile brought the men closer to a crucial fork in the road near the home of Abraham Roberts where the route split toward either Harrisburg or Nacogdoches. Many knew that the fate of the campaign hinged on what decision was made here.

Some tried their best to influence General Houston's decision. Colonel Robert Coleman, an aide-de-camp, informed Houston that he felt "that an attempt to take the left hand road at Roberts' would throw everything into confusion." The left-hand road led toward the Trinity, and in Coleman's mind would translate to continued flight from the enemy. He felt that the army would then further fragment and the men would call upon someone else to lead them to the right.[42]

"The General only remarked that he would reflect on what the Colonel had said," wrote Coleman.

After crossing the swollen creek on the evening on April 14, General Santa Anna's advance force had marched until about 9:00 p.m. The men, exhausted from towing their heavy cannon through muddy roads, collapsed "in a small grove, where we passed the night without water."[43]

Stragglers continued to catch up to Santa Anna until 8:00 a.m. on April 15, when His Excellency set his troops in motion again. "At about noon we reached a plantation abundantly supplied with corn, meal, sheep and hogs," wrote Colonel Delgado. "It had a good garden and a fine cotton gin. We halted to refresh men and beasts."

The Mexican forces had reached the intact plantation of William Stafford. After resting, Santa Anna ordered the plantation and its gin houses burned down. His troops moved on at 3:00 p.m. Santa Anna moved ahead of his main forces with his staff and escort, leaving General Castrillon in command of the infantry. After an exhausting eight-hour march, the Mexican troops reached the vicinity of Harrisburg at night.

Santa Anna searched the plantations as he approached Harrisburg, hoping to find signs of President Burnet and his cabinet. They reached one plantation late and inquired of the old man there where President Burnet might be found. The old man, who professed to being too elderly to fight, told him that he had read in the newspaper that they had been at Harrisburg several days before. According to First Sergeant Francisco Becerra, Santa Anna did not harm the old man or his family, but "immediately issued orders for a start before dawn in the morning."[44]

Colonel Delgado's diary records the actions of this night and the following day.

> His Excellency, with an Adjutant and fifteen dragoons, went on foot to that town, distant about one mile, entered it, and succeeded in capturing two Americans, who stated that Zavala and other members of the so-called government of Texas, had left the morning before for Galveston. A party of the infantry joined us on the following morning at daylight.
>
> On the 16th, we remained at Harrisburg to await our broken-down stragglers, who kept dropping in till 2 or 3 o'clock P.M.[45]

Santa Anna wrote that on April 15 he captured "one Frenchman and two North Americans working in a print shop" in Harrisburg. They had surprised and captured three men working on the *Telegraph and Texas Register*, the only newspaper of Texas. The printers informed Santa Anna that Gail Borden Jr., one of the paper's two editors, had just left town an hour before.

They also informed him that Burnet, Zavala and the rest of the cabinet had departed at noon that day on the steamboat *Cayuga* for Galveston Island. These captives believed that President Burnet's cabinet was moving toward New Washington, located on a peninsula where San Jacinto Bay joins Galveston Bay. Now known as Morgan's Point, New Washington was about twenty miles east of Harrisburg.[46]

The other good intelligence the printers gave Santa Anna was on the movement of Sam Houston's rebel Texian army. He was told that Houston had roughly eight hundred men, who had camped until recently at Groce's plantation. Further, Houston now had in his possession two small cannon which had passed through Harrisburg just days before. The Texian army was roughly fifty miles northwest of Harrisburg, moving toward the Lynchburg ferry on the San Jacinto River.

In anger at having just missed the Texas cabinet, Santa Anna ordered the printing presses destroyed and thrown into the river. These very newspaper presses had cranked out the first issues of the *Telegraph and Texas Register*, and most recently the brand-new Texas Declaration of Independence.

From Harrisburg, President Burnet's cabinet would have to move along Buffalo Bayou in the steamer *Cayuga*. This bayou then dumped into the San Jacinto River and finally San Jacinto Bay before it could reach New Washington.

Knowing of Houston's whereabouts and those of the Texas Cabinet, Santa Anna ordered Colonel Juan Almonte out with fifty dragoons to "reconnoiter as far as the pass at Lynchburg and New Washington." Santa Anna hoped to still catch Burnet at New Washington and to intercept Sam Houston at Lynch's Ferry. Almonte's scouts would soon report back that Houston's men appeared to be withdrawing "in the direction of the Trinity River through the pass at Lynchburg."

———————

The Texas Army made camp on April 15 at Samuel McCarley's homestead, stopping after nightfall within three miles of the forks of the road. McCarley's plantation was along the main road near the edge of the prairie the men had crossed. This plantation was about three miles from his nearest neighbor, Abraham "Abram" Roberts, at whose home the crucial fork in the road would be reached. A historical marker locates McCarley's on present FM 2920 (Waller-Tomball Road) at the intersection of A.J. Foyt Road in present Harris County.

The site of the Texas Army's campground during the night of April 15–16 was at the plantation home of Samuel McCarley. Today a historical marker on FM 2920 (west of present Tomball) in Harris County marks the location. *Author's photo.*

Private John Plunkett, an Irishman of Captain Calder's company who had lived briefly in Massachusetts, wrote of the campaign marches three months later. Plunkett found his army

> traveling these vast prairies, the canopy of Heaven our covering, depending on beef for our sustenance, which we killed on our march. When dealt out to us sometimes scantily, we cut a small stick, sharpened it at both ends, one end we stick in the ground, the other we put the meat on before the fire and turning it as it cooked. We sometimes had frying pans but on the march frequently had to leave them, not having teams sufficient to carry our baggage.[47]

Once settled into camp on the evening of April 15, the Texas soldiers used McCarley's fencing to start fires, while the civilians straggling along with them struggled to burn green wood.

Colonel Robert Coleman later claimed that he spoke with General Houston that evening and that Houston confided in him that he intended to take the Harrisburg road in the morning. Houston stated that he had "been ordered to do so by Col. Rusk, the Secretary of War; and that in so doing he yielded his own judgement in obedience to his superior." Coleman spread the word about camp, but found that "the soldiers were suspicious, and much discontent prevailed."[48]

Contrary to Coleman's version, it is not likely that these two had this conversation. Sam Houston admittedly kept his thoughts to himself throughout most of the San Jacinto campaign. In support of this, Houston later gave some insight into his campaign strategy.

> The commander-in-chief was the only one of the officers who had ever witnessed an array of hostile armies, or been in a general battle; and it is not probable that he would surrender his opinions to those on whom no responsibility rested. If victorious, the victory would take the name of the place, if it were a defeat it would bear the name of the General, but not that of his subalterns![49]

CHAPTER 11

The Road to San Jacinto

> In our march from Donohue's we came to a fork in the road, one leading to Harrisburg, the other to San Jacinto, eastward.
>
> —*Captain William Heard and Sergeant Eli Mercer,*
> *Company F, First Regiment of Texas Volunteers*

Breakfast came early at the Texan campfires around Sam McCarley's plantation on April 16. The army then quickly packed up and resumed the march eastward along the muddy road from Groce's plantation. Captain Conrad Rohrer's artillery and provisions wagons led the procession this day, due to the poor road conditions from the heavy rains that had been falling.[1]

About two miles south of McCarley's the road led through a dense thicket on the prairie. The two cavalry companies, serving as flank guards during the daily marches, were forced to fall into line to march through this thicket. A number of men, as many as fifty, slipped from their companies and concealed themselves in this thicket. Private William Zuber noted that one of the deserters included the orderly sergeant of Captain Gillaspie's company. In camp that night, his captain would appoint Richard Chadduck to fill this open spot.

At a point about fifteen miles east of Donoho's and three miles from McCarley's, the Texas Army reached a crucial fork in the road. One route would lead them across the San Jacinto River toward Nacogdoches and eventually the United States, while the other road curved southeasterly for Harrisburg and the Gulf Coast.

The fork was located near the Abram Roberts' homestead, a little community that became known as New Kentucky. A historical marker in the little New Kentucky Park can be found today near the intersec-

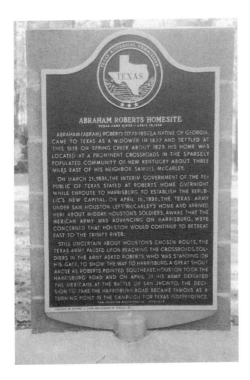

This historical marker in New Kentucky Park in Harris County is near the controversial fork in the road where Houston's army turned toward San Jacinto.
Author's photo.

tion of 2920 (Waller-Tomball Road) and Roberts Cemetery Road in Harris County.

Many of the army leaders knew that this fork in the road would mark a crucial decision for Sam Houston, and his choice would indicate his true colors. According to Captain Jesse Billingsley, some of the company commanders had already decided the course they would choose.

> So great became the excitement among the Captains commanding companies, that many of us signed an agreement to support each other and take the road leading in the direction of the foe, whatever the order might be.[2]

Colonel Sidney Sherman of the Second Regiment claims that Secretary of War Thomas Rusk was responsible for the decision to turn for Harrisburg. Sherman wrote in 1847 that he believed Houston was heading for the Trinity River, against the better wishes of most men, until Rusk "issued him a peremptory order, requiring him to take the Harrisburg road." Sherman felt that Houston "always contended he could not meet the enemy without the aid of his Red Landers." Sherman felt assured in this belief, due to the fact that Houston had sent his couriers to the Trinity to halt further oncoming troops.[3]

This turn at the fork in the roads caused word to swiftly spread through the men that Sam Houston had finally decided to fight! As with many other curiosities of the San Jacinto campaign, the famous turn at the fork in the road is another event which is subject to many interpretations.

Many felt that the army decided which way to turn and Houston had no choice. Some later claimed that Rusk gave Houston orders to make the turn. Houston had, of course, just received the intelligence from Secretary Carson which urged him to fall back to the Sabine River.

Still another scenario is possible. Houston may very well have allowed the psychology of the moment to work in his favor. As the more determined swung toward Harrisburg, he may simply have allowed the masses to follow, thus seemingly allowing the men the free choice to fight. They were thus choosing victory or death, much as had Travis at the Alamo. Certainly, Houston had the intelligence that Santa Anna was bound for Harrisburg. Houston was also taking great troubles to haul the cannon through the mud, not something he would be as inclined to do if he planned to keep fleeing for the east.[4]

In keeping with his philosophy, Houston commented to no one what his true intentions were.

Dr. Labadie noted that Abram Roberts was standing by his gate as the army passed and he pointed out the road to the right which led down to Harrisburg. A shout was raised, "To the right, boys, to the right." At this shout, the little Texas band struck up a number and marched to the right. "The advance guard, then a quarter of a mile ahead, between the two roads, seeing the music take the right, wheeled also to the right," wrote Labadie.[5]

Captain Robert Calder's company was among the advance guard this day. He did not recall any mutinous conduct or any altercations around the decision. His only knowledge was that "after a short halt at that point, I received an order to take the right-hand road."[6]

A number of men present felt that Houston's decision was influenced by others. James Robinson, the former acting governor of Texas turned cavalryman, felt that Houston "manifested the strongest determination to retreat to the Redlands" across the Sabine River. At the fork near Roberts, he was prevented from so doing by the urging of Colonel Rusk and the previous orders to fight from President Burnet.

Near the homestead of Abram Roberts, the Texas army reached the so-called "fork in the road." One road led northeastward toward Nacogdoches and the United States, the other toward Harrisburg and San Jacinto.
Oil painting courtesy of the San Jacinto Museum of History, Houston.

"President Burnet's order, and the command of Gen. Rusk, were powerfully aided by an almost united resolution by the men, to meet and fight the enemy," wrote Robinson.[7]

Colonel Sherman's recollections reinforce Rusk having given the command to take the Harrisburg road. "General Houston told me that Rusk had given him orders to take the Harrisburg road," Sherman wrote in 1859, "and he was bound to obey him as his superior officer and requested me to inform my regiment to that effect."[8]

Houston would later flatly deny receiving orders to turn at the fork in the road. Whose decision to make the actual turn is again subject to interpretation. Perhaps he actually yielded to the advice of Rusk. "I crossed the road to the Trinity, at right angles on my march to Harrisburg," wrote Houston in 1855. "Col. Rusk had been made acquainted with my plans, as also Col. Hockley."[9]

Captain William Heard and Orderly Sergeant Eli Mercer of the First Regiment's Company F wrote that the men helped compel Houston's road decision.

> We believe that Gen. Houston intended to take the road to the Trinity when we arrived at the fork at Donohue's, because he had sent Major Digges, with another individual, to Robbins' Ferry on the Trinity, to stop all recruits coming to the army at that place. The men, believing this to be his intention, made no secret of their dissatisfaction, and there was an arrangement among them that, in case he took the road to the Trinity, with his regulars,

the volunteers would call out for a leader to go at their head to Harrisburg to meet the enemy, all of which we believe was known to Gen. Houston, and which, we think, was the cause of his turning in that direction.

In our march from Donohue's we came to a fork in the road, one leading to Harrisburg, the other to San Jacinto, eastward. Gen. Houston and a part of the army had passed the fork, taking the latter route, when the army came to a halt, and well nigh to mutiny, the volunteers wishing to cross at Harrisburg and meet the enemy, and we believe Gen. Houston was going eastward.[10]

Shouts of joy were passed among the ranks as men followed the musicians down the right-hand road. A small squad marched ahead with the eager musicians until Major Lysander Wells galloped ahead and ordered them all to halt until the wagons, cannon and medicine cart could catch up.

For those close enough to witness the passing of the crucial fork, it was a clear signal that Houston was now prepared to fight. Dr. Anson Jones: "At Donohue's he was compelled, by the unanimous sense of the army, to deflect from the road, and go to Harrisburg."[11] Captain Amasa Turner felt that the chance of meeting the enemy "revived our drooping spirits."

True to Heard and Mercer's testimony, orders had been sent ahead to the East Texas volunteers. Colonel Rusk sent orders with Major George Digges and Colin DeBland on April 16 to concentrate troops

Captain William Jones Elliot Heard (1801–1874) was in command of the "Citizen Soldiers," officially Company F, First Regiment. Captain Heard, one of many who was later critical of Sam Houston, wrote that the general was compelled by others to take the fork toward Harrisburg.
Courtesy of the San Jacinto Museum of History, Houston.

at the Trinity River at Robbins' Ferry. The only troops which were to be marched immediately to join General Houston were those "you may meet on this side of the Trinity."[12]

Contrary to Heard's and Mercer's beliefs, Rusk's orders to Digges clearly show that he and Houston were of the mind-set to fight. "The enemy are beyond a doubt moving towards Galveston and Anahuac," wrote Rusk. "They may however send some portion of their forces towards the Trinity." He felt that this tactic would be to "effect a crossing at Nacogdoches or to divide our present force" into being too splintered in numbers to be effective. Rusk called for more volunteers to turn out to defend East Texas. "If they do as they should, the enemy cannot possibly cross [the] Trinity."

Nowhere in Thomas Rusk's April 16 orders to Major Digges does he even remotely suggest that the main body of the Texian army was considering marching to the Trinity to help defend that crossing. "I am decidedly of the opinion that a very few days will bring our armies into contact and I have no fear or doubts as to the result."

Dr. Labadie wrote that about six miles down the road to Harrisburg, Houston ordered Major Willie Williamson to "go with all possible speed to the Red Land Company, with directions that they should join the army, as it had now changed its course to Harrisburg." This reference was most likely to Captain William Kimbro's company, which had been stationed on detached duty during the previous two weeks. Labadie wrote that ranger commander Williamson was "dressed in buck-skin and a coon-cap ornamented with some half a dozen old coons' tails that were dangling on his shoulders."[13]

With the Twin Sisters now a part of the army, movement down the road from Donoho's was only as fast as the cannon could be moved. One of the fleeing civilians with the army was Pamelia Mann, who had brought along her two wagons and oxen teams from Groce's. Her husband Marshall Mann was away during the Runaway Scrape. With two sons from two previous marriages, Pamelia Mann had managed to operate an inn at Washington-on-the-Brazos until the flight of the government had forced her to move on to safety. While at Groce's, General Houston had managed to get a yoke of oxen from her to help pull the two cannon.

Due to the great spring rains, the roads were in horrible shape. Moving the cannon without oxen would be an incredible labor.

Upon departing McCarley's, Mrs. Mann announced, "General, if you are going on to the Nacogdoches Road, you can have my oxen, but if you go the other to Harrisburg, you can't have them, for I want them myself."[14]

General Houston wisely said to the lady that he was taking the Nacogdoches Road, although he did not state how far down that road he would be traveling. About six miles down the road came the crucial fork. The road to Harrisburg turned to the right, almost a right angle down east.

The Texas Army made it about ten miles down the road to Harrisburg when Mrs. Mann overtook General Houston. The prairies were full of water from the rains and it was now very warm. Mrs. Mann was equally hot as she rode up.

"General, you told me a damn lie," she snapped. "You said that [you] was going on the Nacogdoches Road. Sir, I want my oxen!"

Houston politely replied, "Well, Mrs. Mann, we can't spare them. We can't get our cannon along without them."

"I don't care a damn for your cannon," she retorted. "I want my oxen!"

Private Bob Hunter noted that Mrs. Mann had a pair of holster pistols on her saddle and a "very large knife on her saddle." Jumping down from her horse, the determined woman cut the rawhide tug holding the chain to the oxen with her knife. "Nobody said a word," wrote Hunter.

Mrs. Mann jumped on her horse and rode away with her oxen. Captain Rohrer, the wagon master, rode up to General Houston and said, "General, we can't get along without them oxen. The cannon is done bogged down."

Houston replied that they would have to get along as best they could. Rohrer then announced that he would go and get the oxen back from Mrs. Mann and away he rode with another of his teamsters. As Rohrer rode off, Houston reportedly hollered, "Captain Rohrer, that woman will fight."

"Damn her fighting!" shouted Rohrer.

According to Private Hunter, Sam Houston then dropped down from his horse and announced, "Come on boys. Let's get this cannon out of the mud." The mud was near the commander-in-chief's boot tops as he put his shoulder to the wheel. Eight or ten other soldiers quickly joined their leader and forced the iron cannon up from the mud.

Anyone who had questioned Houston's intention to fight could now see that the general meant business. Certainly he would not have the army labor to haul the heavy cannon through the mud if he did not soon hope to mount an attack on his enemy.

Private James Winters of Captain Ware's company later gave his account of this episode.

> I never heard any talk as to Houston's not designing to fight; or of officers or men insisting on his taking the road to Harrisburg; or of any one doubting his intention to do so. We went as straight as we could go towards Harrisburg. Mrs. Mann did take her oxen from the ammunition wagon before we got to camp at McCurley's. She needed them herself. They had been pressed into service by our wagon master.[15]

The army continued its slow pace throughout the afternoon, covering another six miles before stopping to make camp for the night in some heavy timber near a creek. Camp was made near Matthew Burnett's place among the oaks and towering pines. The ground was heavy with pine straw and dense brush along the steep banks of the deeply cut channel of Cypress Creek.

The site of this Texan campground is now located near Highway 290 in Telge Park, marked by a historical marker, just east of Telge Road on Pleasant Grove Road.

The weather was poor and the report of thunder could be heard in the distance. Some mistook the occasional booming for an enemy's cannon.[16]

Private Stephen Sparks and others were detailed during the day to drive cattle ahead of the army to Burnett's place and to have some butchered by the time the army arrived. They arrived at the Burnett house by mid-afternoon. To the protest of some of his companions, Sparks proceeded to kill a dozen chickens and cook them on the family's stove, along with bacon and cornbread. The men ate and, upon the arrival of the army in the late evening, Sparks called in the officers to share in their little meal.[17]

General Houston was furious that the family's personal effects had been used. "I will have to punish you," he admonished Sparks. Rusk, Sherman and other officers joined Houston in eating some of the chicken, after which the general let Sparks off with a stern warning against ever using citizens' property again.

About the camp that night, there was much discussion of an engagement with the enemy. The army had taken the road toward Harrisburg versus fleeing all the way to the United States. According to Colonel Coleman, "a new commander was spoken of. It was evident to the men that their General was marching contrary to his wishes, dragged in that direction by the Secretary of War, and the will of the army." Despite his own personal bias, Coleman defended Houston on this occasion to those who spoke out, telling them that their commander-in-chief had been "placed in his situation by the authorities of the country."[18]

Captain Rohrer made it back into camp that night empty-handed. He announced that Mrs. Mann refused to give up the oxen team. Several of the soldiers noticed that his shirt had been torn in several places. Rohrer stated that she had asked for some of it for baby rags, but others snickered that the tough woman had torn it off him.[19]

Private James Winters recalled, "The boys had a good joke on the wagon master, and they did not forget to use it."[20]

President Burnet narrowly escaped capture by Colonel Juan Almonte's dragoons. Instead of riding the steamer *Cayuga* all the way around San Jacinto Bay to reach New Washington, Burnet apparently left the steamer at Lynchburg. There, he, his wife Hannah Este Burnet and several cabinet members took horses and crossed the San Jacinto aboard the ferry. They stayed briefly at the farmhouse of Dr. George Moffitt Patrick, who had helped to organize Captain Moseley Baker's San Felipe company in March. They then proceeded to ride the remaining ten miles to New Washington. There they found a flatboat busily hauling supplies from the warehouse of Colonel James Morgan out to the Texas schooner *Flash* in Galveston Bay.[21]

At this same time, Colonel Almonte's fifty troops were rapidly approaching New Washington. En route, they had encountered young Texan courier Mike McCormick. His mother, forty-nine-year-old Irish widow Peggy McCormick, owned a ranch between San Jacinto River and San Jacinto Bay. Almonte's dragoons followed McCormick toward New Washington, where the young man was carrying messages for President Burnet.

"We were severally employed in the warehouse, and loading boats, for some time, not dreaming of immediate danger," recalled Dr. Patrick. As young McCormick raced up, he yelled out, "Make haste, Mr. President! The Mexicans are coming!"[22]

Burnet had directed his indentured servant to bring a large skiff to the water end of the warehouse. The man was busily loading this boat

President David Burnet and his Texas cabinet narrowly avoided capture by Colonel Almonte's soldiers at New Washington on April 16. Because Burnet's wife was in the boat, Almonte restrained his men from firing upon them.
Oil painting courtesy of the San Jacinto Museum of History, Houston.

with trunks and other supplies at the moment the alarm was shouted. The servant quickly brought the boat around to the beach for the cabinet to board. President Burnet scooped up one of his small children and Dr. Patrick the other. They put the children and Mrs. Burnet aboard.

They shoved off in the skiff while David Thomas and other cabinet members climbed aboard a large flatboat loaded with Colonel Morgan's property. According to Dr. Patrick, this flatboat "hastily shoved off, two negroes at the oars. At this moment, the Mexicans were descending the hill, and not more than one hundred and fifty paces from us. We had not made more than thirty or forty yards from the shore when the enemy dismounted on the beach."

McCormick wheeled his horse and dashed for safety through the woods as Colonel Almonte's soldiers raced for the shore. The president of Texas, his servants and companions pulled hard on the oars. The large skiff and the flatboat worked out into the bay as the Mexican cavalrymen took aim on them.

David Burnet, according to Dr. Patrick, refused his wife Hannah's frantic pleas to be seated. He instead remained standing "from the time we left the shore until we had proceeded perhaps a mile," offering himself as a target over his children. "We effected certainly a narrow and providential escape."

Only the gentlemanly spirit of Colonel Almonte spared the Texas leaders. He ordered his men to halt their firing, as he would not have

Colonel Juan Nepomuceno Almonte (1803–1869), circa 1860, was a former international diplomat of Mexico who had been educated in the United States. Almonte was General Santa Anna's trusted English-speaking aide who led the division which attempted to capture President Burnet.
Courtesy of the San Jacinto Museum of History, Houston.

them accidentally kill the woman in the boat. Burnet's cabinet thus escaped capture by the Mexican army and he was able to make his way across to Galveston Island, where the Texas government took up station.[23]

Almonte's scouts would soon report back that Houston's men were withdrawing "in the direction of the Trinity River through the pass at Lynchburg."

Almonte's men were not completely at a loss. They did take control of Colonel Morgan's warehouses, which were stocked with food and other provisions. He sent word to Santa Anna to hurry his troops to join him at New Washington.

Santa Anna's men had lingered in Harrisburg through April 16, looting and burning all the buildings. His Excellency would later claim, however, that the Texian troops destroyed Harrisburg before his arrival. "This town was no longer in existence because the enemy had burned it," wrote Santa Anna. "They had interned the inhabitants as had been done in Gonzales."[24]

General Houston's men, of course, were behind Santa Anna's main force and had not yet reached Harrisburg before the Mexican troops. A small group of Houston's spies, however, did happen upon some of Santa Anna's men as they were camped along the bayou near Harrisburg. According to Colonel Pedro Delgado, these Texans began firing across the water at Santa Anna's men around 5:00 p.m.

On the opposite side of the bayou [from Harrisburg], we found two or three houses well supplied with wearing apparel, mainly for women's use, fine furniture, an excellent piano, jars of preserves, chocolate, fruit, &c., all of which were appropriated for the benefit of His Excellency and his attendants. I and others obtained only what they could not use.

After the houses had been sacked and burnt down, a party of Americans fired upon our men from the woods; it is wonderful that some of us, camped as we were along the bank of the bayou, were not killed. The Quartermaster Sergeant of Matamoros was seriously wounded.[25]

Having escaped capture by Almonte's men, President Burnet put out another call for support from his fellow Texans. From Galveston on April 16, Burnet called on the Texan citizens to contribute to the funding of the war effort by donating parts of their land holdings to be sold to raise money to provide for the army. Following the revolution, if Texas had not fallen, those citizens contributing land would be repaid at eight percent interest. The first citizen to make such an offer to Burnet had been Ritson Morris, who on April 12 offered half of his league on Galveston Bay to support the revolution.[26]

Houston Marches to Harrisburg

During the night of April 16–17, an express arrived in General Houston's camp with the news that Santa Anna's men were in Harrisburg, only about twenty-five miles distant. "Upon receipt of this information, all dissension ceased in camp," wrote Colonel Coleman. "The men were of one mind, to march down and fight the enemy."[27]

The camp was broken early and the Texas Army was on the move in the early morning hours of April 17. Houston sent out his scouts throughout the day to check on the enemy's movements.

The army moved about fifteen miles this day, slowed by mud and poor conditions. Camp was made that evening "in the edge of the pine woods about six miles north of Harrisburg."[28]

Captain Kimbro's San Augustine company made it to the Texan camp during the night hours of April 17–18 with Major Williamson, who had been sent back by Houston to recall them. By request of Kimbro, his company was allowed to rest the following morning until 11:00 a.m., with orders to then follow as the rear guard of the main army and to join Houston at Harrisburg again that night.[29]

General Houston's troops were again up early on April 18 and marching along the muddy road toward Harrisburg. Since departing

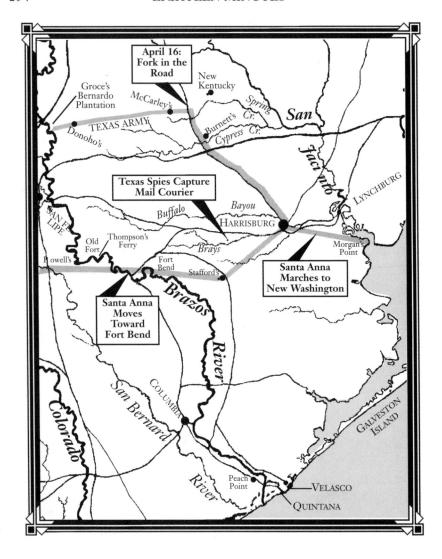

Gonzales on March 13, the Texas Army had marched some two hundred miles. They reached the town around noon and found only charred skeletons of the former homes and shops. Camp was established within sight of town, but about eight hundred yards below on the left bank of the bayou.[30]

According to Dr. Labadie, "We arrived opposite Harrisburg about noon, when the smoke at the town told us too plainly to be mistaken, that the enemy had been there before us, and set fire to its buildings."[31]

Captains Karnes and Smith went out with their scouts, crossing Buffalo Bayou in search of the Mexican army. The Mexican army had departed town less than twenty-four hours previous. In the new camp below Harrisburg, some men literally collapsed in exhaustion for a brief rest. They had traveled about sixty miles in two days, marching in wet clothes through muddy roads.

Private Stephen Sparks of the Second Regiment's First Company recalled the men sharing a common thought. They were "tired and hungry, so we all scattered to look for something to eat."[32]

Old Whip and Miss Emily

Santa Anna's plan was to prevent Sam Houston from crossing the Lynchburg ferry and to crush his forces there. On April 17, he moved from Harrisburg around 3:00 p.m. toward New Washington with some of his troops. He had ordered Colonel Pedro Delgado to "burn the town" as they left, thus leaving Harrisburg in ashes.[33]

According to Lieutenant Colonel José María Castillo y Iberri, he was also ordered to set fire to the town because Santa Anna was "greatly annoyed at having failed" in his plan to capture the Texas Cabinet. Iberri told another officer that "His Excellency lent a hand in its destruction."[34]

As his troops crossed the bayou at Harrisburg, Santa Anna received a courier from Colonel Almonte with news of President Burnet's escape.

Santa Anna had with him "seven hundred foot soldiers and fifty horses," enough men to make him feel "superior in number to the enemy," whom his best intelligence had pegged at about eight hundred men. Writing to General Filisola on April 17, he related that his spies found that Houston had moved out from Groce's Landing toward Nacogdoches. "Since he is escorting families and supplies in ox-drawn wagons, his march is slow," wrote Santa Anna.[35]

His Excellency had no idea that Houston's men were actually following so closely behind him at this point.

Santa Anna also ordered Filisola on the Brazos to suspend the movement of General Cos on the port of Velasco. Cos was "to send at once under his command five hundred chosen foot soldiers to join me as quickly as possible." Santa Anna sent these orders to Cos with a rapid courier, his aide-de-camp, Lieutenant Colonel Castillo y Iberri.[36]

El Presidente's troops pushed forward for New Washington, crossing Buffalo Bayou on a tributary known as Vince's Bayou. Across this body of water was a sturdy cedar bridge built by the Vince brothers only months before. When the mules pulling the heavy Golden Standard refused to cross the bridge, Santa Anna ordered General Castrillon to circumvent the bayou via a nine-mile route over boggy, high-grassed prairies. Castrillon dutifully hauled the cannon on his lonely vigil "with an escort of only one company of infantry."[37]

Santa Anna's advance force was greeted by "a violent storm" that set in around 10:00 p.m. The driving rain and darkness soon caused his troops to wander from their course, so His Excellency "ordered a halt, requiring every man to stand in the ranks, without shelter from the rain."

En route to New Washington on the morning of April 18, the Mexican army moved across the large ranch of William Vince near the San Jacinto River. There, the army relieved Vince's housekeeper and her young son of a prized studhorse. This large, black thoroughbred stallion, called "Old Whip," belonged to William's brother Allen Vince. Colonel Juan Bringas, an aide to Santa Anna, took Old Whip as his new mount.[38]

The remainder of the main Mexican force under Santa Anna reached New Washington by noon on April 18. "We found flour, soap, tobacco, and other articles, which were issued to the men," wrote Colonel Delgado. General Castrillon and his men arrived with the Golden Standard cannon around 5:00 p.m.[39]

General Filisola and the main body of the Mexican army remained encamped at Thompson's Point, or the current Fort Bend area, awaiting further orders. Among the senior officers present were Generals Cos, Tolsa, Woll and Ramirez y Sesma. Lieutenant Colonel Castillo y Iberri reached camp on April 18 with the new orders from Santa Anna concerning General Cos bringing five hundred reinforcements.

General Cos marched out that afternoon with a little more than five hundred men, but no artillery. He took the Guerrero Battalion under Colonel Manuel Cespedes, the remnants from the Aldama and Toluca battalions under First Adjutant Felipe Romero, and two companies from the Guadalajara battalion under Captains Vallejo Rocha and Jose Lisola.[40]

Santa Anna's men found New Washington deserted by most of its settlers. The Mexican looters, however, did find some of Colonel James Morgan's remaining indentured servants and a young "yellow boy" named Turner. Among the servants was a beautiful mulatto girl named Emily. Legend has it that Santa Anna first spotted this attractive girl at the wharf as she was assisting with loading a flatboat with supplies.[41]

Emily D. West, less than thirty years of age, was originally from New Haven, Connecticut. She had entered into an indentured servant contract with Morgan in New York in 1835 and had come to work on his Gulf Coast Texas plantation. Taken into custody of the Mexican army on April 18, Miss Emily would play a crucial role in the San Jacinto campaign by some accounts.

Morgan's Point was a parcel of land extending into the bay where Colonel Morgan kept his plantation. Near the mouth of the San Jacinto River, his land was known for its orange groves and herds of cattle.

Once complete with their looting, the Mexican soldiers burned the town of New Washington to the ground. The boy named Turner who had been captured was an intelligent printer's apprentice. Turner was taken aboard one of the flatboats with a guard detail. Loaded with bread and other supplies, this boat sailed from Morgan's Point up San Jacinto Bay toward Lynch's Ferry.

General Santa Anna's forces marched out from New Washington and rendezvoused with Colonel Juan Almonte's force. El Presidente found a German schooner lying off the banks of New Washington. Stranded by lack of winds, the vessel was appealing to Santa Anna. Considering that he might use it to sail to Copano Bay, he had Colonel Almonte's men prepare boats and rafts to seize the vessel on April 19. To the dismay of the Mexican soldiers, "a steamboat arrived and opened fire."[42]

This "steamboat" was apparently one of the four armed schooners of the Texas Navy, which operated out of Galveston under the discretion of Secretary of the Navy Robert Potter. With this vessel destroyed and his new scheme spoiled, Santa Anna returned his thoughts to surprising Sam Houston at the Lynchburg ferry.

Spies Capture Santa Anna's Mail

The best thing going for the Texas Army was the resourcefulness of its spies and their uncanny ability to gather intelligence on their enemy. While his army took an early afternoon rest at camp near Harrisburg on April 18, Sam Houston's top scouts were making another key find.

Erastus "Deaf" Smith (1787–1837) was considered by Sam Houston to be the ablest of the Texas Army's scouts. Among other feats during the campaign, Smith helped capture a Mexican courier on April 18 who was carrying dispatches for Santa Anna. *Texas State Library and Archives Commission.*

Captain Henry Karnes was out on patrol with a small scouting force which included Deaf Smith and William Pearce. They had crossed Buffalo Bayou and rode roughly twelve miles along the road leading toward the Brazos River. The men under Karnes and Smith had brought the Alamo survivors to Gonzales on March 13 and had taken an enemy prisoner a week later. Four weeks later, their knack for providing information to General Houston proved invaluable once again.

On the road toward the Brazos, Captain Karnes' party met and captured three Mexican horsemen who were carrying mail for Santa Anna. These men put up little fight, but their capture was highly important. One of them was Captain Miguel Bachiller, a special courier or *correo* from Mexico City. Another of the captives was a Mexican guard for Bachiller. The third man was actually a former member of Captain Juan Seguin's Tejano company who had been given a furlough to go to San Antonio to provide for his family. This man had been captured by General Sesma's men and impressed as a guide.

The spies found that the courier's deerskin wallets, or saddlebags, were inscribed with the name "W. B. Travis." Stamped into the underside of one of the saddlebags, this name indicated that the saddle had once been the property of the Alamo's late Lieutenant Colonel Travis! Even more important was the discovery of a number of letters intended for Santa Anna.

Dr. Nicholas Labadie noted that the captured Mexican army courier was brought into camp "about 8 o'clock, that night." Private Bob Hunter recalled seeing two riders, Ben Fulshear and James Wells, lead one of the captured Mexicans into camp about nightfall. Private William Zuber saw two of the prisoners "with their elbows slightly back and tied with cords." He considered the Mexican captain "a fine-looking man, of genteel appearance."[43]

Not one to pass up good souvenirs, Deaf Smith had traded clothes with one of his courier prisoners. At their first sight in camp, Smith and his prisoners, "caused a general laugh and hurrah," wrote Sergeant Moses Bryan.

> Smith had on the Mexican courier's fine suit of leather, all braided and fixed up in uniform style. A broad brim Sombrero, a heavy bead band and trinkets attached, fine shoes and socks, but the suit was too small and too tight and pants not reaching nearer than six inches of the top of the shoes.[44]

Sergeant Bryan found that the poor courier "had on Deaf Smith's old ragged coat and ragged pants," which were too big and too long for him. Wearing Smith's old shoes, his toes stuck out through the holes in them. "The men and officers came in squads to see Deaf Smith in his new suit and to sympathize with the forlorn-looking courier." Amidst the shouting and the laughter, Captain Bachiller looked as though "he would like for the earth to open and swallow him."

Funny as he appeared, Smith most likely had a greater purpose in such a disguise than in merely amusing his comrades. To avoid being fired on by enemy forces, he had taken on the general appearance of a Mexican officer for the ride back to the Texan forces with his prisoners.

"I was called as interpreter by Gen. Houston, to question the captain," recalled Sergeant Bryan. "He stated that Santa Anna had left the Brazos with 500 infantry, 100 cavalry, and one brass 12 pounder."[45]

Colonel Rusk called for the Tejano officers of his army to assist in translating these letters. Sergeant Tony Menchaca read one General Filisola to Santa Anna dispatch which indicated to Houston that Santa Anna's divisions were separated at the present time.[46]

Major Lorenzo de Zavala Jr., the Vice President's son, helped translate other dispatches for General Houston which further revealed the strength and positions of Santa Anna's forces. De Zavala sat near Houston, carefully reading each scrap of mail. Captain Robert Calder recalled that the captured Mexican mail included "letters from husbands to wives, from lovers to mistresses, all speaking confidently of an early return home."[47]

Sergeant William Swearingen wrote on April 22 that these letters included

> a letter from Cos to Santa Anna stating that he would start the next morning from Fort Bend with 650 men to join him at Lynch's Ferry on Buffalo Bayou. Gen. Houston then knew that Santa Anna had gone by way of New Washington on the bay to destroy that place and then to march up the bayou to Lynch's Ferry and join Cos and march on to Galveston and take it before Houston could find out where he was.[48]

The captured mail indicated that Santa Anna's main division was still unaware of Houston's exact location and that his men numbered only about six hundred. With more than eleven hundred men at his disposal, Houston obviously knew that he had the upper hand if he could attack before Cos' reinforcements arrived. He also knew that Santa Anna himself was in command of the troops near New Washington and could be a valuable prize if captured before his division was joined by others.

Colonel Coleman felt that "the spirits of the General revived, he became more cheerful, and no one was insulted by him in this camp."[49]

Colonel Sidney Sherman was ordered that evening to cross the cavalry over Buffalo Bayou with the thought that the Mexican army might still have other forces lurking about the area. Approximately 150 mounted men were taken on a volunteer basis to probe the enemy's strength near Vince's Bayou. Captain Henry Karnes' company went first, swimming their horses across the swollen bayou and sending their baggage across on a raft that had been constructed for moving goods over water.[50]

Major James Perry was among the officers who crossed the bayou with Captain Karnes' company, although most of General Houston's staff remained behind.

One of those volunteers crossing Buffalo Bayou to attack Santa Anna was Private Stephen Sparks of Captain Arnold's Nacogdoches company.

> I was one of the volunteers, and we began to try to swim our horses, but whenever we got to where the light shone on the water (all along the oppo-

site bank the buildings were still burning) our horses would turn back, and we could not force them across. At midnight the order was countermanded.[51]

The task proved very tedious with the horses in the high waters in the darkness. Shortly after Karnes' men had crossed, and before the balance could follow, Colonel Rusk sent orders to discontinue crossing the men. He had ascertained that by crossing at Harrisburg, Karnes' men would have yet another difficult bayou, Sims Bayou, to cross, on their route to Lynchburg.

Karnes' company found itself on a lonely vigil on the opposite bank of the bayou that night. Standing his first guard detail on the night of April 18 at Lynchburg was young Private Walter Paye Lane. A nineteen-year-old from Ireland, Lane had come to the United States with his family and settled in Ohio. He was working in Louisville, Kentucky, when he happened to meet General Stephen F. Austin and Dr. Branch T. Archer. Learning of his desire to come to Texas, they gave him letters of introduction. Lane made his way to San Augustine, where he arrived in time to join the company of Captain Kimbro on March 1 and be elected second sergeant.[52]

With his letters of introduction and his dispatches from Kimbro, Lane thus arrived in front of General Houston at Groce's and was assigned to the army. He was assigned for a time to the company of Captain William Patton and later became part of Captain Henry Karnes' cavalry.

The threat of the Mexican army's presence was all too real for a nineteen-year-old boy. He describes his first guard experience near Buffalo Bayou.

> I was detailed as a sentinel that night—my first military experience. The sergeant [Robert Goodloe] stationed me one-half mile from camp in a wood; told me to keep awake, as the Mexicans might be on me at any minute. He said, "You can hear their drums now." I did.
>
> I was pondering the situation, in front of the enemy, didn't know the way back to camp, and it was dark as pitch. Just then, I heard a rush in front of me. Here they come, I thought. I got behind a tree, cocked both barrels, and cried, "Give the countersign, or I fire." A cow marched by me. I almost dropped in my tracks.

CHAPTER 12

"Determined to Conquer or Die"

April 19

> We view ourselves on the eve of battle. We are nerved for the contest, and must conquer or perish. It is vain to look for present aid: none is at hand. We must now act or abandon all hope! Rally to the standard, and be no longer the scoff of mercenary tongues! Be men, be freemen, that your children may bless their fathers' names!
> —*General Houston to "The People of Texas," April 19, 1836*

Sam Houston prepared his army for crossing Buffalo Bayou on April 19 for Lynchburg. He would not move the cumbersome baggage wagons and camp gear with him. Fully expecting a fight soon, he preferred to keep his men quick on action. The mail captured by Karnes and Smith gave Houston the confidence that he must attack quickly while Santa Anna was still isolated.

Aside from baggage and camp gear, General Houston would also leave behind in camp those men who had taken sick during the campaign. Dr. James Phelps was attending to about a dozen men who were sick with diarrhea at the Harrisburg camp. Many other men were sick with measles, fever or flu-like symptoms. They would serve no value in combat.

As the army prepared to move out, Doctors Nicholas Labadie and John Davidson loaded their saddlebags onto Davidson's horse, Labadie having been forced to give up his own horse to a cavalryman. They filled their medical bags with bandages that had been made from rags.[1]

Doctors Phelps and Anson Jones were detailed to stay behind at Harrisburg with the sick. Jones, however, had been adamant when assigned as a doctor that he would still be allowed to fight.

> I resolved as I have done on subsequent occasions, to "disobey the order." I, therefore, having attended to my daily routine, handed over my sick to the

hospital surgeon, and joining the army at the crossing [of Buffalo Bayou], about sundown, and proceeded with it to Lynchburg.[2]

Two company commanders were among those too sick to cross Buffalo Bayou. Captain Henry Teal, commanding Company A of the regular army, was left sick with the measles on April 19. His company was turned over to the acting command of Captain Andrew Briscoe, who had previously commanded a small mounted spy unit during the San Jacinto campaign.

Captain William Hill was also left behind sick at Harrisburg. First Lieutenant Robert Stevenson became acting captain in his place. Born in Ireland in 1805, Stevenson had been recruited on the Colorado River on March 20 by Captain Joseph Lynch. On Lynch's muster roll, Stevenson was listed as a merchant by trade, towering above the average Texan at six feet, six inches tall, "of fair complexion with hazel eyes and fair hair." He had come to Texas with his family in 1832 from Tennessee, where he had been very familiar with the late Davy Crockett.[3]

A third Texan company under new command was that of Captain William Patton, who had been selected to serve as one of General Houston's aides-de-camp. In his absence, First Lieutenant David Murphree was promoted into command of the Columbia company—which was officially the Fourth Company, Second Regiment. Twenty-four-year-old Murphree, the oldest of eleven children, was a Tennessee native who had fought during the Bexar siege. He had enlisted in Patton's company on March 16 and had been promoted up to first lieutenant on April 10.[4]

Eight of the twenty-six companies present at Harrisburg on April 19 had undergone at least one command change during the San Jacinto campaign.

By leaving behind some of his doctors and a large number of sick men, General Houston was thereby forced to give the unpopular order for each regiment to station some guards to protect this camp from the enemy's capture. Major Robert McNutt, third senior officer of the First Regiment, was placed in command of the camp at Harrisburg. In McNutt's place, Captain John Allen would serve as acting major of the First Regiment's command staff. McNutt's former company, now under Captain Gibson Kuykendall, would also remain behind.

Those selected to remain behind at camp were not pleased, as Private James Kuykendall recalled.

As my brother's company was one of the first in the field, its detail to "keep camp" when there was a prospect of a fight seemed unfair. Cols. Burleson and

Somervell and Sergt-Major Cleveland, at the request of my brother, urged Gen'l Houston to excuse said company from this service. The Gen'l refused to do so.[5]

Private William Zuber wrote that the Harrisburg detachment "amounted to about 150 men capable of fighting," obviously not counting the seriously ill. He counted "about 50 men prostrate with measles."[6]

In addition to Captain Kuykendall's Company E, Captain Peyton Splane's Company J of the First Regiment was left under Major McNutt. Colonel Sherman left one complete company from his Second Regiment. The Washington Guards ranger unit formed by Major Williamson, under command of Captain Joseph Chance, was assigned to Major McNutt.

More than eighty men who had served as Texas Rangers under eight different captains during the Texas Revolution would either guard the baggage at Harrisburg or march with the army for Lynchburg. This includes W. T. Sadler's eight former rangers, several rangers formerly under Captain Louis Franks and the twelve-man ranger unit under Captain Stephen Townsend.

Two ranger battalions remained in existence as of mid-April 1836. The first was under Major Willie Williamson. By April 17, Captain John Tumlinson and a few of his men had caught up with Major Williamson and the two rangers who had kept company with him, Ganey Crosby and Jimmy Curtis. Tumlinson had taken leave from the main body of his company during the Runaway Scrape to help escort his and other families to safety ahead of the Mexican army. The military papers of Private Ganey Crosby show that he was discharged from service by Captain Tumlinson on April 17 to join the regular army. Crosby was immediately enlisted by Lieutenant Colonel Joseph Bennett into Captain James Gillaspie's Company F of the Second Regiment.[7]

Tumlinson and at least two other of his men, Jimmy Curtis and Henry Redfield, joined First Regiment companies at Harrisburg. Major Williamson joined Captain William Smith's cavalry company as a buck private. At least two other officers of Williamson's ranging battalion, Captain Isaac Watts Burton and Lieutenant Thomas Robbins, temporarily abandoned their commissions and joined the cavalry at Harrisburg.

Many of the rangers who rode out with Sam Houston to seek battle would not give up their commissions. Captains Burton and Tumlinson would soon resume command of their men. For example, Private Sylvanus Cottle had enlisted under Burton on February 4. Although assigned to Captain Chance's baggage guard at Harrisburg, Cottle's military papers show that he was constantly under Captain Burton's supervision in the ranging service through October 1836.[8]

Captain Townsend left most of his small ranging company at Harrisburg, joining the cavalry with his brother, Spencer Burton Townsend. Another of Townsend's men, Private James Bird temporarily joined Captain Heard's Second Regiment company.

Public debt papers show that Townsend (despite his brief service with the cavalry) was continually in command of his rangers through May 12, 1836. His brother, Moses Townsend, was later paid for serving three months and twelve days in

> Capt. Stephen Townsend's company in the year A.D. 1836 [and] service in guarding the baggage wagons in the Battle of San Jacinto.[9]

The second ranger regiment in commission during April was headed by Lieutenant Colonel Griffin Bayne. His superior, Colonel Jesse Benton Sr., was working on a military road to the Red River and recruiting rangers during this time. Lieutenant Colonel Bayne had recruited men from Robertson's Colony for the ranging service during March and April.

Captain William C. Wilson's ranger unit had been formed on March 1. Other recruits joined Bayne's group as it moved for the Texas Army. By April 13, Bayne's rangers had joined with the ranger company of Captain Isaac Burton, whose men were under Major Williamson's direction.[10]

The majority of these rangers under Lieutenant Colonel Bayne would not see any action during the San Jacinto campaign. Although Captain Burton and a few of his company did join the Texas Army at Harrisburg, most of his company remained with Bayne. At least a few of Captain Wilson's rangers appear to have accompanied Burton to the main army. Private Daniel T. Dunham, who had entered Lieutenant Colonel Bayne's ranging corps on March 27, had left the rangers by April 18 to join the artillery company of Captain George Poe. Papers of Francis Weatherred indicate that he also served for a time under Jesse Benton's ranger corps before joining Captain Poe's company.[11]

General Houston found the rangers to be an easy target to deploy as camp guards at Harrisburg. The number of ranger officers who temporarily joined other companies as mere privates clearly indicates how unpopular it was to be forced to remain behind.

According to Alfred Kelso of Captain Heard's company, every man who wished to stay behind at camp was given the opportunity. "They wanted no man to go into the battle that could not stand up to the point of the bayonet," wrote Kelso on April 30.[12]

Aside from those too sick to walk, there were no takers. All were eager for battle. The companies of Captains Kuykendall, Splane and Chance were the only three complete units which were ordered to stay behind. The other camp guards were picked in small numbers from their regiments.

From Captain James Gillaspie's company, ten men were ordered to stay behind as guards. Gillaspie expected many men to be willing to stay behind as guards, thus avoiding battle. He was mistaken. Like the other captains, he was thus forced to make the hard choice of picking out the men to leave behind. Among those he selected was teenager William Zuber, partially for his age and partially for a faulty weapon that he carried. Having joined against his parents' wishes for the specific purpose of fighting, Zuber succumbed to tears when Gillaspie refused to let him join those fighting.[13]

Being left behind was not a secure feeling. "If Cos, with 600 or more men, should arrive in Harrisburg the next night as we expected him to do," thought Private Zuber, "he would probably cross the bayou and treat our little detachment left behind to the enjoyment of as much fighting as they desired."

From Captain Amasa Turner's regular company, Private Ellis Benson was selected as one of the guards for the Harrisburg camp. Benson protested, telling his captain that he had "swore an oath" to fight and that he intended to fight. Apparently applauding his determination, Turner let Benson trade places with another man. Benson and three others from Turner's company volunteered to help fight with the artillery.[14]

Sam Houston reportedly also considered keeping the artillery pieces behind to guard the camp. Lieutenant Colonel James Neill, the fiery thirty-eight-year-old Scottish veteran in command, protested so steadfastly, however, that his Twin Sisters cannon were finally allowed to accompany the army. Major McNutt later claimed that he was given orders that, in case he was hard attacked by the enemy, that he should shoot his two Mexican prisoners and blow up the Texan ammunition wagon.[15]

Captain Juan Seguin's Tejano company was also among those given orders to remain at Harrisburg. Sergeant Tony Menchaca was not pleased with this situation.

> Houston ordered Sherman to have the Mexican company left at camp, that they knew but little about fighting, but were good at herding. General Sherman went to the Mexican company and asked for Captain Seguin and was told he was not there. Then General Sherman instructed me that as soon as Captain Seguin came, to tell him that his company was ordered to remain and guard horses and equipages.[16]

Menchaca questioned this call, but Sherman firmly told him that these were Houston's orders. Upon Captain Seguin's return, he and Menchaca marched to see the commander-in-chief. They asked him why they had been selected to remain in camp.

Sergeant Menchaca spoke his mind, telling General Houston that "he could not deprive me of my commission." He had joined the Texas Army to aid them in their fight "and that I wanted to do so even if I died facing the enemy. I did not enlist to guard horses and would not do such duty."

Finally, Menchaca stated that if deprived of fighting, he would "go and attend to my family, who were on their way to Nacogdoches without escort or servants."

General Houston, respecting the heartfelt speech, answered Menchaca that he had spoken like a man. Smart enough not to turn away such a strong sense of patriotism, he opted to give the Tejano company the chance they desired.

"You have a willing heart," said Houston. "I do not see why you should not be allowed to fight."

On April 19, President Santa Anna and his eight hundred troops were on a course that he hoped would quickly bring him face-to-face with the rebel leader Sam Houston.

From the New Washington and Galveston area, he had decided upon the likely course of the Texas Army. Santa Anna decided that he would march for Lynch's Ferry on the banks of the San Jacinto River the following morning. This ferry could be approached by two roads, one from the remnants of Harrisburg and the other road from New Washington. Both of these roads merged close to the ferry.[17]

On the northeastern banks of Lynch's Ferry sat the community of Lynchburg. From Lynchburg, the road opposite the ferry continued northeasterly a short distance and then turned due south toward the coastal community of Anahuac. Santa Anna proceeded through this general area back toward Lynchburg, hoping to meet the Texans and cut off their line of retreat.

Perhaps disgusted with Colonel Almonte for allowing President Burnet to escape New Washington, Santa Anna put Captain Marcos Barragán in charge of fifty scouts on the night of April 19. While Barragán's men pushed ahead to scout for signs of Sam Houston's army, the general's main body completed looting New Washington.

"Remember the Alamo"

Before leaving Major McNutt's command at Harrisburg on April 19, Colonel Rusk wrote another appeal to "the people of Texas" in which he strongly called again on citizens to turn out to fight. "Rise up at once, concentrate, and march to the field!" In his ever-patriotic flare, Rusk concluded his appeal with, "What is life worth with the loss of liberty? May I never survive it!"[18]

Sam Houston added his own note at the bottom of Rusk's letter. "We view ourselves on the eve of battle. We are nerved for the contest, and must conquer or perish." He made a final appeal for more help, calling, "Be men, be freemen, that your children may bless their fathers' names!"

Colonel Robert Coleman wrote that "about 300 men" were left at Harrisburg. Another "800 took up their march in pursuit of the enemy" on the morning of April 19.[19]

The majority of the troops hiked along the flooding Buffalo Bayou, more than three hundred yards wide in places, to find the easiest crossing point. Rusk would not have the men cross in the difficult spot where Captain Karnes had gone over the previous evening. The army was marched below the mouth of Sims Bayou before reaching an easier point for crossing.

The anticipation was now more than some could stand. "No difficulty could now restrain the long pent up ardor of our gallant band," wrote Captain Jesse Billingsley. "Water and fire combined could scarcely have deterred them then."[20]

General Houston sent orders to Henry Karnes "with his detachment of command" to remain on the east side of the bayou while the army passed across. "He will then unite with the main army so as to cooperate. Great caution must be observed to conceal our movements from the enemy."[21]

Before the crossing was made, General Houston delivered his first formal speech of the campaign while perched atop his large horse. The men formed a square formation so that he and Colonel Rusk could sit on their horses in the center. Private John Harvey of the Nacogdoches Volunteers noted that Houston "formed us in solid column, rode into our midst and delivered to us one of the best speeches."[22]

Corporal Isaac Hill of Captain Baker's company recalled that Houston said, "if there was a man in the ranks who did not feel like fighting, he had permission to remain with Major McNutt."[23]

"The army will cross and we will meet the enemy," said Houston. "Some of us may be killed and must be killed." Houston promised that they would have "full satisfaction" for all that they had endured on the campaign thus far. He concluded by urging his men to "remember the Alamo, the Alamo! the Alamo!" The First Regiment's Lieutenant Colonel Alexander Somervell remarked, "After such a speech, but damned few will be taken prisoners—that I know."[24]

The troops roared back with, "Remember the Alamo!" Thus a battle cry was born.[25]

Private Patrick Usher, who had recently joined Captain Moseley Baker's company, was "impatient, weary of wading through mud and water, often hungry and angry." Sam Houston's moving speech on April 19 had helped him to quickly forget his troubles. "Had General Houston called upon me to jump into the whirlpool of the Niagara as the only means of saving Texas, I would have made the leap."[26]

The Secretary of War, Colonel Rusk, next spoke to the assembled army in an equally inspiring speech. Being one of only ten signers of the Texas Declaration of Independence present at this point of the San Jacinto campaign, Rusk was annoyed that more of his fellow patriots were not present. "I look around and see that many I thought would be first on the field are not here," he said. Those that had kept their promise to raise troops and join the fight from the Convention besides Rusk were General Houston, Captain Briscoe, Colonel Robert Coleman, Dr. William Mottley, Major James Collinsworth, Dr. Thomas Gazley, William Scates, Edward Oswald Legrand and John Wheeler Bunton.

Prior to crossing Buffalo Bayou on April 19, General Sam Houston and Colonel Rusk delivered motivational speeches to their troops from horseback.
1892 "Equestrian" oil painting by Stephen Seymour Thomas, courtesy of the San Jacinto Museum of History Association.

Corporal Hill said that Rusk offered "a short but very stirring speech." Dr. Labadie found it "a most eloquent speech inspiring all with an enthusiastic and eager desire to meet the enemy." Rusk cried out at one point, "May I not survive if we don't win this battle!" Sergeant Moses Bryan wrote that Rusk made "a cheering and soul stirring speech, which met great applause from the army." Sergeant Menchaca believed that "Rusk addressed the troops with such force and effect as to make every man, without a single exception, shed tears."[27]

Colonel Rusk also called upon the men to remember the Alamo and remember Goliad. In the height of his speech, he abruptly announced, "I have done." Apparently, he felt it a waste of words to work the men up any further. Most, after all, had been wanting to fight for weeks already.[28]

Although Captain Peyton Splane's company was assigned to guard the baggage at Harrisburg, ten members of his company had managed to temporarily merge with other units in order to fight. One such man was Lieutenant M. H. Denham, who had joined Captain Robert Calder's company as its acting second lieutenant in place of Lieutenant Allen Larrison (who was briefly detached but managed to rejoin his unit the next day). As his men prepared to cross Buffalo Bayou, Denham felt that the Texas Army was "determined to conquer or die."[29]

The speech session soon broke up with cheers of "Remember Goliad!" "Remember La Bahía!" and "Remember the Alamo!"

The army crossed Buffalo Bayou shortly after Houston's and Rusk's speeches. The men were instructed to take with them rations for three days, although most had little left to bring along.

Private James Winters recalled the crossing.

> We crossed the bayou about two miles below Harrisburg, just below Sims' Bayou. We fixed up the old ferry boat with flooring from Mrs. [Isaac] Batterson's house and some new lumber which we found there, and took over the cannon. It took all day to cross.[30]

The crossing site is today marked by an 1836 Centennial Marker titled "Texas Army Crossed Buffalo Bayou." It is located on Lawndale Avenue in Pasadena, about two miles west of Richey.

The old ferryboat leaked considerably, especially when burdened with the weight of the iron Twin Sisters. Private Alphonso Steele of Captain Gillaspie's company wrote, "We crossed the bayou as fast as we could, for we had but one little old leaky boat to cross in."[31]

General Houston later stated that he was aboard the first boat to cross Buffalo Bayou, but his fellow officers later denied that being the case. "Houston did not cross over Buffalo Bayou in the first boat nor until a large number of troops had crossed," wrote Colonel Sidney Sherman.[32]

Before crossing, Houston took time to write a note to Henry Raguet in Nacogdoches. "This morning we are in preparation to meet Santa Anna," he wrote. "It is the only chance of saving Texas." He conveyed to Raguet that he felt the cabinet's flight to Harrisburg had "struck panic throughout the country." Instead of the thousands of volunteers he expected, he had only "about seven hundred to march with, besides the campguard." Nonetheless, he was determined. "The rights for which we fight will be secured and Texas free."[33]

During the crossing at Buffalo Bayou, Captain Juan Seguin added another Tejano to his Second Regiment company. Juan López, a sixteen-year-old orphan who had joined a body of Texas troops as cart driver, was still unassigned to any company. Seguin recalled later that the young boy was dressed "in Mexican garb" but yet looked "more like an Indian than anything else." He had become acquainted with some of Seguin's men and he joined this company "whom he considered being more his countrymen than the other troops, in reason of their language."[34]

Tony Menchaca recalled that the troops worked their way across the swollen bayou on the raft until 5:00 p.m on April 19. Captain Seguin noted that during the crossing, "General Rusk, the Secretary of War, did not spare his personal labor."[35]

Once across, the men concealed themselves in the bushes nearby as the others crossed. "We lay in the bushes on the road to watch Cos and the 650 men which were expected to pass that day," wrote Sergeant William Swearingen of Captain Turner's regular company.[36]

General Houston's staff was all mounted, with the exception of three whose horses could not be found. While the remainder of the army crossed this day, Major James Perry came under the scorn and suspicion of General Houston again.

Perry had crossed Buffalo Bayou the previous day with Karnes' scouts, prior to the main army's crossing. "He rode on some miles ahead of the army, and in fact, ahead of the spy company commanded by Col. Karnes," wrote Colonel Rusk in 1843.[37]

Perry was discovered by Karnes and Wash Secrest of the spies at an abandoned house, "some fifteen miles from the Mexican army." Karnes and Secrest took Major Perry under their charge and led him back to General Houston. "They reported that he had changed his horse's caparison, also his musket for an escopeto, and they believed he had communicated with the enemy," said General Houston.

Perry claimed that he had gone ahead to learn something of the Mexican army's movements, but he was captured by the Texan advance guards, who brought him back before Houston. Perry protested that he had been taken back before he even had a chance to spot the enemy, much less talk with them.[38]

"I believe you have been in communication with the enemy," announced Houston. He ordered Perry to hand over his pistols and consider himself arrested for the time being. Major Perry obliged and remained under the watch of the guard fire. Once the Texas Army prepared to go into battle, he was allowed to have his guns returned to him.

"The crossing of the bayou took the whole of the day," wrote Robert Coleman, "but by sunset all were ready, and the march commenced."[39]

General Houston led his troops down the road that Santa Anna had previously taken toward Lynchburg. "As soon as it became dark we commenced a rapid march for Lynch's Ferry, calculating that Santa Anna would not cross the bayou until the arrival of Gen. Cos," wrote

Sergeant Swearingen. "At two o'clock a.m. we halted within 2½ miles of Lynch's Ferry."

John Swisher said that "we marched all night in the direction the enemy had taken." Lieutenant Denham also agreed that they "marched till two o'clock in the morning," before a halt was called. At some point, Santa Anna's men had left the road and the spies were unable to follow the trail in the darkness.[40]

Houston's men were exhausted, having crossed the river and marching through mud and water for several days straight. The halt was made during the early morning hours of April 20 at White Oak Bayou, just across the bayou from the smoking ruins of Harrisburg. The fortunate ones dropped to the soggy ground and caught as much sleep as was possible. Others were forced to stay up all night on guard detail.

The ground was wet and a cold norther left men shivering with the chills. Doctors Ewing and Labadie huddled under one blanket alongside a log. "As we knew not what moment an attack might be made, we passed a comfortless and sleepless night, without supper, and with our rifles under our heads to be ready at a moment's warning."[41]

CHAPTER 13

The First Engagement

April 20

The enemy had not long to wait. Col. Sherman, with his characteristic bravery, gallantly led on his little squad of heroes to the charge.
—*Private James Tarlton, Company D, First Regiment*

As had become custom in the past few days, the Texas Army was afforded little opportunity to rest at White Oak Bayou. The guards kept a small fire burning in camp, awaiting the return of an advance guard detail under Colonel Sidney Sherman which was sent to scout ahead. Men literally rested on their weapons during this brief respite.

Private James Winters of Captain William Ware's company was not able to sleep at all. While the scouts moved the two and a half miles ahead to reconnoiter Lynch's Ferry, he stayed up on guard detail. "As soon as we could see, we set out for the ferry," Winters recalled.[1]

Nicholas Lynch, the regular army's adjutant, had until very recently operated this ferry over Buffalo Bayou. He profited for a time in charging the fleeing Runaway Scrape citizens for his ferry's use, until President Burnet had put a stop to it. The ferry was no longer in use, watched over only by torries, sympathizers of the Mexican army who would not commit to either side during the revolution.

This morning was particularly cold for coastal Texas in April. The late norther that had blown in sent a chill through the men, who had slept on the ground in their clothes, now soggy with dew. Many had gone to bed without supper.[2]

Due to the close proximity of the enemy, the blare of reveille was forbidden. The army was therefore summoned to attention by the tap of a drum. General Houston was known to handle this duty on occasion, but it is possible that the tapping was performed this day by drum major George Brown of Captain Roman's company.[3] The men were quick to rouse and prepare, knowing that this day might likely bring their long-awaited rendezvous with Santa Anna.

At daylight, roughly 6:00 a.m., the army was again on the march toward Lynchburg, four hours after halting at White Oak Bayou. Houston insisted that the famished men march first and wait to make breakfast later.[4]

Sergeant Swearingen recounts the march of the morning of April 20.

> At sunrise on the 20th we formed our line of battle and proceeded to the ferry. When we reached the ferry we found Santa Anna had not yet reached there, but was on his way up from Washington. Houston picked his ground, placed his men, gave them his orders, then made them stack their arms in their places and told them to eat their breakfast and be ready to receive them about 11 o'clock a.m.[5]

The men stopped just past a small bayou for their breakfast and stacked their guns. Some of the men managed to find three cows nearby, which were quickly shot down and slaughtered for food. Captain Calder considered them "very poor-looking cattle," which would make but a "meager breakfast" for so many troops. Large numbers of men scurried about to collect kindling wood for the breakfast fires.[6]

The surgeons were the third group to kindle their fire. Using a pot of brackish water, a handful of half-pounded coffee was thrown in to boil. Dr. Shields Booker appeared with a dozen eggs which he had found nearby and these were added to the surgeons' pot of coffee to boil.

No sooner had the fires been started then some of Colonel Sherman and Captain Karnes' spies came galloping up with word that the advance guard of the enemy had been spotted. These spies had encountered the fifty-man patrol under Captain Marcos Barragán in the direction of New Washington. "Before we could cook our meat, a horseman came dashing into camp, with news that the advanced guards of the two armies had met," wrote Private John Swisher.[7]

"To arms, to your arms!" called Houston. With this order, the men dropped their butcher knives and scrambled to break down their camp and kill the fires. Colonel Rusk rode through camp, shouting, "Moments are ages; Santa Anna has burned New Washington, and is advancing on us on the bayou!"

The eggs were quickly pulled from the surgeons' coffeepot. Each man quickly drank his small share of the hot boiling coffee. "When the eggs were found to contain chickens, I surrendered my share to others," wrote Dr. Labadie, "who finding them well cooked, swallowed them quickly."[8]

During the momentary fear that the Mexican army might be rushing down upon them, the Texans found one incident of particular humor. Their commissary general, Colonel John Forbes, became excited and jumped upon his saddle mule. In his haste, he forgot that the creature had its forelegs hobbled, or tied together. The mule jumped around with Forbes on its back. Private Thomas Corry later recalled that Forbes "sat surrounded by laughing men, until one of them walked some fifty feet and cut the hobbles off."[9]

The Texans seized their rifles and prepared for action. An examination of weapons found that many of the rifles required fresh priming to be prepared for action. In order to load fresh, man after man discharged his musket. There was "a perfect roar of musketry, till over 400 were fired across the bayou."[10]

According to Sergeant Tony Menchaca, the troops were ordered to "discharge their arm and clean and reload, for, the time was close at hand when they would be needed."[11]

Dr. Nicholas Labadie, however, recalled that General Houston was not happy with these orders being passed. Silent throughout the early morning, the general now roared. "Stop that firing! Stop that firing!" he shouted. "God damn you, I say, stop the firing!"[12]

In spite of the general's threats, several other muskets were discharged. Holding his drawn sword, Houston barked that he would run through the next man who fired his gun. The men protested that they would not go into battle with wet weapons that had been loaded for two weeks or more. After another defiant discharge, Houston gave up his threat, apparently realizing with disgust that he could not control the excitement of his ragtag army in its zeal to engage the enemy.

The Texian scouts under Sidney Sherman were plentiful enough that Captain Marcos Barragán thought for a moment he had encountered the main body of the Texas Army. Barragán's men wheeled their horses and fled to alert Santa Anna at New Washington. Four Mexican cavalrymen were shot from their horses before Sherman restrained his men.

Although they had the enemy on the run, they might also run afoul of the entire Mexican army. Colonel Sherman wisely pulled his scouts into the woods near New Washington and waited to observe the progress of Santa Anna's troops.

At least two other Texas scouts had a slight encounter with Mexican forces. One small unit under Wash Secrest, Church Fulshear and Jim Wells had been sent to the west toward the present Richmond area to look for General Cos' reinforcements and other enemy troops. Near Stafford's Point, the Texas cavalrymen had a brush with advance patrols from Cos' troops and were forced to make a run for it. Secrest and Fulshear escaped through some bottomlands, but Wells' horse ran against a tree and fell, injuring Wells' shoulder badly. He also lost his gun and horse in the escape. He was able to liberate another horse from Mexican forces the next day and made his way to a vacant house to eat some food. That night, April 21, he saw many Mexican fugitives on the prairie and realized that there had been a battle. Wells finally met Deaf Smith the following day and learned what had happened in his absence.[13]

Some of Sherman's scouts managed to capture a young boy who had been held by Santa Anna's men. Described as a "yellow boy" named Turner who was an indentured servant of Colonel Morgan of Galveston, this youth had been working as an apprentice on the *Telegraph and Texas Register* in Harrisburg. He and another printer were captured and taken with Santa Anna to New Washington. Turner was sent with a patrol toward Lynch's Ferry by Santa Anna, who intended to use the boy to inform Houston "that the enemy was coming in force." During the encounter with Sherman's cavalrymen early on April 20, Turner managed to separate himself from his captors. The new intelligence carried by Turner was soon sent back to General Houston.[14]

Captain Juan Seguin remembered that:

> At daybreak a man was taken prisoner, who, on discovering us, had attempted to escape. He was a printer belonging to San Felipe, and informed us that the enemy were at a distance of about 8 miles, on the way back to Harrisburg. Our scouts came in soon with the information that the enemy were countermarching towards Buffalo Bayou.[15]

Santa Anna's men were on the march from New Washington early on April 20. All the houses in town were set ablaze. "We had burnt a fine warehouse on the wharf, and all the houses in town," recalled Colonel Delgado, "when Captain Barragán rushed in at full speed."

Barragán and some of his men had been sent to Lynchburg Pass the previous morning by Santa Anna to observe the arrival of General Houston.[16]

Captain Barragán raced up to Santa Anna around 8:00 a.m. and excitedly explained his news. His men had had a brush with Houston's force and he had lost several men. Barragán said that the rebel Texans were close on his heels.

In his haste after hearing this report, Santa Anna "leaped on his horse, and galloped off at full speed for the lane, which, being crowded with men and mules, did not afford him as prompt an exit as he wished." Delgado wrote that His Excellency knocked down one soldier and rode over another as he raced to prepare for attack.

Santa Anna's fears were momentarily projected to his troops. Colonel Delgado took command of the artillery and ordnance, restored order to the troops and directed a further search for the enemy. Santa Anna, possibly aided by his supply of opium, soon gained his composure and led the troops toward Lynchburg.

His men carefully moved across the tall grass of the prairies and established a position on a plain in the late morning hours of April 20. The Mexican army was poised on the ranch of widow Peggy McCormick near the San Jacinto River and Buffalo Bayou.

Santa Anna would soon find that Houston's Texas troops had taken possession of a small wooded area near the bayou. To the Mexican leader, the situation seemed ideal. "His situation made it necessary for him [Houston] to fight or go into the water."

The whole San Jacinto campaign had essentially come down to a race for Lynch's Ferry. The winner would have the first choice of establishing his ground to defend. Unfortunately for Santa Anna, the Texian army had beaten him to the vicinity of the ferry by several hours.[17]

In the distance, Houston's men could make out a smudge of smoke in the direction of New Washington. They correctly guessed that Santa Anna was nearby and had set the town ablaze. The enemy must certainly be marching toward Lynch's Ferry, so Houston had a guard detail under Colonel Coleman posted near this crossing.

At about 10:00 a.m., General Houston had his men move into a small grove of live oak timber near the elevated banks of the bayou.

The big trees, draped with Spanish moss, skirted Buffalo Bayou above its junction with the San Jacinto River. "We immediately took possession of a strong position on the bank of Buffalo Bayou," wrote Captain Robert Stevenson, who had assumed acting command of Captain Hill's company.[18]

General Houston found this to be a satisfactory concealment to await the advance of Santa Anna. The prairie before him was covered with waving green grass for nearly half a mile and this prairie was bordered on the left by woods. Swamplands and river formed a border along the right side.

Beyond the timberlines adjacent to the marshes, one stepped out onto the open field. The field was about a mile wide from north to south and perhaps several miles wide from east to west. Tall, wavy coastal grass covered this magnificent plain.

The field on which Houston planned to meet the Mexican army for battle was bounded by waters on two sides. Along the northern boundaries of this field ran Buffalo Bayou, which fell away to the southeast. Buffalo Bayou ran into the San Jacinto River just above Lynch's Ferry. San Jacinto Bay formed the eastern boundary of this field as it flowed down toward Galveston Bay. The promontory of land was lined with timber groves and marshlands. Several significant bodies of water lay just west of San Jacinto Bay along the edges of the field, including Peggy's Lake, which was almost the size of a small bay itself. The coastal marshes were close to the bodies of water. Just beyond them were thick groves of trees.[19]

Houston would remain here while his scouts went out for more detail. The Twin Sisters were placed in the edge of the live oak timber for concealment. The oxen and horses were turned loose to graze.

In this little timber grove in the late morning of April 20, Sam Houston's army was joined by another small company of nine men under Captain Benjamin Cromwell Franklin. A thirty-year-old lawyer educated at Franklin College in Georgia, Franklin was a member of Captain Calder's company during the early days of the San Jacinto campaign. While the army was camped above San Felipe, he was dispatched to Galveston. There, President David Burnet had appointed Franklin a captain in the Texas Army on April 7, although he had few men to actually recruit in Galveston.[20]

Benjamin Cromwell Franklin (1805–1873) was commissioned as a captain of volunteers on April 7 by President Burnet. He fought at San Jacinto as a private in Captain Robert Calder's company and in 1844 wrote an anonymous account of the battle.
(Previously published in Wharton's *San Jacinto: The Sixteenth Decisive Battle*.)

On April 19, a courier crossed the ferry to Galveston, bringing news that General Houston was determined to fight. According to Franklin, the island contained only "the sick, infirm, and women and children upon it, in addition to the members of the government." Including himself, Captain Franklin had but nine total men "capable of bearing arms." President Burnet nonetheless ordered him to join the main army with haste.

> Never were orders more cheerfully obeyed. Accordingly, providing ourselves with arms, ammunition, and one day's provisions, we manned an eight-oar cutter; and in two hours after the arrival of the courier, were on the Bay of Galveston, my eight companions bending stoutly to the aspen breeze, and I in the stern sheets steering. We were all full of anxiety and hope, anxious not to be too late, full of the hope of victory.

Franklin's men had traveled all night across Galveston Bay, arriving the morning of April 20 at the junction of the San Jacinto River and Buffalo Bayou. His men soon found Houston's main army in the timber half a mile from Lynch's Ferry. Franklin's nine extra rifles were well received, as were the six kegs of powder they brought from Galveston, which were very handy for the artillery company.

> Immediately on my landing, I repaired to the general's tent, and, delivering my despatches, looked around me to observe our position. A scene singularly wild and picturesque presented itself to my view.
> Around some twenty or thirty camp-fires stood as many groups of men, English, Irish, Scotch, French, Germans, Italians, Poles, Yankees, Mexicans, all unwashed, unshaven for months, their long hair, beard and mustaches,

ragged and matted, their clothes in tatters, and plastered with mud. In a word, a more savage band could scarcely have been assembled; and yet many—most indeed, were gentleman, owners of large estates, distinguished some for oratory, some for science, and some for medical talent, many would have, and had, graced the drawing-room.

Supply Boat Captured

Colonel Robert Coleman's scouting patrol had an eventful morning. According to George Duncan Hancock, he and Rodden Crain, Dexter Watson, Sanford Holman, Benjamin Thomas and David Brown had been selected from Captain Kimbro's San Augustine company for this scout.[21]

Moving toward Lynch's Ferry around 10:00 a.m., Coleman's party had spotted a small sail coming up the bayou. Kimbro's men hid themselves along the bayou and lay in wait as a small ferry flatboat sailed toward them. Coleman found the approaching vessel to be "a large flat boat under sail, manned by 10 Mexicans, and loaded with provisions."[22]

Coleman's party hailed the men in the boat to come ashore. When the request was not honored, half a dozen musket shots in the general direction of the Mexican boat were enough to send the crew diving overboard. One man remained aboard, lying flat on the bottom. "Don't shoot! Don't shoot!" he cried out. "I am an American." The passenger was told to show himself and he turned out to be another one of the captured *Telegraph* printers who had been taken by Santa Anna at Harrisburg on April 15.[23]

Colonel Robert Morris Coleman (1799–1837) of General Houston's staff led a small scouting party which captured a ferryboat full of supplies on April 20. Coleman was the ghost author of a very detailed 1837 campaign account which was critical of Sam Houston's character. (From DeShields' *Border Wars of Texas*.)

Unable to manage the boat alone, he was assisted by several of Coleman's men who swam over and commandeered the Mexican supply boat. The supplies aboard had been taken from New Washington before the town was burned, and the crew was ordered to sail up the bayou to Santa Anna's forces.

Coleman's party brought the little boat up the bayou near the Texian encampment to a "convenient landing place." Aboard they found flour, coffee, meal and salt, which were very well received, as what meager provisions were available had been left at Major McNutt's camp at Harrisburg.

"It was loaded with flour and supplies, and was also intended to transport Santa Anna and his army across the bayou," wrote Private James Winters. "The supplies were very timely for the Texans."[24]

The men in camp were excited to finally have barrels of flour to make bread with. "I secured a small tin pan full, and having made it into dough, I threw it on the hot embers, and in ten minutes it was bread," wrote Dr. Labadie. Once cooked, his little bread loaf was such a popular item that he only managed to save for himself a piece "scarcely as large as a common biscuit."[25]

Private Alfonso Steele was happy with the captured supplies.

> This was the first bread we had had in some time. We had left our cooking utensils at Harrisburg, so we had nothing to cook bread in. We made it up in tin cups and roasted it in the ashes or rolled it on sticks and cooked it that way. We feasted that day—the 20th.[26]

Colonel Sherman's scouts rode back to the Texas camp with their latest intelligence. Sherman briefed Sam Houston on his morning's actions against the Mexican scout patrol. He also brought the news that Santa Anna's men had moved up from New Washington.

Shortly thereafter, the Mexican cavalry was observed to be in motion across the prairie. The Mexican scouts picked up on the Texans' trail and soon were advancing in the general direction of the thicket where General Houston's Texian army was concealed. If challenged on the open prairie, the Mexicans would hold the advantage in sheer number of men and in superior cavalry forces. If challenged in the timber, the Texas riflemen could use the cover of their live oak thicket for deadly work from their long rifles.[27]

Santa Anna was likely feeling bold, as only a small number of the hidden Texans could be seen. Aware that Sam Houston had his men hidden away in the woods near Lynch's Ferry, he sent forward a force to flush out his quarry. The sounds of trumpets from Mexican musicians grew steadily louder as the troops approached Houston's thicket. According to Colonel Pedro Delgado, Santa Anna "ordered the company of Toluca to deploy as skirmishers in the direction of the woods" in which the Texian rebels were hidden. His musicians reportedly played "Deguello," or the "beheading song," which had been the "no quarter" music played by the Mexican army in March while the Alamo was being overrun.[28]

According to General Houston, it was 11:30 a.m. when the Mexican troops marched against his forces on April 20. Some sixty men anxiously gathered near the Twin Sisters, which were still tucked in the shadows of the tree line. Houston ordered his men to lie down flat on the grass to help conceal the number of Texans present. The general himself appeared "restless and uneasy, walking backward and forward, casting his eyes toward the cannon and toward the advancing enemy."[29]

Colonel Sherman's infantrymen lay hidden in the woods to the left, while Colonel Edward Burleson's First Regiment lay in a strip of woods to the right. Lieutenant Colonel Henry Millard's two regular companies lay near the Twin Sisters in the center of the thicket.[30]

The Twin Sisters were manned by volunteers assigned since the pieces had reached the Texan camp near Groce's. Another eight men from Captain Amasa Turner's and Captain Andrew Briscoe's regular companies had been temporarily assigned to the artillery for the battle. Another man who assisted the artillery was twenty-five-year-old John Ligett Marshall of Captain Baker's company. A San Felipe blacksmith by trade, Marshall said that the men cut up old pieces of iron, chains and horseshoes to make cannonballs for the Twin Sisters.[31]

Commanded by Captain George Poe, Thomas Green and Ben McCullough manned one of the cannon. The second was commanded by Captain Isaac Moreland, Lieutenant William Shaler Stilwell and First Sergeant Thomas Pliney Plaster, the latter a twenty-two-year-old Tennessean who had recently served on the Texas frontiers as a volunteer ranger. Each command team was assisted by a full crew who would sponge, ram, point and haul the cannon into position.

Not a whisper was heard among the Texans as they lay prone in the weeds on the cold, wet ground. The only sound was the ever-increasing

First Sergeant Thomas Pliney Plaster
(1804–1861) was a key gun crew member of one of the Twin Sisters cannon
on April 20.
*Courtesy of the San Jacinto Museum of
History, Houston.*

blare of the Mexican trumpets approaching. Near the Twin Sisters, Lieutenant Colonel James Neill and Captains Poe and Moreland stood waiting.

"Moreland, are you ready?" General Houston called to his friend. Captain Moreland informed the commander-in-chief that the enemy was still too far distant to fire. Moreland's messmate, Dr. Nicholas Labadie, suggested that the guns were too highly elevated to properly bear on the advancing cavalrymen.

Before Moreland's artillerymen could completely lower the cannon's elevation, General Houston barked out, "Clear the guns and fire!"

The Twin Sisters, which had not even been test fired during the San Jacinto campaign due to a shortage of cannonballs, roared to life. Their first shot was too high and failed to do any damage, but it did frighten the Mexican cavalrymen enough to wheel around and retreat toward their main body once again.[32]

Some accounts of San Jacinto have claimed that the Twin Sisters were not the first cannon to fire on April 20. Enough controversy ensued later, however, to indicate that the Texans did fire the first shot.

Some of the infantrymen, lying prone in the grass, were upset that the Texas cannon was fired so soon, for it gave away their element of surprise. Lieutenant Colonel Neill, a seasoned fighter who had served at Horseshoe Bend, would later respond in his defense, "You know I am too old a soldier to fire without orders."[33]

Sergeant Moses Bryan confirms that the Twin Sisters were first to fire and that Houston later denied giving such an order.

> Col. Neill opened on them with the Twin Sisters, which caused the enemy to halt and finally to fall back, as they evidently did not expect to encounter cannon. Here was another disputed point between the General and Col. Neill—General Houston saying that he had not ordered the cannon to fire, and Col. Neill, alleging that he had.[34]

The bark of the Twin Sisters was enough of a challenge to invoke the ire of Santa Anna. Soon after this episode, he sent his own artillery piece, dubbed the Golden Standard, out onto the field to challenge the Texans. At a distance nearly halfway between the two armies, roughly 150 yards from Houston's men, was a thick little island of oak trees. Captain Fernando Urriza's artillerymen towed the Golden Standard to this spot.

There is some disagreement over the size of the Mexican cannon, but all agreed that it was much larger than the Texans' own pieces. Sergeant William Swearingen wrote that the enemy "came in sight" of the Texan's timber grove "with their 9 pounder in the center." Dr. Labadie felt that the enemy sported a "twelve-pound brass piece."[35]

Replicas of the Twin Sisters prepare to fire during a reenactment on the San Jacinto battlegrounds. At each cannon, the gunner stands ready to watch the effects of the shot. The spongers, loaders and rammers have already prepared the shot.
Author's photo, courtesy of the San Jacinto Museum of History, Houston.

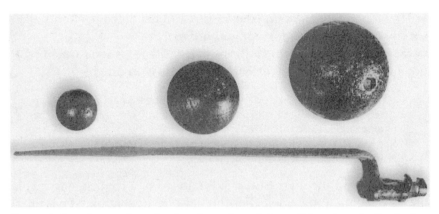

Cannonballs and grapeshot, showing the variety of sizes, all found on the San Jacinto battlegrounds. The Mexican army fired brass cannister rounds, while the Texan gunners used molded lead and even melted horseshoes to form its rounds. This larger cannonball is a 4¼" diameter cast-iron ball, weighing 12 pounds. In center is a 3" diameter 4-pound ball. At left is a smaller 1½" diameter brass grapeshot ball. *Courtesy of the San Jacinto Museum of History, Houston.*

Colonel Thomas Rusk agreed that the Golden Standard was a nine-pounder.

> The appearance of our foe was hailed by our soldiers with enthusiasm. The enemy marched in good order, took a position in front of our encampment, on an eminence, within cannon-shot, where they planted their only piece of artillery, a brass nine-pounder.[36]

The Mexican artillery opened fire first this time, lobbing shots of grape into the trees where the Texans were concealed. The first few rounds whistled by overhead, cutting limbs from the trees above, which fell among Houston's men. After clipping the trees, the first shots splashed harmlessly into Buffalo Bayou and on the opposite bank.

General Houston ordered Lieutenant Colonel Neill's artillery to advance and the two little Texas cannon were rolled forward about ten paces onto the edge of the prairie. Colonel Robert Coleman, for one, wondered whether this was the right move "to display our whole strength before they came within rifle shot."[37]

The next shot of the Twins Sisters, its second firing of the day, landed to the right of the Mexican artillerymen. "We commenced with our cannon, hoping they would charge with their infantry to take them," wrote Sergeant Swearingen. "By that means we could cut them off and if possible take Santa Anna prisoner, or kill him."

Following each cannon shot, the artillery crews hustled to lever their cannon back into position to the gunner's satisfaction. Each repercussion drove the cannon backwards and sent the crews scrambling to prepare their fieldpiece for its next firing.

J. C. Neill's men drew the first blood on the San Jacinto battlefield on April 20. One of the early shots killed two pack mules which were harnessed to the Golden Standard and splintered the Mexicans' ammunition box. Captain Urriza was hit and was severely wounded and his horse was killed by this shot.[38]

After weeks of waiting for true contact with the enemy, both sides were now content to spar lightly. The Texian and Mexican cannon traded shots with each other. Each commander refrained from committing his main body of troops at this time. Miraculously, no Texans were injured during the first half hour of firing. "The grape and canister shot went whistling and rattling through the tops of the trees," wrote Private John Swisher. "We felt no uneasiness from this," for the troops were well protected in their little thicket.[39]

Beyond the enemy artillerymen, Dr. Labadie noted that some enemy soldiers were taking shelter in another island of timber which was located farther away, about four hundred yards from the road which led to the marsh. He saw that the enemy's infantrymen had also taken cover in the tall grass, which was almost waist high. Labadie patiently waited nearly forty-five minutes, stalking forward and hoping to pick off one of the Mexican soldiers with his rifle. The enemy soldiers lay still, watching the artillery exchange, and Labadie finally tired of waiting for a closer shot.[40]

He eased back into the thicket near the Twin Sisters. As he approached, he witnessed the Mexican artillerymen finally land a destructive shot. A grapeshot struck Lieutenant Colonel Neill as he commanded the Texan guns. Neill fell "almost perpendicularly" with a broken hip. Another of the grapeshots passed "within four inches of my head," wrote Labadie. The ball rolled a few feet more and dug into the earth. Picking it up, he "found it a three or four-ounce copper ball."

The Texas infantrymen were held in check during this early skirmishing. Captain Moseley Baker found that "it was with the utmost difficulty that I could prevent my company from rushing on the enemy."[41]

General Houston then ordered Colonel Sherman to lead about half of the mounted men out to an island of timber to take possession of it. This group had been mounted in their saddles awaiting such an order. The men included those of cavalry Captains Henry Karnes and William Smith and some under Captain William Logan, whose company had been largely mounted before joining Houston's army.

Private Luke Bryan, one of Logan's men, rode out with Sidney Sherman.

> On the morning of the 20th of April, we were ordered out to an island of timber. Capt. Logan's company was on the right, I rode by his side, Col. Sherman being a short distance to the right of Capt. Logan.[42]

Upon entering the timber, however, Sherman's men found that Mexican infantrymen were already there, concealed in large numbers. Their numbers were estimated at as many as four hundred. Against overwhelming numbers and unable to fight in such a thicket on horseback, Sherman immediately ordered his men to retreat. The Mexican riflemen opened fire on the retreating Texas cavalrymen, killing several horses and wounding others.[43]

His rifle still in hand, Dr. Labadie had advanced twenty yards from the edge of the Texan thicket on foot and had taken a stance "to see if I could pick some of them off." Instead of Mexicans fleeing from the thicket, he saw Sherman's men beat a hasty retreat back in his direction. He saw a mare ridden by First Sergeant Edward Branch of Captain Logan's company get killed.

Branch's mare fell and he went down with her. "Picking up his rifle, he ran towards me as if for life, causing a hearty laugh, in which he joined," wrote Labadie. Another "fine stallion" belonging to Matthew Mark Moss of Captain Ware's company was also killed.

In addition, Private John Coker of Captain Karnes' company lost a horse that was later valued at $175. John Balch from Captain Wyly's company was later paid for the loss of a horse, saddle and bridle that he had apparently loaned out to one of Sherman's cavalrymen.[44]

As the Mexican infantrymen advanced, General Houston allowed one round of fire from some of his riflemen. "Houston gave orders that those men who lived upon the Navidad and Lavaca and killed deer at a hundred paces offhand should come forward and take a shot at the Mexicans," recalled Sergeant Tony Menchaca. About fifty Texans quickly formed a line and were allowed to fire one solid volley.[45]

Those few Texans who did get to fire enjoyed the action. "We had a good deal of fun mixed with danger that day," recalled Private John Harvey of Captain Arnold's company. "A warm discharge of small arms took place, without, however, any serious effect," wrote Captain Benjamin Franklin. "I waited impatiently for the signal for close engagement, but it was not given."

Captains Poe and Moreland had also turned the Twin Sisters toward this other patch of woods in support of Sherman's retreating men. Shots were fired into this heavy cluster of oaks, with trees being snapped in half above the Mexican soldiers' heads. The accurate shots of the Twin Sisters forced the Mexican infantry "to make a hasty retreat."[46]

Following the Toluca company toward shelter, the Mexican artillerymen soon chose to withdraw the Golden Standard from its advanced position in the thicket 150 yards away. The Texans had thus won the first round at San Jacinto.

Sergeant Swearingen of the regulars wrote that "they fell back to a piece of high prairie in front and immediately commenced fortifying with brush, baggage, etc." Captain Franklin, newly arrived from Galveston with his eight men and posted on the left wing of the battlefield, felt that the enemy's infantry looked "exceedingly grand in the picturesque costume of Mexican soldiers," by comparison to the generally ragged look of Houston's army.[47]

Once Sherman's horsemen had safely retreated from the range of the Mexican riflemen, the action began to dwindle. The firing eventually died off as the range became extreme for both parties. For the Texans, there was a mid-afternoon break.

General Houston used this lull to write an update to President Burnet. He noted the day's action had lasted from 11:30 a.m. to 3:00 p.m., when Santa Anna "withdrew his forces from the field." In estimating the number of troops present, Houston wrote, "His force is reported at 800; ours does not exceed 750." Houston listed only one Texan wounded (Colonel Neill) and an estimated 18–20 Mexicans lost. He penned his note from "Camp Safety," at Lynch's Crossing, San Jacinto.[48]

Many Texans chose to make an afternoon meal from the captured enemy flour, having missed their breakfast and lunch this day. A member of Captain Stevenson's company, John Swisher, was happy to finally get something to eat.

> We went to the bayou, washed our dirty handkerchiefs and mixed the dough on them. We then got sticks about the size of a man's wrist, wrapped the dough around them, and held it over the fire until it was well browned. I thought I had never eaten anything so delicious in all my life as that bread.

Private George Erath felt that it "was a change from our rough living on half-cooked beef and corn ground by ourselves."[49]

While the men found time to eat a late lunch, the general's staff had time to review the action thus far. Their own artillery had proven effective, wounding some of the Mexicans, killing two packhorses, and driving enemy infantrymen back. The little skirmish had cost Sam Houston's army at least three horses killed, several others wounded and Lieutenant Colonel Neill seriously wounded.

Not all of the Mexican officers were pleased with the way President Santa Anna had handled the first skirmish on April 20.

During the cannon exchange of the early afternoon, Santa Anna had ordered Colonel Pedro Delgado to unload his twenty mules' worth of ordnance stores. Captain Barragán was then sent with eighteen mules to fetch the infantrymen's knapsacks, which had been hastily dropped at the roadside during the morning's reconnoitering of the Texian army.[50]

Soon after Delgado had unloaded all of the ordnance stores, Santa Anna selected the area he would make as his campground. The spot lay near the San Jacinto River at the edge of a small thicket. Between the little thicket and the river lay marshlands and a large body of water known as Peggy's Lake.

Lieutenant Colonel Juan Bringas was sent to order Delgado to gather his ordnance stores and move them to the new campground, about one mile from where the ordnance had first been unloaded. Having been left with only two mules after Captain Barragán's departure, Delgado was not happy. Bringas had also ordered the Toluca company to withdraw from the fight with the Texans.

Delgado complained that "should the company of Toluca leave me unsupported, the enemy would probably pounce upon the stores, all of which would go to the devil." Bringas advised his fellow officer to "do the best he could." Besides, added Bringas, it was not worth complaining to His Excellency while he was in such a "raving state of mind."

Sherman's "Little Squad of Heroes"

Colonel Sidney Sherman was perhaps the most determined man to engage Santa Anna. He was eager to follow up on the first successful skirmish of the day. He rode to General Houston's side around 4:00 p.m. with a proposal to seize the Mexican cannon. The enemy's cannon posed a continued threat to the Texans and was protected only by a unit of Mexican cavalry estimated at one hundred men. Sherman recalled:

> The enemy's only field piece was in sight from our camp, and had been annoying us during the day. Late in the evening, I proposed to General Houston to allow me to call for volunteers, and capture their gun.[51]

Given permission, Sherman would personally lead an assault of mounted volunteers upon the Golden Standard. Houston opposed the idea, saying that it would be a great and unnecessary hazard.[52]

Sherman was adamant, however, and continued to argue his case before the commander-in-chief. Sherman won over the support of Colonel George Hockley, whom Houston had more confidence in. Houston finally consented to let Sherman "reconnoiter" the enemy's forces and Sherman immediately proceeded to drum up volunteers. Being that his mission was voluntary, he could not force the two cavalry companies of Henry Karnes and William Smith to participate. Those that were willing were free to join him. Those that saw the venture as suicidal were free to pass their horses to another rider who volunteered.

A study of the service papers of those serving at San Jacinto shows that a number of men from other companies did indeed swap with some of the cavalrymen.

In addition to the volunteers, many of the men who had previously served as scouts and spies were quick to volunteer, such as Captain Henry Karnes, Robert Handy of General Houston's staff, Robert Goodloe, William Taylor, Captain William Smith, the ever resourceful Deaf Smith, John Carpenter, Thomas Fowle, James Cook, Perry Alsbury, Walter Lane, William Crittenden, Moses Lapham, Dr. Fielding Deadrick, his brother George Deadrick and William Foster Young. The latter, a thirty-five-year-old cavalryman known for his honesty, truth and benevolence, was nicknamed "Honest Billy" Young.[53]

Among the volunteers was George Sutherland, formerly of Captain Walker's Brazos River volunteer guards. Matthew Cartwright, a twenty-one-year-old of Captain William Ware's company, took his horse and fell in with Sherman's volunteers. Third Sergeant Oliver T. Brown of Captain Wood's Kentucky Riflemen "was selected as one of the horsemen" by his former captain, Sidney Sherman. From Captain Baker's company, there was Private John Duncan, who had been a

Among those who volunteered to ride into the skirmish on April 20 with Colonel Sidney Sherman was James W. Robinson (1790–1857), a former acting Governor of the Republic of Texas. (Previously published in Wharton's *San Jacinto: The Sixteenth Decisive Battle*.)

Walter Paye Lane (1817–1892) was a nineteen-year-old Irish-born youth of Captain Karnes' cavalry unit. He nearly lost his life during Sherman's April 20 cavalry skirmish, saved only by another man's bravery. (Previously published in DeShields' *Border Wars of Texas*.)

volunteer under Sherman during the morning's reconnaissance "made in the direction of New Washington."[54]

Then there was eighteen-year-old Algernon Thompson, freshly arrived in Texas from New York. He joined the Texas Army near Mill Creek in early April and was placed in Captain Robert Calder's company. On April 20, he had been ordered by Adjutant General John Wharton into the company of Captain William Fisher "for the sake of uniformity of arms," as he carried a musket and bayonet, versus the riflemen of Calder's company. Having no long loyalties to Fisher's company yet, Thompson joined the recruits Sherman was gathering.[55]

There was also James W. Robinson, who had just recently served as the acting Governor of the Republic of Texas. Peter Hansbrough Bell, destined to be the third Governor of the State of Texas, was also among the new U.S. volunteers riding into action with Captain Karnes. Another volunteer was Sergeant James Sylvester, the color bearer for Sherman's old Kentucky Rifles company.

Available horses were pulled from other companies who had men both mounted and unmounted. Second Corporal Ambrosia Rodriquez of Captain Seguin's company had his horse, saddle, bridle and mountings pressed into service and never saw them again.[56]

It is possible that the Rodriguez horse may have gone to another U.S. volunteer, Mirabeau Lamar, the Georgian who had walked until joining the Texas Army. With his borrowed horse, Private Lamar would prove himself to be a true hero before the day was out.

In drumming up volunteers for his mission, Sherman found Colonel Edward Burleson, commanding the First Regiment, to be very supportive of his plan.

> I immediately applied to Col. Burleson, for permission to call on his regiment for volunteers, to mount for the purpose; the cavalry offering to give up their horses to those who would volunteer. The Colonel remarked that I might take all that would volunteer, if I wanted them, and that he would parade the balance of his regiment, and march out to sustain us, if necessary.[57]

Sherman recruited sixty-eight volunteers willing to ride into action. He had asked for support and did receive a token offering from Houston. "Col. Hockley came and informed me that General Houston would order out Lieutenant-Colonel Millard, with his command, to sustain me, if necessary," wrote Sherman.

George Sutherland, later elected a Texas Congressman, was counting on the infantry's support of their mission.

> After we had mounted, I asked Colonel Sherman if we were to be backed by the infantry? He answered, "I expect so"; but he turned round to General Houston, and said, "General, are we to be supported by the infantry?" Houston replied, "Certainly, sir; do you think I would send you there to be killed?"[58]

Wanting to avoid starting a general conflict on this day, Houston had only offered Lieutenant Colonel Millard's regular army companies of Captains Andrew Briscoe and Amasa Turner for support. These two companies did not even reach ninety men in combined strength.

Colonel Sherman, being as circumspect as he was brave, rode to the other leaders of infantry and artillery companies and informed them of his plans, quietly soliciting assistance from them should he need it.

> Before I left the camp, I rode up to Captain Poe, and requested him to keep up his fire on the enemy's cannon, until I should approach so near it, as no longer to allow him to fire with safety; and I informed Col. Millard of the infantry, that I was then ready to move to the attack, and got him to form his command, and march them to a ravine, until the assault should actually be made.[59]

Captain George Poe, one of the two artillery captains present, wrote Sherman several years after the battle. "I distinctly recollect," wrote Poe, "that you told me you intended to take the artillery from the enemy, and wished me to open a fire from my guns to second your attempt; which I did."

Sherman "selected 70 horsemen out of the different regiments to make the attack," Sergeant Oliver Brown wrote two weeks later. Lieutenant Colonel Joe Bennett, second-in-command of the Second Regiment wrote that Sherman rode into acton with "about sixty-eight men." Bennett recalled that Millard's regulars were paraded "for the purpose of sustaining Col. Sherman, in case of necessity, and marched out into a ravine, to wait until he commenced the attack."[60]

Colonel Thomas Rusk, the Texas Secretary of War, and Major Lysander Wells of Sherman's Second Regiment joined the volunteer Texas cavalrymen paraded on the field. "We struck off, at a brisk trot," wrote Wells, "and soon discovered the Mexican mounted men, sitting quietly on their horses, near a thick wood, and about half a mile from our position."[61]

By the time Sherman's mounted men moved out into the field, Colonel Pedro Delgado had succeeded in moving all of his ordnance stores across the prairie to Santa Anna's new campground at the edge of the trees.

During the hour that Sherman was organizing his volunteers, Delgado's only two mules had worked furiously to haul the undamaged supplies into the main camp. Lieutenant Arenal had taken acting command of the Golden Standard once Captain Urriza had fallen wounded earlier in the day. He kept the cannon loaded with grape, but held his fire to conserve ammunition. Delgado had ordered Arenal "not to fire until the enemy came within close range, in order to spare ammunition and to intimidate the assailants."[62]

By 5:00 p.m., the ordnance was safely moved and Colonel Delgado moved his men back toward the main camp. Lieutenant Arenal's men withdrew their cannon at this time also, just as the Texian horsemen under Sherman were seen to be moving onto the battlefield.

Seeing the Texans approaching the retreating cannon, Santa Anna gave orders for the cavalry commander, Captain Miguel Aguirre, to advance his men. Aguirre's men were not to invoke a full battle, but "to face the enemy, without gaining ground."

———————

As Sherman's men advanced across the field, he divided his sixty-eight volunteers into three squads. The left wing was commanded by Major Wells, the center by Captain William Smith and the right by Captain Henry Karnes. Secretary of War Rusk counted one hundred Mexican cavalrymen advancing toward them.

According to Private Walter Lane, riding with Captain Karnes' right wing, the Mexican officers rode out front and verbally challenged the Texans to, "Venga aquí (Come here)."[63]

The Texans took this verbal challenge and the cry to "Charge!" rang out as Texan horsemen spurred their horses forward. As Sherman's volunteers rushed into combat, the Golden Standard began firing again from the spot where it had been hurriedly hauled away to earlier.

"Daringly the rebels threw themselves on my cavalry," General Santa Anna detailed. "For a moment they succeeded in throwing us into confusion."[64]

Major Wells of the Second Regiment later summarized the action.

> *Whiz!* came a shower of grape from their confounded piece of artillery, which they had stationed at the edge of the timber, to the right of their cavalry. At the same time, four companies of infantry came filing out from near the cannon, apparently with the design of cutting off our retreat.
>
> This did not stop us; we drove their cavalry nearly back to their cannon; when their trumpet sounded *no quarter!* we were, in turn, forced back a short distance; but were soon rallied by our gallant Colonel, and again returned to the charge, with the like success.[65]

The Texan horsemen were largely riflemen, which forced some of them to fall back after the first charge to reload their awkward long rifles. The Mexicans, seeing about half of the Texans on the ground reloading their guns, immediately dashed upon them. The Texans defended their fellow soldiers the best way possible until they were remounted and their guns loaded again. Sherman then ordered his men to charge a second time, and they drove the Mexicans back again.

At least two Mexican soldiers were seen to be wounded. Santa Anna, watching the action from the edge of the field, had commanded

Major Lysander Wells (1812–1840) led the left wing of Sherman's cavalry into action on April 20. (Previously published in Wharton's *San Jacinto: The Sixteenth Decisive Battle*.)

his orderly bugler to sound, "No quarter!" This was the deadly "deguello" song also played at the Alamo. Santa Anna ordered two companies of riflemen to join in the fight to support his cavalry.

"Their infantry came to the assistance of their cavalry," wrote Colonel Rusk, "and opened upon us an incessant fire for ten or fifteen minutes."[66]

From a distance, former Kentucky legislator James Tarlton watched the action with Captain Baker's company. "Col. Sherman, with his characteristic bravery, gallantly led on his little squad of heroes to the charge." Private John Duncan, one of the cavalry volunteers this day, felt that Colonel Sherman "exhibited skill and coolness" throughout the action.[67]

There were many acts of bravery. Among the volunteers fighting with Captain Karnes' right wing was "one of Fannin's men, who had been led out to be shot, but made his escape." Major Wells later claimed that this man (likely David Jones) "behaved most gallantly" and was probably all too happy to fire back at those who had slaughtered his friends at La Bahia.[68]

In the height of the action, Sherman's volunteers came under fire from the enemy's cavalry, artillery and finally the two companies of infantry. General Houston finally allowed one of the Twin Sisters to be advanced.

Captain Moreland advanced his gun with seven other men, including Dr. Nicholas Labadie, who was officially unassigned for the battle, and Olwyn Trask. Holding his rifle in one hand, Labadie "took hold of the rope with the other, and we moved forward pretty briskly about

300 yards." It required the full strength of the eight artillerymen to move the iron cannon over the soft prairie ground.[69]

Devereaux Jerome Woodlief, a thirty-year-old Virginian of Karnes' cavalry company, was shot in the hip during the charge with Colonel Sherman. Dr. Labadie left the artillery to assist the wounded man. Leading Woodlief's horse to a large oak, Labadie and Woodlief's companion helped him down from his horse. He was laid out in the grass and his head rested upon a large knot of the oak tree to support him.

The Texans soon suffered a second casualty in this skirmish. Shortly after the Twin Sisters cannon had been advanced onto the battlefield, Olwyn Trask was hit and suffered a broken thigh bone. He was helped across the field to where the surgeons had gathered to assist Woodlief.

After probing Trask's wound, Dr. Labadie announced that "it was either grape-shot or a scopette ounce ball." Doctors Alexander Ewing and Anson Jones, however, felt that Trask had only been hit by a common bullet and decided to examine for themselves. As this wounded man did not belong to his regiment, Dr. Labadie left the others to continued probing the poor man and argue over the size of the shot which had hit him.

Into "The Hornet's Nest"

The first charge of the Mexican cavalrymen had been turned back by timely Texan rifle fire. The fact that the Texian infantry companies had been held back from participating gave the Mexican soldiers enthusiasm to surge forward. Colonel Sherman's men were in the process of reloading their rifles again when Captain Aguirre ordered his men to charge for the second time. With their sabers drawn, the Mexican cavalry bore down onto the momentarily defenseless Texans.

George Sutherland, Matthew Cartwright, and Sergeant Robert Goodloe each had their horses killed under them during this second charge. Goodloe remembered his "horse having been shot from under me on the evening of the 20th." From Captain Logan's company, William Kibbe, originally from Vermont, later certified that he also had a grey horse killed out from under him in the April 20 "evening" skirmish.[70]

The men who lost horses were able to scramble away from the advancing Mexican soldiers. Other men, however, came into serious

Dr. Robert Kemp Goodloe (1813–1879) was one of at least four Texans who had their horses shot out from under them during the April 20 afternoon skirmish. (From Dixon and Kemp's *The Heroes of San Jacinto*.)

danger during this close combat. Colonel Rusk was penned in during the second Mexican advance and might have been captured had not Mirabeau Lamar charged in on his large stallion and knocked down a Mexican horseman on a smaller mount, opening an escape route for himself and Rusk.

San Jacinto veteran Moses Austin Bryan later wrote of Private Lamar's bravery in the *Texas Almanac* of 1872.

> General Rusk went out to reconnoiter the Mexican lines, and before he was aware of it, some Mexican lancers had surrounded him, and were closing on him, when General M. B. Lamar, who had joined us only about two weeks before the battle, saw Colonel Rusk's situation, and made a dash at one of the lancers, run against him, knocking down the lancer and his horse, and making an opening for the escape of Colonel Rusk, the Secretary of War.

Lamar then saved the life of nineteen-year-old Walter Lane, who had been knocked from his horse. Private Lane went into his first battle on April 20 on a fine horse with a double-barreled rifle and a brace of pistols.

> My horse—a powerful animal—had got excited, and having more zeal than discretion, took the bit in his teeth and ran me headlong into the midst of the enemy, much to my disgust. The order was given to retreat. I was unanimously in favor of it, but my horse wanted to go through. A Mexican officer settled the difficulty by cutting at my head with his saber.
>
> I threw up my gun and warded off the blow. My gun was empty. I drew a holster pistol, aimed at his head and pulled trigger. It missed fire; he tucked his head down to avoid the shot, when I hit him over the head with the pistol, knocking him senseless.[71]

In the same instant, a large Mexican lancer charged Lane and knocked him from his horse. The young Texan hit the ground hard and

Private Walter Lane narrowly escapes being overrun by Mexican soldiers after being knocked from his horse. Future Texas president Mirabeau Lamar held off Mexican lancers while Captain Henry Karnes pulled the youth to safety.
"Sherman's First Skirmish." Oil painting by Charles Shaw, courtesy of the San Jacinto Museum of History, Houston.

was momentarily knocked senseless. Seeing him fall, Captain Karnes ordered his company to turn and support their fallen man. Lane then witnessed Mirabeau Lamar ride up and shoot the Mexican lancer who was preparing to finish off his prey. Karnes raced in on his old sorrel mare and ordered Lane to jump on as Lamar held off the attackers.

Just days after San Jacinto, Lane would be promoted for his bravery on the field. "I was elected 2nd Lieutenant of Karnes' Spy Company, quite an honor, too, for a 19-year-old boy, for it was composed of such men as Deaf Smith, Wash and Field Secrest, John Coker, Perry Alsbury, and other famous scouts."

Grateful to be alive, Walter Lane would never forget the bony horse which bore him to safety. "I would know her hide if it was dried on a fence even now, and she had the sharpest backbone it has ever been my fortune to straddle."

Santa Anna later summarized this engagement. "I ordered two companies of chasseurs [infantrymen] out to meet them, and these were sufficient to put the enemy to flight back to the woods." Colonel Pedro Delgado, observing the action on the Mexican side, noted that

Captain Aguirre's cavalry had "forced the enemy back to his camp, on which he retired sluggishly and in disorder."[72]

In his official report, General Houston felt that his cavalry had "a sharp recounter with their cavalry, in which ours acted extremely well, and performed some feats of daring chivalry."[73]

By boldly charging into the Texans as they reloaded, Captain Aguirre's men had caught Colonel Sherman's men ill prepared and had forced them to retreat. The Mexican army had thus won the second round of the April 20 duel.

Houston Restrains Infantry

The results of round two might have ended differently had some of the Texas company commanders had their way. The reserve infantrymen had been held back against their will.

Standing by with his company near the edge of the field awaiting orders to join the action, Captain Robert Calder was moved by the gallantry of Sherman's volunteers. Many of those who fought were youngsters with no cavalry training and often only a rifle or pistol, with no swords. Calder felt that Sherman's engagement "was characterized by a spirit of wisdom and true heroism, that can only be ascribed to fearlessness and true patriotism."[74]

Lieutenant Colonel Joe Bennett wrote that Colonel Sherman "drew off his men from their unequal contest with very little injury." Major Lysander Wells, commanding the left wing, was disappointed in the lack of support the cavalrymen had received from their own regular army.

> Finding ourselves exposed to the incessant fire of an unequal number of cavalry, their artillery, and two hundred infantry, and *our own infantry not having come up* to engage theirs, as expected, we were at length obliged, reluctantly, to retire, leaving two fine horses dead upon the field. We were lucky enough to escape the hornets' nest with only two men badly wounded. Two days after, I was informed, by a Mexican soldier, that Santa Anna, in person, commanded the field-piece throughout the skirmish.[75]

The lack of support from Henry Millard's regulars was expressly ordered by General Houston. The commander-in-chief watched

Captain Andrew Briscoe (1810–1849) commanded a spy unit during the campaign and took acting command of Captain Henry Teal's regular Company A for the battle of San Jacinto. Both Briscoe and Captain Amasa Turner's regular Company B were ordered not to join Sherman's skirmish on April 20.
(Previously published in Wharton's *San Jacinto: The Sixteenth Decisive Battle.*)

Sherman's cavalry advance across the field and challenge the enemy. The general conflict that he warned Sherman not to stir up seemed suddenly inevitable as the Mexican artillery, cavalry and some two hundred infantrymen took up the firing on the Texan volunteers.

Turning to his aide-de-camp, Colonel George Hockley, Houston said, "What are they about? I ordered a reconnoiter only! Call off the infantry!"[76]

Whether he agreed with Houston's order or not, Hockley rushed to Lieutenant Colonel Millard and ordered him not to advance across the field in support. General Houston finally sent Colonel Robert Coleman onto the field to order Sherman to call off his mission.[77]

While Millard's regulars were held in check, other companies were eager to fight. Captain Jesse Billingsley was determined to fight and began marching his Bastrop company toward the field to support Sherman's cavalrymen. Other companies of Burleson's regiment joined in with him. "On passing the place where Gen. Houston and his Aide-de-Camp were standing, he ordered us to countermarch," wrote Billingsley.[78]

This order was ignored by some of the men of Colonel Burleson's First Regiment, who hoped to get the long-awaited action with Santa Anna into full gear. The battle was largely over by this point, however, and Billingsley's men were unable to reach the action.

Although he had not succeeded in taking the enemy's cannon, Sidney Sherman did manage to earn the respect of nearly every Texan present for his bravery. He very nearly succeeded in what might have been his ulterior motive—forcing the enemy, and Sam Houston, into a full-blown engagement. Only the brave actions of Private Lamar had spared the Texans from losing two men in conflict, one of whom was their secretary of war.

Had Houston allowed his infantry to advance onto the field on April 20, he certainly would have encouraged Santa Anna to send in his own soldiers. Only Houston's restraint prevented a full-scale engagement on this date.

Both sides pulled back from the battlefield as evening approached. The Texans had suffered four men wounded during the engagements on April 20. This included Lieutenant Colonel James Neill and Devereaux Woodlief with serious hip wounds and Olwyn Trask with a leg wound that would ultimately prove fatal.

Most accounts of San Jacinto only list three Texan casualties for the battles on April 20. A fourth man, however, was verified to have been wounded in action this day. He was Private Thomas C. Utley from North Carolina, a member of Captain William Heard's company.

In Utley's military service record, Heard, William Fisher and Lieutenant Colonel Somervell all certified that Utley volunteered under Colonel Sherman in the skirmish on April 20 and was wounded by grapeshot from the enemy's cannon. Heard wrote that Utley "was wounded in the arm, I believe the left one between the wrist and elbow." The doctors that night would fix Utley with a sling, which prevented him from participating in any further action at San Jacinto. The painful cannon shot wound would trouble him for life.[79]

In his battle report written on April 22, Colonel Rusk confirms that two Texans were wounded in the morning action and two more men were "severely wounded" during Sherman's evening engagement. While Santa Anna had certainly lost some men in action on April 20, Mexican sources give little indication as to how many. Sergeant Oliver Brown estimated, "We killed about 20."[80]

Trask, Woodlief and Utley were helped across the bayou to Vice President Lorenzo de Zavala's house, which became a makeshift hospital. Jonathan Morris of Captain Billingsley's company was assigned to wait upon Colonel Neill and assist him to the hospital, thus preventing Morris from seeing any further action.[81]

The Texian army had lost two other soldiers during the day on April 20. At Camp Harrisburg, Major Robert McNutt was forced to hold funeral services for two soldiers who had died of their illnesses.

Private William Zuber recalled only one death this day. "The deceased was a young man named Hunter, who had been sick with measles for four weeks," he wrote. "Like Felix Wright, he was buried with military honor but without a coffin."[82]

Private James Kuykendall, another of the soldiers left to guard the baggage at Harrisburg, wrote his recollections of the San Jacinto campaign decades before Zuber. Kuykendall recalled that two men died in camp on April 20. "This day two of our sick died and were buried without the customary military honors."[83]

If there was a second man who died of illness this day at Camp Harrisburg, his name has escaped attention in the records of San Jacinto.

Evening chow for the Texans included captured bread and coffee to go with the soldiers' usual boiled beef. The light from numerous campfires illuminated the night around the San Jacinto battleground as the Texas and Mexican armies camped within one mile of each other.

Captain Juan Seguin, commanding the army's all-Tejano company, later wrote that after the skirmish "we resumed the cooking of our meal." This was "composed of meat only, but had the good fortune to capture a boat loaded with provisions, which afforded some seasoning to a repast that otherwise would have been rather scanty."[84]

In addition to the captured flour, some men made their first meal of whatever scraps they still carried in their pockets or from their saddlebags.

Santa Anna's camp was on an eminence with a marsh and a lake behind him, a thicket of woods to his right which followed the edge of the marsh, and an open plain ahead and to the left. The Mexican leader had his tents pitched under a cluster of hardwoods, while his men worked into the night building a defensive breastwork fortification of saddles and supplies.

Sentinels were stationed about the Texan camp and many took their first chance to really catch up on sleep since marching several days before. The guard detail was doubled for the night, as contact with the enemy was expected at any moment.

Fifty guards were ordered to protect the outer lines of the Texan camps. Most of the men were already exhausted from the past two days of marching and the day's action. Sergeant Benjamin Rice Brigham of Captain Calder's company couldn't stand another night of guard detail. In feeble health already, he had been on duty the past two evenings, and few of the Texans had gotten a wink of sleep the previous night. Upon learning that he was again detailed to guard duty this night, Brigham went to his buddies with tears in his eyes.[85]

"I want to be in the battle tomorrow," pleaded the exhausted soldier. "Will some one take my place?"

Francis Jarvis Cooke, a nineteen-year-old, stepped forward and told Brigham that he was willing. "He threw himself on my blanket and in two minutes was sound asleep," wrote Cooke. "He was among the first killed in battle next day. Thus I gave him his last sleep before his last long one."

Around the Texas campfires, men were certain that the coming morning would bring the long-awaited major clash with Santa Anna. Dr. Labadie found that, "A most profound silence prevailed throughout our camp till morning."[86]

Sam Houston beat reveille himself on the night of April 20. Long after his men who were not on guard detail had fallen into a deep sleep, the commander-in-chief remained awake, planning his moves for the coming day.[87]

Many of his officers were planning their fight for the next day. A growing number were compelled to fight the next day, *with or without* their General Houston. Following his evening skirmish, Colonel Sherman had had heated words with General Houston for not allowing the rest of the army to join the fight.

Captain Billingsley wrote that a letter was started by Captain Moseley Baker "setting forth the convictions of many of the most experienced officers of the army, that Houston did not intend to fight." Captain William Heard, for one, believed that Houston's objective in placing Colonel Sherman in charge of the cavalry on the evening of April 20 "was that he knew [Sherman] would fight, chance or no chance, and that [Sherman] would get killed off out of his way."[88]

The men of the army were thoroughly impressed with Sherman's daring and leadership displayed this day. Dr. John Fitzhugh believed, "General Houston had not in his army an officer who bore himself more gallantly and rendered better service" than Sherman.[89]

Captain Baker felt that Houston would procrastinate until Santa Anna received more reinforcements to the point that it would be "an act of madness to engage with him with the small force now at our command." Baker was reportedly supported in his desire to fight by Colonel John Wharton.

Sidney Sherman and his noble volunteers had not succeeded in taking the Mexican cannon on April 20. They had, however, roused the patriotic fighting spirits of most. With Billingsley, Baker and the majority of captains sharing the same mind-set, there would be no further retreating on this campaign.

"The officers entered into a solemn engagement to fight the enemy on the next day," wrote Jesse Billingsley, "General or no General!"

CHAPTER 14

"Burn That Bridge"

April 21

The camping ground of His Excellency's selection was, in all respects, against military rules. Any youngster would have done better.
—Colonel Pedro Francisco Delgado, Mexican Army

The Texian camp was stirring almost an hour before that of the Mexican army. A mile apart from each other on the cattle ranch of Peggy McCormick, the two armies were eager to end the campaign and its incessant marching. The previous day's inconclusive skirmishing had only further whetted the appetites of those most hungry for action.

The tap of reveille sounded on the drum in the Texian camp at 4:00 a.m. on Thursday, April 21. For a change, reveille was not tapped by the commander-in-chief, but by a former slave from New Orleans named Dick. An indentured servant attached to the army's command staff, Dick tapped out the wake-up call while Sam Houston slept soundly.[1]

The general had given orders not to be disturbed on this morning. As Houston took his first sleep of more than three hours since the campaign had begun, some grumbled that he would sleep all day.[2]

The predawn air was brisk, a very cold morning for this late in the spring for coastal Texas. As the camp came to life, many men displayed "cheerful and animated faces," as they expected combat this day. Dr. Nicholas Labadie felt that the most common expression was, "Let us attack the enemy and give them hell at once."[3]

"The reveille of the Mexican army was heard somewhat before 5 o'clock," wrote Colonel Robert Coleman. "The Texians also arose and stood under arms until it was fairly light, expecting every moment orders from their General to march forward and attack the enemy." General Houston, however, remained fast asleep until after 7:00 a.m.[4]

When he did wake up, he lay on his back, studying the sky. He watched an eagle soar across the clear blue sky and reflected on its meaning. His deep Indian lore had taught him to respect this symbol as a good sign.[5]

Santa Anna felt secure with his camp security on the morning of April 21. Three companies of picked men guarded the woods to his right. The permanent Matamoros battalion held battle formation in the center of camp. To his left, the Golden Standard cannon was held in readiness, protected by the cavalry and a column of companies of specially picked men under command of acting Lieutenant Colonel Santiago Luelmo.[6]

Santa Anna had been up long before sunrise, watching the Texan camp with his spyglass. He was also eagerly awaiting the arrival of his reinforcement troops under his brother-in-law, General Martín Perfecto de Cos.

Not all of El Presidente's staff were satisfied with the location of the army's campground. In his account of San Jacinto, Colonel Pedro Delgado recalled his impressions of their setup on the morning of April 21.

> At daybreak on the 21st, His Excellency ordered a breastwork to be erected for the cannon. It was constructed with pack-saddles, sacks of hard bread, baggage &c. A trifling barricade of branches ran along its front and right.
>
> The camping ground of His Excellency's selection was, in all respects, against military rules. Any youngster would have done better.
>
> We had the enemy on our right, within a wood, at long musket range. Our front, although level, was exposed to the fire of the enemy, who could keep it up with impunity from his sheltered position. Retreat was easy for him on his rear and right, while our own troops had no space for maneuvering. We had in our rear a small grove, reaching to the bay shore, which extended on our right as far as New Washington. What ground had we to retreat on in case of a reverse? From sad experience, I answer—None![7]

Colonel Delgado even took up this subject at one point during the morning with General Manuel Castrillon. A loyal and devoted military man, Castrillon obviously shared some of the same sentiment. He was not one to question military orders and he had learned that Santa Anna would not tolerate officers who questioned his choices.

"What can I do, my friend?" he asked.

As the sun rose, the weather faired and the temperature began to rise. Captain Benjamin Franklin led out one of the early scouting patrols on the morning of April 21 and made a crucial sighting about 8:00 a.m. "I saw advancing from the direction of Harrisburg a dense column of men," he wrote. This force approaching the Mexican campground was the four-hundred-man reinforcement division under General Cos. The word was immediately relayed to General Houston, who had been expecting such reinforcements due to his previous intelligence from the captured mail.[8]

Dr. Labadie and Major Nicholas Lynch, adjutant of the army's regular infantry, walked a quarter mile into the prairie to see for themselves. With Lynch's spyglass, they "plainly saw the soldiers walking by the side of the pack-mules, and judged the mules to number about 200."[9]

The ever resourceful Deaf Smith and his captain, Henry Karnes, were sent by General Houston to further ascertain the enemy's reinforcement strength. Among the folklore surrounding the bravery and resourcefulness of Smith is that he actually entered the Mexican camp in disguise to gather intelligence.[10]

Wearing only a ragged shirt and pants, Smith discarded his shoes and donned Captain Bachiller's large sombrero. With his own darkly tanned skin and his tattered appearance, Smith wandered aimlessly into camp under the disguise of a simpleminded Mexican field hand. Captain Karnes watched the whole episode from the safety of cover as Deaf ambled about the Mexican camp counting men. When questioned, he simply played dumb or mumbled a brief answer in Spanish.

Mission completed, Smith eventually wandered off from the enemy camp, met Karnes and his horse, and rode back to share their latest information with Sam Houston.

Major Robert McNutt was anxious to find an excuse to join the battle before it began. His men had clearly heard the booming of the cannon fire the previous evening. Orders were orders, however, and his were to guard the baggage wagons and the sick men left behind at the camp at Harrisburg.

Still, the word could come at any moment that some or all of his men were needed to join the main army. McNutt resolved to patch up the badly leaking flatboat the army had used to cross Sims Bayou two days before. A party of a half dozen able men was sent to repair the raft.

Their hammering and chopping drew the attention of roving Mexican scouts in the early afternoon. The Mexicans fired upon the repair party from across Sims Bayou, striking Private Henry Freed of Captain Gibson Kuykendall's company. According to the captain's brother, Sergeant James Kuykendall, Freed's left leg was "shattered by a musket ball."[11]

Upon hearing the firing by the bayou, Major McNutt had quickly paraded his men, marching a large party of men down to the boat. "The enemy had become invisible," reported Sergeant Kuykendall, "and in a few minutes we started back to camp."

Private William Zuber, who had cried over being left behind at Camp Harrisburg two days prior, was among those who hoped to engage the enemy's snipers at Sims Bayou. Poor Zuber would be once again disappointed.

> Our guard mustered and marched to the scene of action, and on the way we met the wounded boy [Private Freed] on a horse. So far as we could see, every thread of his bandage was deep red with his blood, but the bleeding had stopped. We proceeded to the bayou, but saw no enemies. Then we returned to our encampment.[12]

Future Texas president Mirabeau Lamar had made a name for himself on the San Jacinto battlefield on April 20. The lowly private from Georgia had saved at least two lives during the cavalry charge and for it he was offered two promotions. Incredibly, he declined the promotion offered to him by General Houston and instead accepted a different promotion, only at the insistence of the men he had fought with the previous day.

Houston asked Lamar to take command of his artillery forces for April 21. After the two in later years became bitter political rivals, Houston explained how his offer was declined.

> Col. Neill was wounded, and Capt. Poe, next in command, was not in camp; therefore I proposed the honor of command on Col. Lamar.
>
> What were his reasons for declining he did not state. That was the last incident which occurred between us that day! He positively refused my offer for him to command the Artillery. He may have thought as the command was small, only eighteen men all told, that he would have to go on foot, and as he had a fine horse he possibly did not wish to dispense with.[13]

Captain Poe, who had fought with the artillery on April 20, had received approval to leave and take care of his family. His wife had showed up on the opposite side of the San Jacinto "in great distress." According to General Houston, he was allowed to go "to her relief and did not get back until after the battle."[14]

He planned to return within a few days. The next most senior member of the artillery, and the oldest man in the artillery, was Captain Isaac Moreland. One of Lamar's political foes in 1839 started a rumor that Lamar had tried to supplant Moreland to command the artillery, but Moreland "to this dart of the assertion" flatly denied any wrongdoing.[15]

The word of Private Lamar turning down General Houston's offer of a battlefield commission apparently spread through camp quickly. Colonel Rusk reportedly then invited Lamar to join him as an aide-de-camp to his staff, to which Lamar agreed.

> I remarked to [Rusk], I should like to go with him, as it would afford me a chance of seeing more of the battle; whereupon, he invited me to accompany him, as an aid-de-camp. We accordingly rode off together, unconnected with any command, when I was called back to the command of the cavalry.[16]

Rusk and Lamar were approached by men of the cavalry who called loudly for Lamar to instead command them. He had, of course, saved both Rusk's and young cavalryman Walter Lane's lives the previous day. Lamar refused until both Captains William Smith and Henry Karnes "galloped up to him themselves and said it was their wish as well as that of the men that he should command."[17]

Captain Benjamin Franklin wrote that Lamar was promoted "in consequence of his daring gallantry of the previous day, his comrades insisting on being led by him to the charge." Franklin was moved

General Martín Perfecto de Cos (1800–1854), brother-in-law of General Santa Anna arrived in the Mexican camp on the morning of April 21 with some four hundred additional troops. Born in Veracruz, Cos had entered service in the Mexican army in 1820. *San Jacinto Museum of History, Houston.*

enough to exchange his little command to join the cavalry under Lamar for the expected action of April 21. He counted sixty-one horses part of Lamar's command this day, "so many horses having been killed and wounded on the previous day."[18]

The news of the arrival of General Cos' additional troops made the Texans feel that battle was imminent on the morning of April 21. Colonel Rusk's report explains:

> About nine o'clock, the enemy received a reinforcement of five hundred men, under the command of General Martín Perfecto de Cos, which increased their strength to fourteen or fifteen hundred men. It was supposed that an attack upon our encampment would now be made; and, having a good position, we stationed our artillery, and disposed of the forces, so as to receive the enemy to the best advantage.[19]

As the morning hours ticked away, Rusk and others came to realize that Santa Anna was not showing signs of attack, but was instead fortifying himself.

Santa Anna's troops were elated at the arrival of General Cos and his reinforcements at 9:00 a.m.

Colonel Pedro Delgado, assigned by Santa Anna to head the artillery and ordnance of the Mexican army, explains a crucial decision that was made upon the arrival of Cos' men.[20]

> His arrival was greeted with the roll of drums and joyful shouts. As it was represented to His Excellency that these men had not slept the night before,

he instructed them to stack their arms, to remove their accoutrements, and to go to sleep quietly in the adjoining grove.

Although Santa Anna was pleased with the "favorable reaction that I noted on the men's faces with the arrival of General Cos," he was disappointed in at least a couple of things.[21]

First, Cos had been ordered to bring five hundred of his best foot soldiers from the Velasco area. Instead, he had pulled less experienced men from the battalions of Aldama, Guerrero, Toluca and Guadalajara and had marched rapidly for the Lynchburg area. In the final push to reach Santa Anna, however, one hundred of the men had been slowed with their "loads in bad shape." Those so delayed were left under command of acting Colonel Mariano García while Cos hurried ahead with the remaining four hundred.

Cos arrived at 9:00 a.m. with men who were beat. Santa Anna later wrote that "General Cos and three hundred recruits from the Guerrero battalion under Manuel Cespedes arrived."[22] Due to their forced march, his men had not slept or eaten for over twenty-four hours. Colonel García and the equipment were still following, but were not expected to reach camp for another two or three hours. Cos explained that his men were in need of food and rest.

Santa Anna was not pleased with the troops that he received with General Cos. His orders had been to send "select infantry." To his disgust, he found that many of those with Cos had recently joined the army en route to Texas and were but "raw recruits."[23]

Lieutenant Denham of Captain Calder's company felt that the Texans must react before more Mexican troops arrived. Denham's thoughts are displayed in a letter he wrote from the San Jacinto battlegrounds two weeks after the battle.

> This crisis was now approaching. The battleground was something in the shape of a horseshoe, and if we delayed in attacking them, other reinforcements were on their march to join them, and if they attacked us and we were defeated, there was no possible chance for us to retreat. We had a chance of defeating them, although so much superior to us in everything—they being Santa Anna's choice troops.[24]

Around ten o'clock, Colonel Wharton made the rounds through camp, visiting each mess. His message was loud and quick: "Boys,

Colonel John Austin Wharton (1809–1838) served as General Houston's army adjutant general. On April 21, he went into battle with the Second Regiment. At his funeral, Texas Vice President David Burnet called Wharton "the keenest blade on the field of San Jacinto."
Texas State Library and Archives Commission.

there is no other word today but fight, fight! Now is the time!" The troops became even more eager, although Sam Houston was still showing no more signs of action.[25]

The waiting was more than some could bear. "The greater portion of the day was spent in inactivity," wrote Private John Swisher, "to the great disgust of some few hot-heads and would-be great men, who had condemned General Houston for not fighting at the Colorado."[26]

During the morning hours, Houston had ordered Colonel Coleman to take out several men to reconnoiter the approaching troops of Cos. He also sent Colonel Wharton on a supply-gathering mission. Wharton proceeded to the other side of Buffalo Bayou to scrounge supplies from Dr. de Zavala's home, which had become the makeshift hospital for the Texas Army. Lorenzo de Zavala Jr., one of Houston's aides, was sent over to supervise the removal of all items that could help to sustain the Texians.

Wharton and Houston later allowed a claim by the Zavalas for $680 due for items they had supplied. "I proceeded to the house of Don Lorenzo de Zavala and took possession of such articles as I could find that I thought to be of use to the army," wrote John Wharton. This included a box of carpenter tools, the family's cooking utensils, and a number of shovels, spades, and axes. Also handy was a quantity of lead, nails and other items that were melted down to form shot and balls for the Texas artillery. Also taken was furniture, cash, wines and other provisions deemed necessary to support the army.[27]

During the mid-morning, Houston gave orders to spy Deaf Smith to ascertain the enemy's camp strength. He asked Smith to ride out from the Texan camp along the San Jacinto River to a rise between the two camps and count the Mexican army's tents.

Smith selected Private Walter Lane, who borrowed a horse for this scout. They dismounted their horses at the rise and then eased up through the tall prairie grass to view the enemy's campground. Lane, who had narrowly cheated death in the skirmish the previous day, found himself once again the object of enemy attention.

> Smith pulled out his field glasses, told me to hold his horse, and commenced counting tents to get an estimate of their numbers. We were three hundred yards off. The enemy ran out a company of soldiers and commenced firing on us. The balls whistled over our heads—greatly to my demoralization—but Smith did not notice them.[28]

Deaf Smith estimated the enemy's forces to be about fifteen hundred men. Only when a group of riders was sent out to intercept them did he announce that it was time to go. As the cavalrymen rode back to camp to share their intelligence with Houston, Lane was relieved to be retreating. "I never obeyed an order more cheerfully in my life."

Numbers, Guns and Flags

Houston considered the arrival of Cos to bring the Mexican troops "to upward of 1500 men, while our aggregate force for the field numbered 783."

Houston's count of 783 men appears to be low, as another 150 Texans were later allowed claims for having been present at San Jacinto on April 21.

The attire of the Texans was as widely varied as the estimates of the total number of men available to General Houston. They were a generally ragged bunch who wore only what they owned or had borrowed during the campaign. Many of the Texas frontiersmen wore buckskin pants, moccasins and an occasional sombrero. "I wore, like all the others, citizen's clothes," recalled Private James Monroe Hill, "and a fur cap."[29]

Twin Sisters cannoneer Ben McCullough, a six-foot, 165-pound Tennessean, wore his homespun Mexia clothes that his mother had made for him the previous November. Private Washington Anderson of Captain Billingsley's company stated that he wore a Casinette suit

Texas Forces at the Battle of San Jacinto
April 21, 1836 (See Appendix C for Complete Rosters)

		Total Men:
Command Staff		
Major General Samuel Houston	14	
Medical Corps		
Dr. Alexander Ewing	10	
Artillery		
Lt. Col. James Neill/Col. George W. Hockley[1]		
Capts. Isaac N. Moreland/George W. Poe[2]	32	
Cavalry		
Col. Mirabeau B. Lamar	1	
Capt. Henry W. Karnes (Comp. G, 1st Reg.)	35	
Capt. William H. Smith (Comp. J, 2nd Reg.)	27	63
Regular Army		
Lt. Col. Henry Millard and Staff	5	
Company A, Capt. Andrew Briscoe	47	
Company B, Capt. Amasa Turner	40	92
First Regiment of Texas Volunteers, Infantry		
Col. Edward Burleson and Staff	4	
A Capt. William Wood	40	
B Capt. Richard Roman	35	
C Capt. Jesse Billingsley	54	
D Capt. Moseley Baker	59	
F Capt. William J. E. Heard	48	
H Capt. Robert Stevenson	49	
I Capt. William S. Fisher	52	
K Capt. Robert J. Calder	45	386
Second Regiment of Texas Volunteers, Infantry		
Col. Sidney Sherman and Staff	5	
A Capt. Hayden S. Arnold	46	
B Capt. William Ware	19	
C Capt. William M. Logan Jr.	36	
D Capt. David Murphree	52	
E Capt. Thomas H. McIntire	33	
F Capt. James Gillaspie	40	
G Capt. Benjamin F. Bryant	23	
H Capt. William Kimbro	38	
I Capt. Juan N. Seguin	24	
K Capt. Alfred H. Wyly	14	330
Companies Unknown Participants	3	

Total Present, Texas Army: 930

[1]Neill wounded on April 20. Artillery led by Lt. Col. Hockley on April 21.
[2]Capt. Poe absent from battlefield on April 21.

Note: Eight men who fought on April 20 not present due to sickness, wounds or furlough.

Baggage Guard/Sick at Camp Harrisburg April 20–21, 1836	
Camp Staff	*Total Men:*
Major Robert McNutt	6
Company E, First Regiment	
Capt. Gibson Kuykendall	66
Company J, First Regiment	
Capt. Peyton R. Splane	33
Chance's Company, Second Regiment	
Capt. Joseph B. Chance	37
Other Men Sick or Detailed as Guards	
Artillery	1
Cavalry	2
Regular Army	1
First Regiment of Texas Volunteers, Infantry	36
Second Regiment, Texas Volunteers, Infantry	65
Unassigned or Company Unknown	8
Total Texans at Harrisburg Camp: 255	
(See Appendix D for Complete Rosters)	

of clothes and a broad-brimmed white hat with a low crown. "Deaf Smith had a suit of buckskin he took from the Mexican courier near Harrisburg," recalled Private John Ferrell. Smith also "wore a Mexican sombrero and rode a Spanish pony."[30]

General Houston wore no formal uniform at San Jacinto. He had his Cherokee coat, buckskin vest and silver-spurred riding boots. He wore a broad cap and a belt pistol while carrying his ceremonial Cherokee sword.[31]

Only one company, Captain William Wood's Kentucky Riflemen, wore uniforms which had been largely paid for by former Captain Sidney Sherman. Only two senior Texas officers are known to have worn proper uniforms. Colonel John Wharton, the adjutant general, wore a sharp blue woolen uniform, complete with brass buttons and a pair of boots. Aside from his military uniform, Wharton wore a Mexican sombrero and carried a gourd canteen. Colonel Sherman wore a long blue cloth round jacket with silver lace. On his side he wore a dress sword.[32]

By best count, General Houston had 930 men present with which to face Santa Anna's troops. Nine men involved in the April 20 skirmish were not with him on April 21. The four wounded men had been sent back across the bayou accompanied by two stewards, Jonathan Morris of Captain Billingsley's company and C. W. Parrott of Captain Calder's company. Also moving to the camp at Harrisburg was William Crittenden, a member of Henry Karnes' cavalry who was too sick to fight, and artilleryman George Washington Seaton, who had been injured in a mishap. The ninth man not present was Captain Poe, having received his brief furlough. By April 21, the number of men sick, wounded or on guard duty at Camp Harrisburg was 255.

General Houston's own count of those present at San Jacinto on April 21 was 783, although this count is known to have missed at least one complete company. Research of audited military claims and land grants, the exhaustive work by Louis W. Kemp, and the continuing research of the San Jacinto Museum of History shows that 930 Texans were likely present. (See "Afterword" for details on this count.)

Counting the exact number of men in each company as of April 21 is difficult at best. Due to injuries and horse losses the previous day, there was a fair amount of company swapping that took place. To replace sick Private Crittenden and the two other wounded cavalrymen, William S. Taylor from Captain Ware's company and Moses Lapham from Captain Baker's unit joined the cavalry for April 21. Private Daniel McKay had apparently also suffered a wounded horse in the skirmish. He was moved into acting Captain Robert Stevenson's unit. In return, Stevenson sent Private Joseph Lawrence to ride with Captain Karnes' company for this day.

Sergeant Robert Goodloe of Karnes' company had lost his horse the previous evening in the skirmish. He now joined his companion William Gant, who had temporarily joined Captain Calder's company in Sherman's regiment. Matthew Cartwright, whose horse had been killed out from under him the previous day, was now on foot with Captain Ware. Dr. Fielding Deadrick, who had lost his pistols while fighting with Captain Karnes in the skirmish the previous day, was attached to Captain Gillaspie's infantry company for April 21.[33]

Private Oscar Farish, a twenty-three-year-old clerk from Virginia, had been a rifleman of Colonel Sherman's Second Regiment. He however, switched companies "for the reason that I had no great confidence in my skill with the rifle, and exchanged for a musket, when I had to go into Captain McIntire's company."[34]

The largest company assembled at San Jacinto on April 21 was Captain Moseley Baker's San Felipe company, officially known as

Company D of the First Regiment, with fifty-nine men. The smallest was Captain Alfred Wyly's with fourteen.

Only Captain Wood's Kentucky company carried a true flag. Featuring a half-nude maiden clutching a banner reading "Liberty or Death," the company's flag had been presented to them by the ladies of Newport, Kentucky, before they departed the United States.

The Mexican army carried at least three flags. The Guerrero battalion and Toluca battalion, both federally funded militia units (*activos*), each carried an ensign. At least one of the *permanente*, or regular army companies, that carried a flag was the Batallon Matamoros Permanente. The latter unit was among the few that could boast of having fought at the Alamo, at Coleto Creek and now at San Jacinto.

Against Sam Houston's 930 men, Santa Anna had roughly 1,250 men with General Cos' new reinforcements.[35] His line troops were largely equipped with .75-caliber East India Pattern "Brown Bess" muskets, which had been the standard issue British infantry firearm since 1722. His Excellency's elite riflemen, known as *cazadores*, appear to have been issued the .61-caliber Baker rifle, a more accurate firearm at longer ranges than the Brown Bess musket. Santa Anna also had well-trained *zapadores*, or "sappers," who were his special reserve force tactical fighters. Finally, his cavalrymen were armed with British Paget carbines, sabers and even lances.[36]

The uniforms of both the Mexican infantry and artillerymen were made largely of a white fabric known as Russian ducking. The officers generally wore blue uniforms, although some wore white trousers with their blue jackets. The dragoons (or armed cavalrymen) wore short red coats and tall black helmets with horsehair plumes.[37]

James Hill, one of the Texas veterans of San Jacinto, would later offer his description of the Mexican troops' armament.

> The infantry had the old fashioned British flintlock muskets, had them very bright and in good order. The cavalry had mostly straight sabres and the escopet and lance. Some had large horse pistols, flintlock.[38]

From a distance, the Mexican army generally displayed a light or white appearance that was splashed with red and blue. This was a sharp contrast to the dirty, worn, dull and dark ragged citizens clothes worn by the majority of the Texian army. Such would be the clash of cultures and colors that would soon mix on the canvas of San Jacinto.

Blacks and Tejanos in Service at San Jacinto

A profile of the Texas soldiers present at San Jacinto shows some interesting statistics. Sixty percent of the men were single and the median age of Sam Houston's troops was twenty-eight. Most were from southern states, with nineteen percent coming from northern states and only five percent having been born in foreign countries. The median date of emigration to Texas was 1834 for Houston's men. One-sixth of his soldiers had arrived between January and October of 1835.[39]

Although most of the Texas troops were Caucasian, there were at least five blacks and twenty-nine Tejanos in service either at the battlefield or guarding baggage at Harrisburg.

For the black men, achieving freedom for the Republic of Texas was especially important. They were free men in Texas or could work as indentured servants, but were not "slaves" as they had been in other areas of the United States. The Tejanos had just as much to lose. They generally despised Santa Anna for not honoring the 1824 Constitution and feared what would become of their land and families under his dictatorship.

Foremost of the Tejano volunteers was the twenty-four-man unit under Captain Juan Seguin. Although few of his volunteers spoke much English, all of his men except one had been born in Texas territory. There were at least five other Tejanos in the army's service on April 21: Major Lorenzo de Zavala Jr. of Sam Houston's staff; Peter Lopez in Captain Karnes' cavalry unit; Martin Flores, a musician from Nacogdoches in Captain Briscoe's regulars; Antonio Trevino of Captain Baker's San Felipe company; and Jose Molino, a Nacogdoches Tejano whose proper name was Jose Palonio Lavigna.

There were numerous other nationalities present on April 21. Joseph Sovereign, born in Portugal in about 1810, was with Captain William Fisher's company. The death certificate filed in Houston in 1877 listed him as "Joe Sovereign, colored, Portugal."[40]

Five blacks served with the Texas Army during the San Jacinto campaign in roles other than servant. Three were involved in the battle. The first, James Robinson, had come to Texas in March as an indentured servant to Colonel Robert Eden Handy. He had been offered a passport to return home, but "begged permission to remain and share the fate of those who met the enemy." Handy, a former cavalryman who served as a volunteer aide-de-camp to General Houston, kept Jim around as a body servant. Handy's sister wrote a letter to President Lamar in 1839 in which she mentioned him: "I refer to Jim, the colored boy my brother took out with him (and whom you may possibly recollect, being in attendance upon him at the battle of San Jacinto). He was a family servant we brought from the South."[41]

Jim Robinson's service was later acknowledged by the Fourth Congress of the Republic of Texas: "This single-minded negro boy, though unacknowledged as a patriot and bound by no ties of interest; still rose superior to every selfish consideration and bravely breasted the storm of Mexican invasion at the gloomiest hour of our fortunes." As later sworn by Chief Justice Wyly Martin, Robinson remained at the Harrisburg encampment on April 21 in obedience to orders.[42]

Captain Martin's own servant, Peter, had also been active during the San Jacinto campaign. He used his own team and wagon to help transport supplies for the Texas Army but remained with Captain Martin and thereby missed the battle of San Jacinto.

Three other blacks did participate in the battle of San Jacinto. The first was Dick, a gray-haired freed black from New Orleans who served as a drummer in the army's little band.

The second was Maxlin Smith, an indentured servant of Major Ben Fort Smith, "who served and did good service in said revolution." Known as "Mack," he was born in Kentucky about 1809, arrived in Texas in 1832 with Major Smith and could neither read nor write during his lifetime. Jesse Billingsley and Pendleton Rector would both later swear under oath that "Mack Smith, Colored, was present and participated on the Side of Texas as a Volunteer in the Battle of San Jacinto." As a freed man in 1875, Smith qualified for a pension from Texas, saying that he "was with Capt. Patton's company and took part with the Texas forces." He noted that he "was engaged with the frees of Texas & did my duty as a soldier faithfully & to the best of my ability." According to a pension document later filed, Smith did not appear on the official muster rolls due to being considered a slave.[43]

The third black man to fight at San Jacinto was Hendrick Arnold, who had successfully guided the Texas Army into San Antonio during its December 1835 siege against General Cos. Arnold was later cited as "one of the most efficient members of Deaf Smith's Spy Company and an active participan[t] in the battle of San Jacinto."

The War Council

At about noon on April 21, General Houston was informed that some of the officers were anxious to hold a council of war. Houston replied that he had no objection and the available senior officers were thus called together. Some of the staff officers—including Hockley, Wharton, de Zavala and Coleman—had been sent out on special assignments and were thus not available for the council of war.[44]

According to Alexander Somervell, Houston discussed during the council of war an idea that had been suggested to him. What about building a floating bridge across Buffalo Bayou for the Texas troops to use in crossing? The bridge would serve as a means of retreat should the Texans be whipped on the battlefield. If his intention was to prevent another absolute slaughter such as the Alamo and Goliad, Houston's idea was not a bad one. His critics, however, again perceived the suggestion as weakness and his creating an option to retreat again.

The captured flatboat, sent to retrieve more axes for cutting trees, had not yet returned by mid-morning. This was just as well, for few men had intentions of retreating this day, much less even working on such a bridge.[45]

According to Houston, the bridge idea had been suggested to him by another. He had even sent officers out to look into the feasibility of such a creation.

> I ordered Cols. Hockley and Wharton to see if there were materials to build one. After some time they returned, and Col. Wharton reported that they thought sufficient materials could be got by pulling down Gov. Zavala's house. My reply was, that I could see no urgent necessity for it, and it was useless to commence it unless it was certain the material would be sufficient for its completion.[46]

The company commanders who caught wind of Houston's bridge idea were much opposed to it. Captain William Heard only found out about the proposed plan from Somervell.

> I never saw any order to build the bridge, nor do I believe he ever issued it; for he knew it would not be done. There was but one order that he could issue, that would have been obeyed at that time; and that was to go and fight. He was not esteemed as the commander immediately preceding the battle; the men were cursing and abusing him, not to his face, but in his hearing: calling him all sorts of hard names, as coward, traitor, rascal, etc.[47]

Captain Jesse Billingsley also opposed the bridge idea, later writing that "no idea could be more repugnant to our men than that of retreating or preparing any way for a retreat."[48] Captain Amasa Turner and his men also refused this proposition.

> It was current in the army that the General was not disposed to fight, but to build a floating bridge across the bayou. This was very unpopular, the men saying, they would not work to build a bridge, but would go out and whip the Mexicans while Old Sam built his bridge.[49]

The point for calling the war council obviously focused on one main thought shared by everyone in the Texas Army: when and how should the enemy be taken to battle? To answer this question, General Houston put the subject to a vote.

The voting members were all field officers: Colonel Edward Burleson and Lieutenant Colonel Alexander Somervell of the First Regiment, Lieutenant Colonel Henry Millard of the regulars, and Colonel Sidney Sherman, Lieutenant Colonel Joe Bennett and Major Lysander Wells of the Second Regiment. Houston's command staff, Houston himself and Secretary of War Rusk would not vote.[50]

The key question posed was, "Shall we attack the enemy in their position, or shall we await his attack?"[51]

Surprisingly, only two of the junior officers present, Bennett and Wells, were in favor of fighting. Burleson, Sherman, Millard and Somervell all cast votes in favor of not fighting right away. Sherman later wrote that, "Major Wells was for attacking immediately, the balance of us were in favor of waiting a reasonable time for the enemy to attack, but all were determined to fight that day."[52]

According to Bennett, Colonel Rusk felt that the Texans did not have enough bayonets to march across a mile-wide prairie in broad daylight against veteran enemy troops. Sherman, Wharton and Lamar felt "that our position was strong and in it we could whip all of Mexico," said Bennett.[53]

General Houston's version of the war council, as written in 1855, agrees. Wells and Bennett were for marching to attack the Mexican army, while the other four field officers voted to "allow them to attack us. If they would not, we should ourselves make the attack that day."

The sentiment of these officers was probably that they fully expected the Mexicans to attack quickly and that they would not have long to wait. Acting Captain Robert Stevenson of Company H, not present for this vote, wrote, "We were then certain of being attacked in the course of the day."[54]

With the vote two to one in favor of waiting to see if the enemy would strike first, Houston announced, "Gentlemen, you are adjourned."

The Texas officers then walked back to their respective commands to spread the word. The long awaited order to fight would be longer yet awaited.

"Cut It Down and Set It on Fire"

While Houston's idea of building a bridge over Buffalo Bayou was not well received, his plan to destroy another bridge on April 21 *was* carried out.

The decision was made to destroy Vince's Bridge, which was located about eight miles southwest of Lynch's Ferry along the only direct wagon road linking Harrisburg and Lynchburg. It has been questioned why Houston would order a bridge destroyed when General Cos' reinforcements had already arrived. The popular version is that he hoped to prevent any further men from arriving. Reinforcements could still reach Santa Anna, but they would be greatly slowed by having to swim the flooded Vince's Bayou or circumnavigate it by several miles.

The decision to destroy Vince's Bridge is one of several dramas of the San Jacinto campaign that has more than one version. Sam Houston in later years wrote that the decision was his and that he had planned for this early in the day.

> Early on the morning of the 21st of April, I sent for Col. Forbes, Commissary-General of the army, and directed him to procure two good axes, and place them at the root of a certain post oak tree, rather out of view of the camp, and at the same time I sent for Erastus (called Deaf) Smith, and ordered him not to pass the line of sentinels that day without my knowledge, as I did not know at what moment I might want him. . . .
>
> So soon as the council of war decided not to attack the enemy, but to let them attack us, I dismissed the council and immediately sent for Deaf Smith [to] select a companion, and meet me at the tree spoken of, both well mounted. In a few minutes he was at the place designated, with a young man named Rivers [Denmore Rives], with auburn hair. I gave them the axes, and directed them to hasten to Vince's bridge, cut it down and set it on fire.[55]

Although General Houston appears to have had the bridge destruction scheme planned out, other San Jacinto veterans would later give credit to the cavalry for hatching this scheme.

In support of this latter claim is the 1858 account written by Private Young Perry Alsbury. Twenty-two years of age, Alsbury had come to Texas from Kentucky in 1823 with his parents and ten siblings as members of Stephen F. Austin's First Colony. From his Brazos County area home, Alsbury had joined Captain Henry Karnes' company of spies on March 1 and was saddled up for action on the morning of April 21.

> On the morning of the twenty-first of April, 1836, Captain Karnes' Cavalry Company, commonly called Deaf Smith's Spy Company, were drawn up in line on the edge of General Houston's position. As well as I recollect, we were between thirty and forty strong. The Mexican cavalry, whom we fought the evening before, at that moment were drawn up in line on the south of our position about six hundred yards distant. I think they were from sixty to eighty strong.
>
> They seemed to invite us again to combat; but prudence, in my humble opinion, dictated to our leaders a different course than to engage them at that moment.[56]

While sitting idly in their saddles, the cavalrymen discussed the day's expected confrontation with Santa Anna. John Coker, a single blacksmith by trade and the left file-leader of Karnes' company, stated that he felt they would soon "have one of the damnedest, bloodiest fights that ever was fought."

Coker then claims to have suggested that they "burn that bridge" to impede the advance of Mexican reinforcements and to "cut off all chance of retreat."

Coker and Alsbury stated that this "proposition was seconded by the whole company." Deaf Smith then agreed to go run the plan past General Houston.

According to Captain William Heard, it was "about 11 o'clock on the 21st" when Smith rode up to General Houston with his bridge burning idea. "Smith insisted on burning the bridge, to prevent any more reinforcements from joining Santa Anna," wrote Heard.[57]

During Smith's exchange with the commander-in-chief, Houston reportedly asked him, "Can you do it without being cut to pieces by the Mexican cavalry?"

"Give me six men and I will try," Smith replied.

Colonel Coleman agrees that Smith was the initiator of the idea to destroy Vince's Bridge.

> I believe Deaf Smith suggested the breaking of the bridge over Vince's Bayou, and that an immediate attack be made on this division; the breaking

of the bridge would for a short time delay the arrival of other troops, and we should be able to defeat this division and be in readiness for another.[58]

Deaf Smith rode back to Captain Karnes' party and stopped near the center facing the company. One cavalryman was quick to question, "What did the General say?" Smith did not answer immediately, but instead surveyed the men with what Young Alsbury felt was "an iron-like countenance."[59]

"I want six men," Smith announced at length. "I am going to burn the bridge. I want six men who are willing to follow me through, or perish in the attempt."

Alsbury was among the volunteers.

> There was silence for several moments, as six of us dropped out of the little line and volunteered to follow our favorite chief. But let me here do justice to the remainder of our companions-in-arms by saying and believing what I say, that there were scarcely a man of our spy company who would not have volunteered to follow Deaf Smith, had each and all been well-mounted. I will here mention the names of all who joined Deaf Smith in the enterprise; yet, before doing so, beg leave to state that I differ from the opinion of my old friend, "Uncle Jack Coker," as we called him, as to the name of one of the party, but, having the most implicit confidence in "Uncle Jack's" honesty I am willing to risk his statement and give the names as he has set them down: Deaf Smith, Denmore Rives, John Coker, Y. P. Alsbury, [Edwin R.] Rainwater, John Garner, [Moses] Lapham, seven in all.

Five of the seven-man party were original members of Karnes' company. John Garner was a private of Captain William Wood's infantry company before joining up with the cavalry on April 21. Garner, of course, had nearly been shot to death after being court-martialed earlier in the month! The seventh man was Moses Lapham, who had joined that morning from Captain Baker's San Felipe company.

Lapham had joined the cavalry after its losses the previous day because many men were "unwilling to fight again on horseback, on account of not being sustained by the infantry the day before."[60] In contrast to Sam Houston's 1855 account that only Smith and Rives had gone to cut the bridge, Lapham wrote in a letter to his family on May 17, 1836, that he had "started at noon with five others to destroy and burn the bridge ten miles above to cut off their retreat."

Under Karnes and Captain William Smith, the main body of the Texas cavalry was used to create a diversion for Deaf Smith's men. To reach Vince's Bridge, the scouts would have to ride about eight miles and pass within gunshot range of the extreme left of the Mexican cavalry. Smith's men hoped to pass the Mexican horsemen without a fight. Young Alsbury recalled that "the remainder of our company followed slowly, under a soldier's pledge, that, were we attacked by the cavalry, they would come to our assistance."[61]

As the main body of the Texas cavalry maneuvered with "the feint of an engagement," Smith and his six volunteers passed the Mexican forces unmolested, striking Buffalo Bayou. The other Texan cavalrymen then turned and headed back to the main camp of the Texas Army, "leaving the enemy to enjoy the belief that we were too cowardly to fight."

Smith's group followed Buffalo Bayou toward the bridge, which was located about eight miles down the road leading to the Brazos River. They rode rapidly down the lane. On the north side of the road, they reached the double log-house of William Vince, where they filed off to the left to avoid a possible enemy ambush if the Mexicans were concealed in Vince's home.

The group threw down the fence where it joined Vince's Bayou, over which the bridge was built. The bridge was 150 yards beyond. Deaf Smith and Young Alsbury passed over the bridge to scout ahead, leaving the other five to "strike fire" and prepare for the bridge's destruction.

Unable to burn the bridge over Vince' Bayou, Deaf Smith and his volunteers destroy the remnants of the bridge in order to slow Mexican reinforcements from reaching the San Jacinto battlegrounds.
Charles Shaw painting, courtesy of the San Jacinto Museum of History, Houston.

The account of Alsbury continues:

> We had gone about half a mile when we noticed in the sandy soil the track of a carriage wheel. Smith, with a countenance of mixed rage and disappointment, exclaimed: "Santa Anna has made his escape! Here is his carriage track, going back, pulled by mules in a great hurry!"
>
> I proposed to him that we should gallop on, about one mile, to a difficult crossing of another bayou [Sims Bayou] where we might get the honor of helping him to cross. He replied: "My orders are to burn the bridge and return as quick as possible."
>
> In a few minutes we were at the bridge, where we found our comrades prepared with fire and plenty of dry rails and wood. In a few minutes the bridge was in flames. If I recollect aright, it was built of cedar.

Although Alsbury claimed that the men burned the bridge, other accounts state that the men tried to fire it but were unable to get the logs to sufficiently burn through. They then cut away a few timbers until the whole structure fell into the bayou.[62]

Santa Anna had neither traveled by carriage nor fled the battleground, as Alsbury had feared. Once the bridge was sufficiently destroyed, Smith and his volunteers turned back for the Texan camp. About three-quarters of a mile from their destination, they reached a deep, dry hollow. Smith ordered a halt and said, "I will ride up the high ground next to camp far enough to see whether any of the Mexican horsemen are near, so that we may avoid them."[63]

The other six watched and saw Smith suddenly drop down upon the mane of his horse and race toward them. He said that the prairie ahead was filled with Mexican horsemen and he felt that Santa Anna had somehow received a whole new reinforcement. Eyeing his men, he asked, "What shall we do?"

Smith's men informed him that they would follow him on whichever course he chose.

"My orders are to return to camp; I will do it or die," Smith announced. Turning a scrutinizing eye over his men, he then offered leave to any man who chose to flee for his life. To a man, all chose to stay and follow their beloved veteran scout, a gesture that Alsbury felt seemed to move old Smith. He asked his men to prepare their guns and to then follow him Indian file through the dry hollow to where it joined Buffalo Bayou.

Smith tersely stated that the men would likely pass within one hundred yards of the Mexican cavalrymen. "When discovered by them," he stated, "we will raise the Texan yell and charge at full speed through their lines." He added that he would likely be killed, but would try to make an opening for the rest to escape through.

Only after racing behind Smith out onto the prairie did the other six realize that their scout was having fun with them. Alsbury felt that the whole incident strongly illustrated "the extraordinary sagacity of that masterly man, Deaf Smith." The courage, keen judgment and fun-loving ways of Erastus Smith were all qualities which helped endear him to men who fought with him in the Texas Revolution, such as Alsbury.

> I must say, and when I say it, do so with candor and truth, that not one of Smith's men but would have preferred the risk of death, rather than an ignominious, disgraceful desertion of the leader we all loved. But to conclude: When fairly on the level which commanded a partial view of both armies, we saw no Mexican cavalry; but knew, from the hearty laugh of our leader, that he had, as he boastingly said, put our fidelity to the test.

CHAPTER 15

"Dreadful Havoc"

April 21

The announcement of the decision to fight acted like electricity.
—*Private George B. Erath, Company C, First Regiment*

Private James Winters noted that General Houston "passed around among the men gathered at the campfires and asked us if we wanted to fight. We replied with a shout that we were most anxious to do so. Then Houston replied, 'Very well, get your dinners and I will lead you into the fight, and if you whip them, every one of you shall be a captain.'"[1]

Deaf Smith's party had long since departed on its mission to destroy Vince's Bridge. The noon hour had passed silently in the Texas camp. Men waited anxiously taking a late lunch near the campfires. Captain Juan Seguin was joined during his afternoon meal by Colonel Tom Rusk, the Secretary of War.

> When he had done eating, he asked me if the Mexicans were not in the habit of taking a siesta at that hour. I answered in the affirmative, adding, moreover, that in such cases they kept under arms their main and advanced guards, and a line of sentinels. General Rusk observed that he thought so; however, the moment seemed to him favorable to attack the enemy, and he further said: "Do you feel like fighting?" I answered that I was always ready and willing to fight, upon which the General rose, saying: "Well, let us go!"[2]

By 3:00 p.m. it was clear to Sam Houston that the enemy was not ready to attack, but instead was fortifying himself. The noon meeting of Texas officers had decided not to attack immediately, but to instead await the enemy's first move.

Company H's Captain Stevenson wrote on April 23 that "Gen. Houston, seeing that they did not intend bringing on the attack, and fearing that they would receive reinforcements, determined to attack them on their own ground."[3]

Some of the officers present would later claim that they helped influence General Houston's eventual decision to call for an attack. According to Colonel Robert Coleman, it was Colonel Wharton, the adjutant general, who advised Houston that the majority of the officers were for fighting immediately, even though four key officers had voted to delay.[4]

Colonel Mirabeau Lamar, who had been one of those most inspired to lead a fight against the enemy soon after joining the army the previous week, was pushing his opinion again. After the noon war council, Lamar claims to have sought out Houston and again expressed his desire to start the battle. According to Lamar, Houston replied that he had always been ready to fight but now his officers were opposed to fighting. "And so are the men," Houston added.[5]

Lamar was shocked at this response. Although four key officers had voted against fighting immediately at the noon council, he knew that the strong majority of troops were all for fighting as soon as possible. Lamar was quick to pass on this news.

> Soon after this, I saw Col. John A. Wharton, and repeated to him what Gen. Houston had said. Wharton inquired, "Do you think he will fight?" My reply was: "He says he will."
>
> Taking leave of me, the Colonel repaired immediately to Gen. Houston, and asked him if he would order a battle provided the army was ready to make the attack. Houston said he would. This I got from Wharton, immediately after his leaving Houston. In a short time there was a general rejoicing through the camp; and Wharton was dashing from point to point, ordering a general parade, and *marshaling the troops for battle.*

Sam Houston later flatly denied speaking with Mirabeau Lamar. He claims that he and Lamar, in fact, had no further conversations whatsoever on April 21 after Lamar had turned down the general's offered command of the artillery.

"Parade Your Companies"

Colonel Edward Burleson decided to take a consensus of his First Regiment captains. Burleson, originally a member of Captain Billings-

Captain Robert James Calder (1810–1885), commander of Company K, First Regiment. Most of his company resided in present Brazoria, Fort Bend and Matagorda Counties. (Previously published in Wharton's *San Jacinto: The Sixteenth Decisive Battle*.)

ley's Mina company, sent Private George Erath out to round up his regiment's company commanders.

This second officer council occurred around 3:00 p.m. according to Captain Robert Calder. Burleson rode along the line of encampment of his regiment and ordered Captains Calder, Wood, Roman, Billingsley, Baker, Stevenson, Heard, and Fisher to meet him at a pecan tree several hundred yards away. Also present were "some of the lieutenants of the regiment," plus Private Erath and Orderly Sergeant Russell Craft of Billingsley's company.[6]

Captain Calder later wrote of the gathering of Burleson's key officers.

> They followed on, and assembled accordingly, when our Colonel told us he wished to take our vote upon the best time for attacking the enemy— whether immediately or at four o'clock the next morning. All the captains but Moseley Baker and myself voted for immediate attack; Baker and myself for four o'clock in the morning. Upon which we were ordered to parade our companies for immediate action.[7]

Captain Heard later claimed that he also voted to wait until morning to attack. He felt that "it was so late in the evening that the wounded would suffer by being out in the night."[8]

Unbeknownst to Heard and Calder, Colonel Sidney Sherman's Second Regiment had also gathered to discuss the time of the attack. They had been called together by Lieutenant Colonel Joe Bennett. "Houston sent me through the camp to see the captains and men and ascertain their feelings about fighting that afternoon," he recalled.[9]

Bennett and Colonel Sherman—surrounded by Captains Arnold, Logan, Seguin, Murphree, Ware, McIntire, Gillaspie, Bryant, Kimbro, and Wyly—found an equally strong desire to attack among their commanders. Colonel Burleson mounted and rode to share his regiment's sentiment with Sherman. Burleson soon returned and announced, "Captains, parade your companies. The other regiment had decided to fight immediately. I don't want mine to be a minute behind."[10]

Lieutenant Colonel Bennett reported to General Houston, telling him "the men were ready to fight. Houston then ordered the troops to be paraded."[11]

"Joy was depicted on the countenance of every man, and there was a rejoicing throughout the camp," wrote Colonel Coleman. "I have never seen sober men animated to the same degree." George Erath wrote, "The announcement of the decision to fight acted like electricity."[12]

Thus at 3:30 p.m. on April 21, 1836, the Texian troops paraded for battle. Sam Houston's official report:

> At half-past three o'clock in the evening, I ordered the officers of the Texan army to parade their respective commands, having in the meantime ordered the bridge on the only road communicating with the Brazos, distance eight miles from our encampment, to be destroyed, thus cutting off all possibility of escape.
>
> Our troops paraded with alacrity and spirit, and were anxious for the contest. Their conscious disparity in numbers seemed only to increase their enthusiasm and confidence, and heightened their anxiety for the conflict. Our situation afforded me an opportunity of making the arrangements preparatory to the attack without exposing our designs to the enemy.

Texas drummers George Brown and Dick, the former slave, called the men to parade with a gentle tapping. Private John W. Hassell of Captain Calder's company wrote that "the drum beat general parade, which was cheering [to] every man."[13]

Within half an hour, Houston's men were fanned out in four divisions directly in front of the mossy hardwood grove in which they had spent the night. Houston estimated that he had 783 men present, although records would later show that approximately 930 Texans were on hand on the afternoon of April 21.

The fate of Texas now rested upon the shoulders of these men. General Houston began his final inspection of the troops, moving from the extreme right wing toward the left. He was mounted on a fine grayish-colored stallion named Saracen.

According to Private Jesse Walling of the Nacogdoches Volunteers, Houston had exchanged his own pony for the gray stallion, which belonged to Private Dexter Watson of Captain Kimbro's San Augustine company. "Sam exchanged horses to get one of a different color, and mounted Dexter Watson's fine gray, and Watson rode the bay pony," wrote Walling.[14]

Sometimes described as white, Saracen was remembered by San Jacinto veterans to be gray in color. "Sam Houston's horse that [he] was on going into battle was a dapple gray," wrote Private James Hill. Sergeant Moses Austin was equally sure that the horse was "gray upon which he went into battle." Finally, Captain James Gillaspie recalled going into battle with Sam Houston "riding a gray horse."[15]

To the extreme right was Colonel Lamar, saddled up with sixty-two other cavalrymen under Captains Karnes and Smith. Private John Ferrell noted that Deaf Smith "wore a Mexican sombrero and rode a Spanish pony" this day.[16]

Next were Lieutenant Colonel Henry Millard's ninety-two regulars under Captains Andrew Briscoe and Amasa Turner. Marching near the regulars was the six-piece Texas band of Dick, George Brown, and fifers John Beebe, Martin Flores, Luke Bust, and Frederick Lemsky. To the left and slightly ahead of these divisions were the thirty-two men of the artillery corps with the two six-pounder Twin Sisters cannon. They were under command of Colonel Hockley, Captain Isaac Moreland and First Lieutenant William Stilwell.[17]

Colonel Hockley, Inspector General for the Army, had been placed in acting command of the artillery forces due to the injury of Lieutenant Colonel James Neill in the previous day's skirmish.

To the left of the artillery, and forming the center of all forces, was Colonel Burleson's First Regiment, eight companies and 386 men strong. Finally, Colonel Sherman's Second Regiment, ten companies and 330 men strong, formed the left wing of the Texas Army. Colonel Wharton, the adjutant general, joined Sherman to help lead the Second Regiment.

The surgeons were momentarily perplexed with how to act during the fight. According to General Houston, "there was no particular assignment of the surgeons made at the battle of San Jacinto." Doctors Booker, Fitzhue, Davidson and Labadie consulted each other on whether they should stay back from the fight or march along. Their surgeon general, Dr. Alexander Ewing, had not given them any direction. The doctors all agreed to fight with their weapons "as circumstances might direct," shook hands all around and marched with their respective divisions. Fitzhue took the center, Davidson the right, and Labadie took to the left with Colonel Sherman's Second Regiment, where his former company under Captain Logan was marching.[18]

Riding past the troops from right to left, General Houston stopped in front of Colonel Burleson's division to listen to company commanders giving motivational speeches.

Captain Moseley Baker, the former editor who now commanded the largest company at San Jacinto, reminded his men that "Travis, Crockett, Bowie and their companions" held out bravely against forces "twenty times their number." Baker told his men he was confident in their ability but "if there be one who is not fully satisfied, he is at liberty to remain at camp, for I do not wish my company disgraced by a single act of cowardice."

Baker's speech at San Jacinto was later written out from memory by Private John Menefee. He later recalled his captain saying:

> Remember, you are fighting an enemy who gives no quarter, and regards neither age nor sex. Recollect that your homes are destroyed; imagine your wives and daughters trudging mud and water, and your children crying for bread, and then remember that the author of all this woe is within a short distance of us; that the arch fiend is now within our grasp; and that the time has come at last for us to avenge the blood of our fallen heroes and to teach the haughty dictator that Texas can not be conquered and that they can and will be free.
>
> Then nerve yourselves for the battle, knowing that our cause is just and we are in the hands of an Allwise Creator, and as you strike the murderous blows, let our watchwords be "Remember Goliad"; "Remember the Alamo."[19]

Baker reportedly also told his men to offer no quarter to the enemy. A token of this measure was displayed in the form of a red handkerchief. A vote was taken on whether the no quarter rule should be followed and only one man, Private John Money, voted against it. "A red handkerchief was therefore hoisted for a flag," wrote Corporal Isaac Hill.[20]

Just behind Baker's company was that of Captain Calder. He felt that Baker's speech was a very moving appeal to the men's patriotism. "Not being an orator myself," wrote Calder, "I requested my company to avail themselves of Captain Baker's sentiments, and so make the effect double."[21]

General Houston also moved along the Second Regiment's lines. Captain James Gillaspie of Company F recalled that "Gen. Houston

In a reenactment on the San Jacinto battlegrounds, company commanders give last minute speechs before the Texians march into battle.
Author's photo, courtesy of the San Jacinto Museum of History, Houston.

passed down in front of the regiment and spoke to every captain belonging to it." At Captain David Murphree's Columbia company, Goliad Massacre survivor Charles Shain said that Houston told them "that such as could not stand the bayonet, must stay behind."[22]

Shain and the other massacre survivors needed no pep talk to find motivation to avenge the loss of their comrades. In addition to the Goliad Massacre survivors, there were two Texans present at San Jacinto who had been in the Alamo shortly before its fall: Captain Juan Seguin and Antonio Cruz, who had been late messengers from the fortress.

General Houston stopped in front of Captain Arnold's Second Regiment company and had a conference with Tom Rusk, deciding that the Secretary of War should stay with Sherman's regiment at the start of the attack. After the battle was joined, Rusk would then ride across the field to report to Houston how the Second Regiment was doing.

Peering across the mile-wide prairie from atop trees, the Texans could see no activity in the Mexican campground. Even stranger, no sentries were noted along the camp's perimeter. Was Santa Anna cleverly and quietly waiting to pounce once they marched forward?

With but one way to find out, Sam Houston trotted Saracen before his paraded companies about 4:00 p.m. and ordered, "Trail arms! Forward!"

———————

Unbelievably, General Houston had finally given the order that hundreds thought might never come. Farmers, lawyers, teachers, politicians, doctors, merchants, rangers, soldiers of fortune, traders, old men and young boys moved out from their mossy thicket onto the plains of San Jacinto.

Sergeant Swearingen of Captain Turner's company wrote that "the infantry was ordered to trail arms and advance until within 50 yards of the enemy before we fired." The order "trail arms" meant for the soldiers to carry their rifle or musket in the right arm, extending downward so that the muzzle was tilted forward and the butt was near the ground.

James Tarlton, of Baker's "no quarter" company, was impressed with the undaunted spirit of the Texans as they finally marched across the field. He had brought volunteers from Kentucky six months before, only to just miss out on the battle for San Antonio. Tarlton was now encouraged by this "handful of raw, undisciplined volunteers, just taken from their ploughs and thrown together with rifles without bayonets, no two perhaps of the same calibre."[23]

Colonel Rusk felt that "all the divisions advanced in good order and high spirits." Rusk noted old Jimmy Curtis, the former ranger, carrying two guns. At fifty-seven years of age, Curtis was the third oldest Texan on the battlefield at San Jacinto. "I asked him what was his reason for carrying more than one gun," remembered Rusk.[24]

"Damn the Mexicans!" Curtis exclaimed. He had recently lost his son-in-law and another relative at the Alamo and planned to kill two Mexicans in return "or be killed myself."

The tall coastal grass on the plains of San Jacinto afforded the Texans the opportunity to move forward without being seen. Private Edward Miles of the First Regiment's Company A recalled that the

Edward Miles came to Texas from Natchez, Mississippi, and fought at San Jacinto with Company A, First Regiment.
H. A. McArdle's San Jacinto Notebooks, Texas State Library and Archives Commission.

prairie before him was "covered with high serge grass."[25] They were also aided by a slight ridge in the middle of the field which, coupled, with the high grass, helped disguise the progress as the Texian army advanced over the mile-wide prairie.

Sam Houston had no idea of the other elements that were working in his favor on April 21. Santa Anna's troops since midday had allowed a laxness to take hold that would do them no favor.

After General Cos' four hundred reinforcement troops had arrived mid-morning, Santa Anna maintained an escort force of thirty-two selected infantrymen on horseback, mounted on officers' horses. These men were to protect Santa Anna's personal escort force and to watch for and protect Colonel Garcia's expected supply train that was approaching from Harrisburg with another one hundred men.

Captain Miguel Aguirre, commanding this special guard force, was sent by General Cos during the noon hour to make an inquiry of Santa Anna. Cos requested that "his troops be allowed to eat and to feed and water the horses since that had not been done since the day before."[26]

General Santa Anna agreed. "The compassionate tone with which they made these requests caused me to agree," he later wrote. He cautioned Captain Aguirre, however, that their needs should be satisfied quickly and that Aguirre should return at once and occupy the guard position that he held command over.

As events turned out, Aguirre failed to return to his position. Santa Anna decided to satisfy some of his own needs as well.

> Since I was worn out from having spent the morning on horseback and had not slept the night before, I lay down in the shade of some trees while the troops were preparing their meals. I had them call General Don Manuel Fernández Castrillón, who was acting as major general, and told him to guard the camp and to advise me of the least movement on the part of the enemy. I likewise charged him to awaken me as soon as the troops had finished eating because it was necessary to act decisively as soon as possible.

Sherman's Second Regiment Draws First Blood

Spyglasses had shown no movement whatsoever in the Mexican camp as the Texan troops pushed forward across the San Jacinto battleground on April 21, 1836. The artillery company hauled the Twin Sisters up the rising slope toward Santa Anna's camp as the wall of Texans, hundreds of yards wide, advanced on the Mexicans. The cannoneers pulled the two heavy cannon with leather straps through the tall prairie grass toward a slight rise in the center of the field.[27]

The Texans certainly moved out silently. An early account by Dr. Labadie states that "the music struck up a lively air as we bid good-by to our camp." This is highly unlikely. Although the Texian band marched with the regulars, most battle participants later related that their music was not started until after the first shots had been fired.[28]

Forward across the battleground marched the volunteer regiment under Colonel Burleson and the regulars under Lieutenant Colonel Millard, while on the extreme right of the Texans rode Colonel Lamar's cavalry. On the extreme left of the advancing Texas forces was Colonel Sherman's infantry regiment.

Sherman's men moved quickly and silently through the mossy live oaks and tall grasses of the little thicket which ran along the edge of the marsh. They advanced with good cover toward the Mexican camp, with almost no chance of being spotted until they were within the last one hundred yards. The tree cover and the slight rise in the ground toward Santa Anna's forces disguised their movements well. All sources, including General Houston's official report, agree that Sherman's Second Regiment on the left wing reached the Mexican camp first.

Sherman's flankers encountered a division of Mexican soldiers in the woods near camp and opened fire. The surprised *soldados* fired shots at the advancing Texans, but quickly fell back to their own camp-ground for protection.[29]

"Captain Arnold's company was the first in the regiment in the charge upon the enemy in battle," wrote Private Philip Martin.[30] "I was the fifth or sixth man from Col. Sherman." Martin's fellow infantryman Stephen Sparks agrees that Hayden Arnold's First Company was first to fire on April 21.

> My captain's company was the front of the regiment, and we marched in double file. We were ordered not to fire until we could see the whites of the enemies' eyes. When we got within 300 yards of the ditch we were ordered to charge, and we charged in double file. There was only one man in front of me who fired before I did, and so I got the credit for firing the second gun on our side. We had out-traveled the first regiment, and had driven [Colonel Juan] Almonte about 200 yards before the first regiment got near Santa Anna's breastworks.[31]

Private Alfonso Steele of Captain Gillaspie's Sixth Company wrote that Sherman's men were ordered to fire "when we got up within sixty or seventy yards."[32]

Marching across the battlefield with Edward Burleson's First Regiment, Captain William Heard witnessed the start of action near a heavy point of woods near the Mexican camp.

> There was a sharp fire took place at that point. In a few moments I looked in that direction and saw the Mexicans running along the edge of the woods, and Sherman and his men after them. This greatly encouraged me and those near where I was. We shouted at the top of our voices: "Yonder they go, boys, and Sherman after them!" This happened when our regiment was some distance from the enemy, and before we had fired a single shot. Sherman and his men pursued them in hot haste, and they crossed the breast-work where it joined the timber. This circumstance had more to do in gaining the victory than any move that took place on that day.[33]

Another First Regiment company commander, Robert Calder, agreed. He wrote that Sherman's Second Regiment "had the honor of breaking the right wing of the enemy before we attacked his centre."[34]

For many of Sherman's men, their first shot was the only volley they had time to fire. The fighting quickly became hand to hand as the Second Regiment swarmed over the right end of the Mexican breastworks. This end of the Mexican camp was occupied by the regiments of General Cos and Colonel Almonte.

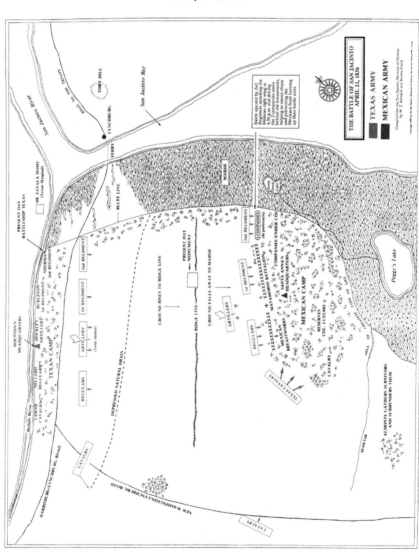

Map of the battle of San Jacinto, April 21, 1836. Compiled by W. T. Kendall and Ronna Hurd, courtesy of the San Jacinto Museum of History Association.

The Mexicans began firing back on the Texans, but they had clearly been caught off guard. Colonel Sherman was given credit for being the first to shout "Remember the Alamo! Remember Goliad!" He would not be the last to hurl these inspirational phrases on April 21.

Colonel Rusk also noted that, "There was a general cry which pervaded the ranks—'Remember the Alamo! Remember La Bahia!' These words electrified all." He felt that the "unerring aim and irresistible energy of the Texan army could not be withstood."[35]

Further behind Captain Arnold's First Company was the nineteen-man Fourth Company of Captain William Ware. The surprise certainly came before Ware's men reached the enemy lines, for Private James Winters states that "before we got in sight of the Mexicans, they began firing at us." After the Second Regiment was fully engaged, Winters recalled that "Rusk started out with us, but turned and went with the artillery."[36]

First Sergeant Edward Thomas Branch, charging with Captain William Logan's Third Company, felt that "no officer stood higher" than Colonel Sidney Sherman as he led the Second Regiment against Santa Anna's campground. He wrote to his commander that "I distinctly recollect seeing you in the timber in the midst of your regiment." Branch's first lieutenant, Frank Hardin, was equally inspired by Sherman's conduct "in the heat of the action." While stopping to reload his gun, Hardin encountered Sherman hurrying to direct the fire of his regiment.[37]

Satisfied with the progress of Sidney Sherman's men in completely surprising the enemy, Secretary of War Rusk moved across the field with his young aide, Dr. Junius William Mottley, riding alongside him. As previously arranged, he intended to report to General Houston on the progress of Colonel Sherman's regiment. As Rusk passed Colonel Hockley's artillery, he noted that the Mexican army had opened fire with its cannon on the Texas cavalry.

As they neared Houston, Mottley was knocked from his horse by a copper-ball rifle shot through the stomach, which would later prove fatal. Rusk wrote that shortly thereafter Mottley's "spirit took its flight to join the immortal Milam and others in a better world."[38]

Unable to help the young doctor, Rusk rode swiftly to Sam Houston. As he approached, the Texas general's horse was hit by a volley of shots. Passing about forty yards from the Mexican lines and in front of the Golden Standard, Houston's borrowed horse suddenly buckled, its gray coat splattered crimson red as five shots found their mark in the animal's chest. It is likely that the horse was hit with grape shot from the Mexican cannon. Houston said that Saracen died almost instantly, "having been pierced with five balls."[39]

As Houston's noble stallion silently collapsed, he literally slid off and landed on his feet. From the First Regiment's Company A, Private Achelle Marre caught a riderless horse for the general and Houston mounted its saddle. The horse was small and Houston's long legs dangled below the stirrups.[40]

Riding his second horse of the battle, Sam Houston pushed forward. With the Mexican army being routed on one side and the main camp fully alerted, the remainder of the Texian forces rushed into the conflict.

Colonel George Hockley, leading the artillery, put it well: "A general conflict now ensued."[41]

Burleson's First Regiment Engages

While Sherman's men were quick to stir up the enemy by sweeping through the woods, he also alerted the enemy as to the others moving directly toward the Mexican camp.

Colonel Lamar's cavalry was in advance of the infantrymen and his horses were fired upon by the Golden Standard, the Mexican cannon. The Mexican riflemen quickly joined in and began to fire upon Colonel Burleson's First Regiment. Joseph Lawrence had joined Lamar's cavalry for the day from Captain Stevenson's company to help offset losses from the previous day. Approaching the Mexican camp, Lawrence felt that the shooting suddenly became intense.

> As we advanced they did not see us until we were within a hundred yards of them. Then they fired a terrific volley of small shot at us. But fortunately they shot over our heads. It seemed at one time that if one had held his hat two feet above his head, it would have caught twenty bullets or more.[42]

Burleson's men had been ordered to fire when within fifty yards of Santa Anna's camp, but they suddenly found the battlefield erupting into gunfire earlier than expected. Flashes of fire and smoke erupted among the breastworks of packsaddles up ahead in the Mexican camp.

Deaf Smith, having seen to the destruction of Vince's Bridge, raced back to the Texas troops just as they were marching across the San Jacinto battlefield. His horse filthy and foaming from hard riding, Smith raced to Houston and announced that the bridge at Vince's had been cut. The general later wrote that Smith said "Vince Bridge was cut down, and set on fire." Houston then sent Smith to spread the word among the advancing lines that there would be no reinforcements. Houston himself "dashed in front of Burleson's regiment, and announced the fact to the army."[43]

Sergeant Swearingen of Company B relates:

> Our riflemen having nearly 100 yards left to go than we had [planned] commenced the action with small arms before we did with our muskets. The musketry and riflemen kept advancing as they fired. When within about 20 steps of the enemy's line we were ordered to charge with bayonets. As soon as we were ordered to the charge and brought our guns to the proper position, the enemy gave way, except about 60 men around the cannon and protected by breastwork of corn sacks, salt, barrels of meal, and boxes of canister shot. They fell by the bayonet and swam in one mangled heap from that time until they reached the bayou.[44]

Captain Calder, leading Company K over the slight rise in the prairie, estimated that Burleson's regiment came under fire "before we were within three hundred yards of them. In the meantime our fire was reserved until we were within sixty yards of their line." Calder wrote that the Texans had moved forward "in regular order and almost perfect silence," indicating that there was no music played until the battle began.[45]

Private Sion Bostick of Captain Baker's Company D recalled, "We moved down a slope slowly, but when we started up a long sloping ridge, we all went in double-quick. Every one of us was yelling: 'Remember the Alamo! Remember Fannin!'"[46]

Burleson's regiment escaped harm from the first volleys fired at them from the Mexican camp. "They overshot us with their muskets," wrote Private Alfred Kelso of Captain Heard's Company F. Private Samuel Hardaway, who had escaped being captured with Fannin in March and had since joined Captain Baker's Company D, agreed that "they seemed to shoot above us." Ed Miles of Captain Wood's Company A felt that "the enemy's shots passed over us like hail."[47]

Reserving their fire, the Texans began descending the slight slope toward the camp and then began to take a few casualties from the enemy's fire. Santa Anna's *soldados* had adjusted their aim and began to hit some of the advancing Texans.

Private Ed Blakey of Billingsley's Company C was mortally wounded as he crested the slight rise. George Erath, running alongside him, picked up Blakey's gun and shot bag, throwing down his own. His own gun had become choked while reloading after his first shot.[48]

Another man of Billingsley's company was shot down while advancing on the Mexican breastworks. Private Thomas Mays, a thirty-four-year-old originally from Tennessee, recalled:

> When in about 250 or 300 yards distant from the breastworks I was cut down by a musket ball, which entered my left thigh (the ball is still in [me]). While on the ground wounded, R. M. Cravens, who had just fired off his gun, stopped near by to reload it, when I requested him to remain with me. He did so, and we laid down with our heads towards the battle, with our guns to protect us.[49]

Once Burleson's First Regiment came under fire, the silence they had maintained instantly converted to a cacophony of simultaneous shouting and shooting. Shouts of "Remember the Alamo" rang out down the lines as the firing began. Captain Calder noted an almost immediate "confusion and panic in the ranks of the enemy."

As the general battle commenced, the Texas field musicians began to play. There were four fifers—Frederick Lemsky, John Beebe, Martin Flores and Luke Bust. The little band also had two drummers, George Brown and Dick, the former slave. They had remained silent during the march across the field until the firing commenced. They opened with "Will You Come to the Bower?" once the shooting erupted.

Some accounts have that the Texas musicians began playing as the army marched forward. Private John Menefee later claimed that the troops "marched upon the enemy with the stillness of death. No fife, no drum, no voice was heard, until at 200 yards," he wrote. Captain Calder's account agrees that the Texians initially advanced in "almost perfect silence."[50]

Menefee's assertion that no music was played until the Texans were close to the Mexican camp is generally accepted by historians. Certainly no element of surprise could have been achieved by six musicians playing drums and flutes! Once the first shots were fired, the musicians then had reason to burst into inspiring tune.

Private John Hassell wrote in June 1836 that Colonel Burleson "ordered Yankee Doodle played" as he commanded his men to move forward at double-quick pace. Private Walter Lane of the cavalry would later insist that the band played an old folk song called "The Girl I Left Behind." While both of these tunes may have been played at some point, the song most commonly accepted as that played during the march into battle at San Jacinto is Thomas Moore's "Will You Come to the Bower?"[51]

The fact that this particular song did not have more military use for the soldiers to step to is indicative of the ragtag little Texas band. The members were from three different companies and certainly this little corps had not practiced much together. "Will You Come to the Bower?" was a popular tune of the time that each man likely knew well enough to play.

According to Colonel Coleman, the Twin Sisters were first fired "when we had approached within two hundred yards." Gunner John Ferrell agreed that "we unlimbered at about 2 hundred yards from the Mexican breastworks." At the same moment, General Houston rode to the center of Colonel Burleson's regiment and cried out loudly, "To the charge! To the charge!" The Texas foot soldiers immediately "set forward in double quick time, and in one minute the action became general."[52]

The roar of the Twin Sisters was inspiring to many of the foot soldiers. "Every man sprang forward with renewed energy," recalled John Swisher. The artillerymen worked rapidly, and the Twin Sisters kept up a steady firing. Swisher felt that "the thunder of their roar is very potent in scaring the wits out of the enemy, and is worth ten bands of martial music in inspiring the troops."[53]

Swisher noted that the First Regiment came under fire while still a considerable distance from the enemy camp. He felt that the Mexican army fired "incessantly" and fought valiantly around their cannon. "During the charge the air seemed to be full of hissing bullets," he wrote. Bullets struck the ground around the feet of the charging men, while others whistled past their ears.

First Lieutenant John Borden of Captain Baker's Company D found some of his men holding their fire until the distance narrowed. During the early firing, Captain Baker was one of the first Texans to be wounded on April 21. Sergeant Moses Bryan later stated, "I had three holes shot in the skirts of my frock coat—the coat flew out as we advanced in a trot. And I heard bullets whistling as they overshot us."[54]

When Captain Baker went down, Lieutenant Borden assumed acting command as he found the battle erupting about him.

> In a very short time, perhaps a minute, the firing became general; smoke from the cannon and small arms rendered it almost impossible to see the shape or size of our enemy. But on we pushed, pell-mell, helter-skelter.[55]

Burleson's regiment would within minutes begin mixing with that of Sidney Sherman's as the Texans rushed upon the Mexican campground.

Captain Juan Seguin's Tejano company fought valiantly. Sam Houston would later write to Seguin's father of "his brave and gallant bearing in the battle of San Jacinto, with that of his men." Commanding "the only Mexican company who fought in the cause of Texas at the Battle of San Jacinto," Seguin also earned Houston's "warmest regard and esteem."[56]

As his company approached camp, they were ordered to fire a volley into Santa Anna's men. Having been ordered to keep low while approaching, Seguin's men lay low and quickly reloaded. Corporal Ambrosio Rodriguez remembered hearing First Sergeant Manuel Flores hollering at his companymen to "Get up! Santa Anna's men are running."[57]

As he led his twenty-four-man unit into battle, Seguin noticed Private Juan López, the teenage orphan boy who had joined his company at the Buffalo Bayou crossing two days prior. López was "entering boldly the fight, brandishing on one hand an old rusty sword, holding on the other a gun stick at the top of which was fastened a red kind of rag." Captain Seguin ordered López to throw down the pole and take the rifle of Private Manuel Tarin, "who declared himself sick and unable to fight." In the boy's Republic pension application, Seguin would later write that young López "fought as bravely as any man in the Army and recd. a slight flesh wound in the left knee."[58]

During the battle near the Mexican camp, one Mexican officer called out for mercy. According to Colonel Rusk, the officer called out to Tony Menchaca of Captain Seguin's company, calling him "a brother Mexican." The enemy soldier pleaded with the Tejano to save his life.[59]

"No, damn you, I'm no Mexican," replied Menchaca. "I'm an American. Shoot him!" Another soldier fired and killed the Mexican officer.

Santa Anna's Forces Overrun

The activities of General Santa Anna at the moment of the Texian assault upon his campground have long been debated among historians. Accounts of Mexican veterans admit that the conditions were very relaxed and that many men were resting from the previous days' long marches.

Henry Arthur McArdle painstakingly contacted numerous battle veterans for their photos and recollections before he painted "The Battle of San Jacinto" in 1898. This 92 x 167-inch oil painting now hangs in the Senate Chambers of the Texas Capitol in Austin. *Texas State Library and Archives Commission.*

General Santa Anna had retired to his own tent to rest. One of the more controversial stories to later circulate was that El Presidente was entertaining young Emily D. West, the indentured servant captured at Morgan's Point three days before. Santa Anna had been without female companionship for more than two weeks. He had taken a "bride" in a mock marriage, performed by a Mexican officer impersonating a priest, in San Antonio before the final assault on the Alamo. The attractive seventeen-year-old rode with the Mexican command on the San Jacinto campaign until April 2. High waters on the Guadalupe River would not allow her heavy carriage to cross, and she was sent back to Mexico City in her carriage, which reportedly included a trunk full of silver.[60]

Santa Anna's men had captured several of Colonel Morgan's indentured servants on April 19 at New Washington, including Emily West. As chaos befell the Mexican army, some believe that the Mexican commander-in-chief was being distracted by Emily West. Her generally accepted description of being a mulatto girl led some to later believe that she was the inspiration for the song "The Yellow Rose of Texas." Sam Houston reportedly knew of the Miss Emily story, although many historians dismiss the whole event as a grandiose piece of Texas folklore.[61]

Colonel Delgado and the other Mexican officers were caught completely off guard as the Texans raced forward. In his diary, he recorded the state of affairs as Houston's men closed in on their camp.

> At this fatal moment the bugler on our right signaled the advance of the enemy upon that wing. His Excellency and staff were asleep; the greater number of the men were also sleeping; of the rest, some were eating, others were scattered in the woods in search of boughs to prepare shelter. Our line was composed of musket stacks. Our cavalry was riding bare-back to and from water.[62]

Colonel Castrillón had just shaved and bathed himself when the commotion erupted. Moments earlier, he had been engaged in conversation with other members of Santa Anna's staff. Santa Anna claimed that Castrillón had carelessly neglected to visit the guard lines a single time while Santa Anna and Cos' men were resting. "Following his example the other leaders and officers did the same thing, and thus part of the troops were asleep, and those who were awake were completely relaxed," wrote General Vicente Filisola.[63]

Santa Anna's personal secretary, Ramón Caro, felt that the president unfairly pushed blame on Castrillón. He felt that the commander-in-chief was equally liable for vigilance against an enemy "who on the day before makes a false attack to feel our strength."[64]

Santa Anna later wrote that he was "sleeping soundly" when he was awakened by the firing. He immediately became aware that his forces were under attack and that "there was unexplained disorder. The enemy had surprised our advance posts." General Santa Anna immediately attempted to organize a defensive force against the Texans.[65]

He organized an attack column under Colonel Manuel Céspedes which consisted of the Guerrero permanent battalion and detachments from Toluca and Guadalajara. Céspedes, joined with a column under Lieutenant Colonel Santiago Luelmo, marched forward to contain the main fire of the Texans. The Mexican cannon was commanded by Lieutenant Ignacio Arenal, who kept up a continual fire against the Texans during the early moments of the battle.

"I Shot Old Betsy Six Times"

During the early minutes of the battle of San Jacinto, the surprised Mexican soldiers managed to put up strong resistance. Their makeshift breastworks offered something of a haven for their riflemen. "Their breastworks were composed of baggage, saddle bags, and brush, in all about four or five feet high," remembered James Winters of Sherman's regiment. "There was a gap eight or ten feet wide through which they fired the cannon."[66]

Once Colonel Sherman's Second Regiment began sweeping into the Mexican camp, these breastworks offered no protection. Few men had bayonets on their rifles, so their firearms became warclubs once the opportunity to reload was lost. The Texans used their muskets and rifles to bash the enemy and many of their guns were broken off at the breech.

Private Michael J. Brake of Captain Logan's company snapped his shotgun in half during the battle. Captain Hayden Arnold's expensive London Younger gun, which he valued at $35, was shot nearly off at the breech. During the continued action, his gun was entirely broken and discarded on the battlefield.[67]

Private Jesse Davis had a close call while fighting with Captain Murphree's Columbia company. Early in the battle, his gun began acting up. Davis took a seat on a fallen log to repair it amidst the fighting and confusion. Hearing a comrade shout to him, he looked up in time to see a Mexican officer advancing on him with a drawn sword. Davis whirled, grasping the barrel of his rifle, and struck the officer a terrific blow on the side of the head. As his victim crumpled, Davis collected the Mexican's sword and moved on into battle, discarding his own broken gun.[68]

The cavalry companies of Captains William Smith and Henry Karnes raced into the Mexican camp to join the hand-to-hand fighting. "In a second we were into them with guns, pistols and bowie knives," wrote Private Walter Lane. "In a short time, they were running like turkeys, whipped and discomfited."[69]

Deaf Smith was as valiant on the battlefield as he had proven as a spy throughout the Texas Revolution. As the Texas infantry advanced across the field, he had galloped ahead and directly up to the breastworks. Secretary of War Rusk happened to catch a view of old Deaf in action at the Mexican lines.

> Just as he reached it, his horse stumbled and fell, throwing him over his head among the enemy. Having dropped his sword in the fall, he jumped up, drew one of his belt pistols, presented it at the head of a Mexican, who was attempting to bayonet him, and the percussion-cap exploded without the pistol's going off. Upon which, Smith threw the pistol at the head of the Mexican, staggered him back, seized his gun, took it from him, and defended himself with it, until the infantry got up to his relief.[70]

Private James H. Nash, a fellow scout of Captain Karnes' company, came to Smith's rescue. Spurring his own horse, he ran down the Mexican officer and allowed Smith to finish off the soldier with the Mexican's own saber.[71]

Rusk noted a number of brave acts of individuals on April 21. One of these was John Robbins, who had given up his horse on April 20 to one of Sherman's volunteers. His horse was killed in the action, and Robbins was forced to fight on foot this day. To further add to his situation, he lost his gun in the heat of battle near the breastworks. Charging through camp, he was seized by a Mexican soldier who had lost his gun also. Colonel Rusk noted the two "stout men" fall to the ground in hand-to-hand combat. "Robbins managed, whilst contending on the earth, to get out a Bowie-knife, which he had in his belt, and quickly ended the contest, by cutting the Mexican's throat."[72]

During the close-quarters duel, Private William Sadler, the former ranger captain who had joined the Nacogdoches Volunteers, was attacked by a Mexican soldier wielding a straight-bladed dagger. In the ensuing wrestle, Sadler won possession of the dirk, which would remain a prized possession of his for many years.[73]

Although some Texans had been shot down while advancing over the center of the battlefield, the larger number of casualties occurred in front of and inside the Mexican campground. Advancing under heavy fire, Colonel Burleson's First Regiment took twice as many casualties as Sherman's Second Regiment, which had advanced under better cover.

Albert Gallatin, first sergeant of Captain Ware's Company B, wrote the *Texas Almanac* in 1872 to confirm that his company fought with Colonel Sherman and that "I was wounded in that battle." From Ware's little nineteen-man company, four men were killed or wounded as they charged the Mexican breastworks.

Second Lieutenant George A. Lamb was shot down and killed while charging with Ware's company. A twenty-one-year-old who had come to Texas in 1834 as an orphan from South Carolina, he was later honored as the namesake of Lamb County, Texas. Second Sergeant William Carvin Winters was shot in the knee and fell. Private George Washington Robinson was also seriously wounded and fell near the enemy's breastworks. Despite losing nearly a quarter of his men in the first moments of battle, Captain Ware's other men fought bravely ahead.[74]

First Sergeant Thomas Patton Fowle of Captain Smith's company was mortally wounded while leading his cavalrymen in the charge against the Mexican encampment. A Boston native who was a scholar of the French, Spanish and Italian languages, young Fowle died on the San Jacinto battlefield.[75]

Private John Hassell of Burleson's regiment considered San Jacinto "an open field fight" in which revenge was the "prevailing feeling or sentiment." He wrote to his father on June 21 with his actions during the battle.

> Our cannons, our muskets, our rifles and pistols played, it appeared to me, the most delightful tune I have ever heard since the world commenced. I had [a] first rate rifle and about this time I was using her, sir, with all my might. She run about forty [inches] to the ground and shot first rate.
>
> I took notice to some of the big yellow bellies and when Betsy would bore a hole in them, the claret would gush out large as a cornstalk. One big fellow, I remember, who I shot in the neck and it appeared that it had near cut his head off. I shot old Betsy six times and a holster pistol one time. In the seven shots I know that I killed four.[76]

Mitchell Putman of Captain Heard's company was wounded in the right arm near the body by an escopeta ball, which caused a partial paralysis of his arm. Another of Heard's men, Leroy Wilkinson, was severely wounded and would die within two weeks from the effects of his wounds.

Captain Stevenson's Company H moved steadily toward the Mexican campground. Private James Hill recalled the enemy's breastworks "beginning at [a] point of timber and extending out a considerable distance in the prairie." Stacked with "brush, blankets, sacks of corn, flour, camp equipage, aparajos [packsaddles]" and other packing, Hill found the enemy's breastworks to be "bulletproof."[77]

Two of Stevenson's men were shot down as the company approached the breastworks. Second Sergeant Ashley Stephens was shot through the calf in each leg, although no bones were broken. Unable to walk, he would lie bleeding on the battlefield for many hours. Private John Tom was also hit in a leg, the force shattering the leg below the knee and leaving his foot dangling.

George Washington Lonis, a member of Captain David Murphree's company, was severely wounded in the chest. Known as "Washington," Lonis fired on the enemy many times before falling. According to Dr. James Phelps, he saw Lonis fall and went to his aid with three other members of Murphree's company. George Wright, James Hayr and Claiborne Rector picked up a blanket from the abandoned baggage of the fleeing Mexican army. These four placed Lonis aboard the blanket and carried him back to the rear of the action, where Dr. Phelps could tend to him.[78]

As they laid him over on his side, Lonis came to long enough to announce, "I fired my gun thirteen times, and I saw twelve of the yellow bellies fall."

Dr. Phelps found that Lonis had been shot through the right lung straight through front to back. Every breath was a bloody, gurgling respiration which Phelps could hear. Although seriously wounded, Lonis would survive and he and his wife settled in Guadalupe County, Texas.

Another of the Murphree company to be hit was twenty-year-old Private Elbridge Gerry Rector. "I was in the battle of San Jacinto and was wounded in the arm and side," wrote Rector in 1902. "The wound in the side is hurting me at this writing." Private Elijah Votaw of Captain Gillaspie's unit "was wounded by a canister shot in the breast."[79]

Benjamin Brigham, the young soldier of ill health who had finally gotten a good night's sleep, was severely wounded early in the battle.

Advancing across the field behind the Twin Sisters, he threw up his arms and cried out to his captain as he fell face forward. His messmate Francis Cooke, who had taken Brigham's guard detail so that he could finally rest before battle, later learned of the loss of his buddy.

> Brigham was my friend and my comrade. We ate together, slept together, fought together. We were two boys about nineteen years of age, fighting for the same cause. I would have done anything for him, and I weep for him to-day, as I wept for him sixty-five years ago when I looked for him after the battle and found he was no more.[80]

Brigham's captain, Robert Calder, considered him a "noble young comrade" who "although a boy in years, his solid sense and judgement would have done credit to most men at maturity of years."[81]

The discipline of the Texans quickly broke down as they raced into the Mexican camp. Every man discharged his firearm as rapidly as possible, then furiously reloaded his gun and fired again. Reloading the muskets required men to stop and work on their weapons. With gun loaded and charged, each man then ran ahead and sought out his next victim. They did not wait for orders to fire again. Nor did many wait for the regiment of companymen to fire in unison.[82]

Private Alfonso Steele had only gotten off his second round by the time he noted some of the Mexicans in camp fleeing ahead of him. He stopped in the timber to reload again and then ran on ahead of some of Captain Gillaspie's company. He raised his gun to shoot another Mexican, but Steele was shot through the body before he could fire.

As he fell, David Rusk of Captain Arnold's Nacogdoches Volunteers called for some men to stay and help him. "No, take them on," implored Steele.

> One of our own men in passing asked me if he could take my pistol, but by this time I was bleeding at the nose and mouth so I couldn't speak; so he just stooped down and got it and went on. After laying there awhile I managed to get to a sitting posture and drink some water I had in a gourd. This stopped the blood from coming from my nose and mouth.

Twin Sisters against the Golden Standard

The Second Regiment routed the newly arrived troops under General Cos, most of whom had been lying down asleep before the shooting began. Some of these inexperienced men rushed into battle without even their guns. While General Cos' reinforcements proved to be outclassed, the *soldados* manning Santa Anna's Golden Standard cannon proved to be fierce fighters. From the center of the battlefield the Twin Sisters fired away, steadily pounding the Mexican forces. The Golden Standard only fired three rounds before a shot from the Twin Sisters hit the Mexican cannon's water bucket, wounding or scaring off most of the gunners.

John M. Wade, a former company commander during the Bexar siege, was working one of the Twin Sisters with Ben McCullough and John Ferrell. It was their gun that carried away the water bucket of the Mexican long-nine and did other damage.[83]

Gunner Ben McCullough later wrote:

> At the battle of San Jacinto, I was in command of one piece of artillery. The fire of it opened upon the enemy, about two hundred yards distant. We advanced after each discharge, keeping it in advance of the breastworks, at which time I had aimed the gun, but was delayed in firing for a moment by General Houston, who passed across some thirty paces in front of the gun, and was nearly that distance in advance of every man in that part of the field.[84]

When Burleson's First Regiment and Millard's regulars had advanced within about one hundred yards of the Mexican breastworks, the Texan artillery corps was slightly in advance of the infantrymen. At this moment, a division of Mexican soldiers under Colonel Manuel Céspedes charged upon Hockley's artillery.[85]

To First Sergeant Lyman Rounds of Captain Briscoe's regulars it seemed that his men were unfairly exposed during the march across the field.

> Although an admirer of Genl. Houston, I think he made a rather unmilitary movement in making the attack. He formed in double file, marched at a right angle on the enemy's left until within musket range, filed to right by flank, so that our Co. (A) had to march the entire length of the Mexicans' line under fire, before we could face to the front and return their fire.[86]

Despite the exposure to his company, Rounds and every member of Colonel Millard's regulars escaped injury on April 21. Every other division of Texans, in fact, suffered casualties except for the regulars!

At the height of the fight, General Manuel Fernando Castrillón, Colonel Juan Almonte and Lieutenant Colonel Pedro Delgado shouted encouragement to their men to fight.

General Castrillón, commanding the Mexican artillery, turned his cannon's attention from Lamar's cavalry in order to assist the charge of Colonel Céspedes and Lieutenant Colonel Santiago Luelmo upon the Texan artillery. The Golden Standard was turned in the direction of Burleson's regiment and quickly readied to fire. The soldier preparing to light the fuse, however, was shot down by a Texas infantryman.

"The First Regiment, at that instant, with the most deafening yell I ever heard, charged upon the breast-work," wrote Colonel Rusk. The Twin Sisters barked angrily at the same moment that Burleson's screaming soldiers charged forward.

"We rushed forward with great impetuosity," wrote Captain Stevenson after the battle, "jumped the enemy's breastworks, the Alamo being our war cry." He added, "Our rifles created dreadful havoc among them, and they gave way in every direction."[87]

The two advancing Mexican columns under Céspedes and Luelmo were crushed and forced to turn tail. Luelmo fell dead and Céspedes, seriously wounded, joined the retreat. The flight of Colonel Céspedes caused some of those manning the Golden Standard to panic as well. Twenty-five-year-old Lieutenant Ignacio Arenal, however, fought bravely until the end with the cannon crew.[88]

General Castrillón stood on, stoically extorting his comrades to fight on. Colonel Rusk noted that Castrillón was "standing on the ammunition boxes, behind the piece, exposed from head to foot." Castrillón tried in vain to sustain his men at the cannon. "When he found that to be impossible, he folded up his arms, stood and looked sullenly, and without moving, upon our troops, who were advancing upon him, until they arrived at or near the breast-work."[89]

According to one of the Mexican eyewitnesses, First Sergeant Francisco Becerra, Castrillón was determined to die fighting. "When it was discovered the army of Gen. Santa Anna was defeated," he recalled, "several of the officers and non-commissioned officers of the command went to General Castrillón and begged him to leave the field." According to Becerra, Castrillón felt that it "was a matter of no consequence should they all be killed, but it was a great loss to Mexico should he fall."[90]

Walter Lane of Captain Karnes' company considered Castrillón "an old Castillian gentleman" who proudly accepted his own fate in the face of superior numbers. Lane claims that Colonel Rusk even implored the Texans not to kill Castrillon, "and knocked up some of their guns; but others ran round and riddled him with balls."[91]

Tom Rusk, in examining the proud artillery general's body after the battle, "found that several rifle-balls had passed directly through his body." Of European Spanish descent, Castrillon was considered by Secretary of War Rusk "to be quite a gentlemanly, honourable man."[92]

Colonel Hockley, designated to lead Captain Moreland's artillery on April 21, found plenty to be proud of. One man cited for conspicuous bravery among Hockley's unit was Private Montgomery Baxter. The rammer and sponger of No. 2 cannon of the Twin Sisters, Baxter had joined the company at the Brazos when it was organized upon the arrival of the cannon. He was cited by fellow companyman Thomas Green as having "acted very gallantly in the battle of San Jacinto." Green further stated that "due to the excessive fatigue of that day," Baxter became sick at the army's campground and died of fever at Harrisburg about a week after the battle.[93]

Colonel Hockley wrote that his men kept up "a hot fire" and proudly noted that their first shot "caused their loud shooting to cease."[94]

The Texans quickly captured the Mexican artillery piece. Captain William Wood certified that Private Achelle Marre, who had come to Texas in January with Sherman's men, was "among the few who took the cannon the Golden Standard" at San Jacinto.[95]

Marre was reportedly assisted in this capture by Private John Bunton, one of the ten signers of the Texas Declaration of Independence present at San Jacinto. Bunton used his rifle to club one of the officers at the cannon while Marre drew a Mexican saber and cut down two more of the Golden Standard's gunners.[96]

Colonel Burleson's First Regiment and Colonel Millard's two companies of regulars "charged upon and mounted the breastwork of the enemy, and drove them from their cannon," wrote Rusk. "The cavalry, under Colonel Lamar, at the same time fell on them with great fury and great slaughter."[97]

The Mexican camp was quickly in disarray. "In ten minutes after the firing of the first gun," wrote Colonel Rusk, "we were charging through the camp, and driving them before us." The enemy took to flight, "officers and all," both on horseback and on foot, with Texans in hot pursuit.

Others estimated that it took slightly longer to break the Mexican resistance. Private Charles Shain of Captain Murphree's company wrote that "Our whole army was across the breast work in fifteen or twenty minutes after the battle commenced. The Mexicans were then running in all directions."[98] General Sam Houston's official report states that it was "about eighteen minutes from the time of close action" until his army had succeeded in completely unnerving their opponents.

The confusion was so complete that Santa Anna himself was seen not to stick around, recalls Captain Calder.

> They were immediately thrown, by the charge of Sherman on their right and our attack on their left and centre, into the wildest confusion. Santa Anna and a portion of his staff, with his cavalry, broke from the field at the first discharge, escaping around our right wing. A ridge was between my position and the ground they passed over, but I saw their heads and a portion of their persons, as they were flying from the camp.[99]

A "Panic Stricken Herd": Flight of Santa Anna

Santa Anna's secretary, Ramon Caro, was disgusted with the "lightning rapidity" in which the Texans had been able to overrun their superior Mexican force. "It is too much to admit that even the cavalry had unsaddled their horses and turned them loose to graze, while the enemy was in sight," he wrote.[100]

Santa Anna, having rushed from his tent, found that even his best attempts to organize a strong stand were lost in the madness. Colonel Delgado claimed to have seen "His Excellency running about in the utmost excitement, wringing his hands and unable to give an order." Delgado noted General Castrillón on the ground, saw that Colonel Antonio Treviño was killed and that Colonel Marcial Aguirre was "severely injured." He tried to rally some of the fleeing dragoons as they raced for the trees beyond camp, "but all efforts were in vain." Delgado felt that "the evil was beyond remedy; they were a bewildered and panic stricken herd."[101]

"With all hope lost and every man for himself," wrote Santa Anna, "my desperation was as great as my danger." A servant of Colonel Juan Bringas, Santa Anna's aide-de-camp, offered the general a horse and urged him to save himself. Reportedly remarking, "The battle is lost," Santa Anna accepted the stallion, leaving his own fine saddle and horse behind in the rush of excitement.[102]

Santa Anna looked about for his personal escort and found only two soldiers from it who were saddling up. These men said that their fellow officers and men were already on the run. Santa Anna then tried to take the road toward Thompson's Pass, where he had last left the division under General Filisola.

Secretary Caro saw Santa Anna "coming already in flight" and he immediately followed El Presidente on horseback. "Thank God we were not among the last who fled," he wrote, "for of those, very few survived to tell the tale."[103]

The Halt Controversy

Sherman's and Burleson's regiments, together with Hockley's artillery, Millard's regulars and Lamar's cavalry, all came together in busting up the Mexican camp with a deadly fury. "Where our two regiments got together, and the Mexicans rallied," wrote Stephen Sparks, "about ten acres of ground was literally covered with their dead bodies."[104]

James Tarlton of Baker's company wrote the next day that "I was enabled to be the third man" who entered the Mexican breastworks. "The destruction of human life was speedy and immense," wrote Private Samuel Hardaway of Baker's company shortly after the battle.[105]

Soon after Dr. Mottley had been shot down, Major General Houston was also painfully wounded on the San Jacinto battlefield, although most did not realize this fact until after the battle. Riding his second horse of the day, he was stoically riding up and down the battle lines shouting, "Fire away! God damn you, fire!"[106]

Private William Taylor, riding into combat with Captain William Smith's cavalry company, felt that Houston was highly visible during the peak of the battle.

> General Houston placed himself at the head of the First Regiment in front of the enemy's breastwork. The cavalry to which I belonged were on the right of it. During the engagement, General Houston was at least thirty paces in front of the interior line, animating his men to the charge at the top of his shrill voice, that was as distinct and as familiar to all as distant thunder.[107]

During the battle, "I met not officers of my staff," recalled Houston, "and spoke to no one of them, from the time the charge was ordered."[108]

Houston was moving across the battlefield and was near Millard's regulars when he was struck. Colonel Rusk later wrote that "Major General Houston acted with great gallantry, encouraging his men to the attack, and heroically charged, in front of the infantry, within a few yards of the enemy, receiving at the same time a wound in his leg."[109]

According to Robert Coleman, the general was wounded after riding "from the 1st regiment to the extreme right of Millard's command." In view of Rusk and the regulars, Houston's second horse was suddenly hit by several shots near the breastworks. As his horse collapsed, he felt a sharp pain in his left ankle as a musket ball struck home. Houston's son, Andrew Jackson Houston, later wrote that "The Texan General was twice dismounted by the enemy's fire. His first horse was killed, having been shot 5 times."[110]

The fact that Houston lost two horses in the opening minutes of the battle of San Jacinto was reported by several participants. Captain Stevenson of the First Regiment wrote in a letter two days after the battle that "Gen. Houston had two horses killed under him, and was shot through the leg." James Winters in 1901 would relate that Houston "had two horses killed from under him, and was on his third one before he passed the Mexicans' works." Dr. Labadie, in speaking with Houston late on April 21, said that Houston told him, "I have had two horses shot under me."[111]

General Houston was hit in the left leg by what was called a copper ball, although it was most likely made of brass. "His second [horse] was shot at the same time that the General's left ankle was shattered by a copper ball from an escopeta," wrote his son. It is interesting to note that most historians have listed Houston as having been shot in the right leg. In 1853, Houston wrote to his wife that "I still suffer slightly in my left leg, from the same cause, that I complained of at home, the San Jacinto wound."[112]

The confusion over which leg Houston was wounded in is the likely result of artist interpretation. The battle accounts of those present do not list which leg Houston was wounded in. For his famous 1886 San Jacinto painting, William Huddle chose to show the Texas general with a bandaged right leg.

Although never confirmed, there were at least a few rumors that Houston was shot by one of his own men. Ellis Benson, fighting with the artillery, agreed that Houston was shot while charging on his horse between the two opposing lines and in front of Texas troops. According to Benson, he was shot in the ankle that was facing the Texan lines.[113]

Colonel Mirabeau Lamar, the poet from Georgia who now commanded the cavalry, also later asserted that Houston could have been shot by one of his own men. In his private papers, he drew a comparison between Houston and the poem *Iliad*.

> With dread that he might defraud the eager band of victory at San Jacinto it was said that an excellent marksman of Captain William S. Fisher's

company in the early part of the action thought it safest to temporarily depose Achilles [Houston] by a touch on the heel.[114]

Houston stumbled and nearly fell before a comrade caught him and helped him to stand on his one good leg. Adjutant Nicholas Lynch soon arrived and, "with the assistance of others, placed the General upon his fine roan charger."[115] Because of how quickly he mounted his third horse of the day and resumed leading his men, few soldiers were even aware that their general had been shot.

In addition to being shot, Houston was also accused after the battle by a number of men of trying to call a halt to the battle. Various versions of this event have been offered by battlefield participants. Several witnesses declared that Houston ordered his forces to halt midway in the battle but that his superior, Secretary of War Thomas Rusk, countermanded the order.

In support of this claim is an account by Dr. Nicholas Labadie, who observed Colonel Rusk riding in full gallop toward the left rear of the forces when Houston ordered the halt. Colonel Coleman wrote that as "the soldiers were storming the enemy's works," and forcing the Mexican soldiers to retreat, Houston had just crossed a ravine some distance from the Mexican campground. "Houston approached and ordered a halt." According to Coleman, Houston felt that "glory enough has been gained this day, and blood enough has been shed."[116]

Captain Heard, leading the First Regiment's Company F, wrote in 1859 that Houston ordered a halt after the Mexican army had been driven from its camp "to a boggy drain." Heard supported Coleman's belief that Houston called out that enough blood had been shed.[117]

The boggy area behind the main Mexican campground was a small bayou feeding into Peggy's Lake. In this soggy muck, numerous horses and mules had bogged down. From this area, General Houston reportedly issued his halt command.

Labadie says Colonel Rusk immediately countermanded this direct order, shouting at the top of his voice, "If we stop we are cut to pieces. Don't stop—go ahead—give them hell!"[118]

Captain Billingsley and Captain Baker both agreed that Rusk implored the men to fight on, in spite of Houston's call to halt. "Well and truly did they respond to his encouraging voice," wrote Billingsley. "The hour, so long delayed, had at length come for vengeance."[119]

Colonel John Wharton reportedly rode up to the general and implored him to continue the fight, as Sidney Sherman's regiment was still hotly engaged in driving the enemy.

Colonel Sidney Sherman wrote a letter to *The Galveston Weekly News* of June 23, 1855, which stated that even Colonel Wharton's influence "did not avail at the time Houston called a halt, for Rusk did, in violation of Houston's positive orders, take the responsibility of ordering the troops to advance." Sherman felt that this halt "would have sacrificed my regiment, as it was then engaged in the timber on the enemy's right." Although Wharton urged the continued advance just as strenuously as Rusk, Sherman felt that the Secretary of War was the only person that could

> with any propriety assume the command. On his doing so, Houston called upon men to bear witness that the responsibility would not fall upon him, and then he left the field. The battle was won, and the Commander-in-Chief has had no use for the witnesses he called upon.[120]

Other participants would later claim that the "halt" order was merely directed at a small portion of the army. Captain Amasa Turner had managed to reorganize a portion of his company after passing through the enemy's breastworks. "In the course of two hundred yards they all got into line, and we joined in the rout, in something like order in my company." During the pursuit beyond the Mexican campground, Turner claimed that Lieutenant Colonel Henry Millard rode up, ordering his company to halt.[121]

As quickly as Turner had halted his company, Colonel Wharton rode up asking, "Regulars, why have you stopped?" Millard spoke to Wharton, and then Millard gave orders for Captain Turner's regulars to march back to the battleground and place a guard around the Mexican camp. Captain Isaac Moreland had reported to Houston that some men were looting and vandalizing the property in the Mexican camp. According to Turner's account, General Houston had hollered at these men to "halt," and had then dispatched Millard to bring a company to act as guardians over the Mexican loot.

Captain Turner therefore felt that Houston had not "ever ordered a halt of the army, or even wished or expected to halt it, but that he articulated the word 'halt,' surrounded by his staff and aides, I have no doubt."

General Houston's own defense of the "halt" controversy agrees with the above events. After the right wing of the enemy had broken and the Mexican camp had been overrun, Houston found his infantry in confusion. He later wrote:

> The Commander-in-Chief cast his eyes to the right and perceived that the Infantry, 200 strong under Col. Millard, was in some confusion. He galloped to the Colonel and asked the cause. He replied, "my horse was wounded," which was correct.
>
> The General faced to the left, and led the Infantry to meet a solid column of the enemy numbering about 500 men, and advancing on the Infantry in good order. When within about thirty yards the General ordered the Infantry (or Regulars) to halt and fire. This fire of the Infantry literally mowed down the enemy and if any survived they fled.[122]

Houston's detailed explanation of this controversy says that he did indeed try to organize men who were pursuing some 240 of Colonel Juan Almonte's men across a ravine beyond the Mexican campground. This bog was some "five to six hundred yards" beyond the battlefield along "the route of the refugees." At the bottom of the ravine was a quagmire in which horses and mules had become stuck. Houston, in his own words, "ordered them to halt and form, and not to advance upon the enemy in disorder." He also ordered Deaf Smith to announce to the fleeing Mexicans that they would be treated as prisoners of war if they would surrender. He then gave further orders to Colonel Rusk to "receive their surrender."

It is at this point of the battle that Rusk would have been close enough to Houston to hear that he ordered a halt, which Houston admittedly did in order to organize these troops near the boggy ditch. Houston next ordered one of the regular companies under Captain Turner to stop its pursuit of the enemy and return to camp to guard the spoils of war from looters. "This order was obeyed, and Capt. Turner's company remained on the field during the night," wrote Houston. "Gen. Houston remained at the ravine until the return of Gen. Rusk, and the[y] return[ed] together over the field of battle to the Texas Camp."

The whole "halt" controversy, therefore, was likely later stirred up by Colonel Coleman's hatred and spread by other political opponents of Sam Houston who chose to agree with Coleman's version. Houston was trying to stop one company and get it under control versus the entire army.

Captain Robert Calder later wrote that if Houston indeed did call a halt, it very well may have been aimed more at organizing the companies before charging again. "I very much doubt if any captain could, at short notice, have formed any five of his men together," wrote Calder. "Under these circumstances, it might appear that such an order was proper."[123]

Lieutenant John Borden, leading Company D of the First Regiment after Captain Baker had been wounded, was not even sure who called for a halt. "Supposing it came from head-quarters, in the absence of my captain," Borden wrote, "I endeavored, as the second in command, to rally the members of our company."[124]

He quickly found this to be impossible. Every man was "fighting and charging Mexicans" on his own accord. "No respect was paid to the order to halt—at least, so little that it had no direct bearing upon the movements either of the enemy or our own men."

Sam Houston would deny to his death that he had ever given a direct order to halt. Rusk later wrote that he only recalled Houston order some men that had become entangled in a bog to halt and reform. Whatever events actually transpired in the heat of battle would not seriously affect the rising popularity of Sam Houston in Texas.

The "halt" controversy did not have any significant effect on the fighting psyche of the troops on the San Jacinto battlefield. Most, in fact, never heard of such an order being called until long after the conflict had ended. Even if an order had been heard over the crack of gunfire and cannon reports, it is doubtful that many would have heeded the call to stop.

The Texans' zeal for revenge, aimed against the Mexican army that had massacred and executed hundreds of Texas soldiers at the Alamo and Goliad, drove them like a pack of hounds frenzied by the action of the hunt. Even after the contest was decided, these men continued to drive their fleeing opponents to an impenetrable area beyond the Mexican campground, and there a general massacre ensued.

CHAPTER 16

"It Was Nothing but a Slaughter"

April 21

> At the end of twelve miles, we all stopped to rest and let our horses rest. When we dismounted, we were so fatigued that we could not stand up and fell around like a company of drunken men.
>
> —*Private Joseph Lawrence, cavalry volunteer*

The Texas Army had approached Santa Anna's camp just after 4:00 p.m. and had overpowered their enemy in just under twenty minutes. General Houston wrote that it was "about eighteen minutes from the time of close action until we were in possession of the enemy's encampment." By 4:30, the enemy was well routed and the battle essentially won, but Houston noted that "the pursuit by the main army continued until twilight."

The fighting was heated in the Mexican campground and the survivors fled. "The officers and men ran promiscuously after the enemy," recalled Private Jesse Walling of the Nacogdoches Volunteers company.[1]

The vengeful Texans showed no mercy, even to the wounded on the ground. Sergeant Moses Austin Bryan, nephew of Stephen F. Austin, recalled one such scene.

> I had a double-barrel shotgun and had shot only four times when we crossed the breastworks. After that I shot no more at the poor devils who were running. I came upon a young Mexican boy (a drummer, I suppose) lying on his face. One of the volunteers brought to Texas by Colonel Sherman pricked the boy with his bayonet. The boy grasped the man around the legs and called in Spanish: "Ave Maria prissima per Dios salva me vida!" I begged the man to spare him, both of his legs being broken already. The man looked at me and put his hand on his pistol, so I passed on. Just as I did so, he blew out the boy's brains.[2]

344

In pursuit of the Mexican soldiers running through the timber, Private Rinaldo Hotchkiss spotted Colonel John Forbes. "A Mexican had surrendered and was begging the Texans not to kill him," said Hotchkiss. Forbes tried in vain to order the prisoner to go to the rear of the action, but the frightened man "did not understand him and continued begging and talking."[3]

Sergeant Tony Menchaca estimated that the entire fight lasted "two hours and a quarter," including the time it took to round up prisoners.[4]

The Texans had suffered relatively few casualties compared to the damage inflicted upon the Mexican army. James Tarlton, the well-educated former Kentucky politician was in awe. "Such slaughter on the one side and such almost miraculous preservation on the other have never been heard of since the invention of gunpowder," he wrote on April 22.[5]

In the woods beyond camp, those being overtaken cried out for quarter. More often than not, the answer was "Remember the Alamo," followed by a lethal blow to the soldier who cried out. Some men even tried to climb trees to hide. As the Second Regiment's First Company pushed on into the woods beyond Santa Anna's camp, William Sadler witnessed friend Dickerson Parker shoot a Mexican soldier out of a tree.[6]

Beyond their campground, the fleeing Mexican soldiers were doomed by the mud bogs and soggy grounds which impeded their flight. Colonel Pedro Delgado of Santa Anna's staff barely escaped with his life.

> On the left and about a musket shot distance from our camp was a small grove on the bay shore. Our disbanded herd rushed for it, to obtain shelter from the horrid slaughter carried on all over the prairie by the blood-thirsty usurpers. Unfortunately, we met on our way an obstacle difficult to overcome.
>
> It was a bayou, not very wide, but rather deep. The men on reaching it, would helplessly crowd together and were shot down by the enemy, who was close enough not to miss his aim. It was there that the greatest carnage took place.
>
> Upon reaching that spot, I saw Col. Almonte swimming across the bayou with his left hand, and holding up his right which grasped his sword.
>
> I was leading my horse, but in this critical situation I vaulted on him and with two leaps he landed me on the opposite bank. To my sorrow, I had to leave that noble animal mired at that place and to part with him, probably forever.
>
> As I dismounted, I sank in the mire waist deep and I had the greatest trouble to get out of it by taking hold of the grass. Both my shoes remained in the bayou. I made an effort to regain them, but I soon came to the conclusion

that, did I delay there a rifle shot would certainly make an outlet for my soul, as had happened to many a poor fellow around me.

Thus I made for the grove barefooted.[7]

This "boggy slough" encountered by Colonel Delgado caused many Mexican horses to bog down and begin sinking. Moving through the timber toward Peggy's Lake, many Texans literally crossed the huge mud bog by jumping across horses and other debris like stepping stones.[8]

"We found that we could jump from one bank to the saddle, and from the saddle to the other bank," wrote Private Stephen Sparks. As the second one to thus hop across, Sparks had the misfortune of brushing his knee against the bayonet of a dead Mexican cavalryman on the far bank.[9]

Slowed momentarily by his knee wound, Sparks soon pushed forward toward Peggy's Lake. From the bulrushes ahead of him suddenly appeared a Mexican woman. Sparks prevented his fellow soldiers from killing her. "Then three other women, who were hiding in the rushes, came running to us, crying and begging that I would protect them, too."

Sparks turned the Mexican women over to Captain Juan Seguin, whose Tejano company was at that moment making its way toward Peggy's Lake.

Many enemy soldiers fled through the woods toward Peggy's Lake behind their camp, where they tried to swim across this body of water to a small island. Peggy's Lake was really a small bay which was separated from the main San Jacinto Bay by only a small strip of land. Texas riflemen cut the fleeing enemy soldiers down as they ran. Incited to feverish intensity, they also began shooting the Mexicans who were swimming for the island. Out of ammunition or without the time to reload, some Texans splashed into the water with their personal bowie knives and hatchets to seek revenge. A few of the more rugged frontiersmen reportedly even removed scalps. Others reloaded and took aim at the heads bobbing across the water.

Santa Anna's troops had shown "no quarter" to the Texans who fought at the Alamo, Goliad and at Coleto Creek. With these atrocities fresh in mind, Texan commanders were unable to control their men. Some officers were content to let their men have their wishes. "We followed the enemy," wrote Captain Heard, "shooting and killing them, for more than a mile."[10]

"Massacre at Peggy's Lake" by Charles Shaw. Many fleeing Mexican soldiers at San Jacinto were chased to the boggy grounds and the bay called Peggy's Lake. There many Texans, with the atrocities of Goliad and the Alamo fresh in mind, slaughtered their fleeing enemies until order could be restored.
Courtesy of the San Jacinto Museum of History, Houston.

Private Allen Caruthers was on a personal mission of vengeance. His brother Ewing Caruthers had surrendered with Fannin's men and had thereafter been executed during the Palm Sunday Massacre. Caruthers later told his son that at San Jacinto he killed at least five Mexicans who had fallen on their knees and raised their hands to beg for mercy. Although his son would consider such senseless killing "nothing but murder," Caruthers justified his action with "I was crazed with anger."[11]

Private Walter Lane, who refused to fire on these victims, said that the Mexican soldiers "took to the water, like ducks, to swim across, our men firing at their heads." He claims that some of the enemy were coaxed back to surrender, only to have the Texans resume firing on them as they neared shore. Lane estimated that "some two hundred" were killed at Peggy's Lake.[12]

Lieutenant Denham, fighting with Captain Calder's unit this day, made it through the battlefield "without a scratch." He found Peggy's Lake to be "a scene of slaughter which defied description." Even the dreaded "famous Lancers were pursued five miles and entirely cut to pieces."[13]

Sergeant William Swearingen wrote the next day that

> It was nothing but a slaughter. They at first attempted to swim the bayou, but were surrounded by our men and they shot every one that attempted to swim the bayou as soon as he took to the water, and them that remained they killed as fast as they could load and shoot them until they surrendered.[14]

Private Bob Hunter, among those detailed to guard baggage at Harrisburg, learned the details of the fight the following day from his comrades.

> General Houston gave orders not to kill anymore, but to take prisoners. [Lieutenant] Eastland said, "Boys, take prisoners. You know how to take prisoners: take them with the butt of your guns, club guns." And [he] said, "Remember the Alamo" and "Remember La Bahia" and club guns, right and left, and knocked their brains out. The Mexicans would fall down on their knees and say, "Me no Alamo. Me no La Bahia."[15]

To James Winters of Ware's company "the Mexicans and horses killed made a bridge across the bayou." The enemy's infantryman dove into the water to hide, "but the minute they would raise their heads they were picked off by our men."[16]

Colonel Wharton tried with little success to stop the bloody massacre. He even went as far as to grab one Mexican soldier and pull him up onto the horse behind him. Wharton announced that this was his prisoner, but the defiant old vengeance seeker Jim Curtis shot the Mexican from his horse.

At the edge of the water, Wharton tried ordering the Texian riflemen to stop their firing. Sergeant Moses Bryan witnessed this attempt.

> Adjutant General Wharton rode up and ordered the riflemen to stop firing. One of Sherman's men, Joe Dickson [Dixon, of Roman's company], who was engaged in shooting the Mexicans, said: "Colonel Wharton, if Jesus Christ were to come down from Heaven and order me to quit shooting Santanistas, I wouldn't do it, sir!"
>
> Colonel Wharton put his hand on his sword. Joe Dickson took a few steps back and cocked his rifle. Wharton, very discreetly (I always thought) turned his horse and left.[17]

One of the senior Mexican officers, Colonel Jose Batres, fell upon his knees and begged Dr. Nicholas Labadie to spare him. A member of Captain Juan Seguin's Tejano company recognized Batres (called Bertrand in Labadie's account) and informed Labadie of his rank. Three other Texans raced up with their weapons leveled at Batres. Labadie shouted, "Don't shoot!" and said that he had taken the officer as his prisoner. The doctor had scarcely spoken when one of his fellow soldiers fired his rifle, "the ball entering the forehead of poor Bertrand, and my hand and clothes are splattered with his brains, as he falls dead at my feet."[18]

Colonel Delgado witnessed the killing of Colonel Batres. Delgado's own life and that of many other Mexican officers would have been lost if not for "the noble and generous" Major John Allen, "who by great exertion saved us repeatedly from being slaughtered by the drunken and infuriated volunteers."[19]

George Erath of Billingsley's company did not enjoy the scene. "No doubt our men were justified, as the Mexican nation deserved punishment for its perfidy, though the soldiers were not responsible for it."[20]

Billy Young rode into battle on a tremendous gray horse with Captain William Smith's cavalry company. During the action near the Mexican encampment he had been wounded. Young did not realize his situation until he began to feel faint. Looking down, he saw that his horse was stained with blood and that blood was running out of the top of one of his high leather boots.[21]

His wound did not prevent him from continuing the pursuit beyond Santa Anna's camp. There, he recalled that, "We drove them into a marsh. I shot 'em till my ammunition gave out, then turned the butt end of my musket and knocked 'em in the head." One of Young's grandchildren, upon hearing him tell this story, suddenly found her grandfather too mortal to keep on the "hero's pedestal" he had long adorned.

Captain Seguin, commanding the only all-Tejano company at San Jacinto, was finally able to spare some Mexican soldiers at Peggy's Lake.

> My attention was called to a Mexican officer, who, emerging from the river where he had kept himself concealed, gave himself up and requested me to spare his life. Being sheltered by weeds and grass, he seemed afraid to leave his retreat, owing to the fire which was kept up against the fugitives. I ordered those who were close to me to cease firing, which order was extended along the line to a considerable distance. Then, the officer who had addressed me came out, followed by Colonels [Juan María] Bringas, [Juan] Almonte, Dias, and quite a number of other officers.[22]

"Colonel Forbes Done It!"

In the late minutes of the San Jacinto battle, Colonel John Forbes, Commissary General of the Texas Army, approached the area near Peggy's Lake where the greatest slaughter had been taking place.

Dr. Labadie wrote that, "It was here that one or two women were killed by some one aiming at their heads, probably mistaking them for men, and two or three others taken prisoners."[23]

Further scrutiny of this battle would reveal that of a handful of women who had been cooking and otherwise serving for the Mexican army, all were taken safely as prisoners with one exception. One Mexican woman of perhaps thirty years of age was killed by Colonel Forbes during the prisoner roundup.

This act was witnessed by Privates Thomas Corry and Robert M. Cravens, who spread the story around the Texas camp that night. Corry, fighting with Captain Murphree's Second Regiment company, found himself near Peggy's Lake late in the battle. The spot was some 250 yards southeast of the center of the Mexican breastworks. "Scattered Texas soldiers were shooting Mexicans that were swimming across the bay or hiding in the marsh," he recalled.[24]

Opposed to such needless killing, Corry, his gun still in hand, turned back toward camp and ran across Colonel Forbes, an old acquaintance of his from his younger days in Cincinnati. Corry later testified as to what happened next, about an hour before sundown.

> He had his drawn sword in his hand. We stopped together and he congratulated me upon the glory of the victory, and upon my own escape from injury. Almost instantly there came from the timber into the prairie where we stood, two men—carrying muskets and bayonets—in the uniform of Texas regulars, bringing with them two prisoners—a man and a woman.
>
> Barely had they joined us, when Col. Somervell or Col. Burleson, I do not remember which, who was galloping at two or three hundred yards distance, cried out; "Kill them, God damn them. Remember the Alamo."
>
> The two regulars immediately attacked the man with their bayonets. There was a momentary struggle in which I tried to save the man's life. At the same time Col. Forbes thrust his sword through the woman's breast, the blade entering in front, and coming out at her back. As the sword was withdrawn she fell forward upon her face, quivering, died, and without a groan.
>
> This dreadful deed paralyzed me, and the man was killed. I said to Forbes, "Damn you, you have killed a woman."

According to Corry, Forbes' only reaction was to touch the woman's shoulders with his fingertips and utter a sarcastically sorrowful, "tut, tut" sound.

Corry then "walked off from this horrid scene without any delay." He did not recall the names of the regular army soldiers, only that they were "young men." He judged the victim to be a young woman "about 25 or 30 years of age."

The other witness, Private Robert Cravens of Billingsley's company, told Private Tom Mays "that he saw John Forbes kill a Mexican woman on the day of the battle of San Jacinto in the evening." In camp later, Mays would witness soldiers accuse Forbes "of killing a Mexican woman to his face, and he never denied it."[25]

In depositions taken later, several would claim that they thought Forbes had not taken part in the main battle. As commissary general of the army, he was considered by Corry to be "a non-combatant, and when I met him, was coming from the direction of our camp, and from where no fighting man could find anything to do."

Cravens and Mays, wounded early in the battle, claimed that they had seen Forbes lying down in the tall grass near the little rise in the hill that led toward the Mexican camp. Once the shooting had died down, they claimed that Forbes then moved toward the main area of action near Peggy's Lake. Cravens helped the wounded Mays onto a horse and had then followed after the commissary general.

Captain Billingsley later testified that members of his company informed him that "John Forbes hid in the grass and did not participate in battle until after the shout of victory was heard in our ranks."[26]

Private Corry, disgusted with the senseless killing, made his way back to camp. He relayed the events to the first man he met, Dr. Shields Booker, whom he encountered "within a quarter of a mile of the place." Corry said that Forbes had done the killing. "The Doctor damned Forbes, and said he would spread it all over the camp," recalled Corry. "He did tell it, and so did I."[27]

Captain William Heard found that the accusation spread through the Texian camp that night. He heard that Forbes had killed a woman on the battlefield "and that she had been run through with a sword or bayonet."[28]

Captain Robert Calder later wrote in defense of Forbes.

> If Colonel Forbes did kill the woman, it was doubtless to him a painful mistake, growing out of her dress approaching so near to that of the other sex that the difference could not be distinguished at a short distance; for, within the knowledge of the writer, a woman dressed in that manner was that day removed from a perilous position on the banks of the lake, by Colonel Sherman and Major Wells, to a place of greater security, and for the reason above stated—that her dress made it difficult to determine her sex at a short distance.[29]

Colonel Sherman soon came upon the woman's body near Peggy's Lake and made inquiries.

> I rode up on high ground to the edge of the prairie, the enemy's left having been pursued by the balance of our troops on the outside of the timber. On reaching their line of retreat, I discovered several of the enemy laying dead upon the ground, and several of our men standing near. I also discovered a body of Mexicans surrendering to a party of our troops at some distance to my right in a small island or point of timber.
>
> While sitting upon my horse waiting for them to march up, I saw laying dead about thirty yards from me, near the timber, on her face, what I at once took to be a woman, from her dress and long hair. I rode up to it and asked some of our men standing near by, if that was not a woman.
>
> (Pointing to her at the same time), they answered that it was a woman. I then asked, "Who killed her?"
>
> Several answered at the same time, "Col. Forbes."
>
> I then asked why he killed her. The same men replied that he (Col. Forbes) was anxious to bloody his sword. I requested one of the men to turn the body of the woman over, which he did. I then had no doubts of her being a woman.[30]

In the victorious Texian camp that night, the jubilant men showed no mercy on Colonel Forbes. Long after the drummers had beaten tattoo that night, and for many nights thereafter, the cries could be heard around camp, "Who killed the woman?"

From the other side of camp, others would holler out, "Colonel Forbes done it!"

In further ridicule—in reference to Forbes' attempt to flee on the mule on April 20 whose legs were still tied up—another voice would call out, "Who got on the hobbled mule?"

"Colonel Forbes!" would come the cry.

Certainly, the murder of the Mexican woman was a horrible act committed during the rush of battle. It was a mistake for which John Forbes would long suffer.

Pursuit to Vince's Bridge

Peggy's Lake was an especially bloody slaughtering ground. Once the Mexican soldiers commenced fleeing for their lives from camp, they were hotly pursued. One large group of cavalrymen and Mexican officers fled down the road leading toward Vince's Bridge. Among these key officers racing away on horseback were General Cos, secretary Ramón Caro and Major General Santa Anna.

Deaf Smith's spies knew that the fleeing Mexican cavalrymen were in for a bad surprise when they reached Vince's Bridge. Aware that Smith's men had just destroyed this crossing, Captain Henry Karnes called for all of those men with loaded weapons and a good horse to join him in pursuit of their fleeing enemy.

From various companies, this group comprised Karnes, Smith, Wash Secrest, Field Secrest, Lieutenant James Cook, Shel Turnage, Lieutenant Thomas Robbins, Jack Robbins, Joseph Lawrence, Elisha Clapp, Thomas House, William Pearce, William Taylor, Benjamin Franklin, Thomas Hughes, Moses Lapham, Perry Alsbury and Dr. Horace Alsbury. Taylor felt that there were "eighteen in all." This force included "a man who had escaped from Fannin's massacre."[31]

Perry Alsbury later wrote that he was one of the pursuit party "who followed the distinguished Santa Anna and the remnant of his staff cavalry back to the site of the bridge I had left in flames some three hours before." The bridge's destruction "insured the capture of Santa Anna," felt Alsbury.[32]

Private Taylor later detailed the pursuit of the cavalry.

> The distance of Vince's Bridge from the battle-ground was about four miles, over a very wet, muddy plain, and, for perhaps a quarter of a mile, knee-deep to our horses in mud and water. Two or three miles from the battle-ground, some three or four Mexicans struck off (leaving the balance), in the open prairie, in the direction of the head of Vince's Bayou.
>
> Elisha Clapp, having a very fleet horse, started in pursuit of them, and soon coming up with them, fired his rifle, killing one of them. The others, seeing that his rifle was discharged, turned to give him battle, when Clapp was compelled to retreat, not being able to cope with three Mexicans, with an empty gun. The one nearest to him discharged his escopet at him, but the ball missed him, though, judging from the whistling, Clapp afterward told me though it passed within six inches of his head.[33]

Clapp returned unhurt. These three Mexican soldiers escaped and eventually made their way to General Filisola. The other Texans continued to ride toward Vince's Bridge.

Private Taylor later wrote that Karnes' eighteen men "took no prisoners in this pursuit." One of the Goliad Massacre survivors was present and he was likely a key inspiration for the vengeful Texans who here returned the favor to the enemy who had slaughtered Fannin's men. Private Moses Lapham wrote on May 17 that his party "killed a dozen or more" of the fleeing cavalrymen and officers.[34]

"We felt compelled to kill them," reasoned Taylor. "We saw it was impossible for us to take prisoners, and we had but little disposition to do so." The road from the Mexican battleground to Vince's Bridge was strewn every few hundred yards with the bodies of these Mexicans who were slaughtered in their flight. "We gained on them and shot our carbines at them, dropping them off their horses," recalled Joseph Lawrence. Benjamin Franklin wrote that he "gave pursuit to the fugitives, which chase did not cease until our arrival at the bridge."[35]

Jack Robbins pursued two Mexicans near Vince's Bridge. Racing on foot away from his comrades, he shot down one of the enemy soldiers. The other Mexican, a strong man, then turned and tackled Robbins. The alarmed Texan cried out for help as he wrestled with his enemy. Robbins managed to draw his knife from his belt and thrust it into his opponent. Private Taylor, coming to his relief, found Robbins "still lying under the Mexican, who was then in the agonies of death from the effects of the fatal wound by the knife."[36]

As the Texans approached within a half mile of Vince's Bridge, Captain Karnes halted his men in order to regroup. In the process of stopping to reload rifles and to execute the little groups of Mexicans who tried to surrender, his little party had become quite strung out. After pursuing fleeing Mexican cavalrymen for miles and engaging in physical conflict with others, the pack of Texians was exhausted. "When we dismounted," said Lawrence, "we were so fatigued that we could not stand up and fell around like a company of drunken men."[37]

Karnes let his men pause only momentarily to regroup and reload. He knew that the bridge was down, which would quickly halt those flying before his men. The swollen bayou would likely compel the terrified Mexicans to turn and face their aggressors. Karnes felt that Santa Anna was certainly among this pack and must be killed or captured. William Taylor continues:

> We then followed in a body, prepared for and expecting a fight; but, when they reached the bridge and found it gone, they immediately scattered in all directions, some going up and others down the bayou. When we discovered this, every man of us put spurs to his horse, and started after them as fast as possible.[38]

Some of the enemy were overtaken, as their horses had become exhausted from being bogged down in the mud. Even though some fell to their knees exclaiming, "Me no Alamo!" or "Me no La Bahia!" they were each shot down.

The Texans came much closer than they at first realized to catching Santa Anna himself. The commander-in-chief, having fled the battlefield on horseback as the Texans overran his camp, narrowly escaped, as he later wrote.

> They followed me, and after a league and a half, on a large creek where the bridge had been burned they caught up with me.
> I lost my horse, and with difficulty I hid myself among some small pine trees. The approach of night gave me the chance to evade their vigilance, and the hope of rejoining my army and of vindicating the honor of our arms gave me courage.[39]

Fleeing with Santa Anna was his personal secretary, Ramon Caro. He followed his leader to the burned bridge. "We retraced our steps a short distance and entered a small thicket, where he dismounted and left me." Caro quickly fell in with several other survivors, including Captain Marcos Barragán and Lieutenant Colonel José María Castillo y Iberri. Barragán succeeded in crossing the bayou and escaping, but Castillo y Iberri was later captured. Ramon Caro was cut off by Texans who began entering the woods, searching for the Mexican soldiers. Terrified of death, Caro found some thick brush and hid himself for the night.

Within a few hundred yards of the bridge, the Texans discovered an officer riding the fine black stallion known as "Old Whip" that had been stolen from the William Vince ranch. The officer dismounted and was asked by Captain Karnes if he was Santa Anna. "He replied that he was, supposing that quarter would be given to Santa Anna." Karnes swung at him with his sword, scoring a glancing blow off the imposter officer's head.

The Mexican officer shouted that he was not Santa Anna and he jumped into the bayou to escape. Several of the Texans were quick to end his swim with their pistols. William Taylor later wrote that "I assisted in killing the Mexican officer that was mounted on Vince's black stallion, near the neck of Vince's Bridge before the sun went down."[40]

Karnes' party came to the wreck of Vince' Bridge about the time that the sun was setting over San Jacinto. In a little thicket close by, they found four horses which had been abandoned as their riders waded across through the water and mud. With the fall of darkness, Karnes knew that it was futile to search the woods for these men.

Dr. Alsbury, who spoke Spanish, was asked to call out for Santa Anna in the thicket. Alsbury hollered to the Mexican president that his life would be spared if he would come out and surrender himself. There was no answer, but Karnes felt that Santa Anna was certainly hiding nearby. Taylor:

> Captain Karnes then dispatched a runner to camp to convey the news that we had Santa Anna in a thicket near Vince's Bridge, and that we had not men enough to guard the thicket till morning, and that more men should be sent immediately to help us. Our force, then consisting of fourteen, was disposed of to the best advantage to guard the thicket; but the number not being sufficient to surround it, we left a space open on the side toward our camp, so that should he get out during the night, he would have to beat about in the direction of the battle-ground, where he would be least likely to escape.
>
> In this condition we remained on post till daylight.

Captain Karnes sent Smith back to the Texas camp to ask for volunteers, as he was certain Santa Anna would be found in the thicket after dawn.

Deaf Smith rode back to the Texan camp about an hour after dark upon "the large black stallion on which Santa Anna had fled the battlefield." As Smith rode into camp on Old Whip, Captain Calder noted that "the horse was covered with mud," and that "our noble old scout, Smith, was in high spirits." Smith felt that Santa Anna could be captured the next day if enough mounted guards could be secured to prevent the Mexican leader from escaping across the prairie during the night.[41]

Smith estimated that he would need one hundred men to properly contain Santa Anna. Colonel Burleson offered to give him only the men who would volunteer, and to this he had countless offers. Calder's entire company volunteered, from which he selected twenty-five men to join the guard detail.

Late Arrivals to the Fight

Lorenzo de Zavala only arrived in time to catch the tail end of the battle of San Jacinto. He had accompanied John Wharton across the bayou to the Zavala homestead turned makeshift field hospital. "I saw from my house, our men moving rapidly, as though to engage the enemy," he wrote. "I immediately crossed over the river without knowing the issue of the fight and joined the Army. The affair was almost over."[42]

Other men claimed to have joined the battle during its progress. Some of the late arrivals were ruefully dubbed "torries," or those who had waited to determine the outcome before deciding which side they would claim.

At Camp Harrisburg, the sick and the baggage guards could plainly hear the sounds of battle. "We heard a cannon fire, and another and another. Three fired in succession, and stopped," wrote Private Bob Hunter. "About two minutes, another fired and the little Twin Sisters commenced. They popped like popcorn in an oven. We could hear the small arms very plain."[43]

Captain Conrad Rohrer and a few men did manage to find action on April 21. Earlier in the day, Major Robert McNutt had marched to the bayou with a large number of his troops to search for the Mexican snipers. They did not encounter any troops. After returning to camp, Private William Zuber noted that, "Our wagonmaster, Rohrer, hastily mustered a few men and went in search for enemies."[44]

Rohrer had located a small encampment of enemy soldiers on the opposite side of Sims' Bayou and attacked. He claimed to have killed as many as eight Mexican soldiers with his small party at about the time that the main battle of San Jacinto was erupting a few miles away. When Rohrer's men returned to report to Major McNutt, the "booming reports of artillery" and the "continuous roar of small arms" could be heard at Harrisburg. Clearly, Sam Houston had finally entered into an all-out engagement with Santa Anna.[45]

Upon the commencement of the battle of San Jacinto, Major McNutt allowed a number of his guards to seek out battle. Under First Lieutenant George Casey of the regulars and wagon master Conrad Rohrer, McNutt sent this patrol to "the opposite side of the bayou" to attack the enemy party previously encountered by Rohrer's teamsters.[46]

Sergeant James Kuykendall later related that his company's first lieutenant, Francis Miller, and at least two dozen others comprised this party from Harrisburg. "Guided by Ro[h]rer, we began to move towards the camp of the enemy about dusk," wrote Kuykendall. After creeping to within two hundred yards of the Mexican campsite in the darkness, the Texan party paused. "We were halted and told to lie down; our officers having determined to defer the attack until daybreak."[47]

Daybreak would show the men whatever enemy soldiers had once been in the Sims Bayou camp had long since fled, likely once the main battle had erupted the previous evening.

Aside from the scouts that went out from Camp Harrisburg, other men would try in vain to reach the battlefield on April 21. Among them was Dr. William P. Smith of Captain Peyton Splane's company. Smith was acting under a commission from President Burnet and Secretary of War Rusk to be a regimental surgeon.

> I, as one of the surgeons of the Army, was left at Donoho's in charge of some sixty sick with the measles, being the sick of both regiments. So soon as I got them in a condition so that some could go to the settlements, to regain their health, Capt. Hill, of Washington Co., and myself, took those who were able to join the Army, and dashed on as rapidly as possible.[48]

To their chagrin, Smith, Hill and others were unable to reach the plains of San Jacinto in time to join the action.

Still others en route over water were denied the privilege of joining the fight for Texas independence on April 21. Another sailing ship with United States volunteers had reached Galveston Bay the previous day. Captain William C. Graham had entered into service for Texas on October 22, 1835. He had an eighteen-man company mustered into service by April 15, 1836, on which date his men sailed from New Orleans. At Galveston, Graham found Captain Jacob Eberly, whose men had just reached Galveston under special orders from Major Edwin Morehouse.[49]

Captains Eberly and Graham were determined to join the main Texas Army, likely encouraged by the sound of cannon fire that carried for miles on April 20. Their men boarded the 85-foot-long steamboat *Laura*, which had been built in Louisville, Kentucky, and was capable of hauling 65 tons of cargo. The *Laura's* skipper was Captain Thomas Wigg Grayson, the former skipper of the *Yellow Stone*.[50]

"About the 20th of April, I started up Galveston Bay on the *Laura* with Capt. Graham's and Eberly's companies to find the Texas Army, from who we had not heard in some time," Grayson documented. Although relatively small, the *Laura* still drew more than five feet and on April 21 she "grounded on Red Fish Bar in Galveston Bay."[51]

Captain Grayson's boat would eventually work free, but it would be far too late for the anxious soldiers aboard her to reach the battle of San Jacinto.

Private Alfonso Steele lay severely wounded in the woods near Santa Anna's abandoned campground. His loaded musket still lay where he had been aiming to fire, but another soldier had taken his pistol. A fellow soldier brought him more water and tended to him. At that moment, two frightened Mexican soldiers ran toward them.

> When they got in about twenty steps of us they saw us and threw up their hands and began to "jabber" something. I said to the fellow with me, "Shoot one of them Mexicans." He said, "I can't do it; they want to surrender."
>
> I said, "I don't want any more prisoners; hand me my gun and I will shoot one of them." He handed me my gun (which was lying where I had fallen) and I shot one of them down; the other ran off.[52]

Steele's companion went after a horse, which he used to move the wounded teenager out of the wooded area to the main battlefield. Blinded by pain and blood loss, Steele sat down among the bodies of slain Mexican soldiers to rest.

Lying among the Mexican bodies, Steele was very nearly finished off by his own army. He noted some of Millard's regulars who had "stayed at the breastworks and were busy sticking their bayonets

Alfonso Steele (1817–1911) was barely nineteen years old when he was severely wounded on the San Jacinto battlegrounds while fighting with Captain James Gillaspie's company. Steele would survive, and at the time of his death in 1911, he had become the last survivor of the battle of San Jacinto.
Texas State Library and Archives Commission.

through wounded Mexicans." One of these regulars approached Steele with his bayonet held ready to strike, when artilleryman Tom Green shouted at the man to halt.

"Damn Your Manners"

Colonel Sidney Sherman and his men began taking prisoners of those Mexicans who chose to surrender. Sergeant Robert Goodloe stood with rifle and bowie knife in hand protecting two young Mexican drummer boys. Some of the regulars wanted to run their bayonets through the Mexican youths, but Goodloe held off the bloodthirsty bunch until Colonel Sherman properly took the young men as prisoners. "You saved my life," recalled Goodloe to Sherman later.[53]

Hundreds were quickly rounded up about the camp, including Colonel Juan Almonte, the English-speaking aide of Santa Anna's. Almonte's men surrendered to Noel Bain and other members of Captain Billingsley's company three miles from where the fight first began in their own camp.[54]

Those who captured Almonte did not at first realize who they had. Almonte and more than two hundred men came out of the woods and surrendered en masse. At this place, there were only about a dozen Texans, and none that could speak Spanish well.

Colonel Rusk, who was present as these Mexican soldiers surrendered themselves, noted that Almonte soon gave himself away.

> The prisoners were standing in a body, and they were asked, in the Spanish language, if any of them could speak English. Almonte answered, in Spanish, that they could not. They were then told, in Spanish, to form, two and two deep, and march with us to camp. They formed, and commenced marching accordingly. Our few men were distributed around them, as a guard.
>
> Most of us were very fatigued, and such was the condition of the Mexicans also. As we proceeded along in this way, one of our men, who was so much tired that he could scarcely walk, being incommoded by a Mexican who was walking immediately before him, and who had dropped out of the line of the prisoners, observed to the intruder, in English, "God damn you, if you don't get back into line, I'll [stab you] with my bayonet."[55]

Almonte quickly advised the Mexican soldier of the threat made against him. Colonel Rusk, noting that this officer understood English very well, spoke out: "You must be Colonel Almonte."

"You speak well," Almonte replied.

Colonel Rusk then rode up and shook Almonte's hand and expressed pleasure in meeting him.

One of those captured was First Sergeant Francisco Becerra, who had been wounded during the fighting. According to his account, Santa Anna and General Castrillon had quarreled prior to the battle about the disposition of the Mexican troops. Castrillon, who had died heroically amid a hail of musket balls, had even predicted defeat. As for Becerra, he would recover from his wounds and remain in Texas after the revolution, working for Texan families to make a living. By March 1839, he was fighting with the Texans, having joined a Texas Ranger company that would fight Cherokees that year![56]

Once the slaughter at Peggy's Lake was finally halted and the men had a few minutes to calm down, a wave of elation swept over the Texans as they realized fully what they had done. The Mexican army was finally whipped! Their weeks of trudging through mud and water and marching without food ahead of a vastly superior enemy army was finally over. They had stood their ground. In fact, they had raced across the grounds into the enemy's own camp and decimated their foes.

The Texian army was called back from Peggy's Lake by the beating of the drums of Dick and George Brown. This beating for assembly slowly recalled most of the companies.[57]

General Houston remained on the battlefield until he was very certain that the victory was attained. Long before the mayhem at Peggy's Lake was brought into order, he tried in vain to reorganize his troops, but the vengeful Texans were not to be controlled easily.

Colonel Wharton was eager to lead other men on to attack Santa Anna's reinforcements. He brought his thoughts before the general in the battle's waning moments, but Houston had had enough. "Col. Wharton, you have commanded long enough," he snapped. "Damn you, go about your business!"[58]

Houston's efforts in restraining his men were no doubt due to his fear that another battalion of Mexican soldiers might reach the battlefield at any time. With his men widely scattered—firing all their ammunition and breaking their muskets to splinters in bashing skulls—Houston later stated that one hundred well-disciplined enemy soldiers might overpower his forces at that moment.[59]

Private James Winters recalled that the wounded General Houston could not even command the attention of his troops in the midst of their celebrating and backslapping.

> After the fight was ended, Houston gave orders to form in line and march back to camp, but we payed no attention to him, as we were all shaking hands and rejoicing over the victory. Houston gave the order three times and still the men payed no attention to him. And he turned his horse around and said, "Men, I can gain victories with you, but damn your manners," and rode on to camp.[60]

En route to camp, Houston was met on the battlefield near the breastworks surrounding the Mexican camp by Colonel Sherman. Sherman was returning from the area of Peggy's Lake, where he had stayed as his men rounded up prisoners after the firing finally ceased. He found Houston "sitting on his horse under the protection of Capt. Turner's company."[61]

Sherman recalled, "General Houston rode up and offered me his hand, congratulating me on our success."

Houston then remarked, "I hope that you are satisfied now," alluding to Sherman's complaint against the general's reluctance to support the cavalry attack the previous day.

"I am satisfied *with this day's work*," replied Sherman as the two rode in company back into the Texian camp.

Sherman, having heard that Houston had been wounded during the battle, inquired of his condition. The general casually replied that it was "a mere scratch."

Near the Mexican camp, the sun had already set behind the trees and the battlefield was heavy in shadows. According to Captain Turner, General Houston noticed Colonel Rusk approaching with several hundred Mexican prisoners. Due to the poor light, and perhaps dizzy with pain from his own loss of blood, Houston reportedly cried out, "My God, all is lost!"[62]

Turner quickly handed Houston his spyglass to show that Rusk was in charge of the Mexicans. Turner's first lieutenant, Bill Millen, then chided, "General, Colonel Rusk has a very respectable army, eh, sir?"

Once in camp, however, General Houston suddenly found himself "exhausted from loss of blood." Before dismounting his borrowed horse, he ordered, "Double sentinels and patrols."[63]

Captain Calder worked on collecting his scattered company after the slaughter was halted at Peggy's Lake. His men felt great "joy and enthusiasm" with their important victory. He was fortunate to have lost only one man, Benjamin Brigham. By dusk, a party of men "had found the corpse of our dear messmate and conveyed it into camp," recalled Calder. His men had become "endeared to each other by the associations of a two months' campaign."[64]

Calder was present when Rusk and Houston reached camp. "Rusk insisted on helping the general from his horse, and called on me to assist him," said Calder. Before he could do so, David Rusk moved in to help his brother ease Houston off his borrowed horse.

"General Houston appeared to suffer a good deal of pain, when being removed, but called repeatedly for Almonte to be brought before him," wrote Captain Calder.

Surgeon General Alexander Ewing removed Houston's bloody left boot and found that his ankle was shattered. The wound was later diagnosed as a compound fracture of the left tibia and fibula, just above the ankle.

Colonel Almonte told him that Santa Anna had fled the battleground toward the Brazos River. Houston knew that San Jacinto would not be a real victory without the Mexican leader.

"The Hand of Providence Was with Us"

Despite the escape of Major General Santa Anna, the action on April 21 had been a monumental battle in which the Texans had surprised and virtually wiped out their Mexican resistance. Sergeant William Swearingen wrote the next day that the Mexicans had lost "between 620 and 700 killed on the field and in the bayou. Ten of his field officers was killed." Of those captured, Swearingen noted that "half of our prisoners [are] wounded."[65]

Sam Houston's battle report shows that 630 Mexicans were killed and 730 were captured, of which 208 were wounded. His best estimate, therefore, was that the Texian army had fought at least thirteen hundred troops. Of the Mexicans killed, Houston wrote that there were "1 general officer, 4 colonels, 2 lieutenant-colonels, 5 captains, [and] 12 lieutenants." The wounded officers included "5 colonels, 3 lieutenant-colonels, 2 second lieutenant-colonels, [and] 7 captains." Colonel Thomas Rusk's battlefield estimate was similar.

> The loss of the enemy is computed at over six hundred slain, and above six hundred prisoners; together with a *caballada* of several hundred mules taken, with much valuable baggage. Our loss, in point of numbers, is small, it being seven slain and fifteen wounded.
>
> This glorious achievement is attributed, not to superior force, but to the valor of our soldiers and the sanctity of our cause. Our army consisted of seven hundred and fifty effective men. This brave band achieved a victory as glorious as any on the records of history, and the happy consequences will be felt in Texas by succeeding generations. It has saved the country from the yoke of bondage; and all who mingled in it are entitled to the special munificence of government, and the heartfelt gratitude of every lover of liberty. The sun was sinking in the horizon as the battle commenced, but, at the close of the conflict, the sun of liberty and independence rose in Texas, never, it is to be hoped, to be obscured by the clouds of despotism.[66]

Texas losses during the battle were seven men killed outright, four so badly wounded that they would shortly die, and thirty others wounded. Sergeant Swearingen on April 22 noted, "Our loss was 4 men killed and 23 wounded. Three have since died and there is one more that will die in two days at most."[67]

Those who died outright on the battlefield were Private Blakey of Captain Billingsley's company, Dr. Mottley, Lieutenant Lamb of Captain Ware's, Sergeant Brigham of Captain Calder's, Lieutenant Hale from Captain Bryant's, Private Cooper of Captain McIntire's and Sergeant Fowle from Captain Smith's cavalry company. Captain

Billingsley's company suffered the highest number of casualties, with one man killed and six wounded. Captain Ware's company was the hardest hit percentage-wise, with four out of nineteen men wounded or killed in action.

Among the more severely wounded was Private John Tom of Captain Stevenson's company. He was found alive on the battlefield after dark by companymate John Swisher, who was returning from his pursuit of fleeing Mexican soldiers.

> A blanket was obtained, upon which the wounded soldier was laid. A man at each corner of the blanket had no difficulty in bearing the weight, but as soon as it was raised the poor fellow gave a cry of agony; his leg had been shattered just below the knee and the foot was dangling, which gave the most excruciating pain to every movement. It fell to my part to support the foot, and in doing this I had to stoop nearly to the ground; if I raised or lowered it an inch it caused a groan. This was the most tiresome task I ever undertook. It was impossible for me to go over a hundred yards without stopping to rest, consequently it was near ten o'clock at night when we reached camp.[68]

Sergeant Swearingen wrote a letter back to his family in Kentucky the next day which summarizes the good fortunes enjoyed by the Texian army on April 21.

> To see the number, the position and the termination and the time in which it was done (time 18 minutes) it at once shows that the hand of providence was with us.[69]

Private Washington Anderson (1817–1894) of Captain Jesse Billingsley's company was shot in the ankle on April 21. Billingsley's Company C, First Regiment suffered the highest number of casualties with seven.
Courtesy of the San Jacinto Museum of History, Houston.

With the rout complete, the Texans seized all of the goods left behind at the Mexican campground. Leading some of the Mexican officers back toward camp, Captain Juan Seguin was led by an officer, Lieutenant Augustin Sanchez, to a place where a large sum of money had been concealed. Captain Seguin reached the Texas camp at dark and presented his prisoners to General Houston. Seguin was congratulated and then he told Houston of the discovery of the large sum of money. "Colonel Forbes was at once detailed to go and bring it in," wrote Seguin.[70]

Captain Robert Calder wrote that some of his men came upon the Mexican trunks while searching for the body of their downed companion, Benjamin Brigham, in the late afternoon. They came upon some baggage and officers' cloaks, among which were "three or four pretty heavy boxes securely fastened up." Calder and his companions raised one and immediately judged it to be full of money.[71]

Calder never opened the chest, and could only relate that he heard estimates ranging as high as $12,000 as to its contents. Leaving brothers Charles and Washington Reese behind to guard the money chest, Captain Calder left to find a field officer to inform of the money. He found Colonel George Hockley, who immediately made out a guard detail to watch over this booty.

Colonel John Forbes, commissary general of the army, would later be accused of taking some of this money. Calder for one, did not believe such charges of "a gentleman and meritorious officer," feeling that if any money was indeed taken, "I would far sooner believe that it traveled into the pockets of some of those worthies who were crawling around in the bushes watching the event of a battle to determine their nationality, and who were the first to come into camp to congratulate us on our victory."

General Houston's official report shows that approximately six hundred muskets, three hundred sabers, two hundred pistols, several hundred mules and horses, and about $12,000 were rounded up from the conquered Mexican army at San Jacinto.

Estimates of the Mexican money captured after the battle range from between $12,000 to $45,000. Many of these estimates came as a result of Nicholas Labadie's 1859 *Texas Almanac* article, in which he accused commissary John Forbes of pilfering large amounts of the Mexican spoils.

General Houston's official battle report of April 25 states that they had captured "near twelve thousand dollars in specie." Another early estimate was that of Sergeant Oliver Brown, who wrote on May 4 that the Texans had captured "$16,000 in gold and silver, and sundries amounting to $2,000."[72]

The Mexican prisoners, many of them wounded, were marched back toward Santa Anna's campground as the sun set. Eventually, as many as seven hundred Mexican soldiers and camp followers were rounded up. A crude stockade of battlefield debris was constructed to create the barrier of their makeshift "prison." The prisoners were made to sit in pairs within this crude confine. Colonel Hockley wrote on May 9 that the Texans had rounded up enemy prisoners amounting "to nearly 600, among whom are six women."[73]

Dr. Labadie noted that both the Twin Sisters and the captured Mexican Golden Standard cannon were loaded and pointed toward the prisoners, "prepared to pour destruction." According to Private Walter Lane of the cavalry, the prisoners were put "in what we called the bull pen, which was a space enclosed with ropes and pack saddles."[74]

Sergeant Tony Menchaca of Seguin's company had taken control of many of the prisoners taken at Peggy's Lake. Lieutenant Colonel Juan Bringas had surrendered to him to avoid execution. Menchaca ordered the Mexican soldiers to carry their own wounded back to the Texas camp. Some did not live to make it.

> It was now growing dusk. Rusk, Allen & Morela[nd] asked me to take the well prisoners and make them cut wood and build fires as it was cold. I made them make 3 fires about 50 yards long in a line and we laid down the wounded beside them.[75]

The light of these fires would assist the Texas surgeons who were aiding fallen comrades during the night. Texas guards also used the ample supply of long white candles confiscated from the Mexican campground. Once the bonfires were built, the Mexicans were brought forward to dry their clothes. Colonel Pedro Delgado was not alone in at first fearing that "we were about to be burned alive, in retaliation for those who had been burnt in the Alamo."[76]

One of Captain Seguin's Tejanos assailed the Mexican prisoners with "a volley of threats, insults and abuse." To Delgado, this one man's abuse was sorely felt, as all of the Mexican prisoners could understand him. He had no doubt that many of the other Texians were delivering threats and insults to the prisoners but, "not understanding their language, we did not feel them."

Throughout the night, more than two dozen heavily armed Texans stood post around the prisoners. "Some wore two, three, and even four braces of pistols," recalled Delgado, "besides a rifle, musket, or carbine." Each sentinel held a burning candle from the ample supply captured from the Mexican campground. The guards had little reason to fear escape. "Where could we go in that vast country, unknown to us, intersected by large rivers and forests?"

The pile of Mexican booty in Santa Anna's old camp was considerable. Colonel Burleson detached two men of Billingsley's company, young George Erath and William Simmons, an "elderly man" from Bastrop, to guard the goods. Burleson instructed them to guard the baggage well. Anything of value was strictly forbidden to be carried away by souvenir hounds. They were allowed to pass out food items to soldiers, however. With this permission, Simmons and Erath were eager to find good food.

> We went inside the baggage pile and found it was Santa Anna's, containing camp furniture of silver, nicely arranged, such as a European prince might take with him into the field. And there were besides all kinds of eatables—a considerable part already cooked. Simmons took a kind of mat off a pyramid about six feet high, and called me to look. It was several dozen baskets of champagne; and just beside it was found another such a pyramid. I was not interested in champagne, nor did Simmons make any immoderate use of it; but he gave the bottles liberally to the stragglers returning to camp, saying that it belonged to the eatables which we had permission to give away.[77]

Erath was troubled during the night by the pitiful cries of some of the wounded Mexicans who still lay near the camp.

General Houston detailed Captain Amasa Turner's regular infantry company to "take possession of and guard the encampment" of the Mexican army. Turner said that "for two days after the battle [I] was not myself in camp" of the Texas Army.[78]

Captain Turner arrived with orders to guard the enemy's military chest. When questioned, Erath and Simmons stated that they had not seen such a chest. Turner's men moved to another area of baggage and did locate a large money chest, estimated by Erath to contain "eleven thousand dollars in specie."

Upon his return, Turner was notified by Erath and Simmons of the champagne that had been found. "The matter of champagne got out some way so that we had plenty of company of officers for the rest of the night," wrote Erath.

CHAPTER 17

Catching "The Old Fox"

April 22

Not until we arrived at camp, did any of the five captors know who the prisoner was, and then only by the Mexican prisoners within the camp.
—*Private Joel Walter Robison, Company F, First Regiment*

Amasa Turner found the evening to be lively as his infantry Company B guarded the enemy's former campground. The jubilant Texans, likely fueled by the captured champagne, hollered out in the night. Among the calls was, "Who killed the woman?"

The reply was invariably, "Col. Forbes!"

Captain Turner became irritated with such disrespect for his fellow officer.

I immediately went to where the men sat around the fires and put a stop to all such exclamations and reprimanded them for repeating or endorsing any such report. My First Lieutenant, William Millen, did the same, and a stop was put to it so far as Company B was concerned.[1]

Turner sent Second Lieutenant William W. Summers with four men back to the main Texas camp, where the Mexican prisoners were being held, to fetch the company's blankets and knapsacks. Summers found that the blankets had all been taken for other uses, but he secured a wagon about 9:00 p.m. The soldiers loaded their knapsacks and planned to use the wagon "to get the military chest and other valuables" from the Mexican campground.

While in the main army's camp, Lieutenant Summers heard from adjutant Nicholas Lynch of the killing of the Mexican woman. Summers informed Lieutenant Millen of this report and announced that he planned to go see for himself in the morning.

Captain Turner was worried that, even if the killing were true, such reports were not good for the army. He felt that "she had probably been killed in the general rout, and without the knowledge of her sex."

Several Texas officers had accompanied Summers back to the Mexican campground with the wagon, including Captain Isaac Moreland, Major James Collinsworth and Colonel Robert Coleman. Colonel Almonte, the English-speaking Mexican officer, was allowed to "collect Santa Anna's private baggage, all of which was put on the wagon and taken to camp on the bayou about 11 o'clock on the night after the battle."

After daylight on April 22, Turner allowed Lieutenant Summers and Private Sam Woods to go in search of the woman's body.

> Summers said on his return that he went right to the place by the directions, and there found the body of a very beautiful Mexican woman, and dressed very fine. He appeared a good deal excited, and had much to say about it. I again thought proper to advise him to say no more about it to any one, but let the matter rest, as there was no proof positive who had killed her; that she had been killed by mistake in all probability. . . .
>
> I saw he was disposed to entertain his own opinions, and we said no more on the subject at the time. The men, after Woods' return, had the subject under discussion when they thought I did not hear them during the day.

Dr. Lorenzo de Zavala's house was a busy makeshift hospital by late evening of April 21. Located across Buffalo Bayou from the battlefield, this homestead was the site where the Texan casualties were transported for attention.

At ten o'clock in the evening, Surgeon General Ewing summoned Dr. Nicholas Labadie over to Zavala's with the final two wounded from the battlefield. Upon his arrival, Labadie found "nineteen in all badly wounded, thirteen of whom were lying on the floor."[2]

One of the two going across with Labadie was Alfonso Steele. Doctors Phelps and Reagan put him on a pallet on the floor. They removed his bloodied shirt, tore it up and made a bandage from it which they tied tightly around his body under his arms.[3]

Labadie joined the other doctors present in operating on the wounded. He was weak, having eaten only a small piece of bread in the past two days. After operating tirelessly for several hours, he was finally provided a bowl of tea and some hard biscuit by Dr. Phelps at

2:00 a.m. This "tasted to me better than anything I had eaten for years, and gave me renewed strength."[4]

Dawn on April 22 showed the full destruction on the San Jacinto battlefield. Captain James Gillaspie and Dr. John Fitzhugh walked the battleground, examining the casualties.[5]

Samuel Hardaway, who had escaped being captured by Mexican forces in late March, wrote:

> The appearance of the battle ground can be better imagined than described. Piles and clusters of their dead and dying lay in every direction. Indeed the ground was liberally covered. But the recollection of the dreadful massacre of our brave companions at the Alamo and Goliad in great manner relieved our feelings from the horrors of the scene.[6]

Sam Houston, learning that the Mexican commander-in-chief had fled the battlefield, correctly predicted that Santa Anna would disguise himself in order to escape. Having departed the battleground on horseback in company with secretary Ramon Caro, Santa Anna and Caro both dismounted their horses once they entered the boggy marshes near Vince's Bridge. General Cos had managed to successfully swim the bayou and he set out for the Brazos River on foot. When his afternoon siesta with Emily West had been interrupted, Santa Anna had fled in what he had readily available: white silk drawers, a linen shirt with diamond studs, red morocco slippers and a fine gray cloth vest with gold buttons.

One of those that had pursued the fleeing Mexican officers and cavalrymen in the late hours of April 21 was Moses Lapham. The enemy "took shelter in [the] thicket along the creek and we guarded it till morning." Lapham eagerly hoped that Santa Anna, "the old fox" himself, would be taken prisoner after daylight.[7]

Word was sent back to the Texas camp during the early morning hours of April 22. "Karnes and Secrest, our spies, with a party of men, consisting of about 20 or 25 Texian soldiers, had surrounded Santa Anna and Cos, with near 50 Mexicans, 10 miles from our camp," recalled Sergeant James Sylvester.[8]

An exhausted and terrified Ramón Caro gave himself up to two Texas soldiers at daybreak on April 22. One of the men was believed by Caro to be a Frenchman, with whom Caro could crudely communicate in his language.

According to William Taylor, Caro surrendered to Captain Karnes. Using Dr. Alsbury as an interpreter, Karnes learned that Santa Anna had escaped from the thicket during the night. Karnes then dispatched a runner to camp to spread the intelligence that Santa Anna was on the move somewhere near Vince's Bayou. Colonel Edward Burleson then moved through camp, gathering up those who would volunteer to help capture the Mexican officers. Within moments, he had raised about fifty mounted men who proceeded to Sims' Bayou near Vince's Bridge.[9]

Caro was taken back to the Texan camp and brought before General Houston for further questioning. After explaining his identity to be that of "the secretary to His Excellency," only Houston's calming influence spared his life. "Had I not been sitting by the side of Houston, more than a hundred bullets would have made me their mark," wrote Caro.[10]

Major General Santa Anna spent the night in tall grass near the bayou and after dawn crossed a waist-deep creek before finding a deserted servants' quarters on the Vince ranch. There he donned some old slave clothes, including a blue cotton round jacket, cotton pantaloons, and an old hide cap. He also used a horse blanket as a serape. He still, however, wore the diamond-studded linen shirt and morocco slippers. With that, Santa Anna set off again down the bayou.

Karnes, Smith and Wash Secrest tried to closely follow the route of the fleeing Mexican officers. Other Texan patrols tried to ferret out the remaining Mexican troops by setting fires on the prairies to burn the tall grass that concealed *soldados*. One fire set to some marsh grass along a bayou resulted in a large group of enemy soldiers being literally smoked out of their hiding place. One who tried to flee was shot down.[11]

Colonel Henry Millard led another patrol, which included a portion of men from the companies of Captains Robert Calder and William Fisher. They conducted a search on the opposite side of Buffalo Bayou for a detachment of Mexicans reported to have been stationed there the previous day. The provisions boat, captured the previous day, moved down the bayou at the pace of the searching horsemen.

Between Peggy's Lake and San Jacinto Bayou, Millard's patrol picked up some twenty-eight Mexican prisoners. Many of them were placed in the provisions boat to be conveyed back to the Texas camp. One of Captain Fisher's soldiers shot and wounded an older Mexican soldier who had thrown up his hands and cried out for water. Captain Calder immediately ran over and "reprimanded the soldier pretty severely, and the indignation of my company was so strongly expressed that the man fell behind and returned to camp alone."[12]

Mexican soldiers continued to surrender and be rounded up throughout the morning of April 22. Colonel Hockley finally detailed Dr. Labadie, who had returned in the early morning from Zavala's makeshift hospital, to take a count of the soldiers and officers captured and of the wounded prisoners.[13]

With the assistance of several fellow officers, Labadie had the enemy soldiers fall into line according to their grade. He noted much hesitation and fear among the Mexicans, "being well apprised, doubtless, of the fate that would have awaited us had we been taken prisoners." Labadie and company counted fifty officers among their prisoners and 280 wounded "privates."

Labadie was ultimately called on to perform surgical duties on the Mexican prisoners. He and some of the other surgeons were reluctant to aid the enemy. Labadie had tended to soldiers at the garrison in Anahuac without pay, but did consent to tend to the Mexican army under a promise of General Houston that he would be compensated with three hundred dollars. By 1858, however, Dr. Labadie had not yet received payment for this service.

Houston in a sworn deposition flatly denied offering any doctor any money for aiding wounded Mexican prisoners. The only word Houston received of Labadie's actions was a rumor given to him on April 22. Another soldier told Houston that Dr. Labadie was

> pulling out the teeth of dead Mexicans, and placing them in a small tin bucket. He asked him what he was at, when he told him that each one of those teeth was worth $5 to him.[14]

Dr. William Carper, who had joined the army at Groce's, later denied this claim against Labadie. After the battle, the two surgeons worked together "among the sick and wounded and also with the wounded prisoners" on the first night. "I did not see anybody extract teeth after the battle of San Jacinto from dead Mexicans," said Carper.[15]

Private William B. Stout later testified that he did witness Dr. Labadie assisting Mexican wounded.

> He came to attend to the Mexicans that were wounded on the opposite side of the bayou. To the best of my recollection, he could speak the Spanish language. He cut out bullets and dressed their wounds. I passed among the Mexicans with him and sometimes assisted in holding an arm or a leg whilst he was operating.[16]

McNutt's Men Arrive

At Camp Harrisburg, Major Robert McNutt's men learned for certain of the victory on the morning of April 22 via an express from Rusk which detailed the battle. General Houston was angry that McNutt's men had not responded to a courier the previous afternoon who had been sent to request more effective men and ammunition. McNutt explained to Houston that Rusk's battle report "was the first information I had received from you since you left the river, except the report of your guns on yesterday evening." He felt that "the bearer of the express sent back for men and arms lost his papers, and must have lost himself, for he never came to me until after the news of victory."[17]

Once the booming of cannon and the cracking of rifles had been heard, McNutt dispatched a scout patrol, under the immediate command of wagon master Conrad Rohrer and Lieutenant George Casey, to the opposite side of the bayou. They had not yet returned, but McNutt reported that Captain Karnes was opposite the bayou from his camp, "occasionally reporting himself by the rifle crack on the flying enemy."

When the dispatch did arrive on the morning of April 22, McNutt's acting sergeant major, Jesse Benton Jr., read it aloud numerous times for the men who were curious of the battle's results.[18]

McNutt's men marched from Harrisburg down the bayou in search of a good crossing. They took most of their camp equipment across on a raft and floated their wagons across. Most of the men crossed in a skiff, while the horses and oxen swam across. They saw one Mexican body floating in the bayou and found many more scattered about as they moved over the San Jacinto battlefields.

Major McNutt's troops reached the battlefield about 11:00 a.m. on April 22. Private Bob Hunter was moved by the carnage. "Where their cannon stood for about 12 or 14 feet, the Mexicans lay 3 or 4 deep."[19]

Hunter and others were ordered to retrieve a money chest of Santa Anna's that was rumored to have been tossed into Peggy's Lake from the Mexican camp. The men cut poles about six or seven feet in length and probed the murky bottom for the elusive chest. They could not find the bottom and cut even longer poles. "We could feel the dead horses, and I expect men, but no bottom, and we gave it up," wrote Hunter.

Also arriving on the battlefield on April 22 were other former members of Captain Bird's company. They had to cross over the destroyed bridge at Vince's, laying down two large logs to walk across the bayou while leading their horses through the water.

Sam Houston, lying wounded in the Texan camp, had little chance to savor his victory. He was surrounded by officers the next morning who were eager to continue their rout of the Mexican army. Major Ben Smith pressed the commander-in-chief to be allowed to lead a division against the enemy near Fort Bend. Colonel Coleman also requested that the troops be allowed to make an offensive, to be led by Edward Burleson.[20]

"Would you march," asked Houston, "and leave your wounded General on the field?"

"I would leave him under a strong guard," replied Coleman.

"When I wish you to march," said Houston, "I will make it known to you; I am weary of your fighting petitions."

Houston then ordered the Mexican baggage to be brought into the Texan camp and divided among the heroes of San Jacinto. Lewis Cox of Captain Ware's company was among those who helped to appraise the value of all the Mexican goods. He was assisted by Jonathan H. Collard, who had arrived on the San Jacinto battlefield the day after the conflict.[21]

This move was popular among the men, but the division of the property would end up taking days.

"A Big Haul": Santa Anna Captured

Colonel Burleson's search party moved en masse to the area of Buffalo Bayou. They heard after leaving camp that Karnes and some of the spies had moved on toward the Brazos to chase key officers. Burleson's mounted party arrived near Sims' Bayou about 10:00 a.m. and consulted on what to do next.

Sergeant James Austin Sylvester (1807–1882) of the Kentucky Riflemen company led the scout patrol which captured General Santa Anna on April 22.
H. A. McArdle's San Jacinto Notebooks, Texas State Library and Archives Commission.

Burleson decided that about thirty of his party would continue to patrol and search. Knowing that the pursuit had moved further from camp, he opted to send about twenty of the riders on back to camp.[22] This group of thirty was then split into several smaller groups of five and six to further carry out the search for Santa Anna.

One of these subparties was placed under the direction of Sergeant James Sylvester from Captain Wood's Kentucky Rifles company. He had from Colonel Burleson "positive orders not to kill any Mexicans, but to bring them into camp." He proceeded on horseback near the destroyed Vince's Bridge with five other men: Privates Sion Record Bostick, Alfred Miles, Charles P. Thompson, Joel Walter Robison and Joseph D. Vermillion.[23]

Twenty-nine-year-old Sylvester had been a printer by trade in Kentucky before joining up with Sidney Sherman's volunteers. There was also twenty-year-old Joel Robison, who had come to Texas with his family in 1831 and fought in the battle of Velasco, along with his father, the following year. Of Sylvester's bunch, Charles Thompson had resided in Texas the longest, settling in the Matagorda County area in 1829. The others had come specifically to fight in the revolution, including Vermillion, who had arrived in Velasco in January after being recruited in New Orleans by Captain Amasa Turner.

"From the bridge we started down the bayou," wrote Robison, who had fought with Captain Heard's company at San Jacinto. Around 3:00 p.m., Sergeant Sylvester's scout patrol happened upon a small herd of four or five deer. They were seen "on the west side of a branch" in a prairie that fed into Buffalo Bayou. Sylvester quietly called to his patrol to "remain where they were, and I would try to kill one of the them."[24]

Sergeant Sylvester then "rode on within 40 or 50 yards of the branch, where I halted my horse under a lone tree, which stood in the prairie." He crept cautiously toward his prey and raised his rifle to take aim. Before he could squeeze off his shot, the deer suddenly displayed their white tails and bounded away with their flags flying. "I immediately looked to my right, when I spied a Mexican bending his course towards the bridge."

Sylvester watched the man stoop for a moment to gaze around and then move cautiously forward again. Calling to his companions in the rear, Sylvester moved back to his horse and motioned the others toward the spot where he had seen the man.

"As soon as I called to them, he spied me, and immediately secreted himself in the grass," wrote Sylvester. The other members of his scout team rode up and they began combing the tall grass where the Mexican soldier had hidden himself.

> The grass was high enough to hide him entirely from our view. When we arrived at the spot, he was lying on his side; with a blanket over his face. I called to him to rise. When he only took the blanket from his face, I called to him a second and third time to get up.
>
> When he rose and stood for a moment, and finding himself completely surrounded, he advanced towards me and desired to shake hands, which I immediately offered to him. He shook my hand, pressed it, and kissed the back of it and asked where our brave Houston was.

Another one of Sylvester's scout party, Private Sion Bostick, wanted to merely kill this enemy soldier and move on. Bostick's recollections:

> As we rode up, we aimed our guns at him and told him to surrender. He held up his hands, and spoke in Spanish, but I could not understand him. He was dressed like a common soldier with dingy looking white uniform. . . .
>
> I was the youngest and smallest of the party, and I would not agree to let him ride behind me. I wanted to shoot him. We did not know who he was. He was tolerably dark skinned, weighed about one hundred and forty-five pounds, and wore side whiskers.[25]

Sergeant Sylvester was unable to communicate effectively with the Mexican prisoner. He therefore had no idea that he had happened upon the major general of the Mexican army! Fortunately, another of

Private Sion Record Bostick (1819–1902) was among Sylvester's scout patrol. Only upon return to camp with their prisoner did Bostick realize "we had made a big haul."
San Jacinto Museum of History, Houston.

his men, Joel Robison, could speak Spanish. Robison immediately became the acting interpreter.

> I was the only one of the party that spoke the Mexican language. I asked him if he knew where Santa Anna and Cos were. He said he thought they had gone to the Brazos. I asked him if he knew of any other Mexicans that had made their escape from the battle. He said he thought there were some up the ravine in a thicket. I told him we would take him to the American camp. He was very willing to go, but complained of being very tired.
> I asked if he was an officer. No, he said he belonged to the cavalry, and was not accustomed to being on foot—that he was run very close by our cavalry the day before, and was compelled to leave his horse.[26]

Santa Anna complained of pains in his chest and legs, telling Sergeant Sylvester that he was not able to walk. Alfred Miles decided that he could walk for a while and offered his horse to the Mexican prisoner. "We proceeded some two or three miles," wrote Sylvester. "Mr. Miles overtaking us, demanded his horse of him, which he refused to give up."[27]

At the insistence of Sylvester, Santa Anna reluctantly gave the horse back to Miles. He was eventually allowed to ride for some of the trip behind Joel Robison. The young Texan found that the prisoner was very inquisitive on how many Mexicans had been killed, how many Texans fought in the battle, how many prisoners had been taken and when the prisoners would be shot. "I told him I did not think they would be shot," wrote Robison. "I had never known Americans to kill prisoners of war."[28]

According to Sylvester, he and Joseph Vermillion parted company with their little group as they rode into the Texan camp. Thinking that they had merely captured another Mexican soldier, Sylvester allowed Robison, Miles, Bostick and Thompson to take their man to the prisoner area. Robison says that the first officer they encountered upon reaching camp was Colonel John Forbes.

Only when the Texan patrol brought Santa Anna near the prisoner area did the truth slip out. Mexican officers yelled for the men to "Shut your mouths!" but it was too late. Two of Captain Arnold's company, Howard Bailey and Stephen Sparks, were standing near the prisoners when the captured general was led in. "There was a stir among the prisoners," wrote Sparks. "They were jumping to their feet, and clapping their hands, and saying, 'Santa Anna.'"[29]

Sergeant Moses Austin Bryan noticed the same reaction near the prisoners' bull pen. "Some of the Mexican officers said, 'Ini la boca!' meaning, 'Shut your mouth!' This let it out that it was Santa Anna." James Winters was busy digging a large grave to bury the fallen Texan soldiers when Robison's men brought Santa Anna into camp. "They passed by us and halted at our guard lines," Winters recalled. "The Mexican prisoners clapped their hands, and gave other signs of joy, shouting, 'Santa Anna, Santa Anna!'"[30]

Private Edward Miles of Captain Wood's company was on camp guard duty. "Our whole camp, prisoners and all, was by such an event thrown into a great fever of commotion and excitement," he wrote.[31]

"Not until we arrived in camp," stated Joel Robison, "did any of the captors know who the prisoner was." Private Bostick, another of the captors, felt, "We knew then that we had made a big haul." Learning who they had captured, Bostick was angry "for not killing him out on the prairie."[32]

Tending to another Mexican prisoner in the compound, Dr. Labadie saw Sylvester and company ride in with their prisoner. He noted that Santa Anna wore a "glazed leather cap, a striped jacket (volunteer roundabout), country made, coarse cotton socks, soldier's coarse white linen pants, bespattered with mud." Private John Swisher, also on guard duty, noted that Santa Anna was "disguised in a blue cottonade round-jacket and pants."[33]

This early enlarged Kodak shows the large post oak under which Sam Houston was lying when Santa Anna was brought before him. This photo was sent to San Jacinto researcher Henry McArdle by Lorenzo de Zavala Jr. in the late 1800s. Buffalo Bayou lies in the background of this early photograph.
H. A. McArdle's San Jacinto Notebooks, Texas State Library and Archives Commission.

According to the story he related to his own children, William Sadler approached the prisoner and pulled back his ragged cotton jacket to reveal the fine linen shirt with jeweled studs underneath.[34]

James Sylvester was later honored as being the leader of the group which captured Santa Anna. Months later on August 3 in San Augustine, he was presented with a pamphlet containing the names of the men who had participated in the battle of San Jacinto. General Sam Houston personally endorsed the back of this pamphlet to him as a token of his gratitude.

> Presented to James A. Sylvester by General Sam Houston as a tribute of regard for his gallant and vigilant conduct, first in the battle of San Jacinto and subsequently in the capture of Santa Anna, whose thanks were tendered in my presen[ce] to Captain Sylvester for his generous conduct towards him when captured.

The destruction of Vince's Bridge on the morning of April 21 by Deaf Smith and his men turned out to be a very significant factor for the Texans. Some have argued that this only caused a minor hindrance for any support troops marching in, who could have simply marched several miles along the bayou to find another crossing point. In the case of Santa Anna, however, the lack of a bridge halted his flight on April 21 and caused him to take up hiding in the woods. His own fear of water prevented him from swimming across and thus set up his own capture on April 22.

Had he escaped and made it to General Filisola's reinforcements, the days following the battle of San Jacinto might have played out differently.

Interrogation

The most important prisoner of Texas, Major General Santa Anna, was turned over to Colonel John Forbes. In company with Colonel George Hockley and Joel Robison, Forbes led Santa Anna to meet Sam Houston.

At the time, "I was lying on my blanket on my left side in a doze," General Houston recalled.[35] The Texian commander-in-chief was stretched out beneath a large oak tree in camp, with his wounded left leg propped up. Forbes later recounted this meeting of opposing generals.

> [We] passed through Col. Burleson's quarters at the head of which Genl. Houston's tent was pitched. On our arrival, we found the Genl. outside of his tent stretched on a mattress at the foot of a large tree, apparently asleep, resting on his left side and his back towards us. We ranged up alongside and I put my hand on his arm to arouse him. He raised himself on his elbow and looked up. The Prisoner immediately addressed him, telling him who he was and surrendering himself to him, a prisoner of war.[36]

Houston looked at Santa Anna intensely, but made no reply, as he could not make out the Spanish language well. Turning to Colonel Forbes, Houston requested him to "proceed to the guard fire." Forbes was asked to return with "a young man who was reported to be the private secretary of Santa Anna and who could talk English fluently."

Among those present as Santa Anna was brought before Houston was Private Henry Brewer of the Nacogdoches Volunteers. "General Houston, in a short respite from pain, had fallen asleep," wrote Brewer. "He awakened, as Santa Anna and the crowd came up to the spot where he lay. The captive President betrayed no emotions of fear."[37]

Benjamin Franklin, standing near the large oak with fellow cavalrymen Lamar and Karnes, watched as the prisoner, "bespattered with mud, was ushered before us." Santa Anna stood before a growing crowd of hostile Texans. "Five hundred men with guns in their hands and vengeance in their eyes were glaring at him," wrote cavalryman Walter Lane.[38]

Some called out, "Shoot him!" and "Hang him!" According to James Winters, General Houston ordered those shouting the threats to be moved away. He ultimately had Colonel Hockley disperse a guard to control the growing crowd.[39]

Colonel Coleman wrote that Santa Anna bowed a few times and then "addressed the General in Spanish."[40]

"What does he say?" inquired Houston.

Several men helped to translate Santa Anna's early dialogue before Mexican translators could be had. One of those best suited to understand Santa Anna during the early exchanges was Sergeant Moses Austin Bryan. In his recollections, the general's confession in English translated to "I am Antonio López de Santa Anna, President of Mexico, Commander-in-Chief of the Army of Operations and I put myself at the disposition of the brave General Houston. I wish to be treated as a general should when a prisoner of war."[41]

Colonel Forbes returned with Ramón Caro. "The young man on seeing the prisoner assured Genl. Houston that the prisoner then before him was truly Genl. Santa Anna," wrote Forbes. Sam Houston wanted further proof that he did indeed have the leader of Mexico before him and sent Forbes back to the guard fire to retrieve Colonel Juan Almonte from the bull pen.[42]

While Almonte was being summoned, Sergeant Bryan and others continued to inform General Houston of what Santa Anna spoke. Private Brewer recalled that Santa Anna tried to compliment Houston.

> Perceiving that flattery fell with no unpleasing force upon his ear, he omitted no opportunity of profiting by this discovery. His compliments were gracefully turned; not, however, entirely divested of the ridiculous bombast of his nation. He said, on one occasion, that, "He was born to no common destiny who was the Conqueror of the Napoleon of Mexico." A man of infinitely less vanity than Houston, might have been betrayed by this courtly flattery.[43]

Robert Coleman of Houston's staff also found that Santa Anna tried hard to flatter Houston. He later recorded El Presidente's banter as:

> The battle that was fought yesterday, Sir, is only to be compared with that of Waterloo. That you are the Wellington of the times, all must admit; great indeed, Sir, must be the destinies of that man who could conquer the

"Napoleon of the South." Twenty-four times have I fought, and twenty-four times have I conquered the most distinguished Generals that Spain and Mexico could produce; but on San Jacinto's plains, Sir, I found myself unable to contend with undisciplined Texians, led on by such wisdom and valor.[44]

Santa Anna proceeded to explain the reason for his disguise and flight from the battlefield. He claimed that he hoped to evade recognition until he could be brought before General Houston himself. After attempting to flatter General Houston, he next spotted Sergeant James Sylvester, who had worked his way into the crowd to observe. The Mexican army's leader made the effort to publicly thank the sergeant for his humanity after the capture.

He pointed myself out, as being his captor, and immediately returned his thanks for my kindness, when I took him prisoner; and if it was ever in his power (which he hoped it would be), that he would reward me handsomely for it.[45]

Captain Robert Calder joined the throng as the verification of the captive took place. Calder's patrol party had been alerted by Major Wells that Santa Anna was captured. He could not resist getting a view

"The Surrender of Santa Anna," 1886 oil painting by William Henry Huddle. This early interpretation of the surrender shows General Houston with a wounded right leg, although he had been shot in the left. Dr. Ewing works on Houston's ankle while scout Deaf Smith cups his ear to listen to Houston.
Texas State Library and Archives Commission.

of "the Butcher of the Alamo," and moved in close for what he found to be truly "an interesting scene."[46]

Colonel Forbes soon returned again from the guard fire with Colonel Almonte, the senior Mexican army officer who spoke fluent English. En route, he encountered Colonel Thomas Rusk and Lorenzo de Zavala Jr., a member of Houston's staff. Even after secretary Caro had identified Santa Anna, Private Brewer felt that Houston "displayed doubt, if not incredulity, as to the identity of the character before him." Once Almonte arrived, "he bowed with great respect, upon coming into the presence of the captured General."[47]

Rusk noted that Santa Anna embraced young de Zavala and tried to invoke the past friendships of de Zavala's father to his goodwill. The younger de Zavala courteously greeted the Mexican dictator but gave a terse stare which "seemed to wither Santa Anna." With the arrival of Rusk, de Zavala and Almonte, Forbes wrote that now "the Prisoner was fully recognized and identified."[48]

Sergeant Bryan relinquished the early translation duties to Colonel Almonte after his arrival. Colonel Rusk then took over the interrogation of President Santa Anna, using Almonte to relay his questions during the next two hours. "Throughout the whole, General Santa Anna's demeanor was dignified and soldier like," wrote Forbes, "but a close observer could trace a shade of sadness on his otherwise impassive countenance."

"Rusk asked what excuse Santa Anna had to make for the massacre of Colonel Travis and his men," wrote Sergeant Bryan. Santa Anna stated that it was customary to "put all to the sword" when such a small force refused to surrender and thereby forced many casualties upon the superior attacking force.[49]

Secretary of War Rusk moved the interrogation into the more serious business of negotiating a formal armistice with the captured leader of the Mexican army. Had Santa Anna been killed on the battlefield or after his capture, Sam Houston would have lost a powerful diplomatic ace in the hole. By choosing to keep him alive, he now could attempt to negotiate the peaceful surrender of the other Mexican forces still in Texas.

Private Brewer felt that Santa Anna "displayed great diplomatic skill in the negotiation which was carried on, firmly (at first) opposing every measure by which Mexico was likely to suffer, and Texas to be benefitted."[50]

Colonel Rusk asked Santa Anna to order General Filisola's troops to evacuate Texas. Santa Anna felt that Filisola's men would refuse without his direct orders. Rusk then replied that if the Mexicans under Filisola would not voluntarily depart the country, then the Texans "were determined to drive them" out.

At length, Santa Anna agreed to issue the orders to have his troops fall back. He asked that his personal secretary, Ramón Caro, be allowed to assist with writing up the official orders on his own stationery. Rusk allowed Caro to return to the battlefield under guard to retrieve Santa Anna's necessary effects and official correspondence papers. During this venture, Caro saw just how devastating his army's loss had been.

> I was informed that, accompanied by one of Houston's aides, I should go back to the battlefield to search for and bring back the portable *escritoire* and other belongings of the private secretarial staff of His Excellency.
> We left for the purpose, taking with us one of our soldiers to bring back whatever we found. To me alone was reserved the sharp pain of beholding our battlefield after the action.[51]

Caro and his guards found Santa Anna's *escritoire* and returned to the Texan camp. Caro was also granted permission to bring back Santa Anna's bed. Thus, from the first night of his imprisonment, the Mexican president "did not have to sleep on the ground as did everybody else, including Houston."

Under the harsh questioning of Houston and Rusk, Santa Anna's nerves had frazzled. From Caro he also received his own medicine box. Some accounts of his interrogation claim that he took a quick dose of some opium from this box to help restore his calm.[52]

Caro took his position at the writing table and began penning His Excellency's orders. A set of three orders was written out to General Filisola on official stamped paper to show authenticity. Santa Anna ordered Filisola to have General Gaona fall back to Bexar and for General Urrea to withdraw his troops back to Guadalupe Victoria. "An armistice has been drawn up with General Houston while negotiations are under way to bring the war to an end for ever," wrote Santa Anna. He also informed Filisola that the army "from now on is under your orders."

The second directive was for Filisola to order his various brigade commanders to insure that no damage be done to personal property of

Texans while the Mexican army retreated. Finally, Filisola was to release any prisoners "and send them forthwith to San Felipe de Austin."
He signed the orders with "God and liberty" from "camp of San Jacinto, April 22, 1836."[53]

After this main agreement was drawn up, Colonel Juan Almonte,
according to eyewitness Isaac Hill, asked General Houston how the
historic document should be dated.[54]

"Lynchburg, I believe is the name of the place," Sam Houston
replied.

"San Jacinto, General," corrected Colonel Wharton, "Let it be
San Jacinto."

CHAPTER 18

The Spoils of War

April 23

As far as I can learn, the war is over.
—*Lieutenant M. H. Denham, First Regiment, May 3, 1836*

Deaf Smith was given copies of Santa Anna's truce agreement and the dispatches he had written to his subordinate officers. With two companions, the tireless Texas spy rode off with this paperwork into the night of April 22.

During the following morning, they overtook another Mexican courier on the road between Harrisburg and Fort Bend. Smith confiscated the dispatches carried by this man and gave him a copy of Santa Anna's letter to General Filisola. The courier was ordered to deliver this message directly to the Mexican command at Fort Bend.

Smith and his fellow scouts followed the man for some time until coming upon another small Mexican man traveling on foot. He was carrying an ear of corn and a fine china pitcher of water. He had no way of knowing at this moment that he had made yet another significant haul, capturing General Martin Cos.[1]

Smith turned back for the Texas camp, taking this man as prisoner. En route, his patrol met up with fellow scout Jim Wells, who had been thrown from his horse and injured on April 20 during a brush with a Mexican patrol. According to Wells, Smith brought Cos to Stafford's Point, where he acquired a horse for the prisoner to ride back to the Texian camp. Just as Sylvester's men had no idea when they had captured President Santa Anna, Smith had no idea that he was hauling in Santa Anna's brother-in-law. The prisoner told Smith that he had been in battle on April 21 but had escaped after dark that night, abandoning his horse at a burned bridge.

When Smith rode back into camp with his prisoner, he was quickly identified as General Cos. Dr. Nicholas Labadie, making a list of prisoners at the time, found that there was a great "eagerness of our men to see General Cos." Another of the Mexican prisoners, Colonel Pedro Delgado, later wrote, "The presence of the General had created such a sensation among the conquerors that they crowded and quarreled for a sight of him."[2]

The arrival of Cos on April 24 made a total of forty-eight Mexican officers who were prisoners. To avoid the curious stares of the Texans, Cos soon spent much of his time lying down, his head wrapped in a blanket to disguise his identity. Reflected Delgado, "Scoundrels were not wanting who would have murdered him."

Colonel Thomas Rusk had completed his official report of the battle of San Jacinto by April 23, while Sam Houston still labored away at his own version. The secretary of war selected a courier for the important mission of getting the news of the San Jacinto victory to Galveston and to President David Burnet.

He picked Benjamin C. Franklin, who had brought a small command to the army from Galveston just days previous. Franklin invited his friend and messmate, Captain Robert Calder, to join him. "I easily obtained the five days' furlough," Calder reflected.

> Two other individuals, Captain Bob Moore and another man, whose name I have forgotten—both privates in other companies—interceded with me to get them furloughs to go with us, saying they would work the boat. As Franklin and myself were not accustomed to such labor, the furloughs were obtained and we started.[3]

Forty-one-year-old Robert D. Moore, a private of Captain Moseley Baker's company, was promoted to captain of the guard at Velasco in May. Only a small open boat was available, which these four men used to navigate Buffalo Bayou down to San Jacinto Bay and across the massive bay to Galveston. Calder and Franklin let Moore and his companion handle the oars. Delivering Rusk's battlefield correspondence would prove to be a long and arduous journey.

In camp, Major General Santa Anna was kept separated from the other Mexican prisoners. Private Henry Brewer of Captain Arnold's company noted that Santa Anna displayed great courtesy while a prisoner. He was kept near General Houston's tent. "It was his invariable custom to send his compliments to Gen. Houston," wrote Brewer, "and to inquire into the state of his wound, every morning."[4]

On April 23, permission was granted for Santa Anna to have his tent erected near that of General Houston. This tent was shared by Santa Anna, secretary Ramón Caro and Colonel Juan Almonte, the senior surviving staff officers who were the subject of the armistice. Colonel John Wharton returned a personal trunk to Caro, "which though it had been broken into and 180 pesos that I had in it had been stolen, still contained some clothes." From this trunk, Santa Anna was able to select other clothing besides his escape costume.[5]

The greatest commotion on the San Jacinto battlefields on April 23 came with the late afternoon arrival of the steamboat *Cayuga*. Aboard her were Vice President de Zavala and Colonel James Morgan, who had departed Galveston that morning for Harrisburg, still unaware of the battle. En route, they had stopped at Morgan's place at New Washington. He found his warehouse burned and his plantation wrecked by Santa Anna's troops.

Morgan and de Zavala received their first news of the San Jacinto victory while at Morgan's plantation from his servants. Morgan likely encountered Emily West, his indentured servant who had detained Santa Anna on the battlefield. There is no record of anyone seeing Emily immediately after the battle, so it is logical to assume that she made her way back the seven or eight miles to Morgan's plantation soon after the battle.[6]

From New Washington, the *Cayuga* moved on up San Jacinto Bay to Buffalo Bayou. Among those on board her was land agent John Linn, who recorded that their boat was met at Lynch's Ferry around 5:00 p.m. by Colonel Rusk and a party of Texian soldiers. The *Cayuga* then traveled up Buffalo Bayou to the Texas camp.

From the prisoner pen, Colonel Delgado found the steamboat's arrival to be a lively affair. "The artillery on board, consisting of two guns, fired a salute of five rounds," he recalled.[7] The troops lined up as de Zavala was triumphantly led to General Houston's tent. The steamer proceeded to unload much-needed supplies to quartermaster Valentine Bennett.

Vice President Zavala was shocked at the condition of the battlefield. He found the body of his old friend General Castrillon lying stripped along with other bodies around where the heavy fighting for the Golden Standard had taken place. De Zavala had his servants carry

Castrillon's body across the bayou to his ranch. He buried General Castrillon in the de Zavala family cemetery, the only known Mexican officer to receive a proper burial after San Jacinto.[8]

Shortly after the *Cayuga*'s arrival, there was a mishap in the Texian camp in the late afternoon of April 23. Among the spoils of war was a large quantity of gunpowder in sacks and packages, piled up within the enclosure. In hauling the powder sacks to the enclosure of munitions, small quantities of powder had leaked out all over the ground, upon which lay other muskets, pistols and general baggage.

Colonel Delgado noted that the Texans had piled up seventy or eighty loads of ordnance stores in camp, along with piles of loaded muskets and cartridge boxes. "Some of the Americans went about that combustible matter, and even handled it, with their pipes in their mouths."[9]

About 3:00 in the afternoon, a fire started among the Mexican baggage. Private Bob Hunter, detailed to guard Santa Anna, witnessed the resulting explosions.

> The baggage was all gathered up and piled all in one big pile: saddles, blankets and all kind of clothing, gun powder, arapahoes or pack saddles. There was [a] small boy looking at the pistols and snapping them, and the guard told him that he might do some damage and to leave. The boy said that they were not loaded and one went off amongst the guns.[10]

The young soldier toying with the firearms was Private John Ferrell, according to Lieutenant Martin Snell of Captain Briscoe's regular company.

> Col. Forbes was assisting in taking an inventory of the spoils at the time of the explosion. Col. Handy was writing near him. John P. Ferrell, then a young man like myself, was with me in the enclosure and accidentally discharged a pistol, which wounded Col. Handy and fired the loose powder on the ground, which communicated with the loaded muskets and pistols lying about on the ground, creating quite an excitement in camp.
>
> The fire was promptly extinguished by Col. Forbes and others. Had the fire communicated with the large amount of powder stacked in the enclosure, much damage may have originated therefrom.[11]

Snell felt that the fire had spread quickly due to many "Mexican cartridges scattered over the ground crushed by [being] tramped on." Pri-

John P. Ferrell (1819–1874) was a seventeen-year-old private of Captain Isaac Moreland's artillery company. On April 23, Ferrell accidentally discharged a pistol, which started a dangerous fire in a pile of ammunition and supplies.
H. A. McArdle's San Jacinto Notebooks, Texas State Library and Archives Commission.

vate Hunter said that after Ferrell accidentally ignited the loose powder, the resulting explosions were "for a few minutes like a little battle."

The ball from Ferrell's shot "grazed the chin of Col. Handy, as he was writing, entering his left arm, while he sat taking an inventory of the articles," wrote Dr. Nicholas Labadie, who was near the pile searching for bandage material. Labadie felt that "over twenty cartridge-boxes" exploded in the resulting fire before enough water was fetched to douse the small fire.[12]

Hunter and others were startled enough to grab their guns at the sound of firing. The Mexican prisoners and even the guards ran as the powder and ordnance began popping, "expecting at every moment the fatal explosion." Seeing that the fires had been extinguished with water, feet and blankets, the guards herded the prisoners back into their pen.[13]

Other than Handy, no one was injured in the explosion caused by Private Ferrell. General Houston used the occasion to make an example of the seventeen-year-old soldier, however. He informed Ferrell that he would be shot at nine the following morning for his recklessness.[14]

Houston had the guard detail bring Ferrell before him half an hour before the execution was to be carried out. Only then did the general let on that he had been bluffing, as he told Ferrell that "young men are too scarce to be shot like dogs."

Sergeant Moses Bryan, the Spanish-speaking nephew of Stephen F. Austin, stood guard over Santa Anna's tent during the night of April

23. Bryan listened as Santa Anna chatted away with other Mexican officers who were allowed to visit him.

> I was sergeant of the guard around the tent the second night. Colonel Almonte, Colonel Nuñez, Santa Anna's brother-in-law, and Corre [Caro], Santa Anna's secretary, occupied the tent with Santa Anna. They talked all night about the condition of the army, the navy, and what would be the result in the City of Mexico on hearing of the disastrous defeat and their capture.[15]

By morning on April 24, Santa Anna and Colonel Rusk were busy once again, negotiating on treaty details.

Now the third day after the battle, conditions about the Texian camp had gone downhill. "The slain Mexicans were a ghastly sight," wrote young William Zuber. "They sent forth a sickening stench. As their number equaled that of our army, our men could not bury them, and they rotted on the field."[16]

The aroma increased daily, but still General Houston maintained his camp close to the San Jacinto battlefield. Colonel Delgado noted that his place among the Mexican prisoners was joined by others on April 24. He later wrote that "several patches of officers and men were brought in by the numerous scouting parties" on April 24.[17]

The most significant catch after Santa Anna was Deaf Smith's delivery of General Cos. Other patrols managed to catch other key Mexican officers. Colonel José María Romero, having also fled the battlefield, was apprehended on April 25 and Lieutenant Colonel Eulogio Gonzales was taken on April 26.[18]

General Vicente Filisola, occupying his makeshift headquarters on the Brazos River, received the first news of the defeat on April 22 via a courier from acting Colonel Maria Garcia. Garcia was the leader of the one hundred men from Cos' division which did not reach San Jacinto in time. Santa Anna had obviously been killed or captured, as no word had been heard from him since the battle.[19]

Filisola withdrew his troops back near San Felipe and sent word for the eleven hundred men under General Urrea in Brazoria and Colonel Salas in Columbia to join his force of 1,408 men. Including corps and branches stationed in Béxar, Copano, Goliad, Matagorda and other areas, General Filisola had more than four thousand troops still dispersed in Texas as of April 24.

On April 25, Filisola reorganized his army into three brigades under Generals Gaona, Tolsa and Urrea, and General Ramirez y Sesma was named second-in-command to Filisola. The bitter news of Santa Anna's defeat was finally sent to Mexico on this day by Filisola.

On April 26, Filisola's brigades set out for Guadalupe Victoria. Heavy rains and swollen creeks made the march treacherous for his troops, many of whom were suffering from the lack of proper provisions and clothing. A soldier caught up with General Filisola at 2:00 p.m. on April 27 with a dispatch from Santa Anna.

Santa Anna reported that he was a prisoner of war of the Texans and he ordered Filisola to order Gaona to countermarch to Bexar "to await my orders." Urrea was also ordered to withdraw his division to Victoria.

Filisola sent his reply back to Santa Anna on April 28 from San Bernard Creek that he had "executed the maneuvers that seemed proper to me for pulling the army together." Filisola and the other commanding generals sent their pleasure in finding that Major General Santa Anna was still alive. General Adrián Woll and three other soldiers were sent to San Jacinto—where Santa Anna was working on his armistice—with Filisola's reply and to ascertain firsthand their general's armistice with Houston.

Santa Anna had drafted a second message to General Filisola by the morning of April 25. This dispatch ordered the Mexican troops to retire to the Rio Grande and was to be handed to Filisola in person. Colonel Edward Burleson was selected to carry out this mission. He set out with Deaf Smith, Captain Henry Karnes and three hundred mounted men on the morning of April 25 for Filisola's camp.[20]

Filisola's men were caught just before they reached the Colorado River. While camped on the San Bernard, Texas scouts happened upon the Mexican campground by chance. Second Lieutenant Walter Lane, promoted from private for his bravery in the cavalry at San Jacinto, wrote that "Colonel Burleson and some others swam their horses over" the river. They delivered the dispatch to Filisola, who stated that he would respond the following morning.

By 9:00 a.m. the following morning, there was no word from Filisola. Another party of officers crossed the San Bernard to investigate. "Deaf Smith came back and said that Filisola had retreated during the night and his camp was vacant," recalled Lane. The enemy had retreated so hurriedly, in fact, that they left tents, weapons, wagons and even a number of their own sick and wounded men.

Burleson's men broke camp and continued to follow the Mexican army as it slowly moved toward Matamoros.

The Booty Auction: April 26

The smell of rotting flesh grew worse by the day. Peggy Mc-Cormick, the widow of one of Austin's Old Three Hundred settlers, lived on the land on which the San Jacinto battles were fought.

The fiery Irish woman sought out Sam Houston where he lay wounded and furiously demanded that he "take them dead Mexicans off my league." McCormick said that their bodies would "haunt" her as long as she lived.[21]

Houston tried to soothe the woman, telling her that her land would soon be a historical landmark.

"To the devil with your glorious history!" snapped Ms. McCormick. "Take off your stinking Mexicans."[22]

The army did move camp by April 26 to Dr. George M. Patrick's house, five or six miles above the battlefield. Private Thomas Corry recalled that "we went to get away from the stench of the battle ground."[23]

Prisoner Pedro Delgado felt that the Texians "had not the generosity to burn or to bury" the corpses of his comrades. At the site of the new camp, he found that there were two or three frame houses, which were quickly "occupied by the conquering and conquered

The restored standard of the volunteer Batallon Guerrero was among four flags of the Mexican army taken at San Jacinto. The Guerrero flag is now part of the Flag Collection at the Texas State Library in Austin.
Texas State Library and Archives Commission.

Flag of the Batallon Matamoros Permanente, one of the regular companies of the Mexican army. Before being decimated at San Jacinto, the Matamoros battalion had fought at Coleto Creek and the Alamo.
Texas State Library and Archives Commission.

Generals." Aside from General Santa Anna, the other Mexican prisoners were penned into a temporary stockade again under some trees.[24]

At Dr. Patrick's, the booty captured from the Mexican army was divided among the Texas soldiers. The spoils of battle were sizable. Mules, horses, saddles, camp equipment and tools were seized in addition to the money. "There was one brass cannon, a nine pounder, and balls, a large quantity of muskets, cartridges, swords" and other munitions, according to Lieutenant John Borden.[25]

As commissary general, Colonel John Forbes was in charge of keeping the books and accounts of items consumed by the army. He was placed in charge of all captured Mexican property. "Genl. Houston issued an order that everything captured should be delivered up, and that any person retaining anything should be deemed guilty of theft," recalled Captain Jesse Billingsley.[26]

Houston was not directly involved in this activity, as he still lay wounded. His wound had become infected and he had taken fever, leaving him in little shape to sort out financials.

According to Dr. Labadie, $12,000 had been captured from the enemy, and it was to be divided. He contended that Colonel Forbes and those who assisted him did not equally divide up the money.

> The money had been counted so often, and by so many, that it naturally stuck to their fingers, till but $7000 were left. I was told that General Houston cursed them in his peculiar way for their rascally conduct, and swore the money should be counted no more. His cursing, as usual, did very little good; and, as usual also, those who did the least toward securing the victory, appropriated to themselves the largest share of the spoils.[27]

Private George Erath, who helped guard the booty overnight on April 21, did "not believe the rumors of embezzlement. It is my opinion that everything was handled fairly and squarely."[28]

Of the captured money, three thousand was voted to be given to the Texas Navy, and the rest was split between the San Jacinto heroes. Sam Houston's counting of the men present at San Jacinto was 783, amongst whom the remaining $9,000 was to be split. This would be about $11.50 per man.

This math would not prove so simple, however. The actual number of Texans who had participated in the battle of San Jacinto was actually about 930 by best count. The first postbattle muster rolls did not account for all men. Captain Alfred Wyly's Second Regiment company, for example, was left out entirely.

This ornamental martingale, a portion of the harness from General Santa Anna's horse, was auctioned off to Colonel Sidney Sherman after the battle. It is made of dark leather with a large silver center emblem which contains a five-pointed star in its design. *Courtesy of the San Jacinto Museum of History, Houston.*

Many of the names of those recorded were improperly spelled on the first list. Captain Billingsley remembered that "seven or eight names in my company" were spelled wrong. Colonel Burleson, determined to make out a correct roll for his First Regiment, ordered his private secretary, William Gorham, and Billingsley's orderly sergeant, Russell Craft, to make out a proper roll for the First Regiment. Billingsley maintained this muster roll until it was requested to be included in the state's archives.[29]

If the money was to be divided among those present at the battle and assigned to Camp Harrisburg, the number of Texans present rose to 1,185. Dividing the remaining $9,000 among everyone would drop the individual take to about $7.60.

On average, private soldiers were given about nine dollars, with which they could buy anything they wanted at the auction of captured Mexican goods. Some Texans received a little more and some nothing at all if they were away on duty at the time of the auction.

"Our company left the army shortly after the battle and I did not receive any," said seventeen-year-old Private Josephus Irvine of Captain Bryant's company. Irvine found that the money for "members of Capt. Bryant's was deposited with Lieutenant Col. Bennett."[30]

The rumblings that the money was being pilfered did not sit well with some men. Captains Moseley Baker and Jesse Billingsley decided that the spoils should be distributed fairly. They announced to Colonel Forbes that if he would not do it, they would march their companies over, seize the money and "distribute it ourselves to the army." That night, Forbes reportedly began distributing the money to the captains that approached him.[31]

Billingsley did not feel that the money was fairly handled.

> The pro rata to each soldier (there was no distinction between officers and privates) was sixteen dollars, and that at the sale which was to take place, each soldier could purchase to the amount of sixteen dollars without paying any money on his purchases. Said sale did take place under an order to this effect, and Forbes kept the account of the same in his marker, and settled with him for my company, and this is one of the reasons why I think he had charge of said articles.
>
> Several boxes of money were captured from the Mexicans—how much it amounted to I do not know. I saw one box counted and I think it contained two thousand dollars. This count was made when I drew the money for my company. Forbes and his clerk had the number of men of the army and made the pro rata, and said that there was due each person twelve dollars and twenty-five cents, and paid that amount for each of the men of my company over to me.

> I have been informed by persons since then, who were in the army, that some companies drew nothing, whilst others drew less than I did. I was the first man who drew any amount, and have been informed that I drew more for my company than any other person did for theirs.[32]

Those men present at the battlefield when the distribution was made generally received more than those who had gone after the Mexican army. Colonel Sherman's recollection was that "each man was to receive about eleven dollars." Private Paschal P. Borden of Captain Baker's company stated that his company "received about eleven or twelve dollars." Dr. William Carper received $11.25.[33]

Captain James Gillaspie said that his Company F of the Second Regiment received "four or five mules" from the quartermaster on the battlefield. Days later, from Lieutenant Colonel Bennett, Gillaspie received "eleven dollars and seventy-five cents for each man." Captain William Heard testified that the soldiers of his Company F of the First Regiment "received $10.25 each."[34]

Sergeant Robert Goodloe recalled that Captain Karnes' men "did not receive but four dollars." Working in advance of the army on scouting duty, Karnes' men were not paid until they arrived in Victoria long after the battle. Captain Turner's regulars also received their share belatedly, and again not the same amount. "My company received six dollars to the man," stated Turner.[35]

General Houston did not participate in the auction, although Adjutant General John Wharton purchased four hundred dollars' worth of goods for him. Of the total money found, Houston said, "I understand that $12,000 had been found in the Army chest of Santa Anna."[36]

That a number of the spoils were purloined or stolen, "I have no doubt," said Houston. Lieutenant Colonel Bennett charged Sidney Sherman with purloining some of the spoils. Houston said that Bennett, "pledged himself to substantiate it, but Sidney Sherman chose to rest under the imputation, or was quiet under the charge for a number of years."[37]

Sergeant Thomas Brooks of Captain Arnold's First Company witnessed Colonel Sherman "take a sword up and carry it to his tent." Brooks had first spotted the sword among the spoils and was admiring its heavy gold hilt and scabbard.

> When Col. Sherman walked up, I said to Col. Sherman that that was a fine sword, and that when it was sold, if it went at five hundred dollars, I would have it. Sherman picked up the sword and looked at it for some time and said that it was a fine sword, and laid it down.

The day after, I believe, I saw Col. Sherman go and pick up the sword and walk off to his tent, and I waited to see if he brought the sword back, and on seeing him without the sword, I said, "Col., some person has taken my sword."

The Col. said he reckoned not; and I said to Col. Sherman, "It is you, Col., that has taken my sword." The Col. smiled and walked off.[38]

Houston recalled that Sherman was the only officer directly accused of taking from the spoils. Specifically, he was told that Sherman had taken a plate belonging to Santa Anna and "a very fine sword." Houston later explained:

I intended to order an investigation, being friendly to him and having aided in his promotion, I deemed it due to his reputation. I mentioned it to an officer in whom I had confidence, and he dissuaded me from doing it. Thus the affair rested without investigation.[39]

The booty auction was held on April 26. Men bought Mexican horses, mules, saddles, spurs, baggage, clothing, and any item of value plundered from their enemy's campground. Colonel Sherman purchased $341.25 worth of property at the auction. Santa Anna's saddle was auctioned for eight hundred dollars. All of the fine items and silver found with the military chest brought in another sixteen hundred dollars.

"I got for my part an old saddle," recalled Private Rinaldo Hotchkiss of Captain Kimbro's company. "There was a good deal of gambling amongst the men" for other spoils. Sergeant Moses Bryan of Captain Baker's unit also received "a common Mexican saddle" for his portion." Lieutenant Martin Snell purchased a Mexican blanket for about eleven dollars during the auction, accounting for his share of the money.[40]

"How strange these men are!" thought Colonel Delgado as he watched the booty auction from the prisoner pen. "Many of them act and feel like the wild Comanche."[41] The Texans had draped their newly purchased mules and horses with red and green cords taken from the caps of Mexican soldiers. Others had decorated their saddles with glittering epaulets taken from officers' gear and equipment. Delgado felt that the Texans were so adorned with mismatched colors and glitter as to look like "bull-fight clowns."

The Texans bought horses and mules alike and saddled them for their own. "It was quite amusing to see these gentlemen putting riding saddles on some fractious and wicked mule, which knew nothing beyond the pack," recalled Delgado. The first mule rider did not properly secure his saddle. His friends held the beast until he had mounted and then turned the frightened mule loose. "You should have seen the brute scampering over God's own green fields," wrote Delgado, "scattering about its trapping and ornaments," and even throwing its rider.

In the auction of property, General Houston found the certain large black horse known as Old Whip to his liking. When William Vince showed up in camp protesting that it was his horse that had been taken by the Mexicans days before San Jacinto, Houston stated that it "had been captured on the battle field and given to him." He planned to pay for it, as this horse was not among the booty divided up among the men. Vince protested to President Burnet, who eventually helped Vince rightfully secure his horse from Sam Houston.[42]

Burnet Is Notified

Captain Bob Calder and Benjamin Franklin spent four days in trying to reach President Burnet with the news of San Jacinto. Assisted by Private Bob Moore and another soldier, they had departed in a rowboat on the morning of April 23.[43]

They camped the first night at Spillman's Island, about five miles down from New Washington. During the second day, the men fought strong winds and high waves with their leaky skiff. Moore and his companion suggested that they "lie up until a change of wind made it practicable to cross the bay from the mouth of Buffalo Bayou to the island direct." Captain Calder felt that this idea "met with no favor from Franklin or myself." They therefore hugged the coastline and guided their craft through shallow water.

By the third day, April 25, they had reached Redfish Bay, about twenty miles from Galveston. The waters calmed and by sundown of the fourth day, April 26, the quartet had rowed to Virginia Point, where they had a full view of Galveston Bay.

There they could see three ships of the Texas Navy, the flagship *Independence*, the *Flash* and the *Invincible*. The men made camp for the night on the beach under wet blankets and resumed rowing for the Texas Navy after dawn on April 27. They pulled alongside Captain Jeremiah Brown's *Invincible* and shouted the news of the victory at San Jacinto.

"His men literally lifted us on board in the midst of wild excitement," recalled Captain Calder. "Brown took off his hat and gave us three cheers." The *Invincible* even fired off three rounds from "Long Tom," the ship's eighteen-pound gun, before control was restored. Calder's party was treated to the best drinks on the ship.

They were next moved over to the flagship *Independence*, where the story was retold to Commodore James Hawkins and the partying ensued again. "We imbibed enough of first rate whiskey to have felt the effects very sensibly if we had been under less excitement, or had our determination been less to carry out our mission as the heralds of victory," wrote Calder. Finally, the couriers of San Jacinto were ferried ashore in one of the navy's gigs to take the news to President Burnet.

The dispatch written by Colonel Rusk asked that President Burnet come to the Texian camp immediately. From Galveston, the quickest mode of transportation was the steamboat *Yellow Stone*, which had carried the Texas Army across the Brazos on April 12 and 13. Timber was scarce and it took several days to round up enough wood to burn for the return trip. Burnet and members of his cabinet boarded the steamboat on May 1 and began the trip upriver to the camp near Buffalo Bayou.[44]

The Forbes Trial

The taunting of Colonel Forbes for killing the Mexican woman continued in the Texas camp after dark each night. Third Sergeant Campbell Taylor of Captain Billingsley's company later stated that he "saw a dead Mexican woman on the battle ground after the battle." Taylor also recalled that John Forbes continued to be harassed each evening.

> It was a general cry through the camps, "Who killed the Mexican woman?" to which was replied, "Col. Forbes;" then it was cried out, "That's a fact." It was cried out, "Who lay in the grass?" replied, "Col. Forbes," and replied further, "That's a fact." I was in the army about a week after the battle, and every time Col. Forbes made his appearance this was the general cry of the soldiers."[45]

Enough people held a guilty opinion of John Forbes that he was compelled to do something about it. Captain Amasa Turner had reached the Texas camp on the night of April 23 after his company was released from guarding the Mexican campground. He met with Adjutant Nicholas Lynch and Lieutenant Colonel Henry Millard on the subject of Colonel Forbes. "Col. Millard said that there was no evidence that Col. Forbes had killed the woman," said Turner. He found, however, that Lynch "entertained a different opinion."[46]

Colonel Sidney Sherman had seen the dead woman lying on the ground and made inquires about her death. He was told that Forbes had killed her. Sherman recalled that Sam Houston sought him out and "remarked to me in a laughing mood" that Forbes was "greatly annoyed by the troops" and their constant badgering. Sherman was appointed via verbal order to organize a court of inquiry on April 28 to study the matter. The proceedings were not conducted under army regulations and Sherman "had no power to acquit or condemn, but merely to ascertain if there was sufficient grounds for calling of a court martial."[47]

"So soon as the report reached the ears of Col. Forbes, he called upon me, and requested a Court for the investigation of the report," recalled General Houston. "I ordered a court of inquiry."[48]

During the inquiry before Sherman's court, with Lieutenant James Tinsley serving as judge advocate, Colonel Forbes admitted to killing the Mexican woman. "He did admit the killing of the woman," reported Sherman, "but claimed that he was excusable for so doing in battle."[49]

The two key witnesses to the alleged murder, Thomas Corry and Robert Cravens, were not called to make specific charges against him during this military trial. More than likely, Forbes was able to have this hearing done quietly and privately with only the knowledge of a few officers. In his own defense, Forbes called but one witness, according to Sherman.

> He had but one witness before the Court for examination; that was a Mexican woman, a prisoner, the wife of a muleteer. She testified to Col. Forbes' humanity and kindness extended to herself and other women made prisoners; spoke of his caressing her fondly; this was the point in her testimony; this created some amusement.
>
> She stated that she had always found Col. Forbes to be a good and kind man and did not think he would kill a woman intentionally.

Dr. Labadie's 1859 account of the San Jacinto campaign, published in the *Texas Almanac*, claimed that "his accusers were advised not to come forward." There is no evidence to support this statement, however. No one specifically recalled any pressure being put on anyone not to testify.

Colonel Sherman felt that the Mexican woman's testimony proved that Forbes had not intentionally killed the other woman. "For the want of any other testimony, the Court of inquiry could not come to any other result."

As for pilfering money, no one could ever specifically attest to seeing Forbes take anything. Captain Amasa Turner later speculated that his position as commissary made him "very unpopular with some of my command, both officers and men. I think some of them were not disposed to do him justice in anything."[50]

The court of inquiry filed its ruling on April 28. After a "strict, thorough and full investigation of all matters bearing upon the case, they find no evidence whatever in support of such charges, or any ground of censure against him in the action of the 21st. inst."[51]

"The decision was that Col. Forbes was acquitted of every imputation of unsoldier-like or improper conduct," said General Houston. "I endorsed my approval thereon, and Col. T. J. Rusk, as Secretary of War, endorsed his sanction."

The wounded Texas soldiers recovered in most cases. Those who had not expired on the battlefield continued to be treated in the makeshift hospital at Lorenzo de Zavala's home on Buffalo Bayou. Privates John Tom and Alfonso Steele, two of the more seriously wounded, continued to improve. The lack of good food was an irritant to Steele.

> My diet was crackers and sweetened vinegar. They fed me on that until I got so weak I couldn't get up. I came to the conclusion that they would starve me to death if I didn't get something to eat.[52]

John Tom's leg wound had been considered so severe that some thought he might not survive. He did pull through, later serving as sheriff of Guadalupe County and as a representative in the state legislature.

Several of those wounded on the battlefield did eventually succumb to their wounds. Sergeant Ashley Stephens, shot through the calf of both legs, took a turn for the worse and died on the ninth day after the battle.[53]

Another who eventually perished due to his San Jacinto wounds was Olwyn Trask, who had had his leg bone shattered during the April 20 skirmish. He lingered on in great pain for some time. Doctors Phelps and Labadie debated on whether or not his leg should be amputated. Some of Trask's friends arrived a few days after the battle to take him away. General Rusk gave orders to Labadie to accompany Trask and his friends, along with as many other wounded men as possible, aboard the steamer back to Galveston to report to Colonel Morgan.[54]

Labadie felt that Trask had been hit by the four-ounce copper balls, or "grape," from the Mexican cannon and that at least one of these copper balls was lodged in his leg. Labadie compelled the new attending doctor in Galveston to do the amputation, but Trask died after three weeks of suffering. His father, having heard the news of his son's serious wounds, was en route from New York to Galveston at the time of Trask's death.

The final Texas victim of San Jacinto was Giles Albert Giddings, who reportedly died of his wounds on June 7, 1836, at age twenty-four. A surveyor from Pennsylvania who had reached the Texan camp on April 9 and joined Captain William Wood's Company A, Giddings had been mortally wounded on April 21. The day after joining the army, on April 10, he had written a patriotic letter to his parents back home.

> Rather than be driven out of the country or submit to be a slave, I will leave my bones to bleach on the plains of Texas. If we succeed in subduing the enemy and establishing a free and independent government, we shall have the finest country the sun has ever shone upon, and if we fail we shall have the satisfaction of dying fighting for the rights of men.[55]

Giddings did live long enough to see that Santa Anna's army had been beaten. His April 10 letter to his parents encouraged them to not be alarmed for his safety, for he felt "no better, and my life no dearer, than those who gained the liberty you enjoy."

From the San Bernard River, General Adrián Woll, who had an excellent command of the English language, and three other soldiers arrived at the Texas army camp with Filisola's reply and to ascertain firsthand their president's armistice with Houston.[56]

Woll and company found Santa Anna on April 30 still working out the details of the negotiation. They approached under the flag of truce and were allowed into the Texas camp. Santa Anna ordered his troops to countermarch, leaving only four hundred men with two light artillery pieces at San Antonio de Bexar with the sick and wounded who could not yet travel.

Woll tried unsuccessfully to inform Houston that he could not make a treaty with a prisoner such as Santa Anna.

"I have," stated Houston, "and it shall stand."[57]

President David Burnet and his cabinet arrived at the Texian camp aboard the *Yellow Stone*, *Flash* and *Cayuga* soon after General Woll. The only change in the acting government was Attorney General Peter Grayson from Matagorda. Grayson, the former steamer captain who had run aground on April 21, had since been appointed in place of the late David Thomas, former Attorney General and acting Secretary of War, who had died of blood poisoning while at Galveston.

Burnet was displeased to find the larger part of the Texas Army inactive and not pursuing the retreating Mexican forces. "I found the President Santa Anna and his suite occupying the only building in the vicinity," wrote Burnet. "Cheerfulness seemed to pervade their countenances."[58]

Colonel Robert Coleman agreed that the soldiers loitering about the San Jacinto area now had "full rations of excellent provision, light duty to perform, and [were] amused almost every day by an auction of Mexican spoils."[59]

Burnet's cabinet worked on the treaty, Burnet using General Houston and Secretary of War Rusk's April 22 original agreement "as a guide in drawing up the first entire formula of a treaty that was ever committed to paper by this infant Republic."[60]

Before the treaty was completed, Burnet elected to have his cabinet moved back down to the Texas coast. He decided that he would take General Santa Anna and the Mexican prisoners with him for safekeeping while the treaty was finalized.

General Sam Houston's doctors finally decided that he needed to be moved to the United States for proper medical attention for his badly infected leg wound. Surgeon Alexander Ewing feared that he might die if he did not receive proper medical attention.

On May 3, as General Houston prepared to depart for New Orleans, twenty-seven of his officers signed a petition requesting him to take the captured saddle and bridle of General Cos to present to Colonel William Christy in New Orleans to show "our heartfelt gratitude towards him for the zeal used by him in our favor in our darkest days." Christy's recruiting efforts were key to providing United States volunteers.[61]

Houston resigned his commission and Thomas Rusk took over as Major General of the Texas Army. "I confide in his valor, his patriotism, and his wisdom," wrote Houston on May 5. "His conduct in the battle of San Jacinto was sufficient to ensure your confidence and regard."

Rusk's resigned position as secretary of war was filled via election by Colonel Mirabeau Lamar. From a lowly volunteer private of the cavalry three weeks before, this Georgia poet had thus reached the highest military position in Texas in less than a month!

The prisoners and officials began boarding the steamboats on the afternoon of May 7. Sam Houston made a farewell speech to his troops. President Burnet, Vice President de Zavala and his cabinet, including Colonel Lamar, went aboard the *Yellow Stone* on the evening of May 7. When the Rusk brothers tried to carry Houston's cot aboard the little steamer, Burnet tried to deny Houston passage—as he was no longer employed by the Republic of Texas. Captain John Ross refused to set sail without Sam Houston until Burnet gave in.[62]

Major General Santa Anna, Colonel Pedro Delgado and the other key prisoners were marched aboard the *Yellow Stone* around 5:00 p.m. on May 7. General Woll, who had arrived the previous week during negotiations, was allowed to leave. Woll "was dismissed at sundown, being hardly allowed to embrace two or three of us, with a few hurried words, as we were surrounded by very strict and insolent guards."[63]

The guards aboard the *Yellow Stone* were largely Texas regulars under Captain Amasa Turner. From the camp, Turner "was ordered to Galveston with my command in charge of the prisoners taken at San Jacinto." A few others volunteered for the duty. Private Thomas Corry, who had lost his horse at San Jacinto, found this to be "the most convenient route for me to reach Matagorda." Dr. Anson Jones followed the group to Galveston, having been promoted to assistant surgeon general and medical purveyor to the army. He resigned his post as surgeon of the Second Regiment to his cousin, Ira Jones. [64]

The Mexican prisoners were packed like cattle on the steamship and forced to spend the night in uncomfortable quarters until the boat could sail at dawn. Delgado:

> After sunset, we were no longer permitted to move, having to sleep on deck, crowded, like bars of soap, on top of each other. Positive orders had been given to the sentinels to blow out the brains of any man that raised his head. Therefore, without obtaining a drink of water, or being allowed to attend to the wants of nature, we laid our heads down, motionless, until sunrise.

> Very early on the 8th, after striking a bell three times, as is customary on these vessels, the machine was set in motion, and we glided down to Galveston.[65]

The *Yellow Stone* arrived at Galveston about noon on May 8. Santa Anna was transferred to the Texas Navy's armed schooner *Independence* for safekeeping. The other Mexican prisoners were kept on deck in the sun for the better part of the afternoon.

The guards grew weary of the waiting and fighting broke out among some of Captain William Wood's Kentucky company. Even the officers were unable to control the general melee that broke out, raucous enough to draw President Burnet from the cabin below. "The rascals were so hotly engaged in their contest that they did not mind the voice of their President and other chiefs any more than the barking of dogs," wrote Colonel Delgado. At length, Captain Allen was instrumental in breaking up the fight and helping to restore order.

Accommodations at Galveston in May 1836 were poor. Without a house for his staff, President Burnet found it "necessary for the Government to seek some place where the ordinary office business could be transacted, and Velasco was selected for that purpose." The cabinet and Santa Anna were thus moved and the final terms of the treaty were taken up once again. Vice President de Zavala had stayed behind at Buffalo Bayou to attend to domestic affairs at his home, which had been greatly depleted by the army's use of it as a hospital. Secretary Potter had also been granted leave.

From Galveston, Houston was put aboard the American schooner *Flora*, which arrived at New Orleans on May 28. He was greeted with a hero's welcome and remained there until he was well enough to journey back to Texas later in the summer.

At de Zavala's home, the balance of the Mexican prisoners remained under charge of Lieutenant Samuel Raymond and twelve guards. On May 14, Raymond sent Sergeant James Sylvester to Colonel Morgan in Galveston to report that they had been left with only "about two days provisions." The men subsisted on whatever beef they could kill and requested that Morgan furnish flour, pork, rice and other necessities.[66]

From early May to mid-August, the Mexican survivors of San Jacinto rode out the hot Texas summer along the Galveston coast before they were eventually released. Pedro Delgado found it to be an "accursed island" with deplorable conditions.

> We had no wholesome water, nor the shelter of shade trees, which we had enjoyed on the coast, and besides, we had to contend with myriads of flies, mosquitoes and sand-crabs, not to speak of continual storms and showers. Such were the swarms of mosquitoes, that it would seem that the whole species in the world had taken Galveston for a place of rendezvous.[67]

Followed closely by the Texas Army, General Filisola and his main body of the Mexican army continued to retreat toward the Rio Grande during early May. Mud, rain and swollen bodies of water made movement utterly horrible for the Mexican army over the next few days. They had reached the Colorado River on May 2, where Texas courier Jim Wells approached the Mexican army with news that he had further dispatches. Assured of their safety, Wells then sent for fellow spy Church Fulshear, who was carrying Santa Anna's further orders.[68]

General Filisola's men crossed the Colorado aboard a crude raft they constructed. He ordered General Ramirez y Sesma to proceed to Matamoros to deliver a detailed account of the army's condition. Fulshear arrived on May 5 with another dispatch from Santa Anna, one that was dated April 30. Santa Anna ordered him to "continue your march to Monterrey." He added that "negotiations under way are about to be concluded" and that he expected to be deported soon to Veracruz.

Filisola's army stopped briefly in Victoria on May 13, but pushed on to Goliad and there paused until May 24 while the final treaty details were worked out. While Santa Anna's troops had been defeated at San Jacinto, Filisola's troops were thoroughly demoralized on the march home. Suffering from lack of provisions, they also dealt with wind, rain, floods and sickness that stripped the Mexican soldiers of any spirit to fight again.

At the port of Velasco, the treaty was read to Santa Anna by Vice President de Zavala. Santa Anna agreed to its terms with condition. He recommended that it be split into two parts, separating some of the stipulations regarding the independence of Texas and her boundaries into a secret document. This second document would not be pushed until Santa Anna could be returned to power and thus secure its final ratification.

The so-called Velasco Treaty contained ten points, chiefly that "Hostilities between Mexican and Texas troops shall cease immediately upon land and sea." Mexican troops would evacuate Texas, crossing back over the Rio Grande. Private property was not to be destroyed during their retreat, and property previously confiscated was to be surrendered to the commander of the Texas forces.[69]

The cabinet was in agreement with the articles, with the exception of Secretary of Navy Potter and Colonel Lamar, the new Secretary of War, who did not sign it. The Velasco Treaty was finalized and signed on May 14, 1836, by Santa Anna, President David Burnet, acting Secretary of State James Collinsworth, Secretary of Treasury Bailey Hardeman and Attorney General Peter Grayson. This treaty was then carried by Captain Henry Teal and Major Ben Fort Smith to General Filisola, whom they overtook near Goliad.

Santa Anna also signed the second, more secretive document in which he swore to use his influence back in Mexico to have the government acknowledge Texas independence.[70]

It would be important to return Santa Anna to his country before his power was lost. He was placed aboard the warship *Invincible* on June 1, but strong winds prevented her sailing from Velasco for two days. On June 3, President Burnet's efforts to return Santa Anna to Mexico peacefully were shattered with the arrival of the steamboat *Ocean*.

The larger part of the troops now in the Galveston area were Americans, who had come to the aid of Texas but had arrived too late for the battle. Aboard this vessel were several hundred newly arrived United States volunteers under General Thomas Jefferson Green, Memucan Hunt and James Pinckney Henderson. Although none of these men had fought at San Jacinto or even served during the campaign, they vehemently demanded that Santa Anna be turned over to them for execution. According to Colonel Robert Coleman, Santa Anna "had actually been put on board ship, in compliance with this resolution, but was taken off the vessel by the citizens and volunteers."[71]

President Burnet, Attorney General Grayson and Colonel John Wharton made determined speeches to try to calm the situation, but to no avail. "The mob headed by Green & Henderson finally prevailed," wrote Colonel Lamar. Captain Jeremiah Brown refused to sail his *Independence* with the Mexican president aboard.

Santa Anna's life was spared, but he would remain a prisoner in Texas for many more months. Thus, Texas did not fulfill its part of the Velasco Treaty by quickly returning its key prisoner.

The Treaty of Velasco insured that the Mexican army would continue its retreat from Texas. Santa Anna was held until the fall, at which time he was taken to Washington to be questioned by the United States government.

Before leaving Texas, Santa Anna requested that his fine gold snuff box be presented to General Houston as a token of his esteem for fair treatment. Dr. Branch Archer presented the box to Houston. In turn, Houston offered El Presidente a replacement snuff box.

> I immediately wrote to Col. Hockley, who accompanied Genl. Santa Anna to the United States, to procure for Santa Anna a very handsome one, which he did in Philadelphia, amounting to $280.00 in value, which amount I refunded to Col. Hockley.[72]

Santa Anna and Colonel Almonte were taken to Washington, D.C., in late 1836 for a conference with President Andrew Jackson. Colonel George Hockley, Colonel Barnard Bee and Major William Patton were selected to accompany the Mexican prisoners. This group left the home of Dr. James Phelps in Brazoria County on November 26, 1836, on horseback. Traveling alternately by horses and by boat, they reached Washington on January 18, 1837.[73]

Shortly after his arrival in Washington, Santa Anna would be on his way back to Mexico.

> General Andrew Jackson greeted me warmly and honored me at a dinner attended by notables of all countries. He placed at my disposal for my voyage to Vera Cruz a battleship, whose commander attended me with great respect.[74]

Santa Anna returned home to his family and remained in seclusion for some time. "I was disillusioned and resentful," he later wrote. "It seemed that my country had abandoned me to my enemies."

The battle of San Jacinto provided Texas independence. Mexico and Texas, however, would continue to struggle with each other until Texas was annexed by the United States in 1845 and the Mexican-American War of 1846–1848 finally settled the dispute. The battle of San Jacinto ended the great Runaway Scrape and allowed settlers to begin returning to their homes. Roughly 650 Texans had died fighting during the Texas Revolution, most killed in the Alamo and at the Go-

This gold snuff box, on display in San Jacinto's museum, was reportedly given to General Sam Houston by Santa Anna. *Author's photo, courtesy of the San Jacinto Museum of History, Houston.*

liad Massacre. In two hours, about the same number of Mexican soldiers died on the fields and in the swamps at San Jacinto.

That the victory was complete and decisive was not questioned. Santa Anna wrote, "Fortune turned her back on me on the occasion when my efforts were to be crowned."[75]

The Texas soldiers spread the good news across the United States in their letters back home. On May 3, Lieutenant M. H. Denham wrote home to Nashville that, "As far as I can learn, the war is over."[76]

Captain Jesse Billingsley later summed up San Jacinto as, "On that day was born a nation of freemen."[77]

The battle summaries written during the first days following the historic engagement were the most heartfelt. James Tarlton wrote home on April 22: "A battle, the parallel to which perhaps cannot be found in the annals of civilized warfare, was yesterday fought."[78]

Captain Robert Stevenson, commanding the First Regiment's Company H, wrote on April 23: "Never was there a greater victory according to the number of men engaged, and the results are glorious for the army and prospects of Texas."[79]

Colonel Tom Rusk, the Secretary of War, was a master at motivating men and had an equally efficient ability to size up every situation. His April 23 postbattle report captures the essence of the San Jacinto campaign.

"It was freemen fighting against the minions of tyranny, and the result proved the inequality of such a contest."

Afterword

The Mexican prisoners remained near Galveston until about August 16, when they were put aboard another schooner and sailed to the coastal settlement of Anahuac. They remained there another week before being marched to Liberty, where they were under supervision of Judge William Hardin.

Some had been put to work on Texas farmland as laborers for servants who had escaped during the Runaway Scrape. All were eventually granted their freedom to return home.

Riding his popularity, a recovered Sam Houston beat out Stephen F. Austin and Henry Smith in a landslide election in September 1836 to become the new President of Texas. Houston took office in October, with Austin his Secretary of State, Smith his Secretary of Treasury and Thomas Rusk his Secretary of War.

His opposing general, Santa Anna, would come out of sulking to command troops in December against invading French forces. Santa Anna was severely wounded by cannon fire and was forced to have a foot amputated. He regained his former glory in Mexico and would serve as president or dictator of the country a number of times over the ensuing decades.

Forbes v. Labadie Lawsuit

Dr. Nicholas Labadie's "San Jacinto Campaign" article in the 1859 *Texas Almanac* created a firestorm of controversy. In it, Labadie alleged that the spoils of war, under charge of Colonel John Forbes, had been pilfered to large degree. Forbes filed a libel suit against Labadie and

413

trial began in the District Court of Nacogdoches County in 1859. Testimony showed that the *Texas Almanac* was prepared and published by Willard Richardson and Daniel Richardson in Galveston. Colonel Sidney Sherman had been given a copy of Labadie's manuscript before publishing and he read it over, making editorial notes. Among them, he claimed that he suggested to the Richardsons to remove the portions that "were not altogether favorable to Col. Forbes."[1]

The suit, seeking $25,000 in damages, took particular offense to Forbes' alleged killing of the Mexican woman on the San Jacinto battlefield. Labadie's article included the statement that "Commissary Forbes was accused of the deed, and arrested, but not tried, as his accusers were advised not to come forward." The suit also took offense to the claim that Forbes had rifled through the pockets of a dead Mexican officer and taken a fine gold snuff box. Labadie charged the commissary department with embezzling roughly $5,000 of the $12,000 originally taken on the battlefield.[2]

Depositions were taken from battlefield witnesses in 1859. General Houston, during his deposition, was critical of the whole Labadie article, calling it a "condensation of concocted calumny and falsehood." Among other sensitive charges, the *Almanac's* article criticized Houston for calling a halt on the battlefield. Houston also swore that, "I believe upon good information that the facts charged in it were fabricated by Sherman, Lamar and other small fry."[3]

The agreement of the suit of *John Forbes v. N. D. Labadie* was filed on November 20, 1866, in the District Court of Nacogdoches County, Texas. Forbes and Labadie on October 18, 1866, adjusted their differences "to their mutual satisfaction" and agreed to dismiss the suit. They agreed that "each party be adjudged to pay the costs by him incurred, and that the same be taxed accordingly by the Court." Labadie's share of the costs was $141.07 and Forbes paid $78.97 for the court's costs.[4]

A written disclaimer was issued by the court which absolved Colonel Forbes of any wrongdoing at San Jacinto. Signed by Nicholas Labadie on July 28, 1866, the retraction stated in part:

> I certainly did not intend upon my own knowledge to charge Col. Forbes with any conduct unworthy of a soldier or of a man of honor.
>
> What is said in relation to him in the article referred to was merely the repetition of a camp rumor. . . .
>
> It is proper for me to state further that the article in question was written somewhat hastily and at the request of the publishers of the Almanac. . . .

At Mr. Richardson's application I gave him permission to make extracts from it for his Almanac, with the understanding . . . to leave out all that related to Col. Forbes, to which he agreed.

Some eight months after, I was much surprised to learn it was not left out, in the first issues of the Almanac. When called upon for an explanation he stated he had ordered his compositor to leave it out, and appeared surprised it was not.[5]

Miss Emily and the "Yellow Rose" Controversy

The most modern, and the controversy most hotly debated by serious San Jacinto historians, is the story of indentured servant Emily West in detaining General Santa Anna on the battlefield.

The first published report of this alleged distraction came in an edited version of William Bollaert's memoirs of Texas which was published in 1956 by the University of Oklahoma. This story told of Bollaert's visit to Texas in 1842–44, where he met many noteworthy early Texans, including Sam Houston.

The edited book contained a footnote which was written into the margin of a page of Bollaert's original narrative. Next to his transcription of the Miss Emily event, allegedly told to him by Sam Houston, was the word "private"—underlined three times. The editors reduced Houston's story to Bollaert to a mere footnote, but Bollaert's footnote was a bombshell.

> The Battle of San Jacinto was probably lost to the Mexicans, owing to the influence of a Mulatto girl (Emily) belonging to Col. Morgan who was closeted in the tent with G'l Santana, at the time the cry was made, 'The enemy! they come! they come!' & detained Santana so long that order could not be restor'd again.[6]

Bollaert's footnote did not at first reveal its source. Historical researcher James Lutzweiler asserts that Sam Houston himself gave the story to Bollaert. Bollaert would only write in his manuscript's notes that the account came from "an officer who was engaged in it (the battle of San Jacinto), in his own words."

Lutzweiler dug deeper into the Bollaert papers while working on his Master's thesis in 1996. It appears that Emily told her story to artillery Captain Isaac Moreland. Houston, in turn, related the story to Bollaert in 1842 soon after visiting with Moreland on his deathbed on June 5, 1842.

Miss Emily, according to suggestions made by writers since this footnote appeared, may have been distracting General Santa Anna with sexual favors during the battle of San Jacinto. This juicy story has led to further suggestions that Emily West provided the inspiration for the popular song, "The Yellow Rose of Texas." When this footnote started the public talk in the 1950s about Santa Anna's alleged encounter on the San Jacinto battlefield, Mitch Miller was bringing back to popularity a minstrel song from the 1850s called "The Yellow Rose of Texas."

Emily West has been misidentified in some accounts as Emily Morgan. She was, however, not Colonel Morgan's slave but instead an indentured servant who had contracted with him to come to Texas from New York to work for him for one year. There is no written account to describe her features or exact age. She may or may not have been a mulatto, as she has often been described. There is a surviving indentured servant contract that Morgan and West signed in New York in 1835. In this, West listed herself as being from New Haven, Connecticut.

This employment contract was witnessed by Simeon S. Jocelyn, a prominent New Haven citizen. An engraver and antislavery philanthropist, Jocelyn was the sponsor of a number of free black organizations and institutions in New Haven. The Federal Census of 1830 shows Jocelyn's household to have seven other persons. Six of them were white and the seventh was designated as a "free colored female" between the ages of 10 and 24. It is likely that this female was Emily West.[7]

There is also a letter signed by Isaac Moreland, an artillery officer at San Jacinto. In this letter, Moreland stated that he met Emily in April 1836 and she told him that she had lost the papers attesting to her free status on the San Jacinto battlefield. Moreland requested a Texas passport for her, which she apparently used to return to New York in 1837.

Santa Anna's army had captured and burned the plantation of Colonel James Morgan just before arriving at San Jacinto. His forces were known to have included a number of women, at least six of whom were taken with the prisoners after the battle.

Sam Houston possibly first heard the story from Moreland, who was serving as a judge in Harrisburg County in 1837 when he signed the passport application for Emily D. West to return to New York.

Who Shot Sam Houston?

Among the many slanderous rumors that would arise during Sam Houston's political career was one that perhaps the commanding general of the Texian army had been shot by one of his own men at San Jacinto.

In President Mirabeau Lamar's private papers, the former cavalry commander later wrote:

> With dread that he [Houston] might defraud the eager band of victory at San Jacinto it was said that an excellent marksman of Captain William S. Fisher's company in the early part of the action thought it safest to temporarily depose Achilles [Houston] by a touch on the heel.[8]

No charges were every formally brought against anyone for shooting General Houston. His position placed him between his own troops and the enemy's breastworks at the time he was struck. While there is the possibility that he could have been struck by "friendly fire," few historians have given this rumor much credit.

Another misconception is where Houston was wounded. He was actually shot in the *left* ankle, although most published accounts of his life or the Texas Revolution erroneously state that he was shot in the right ankle.

One of the earliest depictions of the wounded Sam Houston appears incorrect. William Henry Huddle's 1890 canvas "The Surrender of Santa Anna" shows General Santa Anna being brought before the oak where General Houston lies wounded upon a blanket with a bandaged right leg.

Likely drawing on this illustration as a reference, most all biographies of Sam Houston have stated that he was shot in the right ankle.

Flags of the San Jacinto Campaign

When the Texas Army marched across the battlefield on April 21 to greet Santa Anna, only one company carried a true flag. The companies organized by Captains Moseley Baker and John Bird had some form of colors at their organization, but neither apparently made it past Buffalo Bayou.

Captain Bird's flag had been sewn by the women of San Felipe. His company, however, was largely delegated to other duties before San Jacinto and was not present for the battle. By the time Captain Baker's unit prepared to march into combat, its colors had either left with a deserter or had been left at the Harrisburg camp. Corporal Isaac Hill claimed that Baker's men carried only a red handkerchief as a sign that they would offer no quarter to their enemy.

Captain Sidney Sherman's Kentucky Riflemen, later commanded by Captain William Wood, brought a flag to Texas which had been presented to them by the ladies of Newport, Kentucky. It featured a partially clad maiden clutching a sword, over which was draped a banner reading, "Liberty or Death." Company Sergeant Jim Sylvester carried this flag into battle. The restored original standard now rests in the Senate Chamber of the Texas State Capitol in Austin.

More of the Mexican companies carried flags than did the Texans. Four Mexican flags were taken on the battlefield and three are now part of the Flag Collection at the Texas State Library. The Toluca battalion and the Guerrero battalion both participated in the overthrow of the Alamo. At San Jacinto, both battalions were decimated by the Texians and their standards were captured. The third flag belonged to the "Batallon Matamoros Permanente," a unit of regulars which had fought at the Alamo, Coleto Creek and at San Jacinto.

How Many Texans Fought?

Although the final count will likely continue to be debated, the number is roughly 930. Missing muster rolls or other important documents may surface which provide additional names. Sam Houston's original count of 783 men on April 21 for the battle was obviously at least a little low. The official list of those who fought at San Jacinto was filled out soon after the battle and obviously contains some errors.

Captain Wyly's entire company was originally left out due to error. Other individuals were missed on company muster rolls, often due to their having swapped companies or having joined the unit midway through the campaign.

Algernon Thompson, for example, was transferred on April 20 from Captain Calder's company to Captain Fisher's, although his name did not appear on the postbattle muster roll for either company. He later testified in court that his "orderly sergeant [Benjamin Brigham] was killed in the battle, and the muster rolls of [the] company as reported to the commanding general were doubtless incomplete."[9]

William Gorham filled out the list of the First Regiment's men for Colonel Burleson on April 22, and signed the back of the document as an endorsement. This list also included the men who were sick in camp at Harrisburg. Captain Jesse Billingsley, however, would testify in Travis County in 1855 that the First Regiment's list did not include Jonathan D. Morris of his company, who had escorted the wounded Colonel Neill after the April 20 fight. Billingsley also testified that the muster roll neglected James Stewart and George Duty of his company, both of whom were left sick at Harrisburg.[10]

The original San Jacinto rolls, part of the records of the General Land Office in Austin, show a total force of 863 officers and men of the Texas Army. Sam Houston Dixon and Louis Wiltz Kemp's book *The Heroes of San Jacinto* displayed muster rolls for San Jacinto which included 918 men, or 53 more men than were listed on the rolls at the General Land Office.[11]

Kemp, a prime mover in the plan to construct the San Jacinto Monument, compiled biographical sketches of all the San Jacinto veterans. His extensive research would lead to his revising his muster roll even after *Heroes* was published. His work remains with the San Jacinto Museum of History and another copy resides with the Center for American History in Austin.

In his research of who was and was not at San Jacinto, Kemp consulted early Texas newspapers, the Texas Veterans Association records, the descendants of the veterans, veterans' land headright certificates, county deeds and probate records, and the comptroller's military service records of these men. The latter records refer to original certificates now housed in the archives of the Texas State Library. Audited by the Texas Comptroller's department, these certificates authenticated a man's service at San Jacinto. The man's captain or other higher officers certified on these forms that the man in question did fight at San Jacinto. In some cases, men's names were left off of muster rolls and only such comptroller's records helped Kemp establish that they did indeed serve.

Since Kemp's death in 1956, supplemental research has found that a small number of additional names belong on the list of veterans. Researchers for the San Jacinto Museum of History have added a few names to the official battle roster, after verifying their service through audited claims, pension papers or other military documents that seem to bear credit to their service.

The museum's "Honor Roll of the Battle of San Jacinto" lists all the names of the men who either participated in the battle on April 21 or were at the Harrisburg camp on detached service. With the few names I have added in this book's appendices, my best count of all present on April 21 is 930 on the battlefield and 255 detached.

Footnotes in the appendices give explanation for any names I have added or deleted from the museum's Honor Roll. From Captain Arnold's Second Regiment company alone, it appears that two men may have been missed. The Yarbrough family later claimed that both John Swanson Yarbrough and John Swanson Yarbrough Jr. both served in the Texas Army and received papers to attest to this.

The second man who appears to have been missed from Arnold's Nacogdoches company is James Madden. A member of Captain Sadler's rangers who joined the army on the Colorado River, Madden is actually included in the San Jacinto roster on Arnold's muster roll as "James Madon." A note beside his name on the muster roll says, "Discharged 22nd Apl. after battle," indicating that he was present on April 21. Perhaps his name did not survive Kemp's research due to the fact that he never applied for land grants for his service.

Post–San Jacinto Careers

The convention at Washington-on-the Brazos on March 14, 1836, had provided land bounties for those who would aid Texas in its fight for independence. For those men who had been in service of the Texas Army as of March 14, and could prove that they continued to serve until the end of the revolution, they were to be awarded 1280 acres. Those who served faithfully for a period "not less than six months" would receive 640 acres. Those who had served for a period of "not less than three months" were to receive 320 acres.

President Houston on December 31, 1837, further honored the men of San Jacinto by signing an act of Congress granting donations of 640 acres of land to "All persons who were actually engaged in the battle of San Jacinto." This grant was also extended to those army members "who were detailed by special order of the Commanding General to guard the baggage at the camp near Harrisburg."

Sam Houston enjoyed political gain from his hero status throughout his career, twice serving as President of the Republic of Texas. He also served a lengthy term as a United States Senator and was in 1859 elected as Governor of Texas. He campaigned against the secessionists prior to the Civil War and he refused to take an oath of allegiance to the Confederate States of America. Governor Houston was thereafter deposed from office in Austin and he retired to Huntsville to live out his last two years.

The captors of Santa Anna did not share as much good fortune in their post–San Jacinto years. Charles Thompson died in Matagorda County in 1837 and Alfred Miles was killed by Indians at the 1837 Stone Houses battle while serving as a Texas Ranger officer. Joseph Vermillion assigned his land rights to Captain Robert Calder and left Texas. James Sylvester received 640 acres of land in what is present Dallas, Texas, but traded this off for a mule which he rode to New Orleans to resume his printing career with the *Picayune*.[12]

The veterans of the San Jacinto campaign were consistently the early leaders of Texas. The presidents of the Republic of Texas—Houston, Mirabeau Lamar and Anson Jones—had all fought at San Jacinto. San Jacinto veterans were frequently elected to key political positions during the next two decades. Of the senators and representatives who were seated for the First Congress of the Republic of Texas in 1836, one in three had participated in the San Jacinto campaign. Houston and Peter Hansborough Bell later served as governors of the State of Texas.

The First Regiment's Edward Burleson commanded Texas frontier forces for years in some of the bloodiest Indian battles. He later served as Vice President of the Republic of Texas. Sidney Sherman, leader of the Second Regiment, was heavily involved in the early railroads during the 1850s and helped with the successful installation of the first railroad west of the Sabine River. The line's first locomotive was named the "General Sherman."

Captain John Allen, who had spared many Mexican lives at San Jacinto, became the first mayor of Galveston. Colonel John Forbes, after his nasty lawsuit with Dr. Labadie, later served as Lieutenant Colonel on the staff of Texas Governor Richard Coke in 1876. Captain Moseley Baker, who had fled to Texas in 1832 after scamming

$21,000 from the Bank of Alabama, held to his resolution of clearing his name. During 1836, in fact, he paid back everything he owed via bonds. Baker later subscribed $1,000 to build the first church in Houston and even became a Methodist minister.[13]

Several of the Texas Army's senior command met tragic ends. Colonel Robert Coleman, appointed to command a ranger battalion in August 1836, was arrested in early 1837 after one of his rangers died due to negligence by another officer. President Houston held Coleman under arrest pending a formal trial. During this time, Coleman likely had plenty of time and anger to use against Houston in anonymously authoring the biased *Houston Displayed* pamphlet. Coleman died of an accidental drowning in July 1837 while under arrest.

Another Houston aide, Major James Collinsworth, became the first Chief Justice of the Republic of Texas in late 1836. While campaigning against Mirabeau Lamar and Peter Grayson in the 1838 Texas presidential campaign, Collinsworth committed suicide by leaping from a boat into Galveston Bay. Major William Patton, promoted into Houston's staff during the campaign, was shot and killed on the San Antonio River in 1842 by bandits.

Thomas Rusk, who was secretary of war during the campaign and later major general in command of the army, enjoyed a colorful political and military career in Texas. Deeply grieved in 1857 by the loss of his wife, however, he used his gun to take his own life in his Nacogdoches home.

The Indian wars of the Republic of Texas took their toll on San Jacinto veterans. Conrad Rohrer, the defiant wagon master of Sam Houston's army, was shot and killed by Indians less than two months after San Jacinto. Captain John Bird was killed in 1839 near present Temple while commanding a company of Texas Rangers in a fight against hundreds of hostile Indians. Cavalryman John Carpenter and a Caddo chief killed each other simultaneously during a skirmish of the 1838 Kickapoo War.

James Joslin and Alfred Miles were killed in the 1837 Stone Houses fight between Texas Rangers and several hostile Indian bands. Benjamin Franklin Cage, Washington Perry Reese, and Moses Lapham were killed in 1839 during two different engagements with Comanches near San Antonio. Tejanos Jose Maria Arocha and Pedro Herrera fought with Captain Juan Seguin's company. They were killed by Indians in 1838 while serving in Captain Manuel Flores' cavalry company from San Antonio.

Another of the heroes of San Jacinto was later executed for murder. David J. Jones, who had been one of only twenty-eight to escape death during the Goliad Massacre, and another man were accused of murdering two men in January 1838. Jones and his accomplice were both found guilty by the Harrisburg County judge and were hanged to death on March 28, 1838.[14]

At the San Jacinto Day celebration dinner in May 1850, one of those honored was Dick the drummer, the freed black who had served in the Texas band at San Jacinto. The Austin *State Gazette* gave honor "to the patriotic old man," who had brought the battle cry to Santa Anna "by the effective beating of his drum." Dick had also served as a drummer during the Mexican War at the battle of Monterey and Buena Vista.[15]

Many of the San Jacinto veterans were instrumental in insuring that their historic battleground would be preserved. The Texas Veterans Association was formed and held its first convention in Houston on May 13–15, 1873, with about seventy-five veterans present. Among the San Jacinto veterans who would serve as president were Walter Lane, James Monroe Hill, and Stephen Sparks. Moses Austin Bryan served as the association's secretary from 1873–1886.[16]

The Texas Veterans Association held annual meetings during the week that included April 21, San Jacinto Day. The association eventually dissolved at Austin on April 19, 1907, during its thirty-fifth annual convention. The Daughters of the Republic of Texas took over the association's work.

At the 1906 Goliad meeting, six of the last ten known surviving members of the Army of the Republic of Texas were present: William Zuber, Stephen Sparks, Alfonso Steele, Asa C. Hill, L. T. Lawlor and John W. Darlington. These first four were veterans of the San Jacinto campaign. Photos were taken on April 21, 1906, in front of the Presidio La Bahia.

Sparks, the last President of the Texas Veterans Association, died at age 89 in Rockport, Texas, in 1908. The last surviving member of General Houston's army to have fought at San Jacinto was Alfonso Steele, who died at Mexia in 1911 at age 94. The last surviving member of the San Jacinto campaign was William Zuber, who died at age 93 in 1913. Zuber did not fight at San Jacinto, but had been assigned as a guard for the camp at Harrisburg.

The last reunion of San Jacinto and Texas Revolution veterans was held at Goliad on April 21, 1906. In this photo taken in front of the Presidio La Bahia, the veterans are, from left: William P. Zuber (standing) of Austin; John W. Darlington of Taylor; Asa C. Hill of Oakville; Stephen F. Sparks (seated on the cannon) of Rockport; L. T. Lawlor of Florence; and Alfonso Steele of Mexia. Sparks died in 1908 at age 89 and Steele, at age 94, was the last battle of San Jacinto survivor to die in 1911. William Zuber did not fight at San Jacinto, but participated in the campaign, being among those left to guard baggage at Camp Harrisburg. Zuber died at age 93 in 1913. *Texas State Library and Archives Commission.*

The San Jacinto Monument and Museum

The widow Peggy McCormick tried in vain for years to receive compensation from the Republic of Texas for her losses at San Jacinto. She had given up two horses, plus a large amount of corn and cattle to the troops. She burned to death in her home in the 1850s, however, without ever having been paid.[17]

Eight of the Texans who died at San Jacinto were buried on the grounds on which the Texas Army had encamped on April 20. At the heads of their graves were placed wooden headstones with proper inscriptions. Four decades would pass before Judge J. L. Sullivan of Richmond, Texas, inaugurated a successful campaign to erect a proper joint monument near these graves. The Texas State Legislature passed an act authorizing an additional one thousand dollars to help ensure that "substantial iron rails" help finish off this enclosure.[18]

This memorial was unveiled on August 25, 1881, by Captain Robert Calder. One of the victims was young Sergeant Benjamin Rice Brigham, who had been mortally wounded on April 21, 1836, while serving under Calder. By 1881, the old wooden headstones were so badly decayed that only Brigham's grave could be identified. Also present for this ceremony were Temple Houston, youngest son of General Sam Houston, and a granddaughter of Lemuel Stockton Blakey, another of the eight Texans buried near the battlefield.

At least one other San Jacinto veteran had already been interred at the battlefield prior to this marker. Captain William Wood passed away in 1854 in Houston. True to his last wishes, his body was transported on the steamer *Eclipse* down to the battlefield and he was buried with honors before a crowd that included some of the old soldiers of San Jacinto. In 1936, the State of Texas erected a marker on Captain Wood's gravesite on the battlefield.[19]

In 1883, the State of Texas purchased ten acres of the old McCormick League to start a memorial park. This land has grown to more than 400 acres now. Survivors of the battle of San Jacinto were invited to the battlefield in 1894 to help mark out important sites. On June 3, 1901, veteran James Winters visited the San Jacinto battlegrounds at age eighty-four. Representing the Texas Veterans Association, he was by then one of a very few men still alive who had fought in 1836. Winters and William P. Zuber identified additional important locations which were later permanently marked by the San Jacinto Chapter of the Daughters of the Republic of Texas.[20]

The battlegrounds at San Jacinto have changed significantly since 1836. The area is now choked with chemical refineries. The Houston Ship Channel is a major waterway for ocean-bound traffic. This has consumed the old layout of Buffalo Bayou, San Jacinto River and its adjacent bay. Lynch's Ferry is still in operation, connecting the park with Interstate 10. Powerful automobile ferries haul visitors back and forth across the wide ship channel to the battleground.

Rising above the center of the old battlefield is the impressive San Jacinto Monument. Standing 570 feet tall, it is higher than the Washington Monument by fifteen feet and is listed in the *Guinness Book of World Records* as the tallest stone column monument in the world. Atop the 570-foot shaft is a thirty-four-foot star which symbolizes the Lone Star Republic.[21]

The monument's actual shaft was constructed from blocks of cordova shell stone which is more than one hundred million years old and was quarried from Burnet County north of Austin. The structure is 125 feet square at its base, tapering to thirty feet square at the top. The shaft walls are four feet thick at the base and two feet thick at the top. With each stone block weighing in at five hundred pounds, the San Jacinto Monument weighs in at a whopping 70,300,000 pounds.

The project started as a Public Works Administration project on April 21, 1936. Work was completed on time, exactly three years later, on April 21, 1939, at a cost of $1,500,000. The nine-pointed star atop the monument weighs 220 tons and can be seen as a star from any direction due to its unique configuration.

During the monument's construction, an eight-acre, 1800-foot reflection pool was added on the battlegrounds. On the lower floor of the monument is the San Jacinto Museum of History, whose collection spans more than four hundred years of early Texas history. The museum also houses a research library with more than 35,000 rare books, 10,000 visual images and 250,000 documents.

An elevator ride inside the monument takes visitors 489 feet above the battleground to an observation floor. From this floor, one can view the Houston Ship Channel, Buffalo Bayou, the historic battleground, the nearby battleship *Texas*, and the marshlands surrounding the old battleground.

A major restoration effort is currently under way to restore the San Jacinto battleground site to its 1836 appearance. One of the main goals is to give visitors a better understanding of how the Texans man-

This 510-foot boardwalk extends out into the restored marshes behind the San Jacinto battlegrounds. In this area, the largest loss of life to Mexican soldiers occurred.
Author's photo, courtesy of the San Jacinto Museum of History, Houston.

aged to achieve their victory. The first step of this restoration process was reclaiming three hundred acres of the vast marsh which once extended beyond the Mexican army's campgrounds.

The marsh had subsided and became covered with silt over many decades. San Jacinto Day 2002 was celebrated with the grand opening of a 510-foot boardwalk which leads into the newly restored marshes. Visitors along this walk might enjoy the view of some wildlife, but are also passing over the area where so many Mexican soldiers lost their lives to frenzied Texas soldiers who were avenging their comrades lost at the Alamo and at Goliad.

The San Jacinto Monument itself recently received a ten million dollar restoration to repair its stonework. The ongoing work to bring the historic site back to its original appearance includes plans to remove the huge reflecting pond, which actually lies right on the ground crossed over by Sam Houston and his men while marching against Santa Anna.

At the time the heroes of San Jacinto marched over the field, there was a natural rise in the land. The highest point of this rise is right where the monument stands today. This rise and the tall native grasses which once stood knee-high helped Houston's men achieve the element of surprise which proved so devastating to Santa Anna. One of the final steps to the restoration project will be to bring back some of these coastal grasses.

Each April, the San Jacinto battlegrounds are filled with thousands of spectators who come to watch reenactments of the battle. History lovers young and old are able to wander through the Mexican and Texian campgrounds to marvel at the costumes, culture and weaponry displayed by the actors. At 3:00 p.m., the battlegrounds come to life again with the crack of muskets and the booming of the replicas of the Twin Sisters and the Golden Standard. Many of those charging into action are descendants of men who fought in the Texas Revolution.

Open year-round, the impressive San Jacinto Monument is appropriately dedicated to the "Heroes of the Battle of San Jacinto and all others who contributed to the independence of Texas."

Texian Casualties of the San Jacinto Campaign

APRIL 20 SKIRMISHES

Killed or Mortally Wounded

Company J (Smith), Second Regiment:
Olwyn J. Trask, Pvt.   Mortally wounded. Died three weeks later at Galveston.

Wounded

Artillery:
James Clinton Neill, Lt. Col.   Severely wounded in hip during the cannon action.

Capt. Karnes' Cavalry Company:
Devereaux Jerome Woodlief, Pvt.   Severely wounded during cannon action.

Company F (Heard), First Regiment:
Thomas C. Utley, Pvt.   Seriously wounded in left arm by grapeshot from Mexican cannon.

APRIL 21 BATTLE

Killed or Mortally Wounded

Company C (Billingsley), First Regiment:
Lemuel Stockton Blakey   Mortally wounded. Died on the battlefield.

Company K (Calder), First Regiment:
Benjamin Rice Brigham, Sgt.   Mortally wounded; died on the field on April 21.

Company I (Fisher), First Regiment:
James Cooper, Pvt.   Severely wounded. Died from the effects in 1836 per Dixon, Kemp's *The Heroes of San Jacinto*, 13, 255.

Fifth Company (McIntire), Second Regiment:
Mathias Cooper, Pvt.   Killed in action.

Company J (Smith), Second Regiment:
Thomas Patton Fowle, 1st Sgt.   Killed in action.

Company A (Wood), First Regiment:
Giles Albert Giddings, Pvt.　　Mortally wounded. Died on June 10, 1836.

Seventh Company (Bryant), Second Regiment:
John C. Hale, 1st Lieut.　　Killed in action.

Second Company (Ware), Second Regiment:
George A. Lamb, 2nd Lieut.　　Killed in action.

Medical Staff:
Dr. William Junius Mottley　　Mortally wounded.

Company H (Stevenson), First Regiment:
Ashley R. Stephens, 2nd Sgt.　　Severely wounded in both legs. Died about April 30.

Company F (Heard), First Regiment:
Leroy Wilkinson, Pvt.　　Severely wounded; later died.

Wounded

Command Staff:
Sam Houston, General　　Shot in the left leg.

Artillery Company:
William A. Park, Pvt.　　Slightly wounded.

Company A (Wood), First Regiment:
George Waters, Pvt.　　Slightly wounded.
James Cumba, Pvt.　　Badly wounded.

Company B (Roman), First Regiment:
William S. Walker, Pvt.　　Severely wounded.

Company C (Billingsley), First Regiment:
Washington Anderson, Pvt.　　Shot in the ankle.
Jesse Billingsley, Capt.　　Shot in the hand.
Logan Vandever, Pvt.　　Severely wounded.
Calvin Gage, Pvt.　　Slightly wounded.
Thomas H. Mays　　Seriously wounded.
Martin Walker, Pvt.　　Severely wounded.

Company D (Baker), First Regiment:
Orin D. Anson, Pvt.*　　Slightly wounded. Listed on the postbattle casualty list as "C. D. Anderson."
Moseley Baker, Capt.　　Slightly wounded.
Allen Ingram, Pvt.　　Severely wounded.

Company F (Heard), First Regiment:
James Nelson, Pvt.　　Wounded.
Michael Putnam, Pvt.　　Shot in right arm.

Company H (Stevenson), First Regiment:
John F. Tom, Pvt.　　Severely wounded in the leg.

Company I (Fisher), First Regiment:
George Weedon　　Severely wounded.

Company K (Calder), First Regiment:
Joseph Smith Edgar, Pvt.*   Slightly wounded.

Second Company (Ware), Second Regiment:
George Washington Robinson, Pvt.   Severely wounded.
William Carvin Winters, 2nd Sgt.   Severely wounded.
Albert Edward Gallatin, 1st Sgt.   Slightly wounded.

Fourth Company (Murphree), Second Regiment:
George Washington Lonis, Pvt.   Severe; shot in the right lung.
Elbridge Gerry Rector, Pvt.   Shot in arm and side.

Sixth Company (Gillaspie), Second Regiment:
Alphonso Steele, Pvt.   Severely wounded.
Elijah Votaw, Pvt.   Wounded in the chest by enemy grapeshot.

Ninth Company (Seguin), Second Regiment:
Juan López, Pvt.**   Slightly wounded in left knee.

Tenth Company (Smith's Cavalry), Second Regiment:
W. F. James, Pvt.*   Severely wounded.
William H. Smith, Capt.   Slightly wounded.
William Foster Young, Pvt.   Severely wounded.

*Per postbattle casualty report of Colonel Thomas J. Rusk.
**Per Captain Juan Seguin.

OTHER CASUALTIES AND DEATHS
DURING THE SAN JACINTO CAMPAIGN

John Bricker, Pvt.   Killed by enemy cannon shot through the head on April 8.

Roden Taylor Crain, Pvt.   Slightly wounded during battle with enemy forces on April 8.

Henry Freed, Pvt.   Shot in the leg by Mexican patrol near Buffalo Bayou morning of April 21.

_____ Hunter, Pvt.   Died of sickness in Harrisburg camp on April 20.

George W. Scott, Pvt.   Died of sickness on April 6.

George Washington Seaton, Pvt.   Artilleryman accidentally shot in the foot on April 20. Seaton was transferred to Harrisburg.

Felix G. Wright, Pvt.   Died of sickness on March 28.

Mexican Officers Killed and Captured at the Battle of San Jacinto

April 20–21, 1836

Source: Research of Henry Arthur McArdle. The Battle of San Jacinto Notebook, The McArdle Notebooks, Archives and Information Services Division, Texas State Library and Archives Commission.

MEXICAN OFFICERS KILLED AT SAN JACINTO

General:
Manuel Fernando Castrillon

Colonels:
Jose Arenas
Jose Batrés
Augustín Peralta
Antonio Treviño

Lieutenant Colonels:
Francisco Aguado
Mancial Cos
Mariario Hazaran
Carile Larumbo
Santiago Luelmo
Esteban Mora
Manuel Valdez
Miguel Velasquez

Captains:
Marcial Peralta Aguirre
Ygnacio Berra
Antonio Frias
Nestor Guzman
Ramon Herrero

Juan Manjarra
Benito Rodriguez
Alonzo Yanzales

Lieutenants:
Ignacio Arenal
Ygnacio Brasail
Antonio Castro
Pedro Gonzales
Francisco Molina
Juan Antonio Navarro
Jose Ma Puelles
Juan Santa Cruz
Trinidad Santiesteban
Jose Sanza
Luis Vallejo

Sub-Lieutenants:
Basiliso Eskino
Juan Mansano
Victoriano Martinez
Joaquin Peratta
Secundino Rosas
Jose Maria Tornell

433

MEXICAN OFFICERS TAKEN PRISONER
(With Ages in 1836, as Given by McArdle)

President, Republic of Mexico:
Antonio López de Santa Anna — 42

Brigadier General:
Martin Perfecto de Cos — 33

Colonels:
Juan Nepomuceno Almonte — 32
Manuel Céspedes — 38
José María Romero — 38

Lieutenant Colonels:
Juan María Bringas — 35
Pedro Delgado — 43
Eulogio Gonzáles — 34
Manuel Portilla — 32

First Adjutant (Brevet Lt. Col.):
Felipe Romero — —

Captains (Brevet Lt. Colonel):
Lorenzo Arcos — 46
Vincente Avila — 35
Nicolas Enciso — 35
José María Castillo y Iberri — 27
Salvador Mugica — 30
Ygnacio Perez Valiente — 42
Jose Maria Villa Franca — 40
Cayetano Villasenor — 28

Captains:
Miguel Badvilles — 28
Juan Barrandi — 26
Jose Lisola — 49
Nicolas Telles — 26
Fernando Urriza — —

Lieutenants (Brevet Captain):
Mariano Arias — 32
Ysidoro Campos — 35
Telasforo Cavion — 37
Martin Estrada — 25
Jose Maria Ortego — 34
Mariano Gonzales Vega — 30
Yidefonso Vega — 20
Severiano Vencas — 31

Lieutenants:
Geranino Calayud — —
Augustin Sanchez — —

Sub-Lieutenants (Brevet Lt.):
Ygnacio Carrenza — 25
Toribio Casares — 30
Juan Nieto — 19

Sub-Lieutenants:
Raphael Ancansero — —
Manuel Casis — —
Rafael Castillo — —
Jose Maria Castro — 21
Nicolas Diaz — 28
Jose Maria Obregan — 36
Mateo Peraza — —
Miguel Perro — —
Estanislao Pino — 28
Mariano Reyes — 29

Cadet:
Joaquin Aguirre — 19

Chaplain:
Agustin Garza — 44

Roster of Texans Present at the Battle of San Jacinto

April 20–21, 1836

COMMANDER-IN-CHIEF'S STAFF

Major General:
Samuel Houston

Secretary of War:
Thomas Jefferson Rusk, Colonel

Adjutant General:
John Austin Wharton, Colonel

Inspector General:
George Washington Hockley, Col.

Assistant Inspector General:
William Gordon Cooke, Major

Commissary General:
John Forbes, Colonel*

Aides-de-Camp:
Alexander Horton, Colonel
James Collinsworth, Major
William Hester Patton, Major
Lorenzo de Zavala Jr., Major

Volunteer Aides:
Robert Morris Coleman, Colonel
Robert Eden Handy, Major
James Hazard Perry, Major

Musician (unassigned):
Dick (the drummer)

*Promoted April 2 from Major.

MEDICAL STAFF

Surgeon General/Artillery Surgeon:
Dr. Alexander Wray Ewing

Cavalry Physician:
Dr. Lemuel Gustine

General Houston's Physician:
Dr. Junius William Mottley

Surgeon for Regulars:
Dr. William M. Carper

Surgeon for First Regiment:
Dr. John F. Davidson

Assistant Surgeon, First Regiment:
Dr. John P. T. Fitzhugh

Surgeon, Second Regiment:
Dr. Anson Jones

Assistant Surgeons, Second Regiment:
Dr. Shields Booker
Dr. Nicholas Descomps Labadie*
Dr. James Aeneas Phelps

*Originally served under Capt. Logan.

ARTILLERY CORPS

Lieutenant Colonel:
James Clinton Neill[1]
Leander Smith, Major

Artillery Company
Organized April 7, 1836

Captains:
Isaac N. Moreland
George Washington Poe[2]

First Lieutenant:
William Shaler Stilwell

First Sergeant:
Richardson A. Scurry

Second Sergeant:
Thomas Pliney Plaster

Privates:
Soloman B. Bardwell
Montgomery Baxter
Ellis Benson[3]
Alfred Benton
Michael Campbell[4]
Joseph Alvey Clayton[3]
Willis Collins[5]
George Cumberland[4]
Daniel T. Dunham
Tilford C. Edwards[6]

John P. Ferrell
Joseph Floyd
John N. Gainer[4]
Thomas Green
Thomas N. B. Greer
Thomas Hanson
Clark M. Harmon
Temple Overton Harris
Seneca Legg[3]
Benjamin McCullough
Joseph W. Merwin[3]
Ira Millerman[4]
William A. Park[7]
Thomas Jefferson Robinson
George Washington Seaton[8]
Hugh Montgomery Swift
John Marshall Wade
Joseph E. White

[1]Wounded on April 20. Not present for battle on April 21.
[2]Not present for April 21 battle.
[3]Member of Capt. Turner's company.
[4]Member of Capt. Teal's company.
[5]Joined April 13 from Capt. Kimbro's.
[6]Previously served under Capt. Splane and Capt. Bird.
[7]Wounded on April 21.
[8]Accidentally injured April 20. Transferred to Harrisburg.

CAVALRY CORPS

Colonel:
Mirabeau Buonaparte Lamar[1]

Company J, Second Regiment
Organized March 16, 1836
Texas Cavalry

Captain:
William H. Smith

First Lieutenant:
John W. Carpenter[2]

Second Lieutenant:
William Harness

First Sergeant:
Thomas Patton Fowle

Privates:
William Charles Brookfield
Wilson C. Brown
Thomas Young Buford
Elisha Clapp
William H. Clemmons
Andrew M. Clopper
James Douthit
Anthony Foster
Hugh Henderson
W. F. James
George Johnson
William Davis Redd
John Robbins
Thomas Robbins
James W. Robinson

James Shaw
William S. Taylor[3]
James B. Thompson
Spencer Burton Townsend[4]
Stephen Townsend[4]
Olwyn J. Trask[5]
John W. Williamson
Robert McAlpin Williamson
William Foster Young

[1]Promoted after April 20 actions.
[2]Originally served with Capt. Arnold's.
[3]Served under Capt. Ware through April 20.
Served with Smith's in April 21 battle.
[4]Enlisted in Capt. Townsend's rangers February 1. Tranferred into Smith's.
[5]Mortally wounded on April 20.

Cavalry Company, Texas Army
Organized March 20, 1836

Captain:
Henry Wax Karnes

First Lieutenant:
James R. Cook

Orderly Sergeant:
Robert Kemp Goodloe[1]

Privates:
Horace Arlington Alsbury
Young Perry Alsbury
Hendrick Arnold
Peter Hansbrough Bell
Thomas Blackwell
Isaac Watts Burton
John Coker
William Crittenden[2]
James P. Davis
Dr. Fielding Deadrick[3]
George M. Deadrick
Matthew Dunn[4]
James D. Elliott
Robert Eden Handy
Abraham Webb Hill

Abram Wiley Hill
W. P. King
Walter Paye Lane[5]
Moses Lapham[6]
Joseph Lawrence[7]
Peter Lopez[8]
Daniel McKay[9]
Robert Merritt[10]
Noel Mixon
James H. Nash
John C. Neal
William J. C. Pearce
Edwin R. Rainwater
Dimer W. Reaves
Fielding Grundy Secrest
Washington Hampton Secrest
Benjamin Fort Smith[11]
Erastus "Deaf" Smith
William Burrell Sweeny[12]
Shelby C. Turnage
James A. Wells[13]
Devereaux Jerome Woodlief[14]

[1]Lost horse April 20. Fought under Capt. Calder on April 21.
[2]Sick on April 21; sent to Harrisburg.
[3]Transferred to Gillaspie's on April 21.
[4]Transferred from Capt. Hill's on April 9.
[5]Promoted to 2nd Lieut. on April 24 for actions at San Jacinto.
[6]Member of Capt. Baker's. Transferred to cavalry after April 20 battle.
[7]Joined from Capt. Stevenson's April 21.
[8]Per San Jacinto Museum of History.
[9]Transferred to Capt. Stevenson's April 21.
[10]Member of Capt. Chance's. Fought with Capt. Karnes.
[11]Acting Quartermaster and Adjutant General for the Texas Army.
[12]Originally enlisted under Capt. Patton.
[13]Missed battle after scouting patrol action on morning of April 20.
[14]Wounded April 20. Missed main battle.

Note: John T. Garner of Capt. Wood's Comp. A, 1st. Reg. served under Karnes on April 21.

REGULAR ARMY

Lieutenant Colonel:
Henry Millard

Acting Major:
John Melville Allen, Captain[1]

Adjutant:
Nicholas Lynch

Sergeant Major:
John N. O. Smith[2]

Quartermaster:
Pinckney Caldwell, Major[3]

[1]Served as acting Major in place of Major McNutt, detailed at Harrisburg.
[2]Joined the army February 1, 1836. Promoted into command staff.
[3]Joined the army February 15, 1836.

COMPANY A, REGULAR ARMY
FORMED EARLY JANUARY 1836 IN NACOGDOCHES

Captain:
Andrew Briscoe[1]

First Lieutenant:
Martin Kingsley Snell

Second Lieutenant:
Robert D. McCloskey

First Sergeant:
Lyman Frank Rounds

Second Sergeant:
Davis S. Nelson

Third Sergeant:
Daniel O'Driscoll

Fourth Sergeant:
Charles A. Foard

First Corporal:
Lewis Richardson

Second Corporal:
Henry R. Craig

Third Corporal:
Isaac H. Bear[2]

Musicians:
John N. Beebe
Martin Flores
Frederick Lemsky

Privates:
Daniel Benton
John W. Cassidy
George Darr
Alfred Dutcher

Peter S. Elliott
Thomas M. Farley
Thomas J. Flynn
Abner Glidwell
David Grieves
Robert Henderson
John Karner
George Washington Lang
Charles Larbarthrier
John Marner
Alonzo Marsh
Charles Mason
Robert W. Montgomery
John M. Morton
John O'Neil
William Patton
Edward Pearce
Asa Rheinhart
Daniel Richardson
John Sanders
George Smith
John T. Smith
Dennis Sullivan
William L. Swain
John N. Taylor
William Pike Tindall
John Van Winkle
James Walmsley
George Webb
James Wilkinson

[1]Took command on April 18 after Capt. Henry Teal came down with measles.
[2]Promoted April 19.

COMPANY B, REGULAR ARMY
NEW ORLEANS VOLUNTEERS: ORGANIZED FEBRUARY 4, 1836

Captain:
Amasa Turner

First Lieutenant:
William A. Millen

Second Lieutenant:
William W. Summers

First Sergeant:
Charles Stewart

Second Sergeant:
William C. Swearingen

Corporal:
Robert Moore

Corporal:
Thomas Wilson

Corporal:
Asberry McKendree Snyder

Privates:
John Belden
Prospero Bernardi
Robert B. Bissett
George Washington Browning*
Christopher Columbus Bruff
Thomas Jefferson Callihan
John Christie

Charles Clarkson
William Colton
John Dalrymple
Amos B. Edson
James J. Eldridge*
John Harper
David Harvey
Thomas Hogan
John R. Johnson
James Lealand
Ferdinand Leuders
John F. Lind
William Massey
Joshua Minnitt
Samuel Moore
Henry Mordorff
Francis Nealis
Samuel Paschall
Eli Phillips
Henry Shesten
Abel Sigmon
James Monroe Smith
John Smith
Charles C. Tyler
Felix Wardziski
Samuel Woods*

*Originally with Capt. Roman. Fought with
Capt. Turner's at San Jacinto.

FIRST REGIMENT TEXAS VOLUNTEERS
ORGANIZED MARCH 12, 1836

Colonel:
Edward Burleson[1]

Lieutenant Colonel:
Alexander Somervell[2]

Adjutant:
James W. Tinsley, Major

Sergeant Major:
Horatio N. Cleveland

[1]Elected to command March 12, 1836.
[2]Elected Major of First Regiment on March
12, 1836. Promoted to Lieutenant Colonel
on April 8, 1836.

COMPANY A, FIRST REGIMENT TEXAS VOLUNTEERS
"KENTUCKY RIFLES": FORMED IN KENTUCKY DECEMBER 18, 1835

Captain:
William Wood[1]

First Lieutenant:
Joseph Rhodes

Second Lieutenant:
Samuel B. Raymond

First Sergeant:
John C. Allison

Second Sergeant:
James Austin Sylvester

Third Sergeant:
Oliver T. Brown

Fourth Sergeant:
Nathaniel Peck

Privates:
Irwin Armstrong[2]
William M. Berryhill
Uriah Blue
Seymour Bottsford
Luke W. Bust[3]
James Cumba
Elijah Valentine Dale
Abner C. Davis
Horace Eggleston
Jacob Eyler
Simon Peter Ford
John T. Garner[4]

Giles Albert Giddings
James Greenwood
William Griffin
Thomas A. Haskins
William C. Hays
Robert F. Howell
John D. Loderback
William Wallace Loughridge
Achelle Marre
Edward Miles
Benjamin S. Osborne
James R. Pinchback
John W. Rial
Manasseh Sevey
Ralph E. Sevey
William B. Stout
Edward W. Taylor
John Viven
George Waters
James Welch
Ezra C. Westgate
Walter Winn

[1]Took command on March 13 after Capt. Sidney Sherman was promoted.
[2]Tranferred in from Capt. Roman's.
[3]Company musician.
[4]Fought with Captain Karnes' cavalry company on April 21.

COMPANY B, FIRST REGIMENT TEXAS VOLUNTEERS
RECRUITED IN NEW ORLEANS—ORGANIZED JANUARY 29 AT VELASCO

Captain:
Richard Roman[1]

Second Lieutenant:
Nicholas Mosby Dawson

Orderly Sergeant:
Alexander S. Mitchell

Second Sergeant:
James Wharton

Third Sergeant:
Samuel L. Wheeler

First Corporal:
Abraham R. Taylor

Corporals:
Charles A. Clarke

James D. Egbert
William P. Moore

Privates:
John Angel
Joshua Barstow
Isaac B. Bradley
George J. Brown[2]
Benjamin L. Cole
James S. Conn
James W. Dixon
William Dunbar
Harvey Homan
James Mathew Jett
Stephen Jett
Alfred S. Jordan

Shelly W. Lamar
Edward Lewis
John W. B. McFarlane
Andrew M. McStea
Hugh Miller
William P. Newman
James P. Ownby
William Richardson
Daniel Tindale
James Vinator

C. W. Waldron
William S. Walker
Francis F. Williams
Joseph Wilder

[1]Company originally formed under Capt. John Hart. Roman promoted into command February 13, 1836.
[2]Served as company drum major.

COMPANY C, FIRST REGIMENT TEXAS VOLUNTEERS
"MINA VOLUNTEERS": ENROLLED MARCH 1 AT BASTROP

Captain:
Jesse Billingsley

First Lieutenant:
Micah Andrews

Second Lieutenant:
James A. Craft[1]

First Sergeant:
Russell B. Craft

Second Sergeant:
William Harrison Magill

Third Sergeant:
Campbell Taylor

Privates:
Washington Anderson
Willis Avery
Noel M. Bain
Jefferson A. Barton
Wayne Barton
Andrew Jackson Berry
Lemuel Stockton Blakey
Garrett E. Boome
John Wheeler Bunton
Aaron Burleson
Preston Conlee
Sampson Connell
Robert M. Cravens
William Vanoy Criswell
Leander Calvin Cunningham
James Curtis Sr.[2]
Thomas P. Davey
Thomas Mason Dennis
George Bernhard Erath
Calvin Gage
S. Joseph Garwood
Lewis Goodwin
Thomas A. Graves

George Green
Jesse Halderman
John Harvey Herron
Ahijah M. Highsmith
John Hobson
Prior A. Holder
Robert Hood
Lucien Hopson
Joseph Martin
Thomas H. Mays
Samuel McClelland
McDougald McLean
Jonathan D. Morris[3]
Samuel C. Neill
Dempsey Council Pace
James Robert Pace
George Self
William Simmons
Jacob Standerford
Jacob Littleton Standifer
William Bailey Standifer
James Stewart[4]
Logan Vandeveer
Martin Walker
Charles Williams
Walker Wilson

[1]Elected to position March 2, 1836.
[2]Joined April 17 from Captain John J. Tumlinson's ranger company.
[3]Assigned to assist the wounded Lt. Col. Neill after April 20 battle. Missed the battle on April 21.
[4]Listed on the San Jacinto Museum of History's "Honor Roll," but Stewart was later reported as sick at Harrisburg per Capt. Billingsley.

COMPANY D, FIRST REGIMENT TEXAS VOLUNTEERS
"SAN FELIPE COMPANY": ENROLLED MARCH 1, 1836

Captain:
Moseley Baker

First Lieutenant:
John Pettit Borden

Second Lieutenant:
John Freeman Pettus

First Sergeant:
Joseph Baker

Second Sergeant:
Edward Cratic Pettus

Third Sergeant:
Moses Austin Bryan[1]

First Corporal:
James Madison Bell

Second Corporal:
James Freele

Third Corporal:
Isaac Lafayette Hill

Privates:
Jerome B. Alexander
Orin D. Anson[2]
Daniel Davis D. Baker
John Beauchamp
Thomas Henry Bell
Wilhelm Christoph Frederick Bernbeck
Paschal Pavolo Borden
Sion Record Bostick
John Carr
Jeremiah D. Cochran
George Washington Davis
Samuel Davis
John Duncan
John Flick
John Ray Foster
Styles J. Fowler
Hugh Frazer
George Washington Gardner
Thomas Gay

Augus Greenlaw
Samuel G. Hardaway[3]
William J. Hawkins
Allen Ingram
James H. Isbell
William Isbell
W. R. Jackson
Robert Justus Kleberg
Matthew Kuykendall
John Ligett Marshall
Joseph McCrabb
John Sutherland Menefee
Samuel Millett
William N. Mock
John Hamilton Money
Robert D. Moore
Nicholas Peck
Louis von Roeder
Paul Scarborough
George Sutherland[4]
Valentine Wesley Swearingen
James Tarlton
Antonio Trevinio
Patrick Usher
Joseph D. Vermillion
James E. Watkins
Phillip Weppler
Matthew R. Williams
McHenry Winburn
Abner W. Woolsey
James Allison York

[1]Also served as Colonel Rusk's staff secretary and translator.
[2]Originally under Captain Roman. Fought with Capt. Baker at San Jacinto. Wounded on April 21 and listed on the San Jacinto rolls in 1836 as "C. D. Anderson."
[3]Joined on April 2 from Major Ward's Goliad command.
[4]Volunteered to fight with Colonel Sherman on April 20.

COMPANY F, FIRST REGIMENT TEXAS VOLUNTEERS
"CITIZEN SOLDIERS": FORMED FEBRUARY 1, 1836

Captain:
William Jones Elliott Heard[1]

First Lieutenant:
William Mosby Eastland

First Sergeant:
Eli Mercer

Second Sergeant:
Wilson T. Lightfoot

First Corporal:
Alfred Kelso

Second Corporal:
Elijah G. Mercer

Privates:
Thomas Jefferson Adams
Leander Beason
John Begley
James Bird[2]
Fidelie S. Breeding
Francis E. Brookfield
John Hickerson Burnam
William Owen Burnam
William Daniel Durham
Joseph Ehlinger
Steven Tucker Foley
John Hallett Jr.
Thomas Monroe Hardeman
Charles M. Henry
Joseph Highland
Josiah Hogan
Joseph Hyland
Allen B. Jones
Daniel R. Kincheloe

James Seaton Lester
John Edward Lewis
William W. Lightfoot
John McCrabb
Hugh McKenzie
Robert McLaughlin
Daniel Miller
James Nelson
Patrick B. O'Connor
William Carroll Pace
Mitchell [Michael] Putnam[3]
Nathaniel Reed
Jesse Robinson
Joel Walter Robison
Thomas Ryans
D. Andrew Sanett
Maxwell Steel
Charles P. Thompson
John Jackson Tumlinson Jr.[4]
Thomas C. Utley[5]
William Waters
Christian Gotthelf Wertzner
Leroy Wilkinson
Andrew Zumwalt

[1]Took command on April 2 when Captain Thomas J. Rabb left during the Runaway Scrape.
[2]Member of Capt. Stephen Townsend's rangers from Feb. 1–May 1, 1836.
[3]Wounded in right arm on April 21.
[4]Captain of rangers from Jan. 17–Aug. 16, 1836.
[5]Wounded on April 20. Absent from the battle of April 21.

COMPANY H, FIRST REGIMENT TEXAS VOLUNTEERS
FORMED MARCH 1, 1836 IN WASHINGTON COUNTY

First Lieutenant, Commanding:
Robert Stevenson[1]

First Lieutenant:
Henry H. Swisher[2]

First Sergeant:
Clement Rainey

Second Sergeant:
Ashley R. Stephens

Fourth Sergeant:
William H. Miller

Privates:
Moses Baine
William Robert Bowen
William Jarvis Cannan
Allen Caruthers
Lewis Chapman Clemmons
John Robert Craddock
Nicholas S. Crunk
Walter Riddle Dallas
Moses H. Davis
Abraham Dillard

Berry Doolittle
James Harrison Evetts
John G. Evetts Jr.
James Farmer
John Gafford
Frederick Browder Gentry
John Graham
James Gray
Mayberry B. Gray
John Grimes
Jacob Gross
William Washington Hawkins
Francis K. Henderson
James Monroe Hill
Prosper Hope
John Campbell Hunt[3]
John Ingram[4]
Dr. James D. Jennings[5]
David J. Jones[6]
David Smith Kornegay[7]
Alexander Lessassier
John Lyford
Daniel McKay[8]
Nathan Mitchell
George Washington Petty
James Powell
Henry P. Redfield[9]
Uriah Sanders
John S. Stump

John Milton Swisher
John Files Tom
Elisha S. Whitesides
James G. Wilkinson Jr.

(Note: Joseph Lawrence transferred to Capt. Karnes' company on 4/21.)

[1]Recruited March 20 on the Colorado by Capt. Joseph P. Lynch. Stevenson was acting commander of Company H at San Jacinto for Captain William Hill, who was sick at Harrisburg. Captain Hill had assumed command of company from Captain Lynch on March 13.
[2]Promoted April 3, 1836.
[3]First Lieutenant of Captain Chance's company. Fought with Hill's on April 21.
[4]Recruited March 20 by Capt. Philip Coe.
[5]Member of Captain Chance's company who fought with Hill's on April 21.
[6]Goliad Massacre survivor who joined Texas Army on April 11.
[7]Recruited March 15 by Capt. Philip Coe.
[8]Transferred into company from Captain Karnes' after losing horse in April 20 battle. In return, Stevenson sent Joseph Lawrence to Karnes.
[9]Member of Capt. Tumlinson's rangers who joined Capt. Chance's company but fought at San Jacinto.

COMPANY I, FIRST REGIMENT TEXAS VOLUNTEERS
"VELASCO BLUES": ORGANIZED MARCH 8 AT VELASCO

Captain:
William S. Fisher

First Lieutenant:
Robert W. P. Carter[1]

Second Lieutenant:
Robert J. W. Reel

Orderly Sergeant:
Edward S. Jones

Privates:
William L. Armour
Reason Banks
Mathias A. Bingham
Samuel Pearce Birt
Henry Bond
Moses W. Brigham
James Cooper
Robert Crittenden
William Day
Joseph Doan

George Fennell
Benjamin Franklin Fry
William Gill
Luke John Gillespie
Alexander S. Graves
Andrew Jackson Harris
Denward James
James Joslin
George W. Leek
John Lewellyn
George W. Mason
Jacob Maybee
John D. McAllister[2]
Joseph McAllister
Samuel W. McKneely
Alfred H. Miles
Hugh Morgan
Adam Mosier
Eliakin P. Myrick
Eli Noland

Wesley Walker Pace
James S. Patterson
Daniel Perry[3]
Thomas A. Sebastian Pratt
Nathaniel Rudder[4]
William L. Sergeant
John Milton Shreve
Joseph H. Slack[3]
Joseph Sovereign
John F. Stancell[3]
Charles C. Stebbins
John W. Stroud
Thomas Taylor
Algernon P. Thompson[5]

Henry H. Tierwester
George Weedon[6]
Rufus Wright

[1]Promoted to replace First Lieutenant William H. Steele.
[2]Former member of Capt. John Bird's.
[3]Member of Capt. Daniel Perry's from March 6–April 2, 1836.
[4]Member of Capt. Peyton Splane's who fought with Fisher's at San Jacinto.
[5]Member of Capt. Robert Calder's who transferred into Fisher's for the battle.
[6]Permanently wounded at San Jacinto.

COMPANY K, FIRST REGIMENT TEXAS VOLUNTEERS
"BRAZORIA COMPANY": ORGANIZED AT GONZALES MARCH 12

Captain:
Robert James Calder

First Lieutenant:
John Sharp[1]

Second Lieutenant:
Allen Larrison[2]

Acting Second Lieutenant:
M. H. Denham[3]

Orderly Sergeant:
Benjamin Rice Brigham

Privates:
Elder B. Barton
Henry Percy Brewster[4]
Augustus J. Butts
Francis Jarvis Cooke[2]
Thomas Cooke[2]
James Connor[2]
Robert Crawford[3]
David Deadrick[3]
Henry Dibble[2]
Joseph Smith Edgar[3]
Henry Fields
Benjamin Franklin Fitch
Charles Forrester[3]
Thomas M. Fowler
Benjamin Cromwell Franklin
William W. Gant[3]
James Green[2]
William Hale[3]
John Hall
E. B. Halstead
John W. Hassell
William C. Hogg[5]

George J. Johnson
James Johnson[3]
Walter Lambert
Charles Malone
Pleasant D. McNeel
Andrew Granville Mills
Benjamin Franklin Mims
S. B. Mitchell
William Murray
Thomas O'Connor
C. W. Parrott[6]
John Plunkett
Charles Keller Reese
Washington Perry Reese
William P. Scott[3]
John Smith
Joseph A. Spicer
Henry S. Stouffer[7]
Joshua Threadgill

[1]Elected March 24.
[2]Member of Captain Larrison's company which combined with Calder's on April 3.
[3]Member of Captain Splane's. Fought with Calder's at San Jacinto. Denham was First Lieutenant of Splane's.
[4]Personal secretary to General Houston. Member of Capt. Teal's, but fought with Capt. Calder's.
[5]Changed his name legally in 1842 to William Howard.
[6]Assigned as hospital steward on April 21. Not present for main battle.
[7]Also served as adjutant for General Houston during campaign.

SECOND REGIMENT TEXAS VOLUNTEERS
ORGANIZED APRIL 8, 1836

Colonel:
Sidney Sherman

Lieutenant Colonel:
Joseph L. Bennett

Major:
Lysander Wells

Adjutant:
Edward B. Wood

Sergeant Major:
Bennett McNelly

FIRST (A) COMPANY, SECOND REGIMENT
"NACOGDOCHES VOLUNTEERS": ORGANIZED MARCH 6, 1836

Captain:
Hayden S. Arnold [1]

First Lieutenant:
Robert W. Smith

Second Lieutenant:
Isiah Edwards

First Sergeant:
Thomas D. Brooks

Second Sergeant:
Samuel Leeper

First Corporal:
William P. Kincannon

Second Corporal:
Samuel Phillips

Privates:
Collin Aldrich
Howard W. Bailey
John T. Ballard
James Edward Box
John Andrew Box
Nelson A. Box
Thomas Griffin Box
Henry Mitchell Brewer
Henry Larkin Chapman
Daniel L. Doubt
John Crawford Grigsby [2]
William Calvert Hallmark [2]
Elias Edley Hamilton
John W. Harvey
Peter W. Holmes
William Stephens Kennard
James Madden [2]

Philip Martin [2]
John McCoy
John W. McHorse
Stephen McLaughlin
George Richie Mercer
James Mitchell
Jose Molino
John Moss
Robert Nabers
William Nabers
Dickerson Parker [2]
Levi Pruett
Martin J. Pruitt
David Rusk
William Turner Sadler [2]
Stephen Franklin Sparks
John B. Trenary
Jesse Walling
Madison Guess Whitaker
William F. Williams
John Yancy
John Swanson Yarbrough Sr.

[1] Promoted to Captain after promotion of Major Leander Smith on April 1.
[2] Member of Capt. Sadler's rangers prior to April 1. James Madden shown on Arnold's muster rolls but not on official San Jacinto rosters.

Note: John W. Carpenter also served under Capt. Sadler and joined the Nacogdoches Volunteers. Carpenter then joined with Captain William Smith's cavalry company.

SECOND (B) COMPANY, SECOND REGIMENT
ORGANIZED MARCH 12, 1836 IN WASHINGTON MUNICIPALITY

Captain:
William Ware

First Lieutenant:
Job Starks Collard

Second Lieutenant:
George A. Lamb

First Sergeant:
Albert E. Gallatin

Second Sergeant:
William Carvin Winters

Privates:
David M. Bullock
Mathew Winston Cartwright*

William P. Cartwright
Lewis Cox
James C. DeWitt
Christopher Columbus Edinburg
George Washington Lawrence
Matthew Mark Moss
George Washington Robinson
John Sadler
Jesse G. Thompson
James Wilson
James Washington Winters
John Frelan Winters

*Fought with cavalry on April 20 and lost his horse during battle.

THIRD (C) COMPANY, SECOND REGIMENT
"LIBERTY VOLUNTEERS": ORGANIZED MARCH 6, 1836

Captain:
William Mitchell Logan Jr.

First Lieutenant:
Benjamin Franklin Hardin[1]

Second Lieutenant:
Benjamin J. Harper

First Sergeant:
Edward Thomas Branch

Sergeant:
William Kibbe

Privates:
Thomas Belknap
Ephraim Bollinger
Peter Bollinger
Michael J. Brake
Luke O. Bryan
Patrick Carnal[2]
Michael Chavenoe
David Choate Jr.
David Cole
Cornelius De Vore [Devore]
William Duffee
Joseph Ellenger
Joseph Farwell
Lefroy Gedry
David Hutcheson McFadin

Pierre Menard Maxwell
Thomas Orr
Michael Peveto Jr.
John Pleasants
William Robinson
John Ruddell
David Scott
John Slayton
James Smith
William Smith
William C. Smith
William M. Smith
John Allen Stephenson
Edward M. Tanner
Cyrus W. Thompson
Hezekiah Reams Williams

[1]Promoted after First Lieutenant Edward B. Wood was promoted to adjutant of Second Regiment.

[2]Substitute for Geraldous S. Thomas. Although listed on the San Jacinto "Honor Roll," Thomas' audited military claims indicate that he was not present.

Note: Captain Benjamin Harper's Beaumont (Jefferson County) company merged with Capt. Logan's on March 6 when Logan's was created in Liberty.

FOURTH (D) COMPANY, SECOND REGIMENT
"COLUMBIA COMPANY": ORGANIZED MARCH 13, 1836

Captain:
David Murphree[1]

First Lieutenant:
Phineas Ripley

Second Lieutenant:
Peter Harper

First Sergeant:
John Smith

Second Sergeant:
Pendleton Rector

Third Sergeant:
A. W. Breedlove

First Corporal:
George L. Bledsoe

Privates:
Milton B. Atkinson
Alexander Bailey
John A. Barkley
Robert Barr
Dr. John Walker Baylor
Andrew Jackson Beard
James C. Boyd
James Bradley
William Brenan[2]
Benjamin Franklin Cage
John Chenoweth
Lewis L. Chiles
Thomas F. Corry
Hinton Curtis
Edmund Calloway Darst
Richard Brownfield Darst
Jesse Kencheloe Davis

Colden Denman
Edward Gallaher
James B. Grice
James S. Hall
James Harris
James Hayr
Nathaniel C. Hazen[2]
Charles F. Heck
William Houston Jack
Amos D. Kenyon
Abraham Lewis
George Washington Lonis
Joseph Manton McCormick
Thomas McGay
Daniel Murphy[2]
St. Clair Patton
Sidney Phillips
John Pickering
Claiborne Rector
Elbridge Gerry Rector
Charles B. Shain[2]
Maxlin "Mack" Smith[3]
James H. Spillman
Thomas Jefferson Sweeney
John B. Taylor
Francis Walnut
Leiper Willoughby
George Washington Wright

[1]Capt. William Hester Patton promoted into General Houston's staff
[2]Goliad Massacre survivor.
[3]Servant of Benjamin F. Smith.

FIFTH (E) COMPANY, SECOND REGIMENT
ORGANIZED MARCH 18, 1836 IN WASHINGTON MUNICIPALITY

Captain:
Thomas H. McIntire

First Lieutenant:
John Porter Gill

Second Lieutenant:
Basil G. Ijams[1]

First Sergeant:
Robert D. Tyler

Second Sergeant:
John Wilkinson

First Corporal:
Elkin G. Coffman

Privates:
Moses Allison
Jethro Russell Bancroft
George Barker
William Bennett

William Boyle
John B. Callicoate
Joseph Campbell
John F. Cheairs Sr.[2]
John Cheevers
John Clark
Mathias Cooper
Thomas Cox
Travis Davis
Oscar Farish
Lucien Hopson
Isaac L. Jaques
Connell O'Donnell Kelly
John L. "Jack" Lowary

Cyrus W. Lupton
Isaac Maiden
Ambrose Mays
Placide B. McCorlay
David Odem
Samuel W. Peebles
George Washington Penticost
Samuel Shupe
Freeman Wilkinson

[1]Transferred into company on April 7 from Capt. Jacob Eberly's.
[2]Member of Capt. Arnold's who fought with Capt. McIntire's.

SIXTH (F) COMPANY, SECOND REGIMENT
ORGANIZED MARCH 1, 1836 IN WASHINGTON MUNICIPALITY

Captain:
James Gillaspie[1]

First Lieutenant:
Matthew Finch[2]

Second Lieutenant:
A. L. Harrison

First Sergeant:
Richard H. Chadduck

Privates:
Ganey Crosby[3]
Socrates Darling
Willis L. Ellis
Hezekiah Faris
William L. Ferrill
William Fullerton
Michael R. Goheen
Elzy Harrison
Robert Henry
Benjamin Johnson
Thomas F. Johnson
Francis B. Lasater
Abiah Lolison
William McCoy
William McIntire
Edward McMillan
Andrew M. Montgomery
John Montgomery
Jennings O'Banion

John Peterson
William Peterson
Lawrence Ramey
John Richardson
John Sayres
John Wesley Scallorn
Alphonso Steele
Charles Stephanes
Elijah Votaw
James Walker
Philip Walker
Thomas H. Webb
John Carey White
Ozwin Wilcox
Samuel Wildy
F. Marion Woodward

[1]Assumed command when Captain Bennett was promoted to Lieutenant Colonel on April 8.
[2]Elected March 16.
[3]Joined April 17 from Capt. Tumlinson's ranger company.
[4]Served with Captain Karnes' cavalry through April 20.

Note: Company recruited in February in Washington Municipality (present Walker and Montgomery Counties).

Dr. Fielding Deadrick joined from Captain Karnes' cavalry company and served with Gillaspie's company on April 21.

SEVENTH (G) COMPANY, SECOND REGIMENT
"SABINE VOLUNTEERS": ORGANZIED IN MARCH 1836

Captain:
Benjamin Franklin Bryant

First Lieutenant:
John C. Hale

Second Lieutenant:
Archibald S. Lewis

Privates:
James Clark
William Clark
Adam Coble
William Earl
John Floyd Gilbert
Josephus Somerville Irvine
James Thomas Patton Irvine

John R. Johnson
Benjamin Franklin Lindsay Jr.
Robert S. Love
Alexander McKinza
Joseph Belton Park
William H. Pate
David Roberts
Zion Roberts
Chester B. Rockwell
Robert Benedict Russell
William Bennett Scates*
Rev. James Thomas
Levi H. White

*Joined Capt. Arnold's company after the battle of San Jacinto.

EIGHTH (H) COMPANY, SECOND REGIMENT
SAN AUGUSTINE COMPANY: ORGANIZED MARCH 15, 1836

Captain:
William Kimbro

First Lieutenant:
James Rowe

First Sergeant:
John A. Harmon

Second Sergeant:
William Fisher

Third Sergeant:
Henry Reed

Privates:
William Bateman
W. B. Bennett
John Pelham Border
David Brown
Anderson Buffington
Andrew Caddell
James A. Chaffin
Josh Clelens [Clellans]
Hershel Corzine
Joel Burditt Crain

Roden Taylor Crain
Washington Hamilton Davis
George Washington Forbes
Benjamin Greer*
George Duncan Hancock
H. Hill
Sanford Holman
Rinaldo Hotchkiss
Thomas M. Hughes
George Washington Jones
Joseph Kent
Edward Oswald LeGrand
David Hall Love
Albert C. Manuel
Thomas Maxwell
Daniel H. McGary
Isaac McGary
Andrew Jackson McGown
Joseph W. Proctor
R. Stevenson
Benjamin Thomas Jr.
Dexter Watson
Louis Wilmouth

*Joined from Capt. William Walker's.

NINTH (I) COMPANY, SECOND REGIMENT
ORGANIZED EARLY MARCH 1836 IN GONZALES

Captain:
Juan Nepomuceno Seguin

First Sergeant:
Manuel Maria Flores

Second Sergeant:
Jose Antonio Menchaca

First Corporal:
Nepomuceno Flores

Second Corporal:
Ambrosio Rodriguez

Privates:
Jose Maria Arocha
Manuel Arocha
Simon Arreola
Andres Barcinas

Cesario Carmona
Gabriel Casillas
Antonio Cruz
Antonio Curbiere
Matias Curbiere
Lucio Enriquez
Pedro Herrera
Juan López*
Juan Maldonado
Jose Maria Mancha
Juan Nepomuceno Navarro
Jacinto Pena
Eduardo Rameriz
Francisco Salinas
Manuel Tarin

*Joined on April 19 at Buffalo Bayou per Captain Seguin.

Note: Captain W. H. Smith's Company J is shown with the Texas Cavalry.

ELEVENTH (K) COMPANY, SECOND REGIMENT
ORGANIZED APRIL 5, 1836 AT HARRISBURG

Captain:
Alfred Henderson Wyly

First Lieutenant:
Hezekiah Benjamin Balch

Second Lieutenant:
John Abram Hueser

First Sergeant:
Franklin B. Hickox

Surgeon:
Dr. Tobias Dubromer

Privates:
John Balch
Andrew Fogle

William Gammell
Augustus Henderstrom
Robert Hood[1]
Lewis Kraatz
Joseph Miller[2]
Michael Short
Philip Stroh[2]

[1]Transferred in from Capt. Billingsley's.
[2]Transferred in from Capt. Baker's.

Note: Captain Wyly's company was not listed on the original San Jacinto rolls due to error.

Company Unknown:
Francis K. Hardeman
John Herring
Moses Marritt

Hardeman, Herring and Marritt are listed by the San Jacinto Museum of History's "Honor Roll" as having participated in the battle. At this time, I am unable to precisely place these three men into a particular company. Each of these three is an addition to Louis Wiltz Kemp's original research of San Jacinto combatants. It is likely that John Herring is the same as John Herron.

The "Honor Roll" lists names added since Kemp's research with an asterisk. At least a couple of these are doubtful. One such name is that of Calvin Weaver. His own audited military claims (Calvin Weaver AC, R 111, F 229) show that he was discharged from service by Captain Jesse Billingsley and Colonel Edward Burleson at Groce's on April 12 "on the account of his not being able to do duty."

Another name added to the "Honor Roll" was that of James Cellum. His military papers show that he was a member of the company under Captain William D. Ratcliff (later under Leonard Mabbitt). Mabbitt's company reached the San Jacinto battlefield after the battle. While some of these men such as Cellum were given land for their service during the war that separated Texas from Mexico, it does not necessarily mean that they directly fought at San Jacinto. (James Cellum PE, R 208, F 269-88.)

A third name I have not included from the "Honor Roll" is that of Geraldous S. Thomas. He *did* serve in Captain William Logan's unit during the San Jacinto campaign. His military papers, however, clearly show that Patrick Carnal was allowed to step in as his substitute during the Runaway Scrape and that Carnal fought in his place at San Jacinto.

I have also included John Walker only on the roster of Texans stationed at Harrisburg due to his pension papers (John Walker PE, R 243, F 628-641.) The San Jacinto muster rolls show John Walker to have been attached to Captain Joseph Chance's Washington Guards at Harrisburg. Private William P. Zuber testified in Walker's pension application that Walker was a member of Captain James Gillaspie's company who was assigned to Camp Harrisburg "on the evening of the 19th of April." Walker missed the battle, serving "with the said guard, [and] rejoined the main army after the battle."

Roster of Texans Stationed at Texas Army Camp near Harrisburg

April 21, 1836

CAMP STAFF

Major:
Robert McNutt

Acting Sergeant Major:
Jesse Benton Jr.*

Wagon Master:
Conrad Rohrer, Capt.

Volunteer Physicians:
Dr. Thomas P. Anderson
Dr. William W. Bomar
Dr. William Francis H. Davis

*Officer of Capt. Patton/Murphree's Columbia Company.

COMPANY E, FIRST REGIMENT TEXAS VOLUNTEERS
RECRUITED LATE FEBRUARY; ORGANIZED MARCH 1, 1836

Captain:
Gibson Kuykendall[1]

First Lieutenant:
Francis Miller

First Sergeant:
Sherwood Young Reams

Third Sergeant:
William P. Polk

Fourth Sergeant:
James Hampton Kuykendall

Privates:
John Atkinson
Walter Elias Baker
James B. Blaylock
James H. Bostick
McLin Bracey
Alexander Brown
Jonathan Burleson
James Burnett
Thomas Burtrang
Heil Orton Campbell

John Campbell
Rufus Easton Campbell
Arter Crownover
John Davis
Edward Dickinson
James Carson Duff
Henry Freed
Benjamin Granville
Frederick Miller Grimes
George W. Grimes
Basil Muse Hatfield
Joseph Jackson
Nathan B. Johnson
William P. Kerr
Adam Kuykendall
Brazilla Kuykendall
H. A. Kuykendall
John Kuykendall
Thornton S. Kuykendall
Hiram Lee
Addison Litton
Jesse Litton

453

John Litton
A. Liverall
Joseph Penn Lynch
L. Mantin
Elias J. Marshall
Hugh Lewis Marshall
John Marshall Jr.
Joseph Taylor Marshall
Samuel B. Marshall
Nathaniel A. McFaddin
George Morris
William M. Perry
James B. Pier
Thomas Polk
R. Potts
Perry Price
Robert Price
William Price

John B. Rhodes
Early Robbins
Robert Scott
John Sharp
J. G. Snodgrass
John Stephens
Thomas B. Stevenson
Josiah Taylor
Stephen Townsend[2]
P. John Townsend[2]
Moses Townsend[2]

[1]Promoted April 8 after Capt. Robert McNutt named Major, First Regiment.
[2]Member of Capt. Stephen Townsend's ranger company. This Stephen Townsend was a nephew of Capt. Townsend.

COMPANY J, FIRST REGIMENT TEXAS VOLUNTEERS
ORGANIZED FEBRUARY 22, 1836

Captain:
Peyton R. Splane

Second Lieutenant:
Samuel S. Gillett

Orderly Sergeant:
William Gorham[1]

Second Sergeant:
Wiley M. Head

Third Sergeant:
Preston Pevehouse

Privates:
Calvin P. Abbott
William Barker
Daniel Bradley
Octavious A. Cook
A. W. Cooke
John B. Crawford
Freeman Walker Douglass
Jonathan Douglass
William G. Goolsey
James Gordon

James B. Hinds
Archibald Hodge
James Hodge
William Hodge
Joseph Ranson Johnson
William H. Kenney
William McMaster
John D. Moore
Burrel Morriss
James H. Morriss
James D. Owen
Solomon Calvin Page
Alexander W. Rowlett
John G. Smith
Dr. William P. Smith
William W. Smith
Jesse Williams
Agabus Winters

[1]Sick at upper encampment.

Note: Ten men of Capt. Splane's fought with other First Regiment companies at San Jacinto.

CAPT. CHANCE'S "WASHINGTON GUARDS": SECOND REGIMENT
FORMED BY MAJOR WILLIAMSON, COMMANDING RANGERS; ORGANIZED MARCH 20

Captain: Joseph Bell Chance	Benjamin C. Finley Lankford Fitzgerald	[1]First Lieutenant John C. Hunt and Privates James D.
First Lieutenant:[1]	John A. F. Gravis[4] Garrett Law	Jennings, David J. Jones, and Henry Redfield fought at San
Second Lieutenant: Moses Evans[2]	Theodore Staunton Lee Peterson Lloyd[3]	Jacinto with Captain Steven- son's company.
Orderly Sergeant: John H. Scaggs	James M. Manning[6] James Maury	[2]Enlisted April 7. Elected 2nd Lt. on April 9.
Second Sergeant: Ennes Hardin[3]	Robert Merritt Spencer Morris	[3]Previously in Capt. D. B. Friar's ranger unit.
Privates: George Bond	Richard Rodgers Peebles J. M. Pennington	[4]Previously in Capt. S. C. Robertson's rangers.
David Wilson Campbell[4] Thomas Cannon	Stephen R. Roberts Thomas M. Splane	[5]Enlisted Feb. 4 in Capt. I. W. Burton's rangers.
James K. Chelaup James R. Childress[4]	Thomas Thompson Richard Vaughn	[6]Enlisted Feb. 11 by Capt. Bur- ton for twelve months' service.
John R. Cockrell Sylvanus Cottle[5]	John Walker[7] Josiah Walker	[7]Member of Capt. Gillaspie's company assigned to baggage
Josiah G. Dunn Calvin Brallery Emmons[3]	Robert Winnett Joseph H. Woods	guard on April 19. John Walker PE, R 243, F 629–30.
Edwin B. Emory Massillon Farley	William Riley Woods Gilbert Wright[3]	Source: *Muster Rolls of the* *Texas Revolution*, 208–209.

LIST OF THOSE SICK OR DETAILED AS GUARDS FROM MAIN TEXAS ARMY

Artillery Corps:

Capt. Neill's Company:
George Washington Seaton

Notes:
Accidentally wounded in foot.

Cavalry Corps:

Capt. Karnes' Company:
Jesse Bartlett
William Caruthers

Regular Army:

Capt. Teal's Company A:
Henry Teal

Notes:
Sick with measles. Company A was commanded by Andrew Briscoe at San Jacinto.

First Regiment Texas Volunteers

Capt. Wood's Company A:
Thomas Freeman

Notes:
At camp sick.

Capt. Roman's Company B:
George M. Casey, First Lieut.

Notes:
At camp sick.

Capt. Billingsley's Company C: *Notes:*

John W. Anderson	Detailed to guard sick/baggage.
Albert Black	Detailed to guard sick/baggage.
Jeptha Boyce	Detailed to guard sick/baggage.
David C. Connell	Detailed to guard sick/baggage.
George Duty	Sick at Harrisburg per Billingsley.
Greenleaf Fisk	Detailed to guard sick/baggage.
Isaac Gorham	Detailed to guard sick/baggage.
Isaac Harris	Detailed to guard sick/baggage.
Azariah G. Moore	Detailed to guard sick/baggage.
Elisha Prewitt	Detailed to guard sick/baggage.
George Washington Ricks	Detailed to guard sick/baggage.

Capt. Baker's Company D: *Notes:*

Lancelot Abbott	Sick or guarding baggage.
William Pettus	Sick or guarding baggage.

Capt. Heard's Company F: *Notes:*

Napoleon Bonaparte Breeding	At camp sick. Member of Capt. Stephen Townsend's ranger unit.
Henry L. Lightfoot	At camp sick.

Capt. Hill's Company H: *Notes:*

Isham G. Belcher	
John Bate Berry	
Jacob Castleman	
Willard Chamberlain	
William Warner Hill, Captain	At camp sick.
James Hollingsworth	
James Hughes	
David Levi Kokernot	
Jesse Lindsey McCrocklin	
Sion W. Perry	
Jermiah W. Simpson	
Benjamin Franklin Swoap	
William Townsend	Member of Capt. Stephen Townsend's ranger unit.

Capt. Fisher's Company I: *Notes:*

John Breeding	Sick or guarding baggage.

Capt. Calder's Company K: *Notes:*

William A. Grady	Sick or guarding baggage.

Capt. Bird's Company: *Notes:*

Young Caruthers	Detailed to guard wagons.
John M. Hensley	Detailed to guard wagons.
Robert Hancock Hunter	Detailed to guard wagons.
George B. Peerman	Detailed to guard wagons.

Second Regiment Texas Volunteers

Capt. Arnold's First Company: *Notes:*

Stillwell Box	Stationed at camp.
Alfred M. Hallmark	At camp sick.
William Everett Kennard	

Keeton McLemore Jones
Henry William Vardeman
John C. Walling

John Swanson Yarbrough Jr.*	At camp sick.
Joseph Randolph Yarbrough	At camp sick.

* Not listed on rosters. Both Swanson Jr. and his brother Joseph took part in the San Jacinto campaign (per Beth Walker's "John Swanson Yarbrough, A Man About Texas" article), although only their father, Swanson Yarbrough Sr., fought in the battle. Captain Arnold's roll taker may have missed the younger Yarbrough when a muster roll was created on May 5.

Capt. Ware's Second Company:	*Notes:*
Philip Haddox Coe	Detailed with baggage wagon.
James Hillness Collard, Third Sgt.	At camp sick.
Jonathan S. Collard	Remained at camp.
Evan Conner	Remained with baggage; not detailed to do so.
Thomas Conner	
John Monroe Harbour	Detailed with baggage wagon.
T. J. Harbour	Detailed with baggage wagon.
Lewis Moore	Detailed with baggage wagon.
Morris Moore	Detailed with baggage wagon.
Ransom Olphin	Detailed with baggage wagon.
Wiley Parker	Detailed with baggage wagon.
Daniel Raper	Detailed with baggage wagon.
Benjamin W. Robinson	Detailed with baggage wagon.
John B. Tong	Detailed with baggage wagon.

Capt. Logan's Third Company:	*Notes:*
Stephen William Blount	Detailed to guard baggage.
Patrick Bryody	Detailed to guard baggage.
James Cole	At camp sick.
John J. Holcombe	Detailed to guard baggage.
William M. McFadin [McFaddin]	Detailed to guard baggage.
James McLaughlin*	At camp sick.
William McLaughlin	At camp sick.
Thomas Norment	Detailed to guard baggage.
David Rankin	Detailed to guard baggage.
William A. Smith	Taking care of the sick.
Robert Whitlock	On guard at hospital.
Ransom Willburn	Detailed to guard baggage.
Hezekiah Williams Sr.	Detailed to guard baggage.

*Joined Capt. John Bird's company post–San Jacinto.

Capt. Patton/Murphree's Fourth Comp:	*Notes:*
Robert Brown	Detailed to guard baggage.
Henry Buckley	Detailed to guard baggage.
Emory Holman Darst, Fourth Corp.	Detailed to guard baggage.
Henry H. Haggard	Detailed to guard baggage.
Robert Hodge	Detailed to guard baggage.
Richard Hope	Detailed to guard baggage.
Elisha Mather	Detailed to guard baggage.

George Washington Pleasants   Detailed to guard baggage.
Wesley Tollett   Detailed to guard baggage.
Martin Varner   Detailed to guard baggage.
Nicolas Whitehead   Detailed to guard baggage.
Edward Williams   Detailed to guard baggage.

Capt. McIntire's Fifth Company: *Notes:*
Andrew Crier   Sick or guarding baggage.

Capt. Gillaspie's Sixth Company: *Notes:*
Samuel McFall   Detailed to guard sick/baggage.
William McIntire   Detailed to guard sick/baggage.
Andrew McMillan   At camp sick.
James McMillan   At camp sick.
John Newton   Detailed to guard sick/baggage.
William Physick Zuber   Detailed to guard sick/baggage.

Capt. Bryant's Seventh Company: *Notes:*
William Means   Sick or guarding baggage.
Hardy William Brown Price

Capt. Kimbro's Eighth Company: *Notes:*
James Burch   Detailed to guard sick/baggage.
Valentine Burch   Detailed to guard sick/baggage.
Newell W. Burditt   Detailed to guard sick/baggage.
William Buck Burditt   Detailed to guard sick/baggage.
Godfrey Etheridge   Detailed to guard sick/baggage.
Jonas Hale   Detailed to guard sick/baggage.
David Hill   Sick or guarding baggage.
Samuel McGown   Detailed to guard sick/baggage.
Robert Tippett   Detailed to guard sick/baggage.

UNASSIGNED OR COMPANY UNKNOWN:

Oliver Farnsworth
Seth Ingram   Was "cut off" from main Texas Army by the Mexican army
                                  on April 20, per March 10, 1858, Donation Certificate No.
                                  427.
Thomas Kemp   Goliad Massacre survivor.
Sterling Clack Robertson   Former ranger captain. Served as camp guard per Donation
                                  Certificate No. 7 of May 1, 1846.
Enoch Robinett   Joined army April 3. Detailed as baggage guard at Harrisburg.
James M. Robinett   Joined army April 3. Detailed as baggage guard at Harrisburg.
James Robinson   Indentured servant of Robert Eden Handy. Ordered to stay
                                  at Harrisburg.
Ashbel Savery   "On detached service" at time of the battle. Likely stationed
                                  as camp guard.

Other Companies of the San Jacinto Campaign

March 6–April 21, 1836

Captain:
John Bird

First Lieutenant:
Robert P. Stewart

Second Lieutenant:
John D. McAllister

Orderly Sergeant:
Peter Bartelle Dexter[1]

Privates:
William Allen[2]
Henry Barmer[2]
Berry Beasley[2]
Washington Beasley[2]
George W. Brooks
Nathan Brookshire
Nathaniel Burget[2]
John Callahan[2]
John Carr[3]
Allen Caruthers
Young Caruthers[4]
William Clary
Amos Cooper[2]
James Cothem[2]
Henry C. Dannettell[5]
George W. Davis[2]
Charles Donoho
Patrick Dowlan[2]
Tilford C. Edwards[6]
Richard Faulks[2]
John Fisher

Charles Fortran[2]
Claiborne Foster[2]
Randolph Foster[2]
Churchel Fulshear
Gravis Fulshear[2]
Thomas Hancock[2]
Daniel Harmon[2]
Solomon Haul[2]
John Heiler[2]
Andrew Jackson Hensley
Charles Hensley
James Hensley[2]
John M. Hensley[4]
Johnson Hensley[7]
George Herder
Kenneth Highlman[2]
John House[2]
Joseph House
Mumford House[2]
Ransom House[2]
John Calhoun Hunter
Robert Hancock Hunter[4]
William Hunter[2]
William H. Hunter[2]
John Rice Jones
William Kelly
Samuel McCombs[2]
Samuel McFennell[2]
Pleasant D. McNeel[8]
Robert D. McNeel
Stephen Miller[2]
William T. Millican

459

Bartlett Murray[2]
John Owens
George B. Peerman[4]
Arvelle Perry
Laurence Perry
James M. Rankin[7]
William Rankins Jr.[2]
Leo Roark
George H. Roberts
William Roberts[2]
Bernard Schneider[2]
Robert Sellers[2]
Daniel Shipman[2]
John M. Shipman[9]
Moses Shipman
James Small
Alexander Smith[2]
John H. Smith[2]
William R. Taylor[2]
Meredith Tunget
William Vance[2]
Henry Verm
John Vetrane[2]

John C. Walker
Henry White[2]
T. H. White[2]
Cyrus Wickson
William Wilson[2]

[1]Promoted to Captain about April 20.
[2]Served in company per postbattle muster roll completed by Capt. Bird. See DRT, *Muster Rolls*, 80–81. Other men confirmed via service records, audited claims or pension papers.
[3]Transferred to Capt. Baker's on March 28.
[4]Detailed at upper encampment to guard the baggage and wagons at Harrisburg.
[5]Joined Capt. Baker's on March 28 and days later joined Bird's. (Dannettell AC, R 211, F 430–37.)
[6]Assigned to Capt. Moreland's artillery in April. T. C. Edwards PE, R 213, F 679–87.
[7]Enlisted on March 13, 1836.
[8]Fought with Capt. Calder's company at San Jacinto.
[9]Promoted to First Lieutenant on May 3.

CAPTAIN EBERLY'S VOLUNTEERS
MARCH 20–JUNE 20, 1836

Captain:
Jacob Eberly

Second Lieutenant:
William Preston Stapp

Second Sergeant:
Basil G. Ijams[1]

Privates:
John Adriance
Thomas J. Alsbury
David D. Barry
James Byrne
Samuel Damon
Jacob Fifer
Michael Fox
Thomas Howard
David M. Jones
Washington Lockhart

Hector McNeill[2]
Andrew Northington
Lewis H. Peters
James G. White
John M. White
John T. White
Simon C. White
Edward Williams

[1]Enlisted on March 21, 1836. Transferred to Capt. Thomas McIntire's company on April 7 as Second Lieutenant.
[2]Joined April 10. (Hector McNeill AC, R 69, F 477–81.)

Note: Muster roll is based on author's research of Republic of Texas audited military claims and pension papers. Additional research provided by Donaly Brice.

CAPTAIN WALKER'S VOLUNTEER GUARDS
FEBRUARY 28–APRIL 9, 1836

Captain:
William Walker*

First Lieutenant:
James Moore

Privates:
H. H. Adams
Thomas Jefferson Adams
Abraham Ally
David D. Baker
William Barnes
John W. Baylor
William B. Berry
Thomas Bowman
John Burns
Seth Carey
Charles Cavina
John Chaney
Gustavus Cholwell
J. C. Clark
Gabriel Cole
William G. Cooke
Samuel Damon
Samuel Davis
S. Dolley
Richard Dowdy
Daniel Etherton
William H. Fisher
David George
Freeman George
Holmon George
Jefferson George
Jasper Gilbert
Preston Gilbert
Benajmin Greer
John C. Hale
Elisha Hall
John Huff
W. Hunter
George Hurst
A. Jackson
John B. Johnson
Timothy Jones
A. Kelsey
L. Kelsey
John J. Marshall

Reason Mercer
John F. Miller
Elisha Moore
James Moore
James Nelson
W. R. Newman
Andrew Northington Jr.
P. B. O'Connor
Richard Oena
John L. Osborn
Thomas Osborne
Nicholas Peck
George H. Rault
Nathaniel Reed
Augustus S. Renchalow
Lewis Renchols
Jesse Robinson
James Rowles
John Schwatz
Levi Scott
David Selerigg
J. Y. Silvey
James Silverey
Thomas Slaughter
James H. Stilt
George Sutherland
George W. Thatcher
Isham Thompson
James Thompson
Patrick Usher
John C. Whitaker
Benjamin Whitson
George W. Williams
Andrew Worthington
G. W. Wright
Rayford Wright
Thomas Wright

*Served as Private in Captain William Hill's Company H, First Regiment, April 9–May 30, 1836. (William Walker AC, R 108, F 664.)

Note: 20 of this company left on April 5 to join the army.

Source: DRT's *Muster Rolls of the Texas Revolution*, 127–28.

"Fort Settlement Volunteers"
Formed March 7, 1836 at Fort Bend

Captain:
Wyly Martin

First Lieutenant:
Randall Jones

Second Lieutenant:
Samuel Stone

Sergeant:
Charles O. Edwards

Privates:
William Alley
William Bridge
James Cochrane
John Colder
Mortimer Donoho
Abner Echols
John Fitzgerald
Hiram Goodman
John B. Goodman
Stephen Goodman
William Goodman
William P. Huff
James M. Jean

James Wales Jones
Samuel Jones
Robert H. Kuykendall
Dr. Joseph J. McGee[1]
John F. McGuffin
John V. Morton
William P. Morton
Francis L. Mudd
William Patterson
Wiley Powell
David Scott[2]
Hiram M. Thompson
Jesse Thompson[3]
John D. Thompson

[1] Joined on March 15.
[2] Fought with Captain Logan's company at San Jacinto.
[3] Fought with Captain Ware's company at San Jacinto.

Partial roster constructed from author's research of audited military claims and pension papers.

Captain Kokernot's Volunteers
Formed March 7, 1836 at Fort Bend

Captain:
David Levi Kokernot[1]

Privates:
Milton B. Atkinson[2]
John Dorsett
James Ferguson
David Johnson

Andrew Robison
Thomas W. Smith
James H. Spillman[2]

[1] Stationed with Captain Hill's men at Harrisburg April 20–21.
[2] Fought with Captain Patton/Murphree's company at San Jacinto.

Notes

Abbreviations to the Republic Claims Papers, 1835–1846.
Texas State Library and Archives Commission, Austin.

AC   Audited Claims are those military-related claims submitted to the Comptroller or Treasurer of the Republic of Texas that were audited, approved and paid by the republic government.

PD   Public Debt Claims are claims for services provided between 1835 and 1846 that could not be paid until after Texas' annexation in 1846. These were largely paid between 1848 and the early 1860s, mainly from the 1850 Boundary Compromise money Texas was paid for its lost territory.

PP   Republic Pension Papers were generally filed from the 1870s to the early 1900s by veterans who served in the Texas Revolution and other republic-era military units.

UC   Unpaid Claims are those documents which do not fit in one of the above categories or those whose final payment disposition is unknown.

Kemp Papers   Special research collection of Louis Wiltz Kemp. San Jacinto Museum of History, Houston, Texas. Includes biographical sketches of all veterans of the battle of San Jacinto.

Forbes v. Labadie Libel Suit   The transcripts of this trial have been compiled and typed up by Robert Bruce Blake, whose papers are housed in the East Texas Research Center at Stephen F. Austin State University's Steen Library. Volume One: "The San Jacinto Campaign of 1836." As Given by Depositions in the case of John Forbes vs. Nicholas D. Labadie. District Court of Nacogdoches County, Texas. Volume Two: "Sidelights on the Battle of San Jacinto." Referenced as Forbes v Labadie, R. B. Blake compilation.

CHAPTER 1
"NEVER SURRENDER"

1. Lord, Walter. *A Time to Stand: The Epic of the Alamo as a Great National Experience.* New York: Harper & Row Publishers, 1961, 76–79. Hardin, Stephen L. *Texian Iliad. A Military History of the Texas Revolution.* Austin: University of Texas Press, 1994. Reprint, 1999, 111–17.

2. King, C. Richard. *James Clinton Neill. The Shadow Commander of the Alamo.* Austin, Tex: Eakin Press, 2002, 97–98. See also Hardin, Stephen L. *The Alamo 1836. Santa Anna's Texas Campaign.* United Kingdom: Osprey Publishing, 2001, 30–31.

3. Lord, *A Time to Stand,* 13–14, 111–12.

4. Hardin, *Texian Iliad,* 134–35.

5. Lord, *A Time to Stand,* 141–42; Hardin, *Texian Iliad,* 134–35.

6. Tolbert, Frank X. *The Day of San Jacinto.* New York: McGraw-Hill Book Co., 1959, 5–6.

7. Ibid, 9–13.

8. Hardin, *The Alamo 1836,* 11.

9. Crawford, Ann Fears (Editor). *The Eagle. The Autobiography of Santa Anna.* Austin, Tex: State House Press, 1988, 49–50.

10. Hardin, *The Alamo 1836,* 25–27.

11. Tolbert, *The Day of San Jacinto,* 17–18; Lord, *A Time to Stand,* 119.

12. Hardin, *Texian Iliad,* 136.

13. DeBruhl, Marshall. *Sword of San Jacinto: A Life of Sam Houston.* New York: Random House, 1993, 33–45. *Biographical Directory of the Texan Conventions and Congresses, 1832–1845.* Austin, Tex: Book Exchange, 1941, 107–108.

14. Tolbert, *The Day of San Jacinto,* 28–29.

15. Barker, Eugene C. "The San Jacinto Campaign." *The Quarterly of the Texas State Historical Association.* Vol. 4, No. 4 (April 1901), 239.

16. DeBruhl, *Sword of San Jacinto,* 176–78.

17. Lack, Paul (Editor). *The Diary of William Fairfax Gray. From Virginia to Texas, 1835–1837.* Dallas, Tex: SMU, 1997, 112.

18. DeBruhl, *Sword of San Jacinto,* 182–83.

19. [Coleman, Robert Morris.] *Houston Displayed, or Who Won the Battle of San Jacinto? By a Farmer in the Army* (anonymously published). Austin, Tex: The Brick Row Book Shop, 1964. Reprint. 1836. This pamphlet is credited to Colonel Robert Morris Coleman and was commonly known as early as 1840 as "Coleman's Pamphlet," although he likely used at least one ghost-writer. See page 9 for Coleman's account of Houston's departure from Washington.

20. Walter P. Lane testimony from Forbes v. Labadie papers, R. B. Blake Collection, I:128. John Forbes biographical sketch, Kemp Papers.

21. Lack (Editor), *The Diary of William Fairfax Gray,* 116–17.

22. Brown, Gary. *The New Orleans Grays. Volunteers in the Texas Revolution.* Plano: Republic of Texas Press, 1999, 161. See also Gulick, Charles A. Jr., Winnie Allen, Katherine Elliott, and Harriet Smither. *The Papers of Mirabeau Buonaparte Lamar,* 6 Volumes, 1922. Reprint. Austin, Tex: Pemberton Press, 1968, No. 2169 (W. G. Cooke letter).

23. James, Marquis. *The Raven: The Story of Sam Houston.* Covington, Georgia: Mockingbird Books, Inc., 1977, 189–90. Originally printed in 1929.

24. It appears that Houston did not count Colonel Hockley when he mentioned his other four traveling companions. William Gray's journal reflects that Houston left in the afternoon of March 6, "accompanied by his staff, Capt. Cooke, Capt. Tarleton, etc." According to Major Forbes, Sam Houston traveled with "Col. Hockley, Richardson Scurry, A. Horton and one other man." See Alexander Horton and George Washington Hockley biographical sketches, Kemp Papers and Lack (Editor), *The Diary of William Fairfax Gray,* 117.

25. Alexander Horton biographical sketch, Kemp Papers. *Biographical Directory of the Texan Conventions and Congresses,* 107.

26. James Tarlton biographical sketch, Kemp Papers.

27. [Coleman], *Houston Displayed,* 11.

CHAPTER 2
"ANXIOUS FOR A FIGHT"

1. Menchaca, José Antonio. "The Memoirs of Captain Menchaca, 1807–1836." Edited by James P. Newcomb. Typescript manuscript, in two sections, transcribed in 1957. From the collections in the Center for American History, The University of Texas at Austin. Section I:1–5.

2. Ibid, I:7.

3. Billingsley to *Galveston News*, published Saturday, September 19, 1857; see Billingsley biographical sketch in Kemp Papers.

4. Jenkins, John Holland. *Recollections of Early Texas. The Memoirs of John Holland Jenkins.* Edited by John Holmes Jenkins III. Austin: University of Texas Press, 1958. Reprint. 1995. See pages xvii–xviii, 35–36.

5. Francis K. Henderson and Allen Caruthers sketches, Kemp Papers.

6. Swisher, John Milton (edited by Rena Maverick Green). *The Swisher Memoirs*, 28–29. In the account of J. H. Kuykendall, "Recollections of the Campaign," as published in Barker, "The San Jacinto Campaign," 292, Kuykendall wrote that the Lynch/Hill company did not arrive at Gonzales until March 7. Kuykendall, however, appears to have been mistaken on this date.

7. David Smith Kornegay and John Ingram biographical sketches, Kemp Papers.

8. Bate, W. N. *General Sidney Sherman: Texas Soldier, Statesman and Builder.* Waco, Tex: Texian Press, 1974, 13–14.

9. Sidney Sherman biographical sketch, Kemp Papers.

10. Brown to parents of May 4, 1836; Oliver T. Brown biographical sketch, Kemp Papers.

11. Lack (Editor), *The Diary of William Fairfax Gray*, 87–97.

12. Bate, *General Sidney Sherman*, 31.

13. Juan Seguin biographical sketch, Kemp Papers.

14. Seguin, Juan Nepomuceno. *A Revolution Remembered: The Memoirs and Selected Correspondence of Juan N. Seguin.* Austin, Tex: State House Press, 1991, 79, 107.

15. Groneman, Bill. *Alamo Defenders. A Genealogy: The People and Their Words.* Austin, Tex: Eakin Press, 1990, 97–98.

16. Lucio Enriquez biographical sketch, Kemp Papers.

17. Menchaca, "Memoirs," I:7–8.

18. J. H. Kuykendall, "Recollections of the Campaign," as published in Barker, "The San Jacinto Campaign," 292.

19. *Austin's Old Three Hundred. The First Anglo Colony in Texas. By the Descendants of Austin's Old Three Hundred.* Austin, Tex: Eakin Press, 1999, 69.

20. 1860 *Texas Almanac*, 52.

21. Moseley Baker biographical sketch, Kemp Papers.

22. Foote, Henry Stuart. *Texas and the Texans* (2 volumes). Philadelphia: Thomas, Cowperthwait & Co., 1841, 282.

23. Jenkins, John Holland. *Papers of the Texas Revolution 1835–1836.* Ten Volumes. Austin, Tex: Presidial Press, 1973. See 4:460.

24. John Duncan, James Freele, Robert Justus Kleberg, Louis van Roeder biographical sketches, Kemp Papers.

25. Foote, *Texas and the Texans*, 283.

26. Baker letter published in *Telegraph*, March 12, 1836; Jenkins, *Papers*, 5:22–23.

27. Baker letter to Houston written in 1844; published in Barker, Eugene C. "The San Jacinto Campaign." *The Quarterly of the Texas State Historical Association*. Vol. 4, No. 4 (April 1901), 274.

28. J. H. Kuykendall, "Recollections of the Campaign," published in Barker, "The San Jacinto Campaign," 292–93.

29. Zuber, William Physick. *My Eighty Years in Texas.* Austin: University of Texas Press, 42–44.

30. Steele, Alfonso. *Biography of Private Alfonso Steele (Deceased). Last Survivor of the Battle of San Jacinto.* Privately published pamphlet, 3.

31. Zuber, *My Eighty Years in Texas,* 49.

32. Asbury, Samuel E. (Editor). "The Private Journal of Juan Nepomuceno Almonte." *Southwestern Historical Quarterly,* Vol. XLVIII, No. 1 (July 1944), 22–23.

33. Becerra, Francisco (as told to John S. Ford in 1875). *A Mexican Sergeant's Recollections of the Alamo & San Jacinto.* Austin, Tex: Jenkins Publishing Company, 1980, 24–25.

34. There is evidence that Crockett and five others were captured and executed within the Alamo. Lord, *A Time to Stand,* 206–207; Hardin, *Texian Iliad,* 148–49.

35. Filisola, Vicente. *Memoirs for the History of the War in Texas.* Translated by Wallace Woolsey. Austin, Tex: Eakin Press, 1985–1987, II:179.

36. Crawford, *The Eagle,* 51.

37. Lord, *A Time to Stand,* 207–208.

38. Ibid, 177–80.

CHAPTER 3
HOUSTON TAKES COMMAND

1. Chariton, Wallace O. *Exploring the Alamo Legends.* Plano, Tex: Wordware Publishing, Inc., 1992, 95–99.

2. King, *James Clinton Neill,* 100–101; Chariton, *Exploring the Alamo Legends,* 100.

3. Jenkins, *Papers,* 5:22–23.

4. Seguin, *A Revolution Remembered,* 107.

5. Connell O'Donnell Kelly biographical sketch, Kemp Papers.

6. Williams, Amelia W., and Eugene C. Barker. *Writings of Sam Houston.* Austin: The University of Texas Press, 1938–43, 4:367–68.

7. Jenkins, *Papers,* 5:22–23.

8. Ibid, 5:35–36.

9. Boethel, Paul C. *Colonel Amasa Turner. The Gentleman from Lavaca and Other Captains at San Jacinto.* Austin, Tex: Van Boeckmann-Jones, 1963, 12–13.

10. Haley, James L. *Sam Houston.* Norman: University of Oklahoma Press, 2002, 123–24.

11. Jenkins, *Papers,* 5:38–40.

12. Peña, José Enrique de la (Translated and edited by Carmen Perry). *With Santa Anna in Texas. A Personal Narrative of the Revolution.* College Station, Tex: Texas A&M University Press, 1975. Reprint. 1999, 65.

13. Filisola, *Memoirs,* II:205–208, 149–52.

14. James, *The Raven,* 190–91.

15. Jenkins, *Papers,* 5:69.

16. Jenkins, Recollections, 36–37.

17. Seguin, *A Revolution Remembered,* 107–108.

18. Chariton, *Exploring the Alamo Legends,* 65–68.

19. Jenkins, *Papers,* 5:48–49.

20. According to Houston, his spies "approached within twelve miles" of the Alamo. Jenkins, *Papers,* 5:53. Chariton, *Exploring the Alamo Legends,* 102–103.

21. Lawrence, Joseph. Account of Texas Revolution published in *Hallettsville Planter.* Source: Sons of DeWitt Colony Texas, late 1800s.

22. Seguin, *A Revolution Remembered,* 107.

23. *Texas Almanac* 1872.

24. Jenkins, *Papers*, 5:51–53.

CHAPTER 4
"FLYING IN TERROR AND AGONY"

1. *Texas Almanac* letter of 1872. Heard's company by April was officially Company F of the First Regiment.

2. John W. Hassell biographical sketch, Kemp Papers.

3. Zuber, *My Eighty Years in Texas*, 45–46.

4. Jenkins, *Papers*, 5:57.

5. Kokernot, D. L. "Reminiscences of Early Days in Texas." *Gonzales Inquirer*, August 17, 1878.

6. Jenkins, *Papers*, 5:63.

7. William Hester Patton biographical sketch, Kemp Papers.

8. Elbridge Gerry Rector biographical sketch, Kemp Papers.

9. John Smith biographical sketch, Kemp Papers.

10. Groneman, *Alamo Defenders*, 89–90.

11. Huston, Cleburne. *Deaf Smith: Incredible Texas Spy*. Waco, Tex: Texian Press, 1973, 51–52.

12. Tolbert, *The Day of San Jacinto*, 45.

13. Huston, *Deaf Smith: Incredible Texas Spy*, 53.

14. Jenkins, *Recollections*, 37–38.

15. Swisher, *The Swisher Memoirs*, 30–31.

16. Jenkins, *Papers*, 5:72.

17. Alexander Horton biographical sketch, Kemp Papers.

18. Jenkins, *Papers*, 5:69–70.

19. Connell O'Donnell Kelly biographical sketch, Kemp Papers.

20. Houston to Collinsworth, Brown, John Henry. *History of Texas from 1685 to 1892*. 2 vols. St. Louis: L. E. Daniell, Publisher, 1892–1893, 589.

21. Foote, *Texas and the Texans*, 267.

22. [Coleman], *Houston Displayed*, 12. N. D. Labadie, Labadie, "San Jacinto Campaign." 1859 *Texas Almanac*, 40. James, *The Raven*, 192. Pohl, James W. *The Battle of San Jacinto*. Texas State Historical Association, 1989, 10. Tolbert, *The Day of San Jacinto*, 46.

23. J. H. Kuykendall, "Recollections of the Campaign," as published in Barker, "The San Jacinto Campaign," 293–94.

24. Billingsley to *Galveston News*, published Saturday, September 19, 1857; see Billingsley biographical sketch in Kemp Papers.

25. James, *The Raven*, 192.

26. Foote, *Texas and the Texans*, 268.

27. Horace Eggleston biographical sketch, Kemp Papers.

28. Seguin, *A Revolution Remembered*, 107, 26.

29. Rodriquez, José María. "Memoirs of Early Texas." Memoirs of Judge Rodriquez and his father, Ambrosio Rodriquez were published by the family soon after his death in 1913 and were republished in 1961. Source: Sons of DeWitt Colony Texas.

30. Jenkins, *Recollections*, 39.

31. Labadie, "San Jacinto Campaign," 40–41.

32. Kokernot, "Reminiscences of Early Days in Texas."

33. J. H. Kuykendall, "Recollections of the Campaign," as published in Barker, "The San Jacinto Campaign," 294. 1859 Sherman to Billingsley letter, Jesse Billingsley biographical sketch in Kemp Papers.

34. J. H. Kuykendall, "Recollections of the Campaign," as published in Barker, "The San Jacinto Campaign," 295.

35. Awbrey, Betty Dooley, and Claude Dooley. *Why Stop? A Guide to Texas Historical Road-side Markers.* Houston, Tex: Lone Star Books, Fourth Edition, 1999. Reprint, 1978, 203.

36. Hunter, Robert Hancock. *Narrative of Robert Hancock Hunter.* Introduction by William D. Wittlif. 1936. Reprint, Austin: Encino Press, 1966, 9–10.

37. Nathaniel Townsend AC, R 106, F 168–69.

38. Hunter, *Narrative,* 11.

39. J. H. Kuykendall, "Recollections of the Campaign," as published in Barker, "The San Jacinto Campaign," 295.

40. Jenkins, *Recollections,* 40; Haley, *Sam Houston,* 126.

41. Billingsley to *Galveston News,* published Saturday, September 19, 1857; see Billingsley biographical sketch in Kemp Papers.

42. Private Swisher says that the army "reached Daniel's on the Lavaca about sundown." Swisher, *The Swisher Memoirs,* 31–32.

43. Tolbert, *The Day of San Jacinto,* 48–49.

44. Swisher, *The Swisher Memoirs,* 32.

45. Hardin, *Texian Iliad,* 164–65.

46. Guthrie, Keith. *Raw Frontier. Armed Conflict along the Texas Coastal Bend. Volume One.* Austin, Tex: Eakin Press, 1998, 66–67.

47. J. H. Kuykendall, "Recollections of the Campaign," as published in Barker, "The San Jacinto Campaign," 296.

48. Jenkins, *Papers,* 5:77–78.

49. James, *The Raven,* 193. James does not specifically list the widow's name and says that she had six children. See Groneman, *Alamo Defenders,* 80, and Jenkins, *Papers,* 5:168–70.

50. J. H. Kuykendall, "Recollections of the Campaign," as published in Barker, "The San Jacinto Campaign," 296.

51. Forbes v Labadie, R. B. Blake compilation, II:35.

52. DeBruhl, *The Sword of San Jacinto,* 188; Houston, *Writings,* I:372.

53. J. H. Kuykendall, "Recollections of the Campaign," as published in Barker, "The San Jacinto Campaign," 296. Splane's company is not specifically named, only "a squad of mounted men from the Brazos." The only other company which joined General Houston between Gonzales and the Colorado River was that of Captain Bird, which clearly joined the previous day at Peach Creek. Further support that Captain Splane's company was the one which had joined General Houston on March 15 is that one of his men, James D. Owen, was assisting Henry Karnes' scouts on March 20. See also Petyon R. Splane biographical sketch, Kemp Papers.

54. Dr. Fielding Deadrick biographical sketch, Kemp Papers. See also William P. Smith, Jesse Williams, Jonathan Douglass and Freeman Walker Douglass biographical sketches, Kemp Papers.

55. William W. Gant biographical sketch, Kemp Papers.

56. Asbury, Samuel E. (Editor). "The Private Journal of Juan Nepomuceno Almonte." *Southwestern Historical Quarterly,* Vol. XLVIII, No. 1 (July 1944), 24.

57. Peña, José Enrique de la (Translated and edited by Carmen Perry). *With Santa Anna in Texas. A Personal Narrative of the Revolution.* College Station, Tex: Texas A&M University Press, 1975. Reprint. 1999, 79–80.

58. Ibid, 66.

59. Filisola, *Memoirs,* II:208–209.

60. Jenkins, *Papers,* 5:57.

61. Zuber, *My Eighty Years in Texas,* 51–54.

62. Gillaspie to Rusk, May 29, 1836, in Jenkins, *Papers,* 6: #3195.

63. Zuber, *My Eighty Years in Texas,* 54–55.

64. William H. Smith AC, R 98, F 374.

65. Jenkins, *Papers*, 5:123.
66. Ibid, 5:92.
67. Ibid, 5:123.
68. Ibid, 5:98.
69. Ibid, 5:69, 71, 122.
70. Ibid, 5:122–23.
71. Ibid, 5:124.
72. Andrew Briscoe biographical sketch, Kemp Papers.
73. J. H. Kuykendall, "Recollections of the Campaign," as published in Barker, "The San Jacinto Campaign," 297.
74. Lack, Paul (Editor). *The Diary of William Fairfax Gray*, 123.
75. *The Handbook of Texas*, 2:402; Tolbert, *The Day of San Jacinto*, 41–43.
76. Jenkins, *Papers*, 5:125.
77. Moore, *Savage Frontier*, Volume 1:55–130, 21–22.
78. Paul Samuel Houston biographical sketch, Kemp Papers.
79. Jesse Halderman biographical sketch, Kemp Papers.
80. Moore, *Savage Frontier*, Volume 1:115–18.
81. J. H. Kuykendall, "Recollections of the Campaign," as published in Barker, "The San Jacinto Campaign," 297.
82. Foote, *Texas and the Texans*, 269–270. Scout John Sharp gave the name of one of these scouts as "Murphy." David Murphree, who later commanded a company during the San Jacinto campaign, was listed by some of his soldiers as "Murphy." For example, Thomas Corry later stated under oath in the Forbes vs. Labadie libel trial that he served under "David Murphy." The Columbia company to which Murphree belonged was largely mounted.
83. Henry W. Karnes AC, R 55, F 505.
84. Churchill Fulshear PE, R 215, F 659–61. Churchill Fulshear Sr. sketch in *Austin's Old Three Hundred*, 32–33.
85. Foote, *Texas and the Texans*, 269–270; Jenkins, *Papers*, 5:152. Although General Houston wrote on March 21 that Karnes "had with him at the time but five men," Sharp relates that there were actually nine. Houston's report refers to the fact that there were only six total men at the time Karnes and company encountered Mexican troops on March 20.

CHAPTER 5
SPARRING ALONG THE COLORADO

1. Hardin, *The Alamo 1836*, 58.
2. Hardin, *Texian Iliad*, 165.
3. Charles B. Shain biographical sketch, Kemp Papers. See Shain letter to his father of June 25, 1836.
4. Hardin, *The Alamo 1836*, 65.
5. Shain letter of June 25, 1836, Kemp Papers.
6. Hardin, *Texian Iliad*, 172–73.
7. O'Connor, Kathryn Stoner. *Presidio La Bahía 1721–1846*. Austin, Tex: Eakin Press, 2001, 134.
8. Awbrey, *Why Stop?* 103.
9. Foote, *Texas and the Texans*, 270.
10. Ibid, 270–71. Some sources list Karnes' fight as having occurred on March 19, based very likely on a campaign participant's memoirs written decades later from memory alone. Colonel George Hockley, however, wrote a report to the Secretary of War from Beason's camp on March 21, outlining the battle by Karnes which had occurred "yesterday."
11. Asbury (Editor), "The Private Journal of Juan Nepomuceno Almonte," 26–27.

12. J. H. Kuykendall, "Recollections of the Campaign," as published in Barker, "The San Jacinto Campaign," 297.

13. Jenkins, *Papers*, 5:152.

14. *Handbook of Texas*, II:150. See also R. Jones AC, R 54, F 638.

15. *Austin's Old Three Hundred*, 48–49.

16. Jethro Thomas Bancroft and John L. Lowary biographical sketches, Kemp Papers.

17. Labadie, "San Jacinto Campaign," 41–42.

18. William Mitchell Logan biographical sketch, Kemp Papers.

19. Labadie, "San Jacinto Campaign," 41–42.

20. Paul Samuel Houston biographical sketch, Kemp Papers.

21. Filisola, *Memoirs*, II:210–211.

22. William Bennett Scates biographical sketch, Kemp Papers.

23. Jenkins, *Papers*, 5:150.

24. John Campbell Hunt and Joseph Bell Chance biographical sketches, Kemp Papers.

25. Henry P. Redfield AC, R 87, F 54.

26. Jenkins, *Papers*, VI:#3194, Gates to Rusk.

27. Ibid, *Papers*, 5:150.

28. Winters, James Washington. "An Account of the Battle of San Jacinto." *SHQ*, October 1902, Vol. 6:139–40.

29. Kokernot, "Reminiscences of Early Days in Texas."

30. Townsend/Stapleton family genealogy from www.stapleton.cc website. See also Spencer Burton Townsend biographical sketch in Kemp Papers. Accessed October 2002.

31. Zuber, *My Eighty Years in Texas*, 56–58.

32. Paul Samuel Houston biographical sketch, Kemp Papers.

33. Lyman Frank Rounds biographical sketch, Kemp Papers.

34. Hockley to Rusk of March 23, 1836, in Jenkins, *Papers*, 5:167.

35. Kuykendall, "Recollections," 298.

36. Of these men, I previously listed in *Savage Frontier, Volume 1* Daniel Doubt as the seventh man accompanying Sadler to the army. Of these seven Doubt is most in doubt, with no conclusive proof found as to when he joined Captain Leander Smith's Nacogdoches Volunteers. His records, like most of the Nacogdoches Volunteers, show only that he served from March 6. Most all men who served in this unit show this enlistment date on their audited claims or pension papers, even those men who clearly did not join the unit on March 6 in Nacogdoches. John W. Carpenter, who had been granted land near Fort Houston in 1835 and who later served with the cavalry, is more likely to have been the seventh man under Sadler who joined at DeWees. For more detail on Sadler's company, see Moore, *Savage Frontier*, 1:65–66, 108–110 and Moore, *Taming Texas*, 39–49.

37. Jenkins, *Recollections*, 41; Jenkins, *Papers*, 5:154.

38. Jenkins, *Papers*, 5:152–53.

39. Hunter, *Narrative*, 11.

40. Jenkins, *Papers*, 5:154.

41. Benjamin Fort Smith biographical sketch, Kemp Papers.

42. Calder, R. J. "Recollections of the Texas Campaign of 1836." 1861 *Texas Almanac*, 62–63.

43. Kuykendall, "Recollections," 298.

44. Calder, "Recollections of the Texas Campaign of 1836," 63.

45. Labadie, "San Jacinto Campaign," 43.

46. Foote, *Texas and the Texans*, 273.

47. Calder, "Recollections of the Texas Campaign of 1836," 63.

48. Jenkins, *Papers*, 5:158.

49. Jenkins, *Papers*, 5:167.

50. Kuykendall, "Recollections," 298.

51. Jenkins, *Papers*, 5:167.

52. Lack, *The Diary of William Fairfax Gray*, 142.
53. Jenkins, *Papers*, 5:170–71.
54. Ibid, 5:167, 170.
55. Ibid, 5:168–70.

Chapter 6
Falling Back

1. Baker letter to Houston written in 1844; published in Barker, "The San Jacinto Campaign," 277. See also 1860 *Texas Almanac*, 57–58.
2. Menchaca, "Memoirs," I:9.
3. Calder, "Recollections of the Texas Campaign of 1836," 63.
4. Gambrell, Herbert. *Anson Jones: The Last President of Texas*. Austin: University of Texas Press, 1988 reprint. 1947. Reprint, 61. See also *Biographical Directory of the Texan Conventions and Congresses*, 117.
5. *Biographical Directory of the Texan Conventions and Congresses*, 189. *Handbook of Texas*, II:888–89.
6. Houston speech given in United States Senate on February 29, 1859; James Hazard Perry biographical sketch, Kemp Papers.
7. Foote, *Texas and the Texans*, 278.
8. Jenkins, *Papers*, 5:209–210.
9. Ebenezer R. Hale AC, R 39, F 334.
10. De la Peña, *With Santa Anna in Texas*, 66, 80.
11. Alexander Horton biographical sketch, Kemp Papers.
12. Zuber, *My Eighty Years in Texas*, 61; 1860 *Texas Almanac*, 58; Labadie, "San Jacinto Campaign," 43.
13. Jenkins, *Papers*, 5:254.
14. Barker, "The San Jacinto Campaign," 245.
15. Moseley Baker letter to Houston written in 1844; published in Barker, "The San Jacinto Campaign," 277.
16. Jenkins, *Papers*, 5:200.
17. 1860 *Texas Almanac*, 56–57.
18. Ben C. Franklin to Sidney Sherman, June 29, 1859, in Sherman, "Defence," 27. William C. Swearingen biographical sketch, Kemp Papers. Anson Jones to Sidney Sherman, August 21, 1855, in Sherman, "Defence," 23.
19. Shipman, Daniel. *Frontier Life. 58 Years in Texas*. 1879. Reprint, The Abbotsford Publishing Co., Pasadena, Tex: 1965, 126–28.
20. 1860 *Texas Almanac*, 57.
21. Swisher, *The Swisher Memoirs*, 33–34.
22. Baker letter to Houston written in 1844; published in Barker, "The San Jacinto Campaign," 280. Pohl, *The Battle of San Jacinto*, 12.
23. Foote, *Texas and the Texans*, 280.
24. Zuber, *My Eighty Years in Texas*, 62.
25. Madison G. Whitaker PP, R 245, F 207.
26. Asa Hoxey AC, R 48, F 158.
27. John Harvey biographical sketch, Kemp Papers.
28. Some of Sadler's men show that they joined the Nacogdoches Volunteers on March 6, although this is actually the date that the company was formed. Many men serving under Captain Leander Smith and the company's subsequent commander, Hayden Arnold, were given papers listing March 6 when they clearly were not present for the company's original mustering. William T. Sadler PP, R 237, F 95; Daniel Parker Jr. PP, R 232, F 300. See also Moore, *Taming Texas*, 51, and *Savage Frontier*, I:115–16.

29. Bate, *General Sidney Sherman*, 243. Arnold would assume command from Leander Smith within days.

30. Zuber, *My Eighty Years in Texas*, 62–63.

31. Kuykendall, "Recollections," 298–99.

32. Zuber, *My Eighty Years in Texas*, 63.

33. Boethel, Paul C. *Colonel Amasa Turner. The Gentleman from Lavaca and Other Captains at San Jacinto.* Austin, Tex: Van Boeckmann-Jones, 1963, 21–22.

34. Ellis Benson biographical sketch in Kemp Papers.

35. James Wharton biographical sketch, Kemp Papers.

36. John Forbes biographical sketch, Kemp Papers.

37. Calder, "Recollections of the Texas Campaign of 1836," 63.

38. Kuykendall, "Recollections," 300.

39. Zuber, *My Eighty Years in Texas*, 63–64.

40. Kuykendall, "Recollections," 300.

41. John Walker Baylor biographical sketch, Kemp Papers.

42. Labadie, "San Jacinto Campaign," 44. Zuber, *My Eighty Years in Texas*, 64.

43. Castañeda, *The Mexican Side of the Texan Revolution*, 234–35.

44. Guthrie, *Raw Frontier*, 81–82.

45. Hardin, *Texian Iliad*, 173–74.

46. Guthrie, *Raw Frontier*, 78–83. Duval, John C. Edited by Mabel Major and Rebecca W. Smith. *Early Times in Texas.* Lincoln: University of Nebraska Press, 1986, 89–99.

47. Hamilton, Lester. *Goliad Survivor.* San Antonio, Tex: The Naylor Company, 1971, 3–9. Sowell, A. J. *Rangers and Pioneers of Texas.* 1884. Reprint. New York: Argosy-Antiquarian Ltd., 1964. Sowell on pages 160–68 quotes Cooper's account from the 1881 "American Sketch Book."

48. Jenkins, *Papers*, 5:367–68.

49. Charles B. Shain letter published in June 30, 1836, *Louisville Journal;* see Kemp Papers.

50. Charles B. Shain biographical sketch, Kemp Papers.

51. Nathaniel C. Hazen biographical sketch, Kemp Papers.

52. Daniel Murphy biographical sketch, Kemp Papers.

53. O'Connor, *Presidio La Bahia*, 142–43; Hardin, *Texian Iliad*, 173–74.

54. Jenkins, *Papers*, 5:209.

CHAPTER 7
"INTENSELY HUNGRY, WEARY AND WET"

1. Isaac Lafayette Hill biographical sketch, Kemp Papers.

2. Jacob Eberly AC, R 28, F 322–330. See also Basil G. Ijams AC, R 50, F 201–211.

3. Joseph Urban AC, R 107, F 287–300.

4. Nathaniel Townsend AC, R 106, 103–150.

5. Jenkins, *Papers*, 5:234.

6. Tolbert, *The Day of San Jacinto*, 51–52.

7. Tarlton letter of November 6, 1855, printed in the 1860 *Texas Almanac*, 57.

8. Baker letter to Houston written in 1844; published in Barker, "The San Jacinto Campaign," 279.

9. Labadie, "San Jacinto Campaign," 44.

10. Haley, *Sam Houston*, 130.

11. Baker letter to Houston written in 1844; published in Barker, "The San Jacinto Campaign," 279.

12. Jenkins, *Papers*, 5:216.

13. Hiram Thompson AC, R 104, F 350.

14. Hunter, *Narrative*, 13.

15. Robert P. Stewart AC, R 101, F 85; Nathan Brookshire AC, R 11, F 608; John M. Hensley PP, R 220, F141; George Herder PP, R 220, F 228. George H. Roberts PP, R 235, F 602–604.

16. Seguin, *A Revolution Remembered*, 108.

17. Billingsley to *Galveston News*, published Saturday, September 19, 1857; see Billingsley biographical sketch in Kemp Papers.

18. Pohl, *The Battle of San Jacinto*, 12.

19. Labadie, "San Jacinto Campaign," 43.

20. William C. Swearingen biographical sketch, Kemp Papers.

21. Jenkins, *Papers*, 5:223.

22. Lack, *The Diary of William Fairfax Gray*, 136–140.

23. Baker letter to Houston written in 1844; published in Barker, "The San Jacinto Campaign," 280.

24. Isaac Lafayette Hill biographical sketch, Kemp Papers.

25. Foote, *Texas and the Texans*, 283.

26. Baker letter to Houston written in 1844; published in Barker, "The San Jacinto Campaign," 279; 1860 *Texas Almanac*, 59.

27. Bostick, Sion Record. "Reminiscences of Sion R. Bostick." *The Quarterly of the Texas State Historical Association*. Vol. V (October 1901), No. 2, 91. Zuber, *My Eighty Years in Texas*, 74. William C. Swearingen biographical sketch, Kemp Papers.

28. Isaac Lafayette Hill from *Texas State Historical Association Quarterly*, Vol. 7 and Kemp Papers.

29. Yoakum, *History of Texas*, II:268.

30. Hill from *Texas State Historical Association Quarterly*, Vol. 7 and Kemp Papers.

31. Jeremiah D. Cochran biographical sketch, Kemp Papers.

32. Labadie, "San Jacinto Campaign," 44–45.

33. Kuykendall, "Recollections," 300–301.

34. Jenkins, *Papers*, 5:234–35.

35. Jenkins, *Papers*, 5:344.

36. Lack, *The Diary of William Fairfax Gray*, 144–45.

37. Jenkins, *Papers*, 5:287.

38. Ibid, 5:235–36.

39. Kuykendall, "Recollections," 301.

40. Jenkins, *Papers*, 5:287.

41. Zuber, *My Eighty Years in Texas*, 65.

42. Jenkins, *Papers*, 5:287.

43. William Kimbro biographical sketch, Kemp Papers.

44. *Compendium, 1872 Texas Almanac*, 655.

45. Ibid, 652–53.

46. Josephus Somerville Irvine biographical sketch, Kemp Papers.

47. Jenkins, *Papers*, 5:404; Coleman, *Houston Displayed*, 13.

48. Zuber, *My Eighty Years in Texas*, 67.

49. Jenkins, *Papers*, 5:253.

50. Ibid, 5:254–55, 286.

51. Thomas F. Corry biographical sketch, Kemp Papers. Also Forbes v Labadie trial, R. B. Blake compilation, Volume Two: "Sidelights on the Battle of San Jacinto," 1–9.

52. Jenkins, *Papers*, 5: 253, 286.

53. Labadie, "San Jacinto Campaign," 44.

54. Jenkins, *Papers*, 5:286–87.

55. Zuber, *My Eighty Years in Texas*, 66.

56. Jenkins, *Papers*, 5:268.

57. James, *The Raven*, 196.

58. Jenkins, *Papers*, 5:286.

59. Jackson, Donald. *Voyages of the Steamboat Yellow Stone*. New York: Ticknor & Fields, 1985, 124–27.

60. Ibid, 160–63.

61. Jenkins, *Papers*, 5:295, 309. Jackson, *Voyages of the Steamboat Yellow Stone*, 128.

62. Calder, "Recollections of the Texas Campaign of 1836," 64.

63. Pohl, *The Battle of San Jacinto*, 14.

64. Madison G. Whitaker PP, R 245, F 207. Leander Smith was paid as "Major Artillery" from April 1 to April 17, 1836, Leander Smith AC, R 130, F 218–20.

65. William C. Hallmark PP, R 218, F 640.

66. Jenkins, *Papers*, 5:245.

67. Thomas F. Corry biographical sketch, Kemp Papers.

68. *The Handbook of Texas*, II:812–13.

69. Jenkins, *Papers*, 5:245.

70. Jenkins, *Papers*, 5:288.

71. Filisola, *Memoirs*, II: 205–206.

72. de la Peña, *With Santa Anna in Texas*, 96.

73. Pohl, *The Battle of San Jacinto*, 11; Filisola, *Memoirs*, II: 210.

74. de la Peña, *With Santa Anna in Texas*, 96.

75. Filisola, *Memoirs*, II: 219.

76. Crawford, *The Eagle*, 52.

77. Filisola, *Memoirs*, II: 219.

78. Crawford, *The Eagle*, 52.

79. Jenkins, *Papers*, 5:294.

80. Christopher Columbus Bruff biographical sketch, Kemp Papers.

81. *Austin's Old Three Hundred*, 63.

82. Jenkins, *Papers*, 5:296.

83. William Mosby Eastland biographical sketch, Kemp Papers.

84. Ebenezer R. Hale AC, R 39, F 347–57. Hale had entered service with Perry's company on March 6.

85. Moseley Baker biographical sketch, Kemp Papers.

86. Samuel G. Hardaway biographical sketch, Kemp Papers.

87. Isaac Lafayette Hill from *Texas State Historical Association Quarterly*, Vol. 7 and Kemp Papers.

88. Jenkins, *Papers*, 5:297–300.

89. Ibid, 5:300–301.

90. Ibid, 5:323; Daughters of the Republic of Texas, *Muster Rolls*, 172.

91. DeBruhl, *The Sword of San Jacinto*, 197; Haley, *Sam Houston*, 135.

CHAPTER 8
CAMPING IN THE BRAZOS SWAMPS

1. Jenkins, *Papers*, 5:308.

2. Ibid, 5:309–310.

3. Ibid, 5:404.

4. Lack, *The Diary of William Fairfax Gray*, 144; 1860 *Texas Almanac*, 59.

5. Jenkins, *Papers*, 5:310–311.

6. Calder, "Recollections of the Texas Campaign of 1836," 64; Kuykendall, "Recollections," 301.

7. Swisher, *The Swisher Memoirs*, 36.

8. Hunter, *Narrative*, 13.

9. Swisher, *The Swisher Memoirs*, 37.

10. Jenkins, *Papers*, 5:321.
11. Ibid, 5:313.
12. Ibid, 5:320.
13. Ibid, 5:322–323.
14. Ibid, 5:319.
15. Ibid, 5:321.
16. Ibid, 5:320.
17. Pohl, *The Battle of San Jacinto*, 15.
18. Erath, George Bernard, as dictated to Lucy A. Erath. "The Memoirs of Major George Bernard Erath." *Southwestern Historical Quarterly*, Vol. 26, 255.
19. Swisher, *The Swisher Memoirs*, 35.
20. Erath, "Memoirs," 261–62.
21. Jenkins, *Papers*, 5:330.
22. Ibid, 5:330–32.
23. Linn, John Joseph. *Reminiscences of Fifty Years in Texas*. New York: D.&J. Sadlier & Co., 1883, 247–252.
24. Jenkins, *Papers*, 5:333–34.
25. Henry Dibble and James Green biographical sketches, Kemp Papers.
26. Jenkins, *Papers*, 5:335.
27. Ibid, 5:344.
28. Haley, *Sam Houston*, 132–33.
29. Jenkins, *Papers*, 5:334.
30. Jenkins, *Papers*, 5:380.
31. Alfred Henderson Wyly biographical sketch, Kemp Papers.
32. John Balch biographical sketch, Kemp Papers.
33. Jenkins, *Papers*, 5:364–65.
34. Ibid, 5:343.
35. Ibid, 5:349.
36. Labadie, "San Jacinto Campaign," 45.
37. Gambrell, *Anson Jones*, 64.
38. Labadie, "San Jacinto Campaign," 46.
39. Jenkins, *Papers*, 5:344. Basil G. Ijams AC, R 50, F 201–211.
40. John T. White PE, R 245, F 298.
41. Jacob Eberly UC, R 250, F 519. William Godden, commissary for Major Morehouse's battalion, certified the loss of Eberly's liquors, but the Republic of Texas did not pay him on this claim.
42. Algernon P. Thompson and Dr. James Hazard Perry biographical sketches, Kemp Papers.
43. Jenkins, *Papers*, 5:346.
44. Nathaniel Townsend AC, R 106, F 104–136.
45. Filisola, *Memoirs*, II:220.
46. Tolbert, *The Day of San Jacinto*, 66; Bostick, "Reminiscences," 91.
47. Isaac Lafayette Hill from *Texas State Historical Association Quarterly*, Vol. 7 and Kemp Papers.
48. Jenkins, *Papers*, V:407.
49. Castañeda, Carlos Eduardo (Translator). *The Mexican Side of the Texas Revolution (1836) By the Chief Mexican Participants*. Recollections of General Antonio Lopez de Santa Anna, Secretary Ramón Martínez Caro, General Vicente Filisola, General José Urrea, and General José María Tornel. Dallas, Tex.: P. L. Turner Company, 109.
50. Jenkins, *Papers*, 5:363.
51. Ibid, 5:362.
52. Robinson, Duncan W. *Judge Robert McAlpin Williamson. Texas' Three-Legged Willie.* Austin: Texas State Historical Society, 1948, 144–45.
53. Jenkins, *Papers*, 5:366–67.

54. Ibid, 5:362.

55. Ibid, 5:360–61.

56. Ibid, 5:365–66.

57. Isaac Lafayette Hill from *Texas State Historical Association Quarterly*, Vol. 7 and Kemp Papers.

58. Jenkins, *Papers*, 5:369.

59. Ibid, 5:407; Tolbert, *The Day of San Jacinto*, 67.

60. Isaac Lafayette Hill biographical sketch, Kemp Papers.

61. Filisola, *Memoirs*, II:221.

62. Kuykendall, "Recollections," 301. Tolbert, *The Day of San Jacinto*, 80–82.

63. Jenkins, *Papers*, 382.

64. Ibid, 5:360–61, 382.

65. Ebenezer R. Hale AC, R 39, F 345.

66. Labadie, "San Jacinto Campaign," 46.

67. Jenkins, *Papers*, 5:391–93.

68. Ibid, 5:406–408.

69. Ibid, 5:404.

70. Filisola, *Memoirs*, II:221.

71. Castañeda, *The Mexican Side of the Texas Revolution*, 111; Asbury, "The Private Journal of Juan Nepomuceno Almonte," 31.

72. Pohl, *The Battle of San Jacinto*, 20–21; Tolbert, *The Day of San Jacinto*, 68–69, 89.

73. Asbury, "The Private Journal of Juan Nepomuceno Almonte," 31–32.

74. Jenkins, *Papers*, 5:415.

75. Ibid, 5:417.

76. Ibid, 5:427.

77. Burnet wrote these recollections for the September 6, 1836 *Telegraph* at Houston. See also 1860 *Texas Almanac*, 60.

78. 1860 *Texas Almanac*, 60.

79. Pohl, *The Battle of San Jacinto*, 13.

CHAPTER 9
"I WILL AVENGE THE DEATH OF MY BRAVE FRIENDS"

1. Jenkins, *Papers*, 5:451.

2. Ibid, 5:451.

3. Ibid, 5:428.

4. Ibid, 5:434–35.

5. Ibid, 5:406–408.

6. Haley, *Sam Houston*, 137.

7. James Hazard Perry biographical sketch, Kemp Papers.

8. [Coleman], *Houston Displayed*, 17.

9. Jenkins, *Papers*, 5:436.

10. Jackson, *Voyages of the Steamboat Yellow Stone*, 128–29.

11. Jenkins, *Papers*, 5:436.

12. Day, *The Texas Almanac 1857–1873*, 660.

13. Charles B. Shain account published in June 30, 1836, *Louisville Journal*; see his biographical sketch, Kemp Papers.

14. Labadie, "San Jacinto Campaign," 45.

15. [Coleman], *Houston Displayed*, 13.

16. Zuber, *My Eighty Years in Texas*, 70. Charles B. Shain account published in June 30, 1836, *Louisville Journal*; see his biographical sketch, Kemp Papers.

17. Jenkins, *Papers*, 5:440–41.

18. Ibid, 5:451.
19. Ibid, 5:454–55.
20. Gulick, *Lamar Papers*, III: No. 1645.
21. Jenkins, *Papers*, 5:450.
22. Ibid, 6:100.
23. Wharton, Clarence. *San Jacinto. The Sixteenth Decisive Battle.* Houston, Tex: Lamar Book Store, 1930, 123–25.
24. Jenkins, *Papers*, 5:444–45.
25. 1860 *Texas Almanac*, 61.
26. Pohl, *The Battle of San Jacinto*, 20–21.
27. Paul Samuel Houston biographical sketch, Kemp Papers.
28. [Coleman], *Houston Displayed*, 15.
29. Jenkins, *Papers*, 5:456–57.
30. Sparks, Stephen Franklin. "Recollections of S. F. Sparks." *Quarterly of the Texas State Historical Association*. XII: No. 1 (July 1908), 61–66.
31. Swisher, *Memoirs*, 38.
32. Paul Samuel Houston biographical sketch, Kemp Papers. Foote, *Texas and the Texans*, 295–96.
33. Winters, "An Account of the Battle of San Jacinto," 140.
34. Labadie, "San Jacinto Campaign," 46.
35. Gambrell, *Anson Jones*, 65, quoting from Anson Jones' "Private Memoirs." Jones actually entered the date as April 15, although the army had long since left Groce's by that time. See also Anson Jones biographical sketch, Kemp Papers.

CHAPTER 10
"THE LAST HOPE OF TEXAS"

1. Ramsay, Jack C. Jr. *Thunder beyond the Brazos. Mirabeau B. Lamar: A Biography.* Austin: Eakin Press, 1985, 1–2. Jenkins, *Papers*, 5:216.
2. Kuykendall, "Recollections," 302; Menchaca, "Memoirs," II:2.
3. Jenkins, *Papers*, 5:422–23.
4. Pohl, *The Battle of San Jacinto*, 17; Tolbert, *The Day of San Jacinto*, 86.
5. Asbury, "The Private Journal of Juan Nepomuceno Almonte," 32.
6. Zuber, *My Eighty Years in Texas*, 76.
7. Filisola, *Memoirs*, II:221.
8. De la Peña, *With Santa Anna in Texas*, 102–103.
9. Delgado, Col. Pedro. "Mexican Account of the Battle of San Jacinto." Published in 1870 *Texas Almanac*. See pp. 613–629 of Day, James M. (Compiler). *The Texas Almanac 1857–1873. A Compendium of Texas History.* Waco, Tex: Texian Press, 1967. See also Barker, "The San Jacinto Campaign," 287.
10. Jenkins, *Papers*, 5:461–62.
11. De la Peña, *With Santa Anna in Texas*, 105–106.
12. Jackson, *Voyages of the Steamboat Yellow Stone*, 131–33.
13. Filisola, *Memoirs*, II:221–22.
14. Pohl, *The Battle of San Jacinto*, 16, 25; Tolbert, *The Day of San Jacinto*, 77.
15. Delgado, "Mexican Account of the Battle of San Jacinto," 613.
16. Jenkins, *Papers*, 5:453.
17. Ibid, 5:460–61.
18. Labadie, "San Jacinto Campaign," 47.
19. Jenkins, *Papers*, 5:465–66.
20. Ibid, 5:466.
21. Ibid, 5:468–470.

22. Ibid, 5:489. A search of Republic of Texas audited military claims revealed only one McDermott in service of the Texas Army during the San Jacinto campaign. William McDermott served the military between March 20 and September 21, 1836.

23. Paul Samuel Houston biographical sketch, Kemp Papers.

24. Jenkins, *Papers*, 5:472.

25. Sparks, "Recollections," 67.

26. *Texas Almanac*, "Compendium," 647.

27. Rose, Victor Marion. *The Life and Services of Gen. Ben McCullough*. Philadelphia: Pictorial Bureau of the Press, 1888; facsimile reproduction, The Steck Company, Publishers, Austin, Tex: 1958, 40–43.

28. Swisher, *Memoirs*, 38.

29. [Coleman], *Houston Displayed*, 17.

30. Baker letter to Houston written in 1844; published in Barker, "The San Jacinto Campaign," 281. Isaac Lafayette Hill biographical sketch, Kemp Papers.

31. Zuber, *My Eighty Years in Texas*, 76–77.

32. Ibid, 77–79.

33. Jenkins, *Papers*, 5:484–85.

34. Ibid, 5:473.

35. Ibid, 5:474–75.

36. Zuber, *My Eighty Years in Texas*, 79.

37. Haley, *Sam Houston*, 138.

38. Paul Samuel Houston biographical sketch, Kemp Papers.

39. James, *The Raven*, 202. William C. Swearingen biographical sketch, Kemp Papers.

40. Zuber, *My Eighty Years in Texas*, 80.

41. Labadie, "San Jacinto Campaign," 47. T. C. Edwards PE, R 213, F 687.

42. [Coleman], *Houston Displayed*, 17.

43. Delgado, "Mexican Account of the Battle of San Jacinto," 613–14.

44. Becerra, *A Mexican Sergeant's Recollections of the Alamo & San Jacinto*, 43–44.

45. Delgado, "Mexican Account of the Battle of San Jacinto," 614.

46. Filisola, *Memoirs*, II:222; Tolbert, *The Day of San Jacinto*, 70.

47. John Plunkett to Abiather Holt, July 17, 1836, in Kemp Papers.

48. [Coleman], *Houston Displayed*, 18.

49. Paul Samuel Houston biographical sketch, Kemp Papers.

CHAPTER 11
THE ROAD TO SAN JACINTO

1. Zuber, *My Eighty Years in Texas*, 80.

2. Billingsley to *Galveston News*, published Saturday, September 19, 1857; see Billingsley biographical sketch in Kemp Papers.

3. 1860 *Texas Almanac*, 62.

4. Pohl, *The Battle of San Jacinto*, 22.

5. Labadie, "San Jacinto Campaign," 47–48.

6. Calder, "Recollections of the Texas Campaign of 1836," 64.

7. 1860 *Texas Almanac*, 62, quoting James Robinson letter of January 4, 1847.

8. 1859 Sherman to Billingsley letter, Jesse Billingsley biographical sketch in Kemp Papers.

9. Paul Samuel Houston biographical sketch, Kemp Papers.

10. 1860 *Texas Almanac*, 61–62.

11. Ibid.

12. Jenkins, *Papers*, 5:492.

13. Labadie, "San Jacinto Campaign," 47.

14. Hunter, *Narrative*, 13–14.

15. Winters, "An Account of the Battle of San Jacinto." SHQ, October 1902, Vol. 6:140.

16. Houston-hater Robert Coleman in *Houston Displayed*, 18, claims that General Houston had "cannon fever," fearing enemy cannon when he heard the first boom of thunder.

17. "Recollections of S. F. Sparks," 68–69.

18. [Coleman], *Houston Displayed*, 18–19.

19. Hunter, *Narrative*, 14–15.

20. Winters, "An Account of the Battle of San Jacinto." SHQ, October 1902, Vol. 6:140.

21. Tolbert, *The Day of San Jacinto*, 71–73.

22. Dr. George M. Patrick's letter was reprinted in the *Telegraph and Texas Register* on August 25, 1841.

23. Pohl, *The Battle of San Jacinto*, 26.

24. Filisola, *Memoirs*, II:220.

25. Delgado, "Mexican Account of the Battle of San Jacinto," 614.

26. Jenkins, *Papers*, 5:487–88.

27. [Coleman], *Houston Displayed*, 18.

28. Kuykendall, "Recollections," 303.

29. Labadie, "San Jacinto Campaign," 48.

30. [Coleman], *Houston Displayed*, 19; Kuykendall, "Recollections," 303.

31. Labadie, "San Jacinto Campaign," 48.

32. "Recollections of S. F. Sparks," 69.

33. Delgado, "Mexican Account of the Battle of San Jacinto," 614.

34. De la Peña, *With Santa Anna in Texas*, 114.

35. Jenkins, *Papers*, 5:497.

36. Filisola, *Memoirs*, II:222.

37. Delgado, "Mexican Account of the Battle of San Jacinto," 614.

38. Tolbert, *The Day of San Jacinto*, 73–75.

39. Delgado, "Mexican Account of the Battle of San Jacinto," 615.

40. De la Peña, *With Santa Anna in Texas*, 113, 123.

41. Turner, Martha Anne. *The Yellow Rose of Texas. Her Saga and Her Song. With the Santa Anna Legend*. Austin, Tex: Shoal Creek Publishers, Inc., 9–10.

42. Tolbert, *The Day of San Jacinto*, 76–78. Filisola, *Memoirs*, II:223.

43. Labadie, "San Jacinto Campaign," 48; Hunter, *Narrative*, 15; Zuber, *My Eighty Years in Texas*, 80.

44. Huston, *Deaf Smith*, 68–69.

45. Bryan to Sherman, July 2, 1859, in Sherman, "Defence," 29.

46. Menchaca, "Memoirs," II:2.

47. Zuber, *My Eighty Years in Texas*, 84. Tolbert, 94–96. Calder, "Recollections of the Texas Campaign of 1836," 64.

48. William C. Swearingen biographical sketch, Kemp Papers.

49. [Coleman], *Houston Displayed*, 19.

50. Labadie, "San Jacinto Campaign," 48. Calder, "Recollections of the Texas Campaign of 1836," 64.

51. Sparks, "Recollections," 69–70.

52. Lane, Walter Paye. *The Adventures and Recollections of General Walter P. Lane*. Austin, Tex: Pemberton Press, 1970, 7–9.

CHAPTER 12
"DETERMINED TO CONQUER OR DIE"

1. Labadie, "San Jacinto Campaign," 48–49.

2. Anson Jones biographical sketch, Kemp Papers.

3. Robert Stevenson biographical sketch, Kemp Papers.

4. David Murphree biographical sketch, Kemp Papers.
5. Kuykendall, "Recollections," 303.
6. Zuber, *My Eighty Years in Texas*, 85.
7. Ganey Crosby AC, R 21, F 744.
8. Sylvanus Cottle AC, R 20, F 694.
9. Moses Townsend PD, R 191, F 460–463.
10. William Sherrod AC, R 95, F 405–406; Moore, *Savage Frontier*, 1:117–19.
11. Daniel T. Dunham AC, R 27, F 382; Francis M. Weatherred AC, R 111, F 207–209.
12. Alfred Kelso biographical sketch, Kemp Papers.
13. Zuber, *My Eighty Years in Texas*, 85–86.
14. Ellis Benson biographical sketch in Kemp Papers.
15. Kuykendall, "Recollections," 303–304.
16. Menchaca, "Memoirs," II:3–4.
17. Pohl, *The Battle of San Jacinto*, 26–27.
18. Jenkins, *Papers*, 5:504–505.
19. [Coleman], *Houston Displayed*, 19.
20. Billingsley to *Galveston News*, published Saturday, September 19, 1857; see Billingsley biographical sketch in Kemp Papers.
21. Jenkins, *Papers*, 5:503.
22. Dixon and Kemp, *The Heroes of San Jacinto*, 345; John Harvey biographical sketch, Kemp Papers.
23. Isaac Lafayette Hill biographical sketch, Kemp Papers.
24. Labadie, "San Jacinto Campaign," 49; Erath, "Memoirs," 264.
25. James, *The Raven*, 203.
26. Tolbert, *The Day of San Jacinto*, 97–99.
27. Isaac Lafayette Hill biographical sketch, Kemp Papers; Tolbert, *The Day of San Jacinto*, 99; Bryan to Sherman, July 2, 1859, in Sherman, "Defence," 30; Menchaca, "Memoirs," II:4–5.
28. Labadie, "San Jacinto Campaign," 49.
29. Denham letter from camp at San Jacinto of May 3, 1836; see M. H. Denham biographical sketch, Kemp Papers.
30. Winters, "An Account of the Battle of San Jacinto." SHQ, October 1902, Vol. 6: 140–41.
31. Steele, *Biography of Private Alfonso Steele*, 4.
32. 1859 Sherman to Billingsley letter, Jesse Billingsley biographical sketch in Kemp Papers.
33. Jenkins, *Papers*, 5:504.
34. Seguin, *A Revolution Remembered*, 26.
35. Menchaca, "Memoirs," II:5. Seguin, *A Revolution Remembered*, 108.
36. William C. Swearingen biographical sketch, Kemp Papers.
37. Houston speech given in United States Senate on February 29, 1859; James Hazard Perry biographical sketch, Kemp Papers.
38. Labadie, "San Jacinto Campaign," 49.
39. [Coleman], *Houston Displayed*, 19.
40. Swisher, *The Swisher Memoirs*, 40. Denham letter from camp at San Jacinto of May 3, 1836; see M. H. Denham biographical sketch, Kemp Papers.
41. Labadie, "San Jacinto Campaign," 49.

CHAPTER 13

THE FIRST ENGAGEMENT

1. Winters, "An Account of the Battle of San Jacinto," 141.
2. Pohl, *The Battle of San Jacinto*, 27.

3. George J. Brown biographical sketch, Kemp Papers, citing Wooten's *Comprehensive History of Texas*.

4. Labadie, "San Jacinto Campaign," 49.

5. William C. Swearingen biographical sketch, Kemp Papers.

6. Calder, "Recollections of the Texas Campaign of 1836," 64. Labadie, "San Jacinto Campaign," 49.

7. Swisher, *The Swisher Memoirs*, 40; Erath, "Memoirs," 262.

8. Labadie, "San Jacinto Campaign," 49.

9. Forbes v Labadie, R. B. Blake compilation, II:14.

10. Labadie, "San Jacinto Campaign," 49–50.

11. Menchaca, "Memoirs," II:5.

12. Labadie, "San Jacinto Campaign," 49–50.

13. Harris, Dilue Rose. "Reminiscences of Mrs. Dilue Harris." *Southwestern Historical Quarterly* 4 (October 1900, January 1901), 171–74.

14. Labadie, "San Jacinto Campaign," 50. The 1860 volume of the *Texas Almanac*, page 63, gives this version of the "capture" of Turner:

> Santa Anna was unapprised of his proximity to the Texian main army.
>
> Gen. Houston and the Texian army learned [this] on the morning of the 20th, from a youth captured by the Mexicans at Harrisburg. He was an intelligent boy, employed in the printing office. Santa Anna, after the burning of New Washington, gave him a horse and money to go and find Gen. Houston. On his way from New-Washington, he learned from a negro woman that the Texians were near Lynchburg, on the bayou. Availing himself of the first opportunity, and the speed of his horse, he escaped from the Mexicans, who were in company, and came into the camp, and communicated the fact of the approach of Santa Anna.

15. Seguin, *A Revolution Remembered*, 108–109.

16. Delgado, "Mexican Account of the Battle of San Jacinto," 615; Filisola, *Memoirs*, II:223; Castañeda, *The Mexican Side of the Texas Revolution*, 112–13.

17. Hardin, *Texian Iliad*, 200.

18. Robert Stevenson letter of April 23, 1836; Kemp Papers; James, *The Raven*, 204–205.

19. Pohl, *The Battle of San Jacinto*, 28.

20. Franklin, Benjamin Cromwell. "The Battle of San Jacinto. By One Who Fought in It." *Little's Living Age*, September 7, 1844, 259–265. This article was written anonymously by Franklin in 1837 and reprinted in 1844. His article gives enough clues to verify his identity. He states that President Burnet appointed him in command of a small group of men on Galveston. Records show that Franklin was commissioned a captain by Burnet on April 7, 1836. He fought with Captain Calder's company at San Jacinto, with which he had served for a short time during March. The anonymous author also wrote that he was "despatched to Galveston directly after the capture of Santa Anna." Calder and Franklin were sent to Galveston on April 23 by Colonel Rusk. Franklin's audited military claims show that he was a member of Captain Calder's company from March 5 to May 5, 1836, not mentioning his brief command. In the absence of good muster roll record keeping during the campaign, many other men who joined companies at varying times were similarly issued blanket service vouchers whose time periods matched the company's tenure.

21. Johnson, Francis W. *History of Texas*. Wooten, Dudley G. (Editor). *A Comprehensive History of Texas, 1685 to 1897*. 2 volumes. 1898; reprint, Austin: Texas State Historical Association, 1986. See I:268–274.

22. [Coleman], *Houston Displayed*, 21.

23. Labadie, "San Jacinto Campaign," 49–50.

24. Winters, "An Account of the Battle of San Jacinto," 141.

25. Labadie, "San Jacinto Campaign," 50.

26. Steele, *Biography of Private Alfonso Steele*, 4.

27. Hardin, *Texian Iliad*, 201.

28. Delgado, "Mexican Account of the Battle of San Jacinto," 615; Labadie, "San Jacinto Campaign," 51; Tolbert, *The Day of San Jacinto*, 113.

29. Jenkins, *Papers*, 5:513; Labadie, "San Jacinto Campaign," 51.

30. Denham letter from camp at San Jacinto of May 3, 1836; see M. H. Denham biographical sketch, Kemp Papers.

31. John Ligett Marshall biographical sketch, Kemp Papers.

32. Labadie, "San Jacinto Campaign," 51. James Pohl in *The Battle of San Jacinto* on page 29 mistakenly claims that the Texian cannon did not fire, misinterpreting Labadie's statement of "no execution is done except to cause the cavalry to wheel to the right." Frank Tolbert on page 114 of *The Day of San Jacinto* actually claims that the Mexican cannon was fired first, although it had not yet even been advanced onto the field. Stephen Hardin on page 202 of *Texian Iliad* got it right in claiming the Texians were first to fire. "A line of skirmishers moved against the Texian position, but were brought up short by Lieutenant Colonel J. C. Neill's artillery."

33. 1860 Texas *Almanac*, 63.

34. Bryan to Sherman, July 2, 1859, in Sherman, "Defence," 30.

35. William C. Swearingen biographical sketch, Kemp Papers; Labadie, "San Jacinto Campaign," 51.

36. Jenkins, *Papers*, 6:11.

37. [Coleman], *Houston Displayed*, 20.

38. Delgado, "Mexican Account of the Battle of San Jacinto," 615.

39. Swisher, *The Swisher Memoirs*, 41.

40. Labadie, "San Jacinto Campaign," 51.

41. Baker letter to Houston written in 1844; published in Barker, "The San Jacinto Campaign," 284.

42. Bryan to Sherman, July 6, 1859, in Sherman, "Defence," 36.

43. Labadie, "San Jacinto Campaign," 51–52.

44. John Coker and John Balch biographical sketches, Kemp Papers.

45. Menchaca, "Memoirs," II:6. For Private Harvey's comments, see Dixon and Kemp, *The Heroes of San Jacinto*, 345, and John Harvey biographical sketch, Kemp Papers. For Captain Franklin's account, see [Franklin], "The Battle of San Jacinto," 260.

46. Labadie, "San Jacinto Campaign," 52.

47. [Franklin], "The Battle of San Jacinto," 260.

48. Jenkins, *Papers*, 5:513.

49. Swisher, *The Swisher Memoirs*, 41–42; Erath, "Memoirs," 258.

50. Delgado, "Mexican Account of the Battle of San Jacinto," 616.

51. Sherman, "Defence," 4.

52. Foote, *Texas and the Texans*, II:298.

53. William Foster Young biographical sketch, Kemp Papers.

54. Oliver T. Brown biographical sketch, Kemp Papers. Duncan to Sherman, May 16, 1859, in Sherman, "Defence," 11.

55. Algernon P. Thompson biographical sketch, Kemp Papers.

56. Ambrosia Rodriguez biographical sketch, Kemp Papers.

57. Foote, *Texas and the Texans*, II:298–99.

58. Ibid, II:302–303.

59. Ibid, 299–300.

60. Oliver T. Brown biographical sketch, Kemp Papers. Foote, *Texas and the Texans*, II:300.

61. Foote, *Texas and the Texans*, II:301.

62. Delgado, "Mexican Account of the Battle of San Jacinto," 617.

63. Lane, *The Adventures and Recollections of General Walter P. Lane*, 12.

64. Tolbert, *The Day of San Jacinto*, 117.
65. Foote, *Texas and the Texans*, II:301–302.
66. Jenkins, *Papers*, 6:11.
67. James Tarlton letter of April 22, 1836, from Lynchburg. Published in June 3, 1836, *Daily Commercial Republican and Commercial Register* of Cincinnati, Ohio. Kemp Papers. Duncan to Sherman, May 16, 1859, in Sherman, "Defence," 11.
68. Foote, *Texas and the Texans*, II:302.
69. Labadie, "San Jacinto Campaign," 52–53.
70. Forbes v Labadie, R. B. Blake compilation, II:77. Day, *The Texas Almanac 1857–1873*, 536–37 and 646. Cavalryman William Taylor attested to the loss of Cartwright's horse, valued at $100. William Kibbe AC, R 56, F 715. Kibbe's horse was valued at $85 by L. Bryan and C. W. Thompson.
71. Lane, *The Adventures and Recollections of General Walter P. Lane*, 12–16.
72. Filisola, *Memoirs*, II:223. Delgado, "Mexican Account of the Battle of San Jacinto," 617.
73. Houston's Official Report to Burnet, April 25, 1836.
74. Calder, "Recollections of the Texas Campaign of 1836," 65.
75. Foote, *Texas and the Texans*, II:300–302.
76. Per Hockley's personal description to Foote shortly after the battle. See Foote, *Texas and the Texans*, II:303.
77. [Coleman], *Houston Displayed*, 22.
78. Billingsley to *Galveston News*, published Saturday, September 19, 1857; see Billingsley biographical sketch in Kemp Papers.
79. Thomas C. Utley biographical sketch, Kemp Papers.
80. Jenkins, *Papers*, 6:10–11; Oliver Brown biographical sketch, Kemp Papers.
81. Jonathan D. Morris biographical sketch, Kemp Papers.
82. Zuber, *My Eighty Years in Texas*, 95.
83. Kuykendall, "Recollections," 304.
84. Seguin, *A Revolution Remembered*, 109.
85. Francis Jarvis Cooke biographical sketch, Kemp Papers.
86. Labadie, "San Jacinto Campaign," 53.
87. Hardin, *Texian Iliad*, 206.
88. Billingsley to *Galveston News*, published Saturday, September 19, 1857; see Billingsley biographical sketch in Kemp Papers. Heard to Sherman, June 15, 1859, in Sherman, "Defence," 10.
89. Fitzhugh to Sherman, June 9, 1859, in Sherman, "Defence," 12.

CHAPTER 14
"BURN THAT BRIDGE"

1. Tolbert, *The Day of San Jacinto*, 124; Hardin, *Texian Iliad*, 206.
2. James, *The Raven*, 206.
3. Labadie, "San Jacinto Campaign," 53.
4. [Coleman], *Houston Displayed*, 24.
5. James, *The Raven*, 206.
6. Filisola, *Memoirs*, II:223–24.
7. Delgado, "Mexican Account of the Battle of San Jacinto," 617.
8. [Franklin], "The Battle of San Jacinto," 261.
9. Labadie, "San Jacinto Campaign," 53.
10. Huston, *Deaf Smith*, 77.
11. Kuykendall, "Recollections," 304–305.
12. Zuber, *My Eighty Years in Texas*, 95.
13. Paul Samuel Houston biographical sketch, Kemp Papers.

14. George Washington Poe biographical sketch, Kemp Papers.
15. Mirabeau Buonaparte Lamar biographical sketch, Kemp Papers.
16. Lamar to Sherman, September 24, 1857, from Sherman, "Defence," 3.
17. Mirabeau Buonaparte Lamar biographical sketch, Kemp Papers, quoting from Jacob DeCordova's 1858 sketch of Lamar in *Texas: Her Resources and Her Public Men*, 181–82.
18. Franklin, "The Battle of San Jacinto," 262. Franklin's count of sixty-one cavalrymen for April 21 appears to be right on target. Franklin's audited claims only show his having been a member of Captain Calder's company. They do not reflect his move to Galveston Island, where Burnet had placed him in charge of volunteers, nor him volunteering for the cavalry on April 21.
19. Jenkins, *Papers*, 6:11.
20. Delgado, "Mexican Account of the Battle of San Jacinto," 617.
21. Filisola, *Memoirs*, II:224.
22. Crawford, *The Eagle*, 54.
23. From N. Doran Maillard's *History of the Republic of Texas* (1842), 107. From The Battle of San Jacinto Notebook, The McArdle Notebooks.
24. Denham letter from camp at San Jacinto of May 3, 1836; see M. H. Denham biographical sketch, Kemp Papers.
25. Labadie, "San Jacinto Campaign," 53.
26. Swisher, *The Swisher Memoirs*, 44.
27. Lorenzo de Zavala Jr. biographical sketch, Kemp Papers.
28. Lane, *The Adventures and Recollections of General Walter P. Lane*, 11–12.
29. James M. Hill to McArdle, October 20, 1895, The Battle of San Jacinto Notebook, The McArdle Notebooks.
30. Henry E. McCullough to McArdle, January 14, 1891, The Battle of San Jacinto Notebook, The McArdle Notebooks. Washington Anderson biographical sketch, Kemp Papers. James M. Hill to McArdle, October 20, 1895, The Battle of San Jacinto Notebook, The McArdle Notebooks. John P. Ferrell to McArdle, September 1885, The Battle of San Jacinto Notebook, The McArdle Notebooks.
31. James, *The Raven*, 190.
32. Tolbert, *The Day of San Jacinto*, 88–89.
33. Forbes v Labadie, R. B. Blake compilation, II:77–79. Matthew Cartwright and Dr. Fielding Deadrick biographical sketches, Kemp Papers.
34. Farish to Sherman, July 2, 1859, in Sherman, "Defence," 28.
35. Pohl, *The Battle of San Jacinto*, 32, and Hardin, *Texian Iliad*, 209, both agree that Santa Anna had roughly 1,250 men by late morning on April 21. *The Handbook of Texas*, II:554, gives the count as "about 1,200."
36. Hardin, *The Alamo 1836*, 15–17.
37. "McArdle's Original Draft of His Manuscript," from The Battle of San Jacinto Notebook, The McArdle Notebooks.
38. James M. Hill to McArdle, October 20, 1895, The Battle of San Jacinto Notebook, The McArdle Notebooks.
39. Lack, Paul D. *The Texas Revolutionary Experience. A Political and Social History. 1835–1836*. College Station, Tex: Texas A&M University Press, 1992, 126–28.
40. Joseph Sovereign biographical sketch, Kemp Papers.
41. Robert Eden Handy biographical sketch, Kemp Papers.
42. Schoen, Harold. "The Free Negro in the Republic of Texas." *Southwestern Historical Quarterly*, Vol. XL, No. 1 (July 1936), 32–33.
43. Maxlin Smith biographical sketch, Kemp Papers.
44. Paul Samuel Houston biographical sketch, Kemp Papers; *Houston Displayed*, 25.
45. Labadie, "San Jacinto Campaign," 53.
46. Paul Samuel Houston biographical sketch, Kemp Papers.
47. 1860 *Texas Almanac*, 65.

48. Billingsley to *Galveston News*, published Saturday, September 19, 1857; see Billingsley biographical sketch in Kemp Papers.
49. 1860 *Texas Almanac*, 65.
50. Jenkins, *Papers*, 6:6.
51. Paul Samuel Houston biographical sketch, Kemp Papers.
52. 1859 Sherman to Billingsley letter, Jesse Billingsley biographical sketch in Kemp Papers.
53. Tolbert, *The Day of San Jacinto*, 134.
54. Robert Stevenson letter of April 23, 1836; Kemp Papers.
55. Paul Samuel Houston biographical sketch, Kemp Papers; see also Forbes v Labadie, R. B. Blake compilation, II:30.
56. Alsbury, Y. P. "Burning of Vince's Bridge." Letter of Young Perry Alsbury written January 14, 1858, and published in 1861 *Texas Almanac*, 55–58. Alsbury's letter also contains the sworn agreement of John Coker attesting to the accuracy of Alsbury's statements.
57. 1860 *Texas Almanac*, 66.
58. [Coleman], *Houston Displayed*, 25.
59. Alsbury, "Burning of Vince's Bridge," 56.
60. Lapham to Parents and Brother, May 17, 1836, in Moses Lapham biographical sketch, Kemp Papers.
61. Alsbury, "Burning of Vince's Bridge," 56–57.
62. Labadie, "San Jacinto Campaign," 53.
63. Alsbury, "Burning of Vince's Bridge," 57.

CHAPTER 15
"DREADFUL HAVOC"

1. Winters, "An Account of the Battle of San Jacinto," 141–42.
2. Seguin, *A Revolution Remembered*, 109.
3. Robert Stevenson letter of April 23, 1836; Kemp Papers.
4. [Coleman], *Houston Displayed*, 26.
5. 1860 *Texas Almanac*, 65, quoting Lamar letter in the June 23, 1855, *Galveston News*.
6. Erath, "Memoirs," 260.
7. Calder, "Recollections of the Texas Campaign of 1836," 65.
8. Heard to Sherman, June 15, 1859, in Sherman, "Defence," 10.
9. Tolbert, *The Day of San Jacinto*, 135.
10. Erath, "Memoirs," 260.
11. Tolbert, *The Day of San Jacinto*, 135.
12. [Coleman], *Houston Displayed*, 26; Erath, "Memoirs," 263.
13. John W. Hassell biographical sketch, Kemp Papers.
14. Walling to Sherman, June 1859, in Sherman, "Defence," 7–8.
15. James M. Hill to McArdle, October 20, 1895, The Battle of San Jacinto Notebook, The McArdle Notebooks. Bryan to Sherman, July 2, 1859, in Sherman, "Defence," 31. For Gillaspie, see Forbes v. Labadie papers, R. B. Blake Collection, I:64, 71.
16. Goodloe to Sherman, June 9, 1859, in Sherman, "Defence," 8. John P. Ferrell to McArdle, September 1885, The Battle of San Jacinto Notebook, The McArdle Notebooks.
17. Jenkins, *Papers*, VI:11–12.
18. Forbes v. Labadie papers, R. B. Blake Collection, II:21. Labadie, "San Jacinto Campaign," 54.
19. Moseley Baker biographical sketch, Kemp Papers.
20. Isaac Lafayette Hill biographical sketch, Kemp Papers.
21. Calder, "Recollections of the Texas Campaign of 1836," 66.

22. Forbes v. Labadie papers, R. B. Blake Collection, I:64, 71. Charles B. Shain letter of June 25, 1836, published in *Louisville Journal*; Kemp Papers.

23. James Tarlton letter of April 22, 1836, from Lynchburg. Published in June 3, 1836, *Daily Commercial Republican and Commercial Register* of Cincinnati, Ohio. Kemp Papers.

24. Jenkins, *Papers*, VI:12; Foote, *Texas and the Texans*, II:311.

25. Edward Miles letter, The Battle of San Jacinto Notebook, The McArdle Notebooks.

26. Filisola, *Memoirs*, II:224.

27. James M. Hill to McArdle, October 20, 1895, The Battle of San Jacinto Notebook, The McArdle Notebooks.

28. Labadie, "The San Jacinto Campaign," 54.

29. [Coleman], *Houston Displayed*, 26.

30. Bate, *General Sidney Sherman*, 243.

31. "Recollections of S. F. Sparks," 70–71.

32. Steele, *Biography of Private Alfonso Steele*, 5.

33. 1860 *Texas Almanac*, 338.

34. Calder, "Recollections of the Texas Campaign of 1836," 66.

35. Jenkins, *Papers*, 6:13.

36. Winters, "An Account of the Battle of San Jacinto," 142.

37. Branch to Sherman, June 29, 1859, and Hardin to Sherman, June 28, 1857, in Sherman, "Defence," 25–27.

38. Jenkins, *Papers*, 6:13–14.

39. Paul Samuel Houston biographical sketch, Kemp Papers. Houston's son, Andrew Jackson Houston, wrote in his book *Texas Independence*, page 229, "The Texan General was twice dismounted by the enemy's fire. His first horse was killed, having been shot 5 times."

40. Tolbert, *The Day of San Jacinto*, 143.

41. Jenkins, *Papers*, 6:12.

42. Lawrence account published in *Hallettsville Planter*.

43. Paul Samuel Houston biographical sketch, Kemp Papers; Huston, *Deaf Smith*, 86.

44. William C. Swearingen biographical sketch, Kemp Papers.

45. Calder, "Recollections of the Texas Campaign of 1836," 66.

46. Bostick, "Reminiscences," 92.

47. Alfred Kelso and Samuel G. Hardaway biographical sketches, Kemp Papers. Edward Miles letter, The Battle of San Jacinto Notebook, The McArdle Notebooks.

48. Erath, "Memoirs," 265.

49. Forbes v Labadie, R. B. Blake compilation, II:56.

50. Turner, *The Yellow Rose of Texas*, 25–26; Tolbert, *The Day of San Jacinto*, 141; Calder, "Recollections," 66.

51. John W. Hassell biographical sketch, Kemp Papers. Turner, *The Yellow Rose of Texas*, 25.

52. [Coleman], *Houston Displayed*, 26. John P. Ferrell to McArdle, May 1889, The Battle of San Jacinto Notebook, The McArdle Notebooks.

53. Swisher, *The Swisher Memoirs*, 38–39, 46.

54. Tolbert, *The Day of San Jacinto*, 149–50.

55. 1860 *Texas Almanac*, 70.

56. Seguin, *A Revolution Remembered*, 27.

57. Rodriquez, "Memoirs of Early Texas."

58. Seguin, *A Revolution Remembered*, 26–27.

59. Foote, *Texas and the Texans*, 310.

60. Turner, *The Yellow Rose of Texas*, 12.

61. Tutt, Bob. "New Twists Discovered in Saga of 'Yellow Rose of Texas.'" Originally printed in *Houston Chronicle*, reprinted in *Port Arthur News* on Thursday, March 13, 1997, 4B. See also Tolbert, *The Day of San Jacinto*, 144. Emily West has been described as a free mulatto, or mixed black and Caucasian, woman who was an indentured servant of James Morgan. Gen-

eral Houston is supposed to have heard the Miss Emily story from Lieutenant Colonel James Neill. For more on the Yellow Rose controversy, see Epilogue for section on Miss Emily.

62. Delgado, "Mexican Account of the Battle of San Jacinto," 618.
63. Filisola, *Memoirs*, II:227.
64. Castañeda, *The Mexican Side of the Texan Revolution*, 115.
65. Filisola, *Memoirs*, II:225.
66. Winters, "An Account of the Battle of San Jacinto," 142–43.
67. Dixon and Kemp, *The Heroes of San Jacinto*, 341.
68. Jesse Kencheloe Davis biographical sketch, Kemp Papers.
69. Lane, *The Adventures and Recollections of General Walter P. Lane*, 14.
70. Foote, *Texas and the Texans*, II:310–11.
71. Huston, *Deaf Smith*, 88.
72. Foote, *Texas and the Texans*, II:311.
73. Moore, *Taming Texas*, 67.
74. George A. Lamb biographical sketch, Kemp Papers. *Texas Almanac*, 1872.
75. Thomas Patton Fowle biographical sketch, Kemp Papers.
76. John W. Hassell biographical sketch, Kemp Papers.
77. James M. Hill to McArdle, October 20, 1895, The Battle of San Jacinto Notebook, The McArdle Notebooks.
78. George Washington Lonis biographical sketch, Kemp Papers.
79. Elbridge Gerry Rector biographical sketch, Kemp Papers. Elijah Votaw PE, R 243, F 429–432.
80. Francis Jarvis Cooke biographical sketch, Kemp Papers.
81. Calder, "Recollections of the Texas Campaign of 1836," 66.
82. Steele, *Biography of Private Alfonso Steele*, 5.
83. *Texas Almanac* Compendium, 646.
84. Rose, *The Life and Services of Gen. Ben McCullough*, 40–43.
85. Foote, *Texas and the Texans*, II:308–309.
86. Lyman Frank Rounds biographical sketch, Kemp Papers.
87. Robert Stevenson letter of April 23, 1836; Kemp Papers.
88. Filisola, *Memoirs*, II:225.
89. Foote, *Texas and the Texans*, II:309.
90. Becerra, *A Mexican Sergeant's Recollections of the Alamo & San Jacinto*, 44–45.
91. Lane, *The Adventures and Recollections of General Walter P. Lane*, 14.
92. Foote, *Texas and the Texans*, II:309.
93. Montgomery Baxter biographical sketch, Kemp Papers.
94. George Washington Hockley biographical sketch, Kemp Papers.
95. Achelle Marre AC, R 64, F 501; Achelle Marre biographical sketch, Kemp Papers.
96. Tolbert, *The Day of San Jacinto*, 146.
97. Jenkins, *Papers*, 6:12.
98. Charles B. Shain letter of June 25, 1836, published in *Louisville Journal*; Kemp Papers.
99. Calder, "Recollections of the Texas Campaign of 1836," 66.
100. Castañeda, *The Mexican Side of the Texan Revolution*, 117.
101. Delgado, "Mexican Account of the Battle of San Jacinto," 618.
102. Filisola, *Memoirs*, II:225. Labadie, "San Jacinto Campaign," 58 asserts that this horse was Vince's Old Whip. Battle participants later claimed that this was not true, including William S. Taylor of the cavalry. Taylor, Karnes and others killed another Mexican officer upon Old Whip at Vince's Bridge later in the day.
103. Castañeda, *The Mexican Side of the Texan Revolution*, 117.
104. Sparks, "Recollections," 71.
105. James Tarlton letter of April 22, 1836, from Lynchburg. Published in June 3, 1836, *Daily Commercial Republican and Commercial Register* of Cincinnati, Ohio. Kemp Papers.

Samuel G. Hardaway biographical sketch, Kemp Papers. James Tarlton letter of April 22, 1836, from Lynchburg.

106. Tolbert, *The Day of San Jacinto*, 141.

107. William S. Taylor to William C. Crane, March 8, 1866, The Battle of San Jacinto Notebook, The McArdle Notebooks.

108. Forbes v. Labadie papers, R. B. Blake Collection, II:20.

109. Jenkins, *Papers*, 6:12.

110. [Coleman], *Houston Displayed*, 27. Andrew Jackson Houston, *Texas Independence*, 229.

111. Robert Stevenson letter of April 23, 1836; Kemp Papers. Winter, "An Account of the Battle of San Jacinto," 143. Labadie, "San Jacinto Campaign," 55.

112. Houston, *Texas Independence*, 229. Babineck, Mark. "Houston's 1853 Letter Proves Historians Wrong." *Houston Chronicle*, Sunday, April 21, 2002, 40A.

113. Ellis Benson biographical sketch in Kemp Papers.

114. Tolbert, *The Day of San Jacinto*, 163.

115. Houston letter of August 25, 1855. See Paul Samuel Houston biographical sketch, Kemp Papers.

116. Labadie, "The San Jacinto Campaign," 54. [Coleman], *Houston Displayed*, 27.

117. Major William Heard letter of May 15, 1859, published in the 1860 *Texas Almanac*. Heard could well have been repeating Coleman's previously published bloodshed quote from Houston.

118. Labadie, "The San Jacinto Campaign," 54.

119. Billingsley to *Galveston News*, published Saturday, September 19, 1857; see Billingsley biographical sketch in Kemp Papers. Baker to Houston 1844. Published in Barker, "The San Jacinto Campaign," 286.

120. Sidney Sherman letter published in the *Galveston Weekly News*, September 15, 1857.

121. Amasa Turner letter published in Barker, "The San Jacinto Campaign," 341–42.

122. Paul Samuel Houston biographical sketch, Kemp Papers.

123. Calder, "Recollections of the Texas Campaign of 1836," 69.

124. 1860 *Texas Almanac*, 70–71.

CHAPTER 16
"IT WAS NOTHING BUT A SLAUGHTER"

1. Walling to Sherman, June 1859, in Sherman, "Defence," 8.

2. Tolbert, *The Day of San Jacinto*, 150.

3. Forbes v Labadie, R. B. Blake compilation, II:40–41.

4. Menchaca, "Memoirs," II:9.

5. James Tarlton letter of April 22, 1836, from Lynchburg. Published in June 3, 1836, *Daily Commercial Republican and Commercial Register* of Cincinnati, Ohio. Kemp Papers.

6. Hohes, Pauline Buck. *A Centennial History of Anderson County, Texas*. San Antonio, Tex: Naylor, 1936, 23.

7. Delgado, "Mexican Account of the Battle of San Jacinto," 618–19.

8. Erath, "Memoirs," 266.

9. Sparks, "Recollections," 71.

10. Major William Heard letter of May 15, 1859, published in the 1860 *Texas Almanac*.

11. Allen Caruthers biographical sketch, Kemp Papers.

12. Lane, *The Adventures and Recollections of General Walter P. Lane*, 14–15.

13. Denham letter from camp at San Jacinto of May 3, 1836; see M. H. Denham biographical sketch, Kemp Papers.

14. William C. Swearingen biographical sketch, Kemp Papers.

15. Hunter, "Narrative," 16.

16. Winters, "An Account of the Battle of San Jacinto," 142–43.

17. Tolbert, *The Day of San Jacinto*, 152–53.

18. Labadie, "The San Jacinto Campaign," 54–55.

19. Delgado, "Mexican Account of the Battle of San Jacinto," 619.

20. Erath, "Memoirs," 266.

21. William Foster Young biographical sketch, Kemp Papers.

22. Seguin, *A Revolution Remembered*, 110.

23. Labadie, "The San Jacinto Campaign," 54.

24. Forbes v Labadie, R. B. Blake compilation, II:2–3, 10–11, 95.

25. Ibid, II:52–53, 56–57.

26. Ibid, II:69.

27. Ibid, II:13–14.

28. Ibid, I:99.

29. Calder, "Recollections of the Texas Campaign of 1836," 68.

30. Forbes v. Labadie papers, R. B. Blake Collection, I:42.

31. Taylor, William S. "Pursuit of Santa Anna and His Cavalry after They Had Commenced Their Flight from the Battlefield of San Jacinto." 1868 *Texas Almanac*. This almanac, very rare today, may be found published in Day, James M. *The Texas Almanac 1857–1873. A Compendium of Texas History.* Waco, Tex: Texian Press, 1967, 537–540. Taylor lists one of these men as Thomas House. The closest name to this is Thomas Hughes, a member of Captain Kimbro's company.

32. Young Perry Alsbury biographical sketch, Kemp Papers.

33. Taylor, "Pursuit of Santa Anna," 537–540.

34. Lapham to Parents and Brother, May 17, 1836, in Moses Lapham biographical sketch, Kemp Papers.

35. Taylor, "Pursuit of Santa Anna," 537–540. [Franklin], "The Battle of San Jacinto," 263.

36. Taylor, "Pursuit of Santa Anna," 540.

37. Lawrence account published in *Hallettsville Planter*.

38. Taylor, "Pursuit of Santa Anna," 538.

39. Filisola, *Memoirs*, II:226.

40. William S. Taylor to William C. Crane, March 8, 1866, The Battle of San Jacinto Notebook, The McArdle Notebooks.

41. Calder, "Recollections of the Texas Campaign of 1836," 67.

42. Lorenzo de Zavala Jr. biographical sketch, Kemp Papers.

43. Hunter, *Narrative*, 16.

44. Zuber, *My Eighty Years in Texas*, 95–96.

45. Kuykendall, "Recollections of the Campaign," published in Barker, "The San Jacinto Campaign," 305.

46. Jenkins, *Papers*, 6:9.

47. Kuykendall, "Recollections of the Campaign," 305–306.

48. 1859 *Texas Almanac*, 165.

49. Captain William Graham muster roll of July 25, 1836, courtesy of Edwin G. Pierson Jr. Captain Graham's company would be joined by more recruits after San Jacinto.

50. "Laura." Article from The Handbook of Texas Online. <http://www.tsha.utexas.edu/handbook/online/articles/view/LL/etl1.html. Accessed September 17, 2002.

51. Thomas W. Grayson PP, R 217, F 593–94.

52. Steele, *Biography of Private Alfonso Steele*, 5.

53. Goodloe to Sherman, June 9, 1859, in Sherman, "Defence," 8; Tolbert, *The Day of San Jacinto*, 153.

54. R. B. Walker account in the 1868 *Texas Almanac*.

55. Foote, *Texas and the Texans*, 309–310.

56. Becerra, *A Mexican Sergeant's Recollections*, 15, 44.

57. Erath, "Memoirs," 266.
58. Labadie, "The San Jacinto Campaign," 55.
59. Tolbert, *The Day of San Jacinto*, 156.
60. Winters, "An Account of the Battle of San Jacinto," 142–43.
61. *Galveston Weekly News*, Sidney Sherman in Trial of Forbes vs. Labadie, Nov. 2, 1858; Forbes v. Labadie papers, R. B. Blake Collection, I:41.
62. Captain Amasa Turner account from Barker, "The San Jacinto Campaign," 341–42. Tolbert, *The Day of San Jacinto*, 159–60.
63. Paul Samuel Houston biographical sketch, Kemp Papers.
64. Calder, "Recollections of the Texas Campaign of 1836," 66.
65. William C. Swearingen biographical sketch, Kemp Papers.
66. Jenkins, *Papers*, 6:12–13.
67. William C. Swearingen biographical sketch, Kemp Papers.
68. Swisher, *The Swisher Memoirs*, 46–47.
69. William C. Swearingen biographical sketch, Kemp Papers.
70. Seguin, *A Revolution Remembered*, 110. Seguin was told that the cash amounted to $25,000.
71. Calder, "Recollections of the Texas Campaign of 1836," 68.
72. Oliver Brown biographical sketch, Kemp Papers.
73. George Washington Hockley biographical sketch, Kemp Papers.
74. Labadie, "San Jacinto Campaign," 55. Lane, *The Adventures and Recollections of General Walter P. Lane*, 15.
75. Menchaca, "Memoirs," III:1.
76. Delgado, "Mexican Account of the Battle of San Jacinto," 619–620.
77. Erath, "Memoirs," 26–68.
78. Forbes v Labadie, R. B. Blake compilation, II:87–88.

CHAPTER 17
CATCHING "THE OLD FOX"

1. Forbes v Labadie, R. B. Blake compilation, II:87–91.
2. Labadie, "San Jacinto Campaign," 56.
3. Steele, *Biography of Private Alfonso Steele*, 5–6.
4. Labadie, "The San Jacinto Campaign," 56.
5. Forbes v. Labadie papers, R. B. Blake Collection, I:53.
6. Samuel G. Hardaway biographical sketch, Kemp Papers.
7. Lapham to Parents and Brother, May 17, 1836, in Moses Lapham biographical sketch, Kemp Papers.
8. James Austin Sylvester letter published in *Telegraph and Texas Register* on August 2, 1836; see also his biographical sketch, Kemp Papers.
9. Taylor, "Pursuit," 539.
10. Castañeda, *The Mexican Side of the Texan Revolution*, 118.
11. Winters, "An Account of the Battle of San Jacinto," 143.
12. Calder, "Recollections of the Texas Campaign of 1836," 67.
13. Labadie, "San Jacinto Campaign," 56–57.
14. Forbes v. Labadie papers, R. B. Blake Collection, II:26.
15. Ibid, II:128–131.
16. Ibid, I:122.
17. Jenkins, *Papers*, 6:9.
18. Zuber, *My Eighty Years in Texas*, 96.
19. Hunter, *Narrative*, 16–19.

20. [Coleman], *Houston Displayed*, 28.

21. Lewis Cox biographical sketch, Kemp Papers.

22. James Austin Sylvester letter published in *Telegraph and Texas Register* on August 2, 1836; see also his biographical sketch, Kemp Papers.

23. Ibid. Sylvester wrote in his account that his early party also consisted of David "Cole and Mason of Texas." He does not list Robison or Bostick. He wrote that David Cole was behind the pack at the time and that Mason "left us altogether" before Santa Anna was encountered.

24. 1859 *Texas Almanac*, 166. James Austin Sylvester letter published in *Telegraph and Texas Register* on August 2, 1836; see also his biographical sketch, Kemp Papers.

25. Bostick, "Reminiscences," 92–95.

26. 1859 *Texas Almanac*, 166.

27. James Austin Sylvester letter published in *Telegraph and Texas Register* on August 2, 1836; see also his biographical sketch, Kemp Papers.

28. 1859 *Texas Almanac*, 166.

29. Sparks, "Recollections," 72.

30. Tolbert, *The Day of San Jacinto*, 179. Winters, "An Account of the Battle of San Jacinto," 143.

31. Edward Miles biographical sketch, Kemp Papers.

32. Forbes v. Labadie papers, R. B. Blake Collection, I:55. Bostick, "Reminiscences," 95.

33. Labadie, "San Jacinto Campaign," 58. Swisher, *The Swisher Memoirs*, 47.

34. This story was related to author by his grandmother, Evaline Kolb Moore, and her cousin, former Texas Land Commissioner Jerry Sadler. See Moore, *Taming Texas*, 73.

35. Forbes v Labadie, R. B. Blake compilation, II:38.

36. Forbes biographical sketch, Kemp Papers.

37. Foote, *Texas and the Texans*, II:313.

38. [Franklin], "The Battle of San Jacinto," 264. Lane, *The Adventures and Recollections of General Walter P. Lane*, 15.

39. Winters, "An Account of the Battle of San Jacinto," 143. Labadie, "San Jacinto Campaign," 58.

40. [Coleman], *Houston Displayed*, 29.

41. Ibid, 29. Yoakum, *History of Texas*, II:258–59. Tolbert, *The Day of San Jacinto*, 179.

42. Forbes biographical sketch, Kemp Papers.

43. Foote, *Texas and the Texans*, II:313–14.

44. [Coleman], *Houston Displayed*, 30.

45. James Austin Sylvester letter published in *Telegraph and Texas Register* on August 2, 1836; see also his biographical sketch, Kemp Papers.

46. Calder, "Recollections of the Texas Campaign of 1836," 67.

47. Foote, *Texas and the Texans*, II:312–313.

48. Forbes biographical sketch, Kemp Papers.

49. Yoakum, *History of Texas*, II:258–59.

50. Foote, *Texas and the Texans*, II:315.

51. Castañeda, *The Mexican Side of the Texan Revolution*, 124–25.

52. Tolbert, *The Day of San Jacinto*, 181.

53. Filisola, *Memoirs*, II:235–36; Jenkins, *Papers*, 6:15–16.

54. Isaac Lafayette Hill biographical sketch, Kemp Papers.

CHAPTER 18
THE SPOILS OF WAR

1. Tolbert, *The Day of San Jacinto*, 192–93; Dilue Harris, "The Reminiscences of Mrs. Dilue Harris," 174–75.

2. Delgado, "Mexican Account of the Battle of San Jacinto," 622–23; Labadie, 57.

3. Judge R. S. Calder to J. S. Sullivan, May 31, 1877, in Hayes, Charles W. *Galveston: History of the Island and the City.* 2 volumes. Austin: Jenkins Garrett Press, 1974. See also Benjamin Cromwell Franklin biographical sketch, Kemp Papers.

4. Foote, *Texas and the Texans*, II:315.

5. Castañeda, *The Mexican Side of the Texan Revolution*, 126–27.

6. Turner, *The Yellow Rose of Texas*, 34–35.

7. Delgado, "Mexican Account of the Battle of San Jacinto," 622.

8. Tolbert, *The Day of San Jacinto*, 201.

9. Delgado, "Mexican Account of the Battle of San Jacinto," 622.

10. Hunter, *Narrative*, 18.

11. Forbes v. Labadie papers, R. B. Blake Collection, I:85.

12. Labadie, "San Jacinto Campaign," 61.

13. Delgado, "Mexican Account of the Battle of San Jacinto," 622.

14. Haley, *Sam Houston*, 152–53.

15. Yoakum, *History of Texas*, II:259.

16. Zuber, *My Eighty Years in Texas*, 97.

17. Delgado, "Mexican Account of the Battle of San Jacinto," 622.

18. Castañeda, *The Mexican Side of the Texan Revolution*, 125.

19. Filisola, *Memoirs*, II:231–38.

20. Tolbert, *The Day of San Jacinto*, 203–205.

21. Hunter, *Narrative*, 17.

22. Linn, *Reminiscences of Fifty Years in Texas*, 264; DeBruhl, *The Sword of San Jacinto*, 215; Haley, *Sam Houston*, 154.

23. Forbes v Labadie, R. B. Blake compilation, II:5.

24. Delgado, "Mexican Account of the Battle of San Jacinto," 624.

25. Forbes v Labadie, R. B. Blake compilation, II:108.

26. Ibid, II:70–71.

27. Labadie, "San Jacinto Campaign," 61.

28. Erath, "Memoirs," 268.

29. Forbes v Labadie, R. B. Blake compilation, II:73.

30. Ibid, II:83.

31. Ibid, II:72.

32. Ibid, II:71.

33. Ibid, II:114, 129; I:49.

34. Ibid, I:66, 106.

35. Ibid, II:78–79, 91.

36. Ibid, II:28.

37. Ibid, II:28.

38. Ibid, II:119.

39. Ibid, II:29–30.

40. Ibid, II:50, 103; I:83.

41. Delgado, "Mexican Account of the Battle of San Jacinto," 623.

42. [Coleman], *Houston Displayed*, 32.

43. Calder to Sullivan in Hayes, *Galveston: History of the Island and the City.* See also Tolbert, *The Day of San Jacinto*, 216–18.

44. Jackson, *Voyages of the Steamboat Yellow Stone*, 134.

45. Forbes v Labadie, R. B. Blake compilation, II:64–65.

46. Ibid, II:90.

47. Ibid, I:43.

48. Ibid, II:21–22.

49. Ibid, I:43–45.

50. Ibid, II:92.

51. Ibid, II:137, 22.

52. Steele, *Biography of Private Alfonso Steele*, 6.

53. Swisher, *The Swisher Memoirs*, 47.

54. Labadie, "San Jacinto Campaign," 61–62.

55. Giles Albert Giddings biographical sketch, Kemp Papers.

56. Filisola, *Memoirs*, II:235–38.

57. Hunter, *Narrative*, 17.

58. 1861 *Texas Almanac* in *Compendium*, 402.

59. [Coleman], *Houston Displayed*, 32.

60. 1861 *Texas Almanac* in *Compendium*, 402. See also [Coleman], *Houston Displayed*, 32.

61. Jenkins, *Papers*, 6:152–53.

62. Tolbert, *The Day of San Jacinto*, 222; Jackson, *Voyages of the Steamboat Yellow Stone*, 134–36.

63. Delgado, "Mexican Account of the Battle of San Jacinto," 624.

64. Forbes v Labadie, R. B. Blake compilation, II:86–87, 94.

65. Delgado, "Mexican Account of the Battle of San Jacinto," 624–25.

66. Bate, *Colonel Sidney Sherman*, 118.

67. Delgado, "Mexican Account of the Battle of San Jacinto," 625–26.

68. Seguin, *A Revolution Remembered*, 136–37.

69. Filisola, *Memoirs*, II:244–45.

70. Tolbert, *The Day of San Jacinto*, 226–27.

71. [Coleman], *Houston Displayed*, 33.

72. Forbes v Labadie, R. B. Blake compilation, II:36.

73. George Washington Hockley biographical sketch, Kemp Papers.

74. Crawford, *The Eagle*, 57–58.

75. Filisola, *Memoirs*, II:229.

76. Denham letter from camp at San Jacinto of May 3, 1836; see M. H. Denham biographical sketch, Kemp Papers.

77. Billingsley to *Galveston News*, published Saturday, September 19, 1857; see Billingsley biographical sketch in Kemp Papers.

78. James Tarlton letter of April 22, 1836, from Lynchburg. Published in June 3, 1836, *Daily Commercial Republican and Commercial Register* of Cincinnati, Ohio. Kemp Papers.

79. Robert Stevenson letter of April 23, 1836; Kemp Papers.

AFTERWORD

1. Forbes v. Labadie papers, R. B. Blake Collection, I:47.

2. Ibid, I:7.

3. Ibid, II:27.

4. Tolbert, *The Day of San Jacinto*, 215.

5. Forbes v Labadie, R. B. Blake compilation, II:135–38.

6. Bollaert, William. *William Bollaert's Texas*. Edited by W. Eugene Hollon and Ruth Lapham Butler. Norman: University of Oklahoma Press, 1956. See also Tutt, Bob. "New Twists Discovered in Saga of 'Yellow Rose of Texas.' *Port Arthur News*, Thursday, March 13, 1997, 4B. Reprint of article originally published in the *Houston Chronicle*.

7. Research of James E. Crisp, Department of History, North Carolina State University.

8. Tolbert, *The Day of San Jacinto*, 163.

9. Algernon P. Thompson biographical sketch, Kemp Papers.

10. Jesse Billingsley biographical sketch, Kemp Papers.

11. Dixon, Kemp, *The Heroes of San Jacinto*, 31.

12. Tolbert, *The Day of San Jacinto*, 245.

13. Moseley Baker biographical sketch, Kemp Papers.

14. David J. Jones biographical sketch, Kemp Papers.

15. Schoen, "The Free Negro in the Republic of Texas," 33–34.

16. *Handbook of Texas*, 765–66.

17. Tolbert, *The Day of San Jacinto*, 247.

18. Benjamin Rice Brigham biographical sketch, Kemp Papers.

19. William Wood biographical sketch, Kemp Papers.

20. James Washington Winters biographical sketch, Kemp Papers.

21. Information from the Texas Parks & Wildlife's San Jacinto Battleground State Historic Site website (http://www.tpwd.state.tx.us/park/sanjac/monu.htm). Accessed January 3, 2003.

Bibliography

DOCUMENTS, MANUSCRIPTS AND COLLECTIONS

Army Papers, Republic of Texas. Archives and Library Division, Texas State Library in Austin, Texas.

Forbes v. Labadie Libel Suit. The transcripts of this trial have been compiled and typed up by Robert Bruce Blake, whose papers are housed in the East Texas Research Center at Stephen F. Austin State University's Steen Library. Volume One: "The San Jacinto Campaign of 1836." As Given by Depositions in the case of John Forbes vs. Nicholas D. Labadie. District Court of Nacogdoches County, Texas. Volume Two: "Sidelights on the Battle of San Jacinto." Referenced as Forbes v Labadie, R. B. Blake compilation.

General Land Office of Texas: Records and papers collection.

Houston, Sam, Commander-in-Chief, San Jacinto, To his Excellency, D. G. Burnett [sic], President of the Republic of Texas, April 25th, 1836. Texas State Library and Archives in Austin.

Kemp, Louis Wiltz. Kemp Papers Collection. San Jacinto Museum of History, Houston, Texas. Kemp's research includes biographical sketches of all veterans of the battle of San Jacinto.

Sherman, Sidney, and Mirabeau Buonaparte Lamar, Jesse Billingsley, et al. *Defence of Gen. Sidney Sherman against the Charges Made by Gen. Sam Houston, in His Speech Delivered in the United States Senate, February 28th, 1859*. Galveston: Printed at the "News" Book and Job Office, 1859; reprint, Houston: Smallwood, Dealy & Baker, 1885; copied by George L. Crocket in January 1934. George Louis Crocket Papers, East Texas Research Center, Steen Library, Stephen F. Austin State University. Crocket changed the original spelling of "Defence" to "Defense" in his typescript.

Smelley, Renee Pierce. "The Life and Times of John Swanson Yarbrough." 2001. Family history posted on http://freepages.history.rootsweb.com/~yarbrough/archives.htm. Accessed October 2002.

McArdle, Henry Arthur. The Battle of San Jacinto. The McArdle Notebooks. Archives and Information Services Division, Texas State Library and Archives Commission.

Menchaca, José Antonio. "The Memoirs of Captain Menchaca, 1807–1836." Edited by James P. Newcomb. Typescript manuscript, in two sections, transcribed in 1957. From the collections in the Center for American History, The University of Texas at Austin.

Republic Claims Papers, 1835–1846 (microfilmed). Texas State Library and Archives Commission, Austin.

Rodriquez, José María. "Memoirs of Early Texas." Memoirs of Judge Rodriquez and his father, Ambrosio Rodriquez (an officer of Captain Seguin's company) were published by the family soon after his death in 1913 and were republished in 1961. Source: Sons of DeWitt Colony Texas.

ARTICLES

Alsbury, Y. P. "Burning of Vince's Bridge." Letter of Young Perry Alsbury written January 14, 1858, and published in 1861 *Texas Almanac*, 55–58. Alsbury's letter also contains the sworn agreement of John Coker attesting to the accuracy of Alsbury's statements.

Asbury, Samuel E. (Editor). "The Private Journal of Juan Nepomuceno Almonte." *Southwestern Historical Quarterly*, Vol. XLVIII, No. 1 (July 1944).

Babineck, Mark. "Houston's 1853 Letter Proves Historians Wrong." *Houston Chronicle*, Sunday, April 21, 2002, 40A.

Barker, Eugene C. (Editor). "Journal of the Permanent Council." *The Quarterly of the Texas State Historical Association*, Vol. 7 (1904).

Barker, Eugene C. "The San Jacinto Campaign." *The Quarterly of the Texas State Historical Association*, Vol. 4, No. 4 (April 1901), 237–343. Barker's work included the first-ever printing of accounts written by James Kuykendall, Captain Amasa Turner and Captain Moseley Baker, the latter a lengthy account written to Sam Houston in 1844.

Bostick, Sion Record. "Reminiscences of Sion R. Bostick." *The Quarterly of the Texas State Historical Association*, Vol. V, No. 2 (October 1901), 87–95.

Calder, R. J. "Recollections of the Texas Campaign of 1836." 1861 *Texas Almanac*, 62–70.

Chriesman, Horatio. "Reminiscences of Horatio Chriesman." *The Quarterly of the Texas State Historical Association*, Vol. 6 (1903).

"A Critical Study of the Siege of the Alamo," *Southwestern Historical Quarterly*, Vol. 37, No. 4 (April 1934).

Delgado, Col. Pedro. "Mexican Account of the Battle of San Jacinto." Published in 1870 Texas Almanac. See pp. 613–629 of Day, James M. (Compiler). *The Texas Almanac 1857–1873. A Compendium of Texas History*. Waco, Tex: Texian Press, 1967.

Erath, George Bernard as dictated to Lucy A. Erath. "Memoirs of Major George Bernard Erath." *Southwestern Historical Quarterly*, Vol. 26, 207–269.

(Franklin, Benjamin Cromwell.) "The Battle of San Jacinto. By One Who Fought in It." *Little's Living Age*, September 7, 1844, 259–265. Reprint of an 1837 article carried in *United Service Magazine*. This article was written anonymously by Franklin, although his article gives enough clues to verify his identity. He states that President Burnet appointed him in command of a small group of men on Galveston. Records show that Franklin was commissioned a captain by Burnet on April 7, 1836. He fought with Captain Calder's company at San Jacinto, with which he had served for a short time during March. The anonymous author also wrote that he was "despatched to Galveston directly after the capture of Santa Anna." Calder and Franklin were sent to Galveston on April 23 by Colonel Rusk.

Harris, Dilue Rose. "Reminiscences of Mrs. Dilue Harris." *Southwestern Historical Quarterly* 4 (October 1900, January 1901).

Hegstrom, Edward. "History Gets More Difficult. Looking at Both Sides of San Jacinto's Story Rewrites Texas' Past." *Houston Chronicle*, Sunday, April 21, 2002, 1A, 23A.

Kokernot, D. L. "Reminiscences of Early Days in Texas." *Gonzales Inquirer*, August 17, 1878.

Labadie, N. D. "San Jacinto Campaign." 1859 *Texas Almanac*, 40–64.

Lawrence, Joseph. Account of Texas Revolution published in *Hallettsville Planter*. Source: Sons of DeWitt Colony Texas.

"San Jacinto Day. April 20th Event Celebrates 166 Years of Texas Freedom." Special advertising supplement to the *Houston Chronicle*. Thursday, April 11, 2002.

Schoen, Harold. "The Free Negro in the Republic of Texas." *Southwestern Historical Quarterly*, Vol. XL, No. 1 (July 1936).

Sparks, Stephen Franklin. "Recollections of S. F. Sparks." *Quarterly of the Texas State Historical Association*, Vol. XII, No. 1 (July 1908).

Taylor, William S. "Pursuit of Santa Anna and his Cavalry after They Had Commenced Their Flight from the Battlefield of San Jacinto." 1868 *Texas Almanac*. This almanac, very rare today, may be found published in Day, James M. *The Texas Alamanac 1857–1873. A Compendium of Texas History.* Waco, Tex: Texian Press, 1967, 537–540.

Telegraph and Texas Register. August 2, 1836, and August 25, 1841.

Tutt, Bob. "New Twists Discovered in Saga of 'Yellow Rose of Texas.'" *Port Arthur News*, Thursday, March 13, 1997, 4B. Reprint of article originally published in the *Houston Chronicle.*

Walker, Beth. "John Swanson Yarbrough, A Man About Texas." *Texas Genealogical Society Quarterly*, Vol. 32, No. 3 (September 1992).

Winters, James Washington. "An Account of the Battle of San Jacinto." *Southwestern Historical Quarterly*, Vol. 6 (October 1902), 139–40.

BOOKS

Aldrich, Armistead Albert. *History of Houston County, Together with Biographical Sketches of Many Pioneers.* San Antonio, Tex: The Naylor Co., 1943.

Austin's Old Three Hundred. The First Anglo Colony in Texas. By the Descendants of Austin's Old Three Hundred. Austin, Tex: Eakin Press, 1999, 69.

Awbrey, Betty Dooley, and Claude Dooley. *Why Stop? A Guide to Texas Historical Roadside Markers.* Houston, Tex: Lone Star Books, Fourth Edition, 1999. Reprint, 1978.

Barker, Eugene C. *The Life of Stephen F. Austin: Founder of Texas, 1793–1836.* Austin: University of Texas Press, 1985.

Bate, W. N. *General Sidney Sherman: Texas Soldier, Statesman and Builder.* Waco, Tex: Texian Press, 1974.

Becerra, Francisco (as told to John S. Ford in 1875). *A Mexican Sergeant's Recollections of the Alamo & San Jacinto.* Austin, Tex: Jenkins Publishing Company, 1980.

Binkley, William C. *Official Correspondence of the Texas Revolution.* New York: Appleton-Century, 1936.

Biographical Directory of the Texan Conventions and Congresses, 1832–1845. Austin, Tex: Book Exchange, 1941.

Biographical Gazetteer of Texas. Austin, Tex: W. M. Morrison Books, 1987.

Boethel, Paul C. *Colonel Amasa Turner. The Gentleman from Lavaca and Other Captains at San Jacinto.* Austin, Tex: Van Boeckmann-Jones, 1963.

Bollaert, William. *William Bollaert's Texas.* Edited by W. Eugene Hollon and Ruth Lapham Butler. Norman: University of Oklahoma Press, 1956.

Brown, Gary. *The New Orleans Greys. Volunteers in the Texas Revolution.* Plano, Tex: Republic of Texas Press, 1999.

Brown, John Henry. *History of Texas from 1685 to 1892.* 2 vols. St. Louis: L. E. Daniell, Publisher, 1892–1893.

Brown, John Henry. *Indian Wars and Pioneers of Texas.* 1880. Reprint. Austin, Tex: State House Press, 1988.

Castañeda, Carlos Eduardo (Translator). *The Mexican Side of the Texas Revolution (1836). By the Chief Mexican Participants.* (Recollections of General Antonio López de Santa Anna, Secretary Ramón Martínez Caro, General Vicente Filisola, General José Urrea, and General José María Tornel.) Dallas, Tex.: P. L. Turner Company.

Chariton, Wallace O. *Exploring the Alamo Legends.* Plano, Tex: Wordware Publishing, Inc., 1992.

Clarke, Mary Whatley. *Thomas J. Rusk: Soldier, Statesman, Jurist.* Austin, Tex: Jenkins Publishing Company, 1971.

[Coleman, Robert Morris.] *Houston Displayed, or Who Won the Battle of San Jacinto? By a Farmer in the Army* (anonymously published). Austin, Tex: The Brick Row Book Shop, 1964. Reprint. 1836. This pamphlet is credited to Colonel Robert Morris Coleman and was commonly known as early as 1840 as "Coleman's Pamphlet," although he likely used at least one ghostwriter.

Crawford, Ann Fears (Editor). *The Eagle. The Autobiography of Santa Anna*. Austin, Tex: State House Press, 1988.

Day, James M. (Compiler). *The Texas Almanac 1857–1873. A Compendium of Texas History*. Waco, Tex: Texian Press, 1967.

DeBruhl, Marshall. *Sword of San Jacinto: A Life of Sam Houston*. New York: Random House, 1993.

DeShields, James T. *Border Wars of Texas*. 1912. Reprint. Austin, Tex: State House Press, 1993.

———. *Tall Men with Long Rifles*. San Antonio, Tex: Naylor Company, 1935.

Dixon, Sam Houston, and Louis Wiltz Kemp. *The Heroes of San Jacinto*. Houston, Tex: The Anson Jones Press, 1932.

Duval, John C. Edited by Mabel Major and Rebecca W. Smith. *Early Times in Texas*. Lincoln: University of Nebraska Press, 1986.

Erath, George Bernard, as dictated to Lucy A. Erath. *The Memoirs of Major George B. Erath, 1813–1891*. Austin, Tex: Texas State Historical Society, 1923. Reprinted by The Heritage Society of Waco in 1956.

Ericson, Carolyn Reeves. *Nacogdoches—Gateway to Texas. A Biographical Directory, Vol. I*. Nacogdoches, Tex: Ericson Books, 1977.

Everett, Dianna. *The Texas Cherokees: A People between Two Fires, 1819–1840*. Norman: University of Oklahoma Press, 1990.

Fehrenbach, T. R. *Lone Star: A History of Texas and the Texans*. Reprint. New York: American Legacy Press, 1983.

Filisola, Vincente. *Memoirs for the History of the War in Texas*. 2 volumes Translated by Wallace Woolsey. Austin, Tex: Eakin Press, 1985–1987.

Foote, Henry Stuart. *Texas and the Texans*. 2 volumes. Philadelphia: Thomas, Cowperthwait & Co., 1841.

Gambrell, Herbert. *Anson Jones: The Last President of Texas*. Austin: University of Texas Press, 1988 reprint. 1947. Reprint.

Groneman, Bill. *Alamo Defenders. A Genealogy: The People and Their Words*. Austin, Tex: Eakin Press, 1990.

Gulick, Charles A. Jr., Winnie Allen, Katherine Elliott, and Harriet Smither. *The Papers of Mirabeau Buonaparte Lamar*, 6 volumes, 1922. Reprint. Austin, Tex: Pemberton Press, 1968.

Guthrie, Keith. *Raw Frontier. Armed Conflict along the Texas Coastal Bend. Volume One*. Austin, Tex: Eakin Press, 1998.

Haley, James L. *Sam Houston*. Norman: University of Oklahoma Press, 2002.

Hamilton, Lester. *Goliad Survivor*. San Antonio, Tex: The Naylor Company, 1971.

Hardin, Stephen L. *The Alamo 1836. Santa Anna's Texas Campaign*. United Kingdom: Osprey Publishing, 2001.

Hardin, Stephen L. *Texian Illiad. A Military History of the Texas Revolution*. Austin: University of Texas Press, 1994. Reprint, 1999.

Hayes, Charles W. *Galveston: History of the Island and the City*. 2 volumes. Austin: Jenkins Garrett Press, 1974.

History of Houston County: 1687–1979. Compiled and edited by the History Book Committee of Houston County Historical Commission of Crockett, Texas. Tulsa, Okla.: Heritage Publishing Company, 1979.

Hohes, Pauline Buck. *A Centennial History of Anderson County, Texas*. San Antonio, Tex: Naylor, 1936.

Hopewell, Clifford. *Remember Goliad. Their Silent Tents*. Austin, Tex: Eakin Press, 1998.

Hunter, Robert Hancock. *Narrative of Robert Hancock Hunter*. Introduction by William D. Wittlif. 1936. Reprint, Austin: Encino Press, 1966.

Huston, Cleburne. *Deaf Smith: Incredible Texas Spy*. Waco, Tex: Texian Press, 1973.

Huston, Cleburne. *Towering Texan: A Biography of Thomas J. Rusk*. Waco, Tex: Texian Press, 1971.

Jackson, Donald. *Voyages of the Steamboat Yellow Stone*. New York: Ticknor & Fields, 1985.

Jenkins, John H., and Kenneth Kesselus. *Edward Burleson: Texas Frontier Leader.* Austin, Tex: Jenkins Publishing Co., 1990.

Jenkins, John Holland. *Papers of the Texas Revolution 1835–1836.* Ten Volumes. Austin, Tex: Presidial Press, 1973.

———. *Recollections of Early Texas. The Memoirs of John Holland Jenkins.* Edited by John Holmes Jenkins III. Austin: University of Texas Press, 1958. Reprint, 1995.

Johnson, Frank W. *A History of Texas and Texans.* Edited by Eugene C. Baker. Chicago: The American Historical Society, 1916.

King, C. Richard. *James Clinton Neill. The Shadow Commander of the Alamo.* Austin, Tex: Eakin Press, 2002.

Lack, Paul (Editor). *The Diary of William Fairfax Gray. From Virginia to Texas, 1835–1837.* Dallas, Tex: SMU, 1997.

Lack, Paul D. *The Texas Revolutionary Experience. A Political and Social History. 1835–1836.* College Station, Tex: Texas A&M University Press, 1992.

Ladd, Kevin. *Gone to Texas: Genealogical Abstracts from the Telegraph and Texas Register 1835–1841.* Bowie, Md: Heritage Books, 1994.

Lane, Walter Paye. *The Adventures and Recollections of General Walter P. Lane.* Austin, Tex: Pemberton Press, 1970.

Linn, John Joseph. *Reminiscences of Fifty Years in Texas.* New York: D.&J. Sadlier & Co., 1883.

Lord, Walter. *A Time to Stand: The Epic of the Alamo as a Great National Experience.* New York: Harper & Row Publishers, 1961.

McLean, Malcolm D. *Papers Concerning Robertson's Colony in Texas.* Published by the University of Texas at Arlington. Arlington, Tex: The UTA Press.

Miller, Thomas Lloyd. *Bounty and Donation Land Grants of Texas: 1835–1888.* Austin: University of Texas Press, 1967.

Moore, Stephen L. *Taming Texas. Captain William T. Sadler's Lone Star Service.* Austin, Tex: State House Press, 2000.

Muster Rolls of the Texas Revolution. Austin: Daughters of the Republic of Texas, 1986.

Nance, Joseph M. *After San Jacinto: The Texas-Mexican Frontier, 1836–1841.* Austin: University of Texas Press, 1963.

Nevin, David. *The Texans (The Old West Series).* Alexandria, Va: Editors of Time-Life Books, 1975. Reprint, 1980.

The New Handbook of Texas. 6 volumes. Austin: The Texas State Historical Association, 1996.

Newcomb, W. W. Jr. *The Indians of Texas: From Prehistoric to Modern Times.* Austin, Tex: University of Texas Press, 1961.

O'Connor, Kathryn Stoner. *Presidio La Bahía 1721–1846.* Austin, Tex: Eakin Press, 2001.

Peña, José Enrique de la. Translated and edited by Carmen Perry. *With Santa Anna in Texas. A Personal Narrative of the Revolution.* College Station, Tex: Texas A&M University Press, 1975. Reprint, 1999.

Pierce, Gerald Swetnam. *Texas under Arms. The Camps, Posts, Forts, and Military Towns of the Republic of Texas.* Austin, Tex: Encino Press, 1969.

Pioneer Families of Anderson County Prior to 1900. Palestine, Tex: Anderson County Genealogical Society, 1984.

Pohl, James W. *The Battle of San Jacinto.* Texas State Historical Association, 1989.

Ramsay, Jack C. Jr. *Thunder beyond the Brazos: Mirabeau B. Lamar.* Austin, Tex: Eakin Press, 1985.

Richardson, Rupert N. *Texas, the Lone Star State.* New York: Prentice-Hall, 1943.

Roberts, Madge Thornall (Editor). *The Personal Correspondence of Sam Houston. Volume I: 1839–1845.* Denton: University of North Texas Press, 1996.

Robinson, Duncan W. *Judge Robert McAlpin Williamson. Texas' Three-Legged Willie.* Austin: Texas State Historical Society, 1948.

Roland, Charles P. *Albert Sidney Johnston: Soldier of Three Republics.* Austin: University of Texas Press, 1964.

Rose, Victor Marion. *The Life and Services of Gen. Ben McCullough.* Philadelphia: Pictorial Bureau of the Press, 1888; facsimile reproduction, Austin, Tex: The Steck Company, Publishers, 1958.

Seguin, Juan Nepomuceno. Edited by Jesús F. de la Teja. *A Revolution Remembered: The Memoirs and Selected Correspondence of Juan N. Seguin.* Austin, Tex: State House Press, 1991.

Shipman, Daniel. *Frontier Life. 58 Years in Texas.* 1879. Reprint, Pasadena, Tex: The Abbotsford Publishing Co., 1965.

Smithwick, Noah. *The Evolution of a State/Recollections of Old Texas Days.* Austin: University of Texas Press, 1983.

Sowell, A. J. *Rangers and Pioneers of Texas.* 1884. Reprint. New York: Argosy-Antiquarian Ltd., 1964.

Steele, Alfonso. *Biography of Private Alfonso Steele (Deceased). Last Survivor of the Battle of San Jacinto.* Privately published pamphlet, 1909.

Swisher, John Milton. Edited by Rena Maverick Green. *The Swisher Memoirs.* San Antonio: Sigmund Press, 1932.

Thompson, Karen R. (Editor). *Defenders of the Republic of Texas.* Austin, Tex: Daughters of the Republic of Texas via Laurel House Press, 1989.

Tolbert, Frank X. *The Day of San Jacinto.* New York: McGraw-Hill Book Co., 1959.

Turner, Martha Anne. *The Yellow Rose of Texas. Her Saga and Her Song. With the Santa Anna Legend.* Austin, Tex: Shoal Creek Publishers, Inc.

Webb, Walter Prescott. (Editor-in-Chief). *The Handbook of Texas: A Dictionary of Essential Information.* 3 volumes. Austin: The Texas State Historical Association, 1952.

Wharton, Clarence. *San Jacinto. The Sixteenth Decisive Battle.* Houston, Tex: Lamar Book Store, 1930.

White, Gifford. *1830 Citizens of Texas: A Census of 6,500 Pre-Revolutionary Texians.* Austin, Tex: Eakin Press, 1983.

Williams, Amelia W., and Eugene C. Barker. *Writings of Sam Houston.* Austin: The University of Texas Press, 1938–43.

Wooten, Dudley G. (Editor). *A Comprehensive History of Texas, 1685 to 1897.* 2 volumes. 1898; reprint, Austin: Texas State Historical Association, 1986.

Yoakum, Henderson. *History of Texas from Its First Settlement in 1685 to Its Annexation to the United States in 1846.* 2 volumes. New York: Redfield Publishers, 1855. Reprint, Austin, Tex: Steck Company, 1935.

Zuber, William Physick. *My Eighty Years in Texas.* Austin: University of Texas Press, 1971.

Index

Italicized page numbers indicate artwork.